ECONOMICS OF SOCIAL SECURITY

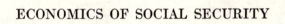

ECONOMICS
OF SOCIAL SECURITY

The Relation of the American Program to Consumption,
Savings, Output, and Finance

SEYMOUR E. HARRIS
Associate Professor of Economics
Harvard University

FIRST EDITION

GREENWOOD PRESS, PUBLISHERS
WESTPORT, CONNECTICUT

To

J. M. KEYNES

PREFACE

This book is the outcome of an interest in the investment of social security funds. The author soon learned that the problem could not be treated adequately without an understanding of other aspects of the social security program. In the process of studying and writing, the author became convinced that there was a need for a study of social security that would utilize the recent developments in theory and especially in the fields of money, fiscal policy, and economic fluctuations. It is, therefore, especially for those interested in these subjects (as well as in social security) that this volume is written.

The author's task was lightened by the important contributions of Mr. Keynes. He, more than anyone else, has demonstrated to the economist not adequately trained in mathematics the importance of putting any concrete program in the general picture. We must consider the repercussions of social security on money, the rate of interest, savings, investment, employment, etc., and the effects of changes in these variables upon the security program. The growing popularity of a general equilibrium approach owes much to him. This study is, then, primarily concerned with the significance of the social security program for the volume and fluctuations of output and employment. Effects on money and finance are of importance primarily in so far as they influence these variables.

The author has profited greatly from the works of Prof. E. H. Chamberlin and Mrs. Joan Robinson on monopolistic competition; of Prof. A. H. Hansen on fluctuations and fiscal policy; of Mr. D. H. Robertson, Profs. J. A. Schumpeter and Gottfried Haberler on economic fluctuations; of Profs. A. C. Pigou, P. H. Douglas, and J. R. Hicks in the field of wage theory and unemployment; of Profs. A. C. Pigou, J. R. Hicks, and Mrs. Joan Robinson on substitution; of Prof. Carl Shoup and his associates in the Twentieth Century Fund studies in fiscal policy; and finally of Dr. E. L. Dulles, Profs. D. A. Brown, P. H. Douglas, and E. E. Witte in the field of social security proper, in which the literature is voluminous. Many others have made important contributions. The long list of writers whose contributions have been useful can more adequately be appreciated in the course of reading the book.

[vii]

PREFACE

Many have helped directly. Of numerous government officials in the Treasury, the Works Progress Administration, and the Social Security Board, the author wishes to mention especially Dr. E. L. Dulles of the last organization, whose comprehensive command of the facts and theories of the security program was of inestimable value. Dr. Paul Webbink of the Social Science Research Council Committee on Social Security also gave valuable aid. Dr. E. L. Dulles of the Social Security Board and Prof. Carl Shoup of Columbia read the manuscript and improved it greatly. The author is also indebted to the following, who read various parts of the manuscript: Prof. P. A. Samuelson of Massachusetts Institute of Technology, Mr. Lyle Schmitter, Miss B. C. Goldwasser, and Miss S. J. Mushkin, the last three with the Social Security Board; Drs. P. M. Sweezy, R. A. Musgrave, W. F. Stolper, and Robert Triffin, all of Harvard.

The author has had three research assistants in the process of writing this book. Mrs. R. G. Gettell worked on this project for a year, and a great deal of credit is due her. She was succeeded by Mrs. Marion Crawford Samuelson, who assisted for almost two years. Mrs. Samuelson contributed research assistance and editorial help. More than to anyone else, the author is indebted to her. Her clear, mathematically trained mind and her faculty of lucid expression have left their impression on this manuscript. Numerous pages are, indeed, her work. In the late stages of preparation, she was succeeded by Miss A. E. Bourneuf, whose thoroughness, accuracy, and interest in getting the manuscript ready for the press lightened the burden considerably. Without her help the volume would still be far from finished. Finally the author is indebted to Mrs. David Lusher for secretarial help at an early stage and to Miss Lillian Buller who has been responsible for the main part of the secretarial work. Miss Dorothy Wescott of the *Review of Economic Statistics* answered many questions for us.

My wife, as usual, read the manuscript and proofs with care and critical insight, to the great benefit of the book.

The Harvard University Committee on Research in the Social Sciences contributed the necessary funds. Without their help, this book could not have been written.

SEYMOUR E. HARRIS.

DUNSTER HOUSE,
CAMBRIDGE, MASS.,
August, 1941.

[viii]

CONTENTS

1. *Direct Effects of Operations of Governmental Funds upon the Rate of Interest.*

   Decline in rate of interest. Analysis of investments of and flow of
   funds to institutions. New issues by the Federal government. The
   social security program and public issues. Size and importance of trust
   funds.

2. *Stagnation, Pay-roll Taxes, and Savings under the Social Security Program.*

   Social security versus the alternatives. Relief and works programs
   financed by loans and social security program by taxes? Savings under
   the social security program. Pay-roll taxes and secular stagnation.
   Savings and income. Excess of savings? Outlets for savings—private
   investment in the thirties. The pros and cons of pay-roll taxes. Public
   investment and consumption. Effects of reserves on rate of interest via
   consumption and investment. Pay-roll taxes from the insurance and
   finance points of view. Pay-roll taxes and the defense program.

3. *Federal Deficits in Relation to the Social Security Program.*

   Significance of the Treasury deficit. Deficiency of private spending.
   Theory of deficits. Public debt and capital investments. Analysis of
   Treasury deficits. Social security program and the Treasury contribution to spending. Future expenditures and deficits. Sources of extra
   revenue. Effect of economic improvement. Estimates made in 1937.

4. *Problems of Integration—Relation of Wages, Benefits, and Relief.*

   Artificial support of wage rates and supplies of labor. Are relief and
   unemployment-insurance benefits preferred to wages? Effect on reservation price of workers. Coordination.

5. *Problems of Integration—the Cost to Be Borne by Insurance.*

   Allocation of costs of economic distress. The share of unemployment
   insurance. Danger of inadequate contributions. Actuarial problems.
   Estimates of receipts and possible benefit payments. Burden to be put
   on unemployment insurance.

[ix]

CONTENTS

[x]

CONTENTS

CONTENTS

CONTENTS

CONTENTS

CONTENTS

CONTENTS

CONTENTS

absence of reserves. Must have rise of taxes or of public debt; or default, disguised or direct.

2. *Are Promises to Be Kept?*

Pay-as-you-go plan raises problem of future revenue. Moved toward pay-as-you-go in 1939. Will necessary amounts be raised by taxes? Failure to pay full benefits now indicates unwillingness to face pay-as-you-go principle. 1939 Amendments move toward equality of benefits over time.

3. *Consensus of Opinion in Favor of Recourse to General Taxation.*

Reasons for Treasury subsidies. Treasury saves on assistance; only way to pay benefits; burden on rich; and coverage very high.

4. *Justice in Taxation.*

With less reliance on reserves and more on general taxpayer more of revenue from well-to-do. Financing of subsidy should be on progressive principle. Contributions and benefits should be associated however—which leads inevitably to reserve.

5. *The Issue of Full Coverage.*

Many against subsidies since coverage not universal. Is universal coverage a prerequisite to subsidies? Not a principle of public finance for disbursements out of general revenue. People in similar circumstances do not always profit equally from Treasury donations; should consider total activities of Treasury. Indirect subsidization of high paid, young insured, and consumers anyway. More justice in direct subsidies.

6. *Future Tax Receipts.*

Taxes have important effects even though redistributed; source of revenue, use to which taxes put, and speed of change in tax structure significant. Pay-roll taxes pay half the cost of old-age insurance. Estimates of yield of personal income and of corporation income and estate taxes on various assumptions.

7. *Summary.*

1. *Effects of the Provision of New Markets for Public Securities on the Cost of Treasury Borrowing.*

Interest rate paid by the government is lowered and rates in other markets apt to be. Factors affecting fall in rate on public securities. Easing of rates might otherwise have been achieved by monetary policy. May discourage debt repayment. Some contend Fund has been subsidized since stipulated rate on its holdings above market from 1935–1939; must be set against lower rates.

2. *Effects on the Magnitude of the Public Debt.*

If government fails to appropriate excess receipts to old-age accounts, its moral obligations grow. Assume it accumulates reserve in securities. If government issues directly to Fund, may stimulate its deficit financing. If securities bought in open market lower interest will also

CONTENTS

CONTENTS

1. *Introduction.*

Individual firm analysis has been applied to whole economy in the
past. Important reservations. Tax may be considered equivalent to rise
in wages and yet on general analysis rise of wages may not decrease
employment. Money and real wages may both rise. Reserve accumulation may affect results.

2. *Wage Theory and Monetary Assumptions.*

Effect of rise in wages on aggregate demand depends on assumptions
as to effects on monetary supplies. High wage theory suggests that taxes
can be absorbed in higher wages. Need general analysis to study incidence. Movements of real and money wages as affecting incidence.
Keynes says fall of money wages will raise employment if it reduces
interest rate. Hawtrey says money supply will increase and interest fall.

3. *Wage Cutting and Demand.*

Pigou finds lower wages increase employment. Assumes nonwage earners maintain money expenditures. Many emphasize adverse
effects of high wages on costs. Schumpeter considers probability
of substitution due to rise in wages—thinks significance of wage rates
overemphasized.

4. *Wages and the Rate of Interest.*

Pigou says lower real wages increase employment; considers effects
on rate of interest. But interest rate is function of supply of money.
Kaldor attacks Pigou; analyzes conditions for decline in interest rate.
With elastic monetary conditions certainly possible for rise in wages to
be passed on to consumer. Keynesian view that with elastic money
supply real wages independent of money wages; conclusions affected by
assumptions concerning substitution.

5. *Level of Wages and Marginal Productivity Theory.*

How is rise in real wages following adoption of social security consistent with marginal productivity? Marginal prime cost curve may
slope downward; labor may gain at expense of other factors; in short
period wage may exceed marginal product; rise of demand may increase
marginal product. Wage may be too high for full employment.

6. *Money and Real Wages and the Burden of Social Security Taxes.*

Keynesian idea that real and money wages vary in opposite directions. American statistical material; behavior of output per man hour,
output per wage earner and total pay-rolls. Cost of living does not seem
to play decisive part. Importance of technological changes in shifting
schedule of productivity. If real wages fall in prosperity, workers will

CONTENTS

CONTENTS

CONTENTS

[xxiii]

CONTENTS

[xxiv]

CONTENTS

CONTENTS

ECONOMICS OF SOCIAL SECURITY

SUMMARY OF THE ISSUES

In the chapter following this, the main problem is the relation of the social security program, which had been introduced under the Act of 1935 and modified in 1939, to related programs of the New Deal. In particular, the issues of a decline in the rate of interest, stagnation, deficit financing, integration with relief and wage policies receive some attention.

This book as a whole covers three main problems: the relation of the security program to output, reserves and finances, incidence and effects of pay-roll taxes. These are the headings of successive parts of this book. It is scarcely necessary to point out that these parts are interrelated. Thus the accumulation of reserves is a relevant issue in the discussion of output, finance, and incidence. Of its relation to output and finance, little need be said here. The incidence of the pay-roll tax is also affected by the accumulation or nonaccumulation of reserves. Thus it may be argued that the imposition of taxes will not require a reduction of wages (exclusive of benefits) or employment if the proceeds are promptly spent. Whether they will be spent will depend, however, in part, upon the system of finance used: reserves or pay-as-you-go.

We now turn to a brief summary of Part I. In 1935, the government, which was excessively concerned with financial problems of later generations, embarked upon its reserve plan for financing old-age insurance. The result was a constant and vigorous barrage of criticism directed against the social security program. Frequently the arguments advanced were fallacious, the estimates of ultimate reserves erroneous, and both friends and critics of the security program united in bringing about the amendments of 1939, which will tend to reduce ultimate reserves to a modest figure. On the whole, these changes are to be welcomed if for no other reason than that the program will now be much more popular throughout the country. It is, however, unfortunate that unsound attacks contributed to the revolt against reserves, and that troublesome financial problems are now substituted for the deflationary issues raised by an accumulation of large reserves.

In Chap. 2, the problem is the deflationary aspects of the social security program. An attempt is made to give the term "deflationary" concrete meaning relative to the problem of reserves. Relevant considerations are the effects upon monetary supply and demand, the alternative uses of money collected and the character and direction of government spending, the state of the budget—is the deflation merely a failure to induce greater inflation? Authority seems to accept the view that the social security program of 1935 had a net deflationary effect. For the years 1936–1938, in particular, the charge has frequently been made that the social security program contributed greatly to the premature downturn. It is, however, necessary to put in their proper perspective numerous other factors: the accumulations of other governmental agencies; the large rise of tax receipts accompanying the recovery; the excessive rise of wages, prices, and inventories; the failure of investment to rise to the level of the twenties—all these played a part as did the social security program.

Undoubtedly, as we shall see, the pay-roll taxes are in large part a tax on consumption—and if taxes on consumption are excessive, then they may well be condemned. Much may be said for pay-roll taxes on other grounds, however, and if possible, it would be desirable to maintain pay-roll taxes and obtain the proper proportion between consumption and nonconsumption taxes through a reduction of the yield of other consumption taxes or a rise of the yield of nonconsumption taxes. Both on grounds of fiscal expediency and on correct insurance principles, the pay-roll taxes should be retained. Furthermore, the pay-roll taxes, to some extent, impinge on savings; and the disbursements of benefits in periods of need contribute toward a net rise of consumption.

In an appraisal of pay-roll taxes, one's conclusions will depend in no small part upon the assumptions concerning the state of employment. On the assumption of *full employment*, much is to be said for consumption taxes. A reduction of consumption will induce a corresponding rise of investment. Furthermore, the net burden of taxation will be smaller if reserves are accumulated at interest; and though reserves may be accumulated through the imposition of taxes other than pay-roll taxes, the probability is that they will be used for this purpose. (It is scarcely necessary to add that the burden of taxes is reduced through recourse to reserves because earnings on reserves are substituted for additional taxes.)

Under conditions of less than full employment, the net effect of pay-roll taxes and accumulation of reserves upon investment is not clear. What will be the effect of public savings upon the rate of interest? What is the elasticity of demand for investment? What are the effects of the security program upon the state of demand? Will the marginal efficiency of capital be reduced greatly by the tax on consumption?

Part of Chap. 2 (Sec. 2.7) is devoted to an analysis of the series of savings and investment. A large part of this section is a digression from the main theme, and the reader may prefer to skip it or read it quickly. The occasion for the examination of these statistical series is the frequent reference to oversavings as the decisive argument against pay-roll and consumption taxes. In recent years, the evidence points both toward large savings by savings institutions and inadequate outlets for investment. It is not, however, easy to find *statistical* evidence of oversaving. The savings-investment pattern of recent years, however, lends some support to those who are critical of consumption taxes and accumulation of reserves.

Oversaving may be attacked through public spending and through the introduction of tax policies which together with deficit spending contribute toward a rise in the propensity to consume. It is possible to provide for pay-roll taxes and sizable reserves and yet through proper tax and spending policies correct the tendency toward oversaving. If these measures are inadequate, it may be necessary to reduce or drop the pay-roll taxes. There are, however, other reasons for adhering to the tax program provided in the legislation of 1935.

The problem discussed in Chap. 3 is the relation of the social security program to savings. Alternative methods of finance may influence the volume of savings through direct effects and through indirect effects via the repercussions upon income. In this connection, it is well to consider the fact that under a current financing scheme the total amount of taxation is greater and the distribution over time more uneven than under reserve financing. Of the direct effects on savings, this may be said. Under the reserve plan, the net volume of saving at first seems to rise. But this issue cannot be resolved without a consideration of the issues of oversaving and the use to which the funds raised are put. The issue is, furthermore, not settled without a more precise discussion of the nature of the taxes. Consumption taxes are likely to result in a rise of savings, and taxes on surpluses in a diminution of savings. These are, however, the first effects. It is possible, for example, that excessive taxation of high incomes will result in a diminution of investment and, on a multiplier principle, in a greater reduction of income.

In order to arrive at any conclusions on the net effect upon savings, it is necessary to consider the effects of compulsory public savings upon the voluntary savings of the low-income classes. Differences of opinion are to be found here. Recent statistical investigations confirm the impression, however, that low-income groups do not cut their private savings to a significant degree in response to a rise of compulsory savings. The distribution of savings by income groups, studies of low-income class budgets, and the volume of savings in recent years via insurance—all these suggest this conclusion. Low-income groups may, however, dissave following the introduction of compulsory-saving schemes.

A rise of savings may be induced via a reduction in the rate of interest (and the accompanying rise of investment and income), which is associated in turn with the antecedent rise of savings (*i.e.*, direct savings by the social security reserves). It is not easy, however, to assess the effects of the accumulation of trustee funds (or all departmental funds) against the improved demand for government securities accompanying the expansion of monetary supplies and in the light of the low and fluctuating marginal efficiency of capital. Furthermore, the relation between a reduction of the rate on government securities and a general reduction in the rate of interest is tenuous. Finally, any net effects upon savings will depend not only on the repercussions of a reduction of rates upon the volume of investment, but also on the effects of a reduction of consumption on the latter.

In a note to Chap. 3, the relation of the prices of consumption (P) to the prices of investment goods (P') is considered. On the assumption that pay-roll taxes and reserve financing induce a reduction of demand for consumption goods and hence a decline in their prices, the question of the relation of prices of consumption and investment goods naturally arises. Mr. Keynes's attempt to prove that P and P' are independent variables has not been very successful; and it may be well to warn the reader that a great deal of space has been given to this problem which is only indirectly related to the issues of this book. This analysis brings attention to the significance for P' of the rate of interest and (via expected incomes) of prices and demand for consumption goods.

Our social security program has been discussed largely on the assumption that excess savings is characteristic of our economy. In an undersaving economy, the arguments for pay-roll taxes and reserve financing become much stronger. Compulsory public savings may put additional resources at the disposal of entrepreneurs. Unwanted price increases may be averted and the volume of investment increased. Pay-roll taxes in the midst of a defense program in 1942–1943 (say) may, for example, be a blessing for the country; the consumption of the masses will then be discouraged to some extent, and more resources will be available for waging war.

What is the relation of the security program to demand, prices, and output? The answers to these questions are the subject matter of Chap. 4. In general, the net effect upon prices of several classes of goods will depend upon the degree of unemployment and the mobility of factors. It is also necessary to consider the manner of finance and the amount of accumulation or decumulation of reserves. Assume, for example, that the funds are obtained from general revenues and in particular from surplus incomes, that decumulation of reserves is taking place, and that the factors of production are fully employed. Then the prices of wage goods are likely to rise, and savings will probably be curtailed. A rise in these prices will tend to attract factors away from investment and luxury-goods industries. Here it is necessary to take account of the degree of mobility of factors and also the effects upon investment demand of a rise in prices of wage goods. Let us assume again that the taxes are largely on surpluses but that oversaving and accumulation of reserves prevail; then the ensuing effect on private savings will be helpful.

Another possible assumption is inflationary methods of finance: in the period of decumulation then, new bonds are thrown on the market in place of old bonds previously accumulated by insurance funds. Under conditions of full employment, the insured old will obtain goods largely at the expense of the masses who account for the greater part of all consumption. In the longer run, others, *e.g.*, consumers of nonwage goods, may also pay through movements of factors.

It should be observed further that the net effect on prices will largely depend upon the manner of finance. A tax on consumption, for example, will divert consumption demand from one group of potential consumers to the insured. Finally, it is well to consider the effect of the program upon capitalist income. Assume that the insurance funds purchase bonds from the market or in purchasing directly from the government indirectly deprive the market of securities. Then a relevant issue is what is the current state of outlets for investment. If private outlets are not available, the effects on capitalist income are unfavorable.

In analyzing the effects upon the rate of interest and the economy, one must go beyond a study of the effects upon savings. Investment policies of the managers of the reserve funds will, via the effect upon the supply and demand for money, also influence the rate of interest. Alternative investment policies are discussed in Chap. 5. It is well to point out at the outset that an increase in the demand for public securities, which is the outcome of the accepted investment policy, may not contribute greatly to a rise of prices of all assets or even of public securities. Much depends upon the elasticity of supplies of old securities and that of new securities. The government may issue additional supplies in response to a rise of price; but under current conditions supplies of *old* issues are inelastic. Finally, the decisive factor in the rise of demand under the New Deal has been the monetary expansion, not the purchases of trust funds.

Three possible methods of investment are discussed. The first is the deposit of security funds with banks. There are distinct limitations on the amount of business deposits that may thus be immobilized. Relevant factors in an analysis of this policy are the incidence of the pay-roll taxes, the capacity of business to recoup losses through sales of assets, and the manner in which the Treasury replenishes the active deposits of banks and business. Thus business may be able to shift the burden in part to consumers and savers, in this manner attracting income and savings deposits, or sell assets to the public or banks. It is not likely that the reserve position of banks will be affected in a serious manner; and this is particularly true if the deposits are put into savings banks. Furthermore, immobilization of deposits by insurance funds is to be considered in the light of the deficit financing and inflows of gold of the thirties.

Another possibility is that the authorities of the Federal Reserve System take over the responsibility of management. The Federal reserve banks may act in the capacity of agents or bankers. In the former capacity, the reserve banks would invest the funds for the trustees of the insurance funds. The disturbance to the money market would be a minimum, for the Federal reserve authorities would assume full responsibility. Others would merely have the reserve banks accumulate the cash of the insurance funds and disburse it as benfit payments are made. In this manner, they would provide the reserve banks with a potent weapon of control. Those who propose this policy should recall the failure to use all weapons in the twenties and even in the early thirties and the costliness of an effective amount of immobilization today.

We come finally to the third method, *i.e.*, investment in government securities. This is, of course, the method required under the Social Security Act. In this connection, it is helpful to consider the repercussions upon the money market of the use of this method of investment in the years following 1922. It would undoubtedly have contributed toward a slackening of the rate of rise in the twenties and toward an improvement in the early thirties. From 1933 to 1936, however, the effects might well have been adverse. It is, however, necessary to consider the sources of the money accumulated and the effects of the inflow of gold and government spending. On the whole, the actual system in operation seems to be the most acceptable one. The lift given to the government-bond market seems, on the whole, to have been a favorable factor though it may have some disadvantages.

We now come to Part II, which is devoted to a discussion of reserves and finances. In the opening chapter (6), the subject under discussion is the evolution of the old-age reserve plan. The occasion for a large reserve, the size of the reserve contemplated and the variables upon which the estimates were based, the reasons for opposition, and the manner in which the program for a large reserve was repudiated—all these receive some attention.

Chapter 7 is a comparison of three alternative plans for providing the required funds under the old-age insurance plan. The first is the so-called reserve plan; the second, a genuine or superreserve plan; and the third, deficit financing, or (more popularly called) pay-as-you-go. It is likely that under the first of these plans, payroll taxes will play a more important part than under the other two plans; for it is not easy to justify an accumulation of reserves out of general revenues. In theory, plan 2 has the strongest appeal. Against the obligations assumed under old-age insurance, it provides tax resources, which are made available once an important part of the public debt is redeemed. It is thus to be preferred to the pay-as-you-go plan, which requires severe taxes later and makes no provision for meeting later obligations now; and it is to be preferred to the reserve plan so long as public debt rises *pari passu* with the accumulation of public securities in insurance funds. That debt repayment is out of the question and a large rise of debt probable and that obligations on account of social security, public debt, and other purposes, *e.g.*, defense, may rise as much as 8 to 10 billion dollars or more annually in the fifties (say) and much more in the early forties suggest the danger of nonfulfillment of promised benefits. A rise of productivity and income comparable with that of the last 50 years and the avoidance of major depressions may, however, eliminate these dangers.[1]

Actuarial aspects of the problems of reserves are discussed in Chap. 8. In order to estimate ultimate reserves, it is necessary to consider the values of numerous variables over a long period of years. It is not surprising that large errors were made. In particular, the actuaries underestimated the large costs resulting from movements of workers from covered to noncovered industries. The fact that many would have a minimum amount of earnings in covered occupations involved the Funds in large outlays. Actuaries also failed to allow adequately for continued improvement in life expectancies. The original legislation subsidized the old and low paid, on the one hand, and those insured in the early years of the program, on the other. Under the amendments of 1939, the present old, the low paid, and finally those who have dependents are treated generously. In later years, however, those who are covered briefly are not treated so generously as under the original legislation. In general, the 1939 legislation provides for relatively large benefits now as compared with those to be paid in the far future and payments that are geared more closely to need than under the original legislation.

Millions of words have been written on the theory of insurance reserves. Fallacies abound, and many of these errors have played a part in the abandonment of large reserves. That the amendments of 1939 have contributed toward a rout of the forces of opposition does not remove the need of distinguishing valid from untenable arguments used to repudiate the program of 1935. Chapter 9 is devoted to a discussion of the theory of reserves.

It is necessary to distinguish accounting from real problems. It does not matter greatly whether the government specifically appro-

---

[1] *Cf.* REDDAWAY, W. B., *The Economics of a Declining Population*, pp. 195, 206–207.

priates the excess of receipts over disbursements to the old-age account or merely acknowledges its indebtedness. What is significant is that the receipts of the government rise relatively to disbursements when reserves accumulate. The government may accumulate the cash, sell securities to the Funds, or buy securities from the market.

What is the reserve system of financing? The answer is that it proposes to make the value of current assets equal to the present value of accrued liabilities, tax receipts being supplemented with earnings from reserves. Present value of accrued liabilities may still exceed the value of current assets. In that sense, the reserve plan of 1935 was operating on a deficit, *i.e.*, the fund was not on a full reserve basis. Under the 1935 Plan, benefits had been underestimated; and therefore under the planned pattern of benefits and taxes, the plan would become insolvent. A rise of tax revenues or a reduction of benefits (or both) was required. Pay-as-you-go financing is deficit financing in the fullest sense. Here large obligations are incurred; and an implied promise is made that the required taxes will be forthcoming. The present value of benefits is very large relative to current assets, or even relative to receipts from *definite* tax proposals for the future.

Much has been made by opponents of reserve financing of the argument that the present young cannot save for the future. These critics should, however, be reminded that the choice of tax program influences the capital and income of the future, that the payment of benefits in the future is dependent in part upon tax capacity, and that a relatively even distribution of taxes is likely to reduce both the total burden of taxation and the danger of a breakdown of the tax system. These points may be interpreted as arguments for reserve financing which must be set against the monetary arguments opposed to reserve financing.

An attack on the "interest-saved" fallacy would scarcely be needed were the argument not used effectively both by popular economists and even by high authority. In a refutation of this position, it is necessary only to assume that public expenditures do not rise on account of the provision of new markets for public securities by the amount of securities purchased by insurance funds. Public debt privately held is then reduced, and to that extent, the taxpayer is not called upon to finance the interest on securities held in insurance funds. What is more, it is necessary to consider the effects upon income of any rise of public expenditures associated with the security program. If income rises, tax capacity rises; and, therefore, some gain may be found even if debt rises *pari passu* with the accumulation of reserves.

Brief comment will be made on several other issues discussed in this chapter. (1) Management of large reserves may provide the monetary authority with a powerful weapon which, if properly used, may be very helpful. (2) Unfortunate effects may follow if all insurance funds accumulate at the same time. It is, however, necessary to consider the business situation; and in depression periods, the net inflow is likely to be modest. Any inflow would, however, be unfortunate. (3) The argument that the poor are asked to pay off the debt is not tenable. They receive in return a *quid pro quo:* a promise of future benefits. If the pay-roll taxes result in an excessive burden being placed on the poor, tax and expenditure programs may be modified in other aspects. A complete repudiation of pay-roll taxes and reserves, and, therefore, of insurance principles, suggests as an alternative the payment of maximum benefits today. Then need, not contribution, would be the criterion of the benefit pattern. The pay-as-you-go school have not been willing to go so far. (4) Many have criticized reserve financing on the grounds that Congress should not today commit future generations. The accumulation of reserves, however, does not commit future generations nearly so much as the pattern of benefits. Reserves may, on the other hand, strengthen the probability of adhering to promises. Moreover, future generations will be able to modify the pattern of benefits and contributions in various ways. Finally, those who criticize the reserve program on grounds that the principles of private insurance have wrongly been applied to social insurance go too far. Reserves of private insurance companies are not to be explained exclusively on grounds of absence of compulsion; and arguments for reserves for public insurance are to be found despite the compulsory character of public insurance.

In Chap. 10, the costs of old-age insurance are discussed. Estimates of an eventual cost under the 1935 Act of 9 to 10 per cent of pay-rolls, or 3.5 billion dollars, have given way to estimates of 13 to 15 per cent, or 5 billion dollars. The anticipated costs rise with the revelation that the number covered will be much larger than had been anticipated; and life expectancies will continue to improve. What is more, any extension of coverage to excluded groups of workers seems at first to suggest increased disbursements under old-age insurance; for the excluded workers are, on the whole, low-income groups, who are treated generously under the social security program. The last is, however, offset by the savings resulting from a reduction of the numbers moving from covered to noncovered, and vice versa: these cases are costly because they are covered briefly. Since 1935, the prospects have grown worse. It is now clear that public debt will continue to rise; that public opinion demands a liberalization of benefits in early years; and that, through liberalization and reduction of tax contributions, the earnings on reserves will be much smaller than had been anticipated. Once benefits attain a maximum under present legislation, the eventual cost of public debt and old-age insurance may be as little as 4 billion dollars and as high as (or even higher than) 9 billion dollars; the latter is a much more likely figure than the former. It is well to compare these figures with costs in 1939 of Federal debt and the social security program of less than 2 billion dollars. If one considers also the probable rise of costs of other parts of the security program, e.g., health insurance, and of other programs, such as defense, farm aid, help to veterans, it is not unreasonable to conclude that a balanced budget may require a rise of revenues from the current level of 6 billion dollars to 20 billion dollars. (This seems to be clearly the case in the immediate future, say by 1942; and it is also likely to hold in the more distant future when perhaps defense expenditures will be less important and outlays for security and debt more important.)

It is possible to estimate roughly the cost of old-age insurance through a comparison of the ratio of productive workers aged 20 to 64 and the number of annuitants aged 65 and over. On given assumptions, these series give the cost of insurance over a long period of time. The eventual costs will be smaller or larger according to whether the conservative estimates of life expectancy of the official actuaries are used or (what seems to be nearer the truth) the more optimistic estimates given in recent studies. The cost may well reach 5 billion dollars; and it may be necessary to obtain three-fifths of the total costs from general revenues.

Financing of the social security program in later years raises difficult problems which are the subject matter of Chap. 11. Unless other expenditures are reduced adequately, it will be necessary to increase tax revenues or debt or repudiate obligations. It is well to raise the question now whether the government will be able to keep its promises to the insured. It has been estimated that over the next few generations 100 billion dollars will be collected, and, therefore, it is held that the saving to business of a billion dollars obtained through the postponement in the stepup of tax rates is a matter of secondary importance. But is it? The point is that the 1 billion dollars have been lost at the first signs of pressure. Some concessions to those who, though friendly to social security, had strong and justifiable fears of deflation might have been made; but the appeasers of business and the financial purists are suspect when they advocate an unbalancing of the social security budget. Furthermore, the marked strides taken toward a pay-as-you-go plan and toward payments on the basis of need, not contributions, also suggest the payment of maximum payments now. Then at least the government would have given a strong indication of an intention to keep promises.

On the grounds of justice and fiscal adequacy, much is to be said for Federal subsidies. The pay-roll tax, moreover, is largely a tax on consumers and is regressive in its effects. Other reasons for support of the pay-roll taxes are to be found; and their adverse effects on consumption may be corrected through changes in the general pattern of taxation and expenditures. One argument frequently invoked against Treasury subsidies, i.e., limited coverage, does not stand up under examination. It would, furthermore, be unfortunate if when Treasury aid were indispensable, inadequate coverage were accepted as an excuse for nonparticipation of the Treasury. This chapter ends with a discussion of tax capacity and some estimates of the amount of additional revenues that might be obtained in order to finance social security and public debt in the future.

In the final chapter (12) of Part II, the problem under discussion is social security and the public debt. (1) The effect of the new markets for government securities upon the rate of interest is considered. In this connection, it is well to observe that the effects of the provision of new markets upon the rate of interest and the effects of monetary policy are not additive. (2) Is the absorption of securities by trust funds and governmental corporations accompanied by an induced rise of debt of equal proportions? The answer is no; and in any case the value of assets acquired is to be put against any rise of debt. In this discussion three cases are distinguished: the sale of securities by the Treasury directly to the Funds, purchase of securities by the Funds on the markets, and purchases of other assets by the Funds. (3) Related to the above is the problem of the effect of new markets upon the repayment of debt. In periods of depression this is not likely to be a significant problem; but in periods of prosperity the temptation may be not to repay debt. It should be observed, however, that the availability of new markets reduces the need for redemption. Pressure will be directed toward tax reduction rather than debt reduction; and, aside from the last issue, the choice of policy should not be affected by the creation of these new markets. (4) The cost of debt reduction is estimated. Over a period of 25 years, a debt of 40 billion dollars might be repaid (and interest charges covered) at a cost of 54 billion dollars as compared with a cost of 25 billion dollars for interest alone. Finally, it is interesting to estimate debt in later years on various assumptions. A possible assumption, though not justified by the history of the last 8 years, is that the debt would rise in future years by the amount of the interest cost. Even on that assumption, the debt would rise to 130 billion dollars in 1980 and 236 billion dollars in the year 2000.

Part III is devoted to a study of the incidence and effects of pay-roll taxes. A summary of this part appears at the end of the book, and, therefore, it is necessary to review the issues here only very briefly. Basing their stand on the marginal productivity theory of wages, the classical economists conclude that a pay-roll tax imposed on the employer would be passed on to the worker through a reduction of wages. Otherwise a rise of unemployment would result. The marginal productivity theory is, however, subject to many reservations; and it is necessary to take into account general demand and supply conditions.[1] In particular, the security program affects productivity via its effects on general demand and supply. It is, furthermore, necessary to make monetary assumptions; and the assumption of an unchanged MV, which has been popular in incidence theory, is not the only possible one, or the most reasonable. On the assumption of elastic monetary supplies, a rise of wages and demand is to be had without adverse effects on the rate of interest or on employment. Furthermore, it will be possible to put part of the cost of the security program on consumers. An examination of the distribution of savings and consumption by income groups will then give some indication of the extent to which the rise of prices will result in a curtailment of consumption on the one hand, and of savings on the other. Modification of accepted theory is especially required when the theory of monopolistic competition is considered. That the demand curve for the product of the individual firm is less than perfectly elastic, the supply curves less than perfectly elastic, and that rents are paid—all these suggest the possibility of putting part

[1] See BLACK, D., *The Incidence of Income Taxes*, 1939, Chaps. X–XI.

of the burden on nonlabor shares. It is also necessary to consider the issues of substitution and complementarity. Even if wage costs rise, it does not follow that the adverse effects on demand for factors will be concentrated on labor. Much depends upon the dominance of substitution or complementarity; and in the discussion of these problems it is especially necessary to consider the elasticities of supply of the factors. Finally, it is well to point out that the pay-roll tax affects firms and industries with varying intensity. The varying proportion of wages to all costs, the system of merit rating, the exclusion of some industries and firms, the seasonality of operations, the distribution of unemployment costs between the security program and other Federal programs—all these are relevant in a discussion of the comparative burdens of pay-roll taxes.

THE SOCIAL SECURITY PROGRAM IN THE AMERICAN ECONOMY

In this chapter, an attempt is made to deal with the social security program of 1935 in relation to other issues. First arises the problem of the rate of interest, for one of the important aims of the New Deal has been to reduce the interest rate. The Social Security Trust Funds and other governmental organizations, in their capacity as buyers of Treasury issues, contribute toward lower rates. In other respects, the effects of accumulations of funds on the rate of interest may be adverse. Consumption may be discouraged and incomes and savings decline. Furthermore, governmental organizations, *e.g.*, the Reconstruction Finance Corporation, not only buy but they also contribute toward sales of securities. It is, moreover, easy to exaggerate the significance of the *trust* funds in the government security markets. When compared with the expansion of deposits, the inflow of gold, and the issues of new securities, the rise in the assets of trust funds has been moderate; and their acquisition of cash is not unrelated to the expansion of deposits and the accompanying inflow of gold and issue of securities.

Second, is the social security program, and in particular the pay-roll tax under the 1935 Act, to be condemned on the ground that it contributes toward secular stagnation? The answer depends in part upon the program that would be substituted for the social security program and its manner of finance. Another (and related) issue is the contribution of the social security program to the volume of savings. Pay-roll taxes may well be condemned on the assumption of oversaving unless remedial measures can be taken to offset the deflationary aspects of the taxes and the net increase in savings. Events move rapidly, however. The adverse effect upon consumption, which is unwelcome in periods of oversaving, may prove to be a blessing when, under the stimulus of the defense program, output approaches the capacity level and inflation threatens.

The discussion turns then to the problem of public deficits and the relevance of the security program. Are deficits required? What are the contributions of the security program to revenues, expenditures, and deficits? Now and later? In three final sections, we con-

[15]

sider briefly (1) the relation of wage rates, insurance benefits, and works and relief payments; (2) the allocation of burdens among the various programs; and finally (3) the Townsend plan.

1. DIRECT EFFECTS OF OPERATIONS OF GOVERNMENTAL FUNDS UPON THE RATE OF INTEREST

That the rate of interest has come down, no one will deny. Numerous series attest to the decline. Many will, however, affirm that the effects of the reduction have not been so favorable as had been anticipated.[1] In its assault on the rate of interest, the Democratic administration has relied upon refinancing of old debts, on the manufacture of money which has been stimulated by the devaluation policy and the inflow of gold, and (at least in the minds of opponents) upon the discouragement of private enterprise. That rates have declined despite the large increase of public issues is to be explained both by the unsatisfactory state of private demand for funds and the unprecedented rise in the supply of deposits. Furthermore, public issues have been sold in part in order to take over assets held by private investors, who were then encumbered with surplus funds. In so far as they then purchased other assets, the adverse effect of new issues on the rate of interest was held in check. In this connection, the figures in Table I are of some interest.

Taking account of investments by the Home Owners Loan Corporation and the decline in the value of home mortgages outstanding, we conclude that over the period 1929–1937 investors and investing institutions reduced their investments in home mortgages by 7 billion dollars; and similar calculations yield the conclusion that in the period 1930–1938, they had disposed of 5 billion dollars of farm mortgages. An examination of the following table will reveal the distribution of losses among the groups of investors.

In this period, the flow of funds to investing institutions continued at a satisfactory rate. They, therefore, had to find additional outlets for their cash. An examination of the amount of securities

---

[1] Many are dissatisfied that the rate has been reduced. The Federal Advisory Council is satisfied that the easy money policy, by lessening the current cost of government financing, has made the people, and even Congress itself, indifferent to the steadily mounting debt. Board of Governors of the Federal Reserve System, *Ann. Rept.*, 1939, pp. 77–78.

THE SOCIAL SECURITY PROGRAM

TABLE I.*—HOLDERS OF MORTGAGES AND OF FEDERAL DEBT IN CERTAIN YEARS

	1. Holders of home mortgages				2. Farm mortgages			
	1929		1937		1930		1938	
	Billions of dollars	Per cent	Billions of dollars	Per cent	Billions of dollars	Per cent	Billions of dollars	Per cent
Total.....................	21.7		17.3		9.2		7.1	
Individuals and others......	7.2	33	6.0	35	...	46	...	39
Life insurance companies....	1.7	8	1.3	8	...	23	...	13
Commercial banks..........	2.5	12	1.4	8	...	} 12	...	7
Mutual savings banks......	3.2	15	2.7	16	...		...	
Savings and loan associations	7.0	32	3.5	20				
HOLC....................	.....	...	2.4	14				
Joint stock land banks..............................					...	7	...	2
Federal land banks and F.L.B. commissioner..........					...	13	...	40

3. Owners of Federal Debt, June 30, 1938

	Billions of dollars	Per cent of total
Total....................................	41.1	
Individual and private corporations...........	11.8	28
Federal agencies and trust funds..............	4.7	11
Insurance companies......................	5.2	13
Banks....................................	19.4	48

* Figures are taken from (or calculated from) *Hearings*, Temporary National Economic Committee (76: 1), 1940, Investigation of Concentration of Economic Power, Part 9, pp. 4094–4098. *Cf.* Federal Housing Authority, *Sixth Ann. Rept. for Year Ending Dec. 31, 1939*, p. 46. Of 688 million dollars of insured mortgages purchased in 1935–1939, Federal agencies accounted for 27 per cent.

of the Federal government outstanding and their distribution gives some indication of the part played by government securities. Private investors substituted Treasury issues for mortgages; and the Federal government accepted mortgages for new issues of its securities.

These changes in portfolios by private investors are further revealed in Table II.[1]

Banks and insurance companies were apparently replacing mortgages with other investments and, particularly, government securities.

[1] *Survey Current Business*, Supplement, 1938, p. 59; *Survey Current Business*, Ann. Rev. Number, 1940, p. 70; N.I.C.B., *Studies in Enterprise and Social Progress*, p. 164; THOMAS, W., *The Banks and Idle Money*, reprinted from *Fed. Reserve Bull.* March, 1940, p. 2; *Hearings*, Temporary National Economic Committee (76: 1), 1940, Investigation of Concentration of Economic Power, Part 9, pp. 3746–3748, Federal Reserve Board, *Ann. Rept.*, 1937, p. 112.

TABLE II.—INVESTMENTS OF BANKS AND INSURANCE COMPANIES, 1930 AND 1938,
AND RISE OF GROSS FEDERAL DEBT
(In billions of dollars)

	1930 monthly average	1938 (December)
1. Life insurance companies (Association of Life Insurance Presidents):		
Mortgage loans..............................	6.1	4.4
All bonds and stocks.........................	5.5	12.9
All government bonds.........................	1.1	5.8
2. Rise of gross Federal debt, fiscal years 1930–8.....	21	
3. Investments of member banks, December.........	11.0	18.9

We shall pass over briefly here the problem of the flow of funds into savings institutions. Part of a table erroneously labeled "Assets of Principal Savings Institutions in the United States, 1920–1938" is reproduced here.[1]

TABLE III.—SAVINGS SERIES, 1930, 1933, AND 1938
(In billions of dollars)

Year	Insurance assets	Commercial banks— time deposits	Mutual savings bank assets	Building and loan association assets	Governmental pension and trust funds*	Postal savings and baby bonds	Total
1930	19.8	19.1	10.3	8.8	1.9	0.2	60.1
1933	21.8	10.4	11.0	7.0	2.7	1.2	54.0
1938	28.8	14.4	11.6	5.7	6.2	2.5	69.1

* For an excellent description of trust funds, see G. G. Johnson, Jr., "The Significance of the Government Trust Funds for Monetary Policy," *Public Policy*, edited by C. J. Friedrich and E. S. Mason, 1940, pp. 214–220. Dr. Johnson points out that the old-age reserve account and the railroad retirement fund affect both sides of the ledger: cash and deficits both rise with an inflow of cash. For the other funds, a rise of cash is had "without affecting the budgetary situation." (*Op. cit.*, p. 219.) One should not infer from Dr. Johnson's statement that in the former case deficits rise *in response to* the inflow of cash. Moreover, the statement is ambiguous and may be misleading. Thus under unemployment insurance, the net effects are similar to those under old-age insurance. The main difference is that a large part of the money collected under the former program is not included under Federal tax receipts. It is, however, used to buy public securities in so far as the money is not currently used.

Assets of life insurance companies rose from 20 to 29 billion dollars from 1930 to 1938, or from 33 to 42 per cent of the total; and governmental pension and trust funds rose from 3 to 9 per cent of the total from 1930 to 1938, while postal savings and baby bonds

[1] Note the inclusion of time deposits of commercial banks as assets of savings institutions. For this table and the figures in the next paragraph of the text see *Hearings*, Temporary National Economic Committee (76: 1), 1940, Investigation of Concentration of Economic Power, pp. 3735, 3738, 4052.

were ⅓ of 1 per cent of the total in 1930 and almost 4 per cent in 1938. A more striking comparison is to be found in the rise of total assets (?) from 54 billion dollars in 1933 to 69 billion dollars in 1938, a rise of 15 billion dollars. These figures are used with reservations, though they throw some light on the popularity of different types of savings institutions. In particular, the inclusion of time deposits is suspect. A change in the volume of time deposits may result, for example, from a transfer from demand deposits because the payment of interest on the latter is discontinued. Whether deposits are to be classified as savings or cash is not correctly determined by the division into demand and time deposits. The argument is not that time deposits should be excluded but rather that it is almost impossible to say what proportion of a rise (say) in deposits (*both time and demand*) is to be considered an increase of savings.

With the exception of the worst years of the depression, savings institutions have continued to attract large amounts of new funds; and the fact that their holdings of mortgages declined following a reduction in the amount outstanding and increased participation by the government in mortgage financing made it necessary for these institutions to seek new investments. One important outlet was government securities. In assessing the net effect of the purchases by governmental agencies of government securities, it is necessary to allow, however, for antecedent creations of deposits by the banking system, which are to be associated with the inflow of gold and deficit financing.

Further evidence of the important part played by (1) institutional savers and (2) new issues by the Federal government are revealed by the figures in Table IV.[1]

It will be observed that the change in the volume of Federal issues was in excess of the net rise of all issues. Furthermore, institutional holdings rose by 15.2 billion dollars, while individual investors increased their holdings by but 500 million dollars. Purchases of securities and mortgages by institutions other than banks kept the rise of deposits in check, however.[2]

---

[1] Securities and Exchange Commission, *Selected Statistics on Securities and on Exchange Markets*, 1939, pp. 21 and A-1 and A-2. Another interesting estimate made in this report is that in 1937, banks and trust companies held in trust 35 billion dollars and that this figure had risen greatly in the years 1933–1937. *Ibid.*, p. 16.

[2] The more these deposits accrue to governmental agencies and the more they use cash thus obtained to purchase government securities, the less the amount of new deposits required to assure a market for a given volume of Treasury issues.

TABLE IV.—SECURITY HOLDINGS OF CERTAIN INSTITUTIONS AND SUPPLY OF SECURITIES IN THE UNITED STATES, 1933–1937
(In billions of dollars)
End of 1932 to end of 1937

1. Net rise of security holdings of reporting institutions..... 17.5
   Insurance companies...................................... 6.7
   Commercial and savings banks.......................... 5.5
   Reserve banks.. 0.5
   Government trust funds and agencies.................. 3.8
   Others... 1.0
   Holdings of *fixed interest-bearing securities* in this period:
   Reporting institutions (see above)..................... +17.7
   Individuals and nonreporting institutions............. − 3.6

2. Supply and Absorption of Securities in the United States

Securities	New issues	Retire- ments	Balance of transactions for foreign account	Changes in total domestic supply
a. All issues........................	39.9	24.7	+1.3	+13.8
b. U. S. government (including guaranteed).......................	22.9	7.2	.....	+15.7

The Part Played by Trust Funds

In the policy of low rates, the social security program has played a part, though not a decisive one. Its significance may be greater in the future, however. First, we shall consider its importance as a sink for public issues, and then the more general aspects of the relations of the security program to the rate of interest. Chapters 2, 3, and 5 deal with some aspects of these problems at greater length. Table V shows changes in a few of the important items.

In the years 1933 to 1940,[1] balances of Federal government trust accounts increased by about 5 billion dollars;[2] and early in 1940, the investments on account of old-age and unemployment insurance

[1] Figures in this and the next three paragraphs for which no source is given are taken from the *Fed. Reserve Bull.*, *Treas. Dept. Bull.*

[2] This figure of 5 billion was obtained by adding (a) the increase in the balance of the unemployment trust fund (1.7 billions), (b) the increase in the balance of the old-age and survivors insurance trust fund (1.7 billions), and (c) the transfers to other trust accounts of the Federal government (1.6 billions). Under (c) the sum of 1.7 billions was subtracted from the transfers in 1936 because this sum was transferred to the adjusted service certificate fund and was paid out by this fund in the course of 1937. On this point see the Secretary of the Treasury, *Ann. Repts.*, 1936, p. 88, and 1937, p. 85. The data for (a) and (b) were taken from the *Treas. Dept. Bull.*, September, 1940, pp. 3, 12, and *Survey of Current Business* (*Ann. Survey* and monthly bulletins), and *Hearings*, Temporary National Economic Committee (76: 1), 1940, Investigation of Concentration of Economic Power, p. 4052.

THE SOCIAL SECURITY PROGRAM

TABLE V.—CERTAIN IMPORTANT FINANCIAL DATA FOR 1933 AND 1940
(In billions of dollars)

	1933	1940	Net rise
Gross Federal debt*	22.5	43.0	20.5
Monetary gold stock*	4.1	19.6	15.5
All bank deposits†	38.5	59.0	20.5
All bank investments†	18.3	28.9	10.6
Total assets of life insurance companies*	16.9	24.7	7.8
Life insurance companies holdings of government bonds (domestic and foreign)*	1.5	6.7	5.2

(In per cent)

	1933	1940	Net fall
Yield on Aaa bonds*	4.5	3.0	1.5
Yield on Baa bonds*	7.8	5.1	2.7
U. S. Treasury bonds*	3.3	2.4	0.9

* From the *Survey Current Business*, current issues and supplements. The 1933 figures are monthly averages. The 1940 figures are for June except for the insurance company data which are for August. *Cf.* Brookings Institution, *Capital Expansion, Employment and Economic Stability*, by H. G. Moulton *et al.*, pp. 56–64. The improvement in high-grade bonds has been steadier than for low-grade bonds.

† From the *Fed. Reserve Bull.*, and Federal Reserve Board, *Ann. Rept.*, 1937. The 1933 figures are for Dec. 31, the 1940 figures for March.

(inclusive of the two railroad funds) were but 3.5 billion dollars. It is clear then that in comparison with the growth of the monetary gold stock, the rise of public debt, and the absorption power of banks and life insurance companies as shown in the preceding table, the trust funds, and in particular the old-age and unemployment insurance accounts, were not of decisive importance. In particular, the growth of the gold stock accompanied and induced a growth of deposits; and the least risky asset available was Federal issues. Trust accounts put part of the deposits at the direct disposal of the Treasury, thus providing an important market for public securities. In fact, the deposits now put at the disposal of the government by the trust funds were probably in no small part deposits that had been created by the government through sales of securities to the banks and through its gold policy. (We are not contending that the gold inflow is associated primarily with Treasury gold policy.)

It would be a mistake, however, to dismiss the trust and other governmental funds, which accumulate balances, as factors of no importance. In the fiscal years 1937–1940, for example, deficits of the Federal government were 11.7 billion dollars and yet the change

[21]

in publicly offered direct debt was but 5.9 billion dollars. Trust and other accounts absorbed 3.9 billion dollars, and working balances were reduced by more than 1.1 billions.[1] In the fiscal year 1938, the Treasury relied largely on consumption taxes to absorb new issues: the deficit was 1.4 billion dollars, and trust funds absorbed more than 1 billion dollars of new issues. (The cash deficit had dropped from 4 billion dollars in the year 1936 to 400 million dollars in 1937.[2]) It was in these years that controversy raged over the deflationary effects of pay-roll taxes. Opponents of social security probably overemphasize the importance of these new markets. In absorbing new issues, trust funds and security reserves have, however, contributed toward the excessive decline in rates on public issues, and they may become a more important factor in the future.[3]

Effects of the social security program on the rate of interest are not, however, limited to the provision of a new market for government securities. It is necessary to take into account the effects of the accumulation of reserves upon the supply of and demand for money and (related to the monetary effects) upon consumption, investment, and income. Some space will be given to these issues in Part I (and to some extent in Parts II and III), and brief comment will be made on them later in this chapter. It may be said that the effects of the program on interest rates *in general* (not on the rate on Treasury issues) is difficult to establish. Much depends on the use to which the money would have been put if the Treasury had not taken it.

[1] See *Fed. Reserve Bull.*, July, 1940, p. 634.

[2] Secretary of Commerce, *Summary Ann. Rept.*, 1940, p. VII. Dr. Johnson finds that despite an excess of expenditures of 3.2 and 1.4 billion dollars in the fiscal years 1937 and 1938, the *net* cash outgo of the Federal government was but 2.4 and .2 billion dollars, respectively. G. G. Johnson, Jr., "The Significance of the Government Trust Funds," in *Public Policy*, edited by C. J. Friedrich and E. S. Mason, 1940, p. 221.

[3] Of an estimated deficit for 1940–1941 of 5.7 billion dollars, it is now estimated that 2.7 billion dollars will be obtained through net receipts of trust funds and governmental corporations and from sales of United States savings bonds. *Federal Reserve Bull.*, September, 1940, p. 911.

2. Stagnation, Pay-roll Taxes, and Savings under the Social Security Program

Social Security versus Alternatives

Since Part I deals with some aspects of this problem, we shall here merely discuss a few general issues. Condemnation of the social security program has frequently rested on the grounds that a pay-roll tax, which largely finances the program, is a tax on consumption and employment. The former meets with the disapproval of those who support an underconsumption or oversavings theory of the depression; the latter is frowned upon by those who condemn any tax that discourages employment in a world of much unemployment. We shall see in Part III, however, that the adverse effects on employment may not be so serious as is generally assumed. In the present discussion, it is helpful to consider the social security program as compared with alternative programs for taking care of the unemployed. Since 1933, the government has relied largely on relief and work programs. In the first few years, relief proved to be the most practical method of help. Beginning with the Emergency Relief Appropriation Act of 1935, the government attempted to provide work for the able-bodied unemployed, relief for the unemployables who now were to become the charges of the state and local governments, unemployment insurance for the temporarily unemployed, and old-age contributory insurance for those employed in covered occupations. Through the Social Security Act, the Federal government also provided grants, which would both reduce the burden now thrust upon local governments and stimulate them to increase their efforts on behalf of the unfortunate. Expenditures on works, therefore, now tend to become a larger part of Federal public assistance.[1]

It may be assumed at the outset that the program introduced under the Social Security Act of 1935 is financed through pay-roll taxes, and that relief and works programs, which are alternative methods of provision of help, are financed through borrowing.[2] If the propensity to consume is too low, then the substitution of aid through the security program may, in the short run, be unwise.

---

[1] See, for example, Gill, C., *Wasted Man Power*, especially pp. 151–189; Williams E. A., *Federal Aid for Relief*, Chaps. 1–2; Withers, W., *Financing Economic Security in the United States*, Chaps. 2–3.

[2] The Federal program is discussed here. It has been estimated that in 1933–1934, states financed 64 per cent of their relief needs through issues of bonds and 20 per cent through sales taxes. Withers, *op. cit.*, p. 83.

Adverse effects following a discouragement of consumption are, however, to be put against the increase of deficits associated with an abandonment of pay-roll taxes under the reserve program; and the ensuing rise in the annual deficit associated with the abandonment of large reserves financed through pay-roll taxes may reach 1 to 2 billion dollars.[1] If annual deficits of 3 billion dollars or more should continue to prevail in periods of peace, then a doubling of the deficit *through the failure to impose any pay-roll taxes* may be as unfortunate as the curtailment of consumption associated with the imposition of the taxes. (Here an extreme assumption is made: Abandonment of pay-roll taxes for many years.) We have a choice of evils: avoidance of deflationary taxes now at the possible expense of much more taxation (and deflation) later.

Methods of Finance of Alternative Programs

Are we justified in our assumption that the alternative (relief and works) programs are financed through loans, and the social security program through pay-roll taxes? (1) Consider the following figures which indicate that the deficit is roughly equal to the amount of expenditures on recovery and relief.[2]

FISCAL YEARS 1934–1939

1. Expenditures on recovery and relief............	$17.9 billion
2. Excess of expenditures over revenues...........	20.0 billion

Actually the former may be larger than the latter, for important categories of expenditures are excluded from the former, part of which might well be included as expenditures for recovery and relief. Thus expenditures for the Civilian Conservation Corps for several years, public works (designated categories), and the Agricultural Adjustment Administration are included under general expenditures. Undoubtedly these items have been transferred on the grounds that they have become normal expenditures. Yet they are properly classified in category 1 over at least part of the period

---

[1] Note the following extreme recommendation. "It seems wise, therefore, to reform the old-age payment system, making it a charge on the General Treasury and to reduce the pay-roll charges for unemployment insurance to a sum which would *defray yearly unemployment benefits in covered industries*, amending the act to provide that the Treasury would make up any yearly deficiency which resulted." (Italics mine—meaning?) Temporary National Economic Committee, Monograph 20, *Taxation, Recovery and Defense*, p. 222.

[2] *Treas. Dept. Bull.*, June, 1940, pp. 13, 15.

1934–1939. It may then be inferred from these figures that the expenditures for recovery and relief have been financed through loans. (2) Part of the social security program, *i.e.*, the assistance items, is financed from general revenues. Part of the required funds for this purpose may be held to be obtained through loans. To that extent the social security program is financed through loans. (3) It is most probable that a significant part of the burden of the unemployment and old-age insurance programs will ultimately be put upon the Treasury. Borrowing and nonconsumption taxes will then provide part of these funds. Finally, it is well to keep in mind the ultimate financing of deficits. Under deficit financing, *total* taxation will be higher, for interest charges are added. Consumption taxes in the *future* may *then* be larger than consumption taxes in the *present* would be if reliance were placed on the security program now instead of on relief programs and deficits now.

In summary, reservations are to be made to the generalization that the security program is financed through taxes on consumption and employment and that the alternative relief and works programs are financed through loan financing. In the short run, however, this generalization is not far from the truth. It is conceivable that relief and works programs will be financed through consumption taxes, and social security largely through loans. That is not the likely outcome, however, though loans *ultimately* have to be financed, and consumption taxes will bear part of this burden.

The Importance of Savings under the Social Security Program

Savings under the social security program are not an unimportant part of total savings. Under the original program an annual accumulation of reserves in excess of 2 billion dollars was not at all out of the question.[1] In many years, of course, net accumulations would have been much lower; in many of these years the unemployment reserves would have disbursed amounts in excess of receipts. Yet accumulations of but 1 billion dollars in periods of underemployment of economic resources raise difficult problems.[2] Accumulations of a billion dollars a year are not out of the question under the amendments of 1939.

---

[1] In 1935, it was estimated that the growth of old-age reserves in the years 1945–1970 would be in excess of a billion dollars yearly and frequently in excess of 1.5 billion dollars. Senate Report 628, *The Social Security Bill*, 1935, p. 9.

[2] *Cf.* HICKS, U. K., *The Finance of British Government, 1920–1936*, p. 295; and JOHNSON, *op. cit.*, pp. 237–238.

How important are these savings? They may be compared with the following:[1]

TABLE VI.—VARIOUS ESTIMATES OF SAVINGS AND CAPITAL FORMATION, 1933–1938

Savings and capital formation	Billions of dollars	Source
1. Total consumers' savings in the year 1935–1936.*	6	National Resources Committee
2. Gross capital formation—average of years 1933–1938	10.4	Kuznets
3. Net capital formation—average of years 1933–1937	1.9	Kuznets
4. Net savings—average of years 1933–1937	−0.5	Goldsmith†
5. Savings by the most important savings institutions, life insurance companies, banks, etc.—average 1934–1938	3.0	T.N.E.C.

* For the year 1938–1939, savings are estimated at 8.0 billion dollars. Temporary National Economic Committee, Monograph 3, *Who Pays the Taxes*, p. 43.

† Net savings here are defined as "the change in the aggregate earned surplus of all household, business and government units in the United States. . . . " Goldsmith, *op. cit.*, p. 236.

Finally, it is well to observe that in the two years 1937–1938 in which social security reserves first became significant, the accumulations in government pension and trust funds rose by 2.6 billion dollars, or roughly one-third of the accumulation of savings by institutions.[2]

Savings under public programs have constituted a significant part of all savings in the last few years, and are large relative to the amount of net capital formation. Under the 1935 program, they undoubtedly would have become more significant, and even under the modified program, they are likely to be of importance in many years of the next few decades. It is necessary to allow, however, for any induced dissaving which follows from compulsory savings of this type. Wage earners may save less; and consumers, if and when confronted with higher prices, may cut savings as well as consumption. These problems receive further treatment in Parts I and III.

[1] KUZNETS, S., "Commodity Flow and Capital Formation in the Recent Recovery and Decline, 1932–1938," *Nat. Bur. Econ. Research, Bull.* 74, p. 2; *Hearings*, Temporary National Economic Committee (76: 1) 1940, Investigation of Concentration of Economic Power, Part 9, pp. 4008, 4052; National Resources Committee, *Consumer Expenditures in the United States*, pp. 53, 69–70; National Bureau of Economic Research, *Studies in Income and Wealth*, Part 4, R. W. GOLDSMITH, Vol. 3, p. 236.

[2] *Hearings*, Temporary National Economic Committee (76: 1), 1940, Investigation of Concentration of Economic Power, Part 9, p. 4052.

The Issue of Pay-roll Taxes in Relation to Oversaving

In some respects the issue of deflationary effects has been given too much attention. Monetary theorists frequently have concentrated on deflationary aspects, paying too little attention to insurance problems. An unholy alliance between the budget balancers, *e.g.*, Senator Vandenberg, and the proponents of deficit financing, *e.g.*, Governor Eccles, has contributed toward the defeat of a plan for large reserves.[1] Purists in finance would balance the insurance accounts through a reduction of taxes, thus contributing toward very large deficits in the future; and those who concentrate their attention on monetary aspects of the problem do not tell us how the required funds are to be obtained in the future.

One may even go so far as to argue that no deflationary effects are to be found in this program broadly considered. Receipts are offset by disbursements. Thus in the calendar years 1937–1939, the social security (and railroad carrier taxes) yielded 2,122 million dollars, and the transfers to all trust accounts were 2,515 million dollars. Retirements, pensions, and assistance (not relief) accounted for outlays of 2,655 million dollars, an amount in excess of the latter figure.[2] A broad view of this situation suggests the conclusion that the program was deflationary in the sense that (1) taxes were being raised currently (and not being postponed) to cover expenditures on pensions, retirements, and the like; and (2) the receipts *under the program of* 1935 were in excess of current disbursements on old-age

[1] For Governor Eccles's views on taxes on consumption, the accumulation of social security reserves, and the need of payment of generous noncontributory pensions, see his address on *Unemployment—What Shall We Do about It*, May 9, 1940 (mimeographed), pp. 17–20. *Cf.* the views of Dr. Altmeyer of the Social Security Board who was doubtful of the deflationary effects, *Hearings*, Ways and Means Committee, House of Representatives, *Social Security*, 1939, pp. 2292–2294.

[2] *Survey Current Business*, Ann. Rev. Number, 1940, pp. 38–39. (For the manner of finance of state and local governments relative to relief needs, see Withers, *op. cit.*, pp. 81–83.)

These figures for tax yields include but a small part of the expenditures under the Railroad Unemployment Insurance Act. Ninety per cent of the total collected is not shown in the daily statements of the United States Treasury from which this table was derived. Furthermore, the expenditures include disbursements under Veterans Administration and the Railway Retirement Board as well as disbursements under the Social Security Act. Benefits from the old-age and survivors insurance trust fund and other Federal retirement systems are excluded. Dr. Dulles of the Social Security Board has given me some valuable help with these figures. They are given in the text as a rough picture of the situation. Figures presented later will be more helpful on this score.

and unemployment insurance. This generalization, *i.e.*, an excess of receipts, is not correctly applied to an over-all picture of Federal receipts and payments for relief, retirements, pensions, and non-relief assistance.

What is the case against pay-roll taxes? It arises in no small part from the thesis that inadequate spending accounts for a condition of secular stagnation; and it may be discussed in terms of the recent tendency in the United States to increase consumption taxes despite a high propensity to save.[1] Many economists support the thesis that the propensity to consume has not been so high in the thirties as it was in the twenties. In Great Britain, on the other hand, the proportion of savings to income has declined in recent years; and the well-to-do have increasingly been asked to contribute toward a social security program which tends to stimulate consumption at the expense of savings.[2] It is to be observed, however, that when account is taken of the burden of taxes upon low-income groups, the net gains of the poor from expenditures on social services may well disappear.[3]

It is, however, not easy to find *statistical* support of the thesis that in the thirties the propensity to save has risen or the propensity to consume has declined or remained low. In this connection the figures in Table VII are of some interest.

What the figures in (1) seem to indicate is that savings relative to income are roughly at the level of the twenties. But, when allowance is made for the increased popularity of savings institutions as channels for the accumulation of savings, the conclusion might be drawn that savings are much less important relative to the na-

[1] See, for example, the well-known writings of Prof. Hansen. *Cf.* W. B. Reddaway, *The Economics of a Declining Population*, especially Chap. IV. The author of this volume accepts the thesis of secular stagnation. He does, however, stress the point that a change in age distribution accompanying a decline in population or in the rate of increase contributes *toward* a higher demand for capital.

[2] *Hearings*, Temporary National Economic Committee (76: 1), 1940, Investigation of Concentration of Economic Power, pp. 3537, 3544, 3553–3559; HANSEN, A. H., *Fiscal Policy and Business Cycles* (1941), *passim;* and Secretary of Commerce, *Summary Ann. Rept.*, 1939, p. XIV; JASZI, G., "The Budgetary Experience of Great Britain," *Public Policy*, 1940, pp. 196–199; REDDAWAY, *op. cit.*, pp. 113–114. (According to the last, the percentage of income saved in Great Britain tends to decline, but the absolute amount of savings remains much the same.)

[3] HICKS, *op. cit.*, pp. 56–59, 269–277; *cf.* however, Political and Economic Planning, *Report on the British Social Services*, pp. 58–59; and CLARK, C. G., *National Income and Outlay*, pp. 142–148.

tional income than in the twenties. This conclusion is confirmed by the figures in column (3).[1]

TABLE VII.—SAVINGS AND GROSS AND NET CAPITAL FORMATION AS PER CENT OF NATIONAL INCOME*

Savings by savings institutions (life insurance, banks, etc.)		Capital formation		
			Gross	Net
(1)			(2)	(3)
1925–1929	5.1	1926–1929	24	12
1934–1938	4.9	1934–1937	21	7

* Calculated from *Hearings*, Temporary National Economic Committee (76: 1), 1940, Investigation of Concentration of Economic Power, pp 194, 4008, 4052.

Savings are a larger part of income when income is high than when income is low. In part the explanation is the change in distribution of income as the total rises.[2] Since per capita incomes have been lower in the thirties than in the twenties, it would be expected that the percentage saved would be less in the former period than in the latter. Given the outlets available in the thirties, the smaller percentage of savings, and the even smaller relative absolute amount of savings in the thirties, may yet be consistent with an excess of savings. If additional evidence is required of the decline in the relative and absolute amounts of saving, the reader is referred to the studies by Prof. Hansen and the National Resources Committee.[3]

In one sense then, the propensity to save may be too high. Both gross and net capital formation are much less than in the twenties though the proportion of the former to national income has not fallen much. The absolute decline later may, however, be the outcome of excessive savings relative to outlets; and when allowance is made for the change in the distribution of incomes since 1929, and, in particular, for the reduction of profits, the maintenance of large *amounts* of savings might be interpreted as a rise in the propensity to save.[4] We come out then with rather inconclusive results. One final point should be made, however. The savings collected by banks,

[1] Dr. Goldsmith, it will be recalled, estimates net savings for 1933–1937 at −2.5 billion dollars, *op. cit.*, p. 236. *Cf.* National Resources Committee, *Consumer Expenditures in the United States*, pp. 68–69.

[2] KALECKI, M., *Essays in the Theory of Economic Fluctuations*, pp. 59–62.

[3] HANSEN, *op. cit.*; and *Structure of the American Economy*, pp. 88–90.

[4] *Cf.* National Resources Committee, *Consumer Expenditures in the United States*, pp. 51, 72, 77.

life insurance companies, and other institutions are to an important degree converted into consumption and to that extent do not contribute toward the flow of savings. These institutions buy government securities, mortgages, and the like; and the sellers of the assets in turn may stimulate consumption or increase their consumption.

The Issue of Outlets for Savings

On the assumption that demand is not adequate to assure full employment or even a reasonably high level of employment, economic practitioners seek a rise of investment or consumption. The former may be achieved through a reduction in the rate of interest and (more important) through a rise in the rate of innovation and reductions of costs achieved in other ways, or through a rise of public investment. (We return to the last in a moment. Here it suffices to say that an increase of public investment financed in a reasonable manner is likely to contribute toward a rise of consumption.)

Private investment has been disappointing in the thirties, even since 1933. Despite the manufacture of vast supplies of money and the accompanying reduction in the rate of interest, investment has not attained the importance that it achieved in the twenties. Numerous explanations may be offered: state and local governments have reduced their outlays for investment purposes; installment credit has contributed relatively little to the *net* volume of investment since 1929; the foreign balance has been disappointing; economies have been found in the process of replacement of plant; and, probably most important of all, construction has suffered a severe decline.[1] Much attention has been focused on the last.[2] There is diversity of opinion on the causes of its decline. Are wage costs too high? Are financing costs too high? Are material costs too high? Does a revival of construction require recovery as a prerequisite?[3] Those who harbor exaggerated hopes would do well to

[1] See *Hearings*, Temporary National Economic Committee (76: 1), 1940, Investigation of Concentration of Economic Power, especially Part 9, *Savings and Investment* (evidence of Prof. Hansen and Drs. Currie and Altman); also *Bull.* 79, *The Volume of Consumer Instalment Credit*, 1929–1938, *Nat. Bur. Econ. Research*, p. 11, and my discussion in Chaps. 2 and 3.

[2] *Hearings*, Temporary National Economic Committee (76: 1), 1940, Investigation of Concentration of Economic Power, Part 11, *Construction Industry.*

[3] Prof. Kreps emphasizes the greater significance of material and financing as compared with labor costs (*ibid.*, pp. 5445–5455, 5568–5587). At one point in his argument at least he seems to make the error, however, of restricting labor costs to

recall that construction in the twenties, and especially residential housing, was at an abnormally high level.[1] Taking the problem of private investment as a whole, one is inclined toward a pessimistic view. Replacement which constitutes the major part of investment can be effected at large savings now;[2] and new industries comparable in their contributions with the railroad and automobile industries do not appear on the horizon. Our defense program may solve many of our problems in the next decade, however, and a possibility of a large improvement in construction is not out of the question.[3]

Pay-roll Taxes—Pros and Cons

A failure of private investment to rise adequately, whether the explanation is the slow rate of innovation or lack of confidence, leaves us with the alternative of policies aimed to increase public investment and the propensity to consume.[4] On the assumption of a dearth of investment demand, much is to be said for a tax system that impinges on savings and stimulates consumption, and particularly so in the light of recent tendencies in American taxation. Here we find the strongest argument against the pay-roll tax. On the acceleration or relation principle, a reduction of consumption, moreover, will have unfavorable effects on the volume of investment. (The discouragement of consumption is associated with the

---

outlays on the site, and leaves out of account the contribution of labor to material costs (cf. p. 5445). Another expert finds that a reduction of 20 per cent in the cost of material and labor would yield greater savings than a reduction of 20 per cent in financing charges (ibid., p. 5590). Mr. Bruere finds in mass production, enforcement of Federal Housing Authority standards, and careful planning the road to a rise in housing activities (ibid., p. 5434), On these issues, cf. pp. 5482–5483.

[1] Cf. Hearings, Temporary National Economic Committee (76: 1), 1940, Investigation of Concentration of Economic Power, pp. 231, 3546, 4009, and especially 4966–4968; and footnote 3 on Prof. Hansen's views.

[2] Hearings, Temporary National Economic Committee (76: 1), 1940, Investigation of Concentration of Economic Power, pp. 3539, 3542, 3674–3679, 4038; cf. FABRICANT, S., Capital Consumption and Adjustment, pp. 159–162, 178–179.

[3] The best treatment of the contributions of construction is to be found in a volume by Prof. Hansen, Fiscal Policy and Business Cycles. Here he emphasizes the interrelation of the 17- to 18-year building cycles and general activity. In the twenties, building made a significant contribution; in the thirties, the long downward phase of the building cycle retarded general recovery; and in the forties, a rise in construction is anticipated, which may make a significant contribution in that decade.

[4] For a good summary of possible remedies, see Reddaway, op. cit., especially pp. 120–135; and J. E. Meade, An Introduction to Economic Analysis and Policy, especially Part I.

introduction of pay-roll taxes.) Economists, however, frequently exaggerate the accelerated effect of a change in the level of consumption upon investment.[1] Whatever the facts on the rise, the effects of a decline of consumption will be limited to the discouragement of new investment and to the rate of disinvestment.

In a discussion of secular stagnation, it is well to refer once more to the significance of the pay-roll taxes and accumulation of reserves for the rate of interest. In the earlier discussion of this introduction, the emphasis was placed upon the effects on the rate of interest via the provision of new markets for government securities. Compulsory public savings in the first instance at least contribute toward a reduction in the rate of interest. It is necessary, however, to take into account the effects upon consumption and investment.[2] Unfavorable effects upon consumption in a period of oversaving may then account for wasted savings. Total demand falls; income declines; and via the reduction of income, savings (net) suffer. The net effects upon the rate of interest may then well be adverse despite the favorable effects associated with a reduced demand for money to satisfy the transactions motive and a rise of supply. This favorable effect is likely to be more than offset by a relative (later) reduction in the supply of money and an increase in the amounts required to satisfy the liquidity motive when consumption and income fall.

These conclusions do not of course suggest that the security program was a mistake, nor even, accepting a stagnation theory, that pay-roll taxes and a moderate reserve should be excluded. In this discussion, the thesis stands out that in a period of stagnation the tax system should not weigh too heavily on consumption.

Nevertheless, much is to be said for the pay-roll taxes. As we shall see in Part III, they do not fall wholly on consumption. Against the deflationary factors, which are considered in Part I, it is necessary to put considerations of insurance and finance. They require an association of benefits and contributions, *i.e.*, pay-roll taxes; avoidance of very uneven distribution of the tax burden over time and of excessive amounts of taxation, which are associated with current financing and repudiation of pay-roll taxes; and protection of the insured through avoidance of excessive burdens later. It is, moreover, possible to devise a tax system that includes pay-roll

[1] On these issues, see Hansen, *op. cit.;* and Part I of this book.

[2] *Cf.* LANGE, O., "The Rate of Interest and the Optimum Propensity to Consume," *Economica*, 1938, pp. 12–32; and Sec. 2.6 of this work.

taxes and yet is properly balanced between taxes on consumption and taxes on incomes. Customs duties and internal revenue taxes may be reduced, and incomes between $2,500 and $100,000 taxed much more heavily. Despite the maintenance of the schedule of pay-roll taxes provided in the Act of 1935, the proportion of consumption or indirect taxes to total taxes could be reduced below the level of the twenties.[1]

The proponents of deficit financing, in particular, have been critical of the pay-roll taxes and the reserve system. The author would be the last one to deny the need of taking into account the monetary aspects of any program. Yet it seems that the monetary repercussions have carried too much weight, and the requirements of the security program too little. Though he would not argue for a reserve of the proportions estimated under the original Social Security Act, he would favor the maintenance of the original schedule of pay-roll taxes; or at least he feels that it would have been better had the stepup in rates in 1940 been reduced rather than

---

[1] *Cf.*, however, Temporary National Economic Committee, Monograph 3, *Who Pays the Taxes?* especially pp. 6–7, 44.

TAXES AS PERCENTAGE OF INCOME—FEDERAL, STATE, AND LOCAL
Incomes
Under $500............................ 21.9
500–1,000............................ 18.0
1,000–10,000........................ Min. = 17.3 Max. = 17.9
20,000 and over...................... 37.8

TAX RECEIPTS
(In billions of dollars)

Tax	Total	(1) Direct taxes*	(2) Property	(3) Other†
Federal...............................	5.5	2.6	...	2.9
State.................................	3.8	0.5	0.2	3.1
Local‡................................	4.7	...	4.3	0.4

* Includes income, corporate-income, capital-stock, excess-profits and estate, inheritance, and gift taxes.

† Customs, excises, pay-roll, stamp, amusement, etc., primarily taxes on consumption. A sum of 6.4 billion dollars under (3), which are mostly taxes on consumption, is to be compared with 3.1 billion dollars of direct taxes, which may be considered taxes on relatively high incomes. Property taxes may be considered in part a tax on high incomes and in part a tax assessed directly or indirectly on consumers.

‡ *Cf.* U. S. Department of Commerce, *Financial Statistics of Cities Having a Population of Over 100,000*, 1937, p. 3. Roughly two-thirds of the total revenue were obtained from property taxes.

Cf. also Twentieth Century Fund, *Facing the Tax Problem*, pp. 228–232. A somewhat similar picture of the regressiveness of the tax system is given; and the burden on low incomes in rural areas seems greater than in urban areas.

eliminated. Maximum rates might have been planned for 1955–1960 instead of 1949. It is possible in various ways to offset the deflationary effects of the pay-roll taxes though it is apparent that dissipation of the revenues thus received would in fact have reduced the reserves of the insured. Why not, for example, use these funds in self-liquidating projects, the government thus maintaining the desired relation of cash income and cash outgo?[1] Again, supporters of the deficit program insist upon the requirement that capital expenditures be amortized over the life of the asset. The operating budget is to carry interest and amortization charges only. Similarly, it might be required that the social security program should provide revenues which, with compound interest, will cover obligations incurred in any period of a year or, say, five years. Similar criteria applied to capital expenditures and to the social security program would require much larger taxes on pay-rolls than are now being levied.

Defense economics should be considered in conjunction with the deflationary aspects of social security. In the years 1935–1940, the tendency has been to be concerned over deficiencies of spending. Hence the criticism of pay-roll taxes. In the next few years, the problem may well be to discourage spending in private quarters. Economies of consumption, if they are to be in significant amounts, must come in part from the masses. Should, under the pressure of excessive supplies of money and strong demand for the factors, a curtailment of consumption be required, then in the overconsumption era of the forties the pay-roll taxes may become a blessing just as in the thirties they were a source of annoyance to the underconsumption school. The social security program may then have the *additional* merit of advancing the defense program.

3. FEDERAL DEFICITS IN RELATION TO THE SOCIAL SECURITY PROGRAM

The Significance of the Treasury Deficit

A failure to raise private investment adequately or (and) the marginal propensity to consume suggests the need of deficit financ-

[1] See, for example, House Report 1421 (76: 1), *Self-liquidating Projects Act of 1939*, pp. 1–5, and United States Housing Authority, *What Does the Housing Program Cost?* (1940), pp. 3–9.

ing by the Federal government. In the early years of the New Deal, the object of deficit spending seems to have been to help the needy or to prime the pump. More recently, government supporters of the spending program have emphasized the deficiency of private spending and the need to offset cyclical and secular deficiencies in private spending.[1]

It is not our purpose to enter into a lengthy discussion of the merits of deficit spending. But it is helpful to indicate the degree of disagreement and to survey the issues briefly.

In his budget message (budget of June 30, 1941), the President made the following comment:[2]

The deliberate use of Government funds and of Government credit to energize private enterprise—to put purchasing power in the hands of those who urgently needed it and to create a demand for the products of factory and farm—had a profound effect both on Government and on private incomes. The national income in 4 years rose 69 per cent, from 42 billion dollars in 1933 to 72 billion dollars in 1937, the largest absolute rise for any 4-year period in our history, not even excepting the rise during the World War. Tax revenues rose from 2 billion dollars in the fiscal year 1933 to over 5 billion dollars in the fiscal year 1937, primarily because the people had more income out of which to pay taxes. The people paid 3 billion dollars more in taxes but they had nearly 10 times more than that, or 30 billion dollars, to spend on other things. This statement deserves a headline.

Rapid progress was made toward a balanced Budget. By the calendar year 1937 excess of Government cash outgo over Government cash income had dropped to 331 million dollars.

Unfortunately, just at the time when it seemed that the Federal Government would be able safely to balance its budget on the basis of a national income of approximately 75 billion dollars, maladjustments in the economic system began to appear and caused a recession in economic activity. The recession was due to a variety of causes stemming in the main from overoptimism which led the Government to curtail its net expenditures too abruptly, and business to expand production and raise prices too sharply for consumers' purchasing power to keep pace. A large volume of unsold goods piled up.

[1] See GILBERT, R. V., et al., Economic Program for American Democracy, pp. 41–49, 56–74; BURNS, A. E., and D. E. WATSON, Government Spending and Economic Expansion, especially Part II; and address by Governor Eccles, Unemployment—What Shall We Do about It? May 9, 1940, mimeographed, pp. 13–15.

[2] Quoted in Temporary National Economic Committee, Monograph 20, Taxation, Recovery and Defense, pp. 53, 56.

If the recession were not to feed on itself and become another depression, the buying power of the people, which constitutes the market for the products of industry and agriculture, had to be maintained. To this end, in the spring of 1938, I recommended a further use of Government credit and the Congress acted on my recommendation.

The soundness of this realistic approach to a fiscal policy related to economic need was again strikingly demonstrated. In place of the 42-billion-dollar decline in national income that occurred from 1929 to 1932, the decline from 1937 to 1938 scarcely exceeded 8 billion dollars. In place of a 4-year period of liquidation and deflation, productive activity turned up within 9 months. By 1939, in terms of dollars, the national income closely approached, and, in terms of real production and consumption, making allowance for the lower level of prices, was equal to that of 1937.

The experience of 1938–39 should remove any doubt as to the effectiveness of a fiscal policy related to economic need.

In a recent study of the problem of government spending, two writers concluded as follows: "The fiscal folly of the 1930's was the tight-fistedness of the Government, and this penny-pinching policy launches the 1940's by reckoning battleship displacement in terms of the jobs for the unemployed on public work."[1]

These authors also emphasize the niggardliness of the spending policy in terms of the expected effects via acceleration. If the spending has been substantially larger, they say, then the effects on capital expansion would have come up to expectations. In fact, they put the maximum additional investment required to attain full employment at 7 billion dollars above the 1937 level. After a survey of the figures of "net contribution" of the Federal government to spending and income figures for the years 1932–1937, the authors conclude that "a good part of the increases in the national income in the period 1934 to 1937 can be accounted for by public spending. . . . " In appraising the decline of 1937–1938, they maintain that "the strategic factor was in fact the sharp drop in spending in the early months of 1937."[2]

Prof. J. M. Clark is of another mind:[3]

To some, the very fact that the assumed unbalance is thought to be permanent seems to argue that Government must fill the gap. A more

[1] BURNS and WATSON, *op. cit.*, p. 158.

[2] *Ibid.*, p. 102, *cf.* pp. 102–106.

[3] National Resources Planning Board, *The Structure of the American Economy: Toward Full Use of Resources*, pp. 25–26. *Cf.* a similar view by N.I.C.B. quoted in Temporary National Economic Committee, Monograph 20, *Taxation, Recovery and Defense*, p. 20.

valid judgment would seem to be the opposite; namely, that such an attempt would be a temporary palliative only, leading to a worse condition in the end; and that only a temporary unbalance could be successfully offset in this way.

Business psychology being what it is at present, the accumulation of deficits seems to have reached a point at which it now deters as much private investment as Government can make, or more. This would be still more strongly true of further deficits on a basis of policy pointing to indefinite future increase, and not limited to a temporary emergency. . . .

. . . If the process did not stop, and if there really is a chronic tendency to underspending to be neutralized, the result would apparently be a cumulative pyramiding of debt, resting on continued confidence in the continued willingness of Government to go on pumping borrowed funds in and out in increasingly astronomical quantities. As a permanent reliance for a sound economic system, this picture seems thoroughly unconvincing. At some point it seems more certain that the sheer arithmetic of the operation would break down the psychology on which it rested. . . .

Our sympathies are on the whole with the spenders. It is granted that they sometimes underestimate the importance of maintaining the confidence of business in the government's economic policies, and, therefore, they underestimate the adverse effects of public spending on private motivation. Furthermore, they occasionally fail to distinguish the milieu in which deficit spending is to be applauded and that in which it is to be scorned. Profs. Burns and Watson, for example, are wrong to insist on a continuance of large deficits in civil fields once the defense program gets under way.[1] Again, since the interest charge is a transfer, they are inclined to dismiss the expenditures on debt servicing as though they were of no account. This is a mistake. A country saddled with a debt of 100 billion dollars is worse off than one without any debt. (The net effects of the expenditures of the 100 billion dollars are left out of account here.) Finally, they cannot have their cake and eat it. Their objective is to raise income; but the attainment of this objective in itself brings in its train new difficulties. The net contributions of the Treasury decline as tax revenues automatically respond to higher incomes. They should not then, on the one hand, praise the spending program and, on the other hand, be critical of the decline in net contributions, which results ultimately from the spending program.

The errors of the opponents are more serious. They overestimate the burden of the interest charge on the Federal debt, which

[1] *Op. cit.*, pp. 155–158.

even today is but 1 to 2 per cent of the national income. Applying the analysis which is appropriate to an economy with full employment to an economy with large unemployment, they fail to allow for the rise of income and the gains in tax capacity accompanying the increase of deficit spending. Additional expenditures may, therefore, be self-financing, providing income that will finance them: the income may come in part out of the new investments and in part through later effects of the new spending. Even if the expenditures are not self-financing in this sense, they may still be justified on account of the favorable effects upon private income and the extension of desirable fields of public activity, which may yield small economic gains or ones that are not easily measured. Who is to say that the amount of expenditures on social welfare of the year 1932 is the optimum amount? Prof. Clark, it seems, leaves many of these considerations out of account.

One final comment. Assume that the debt rising at the rate of 5 billion dollars annually approaches 250 billion dollars in 1980, the interest charge then being 7 to 8 billion dollars, and income remaining at the 1940 level. A serious situation indeed. Yet is the present generation to be condemned for passing on large risks that future generations will have to face 40 to 60 years from now if even larger dangers are averted now?

We turn now briefly to a few accounting problems. It is only necessary to cover interest charges on the public debt and amortization on self-liquidating projects, and even these charges may be postponed.[1] Furthermore, the net rise of debt is not nearly so large as is commonly assumed if proper accounting methods are used. Thus the Federal government spent 50.7 billion dollars in the years 1931–1938. Of this total, 14.5 billion dollars had been invested in assets, and 2.9 billion dollars of the assets had been amortized, net investments valued at 11.7 billion dollars being left.[2] This total is classified as follows:

[1] HANSEN, A. H., testimony, *Hearings*, Temporary National Economic Committee (76: 1), 1940, Investigation of Concentration of Economic Power, Part 9, pp. 3837 *ff*. and pp. 4090–4092; *cf.* also COLM, G., "Comments on Extraordinary Budgets," *Soc. Research*, 1938, pp. 173–177; HICKS, *op. cit.*, Chap. XVII.

[2] *Hearings*, Temporary National Economic Committee (76: 1), 1940, Investigation of Concentration of Economic Power, pp. 4090–4092. The figures for net plant and estimated amortization of plant given on the chart, p. 4090, are not exactly the same as those in the table. Amortization includes write-offs on loans and investments in government corporations and credit agencies. This explains the difference between the figure in the text and the one in the table.

TABLE VIII.—CAPITAL INVESTMENTS OF FEDERAL GOVERNMENT, 1931–1938*

(In billions of dollars)

1. Loans and investments in government corporations and credit agencies (net).. 3.4
2. Total self-liquidating projects............................. 0.4
3. Public works, nonrevenue (excluding work relief)........... 5.3
4. Two-fifths of work relief................................ 3.4
5. Three-quarters of CCC................................... 1.5

Total nonrevenue public works (3–5)................ 10.2
Amortization.................................... 2.4

Net 3–5.. 7.8

Net capital investments (1 + 2 + net 3–5)......... 11.6

* *Hearings*, Temporary National Economic Committee (76: 1), 1940, Investigation of Concentration of Economic Power, pp. 4090–4092.

A statement of the Federal, state, and local positions is even more reassuring:

TABLE IX.—INCREASE IN INVESTMENTS AND DEBT OF FEDERAL, STATE, AND LOCAL GOVERNMENTS, 1931–1938*

(In billions of dollars)

Net construction.. 16.5
Proprietary interest of the Federal government.............. 3.3
General fund balance...................................... 6.3

Estimated total of these increases........................ 26.1
Rise of public debt...................................... 24.8

* *Hearings*, Temporary National Economic Committee (76: 1), 1940, Investigation of Concentration of Economic Power, p. 4149.

Too much should not, however, be read into these statements. A large part of the 16.5 billion dollars of net construction is not self-liquidating.[1] It undoubtedly does contribute indirectly to national income, though its net increase may not be so large as the annual cost of interest and amortization. Whatever its contribution in this sense, however, so long as the government covers interest and amortization out of current revenues and will continue to do so *without serious effects on the economy*, there is no reason for concern.

In assessing the net effect of the government's financial operations, one should go beyond a consideration of the Treasury deficit, *i.e.*, the excess of expenditures (exclusive of debt retirement) over receipts. It has, for example, been pointed out that the Treasury may receive more cash than it disburses and yet show a deficit. Thus, the government may incur a deficit of 1 billion dollars and yet receive (net) 1 billion dollars in cash. Trust funds, for example, may accumulate 2 billion dollars in excess of disbursements. Treasury contributions to the amount of spending are not fully revealed

[1] On these issues, see Colm, *op. cit.*, pp. 168–181. Dr. Colm says, for example, that the contribution to national productivity is of more significance than the issue of self-liquidation (*ibid.*, pp. 173–174).

by an examination of budgetary receipts and expenditures. It is necessary to adjust the budget figures for expenditures that do not contribute toward income and for receipts that are not to be considered deductions from incomes; and in so far as they are not revealed in the budget, it is necessary to consider the net effect of operations of trustee funds.[1] Under this procedure, transfers to trust accounts which are not currently spent are not included as expenditures, and expenditures for refinancing are not included as contributions to income by the Treasury. Accumulations of cash by the trust funds (net) are then, if not already covered as receipts, to be deducted from the contributions of the Treasury.[2] It would be well if we could go farther. For example, one might inquire into alternative uses of money raised by the Treasury: would the money have been hoarded otherwise? If the answer is yes, the Treasury tax (say) does not reduce income. Would the money have been spent if not taken by the Treasury? If the answer is yes, then quite properly, the amount collected is to be deducted from Treasury expenditures in order to obtain the net contribution.

In an analysis of the *cash* or *money* balance, the social security program requires careful consideration. In addition to what has already been said on this issue, Part I is devoted to many aspects of these problems. A discussion of the social security program's contribution to receipts, expenditures, and deficits concludes this section.

The Significance of the Social Security Program for the Treasury Contributions to Spending

1. Let us consider first the receipts and expenditures under the social security program.[3]

It is clear then that over the period 1937–1940, *i.e.*, the period in which financial transactions have been important, the total expenditures for unemployment and old-age insurance have been but 26 per cent of receipts, and even for 1940 but 35 per cent. Under

---

[1] National Resources Committee, *The Structure of the American Economy*, pp. 94–95; *cf*. JOHNSON, *op. cit.*, pp. 221–223.

[2] Two possibilities may be discussed.

　　a. A trust fund collects 1 billion dollars cash (*net*). The account is not included in the budget. Then from Treasury net contributions, 1 billion dollars should be deducted.

　　b. The Treasury collects cash for a trust account and appropriates the amount collected by the trust account. It is not, however, spent by the trust fund. Then these expenditures by the *Treasury* should not be included as net contributions.

[3] Based on material in *Treas. Dept. Bull.*, August, 1940, p. 12.

the Amendments of 1939, they will, however, be a larger part of total receipts. But we leave out of account the favorable effects upon receipts from pay-roll taxes and the savings on disbursements that will result from the defense program; and, as we shall see, the excess of payments under the noncontributing system is a relevant consideration here.

TABLE X.—RECEIPTS AND EXPENDITURES UNDER SOCIAL SECURITY PROGRAM, 1937–1940

Deposits in	Fiscal years	Billions of dollars Rows 1–2	Fiscal year	Billions of dollars Rows 1–2
Receipts, deposits in unemployment trust fund and appropriations to old-age and survivor's trust fund*	1937–1940	4.47	1940	1.47
Expenditures, unemployment and old age†	1937–1940	1.17	1940	0.51
Per cent of expenditures to receipts	1937–1940	26	1940	35

* Unemployment Trust Fund includes deposits by states and also receipts of Railroad Retirement Fund (interest is excluded). Receipts of the Old Age Fund are given by appropriations to this account. The actual receipts are given substantially by appropriations.

† Expenditures are *not* given by appropriations of the Federal government but by actual disbursements under the program (see p. 42).

2. Now we turn to expenditures over the period 1937–1940.[1]

TABLE XI.—EXPENDITURES OF FEDERAL GOVERNMENT AND ANALYSIS OF SOCIAL SECURITY EXPENDITURES, 1937–1940

	Fiscal years 1937–1940		1940	
	Billions of dollars	Per cent of total expenditures	Billions of dollars	Per cent of total expenditures
(a) General Federal expenditures	31.4	....	8.74	
(b) Federal expenditures for social security and disbursements (largely by states) for unemployment insurance	4.08	13.0	1.43	16.4
(c) Benefit payments, both programs	1.17	3.7	0.51	5.8
(d) Grants to states	1.12	3.6	0.36	4.1
(e) c + d	2.29	7.3	0.87	10.0

It is well to observe the following facts:

1. That the expenditures under the social security program relative to all expenditures have been small even in the years 1937–1940 when the program was well launched.

[1] Based on material in *Treas. Dept. Bull.*, August, 1940, pp. 5, 12. General expenditures include expenditures for recovery and relief but not expenditures of revolving funds, transfers to trust accounts, and debt retirement.

2. That the percentage of expenditures for social security to total expenditures is appreciably higher in 1940 than it was in 1937–1940.

3. That for the analysis of the deflationary aspects of the social security program, (b) gives misleading results, but (c), (d), and (e) are of significance. The first, (b), includes as expenditures appropriations to the old-age account although this money has largely not been disbursed. The second, (c) is especially significant, for the relevant variables are receipts from pay-roll taxes and actual disbursements under the two programs which provide pay-roll taxes. Finally (d) and (e) should be considered if *total* expenditures under the Social Security Act are to be included; but part of the required funds come out of general revenue.

In relation to the issue of deflation, the following is also of some interest.

TABLE XII.—RECEIPTS FROM SOCIAL SECURITY TAXES AND NET WELFARE PAY-
MENTS, FISCAL YEARS 1937–1940*

(In billions of dollars)

Receipts:
1. Federal insurance contributions, Federal unemployment
insurance taxes, carrier taxes, deposits in unemployment
trust fund...................................... 5.3
Disbursements:
2. a. Under these programs........................... 2.6†
3. b. Recovery and relief............................. 10.8
4. c. Veterans' administration......................... 2.3
5. Net "welfare" payments (2 + 3 + 4 − 1)............. 10.3

* The author is indebted to Dr. Eleanor Dulles of the Social Security Board for the table from which these figures have been derived.

† *Cf.* (e) in Table XI which is somewhat less inclusive.

It is to be observed that the inclusion *here* of *all* expenditures for recovery and relief may be questioned by some; that, on the other hand, the exclusion from "recovery and relief" of such items as CCC and AAA in the early years of the New Deal may be objectionable to others; that the inclusion of veterans' administration may not be universally approved; and, finally, that receipts and expenditures of state and local governments do not receive attention. Nevertheless, this table brings out the fact that exclusive attention to the old-age and unemployment insurance programs does not yield a complete picture of the issues of deficits and deflation in relation to security programs.

We may consider a somewhat longer period though it is well to keep in mind that the operations under the 1935 programs were not well under way until 1937. Over the first seven years of the New

Deal (1933–1939), the expenditures under the social security program do not seem to have been of great significance when compared with expenditures on relief and public works.

TABLE XIII.—VARIOUS CATEGORIES OF FEDERAL EXPENDITURES, 1933–1939 AND 1931–1938, AS PERCENTAGE OF TOTAL EXPENDITURES

Total Federal Expenditures

Fiscal years 1931–1938........................ 58.1 billion dollars*
Fiscal years 1933–1939........................ 52.8 billion dollars†

Percentage of Expenditures

Fiscal years 1933–1939‡		Fiscal years 1931–1938*	
Item	Per cent	Item	Per cent
Relief and all public works including work-relief...............	34§	Extraordinary expenditures: public works and unemployment relief, loans, subscription to stock, etc.....................	34
Interest on debt................	11		
AAA and other forms of aid.....	11‖		
National defense...............	10	Agricultural adjustment........	4¶
Veterans' administration........	8	Defense......................	10
Social security (inclusive of railroad retirement).............	4.4	Veterans' administration.......	14
		Other ordinary, including social security (does not include interest on public debt or legislative, judicial and civil expenses)....	4**

* Calculated from *Hearings*, Temporary National Economic Committee (76: 1), 1940, Investigation of Concentration of Economic Power, p. 4145.

† Calculated from *Treas. Dept. Bull.*, June, 1940, pp. 13, 15.

‡ All expenditures on relief and recovery were 18.4 billions, or 35 per cent of all expenditures. It should be observed, however, that the AAA, CCC, interest on debt, and some public works are not included under this category but under general expenditures.

§ Includes public works, Works Progress Administration, work relief, and relief.

‖ AAA, CCC and aid to agriculture and home owners.

¶ Secretary of the Treasury, *Ann. Rept.*, June 30, 1938, p. 418.

** It is interesting to compare these figures with similar ones for *all* governments for the fiscal year 1938. *Per cent* of all expenditures (18.2 billion dollars): education, highway and streets, police and other protection, and health and hospitals, 30.0; defense, 8.9; interest, 9.0; relief, welfare, and security, 17.0; net additions (exclusive of interest) to social security funds, 5.5. Temporary National Economic Committee, Monograph 20, p. 49.

Future Expenditures and Deficits

In the future, the issue of expenditures on social security will become much more important. Some space is devoted to these problems in the last two chapters of this book. Ultimate benefits under the old-age insurance program may reasonably be put at 5 billion dollars per year. In making this estimate, an allowance is made for errors on the optimistic side (*i.e.*, receipts relative to disbursements are put too high) by actuaries, for further liberalization of benefits and extension of coverage. Certainly the history of the last few years justifies these revisions. In addition, an estimate of increased outlays of 1 billion dollars is to be made for other parts of the security program. In this connection, the pressure to introduce Federal subsidization of state unemployment insurance funds, the trend toward health and permanent disability insurance, and the continued serious agitation of Townsendites are to be noted. In fact, rumors persist in Washington that the administration would have supported further extension of unearned benefits had not the defense program suddenly required all available resources.[1] Add to these outlays a future debt charge of *but* 2 billion dollars and additional expenditures for defense (in excess of an average outlay of little more than 1 billion dollars in the fiscal years 1936–1940) of *but* 3 billion dollars. In the fiscal year 1940, total revenues were less than 6 billion dollars and social security taxes yielded 1.4 billion dollars. In the future (say in the fifties and later years), the Treasury is required to find additional revenue of 3 to 4 billion dollars to cover ordinary deficits and, furthermore, perhaps 9 billion dollars to cover *additional* outlays on social security (5 billion dollars), servicing of debts (2 billion dollars), and national defense.[2] (In view of the anticipated rise above normal of 5 and 14 billion dollars in the fiscal years 1941 and 1942, respectively, 2 billion dollars additional even for a long period of time is a most modest estimate of the rise of annual expenditures for defense.)

Where is the money to be found? In this discussion, it is assumed that as defense expenditures decline after the forties, the cost of debt servicing, social security, and other services will rise. Two or three billion dollars may be obtained from pay-roll taxes and earn-

---

[1] It is interesting to note that on May 9, 1940, Governor Eccles proposed a universal noncontributory pension, *op. cit.*, pp. 17–18. *Cf.* E. E. Witte, "The Approaching Crises in Old Age Security," *Am. Labor Legislation Rev.*, 1940, pp. 115–123. Prof. Witte makes clear the current strength of the Townsend movement, its support in New Deal circles, and the commitments of the major parties. According to him, a reasonable pension (age 65 and over) of $40 for those unmarried and $60 for married couples would cost the Treasury the total amount collected in all taxes 1939–1940 (5 to 6 billion dollars).

[2] Current estimates put defense expenditures at 6.5 billion dollars in the fiscal year 1941 and as much as 15 billion dollars in 1942.

Over the years 1920–1934, the employers and workers contributed but one-half of the total outlays of the British Unemployment Fund. It is well, however, to consider the large drain of expenditures for relief from this fund. A. C. C. Hill, Jr., and I. Lubin, *The British Attack on Unemployment*, pp. 226–227; *cf.* here N. Y. State, Temporary Emergency Relief Administration, *Aiding the Unemployed*, by H. Kraus, 1935, pp. 21–22.

ings on moderate reserves; and it is conceivable that an additional 5 billion dollars may be obtained from other direct taxes and from improvements in our tax systems. It is not easy to draw any conclusions concerning the possibility of raising large sums of money without recourse to inflation. Much depends upon the extent of the rise of revenues and the change of the tax pattern accompanying a rise of income. In any case, it is well to distinguish the immediate problem of large rises of expenditures for defense over a short period of time and the long-run problem of a large rise of expenditures on defense, public debt, and security. One may even hazard a guess that total expenditures will rise to a sum in excess of 15 billion dollars in the immediate *and in the distant future*.[1]

Possible alternatives are large economies in public expenditures, which are not easily found; a later repudiation of obligations both to bondholders and to those who have a vested interest in government trust funds; and an unexpected improvement of economic conditions, which will yield larger revenues than the government at present can reasonably anticipate. Repudiation of obligations under the social security program may be averted, however, through periodic revisions of contributions upward and benefits downward. Should the pressure of excessive deficits over a period, not of 10 years but of 30 to 40 years, result in a large inflation, however, a disguised repudiation of part of the obligations will be effected. The insured are not easily protected from the effects of an unstable currency though they will probably be treated more liberally than most holders of government bonds.[2] We turn to crucial considerations in the next paragraphs.

The position may not become critical if technological advance continues at the rate of recent years, if full employment is reestablished and, therefore, if losses resulting from long periods of heavy unemployment are averted.[3] Full employment is obtainable, according to various estimates, at an income of 80 to 115 billion dollars. (Price levels are assumed to remain relatively stable.)[4] That the income estimated for 1940 is in excess of 70 billion dollars, despite a continued high level of unemployment, suggests that the unem-

---

[1] These issues are discussed more fully in Chaps. 11 and 12.

[2] *Cf.* International Labor Office, *The Investment of the Funds of Social Insurance Institutions*, 1939, pp. 121–125.

[3] *Cf.* REDDAWAY, *op. cit.*, pp. 195, 206–207.

[4] *Cf.*, for example, National Resources Committee, *Patterns of Resource Use*, preliminary ed., 1939, pp. 31–35; and Hansen, A. H., *Fiscal Policy and Business Cycles, passim*.

ployment problem may not be solved at an income of less than 100 billion dollars. Let us assume, however, that the full-employment income is 80 to 90 billions. Savings of a few billion dollars on relief, insurance, and works may then be achieved; and a rise in direct tax rates which will now be assessed upon larger incomes may well yield the additional income required to cover current deficits plus those associated with increased outlays on social security, defense, and further debt. The total Federal tax charge required to balance the budget may, however, attain a figure of 15 billion dollars or more.

The position is frequently taken that a rise of income automatically induces a rise of tax receipts. Governor Eccles has commented on that fact frequently; and the point has been made relative to the financing of the defense program. It is important to point out, however, that a rise of tax receipts offsets to some extent the stimulative effects of the spending program. If a rise of deficits stimulates, a reduction depresses. One may recall the charge that a reduction in deficits induced the decline of 1937–1938; but this was the outcome of a rise of income.[1]

It may be of interest to refer to some estimates made by experts in 1937 for the forties, which give some indication of the rate at which new demands have been made upon the government. Pessimistic estimates of incomes were put at 60 billions and the rise of debt in the forties at 1.5 billion dollars annually. Optimistic estimates put income at 80 billion dollars and the retirement of debt at 1.2 to 1.7 billion dollars annually. Revenues in the forties will rise greatly above the optimistic estimate of 7 to 7.5 billion dollars; but despite the fact that the income level now (late 1940) is about 80 billion dollars, the anticipated expenditures in the forties may be reasonably estimated at 15 billion dollars or more, not at the optimistic figure of 5.8 billion dollars as estimated in 1937.[2] (Actually, the defense program is likely to raise expenditures in the *early* forties to an amount in excess of 20 billion dollars.)

[1] Governor Eccles points out that at an income of 40 billion dollars, the Federal government obtained 2.1 billion dollars; but 5 years later (1937) the income was 70 billion dollars and the tax yield 6.2 billion dollars. *Economic Balance and a Balanced Budget*, Public Papers of M. S. Eccles, edited by R. L. Weissman, p. 177.

[2] Twentieth Century Fund, *The National Debt and Government Credit*, pp. 141–155; *cf.* also their *Facing the Tax Problem*, Chap. 7. For some comments on the tax capacity of state and local governments see Withers, *op. cit.*, pp. 89–91, 101–103, and M. Newcomer, *An Index of Taxpaying Ability of States and Local Governments;* Social Security Board, *The Fiscal Capacity of the States*, 1938, especially pp. 1–11.

4. Problems of Integration—Relation of Wages, Benefits, and Relief

Programs as diverse as the works program, rural resettlement, the AAA, wages and hours legislation, child-labor protection, housing, refinancing of mortgages, devaluation may all contribute toward the well-being of the unemployed and the underprivileged. Space does not permit a discussion of these programs or adequate comments on their relation to our problems.[1] A few issues only will be taken up. Even the interdependence of different parts of the security program proper is not always evident to investigators.[2]

Maintenance and even increases of wages, despite large amounts of unemployment, has been one of the objectives of the New Deal. The National Recovery Act, the National Labor Relations Act, the Wages and Hours Act, various relief acts, and the Social Security Act, all were to contribute or actually contributed toward the achievement of this goal.[3] In its programs for aid to the unemployed, the Roosevelt government relied in the early years largely on relief, which, it has been held, made it easier for labor to hold out for higher wages. By 1935, the Federal government definitely committed itself to a works program for the employables, a relief program for the unemployables who were to be turned back to state and local governments, and a social security program which

---

[1] Hearings, Ways and Means Committee, House of Representatives, Economic Security Act, 1939, p. 68; U. S. Senate Document, Advisory Council on Social Security, First Report, 1938, pp. 11–12; Burns, E. M., "Financial Aspects of Social Security Act," Am. Econ. Rev., March, 1936, pp. 12–22; Clague, E., et al., "The Economic Aspects of an Integrated Social Security Program," Proc. Am. Econ. Assoc., 1936.

[2] Hearings, Ways and Means Committee, House of Representatives, Social Security, 1939, p. 1857; Norton, T. L., Old Age and the Social Security Act, p. 76.

[3] On these aspects of the policies of the government, see Social Security Board, Ann. Rept., 1939, pp. 104–105; PWA, America Builds: The Record of PWA, especially pp. 1–94; WPA, A Survey of Relief and Security Programs, 1938, pp. 1–49. Trends in Relief Expenditures, 1910–1935, 1937, pp. 11–38, 56–74; WPA, Inventory: An Appraisal of Results of the WPA, 1938, pp. 4–10; WPA, Report on Progress of the WPA Program, 1938, pp. 1–8, 39–47; Ibid., 1939, pp. 1–34, 108–115, 131–135; U. S. Treasury, Report Showing the Financial Status of Funds Provided in E.R.A. Acts 1935 . . . 1938, p. 1; National Resources Committee, Division of Costs and Responsibility for Public Works, 1938, especially Sec. 1 by S. E. Leland; and the monthly reports of FERA; Williams, op. cit.; Gill, op. cit. These items and others referred to in this introduction should be examined for a fuller discussion of wage and hour policies, distribution of costs between Federal and other governments, the relative merits of relief, insurance, and works programs.

was to take care of the old and temporarily unemployed and stimulate state and local governments to assume their new responsibilities. Following the recession of 1937, the government once more proclaimed the principles enunciated in 1935, supplementing these policies with other aggressive measures aimed to increase the amount of credit and purchasing power. In his message of Apr. 14, 1938, the President revealed a three-fold attack: a rise of appropriations; an increase of bank credit; a rise of purchasing power through loans, amendments to the Housing Act, and the like.[1]

In the following figures, one will find evidence of the change of policy announced in 1935:[2]

TABLE XIV.—FEDERAL, STATE, AND LOCAL FUNDS USED FOR RELIEF AND WORKS PROGRAMS

	Billions of dollars	Per cent of total		
		Public works	Works program*	Direct assistance
1933–1935	9.3	29	25	44
1936–1938	15.9	32	47	19

* Sponsors (state and local governments, etc.) have contributed a minimum of 10 per cent of project expenditures of the WPA in the fiscal year 1936 and a maximum of 26 per cent in the fiscal year 1940 (through February). House Report 2186, *Appropriations for Work Relief, and Relief, Fiscal Year 1941*, p. 7.

Undoubtedly any support given to the unemployed encourages them in their efforts to maintain wages. Opponents of the New Deal have, however, made too much of this general line of argument. Relief at the relatively high level of $30 per month is not likely to keep labor off the market.[3] This is not to deny that a significant proportion of those in receipt of relief have not been members of

[1] *Soc. Sec. Bull.*, May, 1938, p. 57.

[2] Calculated from *Hearings*, Temporary National Economic Committee (76: 1), 1940, Investigation of Concentration of Economic Power, p. 225. *Cf.* REED, E. F., "Relation of Unemployment Insurance to Relief in the United States," *Soc. Service Rev.*, 1939, p. 65; WPA, *Report on Progress of the WPA Program*, June 30, 1939, pp. 132–135.

[3] *Cf.*, however, Report Made to the Pilgrim Trust, *Men with ut Work*, 1938, pp. 169–170, 179, 201–212. Here a careful survey of British conditions reveals that a significant number of workers, who receive benefits or aid, refuse to seek work. In fact, the explanation is the payment of assistance which is larger than potential earnings. *Cf.* also BAKKE, E. W., *The Unemployed Man*, pp. 83–88; and Political and Economic Planning, *op. cit.* pp. 31, 163. The difficulty of imposing less satisfactory conditions for the unemployed than for the employed is discussed in the latter.

the labor market for many years. Undoubtedly those who are not members of the labor market make no attempts to obtain work when buttressed by public funds; but they do not seek work in any case. Perhaps similar attacks on the works programs are not without some justification. Even here, however, the payment of a *security wage*, which has been considerably less than full-time earnings in similar occupations in private industry, makes public employment unattractive when private employment is available.[1] Payment of *prevailing* wage rates, when hours of work are kept down to the number required to obtain the security wage, is not likely to contribute greatly to the maintenance of wages at an excessive level. Latterly there has been a tendency to increase the hours required to earn the security wage, thus depressing wage rates below the prevailing rates, and to take other measures to force workers into private industry.[2]

One might conclude from the studies revealing the changing composition of relief recipients that wages are preferred to relief.[3] A study of the Pilgrim Trust of Great Britain is not, however, so reassuring. Since 1929, there has been a shocking rise in the proportion of men unemployed for long periods; and the improvement since 1932 has been much greater in short-period than in long-period unemployment.[4] There is, moreover, evidence in American studies that unemployment for long periods of time is quite common. Thus a Massachusetts study of WPA workers reveals that but 40 per cent

[1] *Cf.* REED, *op. cit.*, pp. 66–67. In a recent month, the wage loss was estimated at four times the payments of relief, unemployment benefits, and wages on works projects.

[2] See Public Resolution No. 24, 76th Congress, *Joint Resolution Making Appropriations for Work Relief and Relief*, 1940, especially Secs. 15–17; *Report on Progress of the WPA Program*, June 30, 1939, p. 13; House Report 2186, *Appropriations for Work Relief*, etc., 1941, pp. 9–11. For a critical appraisal of the WPA program, which arises from a more critical attitude toward public spending, consult the House investigation. (House Report 2187, *Investigation of WPA*, May 15, 1940, especially, p. 4.)

[3] It has been estimated that in one year (1935–1936) the maximum number in receipt of unemployment benefits in Great Britain was 700,000. The number of separate claims was 4 millions, however. Political and Economic Planning, *op. cit.*, p. 118.

[4] Pilgrim Trust, *Men Without Work*, pp. 6–14; *cf.* State of Michigan, *Unemployment, Relief and Economic Security*, by W. Haber and P. L. Stanchfield, 1936, pp. 162–163; *Hearings*, Senate, Special Committee to Investigate Unemployment and Relief, *Unemployment and Relief*, 1938, pp. 117–118; WPA, *Inventory: An Appraisal of Results of WPA*, 1938, pp. 9–10; R. C. DAVISON, *British Unemployment Policy: The Modern Phase*, p. 50.

had been out of work less than 1 year; and throughout the country relief workers in 1935 had on the average been out of work 2 years.[1] This is not to be taken as evidence of an unwillingness to work.[2]

The dangers of abuses arising from unemployment insurance are not great. Benefits are kept at a level substantially below the weekly wages; long waiting periods are required; duration of benefits is limited to a relatively short period each year and are related to past contributions; all state laws require registration at state employment offices as a condition of receipt of benefits; and the waiting period is increased when workers go on strike, refuse suitable work, etc.[3]

We certainly would not go so far as to argue that the availability of relief, work programs, and insurance has no effect on the reservation price of workers. Competition for jobs would, indeed, be keener if the unemployed faced the alternative of starvation.[4] There are two issues, however. The first is, do workers prefer relief or work under the WPA or insurance benefits to private employment? The answer here is no in most cases, though the situation may become worse if large amounts of unemployment continue to prevail for many years. The second question is that if resources under these programs were not available, would they offer their services at lower wages than they actually do? The answer here is yes.[5] It does not follow, however, given the imperfections of the labor market, that they will succeed both in depressing wages significantly and increasing the total wage bill. And it is not clear, as we shall see (Chap. 15), that a general reduction of wage rates will improve the economic situation.

[1] GILL, op. cit., pp. 127–128, p. 179.

[2] Cf. GILBOY, E. W., Applicants for Work Relief, 1940, especially Chap. IX, pp. 155–157. Mrs. Gilboy summarizes American evidence admirably. Cf. also E. F. Reed, "What Turning Relief Back to the Local Community Meant in Cincinnati," Soc. Service Rev., March, 1938, pp. 10–19.

For a recent study of Canadian experience which discusses the incidence of unemployment, e.g., length of time and numbers sharing it, see L. C. Marsh, Canadians In and Out of Work, Part III, especially pp. 369–371.

[3] See especially Social Security Board, Comparison of State Unemployment Laws as of March 1, 1940, Parts III–V; also see E. Burns, "Unemployment Insurance," Soc. Work Year Book, 1939, pp. 449–457. Social Security Board, Principles Underlying Disqualification for Benefits in Unemployment Compensation, Part III.

[4] Cf. SLICHTER, S. H., "The Impact of Social Security Legislation upon Mobility and Enterprise," Proc. Am. Econ. Assoc., 1940, pp. 56–57; WITHERS, op. cit., pp. 115–116; and HILL and LUBIN, op. cit., p. 258.

[5] Cf. WILLIAMS, G., The State and the Standard of Living, pp. 338–339.

It is desirable that potential members of the labor market should be confronted with less satisfactory conditions when unemployed or when employed by the government under relief or recovery programs than when in private employment.[1] Furthermore, a logical structure of payments and working conditions is required under the various programs of government. *Ceteris paribus*, unemployment benefits should ordinarily be higher than relief payments, and less than wages.[2] When need is the primary guide, however, as it is likely to be under relief, a large family with no members employed may well receive amounts in excess of what would have been obtained under the insurance program. Other difficulties arise in coordinating the various programs. Payment under work programs may well be in excess of insurance benefits.[3] The insured then find themselves embarrassed when they are eligible for benefits and find themselves disqualified under work programs.

Another issue is the propriety of including insurance benefits in estimates of income of those who seek relief. In fact, those in receipt of benefits are generally granted relief although the exchange of information is unusual.[4] Finally, anomalies frequently arise under the noncontributory old-age assistance and contributory old-age insurance programs. It has been possible to obtain larger payments under the former than the latter. Recent changes, which have provided a liberalization of benefits under contributory insurance, particularly in the next few years, and a tendency on the part of

[1] *Cf.* WITHERS, *op. cit.*, p. 55; *Report on Progress of the WPA Program*, June 30, 1939, p. 114. Over a period of 4 years (1935–1939), workers on WPA projects have obtained from the Federal government an average amount of $52.50 monthly.

[2] Royal Institute of International Affairs, *Unemployment: An International Problem*, pp. 387–388. In one month of 1938, it was found that unemployment benefits were 50 per cent larger than relief payments in states paying benefits. There are, however, many instances where relief payments are larger than benefits. REED, E. F., "Relation of Unemployment Insurance to Relief in the United States," *Soc. Service Rev.*, 1939, pp. 63–64, 69; also see WILLIAMS, *op. cit.*, p. 100; and WITHERS, *op. cit.*, p. 55.

[3] CLAGUE, E., "The Relationship between Unemployment Compensation and Relief from a National Point of View," *Soc. Sec. Bull.*, June 1938, pp. 8, 13; *cf.* Hicks, *op. cit.*, pp. 49–50. Mrs. Hicks seems to hold the position that wage rates are kept up by the relatively high level of benefits and assistance for low-income groups.

[4] On these issues, see Social Science Research Council, Committee on Social Security, *Methods of Clearance between Unemployment Compensation and Relief Agencies*, p. 13; W. Haber and A. Jacobs, "First Attempts at Coordinating the Administration of Unemployment Compensation and Relief," *Soc. Service Rev.*, 1939, pp. 178–186.

state governments to be ungenerous in providing aid, reduce the possibilities of more generous payments under the noncontributory program than under the contributory program.[1]

5. PROBLEMS OF INTEGRATION—THE COST TO BE BORNE BY INSURANCE

Another problem of integration is the proper allocation of the costs of economic distress to the various programs. At the outset it may be said that one should not put too great a load on unemployment insurance. The analogy of the Blanesburgh Committee (on Unemployment Insurance, 1927) with fire insurance seems to us to confuse the issues. "It is the damage done by the fire, and not the number of fire insurance premiums, which settles the compensation payable by a fire insurance company."[2] In reply, it may be said that the size of the premium has something to do with the payment of damages.

Obviously, the unemployment insurance program should not be required to carry the full load of seasonal unemployment; the semi-permanent unemployed, who have been the victims of technological change or secular movements in demand; the unstable industries; and the unemployed who are not ordinarily attached to the labor market. State administrator Haber, for example, expects too much of an insurance scheme when he proposes that it take care of the seasonally unemployed in the Detroit area. Over the years 1920–1935, an average of 40 per cent of workers employed at the peak of each year suffered unemployment for one month or more.[3] It is

---

[1] See, for example, DOUGLAS, P. H., *Social Security in the United States*, pp. 294–296; *Hearings*, Ways and Means Committee, House of Representatives, *Social Security*, 1939, pp. 808–809, 1133; CLAGUE, E., "The Economic Aspects of an Integrated Social Security Program," *Proc. Am. Econ. Assoc.*, 1936.

[2] Quoted in A. C. C. Hill, Jr., and I. Lubin, *The British Attack on Unemployment*, p. 178. *Cf.* E. W. Bakke, *Insurance or Dole*, pp. 106–107. Is the term "insurance" to be used when payments do not vary with risk and when there is little correlation between payments and benefits?

[3] State of Michigan, Haber and Stanchfield, *op. cit.*, 1936, pp. 13, 147. On this and related issues also consult Social Security Board, *Ann. Rept.*, 1939, pp. 14, 77; Social Security Board *Social Security in America*, 1937, pp. 9–10; W. S. Woytinsky, *Seasonal Variations in Employment in the United States*, pp. 3–8; W. Haber and J. J. Joseph, "Unemployment Compensation," *Appraising the Social*

interesting, however, that under the unemployment insurance program, benefit rights had been exhausted, prior to reemployment, in the automobile industry in Michigan in but 33 per cent of all cases as compared with 46 per cent for all benefit cases. In these years (1938–1939) however, large declines were soon followed by marked improvement.[1]

Equally serious with the danger of excessive burdens for insurance is the danger of inadequate contributions by compulsory insurance programs. (1) Coverage may be restricted. Even in 1939, coverage under unemployment insurance was but 28 millions, or little more than one-half of the gainfully employed.[2] (2) The issue of ungenerous scales of benefits may arise. Unfortunately, the American system allows the states much latitude in the determination of schedules of benefits. Many states have been tempted to increase reserves at the expense of an adequate pattern of benefits. Furthermore, where unemployment is of large proportions, the state has no alternative but to pay modest benefits or increase contributions. A rise of contribution rates much in excess of 3 per cent is not likely to be popular; for states with limited resources and large amounts of unemployment, the dangers are insolvency or niggardly schedules of benefits. It is, therefore, not surprising to find increasing sentiment for Federal subsidies, reinsurance of state funds, and the like.[3] Again, in the process of accumulation of reserves, states are inclined to demand downward revision of contribution rates, not an upward revision of benefits. In 1939, they barely failed in their attempts to introduce discretionary statewide reductions of contributions.[4]

By the end of the fiscal year 1939–1940, the balance of the unemployment trust fund was almost 1,725 million dollars. That the

Security Program, Annals, 1939, pp. 26–27; G. E. Bigge, "Immediate Problems of Unemployment Compensation," *Soc. Sec. Bull.,* September, 1938, pp. 3–7.

[1] STANCHFIELD, P. L., "Adequacy of Benefit Duration in Michigan, 1938–39," *Soc. Sec. Bull.,* September, 1940, pp. 22–24.

[2] Social Security Board, *Ann. Rept.,* 1939, p. 237. *Cf.* Political and Economic Planning, *Report on the British Social Services,* p. 35. In 1936, two-thirds of the occupied British population were covered by unemployment insurance.

[3] On the issue of inadequacy of benefits and methods of coping with the problem, see Haber and Joseph, *op. cit.,* p. 27; J. W. Horwitz, *The Risk of Unemployment and Its Effect on Unemployment Compensation,* Business Research Studies 21, 1938, p. 40; F. Wunderlich, "What Next in Unemployment Insurance," *Soc. Research,* 1938, pp. 38–40; *Hearings,* Ways and Means Committee, House of Representatives, *Social Security,* 1939, pp. 2466–2470; Stanchfield, *op. cit.,* pp. 19–28.

[4] House Report 728 (76:1), *On Social Security Act Amendments of 1939,* pp. 23–26; Senate Report 734, *Social Security Act Amendments,* p. 26; Social Security Board,

assets continued to grow—the rise was 570 million dollars in the depression year (fiscal) of 1938—in both good and bad periods intensified the pressure to reduce contributions and liberalize benefits.[1]

The official attitude was well expressed by Mr. Levine of the Social Security Board.[2] The actuaries who had advised on the pending legislation in 1935 had to be conservative though they had gone too far. Fortified by relatively precise information on pay-rolls, they set the contribution rates and estimated receipts first; and in order to prevent exhaustion of reserves, they were overly cautious in the proposals relative to benefit schedules. Their ignorance of unemployment experience made them overly cautious. Though reserves continued to rise, he continues, it is well to keep in mind the fact that many states were not in a strong position; and by the end of 1938 the reserves had not yet felt the strain of the payments under the benefit schedules of a fully operative program. Mr. Levine's proposal was to liberalize benefits, not reduce contributions. An expert from the *industrial* state of Michigan, however, would not liberalize benefits unless help could be obtained from the outside. Industrial states subject to large amounts of unemployment could not remain solvent if, at current tax rates, they increased benefits. In Michigan, the duration of benefits was inadequate in a year of depression, a conclusion that rested on the early exhaustion of benefits by roughly one-half of the insured.[3]

It is not easy to launch an adequate unemployment insurance program even if the government has good intentions. A thorny problem is set for the actuaries. (Actuarial problems are considered under old-age insurance in Part II, and especially Chap. 8.) They have little experience upon which to proceed; and in fact the term

---

commentary on *Unemployment Compensation Provisions of Social Security Act*, p. IV; and (for a continuance of the agitation in 1940) see Social Security Board, *Current Experience Rating Research*, 1940, pp. 8–9.

[1] *Soc. Sec. Bull.*, October, 1940, p. 77. For similar problems relative to railroad unemployment insurance, see Senate Report 1752, *Amending the Railroad Unemployment Insurance Act*, 1940, pp. 4–5; S. S. Kuznets, "Amendments to the Railroad Unemployment Insurance Act," *Soc. Sec. Bull.*, November, 1940, pp. 13–26.

[2] Social Security Board, *Unemployment Compensation Contributions, Benefits and Reserves*, 1940, "The Problem of Increasing Reserves in Unemployment Compensation," by L. Levine.

[3] *Ibid.*, "Adequacy of Benefit Payments in a Highly Industrial Area," by P. L. Stanchfield.

"insurance" is a misnomer.[1] About all that can be done is to estimate the coverage, the practical rate of pay-roll tax; and having estimated receipts, the actuaries then estimate compensable wage losses. On the basis of the anticipated revenues and compensable wage losses, they then draw up a benefit schedule. They may, for example, provide generous benefits and risk an early exhaustion of reserves. Should a major depression follow or should unemployment rise to a point where solvency of the fund is threatened, the authorities will either borrow from the government or force the unemployed to rely on relief. Another approach is to offer a conservative schedule of benefits, thus maintaining solvency. Limitations of tax receipts and a desire to keep solvent account for the modest benefit schedules now in vogue.[2]

According to estimates made by the Social Security Board, a 3 per cent tax would provide benefits for 11 weeks per year.[3] These results are derived from the experience of the years 1922–1933 and require a waiting period of 3 weeks and payment of benefits equal to 50 per cent of wages. A 5 per cent rate would yield benefits for 24 weeks. That the percentage rise of benefit period is greater than that of the increase of contribution is explained by the concentration of unemployment for relatively short periods. It is clear, however, that a 3 per cent rate yields very modest benefits; and, furthermore, states with heavy unemployment cannot afford to be so generous as the foregoing figures indicate. Thus the average unemployment (percentage of compensable labor force) is put at 27.5 per cent for the years 1930–1933; but the maximum was 36 per cent for Michigan and the minimum 19 per cent for Georgia. An indication of the burden to be borne by stable industries or by unstable industries under experience rating as well as the inadequacy of the 3 per cent rate are revealed by the varying percentage of unemployment by indus-

---

[1] *Cf.* RIETZ, H. L., "Actuarial Aspects of Unemployment Insurance," in *Stabilization of Employment*, American Association for Advancement of Science, 1933, pp. 130–151; and *Social Security in America*, pp. 9–10 and Chaps. III and IV. Mr. Rietz raises the following questions. "Are the cases of exposure to the risk of unemployment independent to a reasonable degree of approximation . . . ? Are statistical data available that would make possible a reasonable approximation to the probability required to predict . . . the number of claims . . . ?" (RIETZ, *op. cit.*, p. 135). He is skeptical of the possibility of application of insurance principles.

[2] See *Comparison of State Unemployment Compensation Laws as of Mar.* 1, 1940, Parts II–V

[3] These estimates were, however, overly cautious as Mr. Levine has indicated.

tries (estimated percentage for July, 1934, by the American Federation of Labor):

Construction	64.9
Railroads	36.2
Manufacturing	27.4
Public service	5.1

Finally, the small contribution that is likely to be made by our current insurance program is revealed in the following estimates: (Possibly unemployment experience of the future will not be so fortunate as for the years 1922–1933. The history of the years 1930–1939 gives little reason for optimism, however.)

REVENUES

1922–1933	Billions of dollars
3 per cent tax	8.7
4 per cent tax	11.9
5 per cent tax	15.0

(Assumption of pay-roll taxes in this period.)

Compensable wage loss for the years 1924–1933 was 31.8 billion dollars. In other words, the yield of a 3 per cent tax over this period of 12 years is roughly (allowance being made for the two years not covered in the figure for compensable wage losses) but one-fourth to one-fifth of the wages lost by those who have been covered.[1]

It is then important that the entire burden of relief and unemployment should not be borne by the unemployment insurance program.[2] On the assumption that the average of unemployment is 10 millions, that benefits (or relief) will be roughly one-half of the weekly wages, or $10 weekly and $500 yearly, the total cost of unemployment relief (or insurance) would be 5 billion dollars. A 3 per cent tax on a pay-roll of 30 billion dollars (three-quarters coverage of the total pay-roll of 40 billion dollars) would yield but 900 million dollars. In one month in 1938, benefit payments, according to one writer, were but 16 per cent of relief expenditures.[3] (The unemployment insurance program was not fully launched by 1938, however.)

[1] Material in the last few paragraphs from Social Security Board, (1) *Social Security in America*, 1937, pp. 57, 60, 80–87; (2) *Actuarial Factors in State Unemployment Compensation Plans*, 1936, pp. 3–14.

[2] From 1921 until quite recently the British made the mistake of loading the unemployment insurance account with excessive burdens. *Cf.* R. C. Davison, *British Unemployment Policy: The Modern Phase since* 1930, pp. 8–9, 54; P. Cohen, *Unemployment Insurance and Assistance in Britain*, pp. 20–42.

[3] REED, E. F., *op. cit.*, p. 65. In this connection, Mr. Meade has an interesting suggestion. He would automatically provide additional consumption when unemployment rises above the standard rate. The mechanism would be the creation of

6. UNEARNED BENEFITS AND THE TOWNSEND PLAN

Under the Social Security Act, old-age assistance is offered on a noncontributory basis. Both the Federal and state governments contribute toward this pension which is paid only when need is demonstrated. Although grants average $20 per month, many states pay considerably less.[1] In fact the rich states, because the Federal government matches state grants, obtain more help from the Federal government than do the poor states. One may well say that the old-age assistance program has not been so successful as had been anticipated; and if it had been more successful, the Townsend movement would have lost much of its appeal. Possibly a system of variable Federal contributions related to state fiscal capacity would result in the payment of more adequate benefits.[2] Federal grants would then be a large percentage of the total grant for the poor states and a small part for the rich states. Another possibility is the payment of a universal pension at the age of 70 irrespective of need. (The British, it will be recalled, have a noncontributory system for ages 70 and over.)[3] Still another solution is the payment to all who reach the age of 65 of an amount (say $20 to $30 monthly) that corresponds to the primary or basic element in the present contributory plan. Under contributory insurance, the annuitant would in addition receive 10 to 15 per cent (say) of his average wages plus 1 to 3 per cent (say) for each year of coverage.[4] In this manner, those who contribute will receive more than they receive now, thus making them feel that relative to the treatment accorded noncontributors they receive an additional amount commensurate with their contributions. The payment of unearned benefits monthly of

---

additional money; and generous payments would be made to all unemployed. *Op. cit.*, pp. 51–56.

[1] Payments vary from $6 to $32 per month and the percentage of those over 65 receiving aid, from 7 per cent in one state, to 54 per cent in another. A. J. Altmeyer, "Social Security in Relation to Agriculture and Rural Areas," *Soc. Sec. Bull.*, July, 1940, p. 10.

[2] GERIG, D. S., JR., "The Financial Participation of the Federal Government in State Welfare Programs," *Soc. Sec. Bull.*, January, 1940, and "Formulas for Variable Federal Grants-in-aid," *Soc. Sec. Bull.* June, 1940; WILLIAMS, *op. cit.*, pp. 205–215; Social Security Board, *Fiscal Capacity of the States: A Source Book*, 1938; WITTE, *op. cit.*, pp. 117–118.

[3] Prof. Hansen made this suggestion to me.

[4] *Cf.* MUSHKIN, S. J., "Financing Expanded Old-age Protection," Social Security Board *Memorandum*, June, 1940.

$30 to $40 (say) to all would in part be a substitute for old-age assistance now being paid and in part would involve the government in additional expenditures.

Finally, it may be said that the pressure from Townsendites is likely to result in further liberalization of unearned benefits. In 1935, the unearned benefits were relatively small; under the amendments of 1939, they became much more important and in particular for the present old, the low-income groups, and those with dependents; and in the future, liberalization will proceed further.

It is not necessary to say much about the Townsend plan. Its problems are those of the pay-as-you-go plan multiplied many times. Since the Townsend plan has played such a large part in the discussions of social security, it is imperative, however, that the main issues be discussed briefly.

There have, of course, been many Townsend plans. Perhaps the one that has attracted the most attention is one which was to be financed by a gross-transactions tax and which promised $200 monthly to approximately 10 millions aged 60 or over. Irrespective of need (with minor reservations), the pension was to be paid on the condition that the money be spent within a designated time.

It is not difficult to criticize this plan. Many have already done so.[1] Perhaps the main issue is that of revenue. Dr. Townsend's estimate of an annual revenue of 24 billion dollars is clearly excessive. It is in error in part because the tax base, *i.e.*, debits to banking accounts in 1929, includes large amounts that were not taxable under the proposed bills, and because the assumption is made that the act of taxation and the volume of transactions are independent variables. In so far as the 2 per cent tax on transactions will reduce both transactions and output (and, finally, the quantity of money), it will have a deflationary effect. In this connection, it is well to keep in mind the fact that money put at the disposal of pensioners is taken from taxpayers who then have less to spend.

---

[1] On the issues discussed here, see, for example, *Hearings*, Select Committee of House, *Old-age Pension Plans and Organizations*, 1937, especially the evidence of Drs. Doane and Hart; House Report 1 (75: 1), 1937, *Old Age Pension Plans and Organizations*, especially pp. 20–32; and *Hearings*, Ways and Means Committee, House of Representatives, *Social Security*, 1939; *Soc. Sec. Bull.*, March, 1939. Numerous witnesses appeared on behalf and against the Townsend proposals. The evidence of Drs. Dewhurst and Hart and the reports of the Twentieth Century Committee and the University of Chicago Pamphlet (the latter two reprinted here) are especially helpful. *Hearings*, Ways and Means Committee, House of Representatives, *Social Security*, 1939, pp. 785–873, 914–942.

The transactions tax would, in another sense, have an inflationary effect if their arguments were correct. The assumption implicitly made by the Townsendites is that the 24 billion dollars of pensions will be a net addition to income, and not a subtraction. But (on the assumption that the 24 billion dollars are obtained) is it possible to *increase* income thus by 30 to 40 per cent without a rise of prices? For the Townsendite, the magic of spending and a rise of velocity suggest a rise of income; but he thinks in terms of MV, not in terms of goods. Townsendites may, however, find support in recent discussions of another issue. Many in Washington today contemplate a rise of income from 70 to 100 billion dollars under the impetus of the defense program; and some even anticipate freedom from inflationary developments. This will hardly be possible, however, in the absence of price control and economies of consumption, *e.g.*, through priorities and rationing. These weapons of control would not be available under the Townsend plan. It is significant, however, that the major part of the finances required for defense are to be raised through loans not taxes. In view of the financial method to be used, the danger to the price level of a rise of income of one-third to one-half in a short time is, therefore, greater under the defense than under the Townsend program; but controls available under the former will tend to reduce inflationary effects.

The great defects of the Townsend plan arise, however, from the failure to raise the required revenue and undesirable effects on the volume of transactions.[1] Reasonable estimates put the revenues obtainable from a gross-transactions tax at 2 to 4 billion dollars. It has been estimated that in a recent year a pension of $60 would have cost 7.3 billion dollars.[2] The cost of pensions will rise rapidly in the future, moreover, as the proportion of old increases.

It is possible then for the state to pay only moderate unearned benefits. In part the resources required may come from additional employment of economic resources. Loan financing would probably be more effective in inducing a *net* rise of real income than a gross-transactions tax. Recently the Townsendites have begun to recognize some of the difficulties inherent in a gross-transactions tax.

---

[1] It is significant, however, that incomes have risen almost 100 per cent since 1932, and yet the price rise has been modest. Given a favorable attitude and appropriate financing, a substantial old-age pension program might have been carried through in 1934 without dire effects.

[2] *Hearings*, Ways and Means Committee, House of Representatives, *Social Security*, 1939, pp. 789–790; *cf.* WITTE, *op. cit.*, p. 118.

Finally, it is well to remind the reader that with limited resources it is important to use funds where they will do the most good. Let us assume that it is possible, without serious effects on the economy, to raise 4 billion dollars more and that provision has been made for the servicing of debts. (In the present world crisis, this is an academic question; for surplus resources will largely be used for defense.) Rather than allow the high-powered Townsend movement to obtain these funds, the money might be used as follows:

Health insurance.................................	1 billion dollars
Relief and work relief, additional..................	1 billion dollars
Youth administration and education, additional.....	1 billion dollars
Additional benefits under old-age assistance.........	1 billion dollars

PART I

SOCIAL SECURITY PROGRAM
IN RELATION TO OUTPUT

CHAPTER 1

ABANDONMENT OF RESERVE PRINCIPLE

1.1. THE IMPLICATIONS OF THE ABANDONMENT OF THE RESERVE PRINCIPLE

As these lines are written, the reserve plan of financing old-age insurance through the accumulation of large "earnings" reserves seems doomed. Congress, following the recommendations of the Social Security Board and the Advisory Council on Social Security, has increased the benefits to be paid in the early years and has postponed the scheduled stepup in pay-roll taxes for 1940. The reserve has been attacked from two sides, and the Treasury, which as recently as 1935 insisted upon self-sufficiency of the old-age insurance program, has reversed itself under this pressure.

The critics of the reserve plan are agreed upon only one thing, that the reserve plan should be abolished. The reasons for this, however, vary and are often inconsistent. One camp, consisting of conservative businessmen led by Republican senators, has been jockeyed into the paradoxical position of opposing what is after all the conservative method of social security financing. Apparently activated by a belief that there is evil magic in the bookkeeping arrangements of the reserve plan and concentrating upon the present burden of pay-roll taxes while neglecting future costs, they have championed a plan that is essentially deficit financing and that is likely to transfer a goodly share of the long-run burden from the low-income, laboring classes to the higher paid members of the business community.

In this respect, they have played into the hands of the ardent supporters of an expansion of the social security program and those New Dealers who disapproved of the President's and the Treasury's conservative method of financing. In contrast to the belief of Senator Vandenberg and others that the accumulation of a reserve stimulates government extravagance, this last group is opposed to the reserve on the ground that it is deflationary, that the excess tax collections are *not* matched by expenditures, and that the privately held debt does *not* grow so rapidly as it otherwise would.

[63]

A strong case can be made against the reserve principle of financing social security under modern conditions. The pros and cons will be presented more fully later. It should be observed, however, that the plan was not defeated in the political sphere on these rational grounds, but rather through a coalition of contradictory and partially irrelevant considerations. In particular, there has been a strong tendency to disregard and minimize problems of future financing. Neither the Treasury nor the Advisory Council has made any concrete suggestions for raising the required future revenues. The Council merely suggests that one-third of the cost of old-age insurance be put upon the general taxpayer. Careful perusal of congressional committee hearings on amending the act confirms the belief that few congressmen who advocate pay-as-you-go have devoted much thought to the problem of the source of future subsidies.

Thanks to the publicity that the reserve plan has received, all are well informed as to the manner in which costs will mount under the old-age insurance program. No one can be unaware of the difficulties that the government faces in financing current expenditures. Yet no group seems seriously alarmed at or interested in the problem of future financing. How can we account for this? In the first place, serious doubts must be entertained concerning the sincerity of certain conservative critics of the social security program. Many fought the introduction of social security or accepted the present program as the lesser of evils in order to head off more drastic proposals. They would welcome relief from current tax burdens even at the expense of jeopardizing the payment of future benefits.

Not all the articulate critics of the reserve plan fall under this heading. The sincerity of the majority cannot be questioned. Yet even they often have failed to take a long-run point of view. They have talked glibly of the mistakes of the reserve plan, have identified the reserve plan only with pay-roll taxation, and have gone along with those whose good faith is open to suspicion.

Although the reduction of reserves through the liberalization of early benefits under the recent amendments must be approved, the failure to increase pay-roll taxes must be regarded as significant in view of the low prevailing rates (1 per cent of pay-rolls from employer and employee). Some doubts may be raised concerning the willingness or ability of the government to raise revenue eventually for the financing of old-age benefits. It is entirely possible that the attitude of Congress toward a tax program foreshadows a future reduction of benefits promised or a failure to fulfill promises made. There is ample precedent in foreign experience for default on social security promises.

1.2. Is the Reserve Problem Solved?

A description of the evolution of the Reserve Plan of 1935 must be deferred to Chap. 6. The apparent abandonment of this plan must not be taken to mean that all reserves are to be eliminated or that a discussion of the principles involved is lacking in relevance and interest. Even under present proposals, provision is made for a contingency reserve. The chairman of the Social Security Board, following the "principle of three" (reserve to equal three times maximum yearly benefit payments), estimates required reserves at 15 billions in 1980. In addition, contingency reserves are provided to cover unemployment compensation.

Moreover, the reserve plan was abandoned under pressure of circumstances prevailing in the thirties. It is entirely possible that future conditions will change in such a manner as to strengthen the case for reserve financing and invalidate arguments against the plan. Social security involves a long-range program. It would be unwise indeed to let current fears of secular stagnation, however strongly founded, commit the nation irrevocably to any one course of action or to close discussion upon important questions of principle and practice. One may, in this connection, point to the defense program, which may require large economies of consumption. Large pay-roll taxes and reserves may be very helpful in inducing these economies.

Finally, the question of reserves deserves attention because of its relevance to fields transcending social security in importance. Throughout the great depression the assets of life insurance companies grew continuously because of a surplus of receipts over expenditures. If the growth of the social security reserve is to be condemned as deflationary, how are we to regard the growth of these funds?[1] As we have seen, the deflationary effects of the govern-

---

[1] *Hearings*, Temporary National Economic Committee (76: 1), 1940, Investigation of Concentration of Economic Power, p. 4052; *cf.* Political and Economic

mental program were at least modified by the unbalanced budgets in other departments so that there is some likelihood that the growth of private reserves served as a greater depressant than did the governmental program.[1] Can one argue that private reserves should be abolished for reasons similar to those given in favor of a pay-as-you-go policy for social security? If not, criteria of differentiation must be defined. Obviously these are all vitally important problems no less in need of analysis now than before.

1.3. REAL VERSUS FINANCIAL ASPECTS OF ALTERNATIVE PLANS

Economic theory like the world it studies passes through cycles of thought. At the present time there seems to be an unwarranted disposition to brush aside questions of finance as matters of secondary or tertiary importance. In some Washington circles it is even suggested that the choice of financial mediums is of no importance.

This swing of fashion is well illustrated by the course of thought concerning war financing. During the First World War it was frequently contended that in relying upon war loans the government was imposing upon future generations the real burdens of the war, and in relying upon taxation, they were requiring sacrifices of the contemporaneous generation. In reaction against this, economists soon began to emphasize the point that whatever the method of finance the generation carrying on the war must make the greatest sacrifice through more work and lower standards of living. That practical men did not share this view is attested by the attempts, frequently successful, to impose heavy tax burdens during the war. If the choice of financial program were deemed of little importance,

---

Planning, *Report on the British Social Services*, p. 165. The latter gives some indication not only of the deflationary effects of one type of private insurance, but also of its costliness.

[1] Introduction, Secs. 2–3. To a considerable extent, however, the growth of private reserves came from a diversion of funds which would otherwise have been saved in other forms. I should also draw attention to the fact that social and private insurance are not independent. One effect of the reduction of taxes and of social security reserves may be an acceleration of the growth of private insurance and hence reserves. Possible future nonfulfillment of social security promises may accentuate this. Therefore, as the pressure of deflation is reduced through the substitution of the pay-as-you-go method of financing old-age insurance, the net deflationary contribution of private insurance may grow.

the authorities would certainly have had recourse to much more inflation and much less taxation.

Similarly, in the early discussions of social security during the thirties financial measures and considerations received great attention. Subsequently, the evolution of thought seems to have followed the familiar war pattern. Economists now are inclined to emphasize the point that each generation must carry its own burden of social security. This has received added support from the adherents of pay-as-you-go, who naturally put emphasis on *real* aspects of the problem.

Let us turn to a closer examination of the early period of emphasis on financial aspects. In the Report to the President it was held that an excess of collections over disbursements in early years on account of old-age insurance would reduce the burden for future generations.[1] Secretary Morgenthau, concerned in 1935 over an eventual cost of 4 billions on account of new benefits under social security, proposed the redemption of the public debt and the provision of useful public works.[2] Both of these statements put obvious emphasis on fiscal aspects of the problem. Retirement of privately held debts through tax collections in excess of old-age benefits would ease future treasury problems through savings in interest. These savings could be used to lighten the financial burden of social security.

Again, it was urged that a deficit (on the basis of actuarial computation of future benefits and contributions) be incurred in the early years of operation lest the young of today support not only the old of today but also the old of the future.[3] It should be noted that this is an argument based upon financial considerations offered at the time by advocates of the pay-as-you-go plan.

[1] *Report to the President of the Committee on Economic Security*, Washington, 1935, pp. 29-32.

[2] *Hearings*, Ways and Means Committee, House of Representatives, *Economic Security Act*, 1935, p. 899.

[3] *Hearings*, Ways and Means Committee, House of Representatives, *Economic Security Act*, 1935, pp. 897-899; *Report to the President of the Committee on Economic Security*, 1935, p. 32; *cf.* Great Britain, *Report of Committee on National Expenditure*, 1931, p. 12.

It was considered proper for the tax collections from current young people and their employers to be expended on current old-age benefits to individuals who, being only recently covered, had through their own contributions and their employers' provided little in the way of their benefits. As a result of such expenditure a smaller actuarial earning reserve would accumulate. Because of losses of interest it would be necessary in perpetuity for future workers to pay higher contributions unless of course a subsidy were later provided.

In the preceding statements the scale may well have been tipped too much in favor of fiscal and financial considerations. Thus, the monetary sum by which the young are alleged to provide annuities for the old is not necessarily an accurate index of the real sacrifice made by the young. As we shall see later, they may even find it possible to maintain their consumption or reduce it by relatively little, to some extent squeezing others with relatively fixed incomes or possibly inducing additional output to provide the goods and services required by the old.

Perhaps because of this overemphasis the recent tendency has been toward increased stress on real considerations. Social security literature abounds with such statements as "You cannot save goods for the future through an accumulation of reserves"; "each generation must bear its own burden of social security whatever the financial program"; etc.[1] This position will be commented on more fully later. Here it is only necessary to point out that this represents an extreme position which if consistently maintained can lead to absurdity. The fact that adherents to this point of view frequently regard the reserve as harmful rather than neutral represents a deviation from this principle and provides a refutation of its logic.

For a number of reasons, financial policies are of great importance for the successful outcome of a social security program. (1) The choice of financial measures will determine whether adequate revenues will be forthcoming and whether adequate benefits will become available for the old and unemployed. (2) The financial policy adopted will determine the distribution of burden as between classes and influence the distribution over time. (3) Different financial measures will affect diversely the level of income and the supply of capital which provide the tax base for social security payments. It is these problems, particularly the last, that are the concern of the present investigation.

[1] "No matter how much reserve is accumulated on the books of the government, the goods and services provided for the aged will be part of the total produced by persons active in industry at the time when benefits are paid. . . . In fact, the Government has no real asset available for storage in large amounts." Quoted by permission from J. D. Brown, "The Old Age Reserve Account," *Quart. Jour. Econ.*, August, 1937, pp. 716–719. *Cf.* M. A. Linton, *The Problem of Reserves and a Possible Solution*, pp. 1–4.; B. E. Wyatt and W. H. Wandel, *The Social Security Act in Operation*, p. 157; Maxwell Stewart, *Social Security*, p. 156; Twentieth Century Fund, *More Security for Old Age*, pp. 146–150.

CHAPTER 2

DEFLATIONARY ASPECTS

2.1. THE ISSUE OF DEFLATION

In this chapter the deflationary aspects of the social security program receive consideration.[1] Because the term "deflation" is so often used rather loosely, it is well in the beginning to devote some space to an examination of its meaning. A decline in MV is characteristic of deflation, and the *demand* for money (as well as the supply) is a relevant factor. A rise in demand not associated with an increase in output, brought about, for example, by an increased demand for liquidity, may be termed a "deflationary influence," for the velocity of circulation is decreased. From another point of view anything that tends to reduce consumption or net investment is, *ceteris paribus*, deflationary. (The effects via the supply and demand for money are likely to be deflationary.)

In what sense can the social security program be interpreted as deflationary? This question can best be answered by considering the case where the Federal budget is balanced. If pay-roll taxes are levied in excess of benefit payments, and if governmental expenditures do not increase, the Treasury has at its disposal a balance with which to retire debt. The bonds purchased from the market or special issues of equivalent amount are placed in the old-age reserve account. The total amount of spending per unit of time will presumably decline because the taxes are collected from active spenders and transferred to the sellers of governmental assets. Although the possession of extra funds by these individuals might to some extent ease interest rates and encourage investment, there is no guarantee that anything like an equivalent amount of real investment will be stimulated.

When the governmental budget is not balanced, the effect of excess social security taxes is clear, but cannot so easily be analyzed. Under the assumption that governmental expenditures do not increase because of the additional tax revenues, the effect is to reduce the amount of borrowing from financial institutions and the public.

---

[1] *Cf.* Secs. 2 and 3 of the introductory chapter.

The outstanding privately held debt, *i.e.*, exclusive of government trust fund holdings, grows less rapidly than it otherwise would have. If the excess of tax collections is sufficient, no recourse to the market may be necessary. Nominally, the budget will appear unbalanced because appropriations to the old-age account are treated as expenditures even though no transfer of cash takes place. In reality, the current budget is in balance in the sense that for the government as a whole tax collections equal *current* expenditures.[1]

In case the government budget is not balanced, the social security program cannot be said to be deflationary in an absolute sense. By and large, money is taken from active spenders and disbursed to active spenders. Nevertheless, it is deflationary relative to a policy of financing deficits by inflationary borrowing. But of course any financial policy is deflationary relative to some other more inflationary policy. It is possible, moreover, although we do not place much emphasis upon this point, that some increase in expenditure must be attributed to the increased demand for public securities for investment by the social security funds, so that the growth of the reserves may not be fully deflationary in even a relative sense.[2] In other words, the Treasury may spend more because it has become easier to borrow.

The important consideration in appraising the deflationary aspects of governmental activity is the use to which the money collected would otherwise have been put and the character and direction of governmental spending.[3] This includes a weighing of

[1] If a "capital" budget embracing a long-run point of view is adopted, the budget cannot be considered balanced. The excess pay-roll tax collections are only sufficient to match the accruing future liability and cannot be used to offset deficits in other branches of the government. Those in favor of liberal spending champion a capital budget when it promotes this end. The same persons are the most severe critics of the reserve plan, which follows the practice of taking account of future assets and liabilities of the social security program.

[2] To the extent that this is true the reserve fails in its purpose of easing the future financial burden of social security.

[3] This is often overlooked by writers when they discuss apprehensively a possible future failure of Congress to appropriate pay-roll taxes to the old-age account. Such a failure would affect only the bookkeeping. The important thing is not whether bonds accumulate in the reserve, but whether there is an excess of taxes over benefits so that privately held debt can be reduced or at least can be kept from growing as rapidly as otherwise. Analogously, a growth of the reserve through the issue of new securities to the fund by congressional fiat unaccompanied by any surplus of pay-roll taxes would not in the slightest degree ease future financing. In this case the interest earned on the reserve, being unmatched by savings in interest to private bondholders,

the secondary contraction attendant upon tax collection and the secondary expansion following expenditure. Thus, a tax on low-income workers used to retire debt would be much more deflationary than an equivalent tax on surpluses used to give benefits to low-income spenders. (The latter may well induce additional expenditures.) And even here a precise evaluation will depend on the use to which sellers of assets put the cash thus obtained.

Monetary effects, it will be observed, are not limited to an increase of hoards. The supply of money may be reduced as business repays bank loans and becomes reluctant to renew or expand loans; a diminution of government bonds outstanding may deprive banks of earning assets and result in a destruction of bank deposits. And the attempt on the part of all to hoard will be abortive in the absence of an increase in the amount of money. The attempt to hoard will result in a diminution of income, expressible as a decline in velocity, until there is no further effective desire to hoard. If the elasticity of demand for money is high because of uncertainty, or if the curve shifts upward, there may be little effective reduction in the rate of interest to offset this process by expanding investment.

Finally, one should not concentrate unduly on the short run. Unless the increase in the public debt is to be permanent (although experience tells us that retirement is unusual), it may be retired later if not now. By avoiding relative deflation now, one may increase the necessity for relative deflation later. In part, the significance of this consideration will depend upon the relative tax capacity in the two periods. (One should perhaps also keep in mind the possibility of repudiation, another alternative to deflation, later.)

2.2. Authority on Deflationary Effects

Agreement is quite general that the social security program is deflationary.[1] Unfortunate effects will follow, according to authority, even if

---

would in fact be spurious. Unfortunately, critics of the reserve have not distinguished between this completely hypothetical case and the actual reserve plan adopted. Cf. Secs. 9.1 to 9.5.

[1] Groves, H. M., *Financing Government*, pp. 383–384. Prof. Groves, a defender of the reserve method, would, however, deal with the problem of deflation (excess savings) in other ways. Prof. J. M. Clark puts the emphasis on the effect on employment. The pay-roll tax is a tax on employment and may have secondary deflationary

the budget is unbalanced; for the government's deficit does not rise *pari passu* with the contraction of spending which accompanies the inflow of reserves.[1] In the previous section it was shown that the necessary offsetting rise of public expenditure is not given by so simple and unqualified a comparison with tax surplus. A variant of this interpretation is to be found in the analysis of Prof. Shoup who emphasizes that bank deposits are reduced below what they would have been.[2] For had the reserve funds not purchased securities, banks would have done so with a consequent rise in deposits.

Similar fears are expressed of periods when the budget is in balance. Under adverse business conditions it is held that purchases of bonds by reserve funds do not induce expenditures on an adequate scale by the sellers of these bonds.[3] Dr. Robinson seems to adopt an extreme position whereby canalization of securities into the reserve funds at the expense of market holdings is to be considered *ipso facto* a deflationary process without regard to what sellers of securities do with their newly acquired cash.[4]

Mrs. Burns goes to the other extreme. She objects to the accumulation even of a contingency reserve on the grounds that in prosperous periods its growth, by releasing funds for investment markets, will be inflationary.[5] It is hardly conceivable that *in our economy* a tax upon active spenders (consumers, workers) used to retire debt could result in an equivalent amount of true real investment. (1) Consumption is discouraged. (2) Even if the sellers of bonds immediately invested 100 per cent of their proceeds, and this is the limiting case, a considerable fraction would undoubtedly go into old issues and merely change capital values. A billion dollars

---

effects. "An Appraisal of the Workability of Compensatory Devices," *Am. Econ. Rev., Supplement*, Mar., 1939, p. 207. Dr. Dulles, however, minimizes the importance of deflationary effects. She emphasizes in particular the large expenditures for social security in all its aspects, the nondeflationary character of taxes used to finance other parts of the programs, and the contributions toward expansion of other governmental activities. "Social Security Program," *Am. Econ. Rev., Supplement*, Mar., 1938, pp. 136–138.

[1] DOUGLAS, P. H., *Social Security in the United States*, 2d ed., pp. 391–393; HANSEN, A. H., *Full Recovery or Stagnation?* pp. 191–192.

[2] SHOUP, C., "Taxing for Social Security," *Annals*, March, 1939, p. 174.

[3] DOUGLAS, *op. cit.*, p. 145. Mr. Roelse does not limit deflationary effects (less spending) to periods of depression. ROELSE, H. V., "Social Security Program," *Am. Econ. Rev., Supplement*, 1938, p. 144.

[4] ROBINSON, G. B., "Nature of Social Security Payments," *Annalist*, Dec. 3, 1937, p. 901.

[5] BURNS, E. M., "Financial Aspects of the Social Security Act," *Am. Econ. Rev.*, March, 1936, pp. 12–22. Others also fear that the effects in periods of prosperity will be inflationary. *Cf.* B. E. Wyatt and W. H. Wandel, *Social Security Act in Operation*, 1937, p. 161; and Maxwell S. Stewart, *Social Security*, p. 266.

invested in the security market would seem to result in less than a billion dollars of real investment.[1]

What is the attitude of defenders of the reserve principle? Although admitting the possibilities of deflation during depression if reserves grow, they would remove the sting through a reduction or even elimination of tax collections in such periods.[2]

2.3. DEFLATIONARY EFFECTS

Much has been made in recent years of the deflationary effects of the social security taxes and in particular of their contributions to the recession of 1936–1938. The reader will recall a brief discussion of that problem in the introductory chapter. Figures for the following in particular were presented there: transfers to trust funds, deficits and net cash contributions of the Federal Treasury, accumulations of the unemployment and old-age trust funds. These figures are supplemented here by a table giving the relevant information for an analysis of deflationary effects of the transfer to trust accounts. It will be noted that the whole story is not given by the accumulations of funds under the social security program, that the operations of other governmental organizations are relevant, and that if the complete picture were to be given the operations of private corporations and insurance companies should be considered.[3] It is also well to recall a point that was made in the opening chapter, viz., that *net income* under the social security program is subject to several interpretations and that a consideration of all security payments and receipts will yield a large *net* contribution to spending by the Treasury for social security broadly considered. The present table does reveal, however, large accumulations by trust funds and, particularly in the fiscal year 1938, an excess of accumulations over the rise of public debt. In 1940, however, the accumulation of the two large funds (column 5) was almost offset by a reduction of cash.

[1] This must be qualified to admit of the possibility that a diversion of funds may in an unstable situation augment a stock market boom and have repercussions greater than its primary impulse.

[2] DULLES, *op. cit.*, p. 137; PRIBRAM, K. B., "The Functions of Reserves in Old Age Benefit Plans," *Quart. Jour. Econ.*, August, 1938, pp. 638–639.

[3] Note that the excess of receipts of the Reconstruction Finance Corporation is roughly one-third of that of the old-age and unemployment funds; 1937–1940. *Cf.* Table I, columns 5 and 7.

These facts may well be considered in conjunction with a decline of the cash deficit, which was 4 billion dollars in 1936, to 400 millions in 1937.

TABLE I.—U. S. TREASURY—FIGURES RELEVANT TO ISSUE OF DEFLATIONARY EFFECTS OF CASH RECEIPTS OF GOVERNMENTAL AGENCIES AND TRUST FUNDS (1936–1940)*

(In millions of dollars)

	(1)	(2)	(3)	(4)	(5)	(6)	(7)	(8)	(9)
Fiscal year ending June, 30	Expenditures: transfers to trust accounts†	U. S. government excess of expenditures over receipts	General fund balance: changes	Gross debt: changes,	Old-age and unemployment reserves: excess of receipts	Issues to social security—total outstanding	Government agencies—excess of receipts. RFC	Government agencies—excess of receipts. Commodity Credit Corporation	Government agencies—excess of receipts. All others
1937	868	3,149	−128	+2,646	560	579	329	112	−127
1938	607	1,384	−338	+ 740	1,037	1,601	9	184	11
1939	685	3,542	+622	+3,275	915	2,511	658	−136	246
1940	747	3,612	−947	+2,528	1,020	3,528	234	− 10	−183

* Data taken from *Fed. Reserve Bull.*, September, 1939, pp. 800–801, and September, 1940, pp. 975–977.

† Not including unemployment reserves (not a trust account).

It is easy to understand then why economists emphasize the contributions of the social security program and the reduction of net contributions by the Treasury to the recession of 1937–1938. One may, however, go too far in this direction. It is particularly important that other explanations of the recession should receive adequate attention; and experts have not been unaware of the importance of other considerations. For the convenience of the reader, a number of factors that have received attention are listed. One final remark before these causes of the recession are given. An important part of the explanation of the decline of the Treasury contributions is the rise of tax yields; and this rise in itself is largely a function of an improvement in the economic situation. It is, therefore, rather paradoxical to explain the business downturn by the rise of tax receipts which is, given our tax system, an inevitable accompaniment of an upturn in business.

In the analysis of the downturn of the year 1937, the following factors have received attention:[1] (This is not in any sense a complete list of factors or analysts!)

[1] HANSEN, A. H., *Full Recovery or Stagnation?* pp. 267–283; SCHUMPETER, J. A., *Business Cycles*, II, pp. 1018–1019, 1032, 1042; *Economic Balance and a Balanced*

1. A decline in Treasury contributions—Hansen, Eccles, Gill.[1] (This is a more general explanation than the deflationary effects of pay-roll taxes.)

2. Excessive inventories accumulated in earlier years—Department of Commerce, Schumpeter, Hansen, Eccles.

3. Bad timing of Federal expenditures and excessive amounts (inclusive of monetary expansion)—Schumpeter.

4. Excessive rise of wages or (and) prices—Hansen, Schumpeter, Eccles, Slichter, Hardy.

5. Failure to supplement the rise of consumption with an adequate expansion of investment—Hansen, Slichter.

6. Heavy taxation (and adverse effects on saving)—Hardy.

7. Inadequacy of capital or savings—National Industrial Conference Board, Hardy, Colm and Lehmann.

2.4. Adverse Effects of the Social Security Program on Consumption

There is no universal agreement with respect to the question of the effects of social security activities upon consumption.[2] Some aspects are favorable and others unfavorable, and each writer chooses to stress the factor that he considers most important. On the whole, attention is primarily fastened on the period of building up reserves

Budget, Public Papers of M. S. Eccles, p. 190; N.I.C.B., *Studies in Enterprise and Social Progress*, pp. 224–225; GILL, C., *Wasted Man-Power*, pp. 219–220; Secretary of Commerce, *Summary Ann. Rept.*, 1940, pp. VII–VIII; COLM, G., and F. LEHMANN, *Economic Consequences of Recent American Tax Policy*, pp. 60–61; HARDY, C. O., "An Appraisal of the Factors, etc.," *Proc. Am. Econ. Assoc.*, 1939, pp. 174–179; SLICHTER, S. H., "The Townturn of 1937," *Rev. Econ. Statistics*, 1938, pp. 103–109; KIMMEL, L. H., *Social Security Finance*, N.I.C.B. Bulletin, Nov. 19, 1937.

[1] *Cf.*, however, HARDY, *op. cit.*, p. 173, and SLICHTER, *op. cit.*, p. 109.

[2] For emphasis on the unfavorable effects on consumption of pay-roll taxes used to accumulate reserves and the resulting deflationary tendencies see, for example, P. H. Douglas, "The Social Security Act," *Econ. Jour.*, March, 1936, p. 8; WYATT and WANDEL, *op. cit.*, pp. 160, 162; STEWART, *op. cit.*, pp. 157, 265. Others have, however, put the emphasis upon the stabilizing effect of the social security program. The flow of purchasing power is equalized over time. E. L. Dulles, *Financing the Social Security Act*, pp. 112–113; J. B. Andrews, "The Investment and Liquidation of Unemployment Reserves," *Am. Labor Legislation Rev.*, December, 1932, p. 143; Social Security Board, *Unemployment Compensation, What and Why*, September, 1937, pp. 10–11.

and on the costs of the program rather than its benefits. The pay-roll taxes are believed to fall primarily upon low-income classes, either on wage earners through a decline in net earnings or on consumers through increases in the cost of living. As a result, their consumption decreases without a compensating increase in the consumption of the wealthy classes.

This analysis ignores the fact that an increasing portion of social security costs will be financed by other than pay-roll taxes. Moreover, as we shall see in the later treatment of incidence, the fact that the tax is levied on pay-rolls does not mean that a significant fraction of its burden will not fall upon the high- and middle-income groups. To the extent that it does so, we may expect from them a sizable cut in savings rather than an equivalent reduction in consumption.

Also, one must not neglect the effects of a pay-roll tax of (say) 9 per cent on the voluntary net savings of the low-income classes. Some portion of the income lost would undoubtedly have gone into savings. Of the income left, less need go into savings because of the coverage provided by the social security program. These effects are neglected by many writers who consider only the average propensity of the poorer classes to save; this may be quite small, with total savings even negative, and yet the marginal propensity to save may be significant. A priori, one might think this a factor of importance. Actually, it must be modified to take account of the allegation of many observers that social insurance schemes call to the attention of workers the insecurities of life and stimulate private thrift. This subject will be discussed again later, although the statistical evidence is not conclusive (Sec. 3.3).

2.5. Favorable Effects of the Social Security Program on Consumption

So far nothing has been said of the favorable effect upon consumption of the disbursement of social security benefits. Recent investigations have revealed that the old have very meager resources at their disposal, and even modest benefits will greatly improve their economic position.[1] Unemployment benefits are received at a time

[1] Shearon, M., "Economic Status of the Aged," Soc. Sec. Bull., March, 1938, pp. 5–16.

when other income sources fail. The diversion of consumption demand from periods of prosperity to periods of depression will not only tend to stabilize consumption, but also may be expected to increase it over time. A minimum consumption standard will be assured in bad times. The disbursements made possible by decumulation of contingency reserves during hard times contribute more to well-being than the process of accumulation will detract.[1]

Disbursements of old-age contingency reserves are not likely to be so highly correlated with periods of declining activity as are disbursements from unemployment reserves. The number of qualified old cannot, except for some induced retirements, be augmented so quickly; likewise, the improvement of business conditions does not witness a decrease in benefits. The tendency, however, for revenues to move cyclically could be intensified by the use of variable rates of taxation.

At best, social security benefit payments cannot, however, be expected to maintain consumption at levels of high employment. Unemployment compensation benefits are only a fraction of wages earned. It has been estimated that if the 1935 Act had been in effect in 1933, unemployment benefits would have provided only 10 per cent of the amount of wage losses associated with unemployment.[2] Payments are made for only a limited period and then only if the worker has been employed for a minimum period in the recent past. Furthermore, it is necessary to keep benefits low enough to assure wage flexibility when recovery demands wage adjustments.[3] Benefit payments under insurance will frequently be smaller than relief and work-relief payments and may even be smaller than noncontributory benefits under old-age assistance. Benefits are related, although not strictly proportionally, to earnings. This raises a problem of equity for a pay-as-you-go system. For under this plan workers will not for many years pay the full cost of their own benefits. Vigorous opposition must be expected to any proposal that

---

[1] HANSEN, A. H., *Full Recovery or Stagnation?* pp. 151–153. *Cf.* Political and Economic Planning, *Report on the British Social Services*, p. 162. Under the unemployment insurance program in Great Britain *net* payments in a year of depression (1931) were £1 million weekly; and in a relatively good year (1935), receipts exceeded payments by £1 million monthly.

[2] LEHMANN, F., "The Role of Social Security Legislation," *Am. Econ. Rev., Supplement*, 1939, p. 220. *Cf.* however, my estimates in the opening chapter, pp. 49–56.

[3] CLARK, J. M., "An Appraisal of the Workability of Compensatory Devices," *Am. Econ. Rev., Supplement*, 1939, pp. 195–196.

provides a larger subsidy for those with the higher incomes, who are presumed to be least in need.

The foregoing analysis must not be taken to mean that the expansive effect of social security payments can be gauged by comparing income to a beneficiary of the social security program with his previous income. The latter sum has little or no expansive effects, for it adds to cost at the same time as it increases purchasing power. Social security payments in excess of revenues financed by decumulation of contingency reserves, on the other hand, are stimulating in the same sense as deficit financing. In addition to favorable secondary effects, there is less reason to fear adverse tertiary effects on business and private investment.

2.6. Consumption and Savings in Relation to Alternative Methods of Finance and Business Conditions

The effects on consumption and savings will depend upon the financial plan adopted, upon the sources of tax revenue, and finally upon private business conditions. If, for example, full employment prevails before and after the imposition of a pay-roll tax large enough to cause the reserve to grow, the sequence of events may perhaps be that envisaged by the classical economists in their treatment of thrift. The tax will curtail consumption. By hypothesis employment remains full, so factors are transferred from consumption purposes to the production of new capital goods. The mechanism whereby this is accomplished is the investment of funds by sellers of government bonds. As a result of such real physical investment, the stock of capital is larger in later years. The *net* productivity of this capital corresponds to the interest earned on the reserve and provides in real terms consumption goods for the future dependent old. The workers of the future are able to consume as much as they would have been able to if there were no old to support. (This is on the assumption that the earnings of reserves are the only source of revenue for the provision of the old at that time.)

This is, of course, a simplified picture and rests on the definite assumption of full employment. It is, however, a refutation of the naive declaration that "you cannot store up goods for the future." Followed to its logical conclusion, this last statement would imply that under all circumstances individual savings through banks, life insurance companies, purchases of securities, etc., serve no useful purpose in the provision of capital.

A pay-as-you-go plan financed by the low-income groups represents largely a transfer of consumption from active workers to dependents. Of course, part of this transfer would have taken place even without a social security program through support of aged by children and relatives. Because the benefit recipients are more needy than the taxpayers, to some extent consumption may be increased through an increased propensity to consume. In full employment this must be at the expense of investment and is brought about directly by reductions of savings or indirectly through raising prices of factors of production, raising cost of living for the wealthy and reducing their surpluses for saving. This indirect effect is the exact opposite of forced savings.

Under conditions of full employment, therefore, a powerful case can be made for the reserve plan. It is appropriate for the active generation to provide part of its future consumption by some curtailment of its present consumption. Moreover, it must not be forgotten that reduced taxes now under pay-as-you-go means increased taxes later; because of interest sacrificed, total taxes over time will be larger under this plan. On the assumption that there is a burden involved in "transfer" expenditure and that this increases more than proportionally with the percentage of the national income taxed, the optimal policy, at least under conditions near full employment, would seem to involve an equalization of burden over time. Since benefit payments grow slowly, this involves the accumulation of a reserve.

Under conditions of less than full employment, the effects on consumption and investment must be modified. Under the reserve plan, consumption will be decreased and there may be no compensating increase in investment. The funds that would otherwise go into governmental bonds may only slightly lower interest rates; and this fact combined with a possible inelasticity of demand makes the probability small that there will be an increase in investment large enough to counterbalance the decline in consumption. Worse than this, the decline in consumption may lower the marginal efficiency of capital so that even less investment will be made. As a result, income will tend to fall and unemployment to increase.

Whether or not investment will increase under conditions of less than full employment is an uncertain matter. The result will depend upon the response of interest rates to increases in savings, the elasticity of demand with respect to the interest rate for investment, and the shift in the marginal efficiency of capital resulting from a decline in consumption.[1] In order to study the result of these complex relationships, we must turn to an analysis of the quantitative aspects of deflation and to the theory of oversaving and vanishing investment demand.

Before we turn to that issue, a brief summary of the best treatment of the subject of the *optimum propensity to consume* will be given.[2] On the one hand, a reduction of consumption induces a curtailment of investment; the ensuing fall in the rate of interest, on the other hand, contributes toward a rise of investment. Dr. Lange concludes as follows:

> The optimum propensity to consume is thus determined by the condition that *the marginal rate of substitution between the rate of interest and total income as affecting the demand for liquidity is equal to the marginal rate of substitution between the rate of interest and expenditures on consumption as inducements to invest.*

As consumption rises the investment curve is concave downward: "The stimulus to invest exercised by each successive increment of expenditure on consumption is weaker. This is explained by the increasing prices of the factors of production. . . . " In the Keynesian system, the income elasticity of demand for liquidity equals 0 and the interest elasticity of demand for liquidity equals ∞. It follows, therefore, that a change in consumption does not affect the rate of interest, and, therefore, the optimum propensity to consume is "*when the expenditure on consumption is such that a further increase does not any more increase the marginal efficiency of investment.*"[3] This happens when the elasticity of supply of the factors of production is zero. In the classical case, the interest elasticity of demand for liquidity equals 0, *i.e.*, a reduction in the propensity to consume stimulates investment by inducing the appropriate fall in the rate of interest.

[1] *Cf.* the excellent discussion on the relation of consumption and the rate of interest to investment in D. H. Robertson, *Essays in Monetary Theory*, pp. 34–38.

[2] LANGE, O., "The Rate of Interest and the Optimum Propensity to Consume," *Economica*, 1938, pp. 18, 24–31. Quoted by permission of the editors.

[3] LANGE, *op. cit.*, p. 31.

2.7. QUANTITATIVE ANALYSIS OF OVERSAVINGS AND INVESTMENT
DEMAND

The reader may well pass over this discursive section, which,
however, is related to important issues of this book. Its main findings follow. Since criticism of pay-roll taxes and reserves frequently
arises from the acceptance of the theory and fact of oversaving, it
seemed desirable to consider the available statistical material. An
examination of outlets for savings reveals that, on the whole, business and construction demand have been disappointing.[1] One is impressed by the increased importance of savings institutions that
collect cash and purchase for the most part the relatively riskless
assets. Unfortunately it is not possible to find statistical verification
of oversavings. The Brookings Institution has been subjected to
just criticism for its attempts to adduce statistical evidence of oversaving. Both an examination of recent outlets for savings and the
views of numerous authorities suggest the conclusion that the danger
of oversaving or underconsumption may rightly be accepted as one
argument against the accumulation of large reserves. It is well to
keep in mind, however, that stagnation is also a function of attitudes
toward capitalism and economic policies. Punitive taxation, excessive demands by labor, and monopolistic practices by business all
contribute toward vanishing demand.[2]

Let us turn to oversaving and to the statistical material that
might conceivably throw some light on this problem. Whether savings and investment are equal or unequal will depend upon the
particular definitions of savings and investment that appeal to the
investigator. The available statistics are not particularly helpful in
solving this problem.[3]

Estimates of savings have been made through budget studies by
numerous investigators, particularly by the Brookings Institution for

---

[1] *Cf.* the discussion of oversaving in the introductory chapter.

[2] *Cf.* Secretary of Commerce, *Summary Ann. Rept.*, 1940, pp. X–XIII.

[3] Dr. Moulton's attempt to find evidence of oversaving in the statistical material
for 1929 has been eminently unsuccessful. An apparent excess of savings of 10 billions
(net productive investments are put at 5 billions and savings at 15 billions) is to be
explained largely by the incorrect inclusion of 7.5 billions of capital gains in savings
(and not in investment) and the failure to include several important types of investment. *The Formation of Capital*, 1935, p. 145. See the brilliant criticism by H. H.
Villard, "Dr. Moulton's Estimates of Saving and Investment," *Am. Econ. Rev.*,
September, 1937, pp. 477–489. Also see National Resources Committee, *Consumer
Incomes in the United States*, pp. 1–2, 34–35.

1929 and the National Resources Committee for 1935–1936.[1] The latter study is based on a very large sample and is therefore to be preferred, although there is remarkable similarity of results in the noncontroversial lower income brackets. Dr. Goldsmith, through a study of the components of savings not unlike the earlier study of Mr. Lough, obtains estimates of both gross and net savings for the years 1933–1937. Drs. Kuznets and Terborgh have made independent estimates of capital formation for the postwar period. Since estimates of gross and net capital formation correspond to those of gross and net saving, a comparison of the series of savings and net capital formation may be useful as a guide to the relative magnitudes of savings and investment. Unfortunately, differences are as easily interpreted in terms of differences in coverage, statistical difficulties, etc., as they are as a verification or failure of verification of any theory of savings and investment. No attempt will be made to go over the ground covered by Prof. Villard and Drs. Goldsmith, Colm, Lehmann, Ezekiel, and others who have made attempts to reconcile the various statistical series. Nor is there the space here to make a complete critical estimate of the various series. All economists must acknowledge a great debt to the workers in this field, especially to Drs. Kuznets, Goldsmith, and Terborgh.[2]

Relevant figures for the year 1929 and for 1933–1938 are presented in Tables II and III. They throw some light on the range of problems now under discussion, not because they reveal discrepancies in the total of savings and investment, but because they reveal present sources of savings

---

[1] LEVEN, MAURICE, H. G. MOULTON, CLARK WARBURTON, *America's Capacity to Consume;* National Resources Committee, *Consumer Expenditures in the United States*, pp. 1–11, 20–21, 55, 68–69; EZEKIEL, M., "An Annual Estimate of Savings by Individuals," *Rev. Econ. Statistics*, November, 1937, pp. 178–191; WARBURTON, C., "The Trend of Savings, 1900–1929," *Jour. Pol. Econ.*, February, 1935, pp. 84–101; MENDERSHAUSEN, H., "Income and Savings of Metropolitan Families," *Am. Econ. Rev.*, September, 1939, pp. 521–538.

[2] GOLDSMITH, R. W., *Studies in Income and Wealth*, vol. III, Part IV, "The Volume and Components of Saving in the United States, 1933–1937;" LOUGH, W. H., *High Level Consumption;* KUZNETS, S., *Commodity Flow and Capital Formation*, vol. I; TERBORGH, G., "Estimated Expenditures for New Durable Goods, 1919–1938," *Fed. Reserve Bull.*, September, 1939; COLM and LEHMANN, *op. cit.*,

Dr. Ezekiel's estimates for savings agree well with Mr. Warburton's; but not with Mr. Lough's. The former two use the Brookings Institution's relation of income levels and savings, however, and rely on income tax data; and in view of similarity of method, such as the inclusion of capital gains as income, their agreement is not surprising. Mr. Lough estimates the volume of savings through a study of the acquisition of important types of assets by individuals. Dr. Ezekiel and Mr. Warburton both find a large rise in savings in 1925–1929, while Mr. Lough's change is relatively less. This may be a reflection on the latter's figures as Dr. Ezekiel maintains, or it may merely indicate the extent to which the inclusion of capital gains resulted in additional savings. For a criticism of Dr. Ezekiel's method, see Goldsmith, *op. cit.*, pp. 241–244.

TABLE II.—SAVINGS AND INVESTMENT: SOME RELEVANT FIGURES FOR 1929*
(In billions of dollars)

A. Estimates of savings and investment	Amount	B. Items in gross capital formation, 1929 §	Amount
1. Gross capital formation (Kuznets)...................	20.0	1. Destined for use by consumers...............	13.8
2. Estimated expenditures for new durable goods (Terborgh)..................	25.5	2. Destined for use by business...................	15.6
3. Savings (Brookings)........	15.0	3. Destined for use by public agencies..............	3.1
4. Consumers' savings (Lough).	9.3	4. Unallocable..............	6.0
5. Savings (Colm and Lehmann)†.................	14.0	5. Inventories (included in 2)	2.4
6. Net capital formation (Kuznets)....................	10.1	6. Excluding all repairs and maintenance and consumers' movable durable	
7. Public issues—*Chronicle* (Eddy)..................	10.2	commodities, total of 1–4 becomes..............	20.3
8. Net new real investment via public issues (Eddy)......	2.2		
9. Net productive capital‡ (Brookings Institution)....	3.2		

* KUZNETS, S., *Commodity Flow and Capital Formation*, vol. I, pp. 494–495; TERBORGH, G., "Estimated Expenditures for New Durable Goods 1919–1938," *Fed. Reserve Bull.*, September, 1939, p. 731; LOUGH, W. H., *High Level Consumption*, p. 306; Brookings Institution, *America's Capacity to Consume*, p. 93; COLM, G., and F. LEHMANN, *Economic Consequences of Recent American Tax Policy*, pp. 17–18; Brookings Institution, *Formation of Capital*, p. 145; EDDY, G. A., "Security Issues and Real Investment in 1929," *Rev. Econ. Statistics*, May, 1937, p. 83.

† Drs. Colm and Lehmann add the totals for public investments and corporate savings (and deduct loans to individuals) to the figures for savings of Mr. Lough. For an attempt to explain discrepancies between these results for savings and Dr. Kuznets's for net capital formation, see Colm and Lehmann, *op. cit.*, pp. 17–18.

‡ In the discussion above (*cf.* footnote on Dr. Moulton on the equality of savings and investment), the net productive capital is given as 5 billion dollars. That total includes, however, net flotation of mortgages.

§ Figures from Dr. Kuznets, *op. cit.*, pp. 484–485.

and the outlets for investment. In 1929, for example (and a feature of the twenties), the large relative contributions to gross capital formation of the flow of commodities destined for use by consumers (*B*-1 of Table II) may now be interpreted as an indication of declining outlets in the future; and the large rise of inventories (Table II, *B*-5 and Dr. Kuznets's original table) in 1929 points in the same general direction.[1]

Dr. Eddy's results (10 billions raised on security markets and but 2 billions for real investment) indicate the extent to which the sale of securities constituted merely an exchange of debts for cash by corporations and an exchange of cash for securities by investors or speculators.[2] The difference between the Brookings Institution's estimates of savings and

[1] For a more comprehensive treatment of the significance of the short (inventory) cycles, one should consult Prof. Hansen's *Fiscal Policy and Business Cycles*.

[2] EDDY, G. A., "Security Issues and Real Investment in 1929," *Rev. Econ. Statistics*, May, 1937.

TABLE III.—STATISTICS ON SAVINGS AND INVESTMENT, 1933–1938*
(In billions of dollars)

	Total†	1933	1934	1935	1936	1937	1938
1. a. Gross savings (Goldsmith, p. 241)	58.5	5.5	7.5	10.0	17.0	18.5	
b. Gross capital formation (Kuznets, p. 2)	49.9	3.7	5.5	9.4	13.8	17.5	12.7
c. Estimated expenditures for new durable goods (Terborgh, p. 731)	68.3	7.6	10.4	12.6	17.7	20.0	16.4
2. a. Net saving (Goldsmith, p. 236)..	−2.5	−6.0	−4.5	−2.0	4.5	5.5	
b. Net capital formation (Kuznets, p. 2)	9.6	−3.5	−2.1	1.5	5.5	8.2	
Goldsmith (p. 237)							
3. a. Individual saving	10.9	−2.8	0.0	0.9	7.4‡	5.4	
b. Business saving	−9.5	−3.3	−2.9	−1.6	−1.0	−0.7	
c. Government saving	−3.7	0.0	−1.5	−1.4	−1.7	0.9	
Individual net saving in liquid form							
4. a. Cash and deposits	8.3	−1.2	2.5	2.6	3.9	0.5	
b. Building and loan associations...	−1.6	−0.6	−0.3	−0.4	−0.2	−0.1	
c. Insurance and pension reserves..	9.4	0.5	1.4	1.9	2.7	2.9	
d. Through absorption of securities.	−2.1	0.5	−1.0	−2.3	0.1	0.6	
e. Durable consumers' goods	−3.1	−2.0	−2.6	−0.9	0.9	1.5	
Kuznets (p. 2)							
5. a. Gross capital formation for business use	33.0	1.8	2.6	6.6	9.3	12.7	6.8
b. Same, exclusive of inventories...	29.4	3.0	4.3	5.4	7.3	9.4	7.1
c. Private durable capital formation	34.7	3.4	4.8	6.3	8.9	11.2	8.9
d. Net flow to inventories	3.7	−1.1	−1.7	1.2	2.0	3.3	−0.3
e. Net capital formation for business use (net flow of producers' durable and net business construction and net flow to inventories)..	5.9	−3.1	−2.5	1.3	3.7	6.5	
f. Net private durable capital formation, i.e., including inventories and plus all residential construction	−3.0	−3.3	−2.2	−0.8	0.4	2.9	

* National Bureau of Economic Research, *Studies in Income and Wealth*, vol. 3, Part 4, R. W. Goldsmith, "Volume and Components of Saving in the U. S., 1933–1937," pp. 236–241; KUZNETS, S., "Commodity Flow and Capital Formation in the Recent Recovery and Decline," *Nat. Bur. Econ. Research*, Bull. 74, 1939, p. 2; TERBORGH, G., "Estimated Expenditures for New Durable Goods, 1919–1928," *Fed. Reserve Bull.*, 1939, p. 731.

† Total 1933–1937, 1938 figures not included even when given in table.

‡ The National Resources Committee estimates individual savings (consumer) in 1935–1936 (1 year) at 6 billions. *The Structure of the American Economy*, pp. 91–95.

investment (net productive investment—Table II, A-9) has received some attention above.

Let us consider statistics for 1933 and later years. That savings of individuals in the years 1933–1937 did not offset dissaving by the government and business (Table III, 3 a–c—Dr. Goldsmith's figures) is an indication of the low state of business demand, which in the past had been a very important outlet for savings. According to Dr. Kuznets's figures, business demand seems satisfactory; but the figures of Dr. Goldsmith are not so reassuring. For the years 1932–1937, the former estimates the net capital formation for business use at 6 billion dollars (Table III, 5e), the latter estimates business dissaving at 9 billion dollars (Table III, 3b).[1] Business does, indeed, contribute importantly to gross capital formation, the explanation of its larger contribution to this than to net capital formation being the large deductions from gross capital which are required to obtain net capital formation. Another significant aspect of these statistics is the extent to which any growth of savings is associated with a rise of cash holdings and inventories and an increase in equities of life insurance companies (Table III, 4a, 4c, 5d; also consult the note at end of this section). According to Dr. Goldsmith, there was net disinvestment for durable consumers' goods; existing stocks depreciated in excess of the value of new purchases (Table III, 4e). The flow of durable consumers' goods averaged roughly 6 billions in this period, however.[2]

At this point it would be well to summarize the issues and to integrate the results of this study with the wealth of material presented in the Temporary National Economic Committee volumes which have appeared since the above was written and which provided much of the raw materials for the discussion of these issues in the opening chapter.[3]

It will be recalled that the deficiency of investment relative to the twenties is to be associated largely with (1) the low level of construction, (2) the decline of the contributions of state and local governments, (3) the failure of installment credit to continue to rise, and (4) the economies to be found in the replacement of capital.

[1] It is not easy to reconcile these differences though Dr. Goldsmith makes an attempt to do so. He does not seem to us to be entirely successful. R. W. Goldsmith and W. Salant, *Studies in Income and Wealth*, vol. 3, "Saving and Its Components," p. 243; *cf.* also p. 287 and S. Kuznets, "Commodity Flow and Capital Formation in the Recent Recovery and Decline, 1932–1938," *Nat. Bur. Econ. Research, Bull.* 74, June, 1939, pp. 6–7, 9–10. In general, this may be said. The concept of saving used by Dr. Goldsmith is a monetary or financial concept. Industry may encounter losses, thus consuming part of its capital. Then the net result given by his study would properly be a reduction of capital (dissaving). But the real capital plant may increase, nevertheless, because new capital may be obtained via the security markets or through additional help from the banks. Dr. Kuznets would then properly conclude that there had been a *net* capital formation. Furthermore, the two writers do not consider exactly the same categories of capital; and various problems of evaluation arise, which may account for differences.

[2] Kuznets, *ibid.*, Table I, row 3, p. 2.

[3] *Hearings*, Temporary National Economic Committee (76: 1), 1940, Investigation of Concentration of Economic Power, especially Part 9, *Savings and Investment*, notably the evidence of Drs. Hansen, Currie, and Altman; and Securities and Exchange Commission, *Selected Statistics on Securities and on Exchange Markets*, 1939, especially pp. 9–21 and Tables I–V.

That business contributions to investment declined is explicable in part by (1) and (4). It is well, however, to keep in mind that the low level of business demand, which is to be inferred from Dr. Goldsmith's figures, is not exactly confirmed by Dr. Kuznet's results.[1] Yet even for the latter, business contributions have been unsatisfactory. In a discussion of these issues, one should be careful to distinguish, however, gross capital formation, which has been large in the period 1933–1938, and net capital formation, which of course is much smaller.

In the opening chapter, some material on new savings and on outlets was presented. Estimates of savings were there limited to amounts saved by individuals, although to some extent savings of corporations were included. In addition to individual savings, it is necessary to consider the inflow of funds from foreign sources which has averaged considerably more than 1 billion dollars a year from 1933 to 1939; and the savings by business units are to be considered.[2] Taking into account these additions, Brookings Institution puts the volume of funds available in recent years at 7 to 8 billion dollars annually.[3] In contrast, all new issues (including real estate mortgages) in the thirties have averaged but 3.5 billion dollars a year, and domestic corporate security issues for "new capital" have averaged little over 1 billion dollars in the years 1936–1938.[4] According to the Brookings Institution, *private* issues including mortgages came to 24 billion dollars in 1926–1928 as compared with 4 billion dollars in 1936–1938. Of new corporate (net) issues, Moody's "productive" issues have averaged a little less than 40 per cent in the years 1935–1938.[5] It is to be observed, however, that Dr. Eddy

[1] KUZNETS, *op. cit.*, Table 1 and pp. 5–10; GOLDSMITH, *op. cit.*, pp. 242–243. The differences are not adequately explained by the latter's failure to adjust inventories for changes in prices and his exclusion of some inventories.

[2] See *Hearings*, Temporary National Economic Committee (76: 1), 1940, Investigation of Concentration of Economic Power, pp. 4038–4041. Savings of corporations were negative in the years 1930–1934. In the following three years, they were positive though not large. It is another matter when depreciation and depletion expenditures are included as savings. In the last three years (1935–1937) they average an amount in excess of 3 billion dollars for all nonfinancial corporations in contrast with an average of 800 million dollars of adjusted business savings (not including depreciation and depletion).

[3] Brookings Institution, *Capital Expansion, Employment and Economic Stability*, by H. G. Moulton *et al.*, p. 40.

[4] *Ibid.*, p. 32; EDDY, G. A., "The Present Status of New Security Issues," *Rev. Econ. Statistics*, 1939, p. 118.

[5] Brookings Institution, *ibid.*, pp. 28, 32, 40; *cf.* Securities and Exchange Commission, *op. cit.*, p. 10.

puts the percentage of domestic *corporate issues for real investment* to all domestic corporate security issues for new capital (the same as the Brookings Institution—*i.e.*, Moody's—figures for new corporate net issues) much higher. His figure is 82 per cent.[1]

Whatever the facts concerning the relative magnitude of "productive" issues and all new issues, the significant point is that new savings are very large relative to *new* issues. An obvious danger is that the savings will be dissipated, thus inducing a cumulative contraction. Support for government investment is easily found in these figures. Proponents of government investment will find additional ammunition in an examination of the methods of finance of corporations: they rely largely on *internal* financing.[2]

The Brookings Institution has not, however, assented to this interpretation of the facts: "Comparisons between the volume of security flotations and *gross expenditures* for plant and equipment (which include outlay for both replacement and expansion) shed no light upon the ability of corporations to finance *capital expansion* without resort to the investment market."[3] Moreover, the Brookings Institution draws attention to new outlets available for the net savings: the rise of population, the improvement in the standard of living, the restoration of productivity to the level of 1929—all these will provide large demands for new capital.[4] Finally, the Brookings Institution puts much emphasis on a reduction in the value of capital assets, which, since 1930, may be put at 20 billion dollars and which in their opinion will stimulate a large demand for savings.[5] Their experts fail here, however, to take into account the decline in the value of assets associated with a general decline of prices and, therefore, not offset by a reduction in real assets available; and, secondly, they leave out of account the economies in capital which make it possible to produce X units of output with much less capital today than yesterday and, even more so, tomorrow than today. Finally, despite the detailed estimates of future capital requirements which are given here and in *The Recovery Program in the United States*, the authors never dispose of the arguments of Prof. Hansen and others that the rise of population and opening of new lands will not contribute nearly so much to new investment as in

[1] *Op. cit.*, p. 118.

[2] *Hearings*, Temporary National Economic Committee (76: 1), 1940, Investigation of Concentration of Economic Power, pp. 3672–3688, 4041, 4044.

[3] *Op. cit.*, p. 189.

[4] *Ibid.*, Chap. 9.

[5] *Ibid.*, pp. 116–117.

the past and that industries of equal importance with the railroad and automobile do not seem to be on the horizon.

That the volume of savings available seems to be so large and the volume of new productive issues so small suggest strongly the danger of dissipation of savings. Even their diversion to public channels may not result in a corresponding rise of investments, for they may be used merely to stimulate consumption. This outcome, however, would be preferable to a dissipation of savings in the sense that the money thus diverted from consumption channels is not put to any use. The canalization of these funds into channels of consumption by the Treasury may be the appropriate policy in part because business has become accustomed to the provision of a large part of its capital needs through the use of its own funds.

In the economics of the thirties, the Treasury has intervened, providing life insurance companies and other saving institutions with outlets for their new savings, contributing in no unimportant manner to the rise of savings through antecedent creations of money. Had the government not provided new assets to satisfy the demand of new savers, prices of other assets would have continued to rise, with a resultant rise in the demand for cash, which frequently follows a reduction in the rate of interest to a low point. Government intervention, moreover, probably contributed toward a rise of spending without which the relative price of assets (other than gilt-edge) would have fallen and liquidity preference would have risen further. A dearth of outlets, despite the contributions of the government, may account in part for the rise in the amounts of cash held by savers (about which something will be said presently). It is also significant that inventory accumulations have contributed greatly to recent periods of prosperity.[1] When capital is embodied in buildings or factories, the rate of disinvestment is not likely to be great for the life of the asset is likely to be long. An inordinate rise of inventories over relatively short periods may well be followed by an annual disinvestment of 1 to 2 billion dollars. As Prof. Hansen has pointed out, the inventory cycle is much shorter than the 7- to 8-year cycle; and, therefore, the continued rise in the course of the latter cycle will be hampered by disinvestment of inventories.

A survey of the issues leads one to conclude that the stagnationists have a strong case. It is of course possible that the low level of investment may be associated at least in part with cost and price

[1] *Cf.* Brookings Institution, *op. cit.*, p. 112.

rigidities and with an inadequate elasticity of demand in the cost-reduction industries; and it is possible that this aspect of the subject is not given adequate attention by those who uphold the stagnation theory. Given these rigidities and inelasticities, however, the reduced demand arising from a decline in the rate of population increase and a dearth of new investments may be decisive.

Our defense program will put off for many years the day of reckoning. Should the defense program peter out, however, governmental intervention along other lines will be required. Pensions to the old and subsidies to the military and to the less well-off in general may stimulate consumption; and help to foreign nations and public works will stimulate investment. It may even be necessary, once the defense program peters out, to consider revisions of our social security program which would reduce the amount of savings. Savings under the revised program will, however, be much less than under the original program. It would be better, however, to revise the whole system of taxation, and at the same time maintain pay-roll taxes.

Space does not permit a fuller discussion of the issues of vanishing demand and oversaving.[1] On the former, the reader is referred to the works of Mr. Keynes, Prof. Hansen, and other protagonists of this viewpoint.[2] Prof. Hansen, for example, has emphasized the importance of the reduction in the rate of increase in population, the dearth of new industries of outstanding importance, and the nature of technological changes in recent years. (The "deepening" of capital is not playing the part that it seemed to play in the nineteenth century.) For a contrary view, the reader may consult the Brookings Institution study discussed above.[3]

[1] For an excellent discussion of oversaving (underconsumption) theories see G. Haberler, *Prosperity and Depression*, Chap. 5. See Chap. 3 for overinvestment theories, especially pp. 31–32.

[2] REDDAWAY, W. B., *The Economics of a Declining Population;* COLM and LEHMANN, *op. cit.*, pp. 10–11, 19–23, 60–61; HANSEN, A. H., "Progress and Declining Population," *Am. Econ. Rev.*, March, 1939, pp. 8–12; and *Full Recovery or Stagnation?* pp. 312–315; WEINTRAUB, D., "Effects of Current and Prospective Technological Developments upon Capital Formation," *Am. Econ. Rev., Supplement*, March, 1939, pp. 15–32; GILBERT, R. V., *et al.*, *An Economic Program for American Democracy*, pp. 20–21, 56–62; GAYER, A. D., "Fiscal Policies," *Am. Econ. Rev., Supplement*, March, 1938, pp. 93–96, 106; STAUDINGER, H., "Stationary Population—Stagnant Economy," *Soc. Research*, May, 1939, p. 144; and the discussion in the opening chapter.

[3] A very critical view of the theory of vanishing demand is put brilliantly by Schumpeter, *op. cit.*, pp. 1011–1050. In particular, he points out that a decline in

One of the by-products of the vanishing demand for investment is a very serious problem of unemployment; and since improvements more and more are effected in organization and through economies of capital, and since the labor requirements per unit of output decline more and more (improvements are both capital and laborsaving), a very large rise of total output of both capital and consumption goods is required in order to prevent further declines in employment and (in view of the rise of employable population each year) even greater increases in unemployment.[1] Again, it should be observed that the tendency to accept an uncritical interpretation of the acceleration principle has tended to strengthen the support of the theory of vanishing demand. This follows because on the acceleration principle modest rises in consumption induce large rises of investment.[2] Our experiences in 1936–1937 have been revealing in this respect; the rise of new investment was disappointing.[3] Recently Prof. Hansen has written as follows:[4] "When all forms of investment are included, however, it is clear that the increase in

investment demand is likely to be gradual, and hence is not an adequate explanation of the disappointing results of the present Juglar cyclical rise; that other factors, *e.g.*, anticapitalistic attitude, high cost policies, are more reasonable explanations; that a saturation of all needs is *prima facie* an absurdity; and, finally, that the theory of vanishing demand frequently rests on the assumption of unchanged production functions, *i.e.*, combinations of the factors of production. *Cf.* Haberler, *op. cit.*, p. 246; Brookings Institution, *The Recovery Problem in the United States*, pp. 177–232; Robertson, *op. cit.*, pp. 37–38, 101–102, 111–113; and finally, A. Sweezy, "Population Growth and Investment Opportunity," *Quart. Jour. Econ.*, 1940, especially pp. 66–78. (Prof. Sweezy, though a stagnationist, considers the significance of a reduction of the rate of increase of population when great unemployment prevails.)

[1] National Research Project, *Unemployment and Increasing Productivity*, pp. 39–40, 43–44; 73; National Resources Committee, *Technological Trends and National Policy*, pp. 77–72.

[2] Economists who have put much emphasis on the acceleration principle erred in particular in (1) underestimating the importance of excess capacity and the possibility of increasing capacity through economies of capital; (2) in minimizing the relation of investment on the one hand and *expected* net income in the future, the latter being dependent, for example, upon estimates of future consumption (as well as present) and present and future costs; (3) in failing to understand the relation of total investment on the one hand and changes in consumption and varying replacement demands on the other. For an excellent summary of the discussion of some of the issues, see Haberler, *op. cit.*, pp. 85–105, and Prof. Hansen's *Fiscal Policy and Business Cycles.*

[3] HANSEN, A. H., *Full Recovery or Stagnation?* pp. 273–274. *Cf.* KAHLER A., "Government Spending, Its Tasks and Limits," *Soc. Research*, May, 1939, pp. 200–201. SLICHTER, *op. cit.*, pp. 101–107; and this work (2.3).

[4] See HANSEN, A. H., *Fiscal Policy and Business Cycles*, pp. 64–65.

consumption was relatively smaller in relation to increases in investment from 1932 to 1937 than had been the case from 1921 to 1929."

Period	Gross investment, billions of dollars	Consumption,* billions of dollars
1921–1929	+ 8.8	+18.7
1932–1937	+14.4	+18.4

* See Hansen, A. H., *Fiscal Policy and Business Cycles,* p. 64.

In concluding this section, it may be said that attempts to prove the statistical relation of savings and investment have not been successful. It is appropriate, however, to estimate the volume of savings and to compare the resulting figures with issues of securities. The low volume of new issues and the liberation of business from dependence on security markets suggest the reality of the problem of discovery of new outlets for investments. A consideration of these series (savings, issues, self-financing) suggests also that public investment may be required if large sums of money are not to lie idle. In the past, government spending has absorbed large amounts of cash not required in private channels, and failing the absorption by the defense program, new outlets may be required in the future. In the light of the savings-investment situation, the tax structure as well as expenditure pattern of the *governments* of the United States may well be scrutinized and revamped once the present crisis is over. The pay-roll tax and the security program are but a small part of this larger picture.

NOTE

We now turn to an analysis of the effects of the embodiment of savings in cash. There is no more effective way of elaboration of this issue than through the use of elementary accounting. We therefore assume as follows:

1. Business borrows 1 B (billion dollars) from banks. Then
   Savings = +1 B (money)
   Dissaving = +1 B (debts)
2. Business builds plants, factories, etc. The public spends one-half of 1 B, thus received, on consumption
   a. Business:
      Savings = +1 B (factories, etc.)
      Dissavings = +500 M (loses cash) + 500 M (reduction of inventories)

  b. Public:
  Income = +1 B (spends 500 M on consumption)
  Savings = +500 M (cash)
  c. Community (business and public):
  Savings. 1. Investment in factories, etc. = +1,000 M. 2.
  Cash = +1,000 M
  Dissaving. 1. Debts = +1,000 M. 2. Consumption = +500
  M

Net result: Public retains 500 millions of cash and increases consumption by 500 millions; business increases plant by 1,000 millions, reduces inventories by 500 millions, and increases cash by 500 millions. It follows, therefore, that the net effect of a rise of 1,000 millions in cash has been an increase of consumption of 500 millions and of net investment of 500 millions. The net increase in saving is 500 millions; and there is a rise of dissaving of 1,500 millions (1,000 millions debt and 500 millions inventories) and a rise of saving of 1,000 millions in cash and 1,000 millions in factories. Unfortunately, studies of savings do not reveal investments in real capital (expansion of plant) as do studies of capital formation. The conclusion is that the net effect of a rise of cash may be favorable to real investment, but that studies of savings do not help us much here.

Excessive concern over changes in cash frequently accounts for the mistakes in the estimates of savings and investments. Mr. Villard, it will be recalled, took the Brookings Institution to task for including in savings the 7.5 billion dollars of capital gains in 1929.[1] The case presented by Mr. Villard may be put as follows:

Individuals save 7.5 billion dollars. They buy securities which have risen in price by 7.5 billion dollars, the sellers thus obtaining an equivalent amount of capital gains. Consider two possibilities:

1. Sellers of securities use the cash to build factories, accumulate inventories, etc., directly or indirectly. Savings (and investment) then are +7.5 billions. (The maximum rise of savings is, however, 7.5 billions. Original savings only are converted into investments.) Sellers of assets do not save; for they merely put the savings of original savers to use.

2. Sellers of securities dissipate their 7.5 billion dollars in riotous living. Savings of original savers = 7.5 billions. Dissavings of sellers of securities = 7.5 billions. Net savings = 0.

Despite the fact that Dr. Ezekiel quotes Mr. Villard's article, he includes capital gains in his estimates of savings in 1929.[2] His assumptions are different, however. He assumes that the purchasers of securities *borrow* 7.5 billions in order to purchase securities. Sellers obtain profits of 7.5 billions. It is conceivable that, as would be evident from our earlier analysis, the net effect might be a rise of saving (7.5 billions cash) and an equivalent

---

[1] VILLARD, *op. cit.*, pp. 484–487.
[2] EZEKIEL, *op. cit.*, pp. 188–191.

rise of real investment. This result is, however, most improbable, and the estimate of savings on this assumption is subject to serious criticism. (1) The year 1929 was not a year in which monetary supplies expanded. (2) The process of production of 7.5 billions of investment goods would be accompanied by a large amount of disinvestment of consumption goods. (3) The creation of money and the output of investment would not be simultaneous.

2.8. Cures for Oversaving

According to the classical analysis premised upon Say's law, there could not be oversaving or inadequate investment demand. The rate of interest was presumed to equilibrate the rate of savings and investment so that all funds withheld from consumption automatically were translated into investment. This suggests that a first cure for oversaving should be a fall in the rate of interest. At the time of writing the *Treatise*, Keynes expressed more confidence in this measure than is now entertained in the *General Theory*. This change is to be explained on the basis of recent experience, particularly in the United States, which revealed clearly that unprecedented reductions in short-term rates were of little avail in inducing new investment.[1]

Another proposed cure for oversaving consists of public investment. The state can take a long-run point of view and pursue an anticyclical policy. Not only can it mitigate fluctuations, but according to this argument, it can hope to raise the average level of employment. When there is continuous underemployment, governmental construction need not divert factors of production from private uses, with the result that the true social cost of governmental projects is small. It can afford, therefore, to make investments which from the pecuniary point of view do not pay at current rates of interest so long as primary and secondary social advantages outweigh social cost.

The foregoing solution may, however, involve continuous deficits. Also, it may be difficult in a capitalistic world to find outlets

[1] It is not always clear whether Mr. Keynes thinks that a reduction in the costs of borrowing will do little good, or whether he simply believes that it is impossible to lower substantially the cost of borrowing by lowering the safe, short-term rate of interest even to zero. *General Theory*, pp. 205–208, 375–376, etc.

for public investment which are regarded as being useful and at the same time do not invade the traditional realm of private industry. A more direct remedy is, therefore, offered, that of discouraging savings and increasing consumption. This is brought about by a reduction of taxes on consumption or on funds that would be spent on consumption. At the same time, heavier taxes are to be placed on incomes that would be largely saved.[1]

One problem must be faced by all who advocate a redistribution of income to increase consumption, that of assuring an increase in the real capital of society.[2] Even Mr. Keynes who urges artificial stimulation of the propensity to consume through wage and tax policy points out the desirability of an increase of capital until it loses its scarcity value.[3] He argues, however, as follows:

> For we have seen that, up to the point where full employment prevails, the growth of capital depends not at all on a low propensity to consume but is, on the contrary, held back by it; and only in conditions of full employment is a low propensity to consume conducive to the growth of capital. Moreover, experience suggests that in existing conditions saving by institutions and through sinking funds is more than adequate, and that measures for the redistribution of incomes in a way likely to raise the propensity to consume may prove positively favourable to the growth of capital.[4]

Mr. Keynes goes too far here. We have seen in Sec. 2.6 that, even under the Keynesian assumption and with underemployment, an increase in the propensity to save will up to a certain point increase real investment through reductions in the rate of interest.[5]

[1] *Cf.* Discussion in the opening chapter.

[2] In this connection the conclusions of the National Resources Committee are of interest. *Cf. The Structure of the American Economy*, Part I, *Basic Characteristics*, pp. 90–91. An equal distribution of income would (if the present relationship of income and savings is maintained) reduce savings to a very low figure. Furthermore, the committee estimates that a rise of consumers' income of 33 per cent today would result in a rise of expenditures on consumption of but 25 per cent and a rise of savings of nearly 100 per cent.

[3] KEYNES, J. M., *General Theory*, pp. 31, 325, 375–377; LEDERER, E., "Is the Economic Frontier Closed?" *Soc. Research*, May, 1939, pp. 153–162; HICKS, J. R., *The Theory of Wages, passim;* HARDY, C. O., "Appraisal of the Factors Which Stopped the Recovery," *Am. Econ. Rev.*, March, 1939, *passim*. Dr. Hardy emphasizes the need of a continued rise of capital to maintain the high level of real incomes.

[4] KEYNES, *op. cit.*, pp. 372–373. Quoted by permission of Harcourt, Brace and Company, Inc., publishers.

[5] In defense of Mr. Keynes, it may be said, however, that he assumes an independence of changes in consumption and the rate of interest. Lange, *op. cit.*, pp. 30–31.

Where this point will be depends on the relative strengths of the response of investment to changes in the rate of interest and to changes in the level of consumption sales.

Nevertheless, one may well argue that the great problem of our age is using fully *and most effectively* (the latter a neglected problem)[1] the resources we now have and that a higher level of employment even with a slower rate of progress is to be desired. Moreover, there is little need to worry about a shortage of capital until interest rates begin to rise; at that time, offsets through monetary policy may be possible.[2]

2.9. CONCLUSION: DEFLATIONARY EFFECTS AND THE WISDOM OF THE RESERVE PLAN

No one can rule out the possibility of oversaving and secular stagnation whether caused by vanishing investment demand or depressive, anticapitalistic policies. Is it necessary then to condemn the accumulation of social security reserves if this danger is real? No decisive answer is possible. Under such circumstances the deflation attributable to the reserve plan must be counted as a disadvantage to be weighed against other advantages, *viz.*, contributions according to benefits, fiscal solvency, etc.

Moreover, it may be possible by policy in other spheres of activity (not to mention the public-assistance program) to offset the deflationary effects of reserve growth. A long-run public investment program combined with a tax policy designed to maximize the national income might be thought desirable. If these measures are at all efficacious, a relatively small accumulation of reserves of (say) 1 billion dollars a year or even less could hardly have fatal effects.

But if the prophets of doom are correct and large unemployment is to be expected in the years ahead, serious doubts must be raised

[1] National Resources Planning Board, *The Structure of the American Economy*, II. *Toward Full Use of Resources*, 1940, p. 5.

[2] As a qualification we should note that investment may be lessened not because funds are inadequate, but because the tax policies envisaged may destroy incentives at the margin. Also in considering the wisdom of increasing consumption, one should not forget the overconsumption theories. These, resting on the assumption of relatively full employment and inelastic money supplies (at the height of the cycle), hold that a rise in consumption will induce a crisis in investment goods industries. *Cf.* Haberler, *op. cit.*, new ed., pp. 77–79, 123–125, 236.

as to the advisability of an unmodified reserve plan. At the last reading of these lines in the spring, 1941, one cannot refrain from mentioning once more the defense program. So long as armament expenditures induce a condition of full employment or one approximating it, the argument for large pay-roll taxes and the accumulation of reserves during the period of defense or war activities gains in strength. The need of economies in consumption increases *pari passu* as the nation, once having reached this state, requires more and more resources for war purposes.[1]

[1] See, for example, PIGOU, A. C., *Political Economy of War*, new and rev. ed. 1940, Chaps. III–V; KEYNES, J. M., *How to Pay for the War*, Chaps. III, IV, VIII; and HARRIS, S. E., *Economics of American Defense*, Chaps. VI, XI.

CHAPTER 3

SAVINGS

3.1. FINANCIAL PLANS AND SAVINGS VIA INCOME

The central problem of this chapter is the effect of social security taxation on the total amount of savings. Although the influence of taxation cannot be evaluated without regard to expenditure, the influence of the latter is primarily discussed in Chaps. 2 and 4 and will be introduced here only where absolutely necessary.

First, it is well to consider how taxation affects savings indirectly through effects upon income. A reduction in income, *ceteris paribus*, is likely to result in a diminution of savings.[1] Later the direct effects on governmental and private savings may be considered.

Reserve financing involves relatively higher taxation in the near future, whereas pay-as-you-go deals lightly with the earlier years at the expense of very heavy taxation in the more distant future. Neglecting the transitional period before 1949 and taking account of benefit amendments and actuarial errors, we may roughly place the cost under the old-age reserve plan at the *constant* level of 6 to 10 per cent of total pay-rolls; under "current" financing the tax burden rises in amount from 1 to (say) 12 to 15 per cent. Under the latter, the amount of taxation is larger in perpetuity by about 5 per cent of covered pay-rolls, and recourse will be had to tax sources other than pay-rolls. The general tax revenues will carry one-third of the ultimate cost of 15 per cent, thus filling the gap made by the reduction of earnings on reserves. Actually, as we shall see, the Treasury will probably be forced to contribute more than one-third.

In the early years, the adverse impact on income and, indirectly, on private savings will be larger under the reserve plan than under pay-as-you-go, whereas in the later years the situation will be re-

[1] Mr. Keynes's statement on the relation between income and marginal propensity to consume has produced a large literature. The reader is referred to the discussions in the *Review of Economic Statistics* from 1937 to 1940 by Mr. Keynes, and Drs. Staehle, Gilboy, Polak, Dirks, and Ezekiel and to articles in the *Quarterly Journal of Economics* for 1938 and 1939 by Mr. Keynes, Drs. Gilboy, and Holden, and the article of Dr. Lange in *Economica*, 1938. The Brookings Institution's study on *America's Capacity to Consume* and the National Resources Committee study on *Consumers' Expenditures in the United States* should also be consulted.

versed. At first thought, one would be inclined to consider this a point in favor of current financing. For are not savings available today worth more than those available tomorrow? In the meantime they bear compound interest and yield new savings. The fallacy involved in this argument is revealed in a consideration of two related facts: (1) when account is taken of direct effects on savings, it is by no means clear that current financing means more current savings, as we shall see later; (2) a dollar of taxation today also has a greater present value than tomorrow's tax dollar because of interest saved in keeping the privately held public debt from growing as much as it otherwise would. Larger taxes today reduce *in perpetuity* the tax burden of the future. If the problems of governmental expenditure and of effective demand could be ignored, this latter consideration would be conclusive because the total of taxes collected earns interest in the foregoing sense, whereas much of the revenue raised by taxation would otherwise be spent on consumption.

Two facts stand out clearly from our discussion: (1) reserve results in a more even tax burden through time, and (2) it results in a smaller total tax burden through time. Again if we neglect the dual problem of expenditure and effective demand, and suppose no change in taxable capacity, the resultant effect on income and savings would seem to be most favorable under a plan that meets these requirements. Furthermore, if it is granted that taxation, even when matched by equal expenditure, involves a transfer burden that grows more than proportionately with the amount of taxation, this policy can be shown to be optimal in the sense of minimizing the total transfer burden over time.

Lest it be thought that we are arguing that a reserve plan is necessarily best, the preceding analysis should be qualified. It neglects completely the problem of expenditure. Many economists might defend this neglect on the ground that expenditure over time on social security is determined by benefit formulas and demographic factors and will be the same under current and reserve financing. This is perfectly true but does not justify the ignoring of expenditure. For the burden of taxation varies inversely with contemporaneous government expenditure. This means that moderate taxation with little or no government expenditure may be much more depressing to income than heavy taxation matched by expenditure.[1] In other words, taxable capacity depends in part upon

[1] We would not argue that the burden on income depends only upon the difference between taxation and expenditure and is independent of the amount of them. In

governmental expenditure itself. It is because these interactions are neglected that analysis along traditional public finance lines seems to be at variance with monetary analysis; when these are given proper weight, many paradoxes are resolved and the relation of the analysis of this section to the preceding chapter becomes clear. The practical importance of these qualifications is to weaken the case for the reserve plan.[1] In other words, the disadvantage of the collection of more taxes under current financing, than under reserves, is offset to some extent by the beneficial effects of the expenditures.

3.2. DIRECT PRIMARY EFFECTS ON SAVINGS

The reserve and pay-as-you-go plans differ also in their more direct effects upon savings. For one thing, current financing will probably involve greater recourse to non-pay-roll taxation of the income tax variety. Instead of falling upon the low-income classes and upon consumption, taxes will be levied on the middle and higher income groups whose propensity to save is high. Quite clearly such a policy lowers the propensity to save, but as we have seen in the previous chapter[2] this does not necessarily mean that net final savings will be less because, according to the Keynesian analysis, income will fall less under progressive taxation.

Here an important reservation must be made. Mr. Keynes's conclusion holds only if no account is taken of the damaging effects of progressive taxation upon the willingness of people to undertake investment, particularly of the risky variety. Even though consumption and sales do not fall, the inducement for the capitalist to invest

---

addition to depending upon their difference, it probably also increases, *ceteris paribus*, with simultaneous increases in the individual items. The latter burden is of a transfer nature and shows itself in its influence on margins, motivations, administrative costs, frictions, etc. The former is related to the monetary problems discussed in other chapters of Part I.

[1] The case for current financing might be strengthened if the foregoing analysis were pushed to its logical conclusion and the following extreme, alternative criteria of desirable policy were set up: (1) surpluses or deficits (real, not nominal) should be equalized through time, except for business cycle modifications; (2) the total amount of surplus over time should be minimized. Pay-as-you-go means constant surpluses at the zero level. Under reserves there are great surpluses in the near future followed by a final equalization of outlay and income.

[2] *Supra*, pp. 76–80.

may be lessened. The damage to income is not at all measured by the amount of tax collected—as it might be in the case of a tax on consumption—for the following related reasons. (1) The tax may discourage investment by an amount many times itself, and no one must pay taxes on investments he does not make. In the limiting case, all higher income could conceivably be made to dry up, the tax collections would be zero, and the burden great. (2) Because of the secondary multiplying effects of investment on income, the decline in income will exceed the decline in investment. Here the Keynesian analysis works in reverse.

Finally, we must consider the direct primary effects upon saving of the accumulation of the reserve itself, leaving for later discussion secondary effects. Tax collections in excess of expenditure, used to keep the debt from growing as rapidly as it otherwise would, lower the propensity to consume and increase the propensity to save.

We may consider in more detail four alternative financial programs: (1) a tax on workers' pay-rolls or other consumption taxes on low-income groups; (2) a tax on pay-rolls assessed upon employers; (3) taxes on surpluses largely levied on the upper-income classes; (4) inflationary methods, *e.g.*, sales of securities to the banks. We may dismiss the last now, for inflation invoked in order to accumulate reserves is on the face of it absurd.[1] Of the others, the first will provide the largest net savings, and the second and third follow in that order. Savings out of workers' incomes, accumulated in reserves, are not likely to be offset by a large reduction of private savings by the workers. Taxes assessed upon employers on the basis of pay-rolls may be shifted in part to higher income classes or may even in part remain upon the capitalistic classes. These groups may in turn protect their consumption standards through curtailment of their savings. Finally, should the taxes be imposed exclusively upon surpluses, any addition to reserves will be offset by a diminution of private savings to a greater extent than under the first two financial programs. Taxes on surpluses are likely to play a larger part in a pay-as-you-go system than under a reserve system. On this account, the volume of savings may suffer more under this system. Non-payroll taxes will contribute more under the current financing program

[1] The possibility of issuance of noninterest-bearing debt or currency inflation might be considered. This keeps the interest-bearing debt from growing and helps future financing without leading to current deflation. However, it is not discussed here, nor will the obvious results of combinations of the preceding financial methods be considered.

than under reserves, because total taxes will be greater and the distribution in time more skewed under nonreserve financing. Under current financing the pressure to levy taxes other than consumption taxes would become very strong.

3.3. QUANTITATIVE EFFECT ON SAVINGS

For the purpose of focusing attention on the relevant variables, one may make some hypothetical guesses as to their respective magnitudes. Assume that workers pay 3 per cent of pay-rolls on old-age insurance and employers pay 3 per cent on old-age and 3 per cent on unemployment insurance. One per cent of pay-rolls may be estimated very roughly at 400 million dollars. Workers then pay 1.2 billion dollars and employers pay 2.4 billion dollars. Hypothetically, *we may guess* that workers and other low-income groups ultimately pay two-thirds of the assessment upon employers.[1] They pay, therefore, 1.2 billion dollars (directly) plus 1.6 billions (two-thirds of 2.4 billion dollars) = 2.8 billion dollars. (It is of course possible that workers will shift part of the tax to entrepreneurs and other capitalist groups. That is not allowed for here.) Suppose they cut their savings by one-seventh of this amount, or 400 million dollars. Other groups who pay 800 million dollars (2.4 billions − 1.6 billions) may be assumed to reduce their savings by three-quarters of the costs assessed upon them, or 600 million dollars. The reduction of private savings is then 1,000 millions = 400 millions (workers) + 600 millions (employers and higher income groups). This must be set against the direct savings of the funds going into the reserve. If we assume that all contributions are put into reserves at this time and neglect secondary effects, this will amount to 3,600 million dollars (1.2 billions + 2.4 billions). Net savings are then 2,600 million dollars (3,600 millions − 1,000 millions).[2]

---

[1] The problems of incidence are treated in Part III of this book so that a few words in justification of this rough estimate must here suffice. When one considers the magnitude of the tax and the total amount of profit, rent, and interest income, one cannot escape the conclusion that the pressure to pass on the tax will be very strong. The attempt will not be completely successful though the larger part of the burden is likely to be shifted in the form of lower retained wages and increases in prices to consumers.

[2] *Cf.* more extensive calculations of this nature in Chap. 17. The reader should

We have considered the reduction in private savings resulting from loss of disposable income through taxation. There remains still the possibility of an induced change in voluntary savings out of retained income as a result of the social security program. On this point, Drs. Colm and Lehmann reach the conclusion that private savings are *not* affected.[1] This seems extreme, although in a dynamic society it is difficult to substantiate any conclusion even when statistical information is available. However, it is perhaps desirable to review briefly the findings of other investigators relevant to this issue.

According to one investigator, who relies largely on correlation studies, the most important variable determining consumption is income, even its distribution being relatively unimportant.[2] The Brookings Institution (and Mr. Keynes, of course) put much more emphasis on the distribution of income; consumption suffers and savings rise when the wealthy increase their share.[3] These views are reconcilable, however. Changes in the amount of income are accompanied by changes in its distribution. That more is saved as incomes rise follows from assumptions concerning the new distribution of income. In his conclusions on the relations of income and savings, Mr. Keynes was aware of the importance of both the amount and distribution of income.[4]

---

take cognizance of the following assumptions in the foregoing calculations:

1. No benefits are being paid.

2. In the calculations at any rate, no allowance is made for rises in prices. In so far as they rise, the effects will be felt in a reduction of purchasing power of the dollar, not in a reduction of money wages. In other words, the secondary reduction of money income of low-income groups will be less than 1,600 million dollars.

3. Direct payments are made by wage earners (1.2 billion dollars). The indirect burden of 1.6 billion dollars is borne, however, not only by workers but also by other low-income groups.

[1] COLM, G., and F. LEHMANN, *Economic Consequences of Recent American Tax Policy*, especially pp. 38–42. According to these authors, the American tax policy accounts for a reduction of annual savings by 2 billion dollars. The net loss of savings is much less. Social security reserves increase by 1 billion, the losses thus being cut by one half. Contrary views on the effects on private savings are to be found in Karl Pribram, "The Functions of Reserves in Old Age Benefit Plans," *Quart. Jour. Econ.*, August, 1938, p. 636; Winston, Strawn, and Shaw, *The Social Security Act*, p. 10; "Report of the Committee on Social Security Legislation," *Proc. Nat. Tax Assoc.*, 1937, p. 70. The last is, however, concerned with another problem, *viz.*, the effects on savings of a progressive tax program introduced to finance social security.

[2] POLAK, J. J., "Fluctuations in United States Consumption, 1919–1932," *Rev. Econ. Statistics*, February, 1939, p. 10.

[3] Brookings Institution, *America's Capacity to Consume*, p. 93.

[4] On these issues see E. W. Gilboy, "Income-expenditure Relations," *Rev. Econ.*

From the more or less accepted views on these issues, one may conclude that if, following the introduction of a social security program (assumption of unchanged incomes), the distribution of incomes became less skewed, consumption would rise. This assumed effect on the distribution of incomes may not follow, however, if the program is financed exclusively through pay-roll taxes. Furthermore, effects will vary according as reserves are being accumulated, maintained, or decumulated. Thus in periods of nonaccumulation (maintenance), a rise in the propensity to consume may well be expected because income is redistributed in favor of the unemployed and the aged. In general, however, the distribution of incomes over time is improved, the effects upon total consumption, therefore, being favorable.

Several other considerations may be introduced here, however. Dr. Ezekiel, for example, concludes that the most secure group *at a given level of income* saves a minimum, and the least secure group a maximum.[1] Since the social security program increases security, the general effect then should be that in response to a rise of savings under the security program, private savings would decline. Should Dr. Ezekiel be right, his views would conflict with the Colm-Lehmann thesis of maintenance of voluntary saving despite the rise of compulsory savings. In this connection, the evidence of the Brookings Institution's studies and that of the National Resources Committee on the predominance of negative savings on the part of those with low incomes and, therefore, the unavailability of savings that might be reduced, should be considered.[2] These groups might, how-

---

Statistics, 1940, pp. 115–118; A. H. Hansen, *Fiscal Policy and Business Cycles*, Chaps. II, VIII, XIX; M. Kalecki, *Essays in the Theory of Economic Fluctuations*, pp. 59–61. In particular, it is well to distinguish conclusions based on current personal budgets from those to be derived from *historical* changes in incomes for identical individuals. A rise of income for *A* from $1,000 to $2,000 and its effects on consumption are one problem; a comparison of income-expenditure relations of *A* who has an income of $1,000 and *B* who has an income of $2,000 is another problem. Still another problem is the effects on consumption if in year *n*, *A* and *B* both have incomes of $1,500 and in year *n* + 1, *A*'s income is $1,000 and *B*'s $2,000.

[1] Ezekiel, M., "An Annual Estimate of Savings by Individuals," *Rev. Econ. Statistics*, November, 1937, p. 187.

[2] *Cf.* Roelse, H. V., "Social Security Program," *Proc. Am. Econ. Assoc.*, 1938, pp. 143–144. For criticism of the investigations of the National Resources Committee on the distribution of income, see R. S. Tucker, "The National Resources Committee's Report on Distribution of Income," *Rev. Econ. Statistics*, 1937, pp. 165–182.

It may be misleading to generalize from the experience of one or two years con-

ever, dissave. Finally one might accept as evidence against the Colm-Lehmann thesis the large rise and increased significance of savings by life insurance companies and similar institutions in recent years. Here again the evidence is not conclusive. It would be necessary to know more about the income classes that save via these institutions today and have done so in the past.[1]

Let us review in greater detail several of the studies that deal with the relation of incomes, savings, and expenditures. Miss Williams finds that savings of those with incomes of $1,200 to $1,500 had declined in a striking manner in the years 1934–1936 as compared with the years 1917–1919.[2] Increased responsibilities assumed by the government for the security of the unemployed may be one of several factors contributing to that development. According to the Brookings Institution's study the aggregate savings of those with incomes of less than $3,000 in the prosperous year of 1929 seems to have been roughly zero.[3]

TABLE I.—SAVINGS AND PER CENT OF INCOME SAVED BY INCOME CLASSES

Income class	Savings, millions of dollars	Per cent of income saved
Under $0	−1,588	−10
$0–$1,000	− 550	− 5
1,000–2,000	801	5
2,000–3,000	1,490	10

Recent studies are not more reassuring. The Brookings pattern of savings by low-income classes is verified by the study of the National

cerning the significance of negative savings. How long can low-income classes (assuming relatively small movements between classes) continue to spend more than they receive as income?

[1] The paradox of large (and increased amounts of) life insurance savings, on the one hand, and the apparent failure of families with less than $3,000 income as a whole to save (net), on the other, requires further thought and investigation. See the interesting Monograph 2 of the Temporary National Economic Committee, *Families and Their Life Insurance*, especially pp. VI, 8–9, 41–49. In a survey of 2,132 Massachusetts families, of which 25 per cent were on relief, the following facts were revealed: 60 per cent of the families on relief carried insurance; industrial insurance, which is very expensive, accounted for 64 per cent of the premiums paid by the low-income groups studied in this survey; the lower the income, the larger was the percentage of insurance costs to income; for a large sample, nonrelief families paid 4.72 per cent of their income and relief families 3.97 per cent.

[2] WILLIAMS, F. M., "Changes in Family Expenditures in the Post-war Period," *Monthly Labor Rev.*, November, 1938, p. 978.

[3] *America's Capacity to Consume*, p. 93.

Resources Committee, which is based on a much larger sample.[1] A study of 897 white families in New York City (average income of $1,745) reveals that, on the average, current expenditures in 1934–1935 exceeded current incomes by $70 per family.[2] A similar study for Chicago reveals that for four income classes ($500 to $749, $750 to $999, $1,000 to $1,249, $1,250 to $1,499) the respective deficits were 33, 12, 6, and 2 per cent of income. Classes with incomes of $1,750 to $1,999 and above had surpluses of incomes over expenditures, the maximum surplus for the highest class considered ($10,000 and over) being 35 per cent.[3]

Obviously, workers are in no position to cut savings when they are not saving. They may, however, increase their liabilities and reduce their assets. In other words, they may dissave. In this connection, the following facts are of interest. In 1938, commercial time deposits plus mutual savings bank deposits amounted to 24.6 billion dollars.[4] Life insurance premiums, according to the Department of Commerce, were roughly 3 billions in the depression year of 1932, or about 22 millions in excess of the total for 1929. Assets of the 308 legal reserve life insurance companies in 1938 totaled 26.2 billions. If insured against the vicissitudes of unemployment and old age, workers may decide to draw on their bank balances, borrow on life insurance policies, and even cash in on surrender values.[5] In this connection, the table on page 86 of *Family Expenditures in Chicago,* 1935–1936, to which reference is made in footnote 3 below, is of some

[1] *Consumer Expenditures in the United States*, pp. 5–6, 19–20; cf. also Gilboy, *op. cit.*, pp. 116–119.

[2] U. S. Department of Labor, Bulletin 637, *Money Disbursements of Wage Earners and Clerical Workers on the North Atlantic Region*, 1934–1936, vol. I, New York City, Part I, Chap. 1, especially p. 29.

[3] U. S. Department of Labor, Bulletin 642, *Family Expenditures in Chicago*, 1935–1936, vol. II, especially Chaps. II, VIII. From an examination of the latter chapter it becomes evident that savings are predominantly invested in insurance for all but the high-income classes. Beginning at incomes of $500 to $749, where insurance premiums constitute 5 per cent of income, insurance accounts for 5 to 6 per cent for higher income classes including through $4,000, and 6 to 10 per cent for higher incomes. The corresponding percentage of insurance premiums to surplus incomes are 24 per cent, 32 to 89 per cent, and 25 to 36 per cent for the three classes. Also see National Resources Committee, *Consumer Expenditure in the United States*. Large negative savings are made by those with income levels of less than $1,500.

[4] The relevant statistical material is not dealt with fully here because the author is at work on a study of savings and investment.

[5] According to F. C. Mills, *Economic Tendencies in the United States*, p. 425, the average rate of increase of savings deposits, aggregate reserves of life insurance companies, and assets of building and loan associations for the years 1922–1929 was no less than 7, 10½, and 15 per cent, respectively. Reduction in the holdings of these assets is the more likely to occur because the increase had been so rapid. Life insurance reserves have continued to grow, however, and savings deposits and assets of building associations are still much above the level of 1922.

interest. Individuals in receipt of low and even fairly high incomes reduce their assets through withdrawals of bank deposits, sales of investments, and reduction of credits with insurance companies. They increase their liabilities through rises in loans due and balances due (largely installment accounts), and in the higher income groups through a rise of mortgage debt. It should not be assumed, however, high as the rise of net liabilities is shown to be for all classes with incomes of less than $1,750, that the *total* dissaving involved is thus covered. A large percentage of those in low-income brackets also dissave in the sense that they spend in excess of their earned income and yet do not increase their liabilities; they obtain relief funds of various kinds, both public and private.

Of more importance than the considerations adduced above are the effects of the social security program upon output and income and, via the latter, upon savings. It therefore follows that the choice of financial methods, their effects upon consumption and investment, and the investment policy followed by the managers of the fund will be vital factors determining the net effects upon savings. These are issues that receive attention in this part of the book and also later. Compulsory savings of a billion dollars each year which may be obtained through the social security program may conceivably contribute toward a rise (or fall) of several times the amount of initial savings.

3.4. Effects on Savings via the Rate of Interest

A net rise of savings tends to induce a decline in the rate of interest. The retirement of debt involves the transfer of funds to investors. Even if the budget is unbalanced so that no debt is retired, the Treasury no longer finds it necessary to float as many new issues. As a result, funds that would otherwise go into these channels are released for private investment so that interest rates are lower than they otherwise would be.

It is scarcely necessary to point out that a reduction in the yield of public securities is not equivalent to a general reduction in the structure of interest rates. In recent years the spread between public and private security yields has been very marked. Moreover, the fact that banks have excess reserves and that issues of government bonds can result in an expansion of bank deposits suggests that the demand for public issues from private sources consistently rises.

In the light of the significance of the improvement of private demand, only a moderate reduction in the yield of governments should be traced to compulsory public savings. The influence on private yields would be still more tenuous.

To the extent that there is a fall in the general interest rate, what is the effect? It is sometimes argued that such a fall will curtail private accumulation.[1] This involves the question of the supply curve of savings and its properties. In later discussions of incidence (Sec. 20.8) a survey of this problem will be attempted. Recently emphasis has shifted to stressing the importance of income rather than interest rates in determining consumption and savings. Many writers have pointed out that at a lower rate of interest some individuals might save a larger share of their income in order to provide the same income at a future date. Much of saving is almost automatically determined by institutional habits, etc. All in all, many economists hold that the supply of savings is probably quite inelastic with respect to the rate of interest.

Such analysis neglects one vital consideration. Much additional saving is done by individuals out of current interest income from securities held. A decline in the rate of yield on these directly lowers the income of the rentier class and through its effects on the distribution of income lowers saving.

Mr. Keynes permits a decrease in consumption or an increase of saving to influence the rate of interest only through the back door of liquidity preference.[2] An increased propensity to save necessarily in the Keynesian system results in a lowering of national income. At the lower income level, less money is needed to satisfy the transaction motive. Money is therefore released for speculative holding, and with unchanged liquidity preference the rate of interest must fall. This rather artificial sequence of events rules out the straightforward interpretation of a fall of interest rates being due simply to the offering of more funds in the security market, the bidding up of the prices of securities, and the lowering of their yields.

Once the rate of interest is reduced, however this may have been brought about, there is a tendency for investment to rise except

---

[1] If equilibrium in the capital market is stable, the contraction of private savings in the most extreme case would fall short of the initial increase of savings so that there remains a net expansion of savings. Otherwise, the rate of interest would not be lower and there would be no curtailment of private savings.

[2] Cf. LANGE, op. cit., pp. 30–31. More recently Mr. Keynes seems to admit that an increase in thrift will tend to lower the rate of interest despite adverse effects through a rise of liquidity preference. Robertson, op. cit., p. 18.

for the fact that income has fallen simultaneously.[1] In any case the fall in interest rates tends to offset the influence of declining income. If the beneficial effect of decreased interest rates is sufficiently great, investment will rise. In this case, savings and investment will be increased by the attempt to save more, although an increased propensity to save one dollar will always result under the Keynesian assumptions in less than one dollar's worth of savings and investment. On the other hand, the short-run marginal propensity to invest may be such that savings will actually decrease in absolute amount because of the decreased propensity to consume. The result depends, as indicated earlier, upon the extent to which money released from transaction purposes lowers interest rates and the extent to which the reduction in interest rates offsets the decline in investment due to decreasing income.[2]

In the American economy of the thirties, interest rates were low partly because of the low level of the marginal efficiency of capital and partly because of monetary ease. To some extent they may have been lower than they otherwise would have been in the later years because of the growth of departmental and trust funds. Because the budget remained out of balance, rates were not lowered in an absolute sense, but only relative to what they would have been with a pay-as-you-go policy. Probably the marginal efficiency schedule was extremely inelastic at this time so that little extra private or public investment was stimulated. The result may have been largely a dissipation of savings, or a diversion of savings through governmental intervention into consumption channels.

We must distinguish between two senses in which planned savings may not materialize. (1) The attempt to save may so reduce income and investment that the result is a decline in output and in realized savings. (2) And (this is less harmful), savings instead of being invested may be used for consumption purposes. As compared with the original Morgenthau plan, which anticipated debt retirement with an accumulation of reserves, this is what happened to the compulsory savings raised by pay-roll taxation. They were used to buy Treasury issues, and therefore, were diverted to a large extent to consumption; but there is no substantial evidence that total governmental expenditure was increased over what it would have been in the absence of accumulation of reserve funds.

---

[1] In discussing the relation of consumption and the rate of interest, Dr. Kalecki contends that long-term rates of interest change little. Kalecki, *op. cit.*, p. 56.

[2] *Cf.* last paragraph of Sec. 2.6.

3.5. The Relation between Consumption and Investment

Repeatedly in the preceding analysis mention was made of the adverse effects of a decline in consumption or income upon the prospects for profitable investment and upon the marginal efficiency of capital. On the basis of the acceleration principle, any rate of decrease of consumption is likely to result in large decreases in investment; and, contrariwise, a positive rate of consumption increase may induce large amounts of investment.[1] "Investment is an increasing function of the rate of *change* in consumption." Earlier, it had been pointed out that we must set against these adverse effects any lowering of the rate of interest through compulsory saving.[2] According to Mrs. Robinson, however, investment is by definition zero in long-run equilibrium. Lowering of interest rates increases the appropriate stock of capital and increases real wages. However, if the elasticity of substitution between labor and capital is sufficiently great, the distribution of income may change so much in favor of the capitalist class with its low propensity to consume that the long-run level of employment will fall. Thus, long-run effects may differ from those of the short run.[3]

Finally, the reader should remember that an initial act of saving may in its final effects imply an increased propensity to consume. A price increase in the security markets and the resulting capital gains, for example, may encourage greater expenditure out of in-

[1] A tendency to exaggerate the significance of the acceleration principle is happily being corrected. The reader is referred to the large literature on the acceleration principle. Prof. Haberler has surveyed the literature and the issues in his inimitable style, *Prosperity and Depression*, pp. 85–105. See in particular J. M. Clark, *Strategic Factors in Business Cycles*, pp. 33*ff*.; discussion between Ragnar Frisch and J. M. Clark, *Jour. Pol. Econ.*, October, 1931, and April and October, 1932; R. F. Harrod, *The Trade Cycle*, Chap. II; A. C. Pigou, *Industrial Fluctuations*, 2d ed., Chap. 9; P. A. Samuelson, "Interactions Between the Multiplier Analysis and the Principle of Acceleration," *Rev. Econ. Statistics*, 1939; A. H. Hansen, *Full Recovery or Stagnation?* pp. 48–52, and *Fiscal Policy and Business Cycles;* Kalecki, *op. cit.*, p. 65. On the possibility of a rise of consumption inducing a collapse in investment goods industries, see Haberler, *op. cit.*, pp. 50–51, 78–79, 134–135. Writers who take this position generally assume conditions of full employment and relatively inelastic monetary conditions. Apparently Prof. Haberler makes an assumption of less than full employment when he argues that a rise in the propensity to consume must be followed by a rise of employment. He specifically makes an assumption of *ceteris paribus* and an elastic liquidity preference schedule (*op. cit.*, p. 236).

[2] Hansen, A. H., *Full Recovery or Stagnation?* p. 157; Haberler, *ibid.*, p. 128.

[3] Robinson, J., *Essays in the Theory of Employment*, pp. 111–127, 131–135, for example.

come on consumption goods. In this connection Prof. Clark's hypothesis that savings in the twenties had the foregoing result is of some interest.[1] Similar results may follow if the new savings account for a corresponding rise of consumption expenditure by the Treasury.[2]

An issue related to the problems of this section, *viz.*, the interdependence of prices of consumption and investment goods is treated briefly in a note at the end of this chapter.

3.6. SAVINGS AND INVESTMENT

This subject can only be briefly touched upon here. Prof. Haberler has already reviewed the vast literature, and some aspects of the problem will be treated more fully in a later study of savings and investment. It will suffice here to say that the controversy over equality or inequality of these magnitudes is largely terminological.[3] For our purpose it is sometimes convenient to define the terms in such a manner as to permit differences in these magnitudes. One may use the unwieldy definitions prescribed by Mr. Keynes in the *Treatise* or the period analysis of Robertson.

Three cases are to be distinguished: (1) $I > S$; (2) $I = S$; (3) $S > I$. An excess of investment over savings means, by the Robertsonian definition, that income is rising. Equality means that income is constant; this may be at either a high or low level. Thus, only at the top and bottom of the cycle is there equilibrium between savings and investment. An excess of savings over investment means that income is falling.

A different but related sense in which these terms are used involves a comparison of savings and investment in the vicinity of

---

[1] CLARK, J. M., "An Appraisal of the Workability of Compensatory Devices," *Am. Econ. Rev., Supplement*, March, 1939, pp. 205–206; *cf.*, however, KALECKI, *op. cit.*, pp. 58–60.

[2] *Cf.* DOUGLAS, P. H., *Social Security in the United States* (2d ed.), pp. 144–145.

[3] Mr. Keynes himself has said, "The significance of both my present and my former arguments lies in their attempt to show that the volume of employment is determined by the estimates of effective demand made by the entrepreneurs, an expected increase of investment relatively to saving as defined in my *Treatise on Money* being a criterion of an increase in effective demand." *The General Theory*, p. 78, quoted by permission of Harcourt, Brace, and Company, Inc., publishers. *Cf.* my introductory chapter (Sec. 2) and 2.7 for a discussion of related issues.

full employment. If at this level saving exceeds investment, the economy will be depressed and will be at underemployment equilibrium. If investment exceeds saving at full employment, price and wage increases must ensue, leading to a cumulative profit inflation.

In this and the previous chapter we have analyzed at considerable length the effect of increased saving under the conditions of cases 2 and 3. Let us now investigate the consequences of a rise in savings by the government when investment would otherwise tend to outstrip savings (case 1). An increase in savings may release factors of production for the capital-goods industries and make possible a redistribution of consumption goods to workers whose incomes are rising, forestalling an untoward price increase and an unwanted inflation. The savers renounce their rights to consumption goods in favor of entrepreneurs and the beneficiaries of the latter's expenditure. Because consumption is immediately reduced by the full amount saved, and since real investment even under these most favorable conditions will presumably be increased by not quite so much as the amount saved, the total effect is to slow down the increase in income and the rate of price rise. Because of saving by the government, there is less "forced" savings through price increases.

This statement must be qualified. In some circumstances artificially induced savings might accelerate the upward movement. Funds directed or released to a booming security market might cause manifold increases in values. As a result, bullish expectations might develop accompanied by downward shifts in the curve of liquidity preference; credit creation might be stimulated. The combined effect might be to keep the rate of interest too low so that the divergence between savings and investment would only be aggravated. Banking authorities attempting to check the excessive activity in investment markets might ultimately be embarrassed by the influx of new savings.[1]

---

[1] *Cf.* STEWART, M., *Social Security*, p. 246. A related aspect requires mention. The accumulation of reserves by reducing the amount of government bonds which the market must absorb may help to prevent a serious decline in the government bond market incident upon good times. How much weaker might the market for governments have been in the spring of 1937 had it not been for the inauguration of old-age and unemployment compensation programs?

The market for governments is not supported at the expense of private investment in so far as the compulsory saving comes out of consumption. *Cf.* J. B. Andrews, "Investment and Liquidation of Unemployment Reserves," *Am. Labor Legislation Rev.*, December, 1932, p. 143.

With the remark that savings are least likely to be dissipated in this case, the discussion of case 1 may be brought to a close. The special form of case 2 which implies that employment is full, income is stable, and that savings can always be transformed without delay into investment is the pure "classical" case. It is dealt with briefly at the beginning of Sec. 2.6, and no more need be said here.

In concluding this section, it may be instructive to consider the effect of a decumulation of the reserve fund. This involves the reverse process of sale of securities from the old-age account to the public and in many respects is indistinguishable from other types of deficit spending. In the first instance, the propensity to consume is increased and the propensity to save is lessened. But just as an increase of the propensity to save is not equivalent to an increase in effective saving but may even be accompanied by a fall in the latter, so a decrease in the propensity to save may not adversely affect net savings. Because government bonds must be sold, the yield on such securities may increase. If the demand for governments is quite elastic, as it seems to be during depression, the increase in interest rates will be at a minimum; moreover, at this time the differentiation of rates between private and public securities is at a maximum so that the increase in the interest rate to private investors may be slight. Against the discouragement to investment of an increase in the cost of borrowing, we must consider the favorable effects of an increase in consumption sales attributable to the expenditure under the program. Then the safest generalization that may be made is that the more prosperous the community and the more rapidly national income is rising (case 1), the better can it stand an accumulation of the reserve and the less desirable is decumulation.

Periods of decumulation of old-age reserves may not, however, coincide with periods of abnormal depression. The reserve will decumulate when population is decreasing, the proportion of old people is increasing, and the percentage of eligibles is approaching its maximum. Nevertheless, to some extent net withdrawals from old-age reserves (or at least a slowing down of the rate of accumulation) will coincide with declining consumption demand, for tax revenues decline in depression and retirements are accelerated. In general, however, the old-age insurance program is likely to complement other cyclical factors, not offset them. Variations in *unemployment* reserves is more likely to prove an important anticyclical factor.

3.7. SUMMARY.

From the standpoint of taxation alone, expenditure and effective demand being momentarily disregarded, the reserve plan is found to be superior to current financing in its effects upon income and savings because the total tax burden over time is lessened and the distribution of burden over time more nearly optimal. When account is taken of the preceding neglected elements, this superiority is lessened. The reserve plan in the period of accumulation results in a larger amount of primary saving because tax collections are in excess of expenditure and because taxation under this plan is more likely to fall upon consumption and is less likely to impinge on the savings of middle- and high-income groups.

In evaluating the magnitude of primary savings, it is necessary to form an estimate of the effect of compulsory governmental saving upon voluntary private saving out of retained income. The existing distribution of savings by income class lends support to the view that the reaction on private savings is of secondary importance. However, recent studies on the fluctuations in capital assets of low-income classes may suggest a contrary conclusion.

An increase in primary savings or in the amount that will be saved out of a given income does not necessarily mean that net savings and investment will increase. The attempt to save may so decrease income that actually less will be saved. Whether or not savings and investment will increase as a result of an increased propensity to save depends upon (1) the extent to which interest rates are lowered by savings, (2) the extent to which investment will respond to a reduction in interest rates, and (3) the extent to which investment is inhibited by a reduction in consumption sales. One must also consider the relation of prices of investment and consumption of goods.[1] The crucial issue in this connection seems to be the relative importance, in the determination of prices of investment goods, of anticipation of incomes (related to changes in demand for consumption goods) and the rate of interest. Savings may be dissipated through a decline in income and may be offset through being drained off into consumption, as in recent government expenditure.

The strength of the factors enumerated above, upon which the secondary effects on saving depend, must be considered relative to the magnitude of saving and investments in the absence of these compulsory savings. When investments tend to exceed savings and

[1] See note at end of chapter.

national income is high and increasing, compulsory saving will be least deflationary. It is even possible (on the assumption of less than full employment) for the upward movement to be unduly accelerated because of lowness of the interest rates. Once full employment is anticipated (*e.g.*, consider the current defense program), the deflationary arguments lose force.[1] When savings exceed investment so that employment is low and/or falling, the accumulation of reserves will contribute toward further oversaving. The decline in interest rates will be small and insufficient to offset the decline in investment opportunities following a curtailment of consumption. In periods of decumulation the reverse process will be operating.

NOTE: RELATION OF PRICES OF CONSUMPTION AND INVESTMENT GOODS

We now turn to the relation of the prices of consumption and investment goods. The higher their correlation, the more likely is it that a reduction of the demand for and the prices of consumption goods will be associated with a reduction in the output of investment goods. This discussion is centered around the full treatment in Mr. Keynes's *Treatise*. (References, unless otherwise stated, as to vol. I of the *Treatise*.) The discussion in this section is not *closely* related to the problems of social security. Without much loss, the general reader may omit it.

The determination of P' (price level of investment goods) is one of the most baffling problems confronting Mr. Keynes. Income is either spent on consumption goods or saved, and therefore the determination of the price level of consumption goods is a relatively simple problem; but in seeking P', one is thwarted by the fact that money saved is not necessarily spent on investment goods, and therefore a simple equation is not available.

First, the author presents what may be designated the "excess-bearishness" analysis (pp. 141–145). He returns to this explanation in Chap. 15; but in the meanwhile he offers what may be termed the money-rate explanation (especially pp. 202–204).

a. The Excess-bearishness Explanation. The price level of investment goods is held to be determined by the attitude of the public toward securities relative to their attitude toward cash or deposits. At this point, it may be noted, securities and investment goods are used interchangeably. When the public becomes bearish, they turn from securities to savings deposits and, therefore, the prices of securities tend to decline.

b. The Capitalization Explanation. Before turning to the capitalization explanation we must consider Mr. Keynes's only serious attempt to reconcile the two theories (pp. 255–256):[2]

[1] For a discussion of the various meanings of unemployment, see W. H. Hutt, *The Theory of Idle Resources*, especially Chap. I.

[2] Quoted by permission of Harcourt, Brace and Company, Inc., publishers.

"In the long run the value of securities is entirely derivative from the value of consumption goods. It depends on the expectation as to the value of the amount of liquid consumption goods which the securities will, directly or indirectly, yield, modified by reference to the risk and uncertainty of this expectation, and multiplied by the number of years' purchase corresponding to the current rate of interest, for capital of the duration in question. . . .

"But in the very short run, it depends on opinion largely uncontrolled by any present monetary factors."

At this point, however, Mr. Keynes distinguishes between securities and investment goods (especially pp. 211–212, 249, 255–256, 267–268). It is indeed significant that the rise in the prices of securities in 1925–1929 was not accompanied by a rise in the price of new investment goods; and in view of the spectacular rise in security prices, the response of the production of capital goods was moderate indeed.[1]

In contending that the rate of interest influences P' directly, Mr. Keynes specifically denies that any explanation along Fisherian lines is tenable. Yet an examination of the question convinces one that the response of P' to movements in the interest rate is a market phenomenon and that the causal relationship is not from interest rate directly to P'.[2] Let us suppose that the long-term rate of interest declines. Why do the prices of bonds or machinery rise? The capitalization theory merely affirms that the present values of future increments of income rise with a decline in the rate of interest. What we are concerned with is the manner in which this rise in the present value of future increments is translated into a rise in capital values. A machine will rise in price only as the decline in the rate of interest stimulates bids for machinery and, therefore, in turn induces a flow of money for the purchase of machinery, the cost of production not yet being affected. Sellers will also ask higher prices, but only because effective monetary demand rises or is expected to rise.[3] The explanation is therefore along Fisherian lines.[4]

[1] Cf. S. FABRICANT, *Capital Consumption and Adjustment*, p. 162.

[2] Cf. ROBERTSON, D. H., "Mr. Keynes' Theory of Money," *Econ. Jour.*, September, 1931, pp. 403–404; HAYEK, F. A., "Reflections on the Pure Theory of Money of Mr. J. M. Keynes," Part II, *Economica*, February, 1932, pp. 24–25.

[3] The following passage recalls the treatment in the *Treatise*. It is, however, a more careful presentation of the position, so careful in fact as to be devoid of practical significance. "*Where everyone is similar and similarly placed*, a change in circumstances or expectations will not be capable of causing any displacement of money whatever;— it will simply change the rate of interest in whatever degree is necessary to offset the desire of each individual, felt at the previous rate, to change his holding of cash in response to new circumstances or expectations." *General Theory*, p. 198 (the author's italics). Quoted by permission of Harcourt, Brace, and Company, Inc., publishers.

[4] Mr. Keynes's attempt to dispense with the quantity theory in his explanation of movements in P and P' has not been very successful. His mistake was to compare

In the second explanation of the forces determining P' (especially pp. 201–205), the rate of interest occupies a dominant position, whereas little attention is paid to the anticipated income, real or monetary.[1] The fact that the very large increases in P' (the price level of securities at any rate) in 1927–1929 may be explained much more easily by the rise in anticipated incomes than by any reduction of rates may be worth noting.[2] Many reasons might be given for this position if space allowed. Mr. Keynes's analysis in any case should have been applied only to fixed capital, not to working capital (pp. 154–155 and 201–203; cf. Part II, p. 363).

    c. The Independence of P and P'.

Mr. Keynes takes great pains to prove that P and P' (price level of consumption and investment goods, respectively) are independent (pp. 136–137, 144, 205).[3] He is not successful in proving his point. The fact that $E/0$ (efficiency earnings) contributes to the determination of both P and P', the price level of consumption and capital goods, respectively (*cf.* pp. 244, 245), makes the claim of independence rather dubious. Furthermore, it is admitted that the value of securities in the long run is derived from the yield of consumption goods (pp. 255–256). Is it likely that the excess-savings factor that accounts for downward movements in P will be in evidence at the same time that the excess-bullish factor will tend to raise P'? Mr. Keynes says in fact that an increase in P relative to costs makes the public more bullish and thus tends to increase P' (p. 144); and when the possibility of dependence is granted, the movements in

---

the total supply of money with the volume of *output* instead of with the volume of *transactions*. Had he considered the latter instead of the former, he would have seen that an explanation along Fisherian lines was possible. A reduction in the price of consumption goods and in the price level of output would then have been consistent with no change in money, velocity, and output. The failure of P' to rise as more money is spent on nonconsumption markets (and this is the failure to offset the decline of prices in consumption goods) is to be explained by a rise in transactions in old assets which accompanies losses on consumption goods. Mr. Keynes, nevertheless, made an important contribution in pointing out that the money not spent on consumption markets may be used to buy old assets instead of new investments. *Cf.* on these issues especially Robertson, *op. cit.*, pp. 400–403; Keynes' reply to Robertson in the same issue, pp. 417–419; Hayek, *op. cit.*, pp. 27–32; R. G. Sawtrey, *The Art of Central Banking*, pp. 345, 374–375; Robertson, D. H., "Saving and Hoarding," *Econ. Jour.*, September, 1933, pp. 403–409.

[1] In the *General Theory*, Chaps. XI–XII especially, the emphasis is quite properly shifted to the expected income.

[2] *Cf.* ROBERTSON, "Mr. Keynes' Theory of Money," *Econ. Jour.*, September, 1931, pp. 403–404.

[3] *Cf.* ROBERTSON, *op. cit.*, p. 398, and Keynes's reply to Robertson, pp. 413–416. At this point, Mr. Keynes makes important concessions on these issues and also specifically argues that movements in P and P' are in the same direction.

prices are usually assumed to be in the same direction (p. 182).[1] Apparently, by independence in the movements of P and P' all that Mr. Keynes means is that the excess bearishness determines P' and the excess-savings factor determines P. But important factors that contribute to the determination of P either directly influence P' or influence factors that determine P', and, therefore, the claim of independence is not proved.

Mr. Keynes in general anticipates movements in the same direction, and in view of the fact that the prices of investment goods depend on the output and price of consumption goods, this position seems strong. It is necessary, however, to dismiss his related point of independence of P and P'; for clearly the similarity of movements suggests dependence. It is of course possible to explain a decline in P by improved technology so that a decline in P might be accompanied by a rise in profits and a rise in P'. This is not, however, the problem that Mr. Keynes had in mind, for he is considering the possibility of a decline in P following a reduction in purchases of consumption goods which is accompanied by a rise in P'. Those who are faithful to a rigid Fisherian type of analysis are more likely than is Mr. Keynes to come to the conclusion that a decline in P will be accompanied by a rise in P'. They frequently assume that the amount of money remains unchanged and, therefore, a decline in the amount of money expended on consumption goods is accompanied by a rise in the amount disbursed on investment markets. This method of attack involves, however, an evasion of one important consideration, viz., the effect on total monetary supplies of a reduction in P.

In his *General Theory*, Mr. Keynes has little to add to what he said in his *Treatise* concerning the price level of consumption and investment goods. The presumption is that he abandons excess saving as *the* explanation of price movements of consumption goods, for he now insists on the equality of savings and investment. Excess bearishness, on the other hand, which had been proposed as the explanation of short-term movements in prices of investment goods, has probably been the inspiration of his liquidity preference, which plays an important part in the analysis of the latest book. Although he does not systematically deal with P' in his *General Theory*, it is quite clear that as liquidity preference increases, *ceteris paribus* P' should fall: the public will prefer cash (liquidity) to noncash assets (illiquidity).

By way of summary. Prices of consumption and investment goods are likely to move in the same direction. This conclusion is strengthened, the more vital the part played by anticipated income in the determination of P'. Any favorable effects on the rate of interest, should they follow a reduction of consumption demand, may then be of secondary importance. Mr. Keynes was undoubtedly

[1] In the *General Theory*, Mr. Keynes treats consumption and investment as independent quantities. Lange, *op. cit.*, p. 23.

correct in emphasizing the similarity of movements of P and P'; but his argument of independence and his recourse to an explanation on non-Fisherian lines were unfortunate.

For our purposes, the positive correlation of prices of consumption and investment goods is of great importance. Should the accumulation of reserves account for a reduction of demand for consumption goods, which in turn would depress their prices, then the decline in prices of consumption goods is likely to induce similar movements in prices of investment goods. Any downward tendency of interest rates associated with a rise of demand for public securities by reserve funds would have a contrary effect, however; and favorable changes in demand for investment purposes will in turn affect consumption demand favorably, $i.e.$, the net effects on consumption demand would not necessarily be adverse. Furthermore, the initial effects on demand for consumption goods associated with a reserve policy for financing social security are to be considered relative to all other governmental policies that tend to raise consumption demand and relative to the state of private demand.

CHAPTER 4

DEMAND, PRICES, AND OUTPUT

4.1. THE PROBLEM

In this chapter we are concerned with the effect upon the economic system of various methods of financing social security. Alternative financial plans are provided by accumulation of reserves or pay-as-you-go, although there still remains a choice between different possible tax sources. According to the drift of current thought the reserve plan is likely to depend more exclusively upon pay-roll taxes, whereas current financing will be forced to turn in part to nonconsumption taxes. Actually, reserves might accumulate out of nonconsumption tax sources. Also, because total taxes over time must be less under the reserve plan on account of interest earned by the reserve, *total* pay-roll taxes may be larger under a pay-as-you-go system. The *present value* of pay-roll taxes, however, may well be larger under the reserve plan. (This follows because, under the reserve plan, relatively large collections would be forthcoming in the early years.)

In this discussion it is necessary to consider the effects of various financial programs upon the demand for different classes of goods, upon the movements of factors of production, and finally upon total consumption, savings, prices, and output. A further discussion of the effects on prices and savings is offered later in the study of incidence. It will be helpful here to treat successively the repercussions of the programs upon these variables in periods of accumulation, nonaccumulation, and decumulation. The problem of distribution of burden, considered in detail in a later part of this book, must necessarily receive some consideration here.

Three classes of goods are distinguished here: *wage goods*, upon which laborers and other low-income groups spend much of their income and upon which part of the upper-class income is spent; *intermediate consumption goods* including nonnecessities, (or, perhaps better, luxury goods) and many durable consumers' goods, *e.g.*, higher education, better houses, refrigerators, Red Seal Victor records, etc.; and finally, *capital goods*. Financial plans should be considered relative to their influence upon prices, movements of factors, and profitability in these different types of industries. The problems considered here are relevant also to a study of unemployment insurance; for although unemployment reserves are not so large, the amplitude of their fluctuations per unit of time may be even greater.

4.2. Unfavorable Effects of Pay-roll Taxes on Wage-goods Industries

At least in the early years after the introduction of compulsory insurance, reserve accumulation is likely to bring larger disturbances of prices and factor movements than would current financing. In later years the latter plan would be more disturbing, though the synchronization of income and outgo is an important offset to later disturbances arising from heavy tax demands. Let us assume the continuance of the reserve plan as provided in the Social Security Act of 1935. Workers and other low-income groups then pay the larger part of the taxes, curtailing their consumption of wage goods.[1] To some extent, prices of these goods may decline and the industries producing them become less profitable, and, under conditions of full employment, factors begin to move to other industries. If factors of production are specific to these industries and quite immobile, unemployment may prevail or rates of remuneration may decline. When full employment before and after the tax is not assumed, there may be no transfer of productive factors to other fields, the result depending upon the declining demand for capital goods incident to a decrease in wage-goods production. This problem is treated in Chap. 3. An unequivocal answer is not easily given. Under the conditions of the thirties an unfavorable effect is likely to follow. To the extent that recent legislation has reduced the rate of accumulation of reserves, however, the depressing effects on demand for wage goods become less important.

Pay-roll taxes are assessed upon employers as well as upon employees; at present employers pay one-half of the total taxes for old-age insurance and almost all the taxes under unemployment insurance. It is therefore necessary to consider not only the effects

[1] To some extent wage earners pay directly; and, as is brought out later, part of the burden takes the form of an increase in the cost of living.

[120]

of taxes paid by workers, but also excise taxes based on pay-rolls and assessed upon employers. The latter attempt to pass on the tax through a reduction of wages or an increase in prices. They attempt to raise prices of all three classes of goods by restricting supply, and in so far as they are successful, the decline in prices of wage goods (due to a decrease in demand in consequence of direct wage taxes) is lessened. Inability to pass the tax on to the consumer may result in direct attacks on wage rates or a reduction of profits and other capitalist incomes.

The problem of incidence is discussed briefly in this chapter and more fully later. Under the implicit assumption that tax collections are used to build up reserve funds, the following generalization can be made: the net effect of taxes on employers and employees is likely to be a *relative* reduction of demand for wage goods,[1] and the demand for intermediate consumption goods and capital goods will suffer absolutely, although not necessarily *relatively*.[2]

The foregoing analysis is applicable not only to the full reserve plan, but also to the present modified pay-as-you-go plan, which provides for the ultimate accumulation of contingency reserves of a possible sum of 15 billion dollars (three times the disbursements). The significant fact to be observed is that in the accumulation period the reduction of spending by low-income groups is not offset by disbursement of tax proceeds. The excess tax collections go to acquire bonds for the reserve fund at the expense of market holdings.

4.3. Recourse to General Taxation—Effects on Output and Condition of the Insured

It has generally been assumed that the pay-as-you-go plan will necessitate recourse to general tax sources for a large part of the required revenues. It is not thought practicable to levy 12 to 15 per cent on pay-rolls for old-age insurance in addition to 3 per cent for unemployment insurance. Even taxation under the reserve plan

---

[1] Of course, a reduction of lower class real income may stimulate the purchase of some inferior wage goods (potatoes, etc.), for workers will be too poor to afford anything else. However, total consumption will no doubt tend to decrease.

[2] If the acceleration principle is strongly operative, it may be necessary to modify this conclusion. Conceivably, a greater relative decline might take place in the capital-goods industries.

might conceivably be of the non-pay-roll variety although the pressure of necessity for this would be less. In later chapters (especially Chaps. 10 to 12) financial aspects are more thoroughly investigated. For the moment we may assume that *general* revenues, as distinguished from pay-roll taxes, will be obtained in part from taxes on high incomes and in part from other forms of consumption taxation.

What if the taxes are primarily on surplus income? Those taxed will reduce their savings and curtail their consumption of intermediate consumption goods. Their purchases of wage goods will not suffer much. In a period of accumulation of reserves, this reduced demand for intermediate consumption goods and for capital goods is likely to affect their prices adversely. If the accumulation period coincides with a period of oversaving, the reduction in voluntary savings may in the long run have a less harmful effect on prices. The compulsory governmental saving results in a relative retardation of the growth of public debt privately held and increases the funds in the hands of those who would otherwise hold government bonds. This adds to the already excessive savings, and the reduction of private savings may be a welcome offset rather than a curse. To this extent the ensuing decline in income is lessened and the resulting damage to demand and prices is reduced.

If the taxes do not fall exclusively on surpluses, there will be an attempt to pass them on to consumers through price revisions and to exert backward pressure upon the remuneration of the factors of production. Output, investment, and employment may be reduced, which will in turn reduce the demand of succeeding periods with the result that the process will continue. In the absence of checks a cumulative decline in output may follow. To some extent, factors may flow into nontaxed fields; on the other hand, capital may be diverted in a variety of ways from real productive investment, and labor resources may be forced on relief.

4.4. PERIODS OF NONACCUMULATION AND DECUMULATION IN RELATION TO THE DIFFERENT CLASSES OF GOODS

Under the rigid 1935 Plan, reserves would accumulate for many years. Under the present plan moderate reserve accumulation will take place. However, the present plan is more nearly one of current financing, and nonaccumulation is the rule. Under the reserve plan a decline in population in the far future would involve gradual decumulation of the fund, whereas if only contingency reserves are built up, pay-as-you-go will require extremely heavy taxation when population declines and the percentage of aged increases.

In periods of nonaccumulation the demand for wage goods is likely to rise even if reliance is largely on pay-roll taxes. In such periods, receipts and expenditure are equal. The disbursements go on the whole to relatively needy beneficiaries who can be expected in good part to purchase wage goods. On the other hand, to some extent the tax burden is borne through price increases and income reductions by the relatively wealthier members of the community.

If taxes are assessed exclusively upon surpluses, the favorable effects upon the demand for wage goods will be at a maximum. It is interesting to conjecture what the effects of reliance upon taxes on surpluses will be in the period when payments to pensioners will be large and when accumulation of reserves has ceased. Prices of wage goods will rise as demand for them rises and taxpayers do not cut their consumption. Pensioners may be confronted with difficulties in obtaining their required wage goods. If unemployment is of large proportions, the problem will not be serious. Stocks may be adequate, and unemployed factors may be attracted by employment opportunities in the wage-goods industries. But if stocks are low, employment at a high level, and factors immobile, the pensioners may find that their benefits purchase much less than was anticipated. Although the wealthy seem to pay, the poor in fact compete for available supplies of wage goods, bidding up prices against one another. As a result of prosperity in the wage-goods industries, the demand for capital goods may be accelerated so that factors cannot easily be attracted away from these industries.

The foregoing analysis leaves out the depressing effects upon output of excessive tax burdens, especially likely to be incurred in the future under a pay-as-you-go program.[1] Even taxes on surpluses may through their effects upon motivations inhibit physical real investment and contribute to unemployment. Ultimately demand for all types of goods may decline. Pensioners will be confronted with a low cost of living, but all classes of the community will suffer.

---

[1] Cf. REDDAWAY, W. B., *The Economics of a Declining Population*, pp. 181–187, 195, 206–207. Here the author considers the effects of a continued rise of productivity upon national income and the burden of debt, and the rise of the yield of estate duties accompanying a rise in the death rate.

It is necessary finally to consider periods of decumulation. (Actually changes are likely to be more gradual than is assumed here.) The considerations relevant to a period of nonaccumulation are also applicable here. In addition, bonds from the reserve funds are converted into dollars through open-market sales, and the proceeds are put at the disposal of pensioners and the unemployed. Net demand for wage goods is likely to rise even more than during a period of nonaccumulation. Let us assume that in 1970 two billions of reserves in public securities are sold for dollars which are paid out to beneficiaries. We may expect a rise in demand for wage goods of almost 2 billions. What must be offset against this? Who buys the securities? If potential consumers purchase them and cut their consumption by an equivalent amount, there will be no net stimulus to consumption. But if, as is more likely, funds that would otherwise be saved go into the market for governments, and the government in turn pays benefits, the supply of capital may be lowered and the interest rate may rise. Against this we must consider the increase in investment demand incident to an improved outlook in wage-goods industries.

Finally, sales of securities may be made to the banks, which will manufacture additional deposits. It may seem at first that there is no offset to the extra 2 billion dollars demand for wage goods. However, if no factors are released from other spheres by a curtailment of purchasing power, and if idle resources do not exist in abundance, prices of wage goods will rise and purchasers will experience a reduction in the purchasing power of their dollars. It should be observed, however, that decumulation of unemployment reserves is likely to occur in periods of less than full employment. To some extent this is also true of old-age reserves. Nevertheless, if population is decreasing, there *may* be decumulation at a time when an increase in effective demand is harmful and can lead only to cumulative price increases and inflation.

4.5. SOME PRELIMINARY REMARKS ON INCIDENCE

At this point it may be well to dwell briefly upon the problem of incidence. A pay-roll tax assessed upon employers who produce commodity A may result in a rise in its price, the total expenditure on A possibly declining or rising. Dropping a partial equilibrium approach, we may ask what the effect will be if simultaneously pay-rolls are taxed in industries producing $A, B, C \ldots Z$. Presumably the prices of $A, B, C \ldots Z$ will all rise. The elasticity of demand for any commodity, say A, will, *ceteris paribus*, be less than if the tax affected A exclusively. For consumers of A are unable to avert the burden by increasing their consumption of competitive commodities B, C, etc.

It is necessary, however, to consider the limitation of income and expenditure. Demand for *each* commodity will not be so inelastic following a rise of prices as has been assumed so far. All commodities are competing in the sense that a fixed income is to be divided among them. In fact, an increase in all prices in the same proportion is equivalent to a decrease in money income, and the usual Engels's laws derived from budgetary studies should be applicable to describe changes in consumption. The rich will presumably cut down on their savings and maintain consumption relatively, whereas the poor who are doing little saving will cut down on consumption and possibly dissave,[1]

4.6. FINANCIAL METHODS AND THE DISTRIBUTION OF THE BURDEN

Although in previous sections we have dealt with the possibility of raising funds by sales of securities in periods of decumulation, we have not as yet explored the possibility of systematic financing through inflationary borrowing. This is, of course, the antithesis of the reserve plan and is the logical extension of the pay-as-you-go arguments. If a fear of deflation makes one fear reserve accumulation and advocate "current" financing (which from the standpoint of a capital budget is really deficit financing), why not go the whole way and advocate borrow-as-you-go rather than pay-as-you-go?

The effects of such a policy are indistinguishable from those of decumulation of reserves, there being no essential difference between issuing brand new bonds to the market and selling bonds that had previously been acquired by the old-age or unemployment reserve accounts. As in all of our analysis, the results of this policy will depend upon the state of business, employment, and effective

---

[1] Although the demand of the poor for each commodity taken one at a time may be inelastic, when all prices increase, the fixity of income makes contraction of consumption imperative.

demand. If employment is already full, the introduction of such a program raises the question of who is to do without wage goods when the insured receive benefit payments. Supplies of these goods being fixed, at least in the short run, prices will rise, and other low-income individuals, wage earners, small tradesmen, farmers, etc., will suffer losses in real income because of the competing purchasing power. In the longer run, mobile factors of production will be attracted to the wage-goods industries. This raises costs of production and prices in non-wage-goods industries and curtails their demand. In this manner other classes also suffer a loss in real income. If unemployed resources exist in abundance and the demand for private investment is slight, the issue of new securities either to banks or to the public will result in a creation of purchasing power, either through the creation of bank deposits or a speeding up of the velocity of circulation. This will expand the production of wage goods through the absorption of idle factors of production. The increased income of these factors, capital and labor, will in turn be spent so that a secondary stimulus is given to wage-goods and other industries. The consumption of the recipients of benefits comes from the expansion of output incident upon a fuller utilization of resources. In the limiting case there need be no price increase at all and no reduction in the real income of other classes through increases in the cost of living.

In summary, the extent of the price rise will be determined in part by the manner of finance. Thus, a system that taxes the lower classes through consumption or pay-roll levies would secure the transfer of wage goods to pensioners with a minimum effect on prices of wage goods. Taxation of surpluses, especially at a time when expenditure exceeds receipts, will not prevent a large relative increase in wage-goods prices, for the wealthy will not curtail their consumption of wage goods. If their savings are cut and the inducement to invest is lowered, the resulting contraction of income and employment may prevent prices from rising.

Therefore it may be said that the wage goods consumed by the insured in a later generation will be provided largely, but not completely, by others living in that generation. We say not completely because the methods of finance used in the interim are of much importance in determining the size of the national income in later years when social security payments attain high levels. Transfers will be made largely from the relatively poor to the insured, and to some extent from others. In addition, output of wage goods may be increased through a diversion of factors from other industries and through a rise in output. The extent to which factors can be diverted will probably be the most important force determining the elasticity of the supply function in most wage-goods industries.

The method of finance used will influence the volume of output, the price level, and the extent to which the various groups make transfers of wage goods to the insured. The less the burden put directly on the masses in later years, the greater will be the rise in prices of *wage goods;* and the more the resort to inflationary borrowing to meet Treasury contributions, the greater will be the rise in *general* prices. Inflation or taxation of surpluses will be of *immediate* help to the masses especially in so far as the rich give up wage goods and output expands. But the sacrifices of the wealthy will be mostly in nonwage goods, particularly in savings. The insured will gain, at first at the expense of the great number of poor consumers (including the potentially employed); in the end, they will also gain through transfers of resources to wage-goods industries. Their gains at the expense of the masses (on the assumptions made in this chapter) become less important, the more universal is the coverage of the program: gains in benefit payments are offset by losses to them as consumers and wage earners.

4.7. INFLUENCE ON OUTPUT THROUGH SAVINGS AND INVESTMENT

In the first instance the accumulation of a reserve is likely to lead to a net increase in saving, for the taxes collected are likely to be in excess of the additional private expenditure induced by a relative increase in prices. In the short run this need not imply a diminution in sales and consumption, measured in real terms. The decline in consumption demand, if unaccompanied by offsetting investment demand, may cause prices to fall with the result that real consumption will not decline *pari passu* as the old-age account accumulates assets. Alternatively, in the short run, prices may be maintained with the result that inventories accumulate. The increase in savings is accompanied by losses elsewhere or by unintended investment in inventories. In the longer run the fall in prices or the accumulation of inventories will affect output adversely.

Of course, if substantial compensating investment resulted in enlarged income to productive factors in other spheres who quickly entered the wage-goods market with supporting demand, there would be no great decline in prices and accumulation of inventories. However, there would necessarily be a transitional delay; also income in the investment field would not all be spent in the next expenditure period upon wage goods. Some factors would still have to shift to capital-goods industries.

In the short run, with total output fixed, those who pay taxes consume less, and prices falling, others consume more. In the long run, total consumption output may decline with or without a concomitant increase in the output of capital goods. If investment is stimulated, the building of more effective industrial plant may contribute ultimately toward an enlarged output of both investment and consumption goods.

4.8. RESERVES AND RENTIER INCOME

If large reserves accumulate, we must consider the problem of effects upon the interest rate. We are not concerned here with the effect of interest-rate changes on investment and national income in general; this problem has been dealt with in previous chapters. Rather our attention is focused upon interest as determining the share of income going to rentiers and holders of securities. Does the loss of income of this class facilitate increased consumption by pensioners in the period of accumulation, or in the period when the earning reserve is stabilized? How is the course of prices changed, and how is the distribution of burden altered by these changes in the interest rate?

As excess taxes are collected, the funds will either purchase government securities from the market, or, in time of unbalanced budget, will acquire new issues. In either case the quantity of outstanding bonds in the hands of the public and financial institutions is less than it otherwise would be. In consequence, prices of such securities are bid up and yields decrease as compared with what would have taken place in the absence of accumulation. The extent of this relative fall depends upon the elasticity of demand for governments, which in turn depends upon the alternatives open to investors. If there were a very broad margin of completely safe new private issues potentially available, then the interest rate would not fall much.[1] On the other hand, the demand for governments might be extremely elastic for a very different reason, *viz.*, the existence of elastic demands for liquidity. In both of these cases, interest rates would not fall much, but in the former there would be little or no deflation, whereas in the latter hoards would increase and the velocity of circulation decrease.

The relative retirement of debt leading to reduction of yields on governments and to the presence of available investment funds in the hands of previous holders of securities will also tend to lower the yields on private securities. This should encourage the flotation of new private issues, particularly in years of prosperity. The extent to which it does so will determine the extent to which interest earned by the fund is a net addition to total security income or merely a substitute for other investment income.

In order to throw light on these knotty problems, let us consider two extreme cases. Suppose that over a long period of time 40 billions of government securities are retired from circulation. In case 1 there is a broad margin of private investments so that the interest-rate structure is not appreciably changed. When private investors give up government bonds, they acquire new private issues. Their current income from receipts is unchanged whereas the social security fund now has extra interest income (*i.e.*, additional in the sense that the supply of private investment now rises) on 40 billion dollars' worth of securities. What is the source of the extra total income? Clearly it must come from the 40 billion dollars of induced private capital formation hypothetically assumed. The net productivity of this equipment gives rise to income in the form of increased potential consumption. Actually rentiers may choose to reinvest part of their incomes more or less at compound interest so that the increased product resulting from the larger capital equipment is used not completely for current consumption but to increase still further the stock of capital.

In case 2, which is the antithesis of the one considered, private investment opportunities are completely absent. The government as before purchases 40 billion dollars of securities. In the act of purchase it may raise prices against itself, but if bonds are constantly maturing, it can acquire securities at face value. Erstwhile security holders hoard funds or simply bid up the value of existing private securities, no real investment taking place. Income is not simply

[1] House Report 7260 (74: 1), 1935, pp. 51–52.

transferred from private holders to the reserve fund; total security income is lessened through reduction of interest rates. This is particularly important after all securities, private and public, have been refunded.

Each of these examples is extreme. Actuality will lie somewhere in between. To some extent the accumulation of the reserve will result in a transfer of rentier income from private individuals to the fund as trustee for workers. To some extent private individuals by investing in productive enterprise will be able to make adjustments to the situation and maintain earnings out of the net productivity of the new investments. Unless the effects upon the distribution of income are extremely prejudicial to the relatively thrifty and wealthy rentier class, the retirement of debt privately held should accelerate the growth of private productive capital.

The foregoing analysis is concerned with the level of capital after the fund has grown. It does not deal with problems of effective demand during the period of accumulation. These problems can be easily examined along the lines of the previous two chapters. In case 1 there is little or no diminution of effective demand, whereas in case 2, unless the reserve grows completely out of taxes on surpluses, the short-run effect upon prices, employment, and national income is downward. As a result, not only may capital not grow, but it may actually decrease when replacement funds are not reinvested. Again, actuality may lie anywhere between these two poles according to the conditions that will prevail in the years ahead.

It should be observed that when the government sells to the insurance funds securities manufactured *ad hoc* for this purpose, rentier income may also be reduced. They are deprived of potential purchases, and substitute investments may not be available.

4.9. Conclusion

The total impact on prices of the various classes of goods, savings, and output will depend upon the choice of financial program. The final effects will depend upon whether a large reserve plan, a small reserve plan, or a policy of borrow-as-you-go is instituted, and will also depend upon whether the tax burden is put largely on pay-rolls and direct consumption or upon so-called surpluses. Who pays now? Who pays ultimately? What sacrifices in consumption or in savings are made by the taxpayer or by the consumer when he is confronted with higher prices? Questions of the degree of employment of the factors of production and the extent of their mobility inevitably arise. The greater their mobility and the lower the level of employment, the less serious are the effects upon prices likely to be when demand is artificially increased through operation of the social security program. Of extreme importance is the state of savings and investment and their relations to each other. Particularly in periods of nonaccumulation or decumulation are prices most likely to rise and dissaving to be greatest.

CHAPTER 5

THE PROBLEM OF INVESTMENT OF SOCIAL SECURITY FUNDS

5.1. INTRODUCTION

In this chapter several methods of investment of social security reserves are considered. We begin with the possibility of investment in bank deposits. These issues are discussed in Secs. 5.4 to 5.7; and there follows in Secs. 5.8 and 5.9 a discussion of the possibility of deposit of trust funds with the reserve banks. These methods of investment are purely of theoretical interest. Sections 5.10 and 5.11 deal with the method actually in use, *viz.*, purchases of government securities. In the first three sections the subjects discussed are the significance of the rate of interest for the economy, the effects upon the rate of interest on government securities of this artificial rise of demand for these assets emanating from trust funds, and the effects of compulsory public savings upon the total volume of savings and investment. The direct effects upon savings received our attention in an earlier chapter; here the problem is the effect via the rate of interest.

If space were available, alternative policies relative to varying economic conditions would be discussed. In an oversaving economy, for example, the sterilization of large amounts of deposits (the first method discussed) would not be appropriate. This method of procedure would not, however, be so harmful when, in response to the inflow of gold and deficit financing, deposits and excess reserves rise at a rapid rate. In a defense or war economy, the rise of monetary hoards (the total monetary effect would still be expansive) may well be desirable. It would be the monetary counterpart of a discouragement of consumption which may be required when the state demands a large proportion of available resources for military purposes. Unfortunately space precludes a full discussion of these issues though they are not by any means neglected. In the present chapter, moreover, some space is devoted to a consideration of the effects of the accepted policy both during a period of business expansion (and debt reduction) and a period of depression (and debt expansion).

We have dwelt on the effects of the accumulation of reserves and of alternative financial programs upon the volume of savings and investment. The rate of interest and expected net income determine the volume of investment, expected net income being the difference between gross income and costs. Expected incomes and costs are probably of more significance than current and past incomes (the latter two in turn influence the volume of expected incomes) in the determination of decisions to maintain or extend investments. The greater the uncertainty, the larger the risks; the more difficult the proper evaluation of risks, the greater the part played by expectations. This statement means that past and current incomes and costs are to this extent less helpful in determining expected incomes and costs. One element in the determination of gross income, *i.e.*, consumption demand, has received attention in the preceding chapter. Another, the rate of interest, will occupy a prominent place in the discussion of the present chapter.

Largely to Wicksell and Mr. Keynes we owe the important place given to the rate of interest in the analysis of the volume of investment. Wicksell was the first to present with some clarity the significance of the relation of the rate of interest, on the one hand, and the net income to be earned from the use of capital, on the other.[1] In his *Treatise* Mr. Keynes emphasized the significance of the rate of interest both as a cost and as a capitalization factor. As the rate of interest declines, investment rises both on account of the ensuing decline of costs and the rise of security prices associated with a higher rate of capitalization. Thus, the value of a capital asset is twenty times its perpetual net income when the rate of interest is 5 per cent, and twenty-five times at a rate of 4 per cent. Mr. Keynes was, however, then inclined to minimize the effects of changes in income and exaggerate the significance of changes in the rate of interest.[2] Mr. Durbin early emphasized the weight to be given to uncertainties relative to changes in the rate of interest; and others have objected to the prominent place given to the rate of interest as against other cost factors.[3] Mr. Keynes, in his *General Theory*, also shifted the emphasis to changes in *expected income*. In setting the marginal efficiency of capital against the

[1] WICKSELL, K. *Interest and Prices*, especially Chaps. 7–9.

[2] *Treatise, passim.*

[3] DURBIN, E. F. M., *The Problem of Credit Policy*, pp. 196–200, and especially J. A. Schumpeter, *Business Cycles*, pp. 602–10, 635–38. The latter emphasizes the shifts of demand, which account in no small part for the unimportance of the rate of interest.

rate of interest as the determinants of investment, however, he continues to put considerable emphasis on the rate of interest. The rate of interest remains an important element in the cost of production; and the marginal efficiency of capital is the *rate of discount* of expected net incomes which will make the value of an investment good equal to its cost.

Two problems are of vital importance in a discussion of the effects of the social security program upon the rate of interest. (1) There is the effect upon net savings, a problem that receives attention in earlier chapters of this book. (2) There is the problem of investment of funds received in compliance with the provisions of the Social Security Act. These two problems are not independent, for the method of investment will influence the volume of income and savings. What is probably the more important effect of investment policies upon the supply of money will be not the indirect influence on savings via income, but rather the direct effects upon the supply of and demand for money. The larger the social security reserves, the more important the need of an intelligent investment policy. Furthermore, the larger the net savings induced, the greater the danger of deflationary effects and, therefore, the more calamitous any further deflation induced (1) by the impounding of social security funds in cash hoards or (2) by unfavorable effects upon bank reserves. For the issues discussed in this chapter, the accumulation of both old-age and unemployment reserves is relevant.

5.2. Effects on Savings and Investment Policy

First, a few comments will be made on the net effects on savings. The social security program will tend to increase savings more (at least in the first instance), the more the burden is put directly or indirectly on workers and other low-income groups.[1] It should also be observed that to some extent savings accumulated in social security reserves deprive other potential borrowers of funds. Thus, life insurance companies and saving banks may lose savings to the government, there being a redirection of the flow of savings which tends to favor the beneficiaries of public disbursements against the beneficiaries, *e.g.*, farmers and home owners, of invest-

[1] *Cf.* Secs. 4.1 to 4.3.

ments by life insurance companies and savings banks. Beneficiaries of public expenditures may of course not be borrowers, and, therefore, not only may the flow of savings be redirected but also the supply may be reduced.

One may, therefore, find some justification for the redeposit of social security funds in savings banks and commercial banks to the extent that the program tends to divert savings from these institutions. (This is of course not what is being done or contemplated.) Assume that 1 billion of savings are lost by savings banks in a period in which social security reserves accumulate 3 billions of dollars. As the government spends the money thus received, the deposits of savings banks will be replenished at least to some extent. Farmers and home owners, nevertheless, may have been affected adversely by liquidation enforced upon the savings banks because of a net loss of deposits. Yet the conditions of the banks' debtors may not become precarious if account is taken of the benefits conferred upon them through the disbursement of social security and other public funds. Moreover, their plight is to be distinguished from that of the savings banks. The latter's losses of cash may be serious, although the probability of this is small in a period of rapid growth of deposits. Should losses be severe, however, the government might well consider measures to compensate savings banks for losses of deposits.

5.3. Effects of Accumulation of Reserves (and Rise of Savings) on Prices of Government Securities and Other Assets

It should not be assumed too readily that this rise of compulsory (and net) savings in the first instance is followed by a reduction in the rate of interest. We are not *here* concerned with the Keynesian sequence of a rise of savings, a decline of income, and a decline of savings. Let us consider the price of government securities, and let us assume that additional money is put into government securities following an accumulation of reserves. The rate of interest on these securities then declines at least temporarily. What next? Present holders of government securities may not respond to the rise of prices by disposing of their portfolios. Inelastic supply conditions prevail in *this segment* of the market. Alternative investments are not available in a period of distrust and uncertainty, and trustee laws frequently prevent liquidation. For this reason, their prices tend to continue to rise. In another segment of *this market*, however, the elasticity of supply may be high. As prices rise, the government may issue new securities. (Observe, however, that the Treasury may issue irrespective of moderate changes in prices so that, within limits, the supplies are then inelastic.) Issues are determined largely by the budgetary requirements; but the total volume of expenditures and the distribution of sources of revenue between taxes and borrowing will be determined to some extent by the demand for Treasury issues. It follows that, from the side of supply, one factor tends to keep prices up (the rate of interest down) and another, prices down (the rate of interest up).

What can we say of demand for Treasury issues? As prices rise, does demand decline? Here we have to take into account the shifts of demand. Other markets for assets may suffer from a desertion of investors, whereas the creation of new money may increase the demand for conservative assets. Demand for conservative issues, moreover, is likely to be inelastic. Why? Because alternative investment markets are not attractive although some shifts in the use of funds from investment to consumption are possible. Shifts of demand, however, are likely to be more significant than is the elasticity within the relevant ranges at a given demand. A continued rise in prices is therefore to be expected as demand rises. If we assume that the two factors operating on the supply side offset each other and that there is a tendency toward higher prices from the demand side, the net effect is likely to be in the direction of lower interest rates and higher prices for Treasury issues. This reduction is, however, translated into a general reduction with difficulty, if at all. The reader will readily observe that a money and investment market not unlike that of the thirties has been the model for this discussion.

We have so far merely concluded that the effect of an accumulation of reserves is likely to be a rise in the prices of gilt-edge securities, and in particular of those of the United States government. Prices of durable assets and of securities depend not only on the long-term rate of interest but also on expected income, the latter element generally having a larger degree of variability for most assets than for United States government securities. Despite any rise in the total supplies of money and any diversion of purchasing power to investment markets—the latter being a likely accompaniment, in the first instance at any rate, of the accumulation of reserves—the rate of interest may not decline on all securities. The public's preference for government securities against cash may increase; but its preference as between cash and less conservative investments may change in favor of the former. A net decline in the prices of all durable assets will then be more likely to follow under these assumed conditions, the more important are these non-governmental assets relative to all assets. It is, moreover, not at all clear then that any decline in the prices of such assets is associated exclusively with a rise in the rate of interest: a decline in expected net income or a reduction in the cost of producing capital goods may be equally important explanations of any downward revision of these prices. What is more, a depression of consumption demand following the taxation of potential consumers under the social security program or an unwise management of social security funds may contribute toward a decline in expected net income. We now turn to the important problem of investment of social security reserves.

First the investment in bank deposits will be discussed. At the outset, it may be well to mention that if these deposits do not pay interest, the argument for this method of procedure loses strength.

5.4. Limits on Investment of Reserves in Bank Deposits

It is probable that several billions will be accumulated in the unemployment insurance fund; and at one time it was estimated that the old-age pension fund would grow to exceed 50 billions. More recent changes (1939) in the act will have the effect of reducing the old-age reserve to a much more manageable size. Current estimates, which take into account the revisions of the act in 1939 and are based on the maximum disbursements, put the ultimate reserve at 15 billions. Is it probable that deposits of billions in the security funds will be made without putting severe pressure upon industry and the money market? Three possible plans of procedure are considered here:[1] (1) that the transfers to the insurance funds

[1] The possibility that the reserves will be invested in productive enterprises directly is not considered here. At some time in the future this is a possibility that may require serious consideration. Foreign funds have been invested in various

are made to their deposit accounts at commercial banks (and incidentally in savings banks); (2) that the funds are kept at the reserve banks for the Treasury; (3) that the funds are invested in securities of the Federal government.[1]

Let us turn to the first plan. At the outset, the reader is warned that later we take into account the relevance of monetary expansion which may develop independently of the program, but also may be associated with it. Under the first plan, transfers will be made directly from business deposits to the insurance-fund accounts at commercial banks. It is apparent at once that there are limitations to the extent of transfers of business deposits to the government accounts with commercial banks. On the assumption that the volume and distribution as between different types of deposits are not influenced by the process of transfer, it may be said that the volume of business deposits sets a maximum limit on losses of these deposits. Actually, an upper limit on losses may be given by the amount that can be transferred permanently without very serious effects on business liquidity and output. In any case the maximum loss cannot conceivably be (on our assumptions) in excess of the current volume of business deposits. Since these transfers are likely, however, to have an adverse effect upon the economy

---

business enterprises and advanced to local governments. See "Statistics of the Working of the Social Insurance Act in France from 1932 to 1935," *Internat. Labor Rev.*, June, 1937, pp. 856–857.

[1] The classical treatment of this subject is by Prof. Hansen. See A. H. Hansen *et al.*, *A Program for Unemployment Insurance and Relief in the United States*, pp. 166–195; also *Hearings*, Senate Finance Committee, S. 1130, *Economic Security Act* (74: 1), 1935, pp. 452–456. Columbia University Commission, *Economic Reconstruction*, pp. 210–237; A. H. Hansen, *Full Recovery or Stagnation?* pp. 137–192.

Prof. Hansen suggests eight possible methods of investing *unemployment reserves* (his discussion is concerned almost exclusively with the investment of unemployment reserves), which may be divided into four classes according to the effects upon banking reserves. Of his eight alternatives the following will be discussed in some detail: (1) deposits with commercial banks, (2) and (3) investments in government securities (the discussion of this method of investment includes two of his alternatives), (4) deposits with reserve banks. We discuss incidentally the procedure of deposits with savings banks.

Three of his alternatives are not discussed, *viz.*, investment in short-term maturities, purchases of securities from reserve banks, and maintenance of insurance funds in cash. Under investments with the Federal Reserve we also discuss the possibility that the Federal Reserve acts in the capacity of agent.

For a discussion of foreign practice see V. Klumpar, "The Investment of Social Insurance Funds," *Internat. Labor Rev.*, January, 1933, pp. 51–65; *cf.* International Labor Office, *The Investment of Funds of Social Insurance Institutions*, 1939, Chap. 3.

rather than otherwise, the volume of all (and business) deposits may in fact be reduced in the process of transfer. Mr. Keynes puts the proportion of income, business, and saving deposits relative to the total of 8, at 1, 3 and 4, respectively. These proportions, if applicable to the American economy, may give us a very rough idea of the volume of business deposits. The total is not likely to be much in excess of 20 billions in 1940. Dr. Currie's figures yield results in agreement with those based on Mr. Keynes's proportions.[1] In so far as the total of business deposits is unusually large relative to business requirements, the continued transfer of deposits to government account will be less keenly felt than otherwise. Unusual monetary conditions that prevailed in the late thirties are a reminder of this possibility.

This method of investment of reserves cannot be dismissed without a consideration of (1) the size of the reserves to be accumulated, (2) the use to which the government puts the money accumulated by the reserve funds, and (3) the success with which business is able to put part of the costs upon consumers or other nonbusiness elements in economic society. Under (1), it may be said that the practical limits of the amount of business deposits that can safely be transferred preclude the investment of reserves of the proportions contemplated under the Act of 1935 in deposits at commercial banks. These limits may also be of great practical importance even if all public insurance reserves do not at any time exceed 10 to 20 billion dollars, a reasonable total for old-age and unemployment reserves under the Act of 1939.

[1] *Treatise*, Vol. II, p. 34; *cf.* National Resources Committee, *The Structure of the American Economy*, Part I, Basic Characteristics, 173b, p. 88 (Currie's figures).

	Deposits (millions of dollars) Dec. 31, 1935	Percentage to total	
		Dec. 31, 1935	Dec. 31, 1933
Business.........................	7.64	34.9	40.6
Finance.........................	4.96	22.7	15.8
Government, etc..................	4.13	18.9	17.9
Consumers and unclassified........	5.13	23.5	25.9
Total........................	21.86		

At the end of 1939, adjusted demand deposits and money in circulation amounted to 36 billion dollars. If we apply the average of Dr. Currie's figures for 1933 and 1935, we obtain roughly 20 billion dollars for business and finance, which we may assume corresponds to Mr. Keynes's business deposits. (Latest figures from *Fed. Reserve Bull.*, 1940, p. 718.)

Under (2) the issue is the use to which the Treasury puts the deposits accumulated at commercial banks. Technically one may argue that if the Treasury keeps the social security funds invested in deposits at commercial banks, then the Treasury is not in a position to spend these funds. Business (and perhaps to some extent private savings and income deposits) now become public deposits. Private accounts are not replenished and, therefore, the transfers are cumulative. It is at least possible, however, that expenditures of the Treasury may rise as (and because) public deposits rise. The Treasury may then borrow additional funds and in turn spend them. Business accounts may then profit from the rise of public expenditures though it is possible that disproportionate gains (depending on the nature of the expenditures and their secondary effects) may accrue to income and saving deposits.

We now turn to (3), which is largely a problem of incidence. In the first instance the major burden of the social security program is put upon business; and with the passage of time this tendency is likely to become stronger. Losses of business deposits may therefore be large; but business will recoup a large part of its losses as it succeeds in shifting the burden to consumers, wage earners, and others. Losses of income and savings deposits to business accounts may then follow.

5.5. DEFENSIVE MEASURES OF BUSINESS

It is necessary to consider what defensive measures business enterprises will take to protect their cash balances. Obviously the measures taken to protect their financial position will also to some extent protect their cash position. The entrepreneur will try to pass the various pay-roll taxes on to the consumer or to the wage earner. In so far as he succeeds in doing so he will also protect his cash position and induce transfers from income and saving to business deposits. Wage earners will receive less income, and consumers may well draw upon their balances of income and saving deposits in order to maintain their real expenditures. By cutting his savings the consumer may, however, contribute toward a decline in investments and ultimately, therefore, to a reduction in business deposits. It is apparent also that business deposits will be maintained at the expense of income deposits only to a moderate degree (especially since the volume of income deposits is probably not much more than one-eighth of all deposits, and since income recipients find it necessary to hold minimum cash balances); but larger transfers from saving deposits are possible.

Are there any other sources that entrepreneurs may tap? The only other one seems to be that of deposits created to fill the gap. (The consideration of the possibility that business holds surplus cash is excluded.) Under normal conditions Funds cannot continue to draw billions of dollars from business deposits without business drawing cash from other sources. Assume that the hoards accumulated in the Funds are kept with the commercial banks. The mere transfer of deposits to the account of the Funds does not enable the banks either on their own account or on the account of the Funds to make additional purchases of assets. If business finds its deposits depleted through these transfers it must, failing other measures mentioned, borrow from the banks in order to replenish cash amounts; and, as has been suggested, a replenishment of cash follows any additional borrowing thus induced by the Treasury. Any rise in the total deposits resulting from private borrowings of this sort need not be a matter of concern, however, for the new deposits replace those in the Funds and, therefore, replace rather inactive deposits.[1] The banks, furthermore, thus purchase assets that might have been purchased by entrepreneurs in the absence of the pay-roll taxes. Clearly the existence of excess reserves is a necessary condition for the foregoing process.

It may be asked, further, how industry finds itself in a position where it can borrow more from the banks? In other words, how can the financial position of industry be reconciled with its cash position? The growth of reserve funds invested in deposits at banks (in so far as it is not compensated for by reductions of income or savings deposits, or in so far as the pay-roll and other taxes are not passed on to wage earners directly or *qua* consumers, and to other consumers without a curtailment of output) is a rough index of losses suffered by industry in consequence of these insurance schemes. (We leave out of account the assessment of taxes upon surpluses, only part of which will affect adversely the volume of business deposits.) The first effects of the collection of taxes are likely to be losses of cash by industry. Entrepreneurs, it may be

---

[1] Prof. Hansen estimates that the rise of inactive deposits associated with a program of unemployment insurance in 1923–1929 would have had the effect of reducing active purchasing power by 10 per cent. Hansen, *op. cit.*, p. 164.

said, will undoubtedly to some extent avert borrowing by getting along with a smaller proportion of cash and a larger proportion of noncash assets. That the proportion of commodity stocks to all assets is likely to rise and that of cash to decline is evident when one considers that the immediate effects of the operation of these plans will probably be—though not to the extent sometimes assumed—a reduction in purchases of commodities. Industry will sooner or later be under pressure to dispose of noncash assets, tempting both consumers and banks; or industry will curtail purchases of assets. Banks will make advances to entrepreneurs or purchase assets from them, thereby to some extent providing industry with the cash that otherwise would have been provided by consumers. Banks will hesitate to lend, however, in so far as the social insurance program impairs the position of industry. Yet the financial losses may not be so large as the losses of cash. Purchase of assets by banks from nonbanking sources may also improve the cash position of industry, but to a considerable extent the burden will be shifted to other than industrial areas (although possibly to firms in possession of surplus cash).

Undoubtedly, consumers will tend to purchase smaller quantities of commodities in the period when the Funds are growing though, as is indicated above, the entrepreneur may then tempt the consumer by making concessions in price.[1] Prices may be higher, but not so much higher as might be inferred from a consideration of the high costs of social insurance. In short, industry confronted with losses of cash as funds accumulate in security accounts at the banks, now in possession of *relatively* large cash assets, tempts potential purchasers, *i.e.*, banks, industrial buyers in relatively liquid positions, and consumers. In so far as the supply of cash is increased and (or) demand is shifted upward, price concessions will not be required.

5.6. RESERVES OF BANKS UNDER THE POLICY OF INVESTMENT OF SECURITY RESERVES IN DEPOSITS

A word should be said concerning the reserve position of banks should social security funds be deposited with commercial banks.

---

[1] Ultimately any rise in investments may stimulate consumer demand.

These deposits may be withdrawn in large volume and, therefore, may require large reserves or at least normal reserves buttressed by large secondary reserves. It is not at all certain, however, that the reserve situation would be serious.[1] (1) These deposits are not more volatile than bankers' deposits, against which reserves of but 13 per cent have been adequate except in the most panicky periods. (In recent years, requirements have been raised as excess reserves have jeopardized control.) (2) Against withdrawals are to be considered the effects of disbursements of social security funds. (This reservation is, however, almost tantamount to a statement that the accumulation of large deposit accounts by the Funds is not likely.) These losses will be recouped in part as beneficiaries spend (and therefore, security deposits are reduced), and in part as these additional expenditures induce still further expenditures.

Not only may the dangers of withdrawals be exaggerated, but the accumulation of security reserves at banks may not have the serious effects suggested above. In addition to the reasons given above, we suggest the possibility of the availability of large volumes of inactive deposits, and of a high level of excess reserves, and emphasize the readiness of the monetary authority to help in periods of accumulation, *i.e.*, periods of losses of income and savings deposits. Once more attention should be directed toward excess reserves. In so far as they are available, any absorption of reserves becomes of secondary importance.

Before concluding this discussion of the feasibility of investment of social security funds in commercial banks, a brief comment will be made upon the alternative of investment in savings bank deposits. Savings banks hold reserves partly in cash and partly as deposits with commercial banks; but their total cash reserve is but a few per cent in contrast with reserves against demand deposits of $17\frac{1}{2}$ and $22\frac{3}{4}$ per cent required (1941) of commercial banks in the larger cities. *Transfers* of deposits from private to insurance accounts at savings banks would put very little additional strain on reserves; for even a *rise* of deposits requires very small additions of cash. (In so far as these deposits are volatile, they would not be put into savings accounts.)

Should the insurance accounts at savings banks grow at the expense of private accounts at commercial banks, the issues become more complicated. Commercial banks lose private deposits and

[1] *Cf.* HANSEN, *op. cit.*, pp. 164–165, 170–171.

gain bankers' deposits (savings banks' deposits at commercial banks); and savings banks gain security deposits and cash (deposits with commercial banks). Commercial banks may now deem an increase of reserves necessary since bankers' deposits, which have increased, are more volatile than private deposits. Savings banks, on the other hand, now find themselves in possession of an additional amount of cash equal to the rise of security funds, of which but a small part is required to buttress their reserve position. They will therefore be disposed to buy additional assets, thus contributing toward a rise of their assets and a reduction of their cash and toward a rise of private deposits of commercial banks (deposits of sellers of these assets increase) and a reduction of their bankers' deposits. Should the commercial banks, however, dispose of the assets now purchased by savings banks, the net effect would be equal declines of both bankers' deposits and assets held by commercial banks. In conclusion it may be said that the accumulation of insurance funds at savings banks is less likely to have deflationary effects than is the accumulation of deposits with commercial banks. In what is perhaps the most probable development here (*i.e.*, transfers of deposits from commercial banks to savings banks and investment by savings banks of additional cash in assets purchased from the market), the *net* effect on the cash position of commercial banks is nil and, the *net* effect on savings banks is a rise of security accounts (deposits) and a rise of assets.

5.7. CONCLUSIONS ON INVESTMENT IN BANK DEPOSITS AND RELATION TO ALTERNATIVES AND TO MONETARY AND FISCAL POLICIES

Investment of reserve funds in deposits of commercial banks may be a tolerable solution of the problem of investment. Perhaps a more satisfactory solution would be the deposit of insurance funds in both savings and commercial banks, the distribution between the two groups of banks and also among individual banks to be determined by their respective losses of deposits associated with the influx of money into the reserves.

Large deposits of social security funds in banks are unlikely, however, for the present. The Treasury is required to invest cash assets of the Unemployment Trust Fund which are not needed to cover current outlay in obligations of the United States government or obligations guaranteed by the government. In the process of investing old-age reserves, the Treasury issues special obligations to the reserve. The proceeds in either case may be deposited with commercial or reserve banks. It is, however, unlikely that the Treasury will refrain in any important degree from using available funds. At least this conclusion is valid so long as deficits continue to prevail and the outstanding debt remains at a high level.

What further conclusions are we to draw concerning the deposit of reserve funds in banks? First consider the drain of business deposits associated with the accumulation of insurance reserves. Two aspects of this problem should be distinguished. The first is the cash position of business; the second, the banking situation. Business may be seriously embarrassed unless it has large surpluses of cash, or can defend its cash position either by shifting the burden of social insurance elsewhere or by obtaining additional cash through sales of assets to banks or to others.

What of the banks? They may lose deposits and cash *temporarily*. Unless they have large surpluses of cash, or profit from the influx of deposits associated with public spending, gold flows, and the like, or receive support from the monetary authority, they may find themselves in a precarious condition. It is obvious, however, that under any system of investment they will receive aid as the cash received by the social security reserve funds is put to use. One alternative method of investment is that under discussion here, *i.e.*, the redeposit of funds in banks as they lose deposits to the government. Perhaps the need of compensation for losses is at a minimum in this case. The banks then obtain inactive deposits in exchange for the active deposits lost. In so far as social security taxes are shifted to workers and consumers, however, the net gain in inactive deposits will be less.

Investment of insurance funds in deposits is not likely to be popular with Congress or the government, however, so long as deficits are large and the public debt remains at an unusually high level. A more popular solution considered briefly later is investment in public securities. We may consider the possibility briefly here for obvious reasons. Banks lose deposits as reserves accumulate. As the insurance funds accumulate cash, the Treasury may sell public securities to the funds. In what manner do the banks have an opportunity to protect themselves as they lose deposits? They may be forced to sell assets. Should they sell public securities to the Treasury, the net effect would be virtually nil: government trust funds provide additional demand, the banks sell additional supplies.

Actually, since the introduction of the security program in 1935, deposits have steadily grown. Losses of deposits by banks on account of insurance payments have therefore not been serious. Losses of deposits have been more than recouped through the influx of gold and expenditures by the government of social security funds and of funds received through sales of securities to the banks.

The investment of insurance funds in bank deposits may be put then *against the alternative of investment in public securities* and in relation to two important developments of the period 1935–1940, *viz.*, deficit financing and the inflow of gold.

1. Investment in bank deposits
   Cash in the insurance funds is invested in bank deposits. (Commercial and savings both, let us assume.)

Insurance reserves accumulate cash.	Insurance reserves redeposit cash with banks
Deposits – (largely active; in part inactive).	Deposits+ (inactive).

   NOTE: no new market for public securities.

2. Investment in public deposits and subsequent use of these deposits to purchase securities from Treasury
   Reserves invested in public securities

Deposits – (same proportions of active and inactive as above).	Deposits+ as reserve funds purchase securities from Treasury and Treasury spends cash thus received.

   New market for public securities.

3. Case 1 (above) considered in the light of the deficit financing of the Treasury in 1935–1940 and the inflow of gold.

	Reserves redeposited
a. Deposits – (as in case 1).	*a.* Deposits+ (inactive).
This corresponds to Case 1	
b. Deposits+	*b.* Public securities+ and cash+

   Losses of active deposits more than made up as the Treasury sells securities to the banks and as gold comes in.

4. Actual developments 1935–1940

a. Deposits – as transfers are made to insurance funds. (transfers to insurance funds and purchases of securities largely synchronized).	Deposits+ as funds purchase public securities from Treasury and Treasury spends this cash.

b. Deposits+ (active and inactive) as Treasury sells securities to banks in carrying through its spending policy and as gold is imported—net result is a large rise of all types of deposits.

5.8. Reserve Banks: Agency and Banker Purchases

We now turn to the second possible method of procedure: the cash is transferred to the reserve banks which either (1) pay out the cash thus received in purchasing various types of noncash assets for the Funds or (2) hold the cash. The agency function for the reserve banks will be discussed first and later the banker function. To the extent that the assets are purchased by the reserve banks from nonbanking sellers, the deposits of banks are replenished and, therefore, the reduction of business deposits is not so great as under the first plan. It is, however, to be noted that income and savings deposits to some extent will profit from these purchases on account of the Funds;[1] and, also, that the *temporary* transfer of cash to the reserve banks and the temporary disturbances may induce some liquidation of assets and some reduction in deposits. In so far as the sellers of assets to reserve banks are banks, cash supplies of banks are replenished, but their noncash assets decline by a corresponding amount, their deposits *then* not being replenished. Furthermore, if the reserve banks do not act in a skillful manner, the loss of cash by the market may force banks to sell assets so that the banks will to that extent be encouraged to sell the assets that the reserve funds acting through the reserve banks acquire. The extent to which the Funds (via the reserve banks) purchase assets held by the banks or the public will also depend upon whether the Funds purchase a type of asset largely in the possession of the banks or one largely held by the public. Ultimately, however, even if the banks are heavy sellers, they may substitute commercial assets, thus filling the gap in deposits and in

---

[1] The issue here is the extent to which business deposits are reduced through the flow of funds into the security reserves as compared with the gains following the outward flow.

particular in business deposits. All things considered, this method of procedure would probably involve a smaller immobilization of cash resources than the investment in bank deposits and less pressure on the cash or working balances of business. It may also be added that the strain on the commercial banks would be smaller under the second plan, for the responsibility of meeting drains would, in the *first instance*, be put upon the central banking system.

It is possible to give this method of investment of reserves a different interpretation. Reserve banks may accumulate cash for the social security reserves whenever cash flows in and disburse cash whenever disbursements are in excess of receipts; and they would not then act as agents for but rather as bankers for the insurance funds. Reserves of member banks would decline in the former period and rise in the latter period. It would not require large accumulations of reserves by the insurance funds in normal times to embarrass the banks of the country. Some economists would welcome the use of this new weapon of control as a check on undue expansion and a stimulus in periods of inactivity.[1]

5.9. Use of Deposits with Reserve Banks as a Weapon of Monetary Control

Those who would deposit insurance funds with reserve banks until payments on behalf of beneficiaries are due might argue as follows: If insurance funds had been deposited with reserve banks in 1923–1929, an important check on expansion would have been

---

[1] Prof. Hansen at one time seems to have urged the use of this weapon as a means of restraining the banks in a period of excessive activity. See *A Program for Unemployment Insurance and Relief in the United States*, pp. 193–194, and *Hearings*, Senate Finance Committee, S. 1130, *Economic Security Act* 1935, p. 455. Now he does not seem to be enthusiastic, and he is fearful of divided control of the money market. He quite rightly insists that the expenditures of these reserves through their effects on *consumption* will have a beneficial effect upon the economic situation in depression. See *Full Recovery or Stagnation?* pp. 167–169, 180–182. Prof. Slichter would supplement the control by reserve banks through *automatic* restraints introduced through the deposit of at least part of the insurance funds with reserve banks. S. H. Slichter, " Making Booms Bear the Burden of Relief—Some Financial Implications of Unemployment Reserves," *Harvard Business Rev.*, April, 1933, p. 334. *Cf.* P. H. Douglas and A. Director, *The Problem of Unemployment*, pp. 487–488; and Massachusetts House Document 1200, pp. 28–29, 142.

introduced, which would have prevented the fiasco of 1929–1932.[1] Even if the managers of the reserve funds had been in a position to transfer only 1 billion (say) to the reserve banks in 1927–1929 and to return 2 billions (say) to the member banks in 1931 or 1932, purchasing power would not have increased in such an unhealthy manner in the boom or contracted so drastically in the depression. These writers, however, fail to consider that the monetary authority did not use its full powers in the boom period; and for the same reason that the reserve authorities did not use all their ammunition, the political managers of the insurance reserve funds would not have used theirs. It is assumed here that the deposit of insurance funds with the reserve banks would be discretionary. Then either the composite effects of the policies of both agencies (the Federal Reserve and the Treasury) controlling the money market would have been equivalent to the effects of the policies of the reserve system operating alone or else there would have been an even more serious division of responsibility in 1928–1929 than there actually was. In the depression period, the monetary authority pushed the policy of monetary expansion to the limit. Responsibility for the continued depression is not to be put on them for any failure to be active at this time.[2]

Another assumption is possible. Deposits of insurance funds with the reserve banks may be made automatic, the reserve banks in turn being prohibited from investing such funds. It is unthinkable, however, that the use of robots in monetary control would be acceptable, whatever the weakness of political control. Should such a system be introduced, economic fluctuations might well be materially reduced; but economic activity might well disappear also.[3] Reserve authorities have indeed been handicapped by the bluntness of some of their weapons of control.[4] These defects have been remedied to a considerable extent, however, by an increased control of lending policies of member banks and by the introduction of limited flexibility of reserve requirements. Furthermore, direct attacks that influence the demand for money, e.g., public invest-

[1] Cf. STEWART, M., Social Security, pp. 266–267.

[2] For a contrary view, see R. G. Hawtrey, Trade Depression and the Way Out, 2d ed., passim.

[3] In congressional circles high hopes were expressed that insurance funds would be invested to promote economic stability and avoid dangers inherent in their uncontrolled investment and liquidation. Hearings, Senate Finance Committee, S. 1130, Economic Security Act, 1935, pp. 4, 17.

[4] See HARRIS, S. E., Twenty Years of Federal Reserve Policy, Chaps. 31, 32, and Part 8.

ments and subsidies for private investment, are becoming more popular.

In summary, the reserve banks may act as investment agents for the insurance funds, holding cash only temporarily for the funds. Disturbances would then be at a minimum. Should the reserve banks buy public securities, this method would not be unlike that which provides for purchases of public securities in the open market by the managers of the Funds or the Treasury acting as agent. Deposits with reserve banks for more than very temporary periods should then be left at the discretion of the monetary authority. Occasionally this added weapon would be useful, although so long as the authorities do not use their available weapons, the onus of proof of this need is on them. At the present time (1940) when excess reserves are 6 to 7 billions, very large deposits of insurance reserves at reserve banks would be required to assure the country against undue expansion. Furthermore, should the reserve banks hold several billions idle for the Funds, the question of financing the interest payments required would be serious. This solution may be considered as part of the problem of sterilization or impounding of cash through sale of securities by the Treasury. Early in 1940, for example, a maximum rise of reserve requirements possible under existing legislation would deprive member banks of but 900 millions, and the disposal by the reserve banks of all their earning assets of but 2.5 billions more.[1] Further safeguards may be obtained through sales of securities by the Treasury which would then impound the cash. In any case, whatever the decision regarding the deposit of insurance funds at reserve banks, automatic hoarding and dishoarding of insurance funds and division of responsibility are out of the question.

5.10. Investment in Government Securities

The third possibility is that of investment in government securities. We may consider first the period in which the scheme is introduced and assume that unemployment insurance alone is provided. Let us assume that an *unemployment insurance* scheme is introduced in 1922, a year that ushers in a long period of prosperity during which the Fund accumulates 4 billions. This sum is promptly

---

[1] *Fed. Reserve Bull.*, January, 1940, pp. 12–13, and statistical material.

invested in government securities. Actually, the government reduced its indebtedness by approximately 7 billions from 1922–1930. If further purchases of 4 billions had been made by the Fund, the yield on government bonds would have been reduced to a low figure. If the yield was reduced approximately 0.3 or 0.4 of 1 per cent with a reduction of outstanding indebtedness by 7 billions despite the attractiveness of common stocks in this period, the disappearance of 4 billions more from the market in the absence of a stock-market boom might well have reduced the rate an additional ½ or 1 per cent.[1] Rates might not have declined so much as might at first have been anticipated, for the reduction of returns on government securities would have resulted in a loss of interest in government securities and a stimulus to the issue of competing securities. To some extent, of course, there are no competing issues available, since, for many purposes, government securities alone are satisfactory. A significant conclusion can be drawn at this point. An accumulation of an insurance fund in the years 1922–1929 might have intensified the securities boom, for it would have further stimulated investments through the release of funds formerly invested in government securities. Against the increase in demand for speculative securities accompanying an accumulation of reserves is to be put, however, any reduction of consumption associated with the social security tax program, which might contribute to a decrease in demand for securities.

Following this assumed case further, we have to consider what would have happened in the depression period, when the managers of the Fund would have been forced to liquidate securities. Of course it would be absurd to expect that the securities would have been dumped on the market in a period when the exchange of noncash assets for cash was the predominant movement, successive sales being made at lower and lower prices.[2] Nor is it likely that the

[1] Secretary of the Treasury, *Ann. Rept., State of the Finances for the Fiscal Year Ended June* 30, 1934, pp. 350, 372.

[2] *Cf.* CLARK, J. M., "An Appraisal of the Workability of Compensatory Devices," *Am. Econ. Rev., Supplement*, March, 1939, p. 196. P. H. Douglas, *Standards of Unemployment Insurance*, pp. 178–180, for example, seems unnecessarily concerned lest the securities be dumped on the market at a time when purchases would be the proper policy. Another writer is perhaps overly optimistic concerning the availability of markets for government securities in periods of depression. See E. L. Bowers, "Social Security Program; Discussion," *Am. Econ. Rev., Supplement*, March, 1938, p. 142. There are surely times in depression when the market dumps public securities and seeks cash, *i.e.*, periods when the former depreciate. At one time the Social Security Board also seemed a little confused on the issue. See *Social Security in America*, 1937,

government would have redeemed these securities, for the Treasury was confronted with a serious deficit. The sensible and not at all improbable method of realizing on these securities would have been to sell them to banks or to the Treasury, the latter in turn borrowing from the banks.[1] On the assumption that the banks would have purchased the securities and would not have reduced credit to other borrowers, the net effect of liquidation of assets in the Fund would (roughly) be an equivalent rise in expenditures. It may of course be necessary for the monetary authority to provide additional cash in anticipation of these sales.

Imagine—the third plan still being followed—the introduction of an insurance scheme in the year 1935. There would be somewhat different repercussions. In such a period the Fund is accumulating resources and, therefore, accumulating government securities. The government exchanges its securities for the cash collected by the Fund and then promptly disposes of the cash. What then are the net effects of the inflow of cash into reserve funds and their investment in public securities? We assume at first that total expenditures of the Treasury rise at least *pari passu* with (though not because of) the growth of this new market for public securities, and that the additional expenditures are financed in part by sales of public securities to the reserve funds. In making the payments to the security funds, potential consumers, investors, and hoarders all make sacrifices. *Net* effects upon consumption, investment, and hoarding will depend then upon the effects of public spending on these variables. (Secondary as well as primary effects of public spending require consideration.) Consumption may, for example, rise if the new ex-

---

pp. 101–102. Its position was that sales of securities to the reserve banks or Treasury would prevent deflation. The crucial issue is of course the manner in which the Treasury obtains the required cash. Sales of securities in unemployment reserves (say) to the public or even to the banks may be unwelcome, for prices may tumble. It may be necessary to sell to the reserve banks or at least provide additional cash in anticipation of sales to the market. *Cf. Soc. Sec. Bull.*, July, 1939, p. 77.

[1] "Particularly when the government is trying to prevent a depression the unemployment reserve funds should not be thrown on the markets. . . ." *Hearings*, Senate Finance Committee, S. 1130, *Economic Security Act*, 1935, p. 17. Also see House Report 615, 74th Congress, 1st Session (1935), "The Social Security Bill," p. 9.

Prof. Slichter suggests that the reserve banks purchase securities in adequate volume to prevent a drop in prices resulting from the liquidation of securities held by the fund. The favorable effect on prices would follow of course directly from purchases by reserve banks and indirectly through the stimulus to purchases by commercial banks now endowed with additional cash resources. Slichter, *op. cit.*

penditures give consumers more than they lose through the process of tax payments. Should Treasury expenditures be directed largely to the financing of losses, however, hoards may profit and spending suffer.

A reasonable assumption is that the creation of a new market for public securities has small, if any, effects upon total expenditures by the Treasury. It follows, therefore, that consumption, hoards, and investment will be reduced in proportion to the contributions of potential consumers, hoarders, and investors, respectively (secondary effects being allowed for), to the social security funds, at least compared with what would otherwise have been the case. In this discussion, it will be observed that no account has been taken of the possibility that the Treasury may hoard the cash obtained through sales of securities to the security funds. It is assumed that both expenditures and public hoards are roughly what they would have been in the absence of the creation of this new market for public securities. As has been agreed in the preceding paragraph, public expenditures, whatever their cause, will in turn influence the volume of saving and consumption. That these expenditures will influence the components of national income is relevant, though Treasury expenditures independent of the provision of new markets for securities are to be distinguished from those associated with the availability of new markets.

5.11. Economic Effects of Present Investment Policies

Under the Social Security Act the Treasury is required to invest funds not required currently in Treasury securities. Purchases of government securities in the open market are not, however, likely to be of large proportions so long as deficit financing remains popular. The practice since 1935 has been to issue special Treasury obligations to the insurance funds.[1] Thus the public through the payment of taxes gives up purchasing power which the Treasury in turn releases when it spends the proceeds of sales of special obliga-

[1] See, for example, *Soc. Sec. Bull.*, June, 1937, pp. 72–86. In the calendar year 1939, the Treasury obtained cash to finance its excess of expenditures over receipts of 3.2 billion dollars as follows: less than one-half through public issues; one-third through receipts of trust funds and the like; and the remainder by a reduction of its working balance. *Fed. Reserve Bull.*, January, 1940, p. 1.

tions to the insurance funds. The government, instead of selling its securities in the open market and depressing interest rates, issues new securities to the social security reserves, thus keeping rates lower than they otherwise would be. It is conceivable, although unlikely, that the Treasury would hoard the cash received in exchange for the special issues.[1] When deficits are large, sterilization by the Treasury is not likely to be too popular. Yet the experience with the gold sterilization policy of the Treasury proves that the Treasury may be willing to make fiscal sacrifices in order to assume monetary control. During most of the period 1935–1940, however, intolerable sacrifices by the Treasury would have been required in order to absorb surplus reserves. Possibly the Treasury if confronted with a situation similar to that of 1935–1940 might hoard the proceeds of funds obtained through sales of securities to the social security funds. It is scarcely necessary to remind the reader at this point that the sterilization of 1 billion dollars of cash obtained through sales of securities to the insurance funds would have the effect of reducing bank reserves by an equivalent amount.

One further point should be made here. Liquidation of securities in order to obtain cash for social security disbursements might proceed in the same manner whether the insurance funds had purchased securities in the open market or directly from the Treasury. Unless inflation prevails or threatens, the correct procedure would probably be sales to the banks. The more securities had been purchased from the banks in the previous period of accumulation and the less new issues had been created, however, the less harmful the ensuing sale to the banks may prove.

An accumulation of reserves by an old-age fund concomitant with the accumulation for unemployment insurance necessarily intensifies the effects upon consumption and investment. It has been estimated that under the Act of 1935, the net accumulation of old-age reserves in the first eight years would have been 5 to 6 billions. Under legislation similar to that of 1935, total collections (net) for old-age and unemployment insurance in the period 1922–1929 might conceivably have reached 9 to 10 billions. Consumption would have been seriously curtailed by the influx of tax revenues; interest rates on gilt-edge securities might have been greatly reduced. It is difficult to estimate the net effect upon investment of the two opposing forces of a reduction of consumption and the diversion of money

---

[1] *Cf.* Douglas, P. H., "The United States Social Security Act," *Econ. Jour.,* March, 1936, pp. 12–13.

from gilt-edge to other investment markets. Our guess would be that the rise of activity in 1922–1929 would not have been so great as that which occurred and might have been altogether too modest. Moreover, purchases of government securities of 10 billions on top of the actual reduction of 7 billions would have seriously reduced available investments for conservative investors.

What of the period 1930–1940 under our hypothetical case? The gain of consumption associated with the disbursement of 4 billions of unemployment benefits is to be set against the loss of consumption to be ascribed to the inflow of 5 to 10 billions (say) of net contributions to old-age insurance. Unfortunate effects on consumption demand would follow. A word now concerning the effects on security markets. In obtaining 4 billions of cash for the payment of unemployment insurance benefits, the Treasury could sell securities in the unemployment fund to the market or to the old-age fund. Old-age reserves could have absorbed 4 billions of securities in the unemployment fund and 5 billions of securities disposed of to cover deficits.

Much may be said for the provisions in the Social Security Act relative to investment of security funds. Among the advantages, the provision of a market for public securities, which is not unimportant in a period of increasing governmental activity, and the relatively small disturbances on the money market are especially to be noted. Yet the Treasury is in a position to sterilize cash should the need for sterilization be great, and can provide additional cash to banks in periods of liquidation of reserves.

Three criticisms may be suggested: (1) the provision of an artificial market for Treasury issues may encourage public spending; (2) individual banks and groups of banks may not be provided with cash through public disbursements in proportion to their losses from the influx of cash to the reserve funds; (3) the market for public securities is favored against other markets. The last may be held to be an advantage, however, if the tendency of prices of governmental securities, aside from the effects of purchases and sales on account of the trust funds, is downward in periods when cash flows in and when the Funds purchase securities, and upward in periods when the Funds lose cash and sell securities. *To some extent*, let us note, a decline (not net, however) in prices of government securities during the period of influx of funds into the security accounts may even be associated with the sale of securities forced upon banks following transfers of cash to the security reserves. Nevertheless, against the policy of investment exclusively in public securities, it may be said that the investment of reserves in bank deposits, for example, would probably result in less upward pressure on prices of government securities and downward pressure on other assets in periods when cash flows into the reserves than would occur if the investments were made exclusively in government securities.

5.12. Conclusion

The case for investment in public securities having been stated briefly, the reader is now reminded of a few conclusions relative to alternative methods of investment.

First, let us consider the deposit of insurance funds with banks. Effects on industry are to be distinguished from those on the banks. The former's cash position may well become intolerable if the burden of the new taxes cannot be shifted, if their surplus of cash at the outset is small, if replenishment of cash is not to be had through advances from banks or through public disbursements of the social security or other funds. Banks also may find themselves in an unsatisfactory state. Their losses of active deposits and, in particular, business deposits may be recouped, however, should industry succeed in passing the burden on to savers and consumers, and should the influx of deposits following disbursements of public funds and (say) the inflow of gold be adequate. A continued drain of business deposits and substitution of insurance deposits would jeopardize industry and make the continuance of banking activities most difficult. Relief might be found, however, in the various ways suggested above.

What is to be said for the designation of reserve banks as investment agents or bankers? In the capacity of agent, the reserve banks could buy and sell assets (largely, public securities, no doubt) for the insurance funds with a minimum of disturbance. As banker, the reserve banks could deprive the money market of equivalent supplies of cash when insurance funds were put on deposit and release equal amounts when the deposits were withdrawn. It is not entirely clear, however, that the monetary authority requires this new weapon of control so long as all available weapons are not utilized fully. In the present state of excess reserves, however, the sterilization of several billions of insurance funds might conceivably contribute toward control of what might become a dangerous monetary situation. The costs of such sterilization would, however, be large and the problem of the assessment of these costs is not easily solved. Furthermore, the sterilization of several billions of dollars might have serious effects upon total consumption and investment demand. This solution on the whole has not much to recommend it. If the agency function is to be conferred on any agency, much may be said for conferring it upon the Treasury or at least upon the Treasury and reserve authorities acting in concert. The Treasury can also undertake a sterilization (and desterilization program). Sterilization (or desterilization) is also possible if the Treasury sells securities to the insurance funds and hoards cash thus acquired. In any case a unified monetary policy is required, and it is therefore necessary that the Treasury and the Reserve Board act together in so far as the investment of these funds has important monetary repercussions.

One final topic requires comment here. An important issue is the use to which the seller of the assets purchased by the Funds puts the cash thus obtained. From this viewpoint, the deposits of funds with banks is the least happy solution; and the sale of securities by the Treasury to the Funds the most promising one. Deposit of insurance funds with banks prevents any purchase of assets and therefore precludes any later purchases of assets by sellers. In fact, liquidation may be induced by the deposit of insurance funds. When the cash is put at the disposal of the Treasury through sales of new issues, the Treasury is likely to spend at least as much as is thus obtained. The answer is not so easy when the reserve banks or the Treasury purchase assets on the market on behalf of the Funds. The extent to which the sellers of these assets would replace them depends, *inter alia*, upon the losses suffered through the imposition of these taxes and the gains obtained through the expenditures of the cash obtained by the reserve funds. Business prospects will of course also influence the attitude of private sellers of assets.[1]

---

[1] In this chapter we have not discussed fully (1) the relative merits of investment in public securities, in variable yield securities and in "productive" investments; (2) the correct yield on assets purchased by trust funds; (3) the relative weights to be given to safety, liquidity, and yields. These issues are largely of academic interest for us. Yields, liquidity, and type of investments have been determined for us by the requirement that funds be invested in Treasury issues. *Cf.* International Labor Office, *The Investment of the Funds of Social Insurance Institutions*, pp. 20–25, 55–60, and Chap. 3.

PART II
FINANCE AND RESERVES

Chapter 6

EVOLUTION

6.1. Alternative Plans—1935

Perhaps the most troublesome problem confronting the experts dealing with social insurance has been that of the financing of the old-age contributory pension scheme. The alternatives proposed by the President's Committee on Economic Security were (1) the accumulation of a vast reserve of no less than 70 billions by 1980,[1] the income from which together with the current contributions would equal the current benefit payments in 1980 and later years; (2) the accumulation of a relatively moderate reserve of 15 billions, the deficit in later years to be met by government contributions which by 1980 would come to 1,400 millions annually; and (3) the accumulation of a reserve of approximately 50 billions. Under the last plan, benefits in the early years of operation would be modest, the pay-roll tax would be relatively high, and the Treasury would be relieved of any financial contributions to the old-age benefit funds.[2]

The first plan was seriously discussed but came to nothing. The investment problems raised by the accumulation of such a vast fund and the chances that the trust fund would be endangered through a reduction in contributions or a rise in benefits led the President's committee to reject it.[3]

[1] Prof. Witte estimates a full actuarial reserve at no less than 88 billions. A sum of this amount has not been given serious thought. *Hearings*, Ways and Means Committee, House of Representatives, *Social Security*, 1939, p. 1785.

[2] *Report to the President of the Committee on Economic Security*, 1935, pp. 30–32; *Hearings* before Committee on Finance, Senate, *Economic Security Act*, 1935, pp. 107–110, 252–253. The details of the alternative plans as given by authorities who cooperated in the early formulation of the program are not always in agreement. *Cf.* E. L. Dulles, "Financing Old Age Insurance," *Soc. Sec. Bull.*, April, 1939, pp. 19–23; *Hearings*, Ways and Means Committee, House of Representatives, *Social Security*, 1939, pp. 1765–1767, 2111–2112; J. D. Brown, "The Development of the Old-age Insurance Provisions of the Social Security Act," *Law and Contemporary Problems*, April, 1936, pp. 194*ff*.

[3] *Report to the President*, p. 32; also see *Hearings*, Senate Finance Committee, *Economic Security Act*, 1935, pp. 203–204, 573–576, 753–761.

The second plan was approved by the President's Committee on Economic Security. It would involve the Treasury in heavy costs only after 1970, requiring public subsidies which would come to 1,400 millions a year in 1980, whereas the first plan would call for annual contribution by the Treasury of 500 millions at the outset, and no subsidy in 1980 and later years. That under plan 2 the Treasury was to be asked to make contributions is explained by the fact that it was proposed to give the insured who participate in the early years annuities, when attaining the age of sixty-five, in excess of what contributions made on their behalf would entitle them to, the Fund to be reimbursed later for these outlays.[1] Under this plan (government contributions in later years), which was at first approved by the committee, the Treasury would borrow from the Fund in the early years on behalf of those who in these years were to receive payments in excess of benefits earned and would repay in later years.

The President's committee, apparently under the influence of the Secretary of the Treasury, had a change of heart, and in the midst of the deliberations of congressional committees on the bill proposed the third plan which called for the accumulation of a reserve of 50 billions, heavy pay-roll taxes, and a reduction of benefits in the early years.[2] The Secretary was more concerned over the possibility of heavy taxation in 1980 than he was over the difficulty of the task of managing a 50 billion dollar investment fund. He was impressed by the increase in the obligations assumed by the Treasury for the financing of the entire security program and above all emphasized the fact that the Treasury was giving up several billions of potential tax revenue in order to assure the nation an adequate security program and therefore could not assume the additional obligations in later years, which would be incurred on account of contributory old-age pensions.[3] This of course was the basis of the plan approved by Congress.

[1] On the problem of subsidization of particular groups, see the next chapter.

[2] It was possible to provide for a larger reserve through a substitution of the aggregate for average wage as a benefit base, a rise of average contribution rates, and an earlier introduction of their stepup. Dulles, *op. cit.*, pp. 19–21; *Hearings*, Ways and Means Committee, House of Representatives, *Social Security*, 1939, pp. 1765–1767.

[3] *Hearings*, Ways and Means Committee, House of Representatives, *Economic Security Act*, 1935, pp. 897–901. *Cf. Hearings*, Senate Finance Committee, *Economic Security Act*, 1935, pp. 110, 251–252, 514–515, 759. Plan 4 mentioned in the text is the one recommended by the House Committee. It is in general a compromise between the Committee on Security's first proposals (plan 2) and the Secretary's

The financial status of the four plans (plan 4 is referred to in the preceding footnote) in 1980 is given in the following table:[1]

TABLE I.—FINANCIAL STATUS OF PLANS IN 1980
(In millions of dollars)

Plan	Net contributions	Interest	Federal subsidy	Benefit payments	Reserve*
1	2,217	2,087	0	3,038	70,822
2	2,217	468	1,388	4,073	15,600
3	2,660	1,502	0	4,146	50,093
4	2,095	975	0	2,792	32,782 (in 1970)

* These estimates of reserves are based on numerous relatively measurable factors; but there are less tangible factors that are not so easily appraised. In addition, taxes, benefits, coverage, and the like are subject to change, the accumulation of reserves being affected accordingly. *Cf.* W. R. Williamson, "Cost Factors in Old Age Insurance," *Soc. Sec. Bull.*, July, 1938, pp. 3–15.

Congress imposed pay-roll taxes for unemployment and old-age insurance which attain a maximum of 9 per cent (exclusive of any

plan (3). See House Report 615 (74: 1), *Social Security Bill*, p. 6. In the Secretary of the Treasury, *Ann. Rept.*, 1937, p. 53, the reserve is put at 50 billions by 1980 and 57 billions by 2015. The widely circulated figure of 47 billions was inserted in the Senate Finance Committee Report of 1935 on the Social Security Bill. It has no legal basis other than that it is based on estimates of receipts and disbursements, which are indicated by the tax and benefit provisions of the 1935 act.

[1] The British have tended to favor policies suggested by the second plan. They shun schemes involving large accumulations of reserves although they are now beginning to be concerned over the large obligations that the Exchequer will have to meet in the future. In a recent period of five years, the accrued obligations on pensions averaged 20 million pounds in excess of provisions for payment of these pensions. In 30 years the cost to the Exchequer will be 80 million pounds annually. Health insurance, on the other hand, has been actuarially sound, though unemployment and the rise in the amount of sickness reported have troubled the trustees of the Fund. For unemployment insurance, deficit financing has been necessary (a negative fund), though as late as 1927 an official commission suggested the accumulation of a fund in prosperous times to be used in depressions. More recently, provision has been made to repay the Treasury for its outlays on account of deficits. In 1937, for example, 1.6 million pounds were repaid to the Treasury and the Fund had a balance of 60 million pounds accumulated to meet future excesses of expenditures over contributions. *Cf. Reports of the Unemployment Insurance Statutory Committee*, 1938, pp. 2–7; *Report of the Committee on National Expenditure*, 1931, pp. 10–11, 173. National Health Insurance, *Report by the Government Actuary on the Third Valuation*, 1931, pp. 39–41; *Report of the Unemployment Insurance Committee*, 1927, pp. 35–37. For more recent developments, see Political and Economic Planning, *Report on The British Social Services*, pp. 38–39, 54–56, 108–111, 119, 132–133; R. C. Davison, *British Unemployment Policy*, Chaps. II–III; W. B. Reddaway, *The Economics of a Declining Population*, pp. 172–182. The last gives an excellent picture of the financial obligations of the Treasury under both schemes for old-age pensions. In general, the cost seems to rise relative to original and even recent estimates.

taxes levied upon workers *directly* under the unemployment-insurance provisions).[1] Their adoption of the reserve principle for financing old-age benefits is largely to be explained by their unwillingness to mortgage future tax revenues beyond the point set by these new pay-roll taxes.

6.2. MAGNITUDE OF RESERVES

How large the reserve under the provisions of the 1935 act would have grown is beyond the knowledge of any expert. In popular and even technical discussion the assumption is generally made that the Fund would have reached a maximum of 47 billions.[2] Yet the only basis for this estimate is a table prepared by the actuarial experts and published by a congressional committee reporting the Social Security Bill.[3] In constructing this table actuaries had to make estimates for the next 50 years of numerous variables, a problem that will receive consideration in Chap. 8.[4] Even if these estimates were not proved to be wrong, other developments might have threatened the growth of the reserve. Congress might have modified rates of benefits or contributions, extended the coverage, increased benefits for those now middle-aged, or failed to appropriate money collected under the tax provisions of the old-age benefit insurance.[5] On this last point, the failure of Congress to keep the Civil Service Fund actuarially sound and its unwillingness, as evident in the provisions of the Social Security Act, to tie its hands relative to future ap-

[1] Pay-roll taxes on account of old-age insurance attain 6 per cent ultimately: 3 per cent pay-roll tax on workers and 3 per cent on employers. The Federal tax for unemployment insurance on employers attains a maximum of 3 per cent. Any state may also levy a tax on workers, but very few states have availed themselves of this privilege.

[2] According to Prof. Witte, the actuaries estimated the reserves at 32 billions at the time of consideration by the House Committee; but the Senate Report published the estimate of 47 billions. *Hearings*, Ways and Means Committee, House of Representatives, *Social Security*, 1939, p. 1759.

[3] *Soc. Sec. Bull.*, July, 1938, p. 14. The Secretary of the Treasury's more recent estimates (*Ann. Rept.*, 1937, p. 53) vary from the above, however. "On the basis of the valuation assumptions given above, it is estimated that the fund will reach $50 billion in about 45 years and after some 35 years more it will become stable at about $57 billion."

[4] *Soc. Sec. Bull.*, July, 1938, pp. 5–15, for example.

[5] *Cf.* ALTMEYER, A. J., *Progress and Prospects under the Social Security Act*, p. 10.

propriations for old-age benefits aroused doubts concerning the continued growth of this Fund.[1] Actually, some of the foregoing possibilities have become realities under the amendments of 1939. Benefits are liberalized, and, at least for the next few years, contributions reduced below the amount provided in 1935. On the question of appropriation, however, the country has been reassured by the provision for a trust fund, and a permanent appropriation of tax receipts.

6.3. EARLY OPPOSITION TO LARGE RESERVES

Sentiment in favor of a pay-as-you-go plan, or at least a modified reserve system, has been strong from the beginning. A few of the authorities will be listed, before a discussion of the arguments that support their position. The committee of experts, for example, had proposed that the maximum rate of tax should be 5 per cent, a rate adequate to cover all costs in the first 25 years. In later years a subsidy would be necessary.[2] According to Mrs. Burns, experts are overwhelmingly in favor of the pay-as-you-go plan, and the crucial question is whether the loss of interest on reserve is to be recouped by a rise in the pay-roll tax from 6 to 10 per cent or by recourse to general tax revenues.[3] On the basis of a careful survey of the situation, the Twentieth Century Fund recommends the continuance of a 1 per cent tax on wages and pay-rolls. When more revenues are required,

. . . the cost of meeting benefit payments should be defrayed equally by a tax on pay rolls, a tax on wages, and an appropriation out of general revenues up to the point where the taxes on pay rolls and wages are two per cent (4 per cent in all), after which the deficiency shall be met out of general revenues. The Committee recognizes that this is a compromise with the ideal of meeting these costs out of progressive taxes based on capacity to pay.[4]

[1] *Social Security in America: Factual Background*, 1937, p. 213; *Soc. Sec. Bull.*, June, 1937, p. 72.

[2] *Social Security in America*, pp. 204–207.

[3] BURNS, E. M., "Social Realities vs. Technical Obfuscations," *Social Security*, 1937, pp. 108–109.

[4] *Soc. Sec. Bull.*, "More Security for Old Age," December, 1937, p. 11. Also see Twentieth Century Fund Committee on Old Age Security, *More Security for Old Age*, 1937, pp. 153–154.

Mr. Linton would provide tax revenues currently adequate to cover withdrawals from the insurance fund;[1] Mr. Stewart would appeal to the general taxpayer.[2] Whereas the number of writers favoring the pay-as-you-go or perhaps a noncontributory plan is very large indeed (only a few are mentioned), it is not easy to find supporters of the full reserve principle.[3] (Many support contingency reserves, however.) Furthermore, foreign experience is clearly against the accumulation of large reserves. The procedure generally seems to have been the accumulation of a modest reserve during the transitional period and a rise of contributions and subsidies by the Treasury in later years.[4]

It should be observed at this point that those who argue against the reserve plan are not necessarily against the accumulation of any reserve. Dr. Dulles has distinguished three types of reserves: (1) A contingency reserve to cover deficits in depression when disbursements continue at a normal rate and revenues decline sharply. (2) A reserve to keep the fund actuarially sound during the years when the proportion of aged rises. (3) A funded or earning type of reserve which will yield income even when the pension load becomes stationary.[5]

Support for a contingency reserve is fairly wide, that support being found even in quarters where the reserve *principle* is not overly popular.[6] One may even go so far as to say that the so-called

[1] LINTON, M. A., "The Problem of Reserves for Old Age Benefits," *Am. Labor Legislation Rev.*, March, 1937, pp. 25–26.

[2] STEWART, M., *Social Security* (1st ed.), pp. 279–280.

[3] The most notable exceptions are Profs. Witte and Groves and Mr. Willcox who defend reserve financing largely on financial grounds, and Dr. Pribram whose support rests largely on the thesis that contributions and benefits should be related. A large reserve will be a by-product of the adherence to this principle. Mr. Robinson has also defended the reserve principle on fiscal grounds. He expresses doubts of the ultimate contributions of reserves to the income of the insurance account, however, so long as deficits increase. The views of these writers will be discussed later.

[4] PRIBRAM, K., "Social Insurance in Europe and Social Security in the United States," *Internat. Labor Rev.*, December, 1937, pp. 755–756; U. S. Department of Labor, *Bulletin 561, 1932, Public Old-age Pensions in the U. S. and in Foreign Countries*.

In January, 1937, it may be noted, concurrent Resolution No. 4 directed the Social Security Board to report to Congress its recommendations concerning an abandonment of the full reserve system. *Soc. Sec. Bull.*, June, 1937, p. 16.

[5] DULLES, E. L., *Financing the Social Security Act*, pp. 27, 34–36.

[6] LINTON, *op. cit.*, p. 26; Twentieth Century Fund Committee on Old Age Security, *op. cit.*, p. 153. (Observe that Congress and the administration applied pressure to obtain a reduction of reserves, and by 1937 the Social Security Board had

opponents of the reserve principle object to a *large* reserve rather than to reserves on principle. Few supporters are to be found for the second type (above) of reserve. It should be remarked, however, that those who base their objections to the reserve program, in operation before 1939, on foreign experience fail to take sufficient notice of the marked and unusual changes in the proportion of old which are likely to occur in the United States during the next few generations. These changes are very large relative to those which have occurred abroad.

The plan envisaged in 1935 provides a composite of the three types of reserves and, therefore, carried little support. If it were not also a funding or earning reserve (type 3), the plan would have been gradually to liquidate the reserve rather than to maintain it at 50 to 60 billions. This liquidation would occur once the pension load had become relatively stable. Objection is generally found against the second and third elements in our reserve, not the first.

Those who support a pay-as-you-go policy, or at least object to the accumulation of a vast earnings reserve, are not, however, content to base their hopes merely on possible miscalculations of actuaries, which receive attention later, or on the possible failure of Congress to appropriate all sums received by the Fund. (Actually, it is well to distinguish the estimates of actuaries from the use made of them.) Supporters of current financing have numerous suggestions, which will have the effect of reducing or eliminating reserves.

In general, support has been somewhat stronger for a rise of expenditures than for a reduction of contributions. Prof. Witte, for example, saw great danger in a reduction of the rate of contribution, which was in any case according to him inadequate to cover benefits, and preferred the alternative of larger benefits.[1] Let us observe, however, that the adherents of more liberal benefits frequently were aware of administrative or constitutional difficulties confronting their proposals.[2] Whatever the views of experts, Con-

---

become compliant. *Soc. Sec. Bull.*, February, 1937, p. 35, and June, 1937, pp. 13, 16.)

Cf. the views of two of the board's experts who seemed to favor a modification of the present system. E. L. Dulles, Memorandum of October 12, 1936, to Mr. Hamilton; H. P. Mulford, *Incidence and Effects of the Pay-roll Tax*, pp. 49–51. Mr Mulford would accumulate but 8 billions until 1956 instead of 22 billions as estimated under the 1935 legislation. He would effect this change through a reduction of contributions by one-half.

[1] WITTE, E. E., "Old Age Security in the Social Security Act," *Jour. Pol. Econ.*, February, 1937, pp. 31–32.

[2] HOHAUS, R. A., "Observations on Financing Old Age Security," *Trans.*

gress in 1939 postponed the scheduled stepup in rates *and* liberalized benefits.

6.4. LATER OPPOSITION AND THE REVISIONS OF 1939

By 1939 the Secretary of the Treasury under much pressure made a diplomatic turnabout. Coverage would be higher than had been anticipated in 1934, and, therefore, recourse to government subsidies would be acceptable. Under full coverage, the argument usually ran, the assessment on the general taxpayer would not introduce substantial inequities. Furthermore, it had become clear by 1938 that the schedule of tax rates had become insufficient to maintain the actuarial reserve contemplated in 1935. In other words, the account would ultimately be insolvent unless changes were introduced. Finally, it was not clear in 1935 that business would require a *gradual* rise of taxes for the financing of social security. The Secretary therefore was now prepared to scrap the plan for a large reserve and to recommend a contingency reserve which should not exceed three times the highest annual benefits in the ensuing five years.[1] His extreme concern over the tax burdens of the future was now translated into an even greater concern over the burdens on the taxpayer of today. In order that the taxpayer might be spared in the next five years and that benefits might be liberalized, the Secretary recommended a change in the distribution of the tax burden, which would have the effect of imposing upon the taxpayer of the future a greater burden than that from which the Secretary had

---

Actuarial Soc. Am., May, 1937, p. 136; BURNS, *op. cit.*, p. 109. Mrs. Burns suggests the possibility of increasing benefits in the early years. This change would have the advantage of interesting potential beneficiaries in the insurance plan, for the benefits would rise relatively to the benefits obtainable under the attractive noncontributory old-age program. A marked rise in the excess of payments over earnings thus suggested under the insurance scheme, however, would, according to Mrs. Burns, be resented by the large numbers excluded from the insurance plan.

Cf. Hearings, Senate Committee on Finance, *Reserves under Federal Old Age Benefit Plan—Social Security Act*, February, 1937, p. 19; DULLES, *op. cit.*, pp. 13–15; WITTE, *op. cit.*, pp. 31–32; LINTON, *op. cit.*, p. 26; HOHAUS, *op. cit.*, pp. 134–135; GREEN, W., "Labor's Demands in Social Security," *Social Security in the United States*, 1937, p. 181; BURNS, *op. cit.*, p. 225.

[1] *Hearings*, Ways and Means Committee, House of Representatives, *Social Security*, 1939, pp. 2111–2114.

attempted to save him in 1935 through his insistence upon the accumulation of a large reserve.[1]

On the expediency of a suspension of the stepup of tax rates from 1 to 1½ per cent in 1940 for both employers and employees as required under the legislation of 1935, expert opinion was divided. It may be said to the credit of the Advisory Council on Social Security as well as the Social Security Board that they fought the political pressure to suspend the rise of the tax rate.[2] Congress, however, submitted to the pressure for the appeasement of business, the Democratic majority finding much support in Republican quarters. Senator Vandenberg would go much further: in his anxiety to help small business (and perhaps jeopardize the security program) he would suspend the entire schedule of tax rates (which reaches a maximum level in 1949) pending subsequent congressional action.[3]

Not only have taxes for the next few years at least been slashed, but under the current legislation benefits have been liberalized in a generous manner. Both the pressure to whittle down reserves and the political necessity of combating the Townsend movement account for important changes incorporated in the amendments of 1939.[4] One additional factor requires mention. The original old-age insurance plan was based largely on the insurance principle. Under

[1] The Secretary merely presented four alternative plans for financing a proposed scheme for liberalizing benefits. These plans included the schedule of taxes embodied in the legislation of 1935, a more gradual stepup of rates in 1940–1942 than under existing legislation, and a suspension of the increase proposed for 1940–1942, after which the present schedule would go into effect. The last became law in 1939. *Ibid.*, pp. 2115–2116.

[2] Senate Document 4, *Final Report of Senate Advisory Council on Social Security* (76: 1), 1939, pp. 26–27; House Document 110, *Message from the President of the United States Transmitting a Report of the Social Security Board* (76: 1), 1939, pp. 11–12; also see *Hearings*, Senate Finance Committee, *Social Security Act Amendments*, (76: 1), 1939, pp. 248–249; J. D. Brown, "Old Age Insurance," in Russell Sage Foundation, *Social Work Year Book*, 1939, p. 287.

[3] *Hearings*, Senate Finance Committee, *Social Security Act Amendments* (76: 1), 1939, p. 10; *cf. Soc. Sec. Bull.*, May, 1938, p. 58.

[4] Strong support for liberalization of benefits was to be found in many quarters. The President, the Byrnes Committee, the Advisory Council, the Social Security Board, and numerous organizations interested in social security presented strong cases for liberalization. Senate Document 4, 1939, pp. 5–22; *Soc. Sec. Bull.*, January, 1939, pp. 4–11; *ibid.*, September, 1939, p. 1. House Document 110, 1939, pp. 2–6. *Hearings*, Ways and Means Committee, House of Representatives, *Social Security*, 1939, pp. 808–809; A. J. Altmeyer, "Three Years' Progress Toward Social Security," *Soc. Sec. Bull.*, August, 1938, p. 6; "How Shall the Social Security Act Be Amended," *Soc. Security*, 1938, pp. 5–8; J F. Dewhurst, "Old Age Security Financing," *Nat. Tax Assoc. Bull.*, May, 1938, pp. 240–245.

the 1939 amendments much greater emphasis is put upon need though Congress does not by any means now entirely dissociate benefits from contributions. One serious lapse from this principle is to be found, however, in the virtual elimination of lump-sum payments; this is perhaps the most serious attack on individual equity. The heir of a single man without dependents, for example, who dies before the attainment of the age of 65, stands to lose or, more accurately, receives much less than had been paid in by the insured.

In general, the benefit pattern in the Act of 1939 follows rather closely the suggestions made by the Social Security Board.[1] Payments to insured who are now relatively old are liberalized, and, in general, payments are to be made more nearly according to need. Though costs in the immediate future rise greatly on account of the more liberal treatment of the present old, the long-run burden put upon reserves on account of heavy payments to those covered for brief periods is reduced through the substitution of the average wage for aggregate wages as the basis of benefits. Supplementary payments are allowed for dependents; and the low paid in general receives more liberal treatment than the high paid. What of the treatment accorded the present young who remain unmarried? An individual, insured for the maximum period in receipt of the maximum insured income and without dependents, obtains a contract on about as favorable terms as he could purchase with *his* payments (not including his employer's) from a private company. In general, workers earning less than $2,000 get much more than they could obtain through purchase of private contracts with their pay-roll taxes. This does not, however, mean, as has frequently been contended or implied in official quarters, that a small minority of the insured who receive relatively unfavorable treatment may not pay part of the benefits of their fellow policyholders. It is necessary to allow for shifting of taxes to them. Through lower wages and higher prices associated with the security program they may also pay for insurance; and, therefore, their total contributions are not given merely by their direct payments.

---

[1] A comparison of the pattern of benefits under the 1935 and 1939 programs is to be found in *Soc. Sec. Bull.*, September, 1939, p. 4; and Social Security Board, *Ann. Rept.*, 1939, pp. 167–173. The Senate Committee's most significant proposal was the one that would enable "all persons who have reached age 65 prior to January 1, 1939, to develop or complete a qualifying wage record beginning January 1, 1939, instead of January 1, 1940." The cost of this change over the years 1940–1954 would be 695 million dollars. Senate Report 734, 1939, p. 15.

Reserves of the future will be much smaller as a result of the changes of 1939. The more important effects will follow from the ·new benefits pattern rather than from what is now a temporary postponement of the rise of taxes of 1 per cent. According to the House Report, taxpayers will save 275 millions yearly for three years from the postponement of the rise of taxes, and benefits in the years 1940–1944 will come to 1.755 billions, or 1.200 billions in excess of the amount that would have been paid under existing law. Total costs, however, over the next 45 years will roughly be equal to those anticipated in 1939 (not 1935) under the Act of 1935.[1]

As we look this over in November, 1940, we are impressed by the probability of further changes along the lines proposed by Townsendites. The defense program makes the progress toward their goal more difficult, however, though the provision of large unearned benefits for the relatively well off among the old (despite ungenerous old-age assistance in many states for those in need) strengthens the pressure for change.

6.5. SUMMARY

That the Secretary was concerned over the possibility of eventual Treasury subsidies of significant amounts accounts in no small part for the introduction of a plan in 1935, which provided large assessments on pay-rolls in the early years and the accumulation of large reserves. Under the reserve plan taxes would, however, be much less later when the load had become relatively stationary than under a current financing plan; and the Treasury would not be asked to contribute. Opposition to the pay-roll tax and to the accumulation of large reserves, pressure for business appeasement, errors in the original estimates especially relative to partial coverage, the influence of those who feared monetary deflation *pari passu* with the accumulation of reserves—all these factors contributed to the complete turnabout of the Treasury in 1939. The net effect was important measures of liberalization of benefits in the immediate future, a suspension of the stepup of contributions, a serious attack on the insurance principle and greater emphasis on need, and an implied promise of Treasury subsidies in the future to replace earnings on reserves.

[1] House Report 728 (76: 1), *Social Security Act Amendments*, 1939, p. 2.

CHAPTER 7

FINANCIAL ASPECTS OF THREE ALTERNATIVE PLANS

7.1. THREE PLANS[1]

Those who favor the reserve plan for financing old-age benefits are inclined to put the emphasis upon fiscal considerations. Let us begin a discussion of these considerations by presenting three possible plans.

1. Mention should be made of the reserve plan incorporated in the Social Security Act of 1935, which has been subjected to severe criticism from all sides. Under the reserve plan in operation (1940) the Treasury levies a tax on pay-rolls attaining a maximum of 6 per cent in 1949. Receipts for many years (including interest on the reserve) are to be in excess of current disbursements, though, under the 1939 amendments, the excess will not be nearly so large as had been contemplated in 1935.

2. The government may levy large taxes (and presumably these taxes would be mainly of the progressive type), the proceeds of the new taxes to be used to pay off the Federal public debt; and when the debt is extinguished, the receipts from these taxes are to be applied toward financing old-age benefits. Debts will be liquidated, thus assuring the financing of deficits on account of old-age benefits at least in part out of the tax receipts formerly available for the financing of the debt services. Thus, as the charge on account of old-age benefits rises, the cost of debt servicing will decline. Under this plan, it will not be necessary to accumulate a reserve other than the disguised reserve associated with a reduction in the cost of servicing of debt. It will be recalled that the costs of old-age insurance will rise in later generations when (1) earnings, upon which benefits are still based to some extent will have been covered for a lifetime, and (2) the number of annuitants will rise greatly. Disbursements in general are likely to be much in excess of receipts from pay-roll

---

[1] These plans are to be distinguished from the three plans discussed in Chap. 6.

taxes.[1] It will then be necessary to have a large earnings reserve or large subsidies from the Treasury. This plan is a superreserve plan, or perhaps a *genuine* reserve plan in contrast to plan 1, which accumulates reserves while the government's debt continues to rise. The use of progressive taxation, we should emphasize, makes the application of the contributory principle difficult.

Proposal 2, let us observe, is in fact a variant of 1. Under the first plan, securities are purchased on account of the Old-age Reserve Fund; under the second, the purchases are made on account of the Treasury. Differences require comment, however. In the operation of the former plan, the debt remains outstanding, the Treasury continuing to be saddled, on paper at least, with debt charges; under the latter, the formal debt is extinguished or at least reduced. Again, under the second plan, both during the period of liquidation of debt and during that of financing deficits for insurance out of earnings of the Old-age Reserve Fund, the *additional* tax load is likely to be put upon the general taxpayer. Pressure to relieve pay-rolls will be strong when the proceeds are being used currently to pay off debt. This relief, if granted, would not be warranted. Let us assume, however, that under plan 2 pay-roll taxes will amount to 1 to 3 per cent or even less (as compared with 6 per cent under the reserve plan) and the revenues required for liquidation of debts and for payments of benefits in excess of receipts from pay-rolls in 1955–1965 (say) and later years will be obtained from other tax sources. Under the second (or superreserve) plan, pay-roll taxes would be levied; but these levies would be smaller than under the reserve plan, for in the first 20 to 30 years they would be merely sufficient to cover current disbursements to the insured and in later years not nearly equal to current costs. Furthermore, once the debt has been liquidated and benefit payments exceed current receipts from pay-roll taxes, the taxes required under the second plan will be imposed not to pay interest on the reserves held in the Old-age Reserve Fund (or on any indebtedness held outside of the Fund) but rather to cover the excess of withdrawals from the Fund over receipts.

Our second plan may not be practical and perhaps should be dismissed for that reason. It does not seem likely that in the next generation serious progress can be made in the liquidation of the public debt through an increase of general taxes. Larger public

[1] DULLES, E. L., *An Examination of the Reserve Problem*, Remarks before the Advisory Council, Nov. 5, 1937, p. 5 (revised).

debts are on the horizon; and the yield from an increase in income and similar taxes is not likely to provide adequate revenue to satisfy additional demands for defense and Social Services and also to reduce debt by a large amount, whereas the use of pay-roll and similar taxes for redemption of debt is not likely to be countenanced.[1]

3. There is the third proposal, the pay-as-you-go plan. Authorities partial to this plan would eliminate reserves through a reduction of pay-roll taxes and an increase of benefits in early years and would finance later deficits through an increase in general tax revenues. The main difference between this plan and the preceding one is that under plan 3 (pay-as-you-go) taxes are increased *pari passu* with the mounting level of benefit payments rather than at the outset. It follows that *total* taxes are much higher under this plan, for large savings on the financing of the public debt are not made.[2] The explanation of the economy of taxation under plan 2 is as follows: a reduction of debt in the years 1940 (say) *et seq.* constitutes a saving of interest charges and (hence) later of taxes.

The pay-as-you-go system

. . . is essentially deficit financing, in which a large part of the costs computed on an actuarial basis are left unprovided for, to be met in the future as best they may. . . . Later, however, higher taxes must be raised from some source or promised benefits be reduced.[3]

The term pay-as-you-go has traditionally been used to mean that a government meets its currently accruing obligations as these obligations are incurred. However, the meaning of the phrase as it relates to the Federal Old-age Insurance plan is that the Government does not meet its currently accruing obligations as they accrue.[4]

Clearly the pay-as-you-go system requires that current revenues on account of old-age benefits equal current disbursements. Collec-

---

[1] The issues of revenues and future debt are treated in Chaps. 11 and 12.

[2] The Secretary of the Treasury has put the essentials of the pay-as-you-go plan well: Any system of taxes having the same present value as Title VIII taxes would do. The question is essentially one of fiscal and economic policy. Each year's taxes may equal the benefits and cost of administration of that year. Taxes would then begin at a very small fraction of 1 per cent of pay-rolls and rise to a point in excess of 11 per cent over a period of 75 years. *Annual Report on the State of the Finances*, 1937, p. 51.

[3] WITTE, E. E., "Old Age Security in the Social Security Act," *Jour. Pol. Econ.*, February, 1937, p. 23.

[4] ALTMEYER, A. J., *Progress and Prospects under the Social Security Act*, p. 9; also see WITTE, E. E., "In Defense of the Federal Old Age Benefits Plan," *Am. Labor Legislation Rev.*, March, 1937, p. 28.

tions will then be relatively small in the early years and very large in later years when disbursements rise and when the load tends finally, to become more or less stationary. The losses resulting from the failure to collect pay-roll taxes in excess of the amount required by current demands on the Fund will be recouped in later years, it is argued, by a recourse to general taxation. Additional funds obtained in these later years through taxation will necessarily be in excess of the taxes renounced in earlier years, for the Fund will have lost interest on the reserve. Moreover, the burden will *probably* be shifted from workers and employees, who would have paid the pay-roll taxes relinquished by the Treasury, to the general taxpayer, who is requested to pay later. Payments are thus shifted in time, *i.e.*, from the present to the future, and to some extent between classes, from the poor to the rich.

7.2. FINANCIAL WEAKNESS OF PAY-AS-YOU-GO

We should like to elaborate further on the relative advantages of plans 2 and 3, for though the former is not likely to find general approval, it has certain advantages over the *particular* pay-as-you-go plan (3) which has wide support. Whereas under plan 2 the *net* public debt (*say* 40 billions) is to be paid off in the years 1940–1965 (the amount liquidated annually rises as the interest charge and the total amount outstanding decline), under plan 3 the debt remains outstanding. Thus under plan 2 the debt is paid off at a cost of 30 billions in the next 25 years (the saving on interest during this period being allowed for) with the result that by 1965 the country (the taxpayer) has been saved an annual debt charge of 1 billion dollars. A rate of interest of $2\frac{1}{2}$ per cent is assumed. It therefore follows that at a cost of 30 billions (allowance being made for savings in interest during the years 1940–1965) the country is saved a perpetual debt charge of 1 billion (no repayment of debt being assumed under plan 3) and, therefore, the Treasury is able after 1965 to divert 1 billion annually from debt servicing to old-age insurance.[1]

It is impossible to escape the conclusion that the weakness of the pay-as-you-go policy lies in the difficulty of assuring adequate benefits in later generations through subsidies out of current tax

[1] The calculations are presented in Sec. 12.4.

revenues. If the supporters of the pay-as-you-go plan are sincere in their affirmations of support of adequate benefits, they ought at least to accept the principle of plan 2: the reduction of debt charges through a rise of current taxes in the present generation and the use of the tax revenues thus made available for the payment of old-age benefit payments in later years. Even if the repayment of the entire debt is not possible, the redemption of part of the debt may be practicable. If repayment of part is not practical as seems certain now (1940), then the possibilities of collecting adequate taxes later to finance a pay-as-you-go plan *and* the rising debt do not seem promising. If the state is unable to increase annual tax revenues by an amount adequate to provide for significant redemption of debt currently, thus preparing for the demands on the taxpayer for contributions toward social security, what reason have we for anticipating a rise of tax revenues of 8 to 12 billions or more yearly for the support of old-age insurance, defense, and servicing of debts in later generations?[1] At the present moment (1940) the repayment of debt or even the nonaccumulation of debt seems out of the question for a few years at least. This question will be taken up again in Chaps. 11 and 12.

7.3. THE ESSENTIALS ONCE MORE

Let us repeat the essential points of the three plans. Under plan 1 (reserve plan) pay-roll taxes are levied up to a maximum of 6 per cent, the excess of receipts over disbursements being accumulated as a reserve. Ultimately, two-fifths of the costs of social insurance (1.4 out of 3.5 billions) are to be provided by interest on a reserve of 50 billions or thereabouts. (The rather optimistic—relative to the excess of receipts—and modest estimates of future costs made in 1935 are used here.) A reserve plan, it is scarcely necessary to add, may be financed out of other tax revenues.

Under plan 2 (debt liquidation) heavy taxes are levied in the early years (as under plan 1), the excess of receipts being used to

---

[1] Current estimates (December, 1940) put the cost of *operation* (alone) of our new defense plant at 5 to 7 billion dollars annually. In the preceding (text) estimates the optimistic assumption is made that as the cost of security rises, the cost of defense will decline.

pay off the public debt. The arguments for the use of tax sources other than pay-roll taxes seem strong here, for the proceeds are to be used in part to liquidate public debt. We may assume that as the public debt is gradually liquidated, the proceeds of these taxes will be diverted to the old-age insurance account. Proceeds from general tax revenues (other than pay-roll taxes) will thus in later years supplement receipts from pay-roll taxes in the financing of old-age insurance. We may summarize plan 2 as follows (the figures are used for illustrative purposes):

1955

Pay-roll taxes yield.................................	2 billion
New tax revenues....................................	1.5 billion
Disbursements for old-age insurance....................	1 billion
Available for debt servicing...........................	2.5 billion

1980

Pay-roll taxes yield.................................	2 billion
New tax revenues....................................	1.5 billion
Available for old-age insurance........................	3.5 billion

Under plan 3 (pay-as-you-go) the tax revenues are increased as the current outlays on account of old-age insurance rise. Thus in the year 1955 (foregoing schemata) total tax revenues for old-age insurance would amount to 1 billion dollars; in the year 1980, the tax charges would be 3.5 billions. In addition, the Treasury would still be encumbered with a large public debt, for it is assumed that no provision has been made for the liquidation of debt in anticipation of heavy charges for old-age insurance. Plans 1 and 2 relieve the future taxpayer by introducing heavy assessments on the present generation. Plan 3 (pay-as-you-go) treats the taxpayer of today leniently, striking the taxpayer of the future a severe blow; or else the plan fails to materialize.

7.4. THE 1935 PROGRAM—RESERVES OR PAY-AS-YOU-GO?

One further point should be made at this juncture. It has generally been assumed that the plan in operation in 1935–1939 would result in the accumulation of a reserve roughly of 50 billions by 1980. (The reader is referred to a discussion of actuarial principles and errors in the preceding and later chapters.) Here let us consider the following, however.

In most discussions of the Social Security Act this provision[1] has been interpreted as requiring financing on a reserve basis, but this interpretation has no foundation other than that this is the maximum authorized appropriation. Under the Act it is possible for Congress to finance old age benefits on a reserve basis, or on a pay-as-you-go basis, or any combination of these plans.[2]

It goes without saying, however, that the diversion of social security funds to uses other than the payment of old-age benefits would have aroused vehement protests. What is said here is of only academic interest now for the amendments of 1939 provide safeguards against failure to appropriate receipts from pay-roll taxes to the old-age Fund. This problem is still, however, of much theoretical interest and may become of practical importance.

The rate of collection is determined by the Social Security Act. A failure to appropriate the amounts collected (with some minor deductions) would be tantamount to the collection of pay-roll taxes presumably for the ultimate payment of old-age benefits and the use of these funds for other purposes. Some may argue that in effect the result is not different if all money collected is appropriated by Congress to the account of the old-age reserves. Thus if the full appropriations are made, money not currently required is likely to be invested in public securities issued by the Treasury and thus used to meet current needs of the government. One important difference is, however, that if virtually all sums collected are appropriated to the old-age account, it receives public securities in exchange for cash, a reserve thus being accumulated; and if the money is appropriated for other purposes, the obligation of the government *on account of future claims of pensioners* is not evidenced in an accumulation of public securities by the Fund. It follows also that if the appropriation to the Fund is made, the Fund receives not only public securities but also interest on these securities, whereas if it is not made, the asset of the Fund is an indefinite obligation of later governments.

We are not arguing that under the 1935 act or later legislation the Treasury will not try to divert old-age funds to other uses; but

[1] "Congress can annually make any appropriation that it sees fit to the old age reserve account, not exceeding the maximum estimated by the Secretary of the Treasury to be necessary to finance the old age benefits on a reserve basis." Witte, *op. cit.*, p. 15.

[2] Quoted by permission of the University of Chicago Press, publishers, from Witte, *op. cit.*, p. 15.

we are implying that the outcry will be so loud as to make the authorities reconsider their move. Congress by refusing to appropriate a large part of the receipts on account of old-age insurance might have put the insurance provided in the legislation of 1935 on a pay-as-you-go basis. Prof. Witte is certainly correct in this interpretation of the law; but it is very doubtful if Congress would use this method of preventing the accumulation of a reserve.[1]

Finally, too much attention may be paid to the issue of appropriation. Of much more importance are the expenditures and commitments of the Treasury in so far as they affect the Treasury's capacity to pay promised benefits. On these and related issues, the reader is referred to Chap. 9 and the earlier part of this chapter.

7.5. CONCLUSION

In some respects the proposal offered under plan 2, *viz.*, repayment of debt and the application of these savings of interest later toward the financing of old-age insurance, seems eminently the most desirable plan. Unfortunately debt repayment is clearly out of the question for years, and even stabilization at the present level seems impossible. Yet the discussion of this plan helps greatly to clear up the issues. It brings attention to the fact, for example, that an accumulation of reserves *pari passu* with a rise of public deficits of the same or greater proportions is not an ideal solution. Whereas the probability of solvency of social security increases with the accumulation of reserves, the government's fiscal position suffers from the growth of *total* liabilities, which, let us add, we do not associate with the accumulation of reserves. (This is not the question of the distribution of government securities between trustee and private accounts. In so far as the accumulation of reserves by the old-age account results in a *reduction* of debt privately held and a *rise* of debt held by that account, the future burden on the taxpayer for the support of old-age insurance is lightened.) A discussion of plan 2 also emphasizes the weakness of the pay-as-you-go plan. The latter not only does not provide for future liabilities through repayment of debt by the Treasury, as under plan 2, but does not provide for

---

[1] It may be added, however, that the management of other insurance funds by Congress is not entirely reassuring. See A. W. Willcox, "Old Age Reserve Account," *Quart. Jour. Econ.*, May, 1937, p. 464.

the accumulation of assets by the insurance accounts as under plan 1.

A few other conclusions emerge from this chapter. If plan 2 (repayment of debt) were practical, the resources made available for the future would be intangible. They would constitute tax capacity that might be used for the purpose of raising revenue for social security. Defaults on insurance might be more tempting under these circumstances than if concrete securities were deposited with insurance trustees. Only an indefinite obligation of the government would remain under plan 1 (reserve) also if Congress failed to appropriate sums collected through pay-roll taxes and used the proceeds to meet current deficits. Finally, observe that under plan 2 the burden of taxes will probably fall to a proportionately greater extent on taxes other than pay-rolls than under plan 1.

CHAPTER 8

ACTUARIAL PROBLEMS

8.1. ACTUARIAL STATUS, 1935–1939

Actuarial problems arising under the legislation of 1935 will be considered first.[1] An understanding of the reserve plan and its financial principles requires an examination of the actuarial principles that underlie the reserve plan of 1935.[2]

Actuarial soundness is used in a peculiar sense. Liabilities, of course, consist of discounted future benefit payments, etc.; but assets are defined as discounted future income to be credited to the account. Future income may be appropriated out of the proceeds of pay-roll taxes; but in addition, appropriations may be made out of general revenues. According to such a definition the account would be actuarially sound even on a pay-as-you-go basis provided only that it is certain that Congress will always appropriate currently enough to make all payments!

A more narrow interpretation of actuarial soundness would require that the payments into the account by any age group should, when compounded at the appropriate rate of interest, accumulate an amount sufficient to cover its benefits.

In connection with the problem now under discussion it appears that the assets imputed to those covered from 1935 to 1939 consisted of discounted future pay-roll tax payments made by or for them; and a similar criterion was used to define assets of the future entrants.[3]

---

[1] For the retirement program of railroad workers, see Railroad Retirement Board, *Ann. Rept.*, fiscal year ending June 30, 1939, pp. 40–44, 213.

[2] For an excellent discussion of actuarial aspects, which has just come to our attention, see *An Examination of the Reserve Problem*, Remarks by Eleanor Lansing Dulles before the Advisory Council, Nov. 5, 1937, especially pp. 1–16. Dr. Dulles, for example, makes clear the dependence of reserves on actuarial calculations (not taxes) under the 1935 act (p. 2) and the factors that account for the rise of costs (notably rise of pay-rolls and numbers of annuitants—see revised chart on p. 5), and gives an excellent description of the actuarial considerations relevant to the pay-as-you-go-plan (*ibid.* pp. 15–16).

[3] The following references are of some help for an examination of these problems: Social Security Board, *Social Security in America*, 1937, pp. 213, 533; Secretary of the Treasury, *Annual Report on the State of the Finances*, 1937, pp. 49–54; 1938, pp. 55–60; *Soc. Sec. Bull.*, February, 1938, pp. 16–17; July, 1938, pp. 3–15; and Social Security Board, *Ann. Rept.*, 1936, p. 81.

The expert committee had recommended that pay-roll taxes be allocated to a special fund and that appropriations be measured by taxes collected; but Congress merged these taxes with the general revenues of the Treasury and assumed the prerogative of appropriating any sums required for old-age benefits in accordance with the rather vague formula drafted into the Social Security Act. Some latitude was given by the formula that the amount appropriated "must be sufficient as an annual premium to provide for old age benefit payments required under Title II".[1] In 1939, uncertainty in these matters was removed through the provision for the establishment of a trust fund and a Board of Trustees.[2]

In the first few years, Congress appropriated all sums collected minus an allowance for administrative expenses, and in the fiscal year 1937 the Treasury actually transferred 58 millions in excess of the amount collected, the explanation of the excess amount appropriated being that the appropriation had been based on anticipated receipts from pay-roll taxes which had not been realized. The Secretary of the Treasury, in his actuarial valuations, assumed that appropriations in the future would be 95 per cent of Title VIII taxes, i.e., pay-roll taxes collected for old-age insurance.[3] Under the Act of 1935 Congress might have solved the reserve problem by failing to appropriate the sums required for the accumulation of a reserve.[4]

Now let us inquire into the actuarial status and the theory of the old-age benefit fund. In his report for 1937, the Secretary of the Treasury has shed some additional light on these matters.[5] Actuarial status is determined by a "comparison of future benefit payments with funds on hand plus future income of the account." Appropriations are assumed to be 95 per cent of Title VIII taxes. The evaluation of June 30, 1937, implies that the taxes voted under Title VIII plus 3 per cent interest on reserve

---

[1] The full provision reads as follows: "There is hereby authorized to be appropriated to the Account for each fiscal year, beginning with the fiscal year ending June 30, 1937, an amount sufficient as an annual premium to provide for the payments required under this title, such amount to be determined on a reserve basis in accordance with accepted actuarial principles, and based upon such tables of mortality as the Secretary of the Treasury shall from time to time adopt, and upon an interest rate of 3 per centum per annum compounded annually. The Secretary of the Treasury shall submit annually to the Bureau of the Budget an estimate of the appropriations to be made to the Account." *Social Security Act*, Title II, Sec. 201.

[2] House Report 728 (76: 1), *Social Security Act Amendments of* 1939, p. 3; *Compilation of the Social Security Laws*, Social Security Board, 1940, pp. 4–7.

[3] More recently the Secretary said that the assumed annual appropriations will equal annual receipts under Title VIII, less an administrative-expense allowance of $1 per year per individual covered by the act. *Annual Report on the State of the Finances*, 1938, pp. 55–56.

[4] *Cf.* Witte, E. E., "Old Age Security in the Social Security Act," *Jour. Pol. Econ.*, February, 1937, pp. 18–19, 28–29.

[5] *Annual Report on the State of the Finances*, 1937, pp. 49–54.

will be adequate to cover benefit payments provided that estimates of mortality, average wages, and other significant variables prove to be justified by history. In his report for 1937 the Secretary observed that the evaluation of June 30, 1937, might prove to be overoptimistic if the old and the low paid, who are subsidized heavily, took advantage of the old-age insurance in larger numbers than was then anticipated.[1] In the report for 1938 the admission was forthcoming that against future income and present assets of 77 billion dollars, present estimates of future benefits were no less than 86.2 billion dollars.[2] On more fundamental grounds, also, accounting methods used by the government have been the subject of criticism. According to one authority the Treasury was to be censured for not showing "such annual amounts as would amortise and provide for the benefits on a single accounting basis, and in not showing the said accruing liabilities elsewhere on the Treasury's accounts." By 1939 the deficit on the old-age account under the 1935 act was, in the opinion of this expert, no less than 2 billions and would attain 10 billions by 1949. Accrued liabilities were, in other words, in excess of assets.[3]

8.2. ESTIMATES OF RESERVES AND REVISIONS

On the basis of estimates of numerous variables for many years to come, the experts in 1935 drew their conclusions concerning the rate of growth and the ultimate size of old-age reserves. Until 1942 reserves would increase and no benefits would be paid; from 1942 to 1965 taxes would continue to exceed disbursements, the reserve finally becoming as large as the public debt; from 1965 to 1980 the

[1] Cf. Soc. Sec. Bull., July, 1938, p. 15.

[2] Annual Report on the State of the Finances, 1938, p. 56. The Treasury actuary, in an official statement early in 1939, said that if appropriations to the old-age reserve account were limited to Title VIII taxes, and tax and benefit provisions remained unchanged, the reserves would ultimately be exhausted. Soc. Sec. Bull., April, 1939, pp. 21–22.

[3] Hearings, Ways and Means Committee, House of Representatives, Social Security, 1939, p. 2097. Cf. G. B. Robinson, "The Old-age Reserve," Annalist, Feb. 8, 1939, pp. 228–229, 254. Dr. Robinson points out that the Treasury appropriates not the annual accrual of liability but the excess of taxes over benefits. Actually, its liability is given by the equivalent of 5.34 per cent of covered pay-rolls. This would correspond to a level-premium rate, i.e. an average rate charged by a private insurance company over the life of the contract. In 1939 some actuaries, according to Prof. Witte, put the level-premium rate at 7.88 per cent. Hearings, Senate Finance Committee (76: 1), Social Security Act Amendments, 1939, pp. 248–249.

reserve would exceed the public debt, and interest on reserves would provide a large part of the annual revenue on old-age account.[1] Even by 1939 these anticipations of 1935 were far out of line with what then seemed to be reasonable guesses.[2] It appeared that public debts would be much larger than had been anticipated in 1935 and reserves, aside from the changes in legislation of 1939, much smaller.

It is not difficult to find explanations of the fact that even by 1939 estimates of 1935 had proved to be seriously erroneous. A mistake in any one of a large number of estimates might seriously impair the usefulness of the actuarial valuation. It was necessary, for example, to estimate the following variables over a long period of time: population, the age distribution of the population, distribution between covered and noncovered workers, average wages, and age of retirement. A bad guess for any of the series mentioned above might have the effect of under- or overstating seriously the ultimate size of the reserve.[3]

We shall indicate here, on the basis of five years of experience with old-age insurance and as a result of new investigations, what seems to have been the most serious miscalculations made by actuaries in 1935. What is said here is not meant to reflect criticism of the work done by the actuaries who labored under the great handicap of inadequate experience.[4] The most serious oversight seems to have been the failure to allow for *significant* movements from unemployment in noncovered industries (and from a state of idleness) to employment in covered industries and in the reverse direction. Not only are the numbers to be covered therefore much larger than had originally been estimated, but, what is more significant, estimates of costs relative to contributions require a sharp revision upward. The explanation for the last point is that men earning an amount in

---

[1] DULLES, E. L., *Financing the Social Security Act*, p. 29; *cf.* MULFORD, H. P., *Incidence and Effects of the Payroll Tax*, pp. 47–48.

[2] For the original assumptions, comments on the revisions required, and original and revised estimates, see especially, *Hearings*, Ways and Means Committee, House of Representatives, *Social Security*, 1939, pp. 2473–2478.

[3] On these matters, see especially *Annual Report on the State of the Finances*, 1938, pp. 55–60; *Hearings*, Ways and Means Committee, House of Representatives, *Social Security*, 1939, pp. 1759–1761, 2473–2478; *Soc. Sec. Bull.*, July, 1938, pp. 3–15; E. L. Dulles, "Social Security Program," *Proc. Am. Econ. Assoc.*, 1938, p. 139; O. C. Richter, "Actuarial Basis of Cost Estimates of Federal Old-age Assistance," *Law and Contemporary Problems*, April, 1936.

[4] See references cited above and several that will be given presently.

excess of $3,000 over relatively brief periods were, under the Act of 1935, eligible for benefits. It follows, therefore, that since the ratio of benefits to contributions in a very rough way varies inversely with total wages earned in covered employments the serious under-

TABLE I.—ORIGINAL ESTIMATES AND REVISIONS OF SEVERAL VARIABLES UNDER OLD-AGE INSURANCE

Source	Original estimate	Revision
1. Williamson[a] (actuary of the Board):		
a. Average wage	$1,100	$900[b]
b. Coverage	25 million	32 million
c. In and out movement	Small allowance	Much larger than anticipated
2. Secretary of the Treasury:[c]		
a. Coverage	25 million	34 millions for June 30, 1938, and 38 millions ultimately
b. Age of retirement	67½	66
3. Norton[d] Age of retirement	67½	65[g](?)
		Added cost = 20 per cent
Burns[e] Age of retirement	67½	65(?)
		Costs in 1980 would then be not 3.5 billion dollars annually but 4.66 billions
4. Witte:[f]		
a. Number of life annuitants, 1980	6 million	13–15 million[h]
b. Costs, 1980, as percentage of pay-roll.	9½–10 per cent	Recent estimates higher—as much as 30–40 per cent higher

[a] *Hearings,* Ways and Means Committee, House of Representatives, *Social Security,* 1939, pp. 2473–2475; also see *Soc. Sec. Bull.,* July, 1938, pp. 3–15.

[b] The average wage over a large number of industries is given as $913, $1,071, $1,237 for the years 1933, 1935, and 1939, respectively. R. R. Nathan, "National Income at Nearly 70 Billion Dollars in 1939," *Survey Current Business,* June, 1940, p. 5.

[c] *Annual Report on the State of the Finances,* 1938, pp. 57–59. A small part of the increase over 1935 is to be explained by the normal increase of coverage.

[d] NORTON, T. L., *Old Age and the Social Security Act,* p. 58.

[e] BURNS, E. M., "The Financial Aspects of the Social Security Act, *Am. Econ. Rev.,* March, 1936. p. 15. The last two estimates do not seem to have been borne out.

[f] *Hearings,* Ways and Means Committee, House of Representatives, *Social Security,* 1939, pp. 1759–1761.

[g] The reduction from 67½ is not a revision of estimate but an indication of the effect of change of age of retirements from 67½ to 65 years. Any estimate here is guesswork.

[h] In the 1939 House Report, the number 65 and over (not *life annuitants,* the variable in the text) are estimated at 22 millions in 1980. House Report 728 (76: 1), *Social Security Act Amendments,* 1939, p. 5.

estimate of numbers temporarily covered and eligible for benefits was found to reduce the contemplated reserve much below the amount of 47 billion dollars. In this connection recent comments of the Secretary of the Treasury are interesting. Even as late as 1939, the Secretary *arbitrarily* (his word) assumed that of the 34 millions insured on June 30, 1938, 24 millions were regularly employed in covered employments, and the remainder were *primarily* employed in noninsured industries. Within five years about 25 millions will be covered through intermittent employment; and ultimately this number will be 40 millions.[1]

Perhaps the most effective method of concentrating attention on the unreliability of the original estimates would be to list some of the revisions of original estimates. (Revisions 1, 2, 4 in Table I are by men who have been intimately associated with the program.)

The population problem will be discussed more fully later. Here the reader is referred to a comparison of the age, sex, and color of applicants for old-age account numbers (10 per cent sample) and the distribution according to these three attributes in the census of 1930. Especially significant are the relatively low average age in the 10 per cent sample and the small percentage of groups of low-wage workers, *e.g.*, negroes. These changes relative to the figures in the 1930 census are significant for the determination of the size of reserves.[2]

8.3. Numbers 65 and Over

It seems appropriate to deal somewhat more fully with one variable that is of significance for the estimation of future costs and, therefore, of ultimate reserves. Actuaries made large errors in their estimates of population over 65 in the future and in the proportion of the aged that would be eligible for benefits. The former miscalculation deserves some criticism. It will be recalled, however, that numerous revisions of the number of annuitants have now been made.

Costs will increase both because the percentage of old will rise and because the percentage of insured old will tend to rise. Contributions also rise as coverage increases though the net effect on the size of the reserve fund is not clear. We return to that problem later. High birth rates and immigration in the early decades of the twentieth century and the improvements in life expectancy account for the future rise of the percentage of old to the total population. Annual increments of new policyholders for many years (exclusive of entry on account of extension of coverage) will

---

[1] *Annual Report on the State of the Finances*, 1938, pp. 57–58. *Cf.* P. H. Douglas, "Pay Roll Taxes and a Coordinated Program for Old Age Protection," *Social Security in the United States*, 1938, pp. 138–148.

[2] *Soc. Sec. Bull.*, September, 1938, pp. 62–67.

be in excess of withdrawals on account of death. For these reasons the percentage of insured and of annuitants to total population as well as of annuitants to insured will rise.[1]

Two tendencies must be sharply distinguished in connection with the relative increase in the number of old people. A relative increase in old people brought about by a reduction in birth rates, crude or real, will have no effect whatsoever upon a correctly established reserve fund. For if in each year there is paid into the reserve fund (through taxes plus subsidies) an amount (including earnings on the accumulation) large enough to equal the cost of later benefits, then it will not matter that there are less young workers entering the system. Each generation stands on its own feet. An analogy may be made to a private insurance company that refuses to accept any new policyholders. As all the old ones die off, they are paid out of the previously accumulated reserves.

An increase in older persons brought about through an *unexpected* reduction in the number of deaths will, on the other hand, impair the actuarial soundness of the Old-age Reserve Fund, for less than the discounted value of future benefits imputable to the present time will be going into the reserve fund. Later when payments must be made, this deficiency will become evident. The actuarial staff of the Committee on Economic Security had used in its estimates of the future the life table for white population in 1930. Use of these life tables tends to result in the understatement of the amount of future benefit payments, for there is every likelihood of improvement in life expectancies.[2]

In order to obtain some estimate of the possible magnitude of this error, we have used Dr. Dublin's estimates of the course of future population by age groups on the assumption that life expectancies will improve up to the point of an average life expectancy of 70 years (as compared with the present rate in the low sixties). The numbers over 65 estimated on this assumption can be compared with the numbers given by the Committee on Economic Security, and the percentage deviations can be computed.

[1] *Cf.* Social Security Board, *Ann. Rept.*, pp. 36–37; *Hearings*, Ways and Means Committee, House of Representatives, *Social Security*, 1939, pp. 1764–1765.

[2] It is clear that the trend of the last 50 years cannot be mechanically projected since once infectious diseases are completely wiped out, no further improvements should be expected. Nevertheless, considering the improvements of medical science and public health, some of which have not yet been universally applied and considering the experience of the most progressive community in this respect, New Zealand, it is clear that life expectancy will increase in the future and approach the level of 70 years.

Recently the Secretary of the Treasury has admitted that direct allowance had not been made for future improvements; but in using life tables for white people, which reflect lower mortality than the ratio for the entire population, the actuaries had made some allowance indirectly. *Annual Report on the State of the Finances*, 1938, p. 59.

The differences are found to be considerable. For the year 1980 Dr. Dublin estimates an old-age group of 26 millions as compared with the committee's estimate of only 17 millions, a percentage deviation of more than 50. The actual figure will probably lie within these limits.[1] In the House Report of 1939 the estimate of numbers 65 or over, which was undoubtedly obtained from official sources, is over 22 millions.[2]

In the light of the trend of mortality rates in the last few generations, life tables for the future should have reflected the recent trend toward a longer life span. Should mortality rates continue to fall and life expectancy to increase, the demands on the Fund in later years will be much larger than may be inferred from the valuation of 1935.[3] Recourse would then have to be had to the accumulation of larger reserves through the imposition of higher taxes currently, or (and) to a rise of taxation in later generations when demands on the insurance accounts rise, or (finally) to a reduction of benefits.

A reduction in mortality rates will have the following effects: (1) Less deaths will occur before the attainment of age 65. Coverage will therefore be larger, and the burden of supporting the old in any period will be distributed more widely. (2) As life expectancy increases, workers in larger numbers will survive beyond their sixty-fifth year, and unless the new survivors die soon after 65 (in which case the claims on the Fund will be small) the Fund stands to lose much. As the life expectancy of those who attain the age of 65 increases, the Fund will suffer. This loss will be offset

---

[1] DUBLIN, L. I., and A. J. LOTKA, *Length of Life*, pp. 154–196. *Cf. Soc. Sec. Bull.*, July, 1938, pp. 8–14. Various estimates of ratios of survival to age 65 are given here. "The United States life tables of 1900–1902 show that of 1,000 persons aged 20, 514 will 'probably' survive to age 65, while the table for 1933 shows that 614 will reach 65, and the hypothetical table, that 769 will attain that age. In this range there is a difference of nearly 50 per cent of the lowest 'probability'." (*Ibid.*, p. 8.)

It is to be observed that variations in these ratios (percentage attaining age 65) are particularly large for young age groups where sufficient experience is not available and where, because of the longer period involved, errors are more likely. Thus the variation for three experience tables at age 20 is 35 per cent and for six tables (including three hypothetical) is roughly 50 per cent. At age 50, the corresponding figures are 12 and 22 per cent. (*Ibid.*, p. 14.)

[2] House Report 728 (76: 1), *Social Security Act Amendments*, 1939, p. 5.

[3] Mr. Williamson admits that "many more annuitants from the covered group will survive to age 65 and will live longer after reaching age 65 than was indicated as probable in the use of the life tables prepared from census data for the Committee on Economic Security. It seems likely that recent mortality improvement may be expected to continue into the future." *Soc. Sec. Bull.*, July, 1938, p. 15; also see pp. 8–14.

Annuity tables give a more plausible situation in regard to life contingencies than the ordinary insurance life tables. "Such a table prepared for persons now aged 20 shows a rate of 713 per 1000 surviving to 65, an increase of more than 15 per cent over that indicated by the 1933 tables." (*Ibid.*, p. 8.)

to some extent by a gain resulting from a postponement of retirement. (Benefits are paid only after retirement.[1])

8.4. SOME PROBLEMS OF SUBSIDIZATION

The following balance sheet (adapted for our purposes) has been taken from the 1937 report of the Secretary of the Treasury.

(In billions of dollars)

a. Covered June 30, 1937		b. Future entrants	
Present value of liabilities......	25.9	Present value of liabilities......	26.5
Present value of assets.........	18.7	Present value of assets.........	33.8
Excess liabilities.............	7.27	Excess assets..............	7.27

The deficiency of assets of the first group, *i.e.*, those covered in 1937 (as compared with the excess of assets in the second group), appears to be the result of two distinct causes to be associated (1) with the failure to impose a maximum pay-roll tax until 1949, (2) with the application of differential rates which favor those whose total lifetime earnings are low.

The first cause may be analytically distinguished from the second by the device of imagining that all benefit payments now and later were to be a uniform (average) percentage of earnings. In this case, completely aside from the differential percentages, there would still be a deficiency to be explained by the fact that from the years 1936–1949 pay-roll taxes at maximum rates are not to be paid. It should be observed, however, that annuitants in the early years are to receive smaller benefits than later annuitants. It follows that the

---

[1] Whelpton and Thompson's studies of future population growth "show such marked possible reductions in the death rates from ages 65 to 80 as to add perceptibly to the prospective duration of monthly benefits under the Social Security Act. . . . An increased life expectancy of as much as 20 per cent could be deduced from some of the Whelpton-Thompson assumptions above age 65." *Ibid.*, p. 9.

On the issues of the present section, *cf.* W. B. Reddaway, *The Economics of a Declining Population*, especially Chaps. 1–2, and pp. 176–177. The author reveals the manner in which estimates of future populations and their age distributions are made; and in discussing British population figures he also elucidates on the "apparent paradox of a rising total with a net reproduction rate of under 0.8"; and finds that the mortality rate (as in the American case) has been overestimated.

deficit, which is associated with small contributions in early years, is to be put against the gains associated with the modest benefits in early years.[1]

The second reason for the deficiency is that the monthly benefit payments are a larger percentage for those who have low total lifetime earnings than for those whose total lifetime earnings are high. At first glance this might not seem relevant, for this provision is a permanent part of the law and will hold even for *future* entrants. Why, it may be asked, will not this same provision create a similar deficiency for the group of future entrants?

The answer lies in the fact that for those at *present covered* total lifetime earnings will be on the average considerably less than for future entrants. For total earnings are equal to average yearly earnings times the number of years of working life covered by old-age insurance. The present entrants are covered only from 1936 on; hence their insured period varies inversely with their age in 1936. As a result *total earnings* as defined for old-age insurance will be smaller for the present insured than for the later participants who normally will become insured at age of entry into industry; and the percentage rate of benefit payments will, therefore, be relatively high for the former.[2] (The rate of benefit is, in general, relatively high for those whose total earnings covered by insurance are relatively low.)

This may be illustrated by a simple example. Consider a man making an average lifetime salary of $3,000 a year. If the Act had been in effect for the last hundred years, he (and his employer) would have been covered all his life and would have paid into the account not only enough to provide his own benefits, but also an amount required to subsidize workers with smaller incomes. The monthly benefit he receives will actually be only about $\frac{1}{16}$ of 1 per cent of his total earnings. But suppose that he is 51 years old when the Act is passed. His total lifetime earnings will be $14 \times 3 = \$42,000$ instead of approximately $40 \times 3 = \$120,000$. On this account he will get a benefit payment which is about $\frac{1}{9}$ of 1 per cent, or almost

---

[1] These remarks apply of course to the program of 1935, not 1939. Under the latter program, the benefits to older workers of today are, for example, more nearly at the maximum level promised for the future. Deficiencies and surpluses similar to those discussed in the text are to be found under present legislation also, however.

[2] The Treasury, for valuation purposes, estimates age of entry into covered employment at 22 for women and 27 for men. In these estimates, allowance is made, for example, for entry into noncovered employments at first and later transfer into covered employments. *Annual Report on the State of the Finances*, 1938, p. 58.

double the rate applicable had he been covered throughout his working life.

As one of the actuaries states the problem, "For the taxes paid, the benefits are a great bargain at the older ages and quite expensive at the younger ages" and "the pensions for any given age at entry are more of a bargain relatively, the lower the wage level."

"The plan proposed by the Secretary was adopted in principle, even though it saddled indirectly the burden of supporting the present aged largely on the young, the well paid, those who will die before reaching 65 years of age, and those who may not retire at 65."[1]

In connection with the problems raised in this discussion, it may be well to reproduce part of a table given in the report of the Secretary of the Treasury.[2]

TABLE II

Age at entry	Percentage of benefits provided by combined taxes of employer and employee in respect to level monthly earnings of:		
	$50	$150	$250
Age on Jan. 1, 1937	Lives covered at Jan. 1, 1937		
20	90	133	159
35	54	78	97
55	12	23	28
Age when first covered	Lives first covered Jan. 1, 1949, or thereafter		
20	111	164	197
30	84	122	149

It is clear from this table that the low paid are treated more liberally than the high paid and the present insured more liberally than the future insured. The subsidy to those who are relatively old now is a costly one, for the excess of payments over earned annuities will be especially large in the next 10 to 40 years.[3] Thus the Fund

[1] Quoted by permission from T. L. Norton, *Old Age and the Social Security Act*, University of Buffalo Press, pp. 30–31.

[2] *Annual Report on the State of the Finances*, 1937, pp. 53–54.

[3] According to Dr. Robinson, a worker of 60 who qualified at age 65 for an annuity of $15 monthly obtains an annuity valued at $1,870 and pays but $60. *Annalist*, Feb. 8, 1939.

loses a sum, the present value of which is relatively large, for the excess payments are made in the near future, the reserve therefore being reduced by the amounts involved plus compound interest. (It is assumed in this discussion that the new entrants in the future will be in their twenties, and therefore the problem of subsidizing the old is largely one for the next generation or two.)[1]

Later entrants as a class then will subsidize the present insured. That is not all, however. Those who are sufficiently young and well paid of the *group insured at present* pay more (*including payments made by employers*)[2] than they receive; and those who receive high wages in the future may (including employers' contributions again) well subsidize not only the low paid and old of the present insured, but also the low paid of their own age groups.[3] In this connection, however, it is well to keep in mind the possibility that the burden in the future will probably be shifted from insured to general revenues.

Women in general, let us note finally, receive more liberal treatment than men. They are employed more intermittently and receive lower wages than do men. Thus for membership covered on June 30, 1938, the percentage of benefits to assumed contributions was 122 per cent for males and 226 per cent for females. For both present and future entrants the respective percentages were 102 and 171 per cent.[4]

8.5. 1939 AMENDMENTS

What changes, relevant for this chapter, have been made under the amendments of 1939?

[1] *Cf.* PRIBRAM, K., "Social Insurance in Europe and Social Security in the United States," *Internat. Labor Rev.*, December, 1937, p. 756.

[2] Under the 1935 act each worker was, however, guaranteed at least as much as *he* had paid into the Fund: he was to receive at least $3\frac{1}{2}$ per cent of the total of wages on which taxes had been paid. E. M. Burns, *Toward Social Security*, p. 34. *Cf.* M. B. Folsom, "Company Annuity Plans and the Federal Old Age Benefit Plan," *Harvard Business Rev.*, *Summer Number*, 1936, p. 418.

[3] "Thus a worker of 20 entering the system in 1949 and earning $250 monthly could, with his employer's contribution, purchase a private annuity of $147.35 as against the $85 monthly maximum under the Federal plan." A. Epstein, *Social Security*, p. 21.

[4] *Annual Report on the State of the Finances*, 1938, p. 56.

1. The benefits in the immediate future are larger. The present old are treated more liberally than under the legislation of 1935, but less liberally absolutely (more liberally in relation to contributions) than the future old. For example, the excerpts (below) from a table submitted by the actuary of the Social Security Board give an indication of relative changes.[1] Assumptions of probable maximum cost, it should be observed, are based upon more conservative estimates of the relevant variables (and hence higher costs) than were made in 1935. The difference between estimates based on these assumptions and the original assumptions made in 1935 are revealed by a study of column (1). Also of interest is the lower level premium rate (long-range cost for the suggested plans) than under the 1935 acts both on earlier and conservative assumptions. In other words, despite higher costs in the present generation, total costs are less under the new (House) plan, which was largely followed in the 1939 act.[2] It is well to keep in mind, however, that the early benefits were increased to some extent in the Senate.

TABLE III.—TOTAL BENEFIT PAYMENTS UNDER SUGGESTED PLAN, EXCLUDING DEATH AND DISABILITY BENEFITS AS COMPARED WITH THOSE UNDER PRESENT TITLE II

A. Estimates Based on Original Assumptions

	Total benefit payments, millions of dollars		Benefits as percentage of pay-roll	
	Present Title II (1935 Act)	Suggested plan	Present Title II	Suggested plan
	(1)	(2)	(3)	(4)
1940	49	58	0.17	0.21
1955	921	1454	2.81	4.35
Level*	....	....	5.06	4.69

B. Estimates Based on Probable Maximum Cost Assumptions

1940	46	70	0.16	0.25
1955	1445	1889	4.15	5.33
Level*	....	....	7.88	6.60

* Level per cent required to support benefits over the whole period.

[1] *Hearings*, Ways and Means Committee, House of Representatives, *Social Security*, 1939, p. 2478.

[2] Mr. Altmeyer puts the total costs under the proposed plan at an amount roughly equal to those under the new plan. It is of course necessary to compare the costs under the two plans on similar and reasonable assumptions. On the issue of total costs, see *Hearings*, Ways and Means Committee, House of Representatives, *Social Security*, 1939, pp. 1781, 2219; Senate Document 4, *Final Report of Advisory*

2. The emphasis on presumptive need as a determinant of the pattern of benefits has resulted in the extension of the insurance principle in one respect: those who die before the age of 65 and without dependents lose. (Benefits are of course related also to former income.) The lump-sum payment, which constituted a guarantee of payment of 3½ per cent of covered wages to those covered too briefly under the original act, is now dropped. Lump-sum payments equivalent to a maximum of six times the monthly primary benefits are granted under the 1939 amendments. It is required, however, that the deceased should not be survived by a widow, child, or parent who is entitled to benefits and that the amount paid should not exceed burial expenses contributed by the recipients of the lump-sum payments. It is also possible for the insured to pay for relatively long periods and lose their status of fully and currently insured. Protests on these violations of the principle of dependence of benefits and contributions resulted, however, in some modifications of the 1939 House bill in the Senate, which tended to reduce the hardships of these provisions.[1]

Officials defend the new principle of insurance and benefits according to need. Some criticisms may be directed against the new benefit schedules, however. The contention that the insured always obtains at least as much as he can obtain at equal costs from an insurance company is subject to several reservations.[2] (1) A surrender value, which can frequently be obtained from private companies, is not obtainable from the government. (2) If the employee is credited

Council, 1939, pp. 13–14; House Report 728 (76: 1), *Social Security Act Amendments of 1939*, p. 7.

[1] On these issues see especially *Hearings*, Senate Finance Committee, *Amendments of Social Security Act*, 1939, pp. 16, 50–63, 71–76, 79, 246–247; *Hearings*, Ways and Means Committee, House of Representatives, *Social Security*, 1939, p. 2164; House Report 728 (76: 1), pp. 8–11, 14, 118–119; *Soc. Sec. Bull.*, September, 1939, pp. 3–12.

A treatment of benefits under the original and revised legislation is also to be found in Social Security Board, *Ann. Rept.*, 1939, pp. 168–173; L. L. Schmitter and B. C. Goldwasser, "The Revised Benefit under Federal Old-age Insurance," *Soc. Sec. Bull.*, September, 1939, pp. 3–12. For definitions of *currently* and *fully* insured status and the privileges under each see Social Security Board, Regulations 3, *Federal Old Age and Survivors' Insurance*, 1940, pp. 3–7.

[2] *Cf. Hearings*, Ways and Means Committee, House of Representatives, *Social Security*, 1939, pp. 2298–2299. According to Mr. Altmeyer, a man earning $1,200 could buy an annuity with 3 per cent of his wages which would yield $25 monthly. Under the proposed bill, he could obtain $36.25 from the government on a similar contract if he were unmarried, and 72.50 if he were married and had two children. For a yearly wage of $2,400, the respective figures would be $50, $50.75, and $76.12.

with the employers' contributions, a substantial number receive less than they would receive from private contracts—the high-paid and those insured for long periods notably. (This is, however, a necessary result of consideration of need.) It is, let us observe, appropriate that at least part of the tax paid by the employer should be considered as a cost on the employee. He pays not only directly through a deduction from his wages, but he may also pay part of the employers' tax through an additional cut of wages or failure to obtain an increase, and through higher prices.

3. Under the legislation of 1939, the principle of the average wage is established, an innovation which in part accounts for the individual inequities associated with the recent amendments. Under the principle of the average wage, the present old receive much more liberal treatment than under the original legislation. They are favored with the status of "fully insured" after a very brief period of coverage, and their benefits are then based largely on their average wage: 50 per cent on the first $40 monthly plus 10 per cent on amounts from $50 to $250. The new schedule is a serious departure from the principle of association of contributions and benefits, and yet it does not constitute a full acceptance of the principle of payments in accordance with need. Annuitants are to receive benefits on the preceding schedule, plus, for each year covered, 1 per cent of the basic benefit, which in turn is derived from the average wage. They will also receive additional benefits for dependents. They will not, in any case, receive an amount in excess of (1) $85 monthly, (2) twice the basic benefit, or (3) 80 per cent of the average wage, whichever is the smallest. Their average wage will be determined by a division of the number of years of possible coverage into the total wages in covered occupations. The present young thus obtain the additional benefits for the additional years covered; and the fund is protected by the provisions for minimum standards for the status of fully and currently insured and by the relevancy of years of *possible* instead of actual coverage in the determination of average wages. Favorable treatment of the present old requires, therefore, sacrifices by present young and middle aged. Costs from 1940 to 1954 are estimated at 8.5 billion dollars under Title II in the 1935 act, and 14.8 billion dollars under the House bill of 1939. (In the Senate and final version the early benefits were liberalized further.)

Association of benefits with the average wage provides a formula under which the relatively old receive liberal treatment and, at the same time, the reserve and the taxpayer of the future are protected against unjustifiable claims. Low-paid workers continue to receive preferential treatment; but the annuitant of the future who is covered for but a brief period will not receive the favored treatment that he would have received under the original Act.[1]

4. Need plays a larger part and contributions a smaller part in the pattern of benefits provided under the legislation of 1939 than under the original Act.[2] The present old, the dependents, the married, and the low paid *in general* gain at the expense of the present young, the annuitant without dependents, and the high paid. One reservation is required, however. Since, after the passage of the transition period, treatment of the insured who receive relatively small amounts of *total* wages in covered occupations is not so liberal as under the original Act, numerous low-paid workers will receive less liberal treatment than under the Act of 1935. The following table is illuminating. On the whole, benefits to the present old are larger relatively to the benefits to future old, and benefits to the low paid (and married) are larger relatively to the benefits to the high paid than under the legislation of 1935. (This table was presented to the House Committee.[3] It is illustrative of the principles of the new legislation.)

TABLE IV.—ILLUSTRATIVE MONTHLY OLD-AGE RETIREMENT BENEFITS UNDER 1935 ACT AND UNDER NEW PLAN

Monthly wage	5 years' coverage			40 years' coverage		
	1935 act	New plan		1935 act	New plan	
		Single	Married		Single	Married
$ 50	$15.00	$21.00	$31.50	$32.50	$28.00	$40.00
100	17.50	26.25	39.38	51.25	35.00	52.50
250	25.00	42.00	63.00	81.25	56.00	84.00

Of the important changes introduced by Congress in 1939, the following in particular are to be emphasized: A further movement in the direction of subsidization of particular groups, *e.g.*, the present

[1] *Cf. Soc. Sec. Bull.*, September, 1939, pp. 6–8; House Report 728 (76:1), p. 10.

[2] *Cf.* House Report 728 (76: 1), p. 7; *Hearings*, Ways and Means Committee, House of Representatives, *Social Security*, 1939, pp. 1007, 2206–2208.

[3] *Hearings*, Ways and Means Committee, House of Representatives, *Social Security*, 1939, p. 2165.

old,[1] the needy, the married; an assault upon the principle of dependence of benefits upon contributions; an affirmation of this principle in a modified form in its application to annuitants of later generations. Future annuitants will have to make good (in the absence of new taxes) the losses suffered through generous treatment of the present old; but the insurance account will be protected from equal drains in favor of those who are now young and will be covered for short periods. Contributions from the insured of the future will provide part of the benefits of the present old and presumably part of their own benefits. More favorable treatment to the relatively less well-off in any one age group will, however, continue to prevail in the future.

No one can doubt but that reserves under the legislation of 1939 will be smaller than under the original legislation; and it is commonly known now that, even under the latter, reserves would not have reached the well publicized amount of 47 billions, nor an amount close to it. Authorities have learned their lesson. They are not inclined to make guesses for the far distant future. On the principle of three, *i.e.*, a reserve equal to three times the maximum annual payment of the next five years, the Chairman of the Social Security Board puts the reserves in 1980 at 15 billion dollars. Accumulations will depend, however, on future policy concerning benefits and upon the contributions of the Treasury. The last question will be returned to later. An estimate of reserves given in the House Report is as follows (round figures):

1940	2 billions
1945	4 (3.5) billions
1955	8 (7) billions

The figures in parentheses are based on liberalization of benefits which the Senate Committee favored.[2]

[1] The principle of the average wage, which is applied under the 1939 act and which favors the present old, is justified by its supporters on the grounds that present old had not been given an opportunity to contribute.

[2] House Report 728, (76: 1), pp. 15–17; *Hearings*, Ways and Means Committee, House of Representatives, *Social Security*, 1939, pp. 1272–1273; Senate Report 734 (76: 1), *Social Security Act Amendments*, 1939, p. 17.

8.6. SUMMARY

It is scarcely necessary to summarize the details of the discussion of this chapter. We begin with a consideration of actuarial status, including the change in that status. Section 8.2 is an attempt to explain why the estimates of 1935 proved so soon to be far from the truth. In particular, the *large* costs relative to contributions for those who are covered for relatively brief periods were unexpected. Another issue is the proportion of old to total population in later generations. In 1935 the actuaries underestimated the proportion of aged; and what is significant is not only the proportion of aged to total population, but the relation of the *anticipated* proportion of aged (and annuitants) to the *actual* proportion: That in the next few generations those beyond 65 become relatively more numerous is explained both by a decline of births and immigration as compared with the early part of the century and by higher probability of life after 65. In Sec. 8.4 the problem of subsidization is considered. Under the 1935 Act, the future insured subsidize the present; the high paid, the low paid; the young, the old; the men, the women. Amendments of 1939 (Sec. 8.5) provide similar subsidies. In addition, the recent legislation puts more emphasis on need and less on the contributory principle than does the Act of 1935. Finally, reserves are likely to be less significant under the legislation of 1939 than under the original act.

CHAPTER 9

THE THEORY OF RESERVES

9.1. ACCOUNTING PRINCIPLES

In response to vigorous criticisms of the reserve principle, defenders have tended to retreat. Some have especially emphasized the point that the accumulation of reserves is merely an accounting device that enables the government to show the true state of the social security account. Confusion often prevails, however. Authorities will on occasion emphasize the accounting aspects in order to divert attention away from the tax and monetary problems involved. Others will emphasize the budgetary aspects, and another authority will jump from one approach to the other. It is held by one authority, for example, that the provision of a reserve is both an attempt to budget costs over a long period of years and a bookkeeping device; by another, that the reserve is an instrument for the redemption of present debt at the rate of acquisition of new debt to the old-age reserve fund; by a third, that the reserve reflects the excess of the then future liability over the then future income.[1]

9.2. THEORY OF RESERVES

Later something will be said concerning the relation of this chapter to the analysis of Part I and to the later chapters of Part II. Here it suffices to remind the reader that the relation of reserves to the volume of output was discussed in Part I. It will be recalled

[1] *Hearings*, Ways and Means Committee, House of Representatives, *Social Security*, 1939, p. 2205; ELIOT, T. H., "Funds for the Future," *Atlantic Monthly*, August, 1938, pp. 225–232; Memorandum of Miss E. Dulles to Mr. Hamilton of the Social Security Board, Oct. 12, 1936, pp. 3–6; WILLCOX, A. W., The "Old Age Reserve Account—A Problem in Government Finance," *Quart. Jour. Econ.*, May, 1937, p. 460; WITTE, E. E., "Old Age Security in the Social Security Act," *Jour. Pol. Econ.*, February, 1937, pp. 22–23.

that the extent to which the accumulation of reserves contributes toward deflation will depend upon the manner of finance and investment; and though the effects on output now and in the immediate future are a vital consideration, they should not be the exclusive factor in the determination of financial methods to be used in the insurance programs. The next few chapters will include a further discussion of fiscal problems. In the present chapter, various issues relative to the nature of reserves are examined. Much misunderstanding has prevailed in their discussion; and the failure to understand the elements of the problem has contributed to some unwise provisions in the 1939 amendments.

It is important in these matters to distinguish accounting from real considerations. In some formulations the former aspect receives too much emphasis. The crucial points are (1) that the government collects revenues in excess of current disbursements on old-age account; and (2) that the taxes are on pay-rolls, though there is no requirement that other sources of revenue should not be tapped. No accounting device can remove the sting of these taxes, and only to a limited extent can proper accounting solve the problems that arise from the accumulation of reserves. Let us, however, consider the accounting problem further.

For our purposes we may take the expenditure of the Federal government in the present and future on social security and for other purposes as given. It should be obvious then that the money collected from these taxes does not vanish. Setting up an account in a particular manner or the choice of any particular bookkeeping procedure does not alter that fact. Then with the same amount of expenditure the result can only be (1) the accumulation of cash, (2) an absolute reduction of debt, or (3) the reduction of debt over what it otherwise would have been. Dismissing the first possibility, we conclude that interest payments for privately held debt will fall *pari passu* with the accumulation of public securities in the reserve funds. As a result, the government will have more to spend, or with a given amount of expenditures the taxes required will be less by the extent of savings on interest payments to private investors. In other words less is required to meet debt charges for privately held debt; and the payment of interest to trust funds is *not* an additional charge and the Treasury has an obligation to these funds for revenue collected for them.

Accounting problems, though not of paramount importance, are not to be dismissed. One method of handling the reserve is to appropriate the excess of receipts over disbursements into a trust fund as is provided in the amendments of 1939. This procedure gives some assurance to the annuitants that the government has not taken lightly its obligations to them. In addition to current revenues, the resources of the reserve fund will be available later. Provision of a reserve, on the other hand, is in the opinion of many an invitation for the government to appropriate assets in the reserves for noninsurance needs whenever the financial pressure becomes overbearing. This procedure will help the Treasury only in the sense that the debt to the insurance fund will not be evidenced by an equivalent amount of public securities held.

These fears suggest an alternative proposal, *viz.*, nonappropriation of the excess of receipts and nonaccumulation of securities (say) in reserves.[1] In that case, it is held, the government will not be able to sell securities belonging to the insurance funds. The reserve is not, however, wiped out: it consists of a debt of the government to the old-age fund, but one that is not recognized in the form of an accumulation of Treasury securities (the Treasury would accept its obligations in an implied promise to pay). In this case the threat to the old-age program is at least as great as under the procedure provided in 1939. Now government securities will be sold to the public as a means of financing new deficits; and, therefore, the capacity to pay old-age benefits later may be reduced just as effectively as if securities were taken directly out of the old-age reserve fund and sold. (Whether the debt of the government to the fund is evidenced in Treasury issues held by the fund or not, the excess of taxes over costs will be put at the disposal of the Treasury. Deficits in excess of this amount will in the long run be covered by borrowing on the market.) When a reserve of securities or other assets is not accumulated, however, a clear-cut breach of faith with pensioners, *i.e.*, an overt act of repudiation through sales of their

---

[1] Large deficits have been incurred in the management of other trust funds. Thus under the Civil Service Retirement and Disability Fund, the Treasury *now* makes an annual regular contribution and a deficiency contribution for services rendered prior to the period of contributions. In the fiscal year 1939, the payments were as follows:

1. Normal costs = 3.50 per cent of pay-rolls by employers
   2.64 per cent by government
2. Deficiency = 5.81 per cent by government

Senate Document 212, *Civil Service Retirement and Disability Fund*, 1940, pp. 6–7.

securities, is not made. Against this advantage, the following is to be considered. Whereas the accumulation of a reserve of securities (even if the only evidence is a Treasury statement) provides a constant reminder of the obligations of the Treasury, the nonaccumulation of securities under a reserve plan fails in this respect. This defect may be corrected, however, by the issue of insurance policies to the insured.

Failure to set up a concrete reserve (not merely an acknowledged or implied obligation of the government to cover future outlays) makes the reserve plan, *i.e.*, financing through an excess of receipts in the early years, and the pay-as-you-go plan similar in some respects. Under the latter, the old-age reserve account for many years incurs obligations against which assets are not stored. Liabilities on the old-age account then continue to grow, and the government's debt to the old-age account, therefore, continues to rise until the point is reached when income equals outgo. In contrast to the plan of accumulation of securities in the reserves, however, the pay-as-you-go plan does not provide directly for debt reduction (absolute or relative) and, therefore, unlike this plan, it does not provide future resources through an increased capacity of the Treasury to pay. This is subject to the important reservation that where the deficits grow as rapidly as or more rapidly than securities in the reserves the government's capacity to pay later does not improve; but the excess of receipts on insurance account will moderate the rise of debt privately held. Thus the collection of taxes in the accumulation period that would not have been collected otherwise contributes toward a reduction of debt; and this is a net gain against the pay-as-you-go plan. Difficulties may remain, however, if the *total* debt continues to rise.

An outline of possible ways of dealing with the problem concludes this section.

1. *Deficits* are incurred in the sense that no provision or inadequate provision has been made to meet future liabilities to annuitants.
   a. No provision is made.
   b. Provision is made, but disbursements are likely to be in excess of original estimates and (or) receipts less than original estimates. By 1937, for example, it was clear that the old-age reserve account was running a deficit in this sense.

2. No deficits are incurred, for when obligations become due adequate revenues will be forthcoming. Three possibilities may be suggested.

   a. No definite tax program is planned now; but the promise of new taxes is implied in the benefit schedule.

   b. A definite tax program is launched.
   The pay-as-you-go plan may conceivably be included under 1a or more likely under 2a or 2b.

   c. One could provide for future obligations through the accumulation of a large reserve and a tax program.
   2c or 1b may be accepted as a description of the reserve plan, which includes a tax program and provision for reserves.

To summarize in a somewhat different manner. The state may accumulate reserves of securities or assets, merely acknowledge debt, provide revenue out of taxes as and when required, or use some combination of these methods. Again, deficits may be incurred in various senses. Assets *now* available may be less than the present value of obligations; assets on hand *plus* present value of expected income may be less than the present value of obligations. Finally, the government may provide the required income in the future (1) through pay-roll taxes, (2) through pay-roll and other taxes, (3) through taxes plus earnings on reserves. Faithful adherence to promises made are most likely under 2c above and least likely under 2a.

9.3. REAL AND FINANCIAL ASPECTS OF RESERVES

Much debate has centered around the question of the contribution of reserves to real resources in the future. In an earlier part of this book we have commented on a tendency to emphasize the financial considerations, which in part accounts for the severe tax program introduced in 1935, and a more recent inclination to emphasize real considerations, which has contributed toward the enthusiasm for the revisions of 1939 (Sec. 1.3). In this section the discussion will be concerned successively but briefly with (1) the increased emphasis on the view that saving for the future is not possible; (2) the effect of the accumulation of reserves on the volume of income and savings; (3) the relation of the manner of distribution of taxes over time to the capacity of future generations to provide social security on an adequate scale; (4) the monetary aspects of reserves in so far as they influence the volume of output, and the like; (5) the financial adequacy of a reserve plan as against the financial inadequacy of a pay-as-you-go plan; (6) a possible way out that combines the monetary advantages of the pay-as-you-go plan and the financial advantages of the reserve plan. These six issues throw light upon the relation of reserves to future amounts of capital and income. Whether adequate real income will be available for annuitants will depend of course upon the capital and income of the future.

First, the relation of accumulations of reserves to the income of the future is discussed.

Numerous writers comment on the absurdity of the accumulation of reserves with the intent of providing for future needs.

. . . it is obvious that no matter what financial jugglery is indulged in, each generation must pay for the security of its own aged. Money can be stored up for the future through hocus pocus, but true wealth must of necessity come almost entirely from current production.[1]

An actuarial reserve can perform its normal function as a savings system when operated by a private institution, they assert, but it cannot do so when operated by the Government or the community as a whole. . . . The goods and services produced this year must be consumed this year or in the near future—as a rule they will be either useless or out of existence a generation from now. . . .

Since the reserve fund is without any real significance as a means of providing for those who will be aged many years from now, say the critics, the only right procedure is not to attempt accumulating it but rather in the early years of operation to pay more liberal benefits than are paid under a reserve plan, or to reduce the rates of the taxes from which the reserve is indirectly built.[2]

Undoubtedly many authorities have labored under the misapprehension that the young of today, through the accumulation of reserves, can put aside commodities (and perhaps services) that they will require in their old age. It is well to warn these writers that essentially each generation bears its own burden of social

[1] Quoted by permission of W. W. Norton & Company, Inc., publishers, from M. Stewart, *Social Security*, p. 156.

[2] Quoted by permission of the Graphic Arts Press, from B. E. Wyatt and W. H. Wandel, *The Social Security Act in Operation*, pp. 156–157.

security. Failure of some supporters of the reserve plan to be cognizant of this vital truth is not in itself, however, an adequate reason for scrapping the reserve plan. Although the material goods required by the young in their old age are not obtained directly by the accumulation of reserves, the repercussions of the reserve plan upon output (present and future) may be favorable (in contrast to the effects of other plans) and, therefore, the drafts upon supplies for the use of the old may be facilitated. These issues have received much space in Part I and therefore are passed over lightly here.

The conclusion under (2) of this section is then that though goods are not "saved," the choice of financial programs and, what is related, the choice between reserves and no reserves or large and moderate reserves will influence the amount of both income and savings now and later. The larger the income and the larger the volume of savings over the next few generations, the larger will be the available capital plant and income which will provide the goods required for social security in later years. The issue of possible deflationary effects of savings has been discussed in Part I, and we shall return to that subject briefly in a moment. What is emphasized here is that depressive taxes will tend to have the same effects as dissaving (subject to reservations in Part I)[1] in that less capital and income will be available in the future; and a judicious choice of financial programs will tend to increase future capital resources and output. In that sense an accumulation of reserves and, therefore, relatively even distribution of taxes over time and a smaller total amount of taxes will have effects not unlike those that follow saving, *e.g.*, an accumulation of goods for the future. Here the assumption of relatively stable taxable capacity over time is required. It is scarcely necessary to add that the nature of the taxes imposed is of significance. Not only may tax A yielding X revenue reduce income by $X/2$ whereas tax B yielding X revenue reduces income by $3/2X$, but tax A may cut savings directly (not via income) by $X/3$ and tax B by $X/2$.

We now turn to the third issue, *viz.*, the distribution of taxes over time. Reserve financing requires, it will be recalled, relatively stable tax burdens over time in contrast to current financing which provides negligible taxes at the outset and very heavy taxes once the peak of disbursements is attained (*cf.* Sec. 7.3).

---

[1] Effects on the marginal propensity to consume may, for example, be favorable and, under conditions of oversavings, may be considered an offset against the adverse effects on motivation.

The desirability of having moderate taxes over a long period of time instead of very low rates at the beginning and compensatingly higher rates later rests upon the postulate that compulsory transfers within an economy, other things being equal, involve a burden that increases more rapidly than the increase in the amount of the transfer. The total burden over time will be minimized if there is an equalization of the burden of the marginal dollar of each year's taxation. Assuming no change, in the level of national income and productivity, suggests that the level of taxation should be constant through time. On the assumption that the level is constant, the reduction of taxes by a dollar now would lighten today's burden. But tomorrow's taxes would have to be increased by a dollar, an extra burden being then imposed. Because of our law of increasing marginal burden, the gain today will be less than the loss tomorrow. This argument neglects the possibility of earning interest upon funds (treated to some extent in Part I) and possible time discounting of future governmental burdens; appropriate modifications of the argument to take into account these factors could be easily made, and they would further strengthen the case for stable distribution of taxes over time. A rise of productivity and income would, however, strengthen the argument for heavier taxes later.

This transfer burden of taxation is ignored by those who argue that it is impossible for a nation as a whole to shift to any degree, by means of any financial transactions, real burdens between generations. In this connection the effects upon savings, which have been treated briefly above and fully in Part I, are also relevant. If there is more or less current real saving, the capital equipment and social product of the future will be larger or smaller. If it could be shown that an increase in current pay-roll taxation would actually result in an increase in equipment, this would be a valid argument in favor of such a policy, for it would shift part of the future burden upon the present generation. If we assume a world of full employment and plentiful outlets for real investment, increased pay-roll taxation and subsequent disbursement of the surplus to private holders of government bonds might be expected to divert resources from the production of consumption goods to that of producers' goods.

In this discussion the monetary aspects have been neglected. They, however, had rather full treatment in Part I. When account is taken of this aspect, the case for a large excess of receipts over disbursements is seriously weakened. Much depends, of course, upon the reactions of those who are taxed directly and of those who in the process of shifting bear the burden as income recipients or consumers. Do they curtail savings or even live on capital, or do they cut consumption? If their savings are reduced, then in the state of investment outlets in 1939, the case for a reserve is not seriously affected. Much also depends upon the manner of investment of reserves by the managers. In so far as consumption is cut and difficulties are encountered in diverting the taxes collected into investment channels, the reserve plan loses some of its appeal.

Currently, private investment outlets seem to be insufficient to bring the economic system to a level of full employment.[1] Deficit spending may, under favorable conditions, compensate for a deficiency of private investment, and on the multiplier principle may contribute to an even larger rise of income. As long as deficits are financed by borrowing, the result is an increase in the national debt and the tax burden on account of interest. Conversely, a program that reduces the national debt and tax burden must be one that reduces deficits or increases surpluses.

We are faced, therefore, with a dilemma. A reduction of the excess of expenditures over receipts associated with the functioning of the reserve plan will necessarily operate to reduce *current* deficits, which may be unfortunate now. (This generalization does not apply once the defense program is fully launched.) The result, moreover, may well be to reduce the current amount of real investment because of the lowering of the national income, still more being added to the burden of future generations. Thus, Mr. Keynes would probably argue that as long as we are not at full employment a tax upon consumption will decrease consumption and decrease real investment as well. When investment outlets are inadequate, individuals pressed by a sense of insecurity try to increase their savings; and the government makes additional provision for their security. Effects on output and income may well be calamitous.

Consideration of the effects of an accumulation of reserves upon consumption, investment, and the supply of effective money may conceivably suggest that the way out is the adoption of current financing of social security. Analysis of the repercussions upon effective demand has clearly increased the support of the pay-as-you-go program. Yet even granting the deflationary (?) effects of the reserve program, one may hesitate to scrap the reserve plan. We do not have in mind here the difficulties of adhering to an insur-

[1] *Cf.* REDDAWAY, W. B., *The Economics of a Declining Population*, Chap. IV.

ance principle if reserves are not accumulated. Financial considerations are paramount at this point. The issue is discussed briefly here (the fifth point in the outline at the beginning of this section) and more fully in a later chapter.

Can we be sure that (even assuming the goods are available in the future) the pay-as-you-go method will succeed in providing the insured with the dollars required to obtain what are considered adequate drafts on the quantities of goods? It is possible (if not probable) that the present generation (and perhaps the next one) may make it possible for succeeding generations to obtain adequate drafts for the provision of social security. This they may do through the accumulation of large reserves that will ultimately yield (on the estimates of 1935) 1.4 billions annually. These calculations are based on the Act of 1935 and the estimates of reserves based on the original legislation. More recent estimates will be given later. If, in later years, the collection of 2 billion dollars through pay-roll or other taxes for old-age insurance can be effected without serious repercussions on the level of output, and if otherwise the collection of 3.5 billions annually for old-age insurance would curtail output in a serious manner, then the accumulation of a reserve would accomplish the fundamental objective of keeping promises made to the insured. A consideration of the defense program, which promises outlays of 15 billion dollars or more in the fiscal year 1942 and annual operating costs of 5 to 7 billion dollars, leaves us at present with the strong impression of understatement of the case.

Finally, the reserve plan may conceivably be applied in such a manner as to remove the sting of its deflationary effects; or the pay-as-you-go plan may be carried through in such a manner as to reduce the net costs in later years. At least (a reserve plan being assumed) supplementary measures may be invoked which will tend to have inflationary effects of an intensity adequate to offset the deflationary repercussions of the reserve plan. Should these supplementary measures prove practical, the country might be saved an excessive burden of taxation in later years or (on the failure to raise adequate revenues) a breakdown of the security program. Various alternatives might be suggested. The state might, for example, increase the *cash* reserves of the money market by an amount adequate to increase expenditures *pari passu* with the diminution of expenditures associated with the accumulation of social security reserves. Banks and the public would then exchange securities for *government* notes. Notes (reserves) of banks would rise, and public securities in their portfolios would decline.[1] Furthermore, as the public exchanged their new notes for deposits, reserves of banks would rise even more. Losses of earning assets by banks would then be a serious matter for them, just as these losses would be serious under a variant of the 100 per cent plan which proposes an exchange of cash for bonds. Under the proposals now being considered, however, in contrast to the 100 per cent plan, the banks could use their cash to buy other assets, and, in fact, both the banks and the public might be impelled by the worsening of their financial position to bid more actively for assets. Their use of cash reserves will contribute toward an induced demand for investment (and possibly even for consumption goods). We need scarcely add that serious problems arise. In the light of the present excess reserves, is it likely that further increases will help? If they will, how much additional reserves of cash will be required? In what manner will the authorities prevent a dangerous inflation when the additional money is once outstanding and employment rises to a high level? And, finally, the expansion of demand for consumption (or investment) goods which is required must be distinguished from a purely monetary expansion.

These suggestions now (in June, 1941) seem of more academic interest than when they were first written several years ago. The defense program will provide the inflationary force that paper money was required to provide in the foregoing analysis; and the deflationary effects are much less to be feared than they were in the thirties.

9.4. INTEREST ON RESERVES A MYTH?

Related to the issues of the last section is the question of the financial significance of the interest on reserves. There are those who deny that the reserves relieve the taxpayer of the future.

But who pays this interest? The answer, of course, is the Government. And it can only obtain this money through taxation. . . . [2]

---

[1] A rise of public expenditures is not assumed here. The state issues money and reduces taxes *pari passu*.

[2] From STEWART, *op. cit.*, p. 185. M. G. Schneider, *More Security for Old Age*, pp. 55–56, seems to hold a similar view, implying that interest can be earned only if investments are made in nongovernmental enterprises or in productive governmental enterprise. (*Cf. ibid.*, p. 151, however.)

> *To say that benefit payments made from such a government bond reserve are derived from interest instead of tax receipts is meaningless since the whole procedure is merely a bookkeeping device.*[1] (Author's italics.)
>
> *Thus the stupendous "reserve" will in no way relieve the taxpayers of the future from assuming their part of the burden.*[2] (Author's italics.)
>
> But if the money which goes into the reserve is used to finance non-income-producing activities, then the interest on the bonds will have to be paid out of *additional* taxes levied on a national income no larger than it would otherwise be.[3] (Italics mine.)

Attacks of this nature on reserves which, in my opinion, are unjustified, have played a not unimportant part in bringing about the Amendments of 1939. Powerful antagonists have used similar arguments. According to Senator Vandenberg the interest payments are merely a disguised subsidy given by the Federal government.[4] Mr. Flynn, in turn, points (1) to the excess of receipts over expenditures on old-age account, which is used to finance current deficits of the Treasury; and (2) to the necessity of obtaining revenue later for the payment of interest on reserves through taxes, concluding then that the reserve principle is "monstrous, weird, fantastic," etc.[5]

It is not difficult to refute the position taken by these critics of reserves:

1. The excess of expenditures over revenue by the Federal government is a relevant issue *only so far as* the accumulation of reserves and the provision of a new market for government securities stimulate further expenditures. In our opinion, the amount of the deficit so far has been related to this factor in a very small measure if at all; our guess would be that it will not contribute greatly to the rise of debt in the future.

[1] BALLANTINE, A. A., "Social Security Reserves and Treasury Manipulations," *Social Security in the United States*, 1938, pp. 152–153.

[2] NORTON, T. L., *Old Age and the Social Security Act*, p. 48.

[3] DOUGLAS, P. H., "Payroll Taxes and a Coordinated Program for Old Age Protection," *Social Security in the United States*, 1938, p. 144. Even Prof. Douglas seems to fall into error here. His conclusion would follow only on the assumption that the bonds purchased by the old-age account represent debt that otherwise would not have been incurred. He does not, however, make this assumption. (In fact on page 145 he says "I see no evidence that public expenditures have been increased thus far because of them, *viz.*, social security taxes.")

[4] *Hearings*, U. S. Senate Finance Committee, *Old-age Benefit Plan*, Social Security Act (75: 1), p. 17.

[5] FLYNN, JOHN T., "The Menace of the Political Spoilsmen," *Social Security in the United States*, 1938, pp. 234–241.

2. It follows, then, that the reserves and the savings on interest are real, for in so far as securities are held in the reserves, they are not held in private quarters. A given revenue then provides interest on securities in reserves and on those held privately, the latter being reduced by the amount held in the former; and in so far as the old-age account obtains interest on reserves, it requires less from the taxpayer, and yet the government contributes no more.[1]

3. It is possible but highly improbable that the supply of government securities will be inadequate. In that case, the reserves would have to find outlets elsewhere. Then it may be even more clear than under (2) that the earnings on reserves are real, not mythical.

4. Assume further that expenditures rise *pari passu* and in direct response to the inflow of funds into the social security accounts. It does not even follow then that the reserves and the earnings on these reserves are fictitious. It is necessary to take into account the effects of the expenditures. These *additional* expenditures may not be wasteful; they may stimulate output and they may yield interest earning assets. In this connection it should be observed finally that in so far as the social security program accounts for a rise of public spending the argument of deflationary effects used by opponents of the reserve plan loses force.

5. Reference is made once more, however, to a point raised by Dr. Robinson and referred to in another section of this chapter. Though the rise of expenditures may be independent of the accumulation of reserves, it may still be true that reserves may not contribute greatly to the successful outcome of the security program. The point is that tax burdens may become excessive with the result that repudiation of debt in some form or other may result. This is not, however, the point made by the Flynn-Vandenberg school. Their arguments are much less subtle than Dr. Robinson's and they are most confused.[2]

---

[1] *Cf.* WITTE, *op. cit.*, pp. 21–22.

[2] A defense of the reserve fund by the author of the Twentieth Century Fund study, *More Security for Old Age*, also seems confused on this point, *Hearings*, Ways and Means Committee, House of Representatives, *Social Security*, 1939, p. 815.

9.5. Some Considerations in Support of the View that Despite Accumulation of Reserves, the Future Burden May Become Intolerable

In an earlier section a few brief quotations were presented that are typical of the recent attitude toward the relationship of the availability of real resources in the future and the accumulation of reserves.[1] Here the view that clearly represents the consensus of opinion on this subject is developed somewhat more fully.

At the outset it is necessary to point out that whether the securities accumulated in one period might or might not be dumped on the market or sold to banks in another is not the essential problem.[2] What is required is that in the process of accumulation and decumulation the wherewithal to obtain the goods and services required by annuitants should be provided.

Numerous arguments are used in support of what may be held to be the accepted position. One point may be dismissed at once, not because it is unimportant but because it has been adequately covered in an earlier part of this book. Undoubtedly the *relative* deflation associated (1) with the discouragement of consumption and (2), in a *stagnation* economy, with the failure to expand monetary supplies more than would otherwise have been the case will contribute to a decline of income and output.[3] In this sense and in so far as this position is valid, accumulation of reserves does not provide goods for the future and may in truth be responsible for a reduction of available supplies.

---

[1] See also H. L. Lutz, *Social Security Financing and Present Fiscal Policies*, Address No. 10 (New Wilmington, Pa.); D. C. Coyle, *Age Without Fear*, 1937, *passim;* Norton, *op. cit.*, pp. 48, 58–59. Prof. Norton even goes so far as to say that the size of the reserve merely determines the distribution of burden between those who pay old-age taxes and those who pay the taxes that finance interest payments of the Treasury.

[2] *Cf.* Lehmann, F., "The Role of Social Security Legislation," *Proc. Am. Econ. Assoc.*, 1939, p. 220.

[3] *Cf.* Shoup, C., "Taxing for Social Security," *Annals*, March, 1939, p. 174. The argument used by Prof. Shoup is along the lines indicated in the text. He emphasizes the failure to add directly to *private* investment. It should be observed, however, that although this is a vital consideration, the differing effects on output and savings of the various possible tax programs are also relevant. *Cf.* E. M. Burns, "The Financial Aspects of the Social Security Act," *Am. Econ. Rev.*, March, 1936, pp. 12–22. Her conclusions and arguments are somewhat similar to those advanced by Prof. Shoup.

Another argument also has much strength. An accumulation of reserves of public securities, whatever its merits in a period in which the fiscal position of the government improves, raises serious questions when the government debt rises even more rapidly than the social security reserves.[1] It is assumed here that the rise of the debt is conditioned by the general political and economic situation and is not related to the availability of an additional market, *i.e.*, social security reserves, for public securities. In other words, the savings on interest are real, not mythical.[2] It is true nevertheless that the "goods" value of the reserve may prove to be inadequate: the government may be unable to raise the revenues required to pay interest on privately held debt *and* on the publicly held debt; or if it succeeds, the cost may be (1) a serious inflation (in which case social security payments in fact would be partly repudiated) or (2), through the imposition of a severe tax program, significant disturbances and maladjustments in the economy will result which will jeopardize output and the security program later. What we mean is that any significant dependence upon financing through the accumulation of public securities may prove to be unfortunate for the social security program, if the fiscal position of the government grows progressively worse.

It may be well to dwell at greater length upon the danger and relevance of inflation. An excessive rise of prices brought on by private expansion is, in this connection, to be distinguished from one that is induced by the state of the public budget. Furthermore, under the latter conditions, the source of the trouble may be the general budgetary situation, on the one hand, or the heavy responsibilities put upon the Treasury by the demands upon the old-age fund, on the other. In so far as (on the latter assumption) the government prepares the country for later demands through an accumulation of reserves (aside from adverse effects during the process of accumulation), the strain put upon the Treasury will be diminished and, therefore, the danger of inflation will be correspondingly less. It is appropriate also to distinguish the effects during the inflationary process from those of the ensuing period of stabilization.

Analysis applicable to the inflationary process will hold in large part for a period of secular increase in prices. A general increase in the cost of living will bring a lowering of the real value of benefit payments fixed in dollars. Similar effects would follow, however, if workers kept their savings

[1] See the comments by Dr. Robinson, *Hearings*, Ways and Means Committee, House of Representatives, *Social Security*, 1939, pp. 2095–2097, and M. A. Linton, "Making Old Age Security Work," *Social Security in the United States*, 1939, p. 206.
[2] *Cf.* BALLANTINE, *op. cit.*

in the form of bank deposits, life insurance policies or annuities, government bonds, or other fixed interest-bearing assets.

On the other hand, the dollar taxes collected by the government will increase, for dollar values of incomes will rise. *Provided that the other expenses of the government did not correspondingly increase*, it could afford to be generous and increase the amount of benefit payments. This possibility is particularly strong in the case of a long-run increase in prices brought about by *inflationary factors other than the government's own spending*. In this case, the real cost of debt service would be constantly decreasing, wages of government employees would tend to lag behind the increase in prices, profits, and taxes so that the financial position of the government might be quite strong.

In the case of a very rapid inflation, possibly engineered by Treasury activities, in which prices are rising so rapidly that tax collections lag behind the increase in prices of the goods and services that the government buys, the position of the Treasury is anything but easy. This explains in part why it is forced to resort to still larger doses of inflation, accelerating the inflationary process. In such a circumstance it might be very difficult, if not impossible, for the government to maintain the real value of social security benefit payments. Such an inflation could, however, be expected to run its course within a very short time.

What would be the status of the social security program after stabilization had taken place? If a large reserve of government bonds had accumulated, these would now be worthless, and it would appear that the financing of social security would become more difficult because of the inflation. In so far as a serious inflation reduces the supply and productivity of the capital of the country, the problem of keeping faith on promises of annuities becomes acute. Inflation, on the other hand, is a manner of repudiation of debt, and, therefore, the Treasury's position improves. In appraising the net effects, one should, therefore, weigh the effects upon private income, which are likely to be adverse, and the effects upon the Treasury's capacity to obtain the required goods for annuitants, which will improve in so far as savings are made on public debt. That is, the Treasury's *relative* position improves in a period in which the country suffers a setback.[1]

[1] In the course of rather extreme inflation episodes after the First World War, those insured under public insurance programs seem to have been treated reasonably well. The state had adjusted benefits in some rough manner to the changes in prices, and had made good a large part of the losses of reserves. *Cf.* International Labor Office, *The Investment of Funds of Social Insurance Institutions*, 1939, pp. 4, 16, 27.

9.6. MANAGEMENT A BURDEN?

We now turn to a related aspect, *i.e.*, the question of management. This can be discussed briefly, for it is treated rather fully in Part I. A reserve of the proportions anticipated under the Social Security Act raises very difficult, if not insuperable, problems of management.[1] (Under the amendments of 1939, these problems become less formidable.) Unwise management undoubtedly would be unfortunate; and if we can take poor management for granted, the reserve plan stands condemned. Effects on output and income would surely then be serious. Are we justified, however, in assuming unwise use of these funds? May we not just as well assume that the net effects of management are nil and, therefore, the choice of plans is to be made on other grounds, or may we not even anticipate that the social security reserve will provide the government with an additional instrument of great potentialities for the beneficent control of economic fluctuations?[2]

Problems of management may be discussed largely in terms of the question of repercussions on the money market. A related question is, however, the effects of monetary management upon investment. The money market, in the absence of offsetting operations, will suffer losses or gains of monetary supplies as the Old-age Fund (or the unemployment trust funds) collects or disburses funds, the corresponding effects being a rise or a decline in the rate of interest. Investment is, however, affected directly as well as through the effects upon the rate of interest via the money market. In periods of accumulation, purchasing power may well be diverted directly from consumption to investment markets; and in periods of decumulation, the reverse movement may occur. As we have seen, however, the effects are not limited merely to diversions of purchasing power: the accumulation and decumulation of funds may well account for important changes in the total volume of purchasing

---

[1] *Hearings*, Senate Committee on Finance, Senate Concurrent Resolution No. 4 (75: 1), February, 1937, p. 16; WYATT and WANDEL, *op. cit.*, p. 149; MULFORD, H. P., *Incidence and Effects of the Payroll Tax*, p. 48.

[2] A body of experts takes a more optimistic view of the management of insurance funds. Managers are bound to associate themselves with the economic and monetary policies of the state which are directed to the general good; and the economic and social aspects of the investment of insurance funds require consideration. International Labor Office, *The Investment of the Funds of Social Insurance Institutions*, pp. 55–60.

power. These problems are treated fully in Part I (especially Chap. 5) where the alternative methods of investment and management of social security funds are discussed. At this point we give merely some indication of the magnitude of the problems involved, and hasten to add that the size of the reserve and the difficulty of its management should not be invoked as important arguments for or against the reserve plan.

Undoubtedly disturbances will be more severe and management a more perplexing problem when the net movement of funds is inward than when the Fund once attains a relatively stable level. This is on the assumption of stagnation, oversaving, etc. In fact, an inflow may be helpful in periods of marked activity, though in such periods the rise of security prices may be stimulated. The unemployment insurance fund will also grow in the prosperous periods, this growth possibly accentuating the difficulties in these years or possibly adding to the beneficent effects of a growth of the old-age reserve. In periods when both funds are growing and a further rise of saving is not wanted, the problems of management are difficult indeed; but in the course of periods when the Unemployment Fund pays out in excess of current receipts, the task of control may be facilitated. It should be noted, however, that an outflow of unemployment funds is likely to occur in depression periods, and therefore be very welcome, for any *net* influx to the *combined* funds, though relatively modest, raises serious problems at such times.

Let us dwell for a moment on the significance of the new monetary weapon made available by the Social Security Act. In the early years, the government is likely on both old-age and unemployment accounts to pay out much less than is collected. Even under the 1939 amendments, significant accumulations would be made. We may assume, for many years at any rate, that the net receipts will be invested in government securities issued for the purpose by the Treasury. Thus the money will be released as it is collected, though the authorities may conceivably find it expedient to hold the social security funds rather than to release them. (The government, for example, may issue certificates to the Fund and hoard the proceeds.) The possibility of impounding a few billions of cash received in social security payments or of releasing an equivalent amount later should be considered.

It may be well to compare (very briefly at this point) this potential weapon with other monetary weapons. (1) There is the "powerful" weapon of open market operations.[1] Federal reserve banks hold roughly 2.5 billion dollars of securities (late in 1940). Sales of these securities (unaccompanied by rediscounting) would deprive the money market of but 2.5 billions of cash. Sales of this magnitude are most unlikely, however, for the effect on the government bond market would be a serious deterrent. (2) Consider the newly acquired weapon of a stabilization fund and the supplementary process of sterilization of gold through sales of Treasury securities. Similar doubts apply to the accumulation of cash through sales of securities by the Stabilization Fund, which, in one aspect, is largely a mechanism for raising dollars through the sale of public securities. (3) This instrument, changes in reserve requirements, is to be taken more seriously. It can be compared in importance with the one now under consideration. Changes in reserve requirements are, however, likely to be made with great caution in the future. In short, the collection of funds for social security offers the Treasury (and trustees) a weapon of great potential strength for the control of money and investment markets. No available weapon seems as powerful.

9.7. RESERVES AND BURDENS

Fiscal aspects are treated to some extent in Part I and mostly in later chapters of this Part. But at present we are interested in financial problems that are peculiarly relevant to a discussion of the theory of reserves.

1. Numerous critics of the reserve principle have bemoaned the heavy burdens required of the poor under a reserve program.[2] One may reply to these critics (1) that since a fundamental principle of old-age *insurance* is an *association* of benefits and contributions the state rightly imposes pay-roll taxes; (2) that if the burden on the poor becomes excessive supplementary levies may be made on the rich; and (3) that even under a reserve plan the revenue required to build up reserves may come from progressive rather than regressive taxes, *e.g.*, pay-roll taxes.[3] We should like to say finally on this point that if the pay-as-you-go school wishes to overthrow com-

---

[1] *Cf.* HARRIS, S. E., *Twenty Years of Federal Reserve Policy*, vol. I.

[2] "How Shall the Social Security Act Be Amended?" *Social Security*, November, 1938, p. 7.

[3] *Cf.* the discussion in the introductory chapter.

pletely the insurance principle and, therefore, discard the pay-roll taxes, then it ought also to support the pay-as-you-go principle to the limit. It would then recommend as generous benefits *now* as in 1980. Though the costs of benefits on this scale would be relatively modest in the next 10 to 20 years as compared with their costs in 1980 when the proportion of annuitants will be much larger than now, most of them do not advocate such large "unearned" benefits. Clearly even the amendments of 1939 do not propose benefits on such a generous level.

2. We come to a related argument, *viz.*, that the poor are asked to pay off the public debt under the reserve plan. This position, which is taken again and again in the literature, is not valid.[1] In fact, the debt is *not* paid off: in so far as the reserve accumulates Treasury issues, the government's creditor now becomes the social security account *instead* of private holders of securities. Furthermore, the insured, who is taxed under the old-age security program (unlike the usual case where the debt is extinguished), obtains a *quid pro quo:* he exchanges cash (and in fact the cash is contributed in part by the entrepreneur) for a stake in the public securities accumulated in the reserves.

3. Another issue that has been raised frequently is that under the reserve plan the young pay not only for their own annuities but also for those of the present old.[2] There may be some truth in the contention that the heavier taxes are now, *relatively* to later (though still below the level of later years), the more the young pay. Several reservations are required, however. In so far as the current financing program involves relatively heavy taxation later, the present young (the future old) will also pay more later, and the heavy taxation is in part associated with a failure to levy adequate taxes in the early years and, therefore, a failure to tax the *present* young adequately. This failure makes necessary much heavier assessments later, for interest on accumulated assets is thereby lost. Furthermore, the burden on the present young follows not so much from the accumulation or nonaccumulation of reserves but rather from the benefit

[1] Brown, J. D., "The Old Age Reserve Account," *Quart. Jour. Econ.*, August, 1937, p. 718; Report of the Committee on Social Security Legislation and Administration, *Proceedings of Annual Conference on Taxation of National Tax Association*, 1937, pp. 57–98; Linton, M. A., "Some Aspects of the Reserve Program," *Appraising the Social Security Program, Annals*, March, 1939, p. 187.

[2] How Shall the Social Security Act Be Amended? *Social Security*, November, 1938, p. 7.

schedule which provides large subsidies to those (the present old) who are insured for a relatively brief period. In one respect, however, the argument may have validity. It may be assumed (though this point has not been made so far as I know) that the annuitants who are now young will pay a smaller proportion of the total taxes if a larger part of the tax burden is shifted to later periods than is contemplated under the reserve plan. In that case, a greater part of the taxes will be paid by groups, *e.g.*, the wealthy, other than annuitants. It still remains true, however, that the total taxes will be greater under a pay-as-you-go plan.

4. Opponents of the plan to accumulate reserves have used the following argument: The government may be as justifiably asked to provide assets against *other* obligations of the future as to be asked to provide reserves against future demands for old-age benefits.[1] We do not agree with this position for several reasons. Obviously, provision of reserves is not possible for all future obligations. Deflationary effects will then clearly become intolerable. Only when there are special reasons (*e.g.*, under contributory plans) can provision for the future through accumulation of assets be sanctioned; and even in these instances significant offsets require consideration. Both because of the rapid rise of costs and the assumed need of associating benefits with contributions, there are special reasons for providing reserves for old-age insurance. Equally pregnant reasons are not to be found for the accumulation for other purposes.

9.8. DO RESERVES COMMIT FUTURE GENERATIONS?

. . . a nation-wide pension plan . . . can, over the years, be successfully operated only upon the principle that each generation will draw from its current production of goods and services for the care of the then aged members of society, only that proportion of such goods and services which under the circumstances then existing it will consider right and proper for the purpose. Any thought that we can dictate years in advance what that proportion shall be is likely to lead us far afield.[2]

First, the question raised by this quotation is to what extent are future generations committed by the accumulation of reserves?

[1] *Cf.* BROWN, *op. cit.*, p. 717.
[2] Quoted by permission from M. A. Linton, *The Problem of Reserves and a Possible Solution*, Provident Mutual Life Insurance Company, publishers, p. 3.

Under the Act of 1935, they are asked (on the assumption of an ultimate reserve of 47 billion dollars) to pay 1.4 billions (interest) to the Old-age Fund, an amount that we may assume would have been paid to other investors if reserves had not been accumulated. These future generations are at liberty to influence the price level if they do not wish to be bound by the earlier decisions of Congress. Changes in prices will of course reduce or increase the real value of *total* benefits and of that part associated with the returns on the reserves. It is not probable, however, that the government in later generations would manipulate prices for the purpose of influencing the real value of benefit payments. Such measures would be akin to burning the house down in order to roast the pig. A more expeditious method would be a downward revision of benefit provisions, though such action may well raise the cry of breach of faith. Another way out is suggested by the amendments of 1939: taxes may be reduced and benefit schedules changed in a manner to reduce the size of the ultimate reserves. In other words, decisions taken in 1935 do not commit future generations.

Whatever commitment is made today for the future is not very precise in terms of goods. Experts today make the decisions for the future in the light of what they know today. In 1935 an attempt was made to commit future generations to the payment of 3.5 billions of old-age benefits, of which two-fifths were to be provided by interest on reserves. (The assumption was that uncompensated errors in the variables upon which the tables of contributions and benefits were based would not be large.) Changes may be made, it need scarcely be said, as the passage of time proves actuaries and others to be wrong. One may be consoled, moreover, by the thought that had similar legislation been proposed in 1850, the history of the next 80 years would probably not have done serious damage to the estimates of 1850.[1] Price history in this period has not been so hectic as to have upset the security program, though the large improvement in real income would probably not have been anticipated. This unexpected rise could have been compensated for by a rise of benefits (and taxes) in later years. In fact, the influx of new entrants would have provided the financial means for a rise of benefits commensurate with the current standard of living.

It is well to add, however, that though the provision of a reserve is not a precise commitment in terms of goods and real income, the

---

[1] See the note at the end of this chapter on a hypothetical history of a social security plan instituted in 1850. *Cf.* International Labor Office, *The Investment of the Funds of Social Insurance Institutions*, p. 4.

promise of benefits is a commitment of a sort. Marked rises of the price level, which are, related to monetary mismanagement, may under some conditions be interpreted as a breach of faith, and similarly if promised payments in dollars are not made. Provision of reserves, unless the accumulation cuts output greatly, makes repudiation less likely, however.

9.9. ANALOGY WITH PRIVATE INSURANCE

Opponents of the reserve plan (and proponents of the pay-as-you-go plan) frequently argue that the reserve principle has wrongly been taken from private insurance procedure and applied to compulsory pension schemes.[1] A private insurance company, it is held, is required to build up a reserve for each policyholder; for, unlike the government, it is unable to compel people to insure for old age or to remain insured, and, furthermore, it is not armed with the power to tax.[2] It, therefore, follows that an excess of claims over current receipts would prove to be most embarrassing if the insurance company were not protected by its reserves. A government plan of a compulsory type, it is held, does not, however, require the protection of reserves: the power to tax and to force insurance upon the public is adequate.

This argument is subject to numerous reservations. 1. Observe that reserves are also held by insurance companies for the purpose of increasing earnings and, therefore, reducing premiums. They serve a similar function under public insurance of a compulsory type. It is, however, true that insurance companies would hold reserves even if earnings were not to be made on their investments. On the other hand, the fact that the rate of interest is above zero contributes toward the accumulation of larger reserves: reserves earn interest and, since therefore, insurance becomes cheaper, the demand for insurance rises and larger reserves accumulate.

[1] National Tax Association, *Report of Committee on Social Security Legislation and Administration,* 1937, pp. 75–76. *Hearings,* Senate Committee on Finance, February, 1937, p. 16; WYATT and WANDEL, *op. cit.,* pp. 149–150; LINTON, *op, cit.,* p. 3.

[2] It may be interesting to note that private pension plans have frequently not accumulated adequate reserves. Their failure to provide adequate reserves may have contributed toward the adoption of the reserve principle in the government plan. *Social Security in America,* pp. 174–177.

2. The use of reserves makes it possible to stabilize taxes under compulsory insurance. This point is of course related to the first. It will be recalled that the pay-as-you-go plan (benefit schedule of 1935) would require pay-roll taxes ranging from a small fraction of 1 per cent to a maximum in excess of 10 per cent, and (according to more recent estimates) possibly up to 15 per cent. This extreme degree of variation is associated, it should be noted, with the nonexistence of reserves and (also) with an unwillingness to tap other sources of revenues. Taxes of 10 per cent or more of pay-rolls are required in later years, when the plan does not provide for an accumulation of reserves or (and) recourse to general tax revenues; and the low rate of less than 1 per cent in the early years is explained by the small disbursements and the nonassessment for reserve purposes.

3. A final point is that too much reliance is placed by the opponents of the reserve plan on the compulsory powers of the government. It is necessary to finance old-age insurance during a period when the number of old and annuitants rises at an extraordinary rate. If contributions by insured (both old and new entrants) are not adequate to cover disbursements, which rise rapidly in the next two generations, the only alternatives are larger rises of the contribution rate in the future, recourse to other sources of revenues, reduction of benefits, or reliance on reserves. And one should speculate on the capacity of the government to raise the 4 or 5 billion dollars (largely through pay-roll taxes?) in 1980, which, according to present estimates will be required under a pay-as-you-go plan for old-age insurance.[1] At that time the pension load will become relatively stable. (Taxes for unemployment insurance are additional.) Once the load becomes stable, it may be added, the case for accumulation of reserves on the grounds of a rise in the proportion of old becomes weak. In fact, a *decline* in the proportion of annuitants might be a reason for consuming reserves.

The case for reserves is then to be put largely in terms of the rising burden of social security in the next few generations.[2] Deficits incurred later may be covered by taxes now or larger taxes later.

---

[1] One of the actuaries responsible for the plan embodied in the 1935 legislation envisages as easily possible a rise of benefit payments to 5 billions in 1980, a sum equal to 15 per cent of pay-rolls. *Soc. Sec. Bull.*, July, 1938, p. 15.

[2] For a somewhat similar view, see P. H. Douglas, *Social Security in the United States*, 2d ed., pp. 386–388. Prof. Pigou expresses himself cautiously: he says smaller reserves are required under a public and compulsory program. A. C. Pigou, *Industrial Fluctuations*, pp. 348–350.

It is because the burden of future taxes promises to be heavy that the accumulation of reserves (through larger present taxes) is suggested as a means of minimizing the burden. Under the defense program an added reason for large pay-roll taxes is that they will check the rise of consumption.

9.10. Conclusion

This chapter which deals with the theory of reserves constitutes an attempt to tie up the issues discussed in Part I with those of Part II. Section 9.1 is an attempt to consider the accounting as distinguished from the real issues. What is the correct manner of showing the state of the insurance account? In what sense are deficits incurred? These and similar questions are discussed in this section.

In the second section the issue is the relation of reserves to the provision of capital and income in the future. The manner of finance and the distribution of taxes over time clearly influence the volume of output. It follows that under a reserve plan, the output of the future may well be greater than under a pay-as-you-go plan. When monetary considerations are introduced, the final outcome is not so clear, however. It may, nevertheless, be possible to reconcile the financial and welfare advantages of a reserve plan with the monetary advantages of the pay-as-you-go plan if supplementary monetary measures are taken to offset any deflationary effects of an accumulation of reserves.

We are not convinced by the oft repeated contention that the saving on interest is not real (Sec. 9.3). Defenders of this position are on vulnerable ground unless they assume, what they generally do not explicitly state, that expenditures rise *pari passu* with (and on account of) the accumulation of reserves. They fail, moreover, to take into account any beneficial effects or offsets to any rise of expenditures.

In Sec. 9.4, more plausible arguments advanced against the accumulation of reserves are considered briefly. Monetary effects may be unfortunate: the burden of government debt may be so great in the future that direct repudiation or indirect repudiation through inflation may be inescapable. This line of thought offers an opportunity to discuss the possibilities and significance of inflation for the old-age program. Another point made by antagonists is left for consideration in Sec. 9.5. One may as reasonably argue that the reserves provide a weapon that may prove very useful for the management of money and investment markets as to assume that the effects of management are bound to be adverse.

Opponents of reserve financing frequently use the following arguments. Under a reserve program the poor are asked to pay off the debt, the poor are taxed excessively, the young pay too much, and provision of reserves is as justifiable for other expenditures of the future as for disbursements on account of old-age benefits. Section 9.6 is an attempt to consider the validity of these points. In Sec. 9.7 another issue raised by the critics of reserve financing is dealt with. It is true that to some extent the provision of reserves commits future generations to our present program, and they may rightly resent these commitments made for them. Benefit schedules, however, commit them more than the manner of finance. These schedules can, moreover, be modified. In so far as commitments are made, the reserves probably offer additional assurance that they will be kept.

Finally, the analogy with private insurance companies requires consideration. Arguments for reserves under compulsory social insurance are not so strong as under private insurance, as the critics contend. It does not follow, however, that the reserves held by insurance companies are independent of the earnings to be made on reserves, nor that, despite the compulsory aspects of social insurance, there are not important reasons for the provision of reserves.

NOTE: HYPOTHETICAL HISTORY OF A SOCIAL SECURITY PLAN
INSTITUTED IN 1850[1]

1. *Growth of Old-age Fund.* If a compulsory old-age benefit plan had been instituted in 1850, embodying features similar to those in the 1935 act, the broad outlines of its development until 1930 would perhaps have been as follows.

The reserve fund starting from zero in 1850 would have increased steadily, probably at an accelerated rate almost up to the present time. The rate of growth may be explained by (1) the natural increase in population, (2) large immigration from abroad, (3) a steady influx of workers from the agricultural (noncovered) field into the covered groups, (4) an increase of money wage rates through most of the period, (5), and related to (3), a rise of the percentage of population gainfully occupied. (An unexpected rise of life expectancy would tend to reduce the rate of growth.)

[1] This note is largely the work of Mrs. Marian Crawford Samuelson.

Each of these causes would tend to result in increases in payments into the Fund with a delayed increase in benefit payments, the reserve account therefore tending to grow. Moreover, since these causes would have been effective through most of the period, the benefit payments would not at any point have attained the current volume of receipts.

2. *Size of Reserves and Public Debt.* According to the Act of 1935, the reserve fund not currently required is to be invested in securities of the Federal government and to bear a specified rate of interest, *viz.*, 3 per cent. Under the Amendments of 1939, the rate becomes the average rate on government securities. If provisions similar to those in the 1935 act had been included in the Social Security Act of 1850, the following difficulties would have been encountered:

The magnitude of the fund would have been *far* greater than the total outstanding debt of the Federal government throughout most of the period. Only in the war and early postwar period (1918 *et seq.*) would the debt have been of comparable size to the Fund. Making the roughest sort of an estimate in order to arrive at hypothetical figures for purposes of comparison, let us suppose that the fund would have grown approximately as follows:

Year	Fund, billions of dollars	Actual Federal debt, billions of dollars
1850	0	
1865	3–4	2.7
1890	10	0.9
1917	22	2.0
1930	35	15.0

These figures are not to be taken very seriously, for they are formed from rough guesses and are premised on various assumptions concerning the fluctuations in the rate of interest. Furthermore, the assumption is made that financial policies of the Federal government would not have been affected if there had been a Social Security fund throughout this period. Nevertheless, the rough figures bring attention to the problem of the investment of the fund. Various possibilities suggest themselves, *e.g.*, investment in state securities or commercial investments. Our present knowledge of the administration of the public domain in the nineteenth century and the difficulties of foreseeing which speculative ventures would turn out well, for example, suggest the complexity of the problems of administration of these funds.

3. *Problem of Solvency of Reserve Fund.* If a social security act had been passed in 1850, there is no particular reason to believe that the present scale of benefits and premiums would have been adopted. It may be of interest, however, to consider the effects on a hypothetical fund of the enactment in 1850 of rates of 1935. In the first place, it is not clear whether

the length of working life has increased or decreased. Against lower life expectancies in earlier generations, we must balance considerably earlier entrance into industry. Life earnings would certainly have been lower than at present, for wages were relatively low. Should the progressive scale of 1935 have been introduced in 1850, benefits would therefore probably have been a higher proportion of premiums than under the present scheme and migration from country to city and similar factors would have contributed toward a low total of covered life earnings. There might, therefore, have resulted technical insolvency of the account, although in this period of *growth* there would undoubtedly have been sufficient cash reserves to meet all liabilities. Against these considerations, however, we may put the steady rise of wages referred to in the next paragraph.

4. *Problem of Price Level and Wage Changes.* Changes in wage rates through time apparently affect the solvency of the old-age reserve account only because of the fact that benefit payments vary regressively with total life earnings. A reduction in the level of wages will increase outpayments relative to inpayments. If the sliding scale is excluded, both premiums and benefits will not be affected by changes in the level of wages, for they are both percentages of wages. On the other hand, the amount of money in the old-age fund will be increased by rising wages and decreased by falling wages, these changes in assets being compensated by concomitant changes in liabilities. A rise in money wages such as has occurred since 1850 might well have resulted in the payment of inadequate benefits (relative to the new standard of living) unless the scale of benefits adopted in 1850 had been periodically revised or unless (which is unlikely) large improvements in wages had been anticipated. Fiscal and monetary considerations (as is argued in the preceding paragraph) point toward an unduly high ratio of benefits to total wages. Technical insolvency would have followed then if benefits relative to payments had been fixed on a sliding scale as generous as that stipulated in the 1935 act. This is perhaps not a reasonable assumption. The opposite danger is that benefits would have been inadequate on the assumption that schedules were not adjusted to a rising standard of living.

We conclude that in the face of a rising standard of living, benefits under a scale likely to have been adopted in 1850, would have been inadequate; but any marked upward revisions, in the light of a vastly improved *cash* position, might have made the Fund technically insolvent. A tendency of receipts to exceed disbursements might have encouraged the application of a sliding scale that ultimately would have threatened the solvency of the Fund.

In retrospect do there not emerge historical changes, unforeseeable *ex ante*, which might have upset the calculations of the authorities? If a reserve plan had been adopted, we should think that the administration of the scheme would have been almost foolproof except for the points enumerated above, *i.e., a.* The investment of the fund.

b. The problem of the adjustment of taxes and benefits to changes in wage rates, a problem complicated by the introduction of sliding rates.

c. Changes in life expectancy. These would be slow and continuous and would seem to require minor modification in rates from time to time.[1]

[1] Data obtained from obvious sources, which are not given in order to save space.

Chapter 10

COSTS OF OLD-AGE INSURANCE

The next three chapters are devoted to financial problems. In this chapter, the issue is largely the cost of old-age insurance and to some extent the cost of other security programs. Guesses into the far future are not very helpful; but a definite program has been sold to the public, and this involves financial commitments for the future. It is not, moreover, easy to envisage the sources from which the necessary money is to come. This problem is, however, reserved for Chap. 11. In Chap. 12, the effect on public debt of the social security program receives more attention than it has received so far.

10.1. Financial Problems of the Future

The Federal government has embarked upon a social security program that will involve increasing future outlays to benefit recipients. Because of increased births during the early part of this century, because of increased life expectancy, and because sufficient time will have elapsed since the installation of the program for most workers to have qualified for an annuity, the outlay in general will tend to increase and by 1980 will be much higher than the costs in the early years, and in absolute figures will be of considerable magnitude. Since the working population in 1980 will not have increased by nearly so much as the old-age group, costs will be heavier not only in an absolute sense, but also relative to pay-rolls.[1] This problem is treated fully later in this chapter. Finally it is well to note that for reasons given above and for other reasons the increase of the old *insured* will be greater than that of the old.

According to original estimates, the cost of the program in 1980 would have equaled about 9 or 10 per cent of pay-rolls and could have been met by a 6 per cent pay-roll tax plus the interest earned

[1] Dulles, E. L., *Remarks before the Advisory Council*, 1937, p. 5.

[228]

(roughly 1.5 billion dollars) on a reserve of approximately 50 billion dollars. Total costs were then put roughly at 3.5 billions or more. The original estimates were drawn up on the basis of optimistic (for the Treasury!) assumptions with respect to life expectancy, on the basis of benefits related regressively to total lifetime covered earnings as provided for in the original act, and under the assumption of limited movements between covered and excluded occupations. Early developments under the act revealed that the third of the preceding assumptions was grossly in error. Actuaries make other errors also.[1] Though only one-half of the gainfully employed may be in covered employment *in any one week*, a very large part of workers at some time of their life are covered, and presumably for long enough periods to qualify for minimum pensions. This fact taken in conjunction with the extremely generous benefits paid to workers with low total covered earnings means that the original estimates of cost, particularly those of the far future, were in serious error. Without any change in the Act it appeared likely that costs in 1980 instead of being 9 or 10 per cent of pay-rolls would actually have reached 12 to 14 per cent or more (*i.e.*, nearer to 5 than to 3½ billions).[2] Under the Amendments of 1939, however, the subsidy to workers covered for a brief period becomes less costly. This generalization does not, however, apply to the early years.

From 1935 to 1939, it became clear that (1) Congress and the public were not in favor of excessive pay-roll taxes in the early years to build up the reserve fund, (2) there was strong sentiment for increases in benefit payments in the immediate future, and (3) the general budget was out of balance and likely to continue to be so for many years. There appeared to be every likelihood that in 1980 there would *not* exist a smaller public debt than in 1936, so that in addition to the social security costs the government would still have to meet interest charges on outstanding debt. What a contrast to the picture painted by Secretary Morgenthau when the Act was first passed![3]

---

[1] *Cf.* Chap. 8.

[2] *Cf.* DULLES, E. L., "Social Security Program," *Proc. Am. Econ. Assoc.*, 1938, p. 136; GRAY, H. A., "Effects of Present Taxation on an Extended Social Security Program," *Social Security in the United States*, 1938, p. 156; BURNS, E. M., "The Financial Aspects of the Social Security Act," *Am. Econ. Rev.*, March, 1936, p. 15; and ROBINSON, G. B., "The Old-age Reserve," *Annalist*, Feb. 8, 1939, pp. 228–229, 254. Estimates of eventual costs of 5 or 6 billions and as high as 18 to 20 per cent of pay-rolls were not uncommon in reliable quarters.

[3] *Cf.* WITTE, E. E., "Old Age Security in the Social Security Act," *Jour. Pol.*

The Act has now been amended. There has been a liberalization of benefits in the early years by the use of formulas involving *average earnings since* 1936, and a change in the form of benefits and the introduction of new benefits (survivor benefits, joint annuities, dependent allowances, etc.). The reader is referred to Sec. 8.5 for a fuller discussion of the changes. Despite the generosity of the Act in early years, the combined effect of these changes is to lower the ultimate (*i.e.*, level premium) costs, if not as compared with the original estimates, at least in respect to corrected estimates of costs under the old Act.

The scheduled increase in pay-roll taxes has not taken place, and there is no guarantee that future ones will not be postponed. This postponement, together with the ever present possibility of a further liberalization of benefits, increases the likelihood of financial strain on the Treasury in later years.

Alternative estimates can be made of the position of the Treasury in 1980 with total benefit payments running from 4 to 6 billions and with a national debt of anywhere from zero to 100 billion dollars. Thus, the combined expense of interest payments to private bondholders and social security old-age benefits may vary from 4 to 9 billion dollars, and even these need not be outside limits. One might also add to these expenditures the outlay on old-age assistance, unemployment compensation, and the increased cost of other social expenditures and defense expenditures, which may well (on the assumption of unchanged prices) add from 5 to 10 billions more to the taxpayers' burden. This compares with a cost on account of public debt and disbursements under the social security program of 1935 which at the present time (fiscal year 1941) comes to about 2 billion dollars. Indeed, before 1940 the total expenditure of the Federal government had never exceeded 10 billion dollars in peacetime. Where can extra revenues be found to meet this growing burden? It is conceivable of course that real income will rise *pari passu* with the increase of assessments on taxpayers, in which case the burden need not become intolerable. Many economists would, however, not be nearly so optimistic. If the budget is to be balanced and additional outlays of the magnitude assumed above are to be met, there must be a rise of revenues from the present level of 6 billion

---

Econ., February, 1937, pp. 29–30, and "In Defence of the Federal Old Age Benefit Plan," *Am. Labor Legislation Rev.*, March, 1937, pp. 28–29; WYATT, B. E., and W. H. WANDEL, *The Social Security Act in Operation*, p. 163.

dollars to 15 billion dollars in the future. A range of expenditures from 12 to 20 billion dollars (prices unchanged) does not seem unreasonable, if allowance is made, *inter alia*, for expenditures for upkeep of the defense plant of 5 to 7 billion dollars.

10.2. Need of Reserves for Revenue

Many contend that a wise distribution of the tax burden can be achieved only through the accumulation of a reserve. One writer even goes so far as to say that "a governmental reserve is designed, not to assure the future solvency of a government that can always resort to the taxing power, but to distribute a given burden fairly and wisely between the taxpayers of different periods of time."[1] One of the major aims of the provisions for old-age benefits, according to the Social Security Board, is "the budgeting of the cost according to an orderly plan which will effect a wise distribution between present and future payments. . . . "[2]

That the cost would be excessive if financed exclusively by payroll taxes (and not in part through earnings on reserves) is most likely. Provision of a reserve accumulated out of pay-roll taxes and used to take securities off the market would reduce the *total* tax burden in later years. (Once more the reader is reminded that the issues discussed in Part I are relevant; but attention is focused here exclusively on financial considerations, the effects of accumulation on income and savings being left out of account.) One authority writes as follows:

The decision [to levy payroll taxes] rendered impracticable "pay-as-you-go" financing of benefits on the scale contemplated by the Act. For while it would be very easy to levy payroll taxes which for a generation would be just adequate to pay currently the benefits fixed by Title II, the percentage of payrolls required would ultimately rise to a figure considered to be out of the question. In other words, to ask the covered working population of 1980 to pay taxes which would equal the cost of supporting

[1] "The Old Age Reserve Account—A Problem in Government Finance," *Quart. Jour. Econ.*, May, 1937, p. 454. "The major purpose of the reserve plan of financing is to distribute the cost of old-age benefit payments in a reasonably equitable manner." *Annual Report on the State of the Finances*, 1937, p. 50.

[2] Social Security Board, *Ann. Rept.*, 1936, p. 14.

the seven-odd million pensioners of 1980 on even the scale contemplated by Title II would be to ask at least the politically impossible.[1]

It is possible to go more fully into the problem of the ultimate burden as a pay-as-you-go plan. Actuaries acting in an advisory capacity had put disbursements by 1980 at 3.5 billions, and more recently one of the semiofficial actuaries has revised the estimate of maximum outlay, contending that the total may well attain 5.2 billions.[2] As 3.5 billions was estimated at 9 to 10 per cent of pay-rolls covered, 5.2 billions would equal roughly 15 per cent of pay-rolls. In other words, the cost in 1980 would equal 15 per cent of pay-rolls and that on the improbable assumption of no upward revisions of benefits. Amendments of 1939, let us observe, increase benefits in the early years but do not involve a rise in the total or ultimate costs over estimates of 1939 under the original schedules. In addition to the old-age taxes, pay-roll taxes of 3 per cent or more for unemployment insurance are to be levied. It is not easy to envisage the source of alternative revenues. That problem is dealt with in a later chapter.

Let us assume that the maximum levy on pay-rolls remains 6 per cent as provided in present legislation (plus 3 per cent or more for unemployment insurance). It would follow, therefore (on the not unreasonable assumption of costs of 5 billions annually for old-age insurance alone by 1980) that additional revenues from other tax sources of approximately 3 billions would be required. Where are this revenue and the additional revenue required for other purposes to come from? Moreover, in so far as coverage is extended and three-fifths[3] of this additional burden are transferred to the general taxpayer, the strain on the taxpayer increases. If coverage is increased through inclusion of groups of noncovered workers and through an unexpected rise of the working population, and if the general taxpayer assumes three-fifths of the total burden (as is assumed above—see last footnote, however), the total charge on general revenues other than pay-rolls may conceivably attain 4 to 6 billions. Savings on old-age assistance would of course be an offset.

[1] Quoted by permission from "The Old Age Reserve Account," *Quart. Jour. Econ.*, May, 1937, p. 447.

[2] *Soc. Sec. Bull.*, July, 1938, p. 15.

[3] Total costs equals 15 per cent of pay-rolls. Pay-roll taxes equal 6 per cent or two-fifths of total. This is subject to one significant reservation. As coverage increased under the 1935 act, costs would have fallen below 15 per cent, and therefore a subsidy of less than 9 per cent would have been required.

These estimates are based on the assumption of a large rise of coverage. Much depends also on future rises of wages. It should be observed that the effects of a rise of coverage, will be, for many years a much larger rise in receipts than in disbursements.

It may well be that recent estimates of costs of 5 billions, or 15 per cent of pay-rolls, are excessive. Actuaries of late have been less pessimistic than they were in 1936–1937 when the errors in original estimates began to stand out. They are even inclined, taking into account changes under the new legislation, to estimate eventual costs below those under the 1935 legislation though not less (in fact much higher) than the costs as originally *estimated* under the benefit schedules of 1935. The cost upon the general taxpayer may not be quite so serious as is here implied if allowance is made for any rise of pay-roll taxes above 6 per cent, savings on old-age assistance, and earnings on the reserve, which, though it will not attain the amount contemplated originally, may conceivably rise to 10 to 15 billion dollars. It is even possible, though not probable, that the general taxpayer, as is frequently suggested currently, will be asked to pay no more than one-third of the total costs.

I conclude nevertheless that an estimate of eventual costs of 5 billions for old-age insurance is not unreasonable. If the ultimate cost proves to be less than 5 billions, this saving (?) will very likely be offset by probable rises of costs under various programs for old-age assistance (despite savings associated with the extension of coverage under old-age insurance), *e.g.*, the present Federal program, or Townsend programs. Additional benefits under various disability programs are also likely to be incorporated in the old-age insurance program. One should, furthermore, allow not only for the extension of coverage but also for the fact that the new coverage will put a heavy drain on reserves. Noncovered workers are largely in low-paid occupations, their contributions under present benefit schedules being low in relation to benefits. Since average lifetime earnings in the important noncovered occupations (farming and domestic service) are low, a rise of x coverage will raise benefits by xa (a = average benefits); but receipts will rise by $xa - xn$ (n being any positive number).[1]

---

[1] An important offset is the saving from a reduction of movements between covered and noncovered workers.

10.3. Estimates of Future Costs

The reader not interested in statistical and technical details may prefer to read this section hastily or to skip it.

It is possible to construct an index of the estimated percentage of pay-rolls required to meet the estimated current disbursements of old-age benefit funds for the period 1860 to 2000. The advantage of this index is that it gives an indication of the marked rise of costs with the passage of time.[1]

Since this percentage is a ratio, it is necessary to compute the two series of benefits and future pay-rolls. The further we go into the future, the more hazardous it is to venture an estimate of pay-rolls. This is also true of benefits, for these depend largely upon past earnings of properly qualified persons over the age of 65.

The ratio between these two series may be easier to estimate than the separate series themselves; for any long-run factor affecting one will tend to affect the other in more or less the same direction. Under the following assumptions an estimate of relatives of this percentage can be computed for future years: (1) that old-age benefits per person in the group over 65 remain the same, and earnings per person in the productive-age groups remain the same, or (2) that these two quantities move in the same proportion. Then the numerical ratio of the population in the group aged 65 or over[2] to the population in the productive-age groups related to a base year will give an index of the required percentage. Let

B_t = benefits at time t, and B_0 at time o.

P_t = pay-rolls at time t, and P_0 at time o.

a = average benefits per qualified person.

b = average earnings per productive worker.

Q_t = number of persons at time t in old-age group, and Q_0 at time o.

E_t = number of persons at time t in productive-age groups, and E_0 at time o.

Then

$$\overset{(1)}{\left(\frac{B_t/P_t}{B_0/P_0}\right)100} = \overset{(2)}{\left(\frac{aQ_t/bE_t}{aQ_0/bE_0}\right)100} = \overset{(3)}{\left(\frac{Q_t/E_t}{Q_0/E_0}\right)100}$$

that is to say,

(1) $\dfrac{\text{Benefits at time } t}{\text{Pay-rolls at time } t}$ divided by ratio of same variables at time o =

(2) $\dfrac{\text{Average benefits per qualified person times number at time } t \text{ in old-age group}}{\text{Average earnings per productive worker times number at time } t \text{ in productive-age group}}$

[1] The index and formulas are the work of Mrs. Marion Crawford Samuelson.

[2] The assumption is that all in old-age group receive benefits.

[234]

divided by ratio of same variables at time o =

(3) $\dfrac{\text{Number of persons at time } t \text{ in old-age group}}{\text{Number of persons at time } t \text{ in productive-age group}}$ divided by ratio of same variables at time o.

Fortunately we have available fairly reliable estimates of the various series (at least maximum and minimum estimates) required for this calculation. I have gathered together population estimates of this kind prepared by Thompson and Whelpton, Louis Dublin, Carr-Saunders (giving illustrative examples of a similar calculation for England) and by the Actuarial Staff of the Committee on Economic Security.[1]

An advantage of such a calculation is the fact that we can form a rough estimate of its bias under the following conceivable circumstances: (1) that in the future there will be a long-time trend of rising money wages and (2) a future long-time trend of falling money wages. In the latter case our estimated burden will be too low, for benefits (depending upon the previously higher money wages) will be inflated relative to the shrinking current wage bill.[2] In the case of condition (1) the bias will be in the opposite direction.

If the considerations discussed in the previous paragraph are left aside, it is possible to state in a general way what the effects of current tendencies of population will be. These tendencies are (1), first and most important, a decline in birth rates per woman of childbearing age such that the population is in effect not reproducing itself. This fact is hidden by the maintenance of fairly high crude birth rates and an actual rate of population increase. This, however, is easily accounted for by the extraordinarily large number of women in the childbearing ages due to a higher birth rate a generation ago. This is temporary and is not likely to endure as can be seen from those Western European countries which are farther along in this sequence of events.[3] (2) The second tendency, of less importance for the general population problem, but still of some interest to us, is the likelihood of some further improvement in the life expectancy of persons beyond middle age.

As a result primarily of the first factor we can expect in the future a smaller number of births than at present, a smaller number of persons in the

---

[1] *Social Security in America*, p. 141; MARSHALL, T. H., A. M. CARR-SAUNDERS, et al., *The Population Problem*, pp. 73–75; DUBLIN, L. J., and A. J. LOTKA, *Length of Life*, p. 265; THOMPSON, W. S., and P. K. WHELPTON, *Population Trends in the United States*, p. 109.

[2] In other words, the ratio of annuitants to productive workers as a measure of the ratio of pensions to pay-rolls for year t relative to the same ratio for year o will require correction. The ratio of benefits to pay-rolls, based on the relatively high wage rates of the past, will be larger when based on the lower wages of the present than is indicated by our formula, which is strictly accurate on the assumption of unchanged wages and benefits or changes of similar proportions of both.

[3] See REDDAWAY, W. B., *The Economics of a Declining Population*, Chaps. I–II.

TABLE I.—VARIABLES RELEVANT TO PROBLEM OF COST OF OLD-AGE INSURANCE

Year	Proportion of population 65 and over to population 20–64, related to base year 1930	Ibid—but based on alternative estimates of population	Ratio of benefits to pay-rolls		Estimated population aged 20–64 (millions)	Covered population aged 20–64 (millions)	Covered population—wage bill (billions of dollars)	Covered population over 65 (millions)	Benefit payments (billions of dollars)
(1)	(2)	(3)	(4)	(5)	(6)	(7)	(8)	(9)	(10)
1860	58	61	0.031	0.033					
1890	81	81	0.043	0.043					
1930	100	100	0.054	0.054	68.5	25.8	24.9	2.5	1.3
1950	152	138	0.082	0.074	86.6	32.6	31.5	4.4	2.3
1980	311	204	0.167	0.110	95.1	35.8	34.7	7.1	3.8
2000	351	...	0.188						

Columns 2 and 4 are based on population estimates of L. I. Dublin and A. J. Lotka, *Length of Life*, p. 265. The authors assume in later years a life expectancy of 70 years and a birth rate of 14 per 1,000.

Columns 3 and 5 are based on population estimates of W. S. Thompson and P. K. Whelpton, *Population Trends in the United States*, p. 109.

The assumption is made that annuities are paid to all covered workers over 65.

Both columns 2 and 3 give an index of the ratio of benefits to pay-rolls *for a system that has long been in operation*. The former, however, is based on much more optimistic estimates of survivors after 65 than the latter which apparently were the estimates used by the official actuaries.

Columns 4 and 5. First, it is necessary to obtain hypothetical values for the ratio of benefits to pay-rolls for 1930. Benefit payments (see remarks relative to column 10) = covered population over 65 (see remarks relative to column 9) × benefit payment per person over 65. Pay-rolls = covered population aged 20 to 64 × average wage per capita (see remarks relative to column 8).

Column 4 is obtained by multiplying relatives in column 2 by the ratio of benefits to pay-rolls for 1930 (0.0538). Similarly, column 5 is obtained by multiplying relatives in column 3 by 0.0538. It should be observed that the use of the former relatives gives a very high ratio of benefits to pay-rolls. Thus in 1980, the ratio based on Dr. Dublin's estimates of population comes to 0.167, whereas that based on the more conservative and official estimate of population comes to 0.110.

Column 6. The figures in this column are taken from Thompson and Whelpton, *op. cit.*, p. 109.

Column 7. The estimated fraction of population which is covered can be derived by taking the number that would have been covered in 1930 as a fraction of the total population in productive-age groups. The required fraction is 0.377 (Senate Report 628, 74th Congress, 1st Session, p. 26).

Column 8. The number of covered workers is multiplied by $967 (wages per capita—*Report of the Secretary of the Treasury*, 1937, p. 52) in order to obtain pay-rolls for future years.

Column 9. Estimates of population over 65 (Thompson and Whelpton, *op cit.*, p. 109) multiplied by 0.377 yield the totals given in column 9. These results are valid on the assumption that the life expectancy of covered workers is equal to that of the rest of the population.

Column 10. The figure for average yearly benefits is multiplied by that for numbers of recipients of benefit, the resultant total giving old-age benefit payments.

productive-age groups, and in the far future a smaller number of older people. The timing, however, will be such that the ratio of the old to the middle groups will increase as well as the ratio of the middle to the younger group. The second tendency indicated above will further accentuate the increase of older persons relative to those in the productive-age group.[1]

We should expect, therefore, an increase in the percentage of benefits to current pay-rolls from the low level typical of a growing population to the level appropriate to a stable population, and then on to a still higher level appropriate to a declining population. This will be reinforced to some small degree by improved life expectancies. In addition there will probably be an increase in benefits due to wider coverage. A rise of benefits associated with an extension of coverage will not require a correction of the results given by the following table (which applies to a system long in operation) except in so far as the proportion of the average wage to the average benefit in year t relative to year o is modified. In so far as the newly covered are relatively low-paid workers, the need for correction is evident. An offset is savings resulting from a reduction in movements from noncovered to covered occupations and vice versa.

Table I is of some interest in this connection. Figures in columns 2 and 3 confirm our expectation concerning the effects of population changes on the future burden of old-age insurance. (This table, it should be observed, is constructed on the assumption that the system *by* 1930 *has long been in operation*. Table II, however, is based on The Social Security Act of 1935, operations beginning, therefore, after 1935.)

On the average, the yearly benefit comes to $536.76. Earnings over a lifetime = $967 (average wage) × 40 (average working life), or a total of $38,680.

One-half of 1 per cent on first $3,000* = $15 per month.
One-twelfth of 1 per cent on remainder* = $29.73 per month.
$$\$44.73 \times 12 = \$536.76.$$

The assumption (Table I) is made throughout that the system has been in operation for a long time. We have not taken the trouble to adjust these figures to the changes made in the Security Act in 1939. These changes will not materially affect the conclusions drawn from this table.

We now turn to Table II which, it will be recalled, relates to the period after 1935. Lest there be any misunderstanding, the reader should be warned that this is based on estimates relative to the 1935 act. Actual developments since 1935 (including the amendments of 1939) reduce the significance of this table. Obviously the estimates for 1940 and later years do not check with the actual figures for 1940 (pay-rolls in 1940 are in excess of 30 billion dollars); and for later years changes in contributions and benefits will modify the figures in all columns. In other words, this table is largely of historical interest.

---

[1] *Ibid.*, p. 37.
* Rates provided by Social Security Act (1935).

TABLE II.—OLD-AGE INSURANCE, PAY-ROLLS, RESERVE APPROPRIATIONS AND EARNINGS, AND BENEFITS*

Fiscal year ending June 30	(1)† Estimated appropriation to reserves (millions)	(2)† Interest on reserve (millions)	(3)† Benefit payments (billions)	(4)† Balance in reserve (billions)	(5) Pay-rolls Col. 1 × $\frac{1}{0.95}$ × $\frac{1}{\text{tax rate}}$ (billions)	(6) Ratio of benefits to pay-rolls $\frac{\text{Col. 3}}{\text{Col. 5}}$
1940	662	39	0.022	1.97	23.2 (23.8)	0.0009
1950	1,783	371	0.505	14.0	31.2 (31.3)	0.0162
1960	1,939	844	1.38	29.5	34.0	0.0406
1970	2,095	1,211	2.30	41.4	36.8	0.0625
1980	2,180	1,406	3.51	46.9	38.2	0.0916

* *Cf.* Senate Report 734 (76: 1), *Social Security Act Amendments*, 1939, p. 17. The estimates for 1950 are as follows:

	Millions of dollars
Net tax receipts..	1,751
Benefit payments..	1,422
Interest on reserves (at 2½ per cent).....................................	136
Addition to fund...	465
Fund at end of year..	5,737

† Columns 1 to 4 are taken from Senate Report 628, 74th Congress, 1st Session, 1935.

I assume that appropriations in column 1 equal future pay-roll taxes minus 5 per cent for administration expenses. We are then able to compute pay-rolls by multiplication of figures in column 1 by 1/0.95 × 1/tax rate (column 5). In parenthesis, another estimate of future pay-rolls for the years 1940 and 1950 is given. These figures are obtained by dividing estimated receipts from pay-roll taxes by the tax rate.

A third table is given which is based upon the assumptions made earlier in the text. (The system begins to operate in 1860; the general revenues cover three-fifths of the burden, etc.) Thus in the first column figures giving the cost of benefits as a percentage of pay-rolls are presented. For the year 1980, the estimate of possible costs (relative to pay-rolls) given in 1938 by the official actuary is used. Estimates for other years are obtained through adjustment of the figure for 1980 by the relatives given in column 2 of the first table. These relatives (of population 65 and over to population 20 to 64 adjusted to year 1930) are based on optimistic estimates of life expectancies. The burden is large because continued improvement in life expectancies is assumed. Yet the results are clearly within the realms of the possible.

In the second column, the estimated cost of old-age insurance in billions of dollars is given. In this column for 1980 a figure somewhat below the estimates for 1980 made by the actuaries is used.[1] The other figures in this column are adjusted by the relatives in column 1. Column 3 (charge on general revenues) presents the charges on general revenues on the as-

[1] *Soc. Sec. Bull.*, July, 1938, p. 15.

sumption made in the text that three-fifths of the costs are charged in this manner and two-fifths through assessments on pay-rolls. Any material rise in coverage might contribute to a further increase in the assessments on general revenues. Recently, experts have frequently suggested that the Treasury contribute out of general revenues. The usual figure given is one-third. At a cost of 15 per cent of pay-rolls, the levy on pay-rolls, on the assumption that no revenues are obtainable from reserves, would come to 9 per cent, a very high figure. A liberal estimate of ultimate earnings on reserves under the 1939 act would be 2 per cent of pay-rolls.

TABLE III.—COST OF OLD-AGE INSURANCE

Year	(1) Per cent of pay-rolls	(2) Total costs (billion dollars)	(3) Charge on general revenues (billion dollars)
1860	3	1.0	0.6
1890	4	1.3	0.8
1930	5	1.6	1.0
1950	7	2.5	1.5
1980	15	5.0	3.0
2000	16	5.3	3.2

The reader may be puzzled by apparent inconsistencies in the three tables. First, observe the following:

PER CENT OF BENEFITS TO PAY-ROLLS

Year	Table I	Table II	Table III
1950	0.082 (0.074)	0.0162	0.074
1980	0.167 (0.110)	0.0916	0.150

Calculations in Tables I and III are made on the assumption of a system long in operation even as early as 1930, whereas Table II gives estimates based on the actual system provided by the Act of 1935. The ratio of benefits to pay-rolls is therefore very small for the year 1950 in Table II. The differences in 1980, however, are to be explained largely by other considerations. Official estimates made at the time of the passage of the Act are given in Table II. Semiofficial estimates (1938) of possible costs relative to pay-rolls for the year 1980 are given in Table III. In Table I, figures derived from optimistic estimates of life expectancies, *i.e.*, a high proportion of pensioners to the working population, are presented. The figures in parentheses in Table I are based on the more conservative life expectancies apparently accepted by the official actuaries in 1935. A reasonable guess is that the ratio of benefits to pay-rolls in 1980 may well attain 13 to 14 per cent or even higher.

Our estimate of costs by 1980 as given and explained in Table I (and accompanying notes) is 3.8 billion dollars. An official estimate of a few years ago of which no explanations have come to my attention is 3.5 billions. In these calculations of monetary cost the conservative vital statistics (relatively low life expectancies) of Thompson and Whelpton have been used. It is easy to see why later estimates of possible costs have already risen to 5 billion dollars. A ratio of 11 per cent for benefits relative to payrolls will yield the more conservative estimate, and the ratio of 0.167 the larger sum. Allowances for longer life expectancies and a rise in the proportion covered, for example, will account for large increases in costs. An offset is the gain resulting from less movement from covered to noncovered occupations and back again.

The legislation of 1939 does not radically change these conclusions. Total costs are not materially different from later estimates under the benefit schedules of 1935. Benefits are, however, distributed more nearly according to need, with the result that dependents share both during the life of the annuitant and after his death.

Chapter 11

FINANCING THE PROGRAM

11.1. Introductory

In the last chapter the problem of the costs of the old-age insurance program was discussed. It is, therefore, quite appropriate at this point to raise the question of the country's capacity to pay the promised benefits. The ultimate outcome will depend in no small part upon the costs of the entire social security program and upon the growth of other public expenditures. If, for example, the cost of old-age assistance rises, and (or) if additional benefits are conferred under the old-age insurance program, and (or) if the state offers increased subsidies to the unemployment insurance fund directly or through relief measures, and (or) if the United States undertakes a costly defense program or war, the possibility of meeting promised obligations in later years becomes less and less likely. Of one point we may feel reasonably certain. Public expenditures in general will tend to rise in the future as they have in the past. It is possible of course that to some extent the state will substitute expenditures for the benefit of the old for other expenditures. In fact, on the principles of welfare economics and of the maximum stimulus to the economy for a given volume of expenditure, much is to be said for such redistribution of public expenditures.[1] A reasoned guess, however, is that new expenditures for the benefit of the old will be largely additional rather than a substitute for other outlays.[2]

Let us assume that the cost of the old-age insurance program will ultimately rise to 5 billion dollars, a not unreasonable estimate. What are the alternative methods of dealing with the large rise of

[1] Even in the years 1911–1931 the rise of expenditures for relief seems to have been much greater than the rise of population and that of *all* public expenditures. *Cf.* WPA, *Trends in Relief Expenditures, 1910–1935* (1937), pp. 11, 13, 46.

[2] It is well to keep in mind the fact that the rise in the proportion of old will be offset by a decline in the relative numbers of young dependents. Economies in the cost of education may, therefore, be forthcoming though the net gains for the budget will not be of the same proportions as the rise of costs of old-age insurance and pensions. *Cf.* W. B. Reddaway, *The Economics of a Declining Population*, pp. 187–191.

expenditures involved? It is to be repeated that the failure to accumulate a large reserve aggravates the financial problem, for at the present moment provision has been made to cover possibly one-half of the anticipated maximum costs of insurance (not including assistance) through pay-roll taxes and reserves.

Five possibilities of dealing with the problem of rising costs of insurance may be mentioned.[1]

1. A reduction of other expenditures.
2. A rise of taxes, and in particular of taxes imposed upon those who do not gain directly from the insurance program.
3. Recourse to borrowing through the sale of securities.
4. The direct issue of paper money to finance deficits.
5. Defaults.

Items 1, 3, and 4 can be dismissed with but a few words. As indicated above, a reduction of public expenditures (1) is not likely. It is not so easy to dispose of the possibility of a continued rise of public debt (3). In fact this is the main issue of the last chapter in which the relation both of general expenditures and of the social security program to the rise of debt is considered. In the present chapter, the assumption is that the annual cost of debt financing is rather modest as compared with reasonable estimates of the future cost of the public debt. The financing of deficits through the issue of paper money (4) is in many respects a more intelligent policy than sales of securities to banks; but political factors present greater obstacles to the introduction of the former policy than the latter. This discussion naturally leads to the possibility of defaults (5). A very large rise of debt or large issues of money may possibly result in a disguised repudiation, *i.e.*, a rise in prices of large proportions. Defaults may also be introduced through a direct cut of promised benefits.[2] It follows then that if tax receipts are not available in adequate amounts, the probable alternative is repudiation, disguised or direct. We turn, therefore, to the issue of revenue.

---

[1] *Cf. Hearings*, Ways and Means Committee, House of Representatives, *Social Security*, 1939, pp. 1767–1768.

[2] *Hearings*, Ways and Means Committee, House of Representatives, *Social Security*, 1939, pp. 2258–2260. Dr. Altmeyer suggests that in view of the fact that Treasury contributions will be required 15 years from now, preparations ought to be made at present. In any case, it would be unfair to cut benefits in the future, thus paying more to the present old who contribute less than the future old. The Twentieth Century Fund, however, is not concerned over the possibility of defaults. *Hearings*, Ways and Means Committee, House of Representatives, *Social Security*, 1939, p. 813.

11.2. ARE PROMISES TO BE KEPT?

We begin with a few general comments. Abandonment of large reserves and adherence to the pay-as-you-go principle clearly raise the issue of the adequacy of revenue in the future. We do not share the optimism of those who say that "the change could be effected quickly and without disturbing the balancing of the fiscal budget if the old age reserve account were placed on a pay-as-you-go basis."[1]

If we are to judge from what has happened so far, the prospects of promises being kept are not too bright. Those who have been concerned over the unfortunate monetary effects of an accumulation of reserves and those who have been hostile to the security program in general (and, let us add, those who were interested in the payment of adequate benefits earlier) have combined to introduce the Amendment of 1939 which clearly marks a distinct advance toward an unqualified pay-as-you-go principle. It is no wonder then that Dr. Douglas Brown, a friend of social security, now remarks that "those who now criticise the large reserve will criticise the federal subsidisation to the old age insurance account."

First, Congress, despite the vote of the overwhelming majority of the Federal Advisory Council, and of the Board, postponed the scheduled rise of pay-roll rates from 1 to 1½ per cent for employers and employees each. Having thus increased the fiscal difficulties of the future, Congress nevertheless has refused to consider or recommend a program for covering the ever-increasing deficits of the future.[2] So far as we have been able to discover, the Treasury has no plans either. The representative of the National Association of Manufacturers in fact fires the first gun for later postponements when he tells Congress that a tax of 1 per cent will finance the costs for the next 15 years.[3] Even the actuary of the Social Security Board makes little of the postponement of the rise of rates. In his words,

[1] Cf. GAYER, A. D., "Fiscal Policies," *Proc. Am. Econ. Assoc.*, 1938, p. 104.

[2] *Hearings*, Senate Finance Committee (76: 1), *Social Security Act Amendments*, 1939, pp. 9, 250; *Hearings*, Ways and Means Committee, House of Representatives, *Social Security*, 1939, pp. 1767–1796. Both the Advisory Council and the Board have gone on record as approving Treasury contributions. The latter in fact makes concrete proposals for progressive taxes. *Ibid.*, pp. 2187–2188, 2201.

[3] *Hearings*, Ways and Means Committee, House of Representatives, *Social Security*, 1939, p. 2070. It is interesting that the group in Congress which insists that interest on reserves constitutes a Treasury subsidy also opposes Treasury subsidies later. They are, however, made necessary by the paring down of reserves. *Ibid.*, p. 2204.

the postponement will cost but 1 billion dollars out of 100 billions to be collected in the next 59 years.[1] (Incidentally does he not leave out of account the interest on the additional sums that might have been collected but actually will not be collected in the years 1940–1942?) What is crucial is that Congress has yielded to the pressure of those who would placate business now and would cut taxes by a few hundred millions annually. What reason have we to assume that Congress will appropriate 100 billions in the next 50 years then if under current conditions it renounces 1 billion dollars of revenue? Strangely enough, Senator Vandenberg and other *purists* in fiscal matters support this movement for a most *unbalanced* budget of the *future*.[2] In the light of these developments, it is not difficult to understand the admonition of the Federal Advisory Council that no benefits should be promised or implied that cannot be met later and that we should not commit future generations to pay more than we are prepared to pay ourselves. The amendments of 1939 mean that this is what we are in fact doing.[3] It would have been better if the rates for 1940 had been increased by at least $\frac{1}{4}$ of 1 per cent over those of 1939. Then Congress would have met the criticisms of those who fear deflation and yet have given evidence of good faith.

Thus we have seen that Congress by its decisions on revenue up to the present has not given evidence of its determination to keep the promises implied in the present schedule of benefits or in any later schedules, which may well provide for even more liberal payments. Its attitude toward benefits is not much more reassuring. Under the program of 1935, benefits to be paid in the near future were to be much smaller than ultimate benefits. Supporters of the program defended these schedules on the grounds that under an insurance plan a close relationship between contributions and benefits was desirable and that the accumulation of reserves which

[1] *Hearings*, Ways and Means Committee, House of Representatives, *Social Security*, 1939, p. 2487. *Cf.* pp. 1770–1771.

[2] He is, it seems, determined to help small business. *Hearings*, Senate Finance Committee, *Social Security Act Amendments*, p. 10.

[3] *Report of Federal Advisory Council on Social Security*, Senate Document 4, 1939, pp. 25–26. Misgivings have been expressed elsewhere also. *Cf.* LINTON, M. A., "Some Aspects of the Reserve Program," *Annals*, March, 1939, p. 189, and NORTON, T. L., *Old Age and The Social Security Act*, p. 57; *Hearings*, Ways and Means Committee, House of Representatives, *Social Security*, 1939, p. 812. *Cf.*, however, *Hearings*, Ways and Means Committee, House of Representatives, *Social Security*, 1939, p. 813.

followed from the ungenerous payments in early years assured benefits to those who had contributed in the course of their working lives. Even at this time, however, many condemned the government insurance scheme which treated old workers less liberally than private insurance schemes.[1]

Whatever may be said of the provisions under the original act, the failure to pay maximum benefits to those over 65 at the outset under the amendments of 1939 can be interpreted as an unwillingness to face the full implications of the pay-as-you-go principle. This conclusion follows from the attack made in 1939 on both the reserve principle and the principle of close association of contributions and benefits. The cost of launching a program providing for maximum payments at the outset would, moreover, be small as compared with the ultimate costs; for the percentage of old now is much less than it will be ultimately and, furthermore, coverage is likely to increase in the future. (Under the 1939 act, however, the principle of the average wage is an important approach toward maximum payments at the outset.) We may conclude, however, that if Congress would enforce moderate sacrifices *now* through the introduction of maximum benefits at once and a *modest* rise of taxes, then the country might feel reassured as to the future of the security program and the willingness to impose large sacrifices later.

One difficulty arises, however, *viz.*, the relation of old-age assistance and insurance. Generous payments at the outset would also have to be paid to the needy old who were not insured. Fiscal difficulties would arise then.

Congress and the Board shrank from the full implications of current financing. It may be said to their credit, however, that the schedules of 1939 make an important advance toward equality of

New plan (1939)			Old plan (1935)	
Benefits* in	Single	Married	Benefits* in	Amount
3 years	$25.75	$38.63	5 years	$17.50
40 years	35.00	52.50	40 years	51.25

* For average monthly wage of $100.

[1] LINTON, *op. cit.*, p. 186. Mr. Linton points out that under the 1935 act, an average benefit of $30 monthly is not attained until 1962. Yet the cost of introducing benefits of this amount *from* 1940 *on* would be roughly one-half of the receipts in the years 1940–1950.

benefits in time. In this connection, the plans shown in the accompanying table, proposed by the chairman of the Social Security Board are of interest.[1]

11.3. CONSENSUS IN FAVOR OF RECOURSE TO GENERAL TAXATION

A survey of the literature leaves one with little doubt that informed opinion strongly favors Treasury subsidies of the old-age insurance account. Not alone the friends of the program, *e.g.*, the Board, the Federal Advisory Council, Dr. Brown, Dr. Dewhurst, Mrs. Burns, and many others, but rather unfriendly critics, *e.g.*, the representative of the nonpartisan social security commission and the National Association of Manufacturers, support Treasury subsidies. Even the House Ways and Means Committee concludes that ultimately a rise of pay-roll taxes or a direct subsidy by the Treasury will be required. In his usual cautious way, the Secretary of the Treasury, however, refuses to make any recommendations.[2]

Numerous reasons are adduced for eventual aid by the Treasury. Among the most frequently mentioned (and which at the same time carry conviction) are the following. The introduction of old-age insurance saves the government large amounts on old-age assistance. Again adequate benefits are not forthcoming without the interven-

---

[1] *Hearings*, Ways and Means Committee, House of Representatives, *Social Security*, 1939, pp. 2165–2166. For similar comparisons in the final Act, see Social Security Board, *Ann. Rept.*, 1939, p. 172.

[2] The following references are an adequate sample for those who wish to obtain a catalogue of the arguments adduced in favor of subsidies. *Hearings*, Ways and Means Committee, House of Representatives, *Social Security*, 1939, pp. 812, 957–958, 1222–1226, 1849–1857, 2070–2075, 2185–2211, 2258–2271; Senate Document 4, 1939, *Final Report of Senate Advisory Council on Social Security*, pp. 23–24; House Document 110, 1939, *Report of Social Security Board (Message of President)*, pp. 11–12; BROWN, J. D., "The Old Age Reserve Account," *Quart. Jour. Econ.*, August, 1937, p. 718. PRIBRAM, K. B., "The Functions of Reserves in Old Age Benefit Plans," *Quart. Jour. Econ.*, August, 1938, pp. 621–622, 632–633; BURNS, E. M., "The Financial Aspects of the Social Security Act," *Am. Econ. Rev.*, March, 1936, pp. 14–15; *Social Security: A Symposium for National Municipal Review* (March–April, 1936), pp. 15, 21; GRAY, H. A., "Effects of Present Taxation on an Extended Social Security Program," *Social Security in the United States*, 1938, pp. 156–157; DEWHURST, J. F., "Old-age Security Financing in Relation to Income Tax Reform," *Nat. Tax Assoc. Bull.*, May, 1938, pp. 240–245; House Report 728 (76: 1), *Social Security Act Amendments*, 1939, pp. 16–17.

tion of the Treasury. It is scarcely necessary to add that the inadequacy is associated by some with the abandonment of the principle of large reserves. Others raise the issue of social justice. In the opinion of these proponents of a Treasury subsidy, pay-roll taxes ultimately are borne by the poor, whereas the Treasury should put the burden at least to some extent on the rich. In this connection, some raise the question of the relation of coverage and subsidies. It is now contended that since coverage is likely to increase, and since in fact coverage is much larger than had originally been anticipated, the argument of inadequate coverage which had been used so much in 1935–1938 against Treasury subsidies now loses force.[1] Thus since the vast majority of workers are to be covered, the insured are not to receive much public aid at the expense of noncovered workers. Finally, two other points made by many who now favor subsidies should not go unmentioned. (1) At least a few of those who view the earnings of the reserve merely as financial wizardry or hocus-pocus agree that it would be better to offer an undisguised Treasury subsidy. (2) Many appeal to foreign experience, foreign programs relying quite generally on Treasury subsidies.[2] It should be observed, however, that in the British case self-sufficiency is the ultimate goal.[3]

Although the consensus of opinion favors government subsidies, the experts differ on the timing of public aid. There is some sentiment, for example, for early aid by the government.[4] In so far as subsidies are introduced the cost in absolute amounts will then be less. Others (including Dr. Altmeyer) would not introduce subsidies until the pay-roll taxes prove inadequate.[5] In this connection, let us observe that the timing of intervention will be related to the later attitude toward reserves. If, for example, the rule of three

---

[1] Cf. DULLES, E. L., Remarks before the Advisory Council, 1937, p. 10. Dr. Dulles objected then to Treasury subsidies on the grounds that they were inappropriate when benefits varied from $10 to $85 monthly.

[2] Hearings, Ways and Means Committee, House of Representatives, Social Security, 1939, pp. 1235–1238; Cf. International Labor Office, Compulsory Pension Insurance, 1933, Studies and Reports, Series M, No. 10; GRANT, M., Old-age Security, p. 153; ARMSTRONG, B. N., Insuring the Essentials, p. 416.

[3] Ibid., 423–424; cf. Hearings, Ways and Means Committee, House of Representatives, Social Security, 1939, pp. 1235–1238.

[4] Hearings, Ways and Means Committee, House of Representatives, Social Security, 1939, pp. 1222–1223; cf. p. 812.

[5] Hearings, Ways and Means Committee, House of Representatives, Social Security, 1939, pp. 2200–2201, 2258; House Document 110, 1939; Social Security Board, Ann. Rept., 1939, pp. 11–12.

(reserves = three times maximum benefits in the next five years) should be abandoned later, the contributions of the Treasury might be postponed further. In that case, less revenue would be required for a number of years, both because transfers to reserves would not be required and because current needs may be met in part out of reserves. Again the National Association of Manufacturers recommends that the rate shall not rise above 2 per cent (in all) until 1955.[1] Failure to increase rates in the next 15 years, however, will involve the Treasury in large subsidies later but if, as this organization suggests, benefits are not increased, the ultimate costs to the Treasury may not prove to be excessive.

11.4. JUSTICE IN TAXATION

Many support the recourse to general revenues on the grounds of social justice. A brief discussion of the issues will not be irrelevant at this point. Let us assume that Congress is sincere in its announced desire to fulfill the promises implied in the benefit schedule. Then it follows that if adequate revenues are to be obtained, revenues obtained from the well-to-do will contribute greatly to financial solvency. It is unlikely that the government will be able to collect a tax (say) of 15 per cent of pay-rolls for old-age insurance. If, on the other hand, a large reserve were provided, the need for subsidies from the Treasury would to that extent be reduced. A safe conclusion on the assumption of sincerity is that a large part of the revenues will be collected from general tax sources, the proportion declining *pari passu* with greater reliance on earnings of reserves; and as the levies on the general taxpayer rise in importance, the safe inference is that the authorities will apply the progressive principle more and more.

Many arguments have been adduced against the pay-roll taxes, which shall not be presented here. The most popular criticism is that the pay-roll tax is a regressive form of taxation.[2] In view of the large proportion of revenues raised by consumption taxes and taxes

---

[1] *Hearings*, Ways and Means Committee, House of Representatives, *Social Security*, 1939, pp. 2070–2075; *cf.* also, p. 1849.

[2] *Cf.* DOUGLAS, P., "The United States Social Security Act," *Econ. Jour.*, March, 1936, p. 14; GREEN, W., "Labor's Demands in Social Security," *Social Security in the United States*, 1937, p. 180; WILLCOX, A. W., "The Old Age Reserve

on the poor, this argument carries considerable weight.[1] Observe, however, that the pay-roll taxes are imposed upon employers (almost exclusively on employers for unemployment insurance) as well as upon employees; and taxes on employers (and possibly on employees) are to some extent shifted to relatively well-to-do consumers and to some extent to those who may broadly be termed the "capitalist class."[2] Another point that is frequently made by opponents of the pay-roll tax has received attention above. We refer to the fallacy that the pay-roll tax forces the poor to pay off the public debt. Our belief is, however, even on the assumption of accumulation of fairly large reserves, that, in so far as it is expedient, the financing of the required Treasury subsidy should be carried through largely on progressive principles.

We ascribe importance, however, to the insurance principle, which requires that the contributions and benefits should be associated at least to a significant degree.[3] It may well be that under the amendments of 1939 the association has become less strong than is desirable. Proponents of the reserve principle frequently take the position that an accumulation of reserves (and the levy of large pay-roll taxes in early years) is to be defended on the grounds that it is an inevitable accompaniment (in the transition period of the next few generations) of a close relation between benefits and contributions. This seems to be a sound position.[4] Those, however, who oppose the accumulation of reserves and are prepared to destroy the desired relationship between contributions and benefits and, incidentally, to jeopardize the solvency of old-age insurance account, ought to go the whole way and dissociate contributions and benefits even farther. They will then pay maximum benefits at the outset, thus giving evidence of serious intentions of keeping promises.

Account," *Quart. Jour. Econ.*, May, 1937, p. 447; *Soc. Sec. Bull.*, December, 1937, p. 11; EPSTEIN, A., *Social Security*, pp. 20–23; DEWHURST, J. F., "Economic Implications of the Social Security Program," *Social Security: A Symposium*, National Municipal League, 1936, p. 15; BURNS, *op. cit.*, pp. 12–22.

[1] *Cf. Hearings*, Ways and Means Committee, House of Representatives, *Social Security*, 1939, pp. 1169–1171; *cf.* introductory chapter also.

[2] *Cf.* RUBINOW, I. M., "State Pool Plans and Merit Rating," *Law and Contemporary Problems*, January, 1936, pp. 78–79.

[3] Especially Pribram, *op. cit.*, pp. 617–621; 632–633.

[4] Possibly the contributory principle might be adhered to and yet the reserves might be dissipated through concessions in other taxes on manufacturers and possibly even on labor.

11.5. The Issue of Full Coverage

In the controversies over financial methods, opponents of Treasury subsidies dwelt at great length and with annoying frequency on the point that when coverage is not universal recourse to general revenues is unjust. This line of argument has played such a large part in the development of policies that it would be well to examine it more fully. It does not appear, moreover, despite the unexpectedly high proportion of workers now covered, that coverage will in the reasonably near future attain a figure at all close to 100 per cent. Confusion arises in the discussion of this issue from a failure to distinguish coverage at any one time from coverage over a worker's lifetime. A worker, for example, may be covered at intervals with the result that he becomes eligible for minimum benefits. Though 80 per cent of all workers *may* thus be eligible for benefits (and these frequently for minimum amounts) probably not more than 50 per cent of the gainfully occupied will be in covered employment at any specific time.[1] In anticipation of future attempts to flay this dead horse, we reply to those who use this argument. Whatever the merits of this attack on Treasury subsidies, we may say parenthetically that the damage done by it was small so long as reserve financing as contemplated under the 1935 act was in operation; but with the scrapping of the 1935 plan, any point adduced against Treasury subsidies is most probably a contribution toward repudiation of social security obligations.

A few typical statements of the pre-1939 era follow:

"The use of other tax funds, in the form of a Government subsidy, to help finance old-age insurance would mean, in effect, that the non-covered portion of the population would be compelled to pay a substantial part of the cost of insuring the covered population."[2]

"The payment of a subsidy is regarded as inequitable on the ground that the old-age benefits plan, which protects only a limited section of the population, would then be supported in a measure by revenues collected from the population as a whole."[3]

Clearly the situation has changed since these remarks were made. Movements from uncovered to covered employments have been much larger than had been anticipated, with the result that the percentage of workers eligible for benefits is much larger than had originally been esti-

---

[1] Under the 1939 revisions, the 80 per cent figure is probably excessive.

[2] Social Security Board, *Ann. Rept.*, 1937, pp. 23–24; *cf. Quart. Jour. Econ.*, May, 1937, p. 447.

[3] Wyatt, B. E., and W. H. Wandel, *The Social Security Act in Operation*, p. 155.

mated. Thus on the basis of the census of 1930, which, however, offers classifications of limited usefulness for our problems, the estimate was that 25 to 26 millions, or 52.4 per cent, of all gainful workers in 1930 would be covered under the old-age provisions of the Social Security Act. Of those not covered the most important single class are the self-employed (in excess of 12 millions); and in addition there are 9.2 millions specifically exempted. The three most important groups of the latter are agricultural and domestic laborers and employees in public service.[1]

Later estimates put the percentage of covered workers much higher. Early in 1938 it was observed that 38 millions had taken out numbers under the old-age insurance program, though many of these were of course not yet accumulating credits.[2] A year later an official estimate put the number who would obtain a job covered by the old-age security plan at 35 millions. From 2 to 3 millions were, moreover, covered under the Railroad Retirement Act and legislation covering Federal government employees.[3] According to Dr. Corson, 32 million workers, who had earned an amount in taxable wages in excess of two-thirds of the 42.8 billion dollars of wages and salaries paid in 1937 for the country, were covered under the Social Security Act.[4] In 1939, the Social Security Board recommended to Congress an extension which would have increased coverage by 1.8 to 2.4 millions.[5] Congress did not, however, take kindly to all these recommendations. The rise of coverage under the 1939 revisions is about 1 million.[6] Dr. Altmeyer, in the course of the hearings, expressed the opinion that the program was on its way toward a coverage of 80 per cent.[7] It is no wonder then that the Secretary of the Treasury could say at this point (thus

[1] WENDT, L., "Census Classifications and Social Security Categories," *Soc. Sec. Bull.*, April, 1938, pp. 3–12.

[2] *Soc. Sec. Bull.*, March, 1938, pp. 82–83. In 1939, the figure reached 44 millions. House Report 728 (76: 1), *Social Security Act Amendments*, 1939, p. 4.

[3] WINSLOW, H. J., and W. K. SHAUGHNESSY, "Estimated Numbers of Persons in Employments Excluded from Old-age Insurance," *Soc. Sec. Bull.*, February, 1939, pp. 18–19.

[4] CORSON, J. J., "Wage Reports for Workers Covered by Federal Old-age Insurance in 1937," *Soc. Sec. Bull.*, March, 1939, p. 3. *Cf.* WASSERMAN, M. J., and J. R. ARNOLD, "Old-age Insurance," *Soc. Sec. Bull.*, April, 1939, pp. 3–4. They find that the number of wage earners in covered employment in 1937 was 60 per cent of the total number of employables aged 15 to 64.

[5] On the unwillingness of Congress to follow the wishes of the President and the Social Security Board on the extension of coverage, see House Document 110, *Report of Social Security Board (Message of President)*, 1939, pp. 9–10; Senate Document 4, *Report of Senate Advisory Council*, 1939, pp. 22–23; House Report 728 (76: 1), *Social Security Act Amendments*, 1939, pp. 3, 17–18; and *Hearings*, Senate Finance Committee, *Social Security Act Amendments* (76: 1), p. 20.

[6] "Old Age Insurance," *Soc. Sec. Bull.*, December, 1939, p. 83.

[7] *Hearings*, Ways and Means Committee, House of Representatives, *Social Security*, 1939, p. 2264. The figure of 80 per cent is excessive as we shall see.

reversing himself completely on financial methods) that coverage would rise to 80 per cent even if no extensions were made and therefore that further subsidies would not introduce substantial inequities.[1]

Having dwelt upon the extent of coverage present and potential, we return to a consideration of the validity of the argument that in so far as coverage is not universal, Treasury subsidies are not to be favored. A few preliminary remarks are relevant here, however. If the attitude of Congress in 1939 is symptomatic and if administrative complexities are not straightened out, it will be a long time before anything like universal coverage is attained. Again, universal coverage or an approximation to it is held to be a *sine qua non* for the appeals to the Treasury; and in so far as coverage is extended the cost to the Treasury is likely to rise. Why? Excluded occupations are to a significant degree the low-paid ones which involve the old-age account in large outlays relative to contributions. It should be observed, however, that the additional burden on the old-age account associated with an extension of coverage is not so great as it at first seems to be. Coverage at any given time has been put at roughly 50 to 60 per cent of the employable population and coverage of the employable population during their *entire* working lives adequate to obtain minimum benefits at 80 per cent.[2] It follows, therefore, that an extension of coverage will increase the taxable wages of many workers, otherwise in receipt of wages adequate to make them eligible, thus (because of the sliding scale) reducing the ratio of benefits to contributions.

On what grounds may one hold that universal coverage is mistakenly invoked as a prerequisite to the appropriation of funds from the general revenues of the state? (1) It is not a principle of Federal finance, as is implied or stated by those who use this argument, that universal coverage is a condition for Federal aid out of general tax revenues. Nor is it an accepted principle that if complete coverage is administratively impossible and direct assessments on those benefited are either unjust or inexpedient, the only alternative is the elimination of expenditures otherwise deemed desirable. Justice Cardozo affirmed for the majority of the Court that Congress

[1] *Ibid.*, p. 2112.

[2] Amendments in 1939 are relevant here. Since the requirements for the attainment of the status of *fully insured* are more stringent after the first few years, the effect under these amendments may well be that the estimate of coverage of 80 per cent which is based on the definitions of coverage of 1935 is excessive. Regulations No. 3, *Federal Old Age and Survivors' Insurance*, 1940, pp. 3–7.

can *spend* for the general welfare and is reasonable in designating old-age aid as coming under this category.[1] In discussing the unemployment insurance case, the Court held, moreover, that the pay-roll tax was valid so long as the exemptions and the restrictions of benefits were not arbitrary.[2]

2. The assumption made by those who appeal to the argument of universal coverage is that people in similar circumstances should be treated in a similar manner. Treasury subsidies are said to be acceptable if the vast majority of the working classes profit from their disbursement. It is, however, true that people in similar circumstances do not always profit to the same extent from Treasury donations. Frequently gains of particular groups at the expense of the taxpayer are determined by the effectiveness of their lobbies rather than by their needs. In applying the principle of equal treatment, moreover, one should consider the expenditures of the Treasury in all its activities. Farmers, for example, obtain aid through the conservation programs and the activities of the FCA; a large percentage of the working population (and perhaps to a disproportionate degree those excluded from old-age insurance) receive help through relief, public works programs, and old-age assistance. Unequal treatment under individual programs to some extent cancels out when the total activities of the government are considered.

3. It is a mistake to assume that aside from Treasury subsidies the old-age insurance program excludes subsidization. The old and poor insured gain at the expense of the relatively high paid and young insured. Again, allowing for the ensuing rises of prices, one may conclude that a small percentage of the insured *may* receive less than they pay and a not insignificant percentage less than they and their employers pay. The program, furthermore, involves subsidization of the insured by consumers in general; and to an important extent consumers and insured are not identical groups.

This brings us to the final point. The introduction of direct subsidies by the Treasury is likely to give us a larger measure of social justice. In so far as taxes of the relatively well-to-do are thus substituted for pay-roll taxes, the uninsured poor will be relieved of the responsibility of paying part of the cost of insurance for the covered population.

---

[1] Senate Document 74 (75: 1), No. 910, *Constitutionality of the Social Security Act,* Guy T. Helvering and Edison Electric Illuminating Company *v.* George P. Davis.

[2] *Ibid.,* Nos. 724 and 797. Albert A. Carmichael *v.* Southern Coal and Coke Company *v.* Gulf States Paper Corporation.

11.6. Future Tax Receipts[1]

This section begins with a brief discussion of the problem of tax capacity. Presumably, if people willed it, any proportion of the economy's resources might be devoted to publicly determined purposes. Social security and interest payments particularly involve only a redistribution of the social dividend; but this is not to deny that the effects of taxes upon motivation might be large. Nevertheless, it is chiefly the impact of a *new* tax which disturbs the economy. Expectations are disappointed, shifting takes time, consumers reduce purchases, and investment is discouraged. The year 1980 is a long way off, and the burden of social security taxes increases gradually. A rise of a given amount of taxes will probably have less serious repercussions if introduced by small steps than if introduced all at once. The consideration that there may always be unused resources in modern economies perhaps strengthens the conclusion that the effects of large rises of tax assessments may not be so serious as is generally assumed. It is assumed here that the net effect of a rise of taxes and expenditures is a rise of effective demand. A generous and assured level of government spending may well increase the propensity to consume. Direct taxes upon consumption, however, might have undesirable effects in this respect; and income taxes might undermine the incentive to invest. Keynesians would be interested primarily in the effect of taxes on the marginal propensity to consume and on the marginal efficiency of investment. A very bad tax system (on the assumption of oversaving) would be one not substantial enough to tax away savings (and raise the propensity to consume) but sufficiently large to inhibit investment through adverse effects on the marginal efficiency of capital and liquidity preference.[2]

It may well be that there has been excessive concern over tax capacity. Clearly, much depends upon the source from which the revenue is obtained, the use to which the money is put, and the time over which the change in tax structure is consummated. Assume that the tax collections of the Federal government are to rise from 5 to 10 to 15 billion dollars from 1940 to 1980. (Prices and

---

[1] Mrs. Marian Crawford Samuelson contributed greatly to this section.

[2] A fair picture of the inconclusive statements that can be made about this subject is given in Carl Shoup, *Facing the Tax Problem*, Chap. 5, pp. 57–68; *cf.* J. Stamp, *Wealth and Taxable Capacity*, Chap. IV.

incomes are assumed to remain unchanged.)[1] Then in so far as the taxes are collected from surplus incomes and expended in such a manner as to increase the marginal propensity to consume, or in so far as the money is expended for transfer purposes, *e.g.*, old-age insurance, and not for exhaustive (or real) purposes, the effects may even be favorable.[2] The time may come, however, when taxes on surpluses will be inexpedient, for the attainment of an adequate standard of living may require large additional savings. At this point, taxes on surpluses may be justified only to the extent that cash is diverted from consumption or hoards and will be harmful in so far as real savings are reduced. At such time, moreover, the allocation of public expenditures for investment rather than consumption purposes may also be appropriate. Finally, a rise of taxes of 125 millions per year over each preceding year for 40 years in all (5 billion by 1980) will injure the economy much less than if the change is effected in (say) 1 to 10 years.

If additional revenue of the order of magnitude of 5 billions or more is to be obtained by the government, then reliance must be had on other taxes in addition to the pay-roll tax. It is likely that the pay-roll tax will yield no more than one-half (and possibly less) of the revenue required for the old-age insurance funds when once a stationery population has been reached. The Treasury will then be confronted with the task of getting several billions from other sources.[3] As we shall see, 5 billions is a very conservative estimate of the additional amounts required. Moreover the results will not be so favorable as they at first seem to be: a rise in the yield of one tax will cut yields elsewhere. It is well then to turn to the personal income tax, which is likely to prove to be the most important single source

---

[1] One might assume that output will be much larger in the future and, therefore, the problem of finance should not be a cause for concern. (*Cf. Hearings*, Ways and Means Committee, House of Representatives, *Social Security*, 1939, p. 1841.) Such assumptions should not be made too lightly, however, in view of the history of the last 10 years. Furthermore, against any rise of output, one should put the increasing demands that are likely to be made on governments. *Cf.* W. B. Reddaway, *op. cit.*, pp. 195, 207.

[2] We use the term as it is used by Prof. A. C. Pigou, *Studies in Public Finance*, pp. 19-20.

[3] *Cf.* GRANT, M., *Old-age Security: Social and Financial Trends*, p. 193. For seven countries with rather advanced security programs, the cost of old-age pensions or insurance costs for a recent year varied between 1.1 and 2.7 per cent of the national income. An estimated ultimate cost of 5 billions (including old-age assistance) is not unreasonable on the basis of present legislation in the United States. On the assumption of a national income of 80 billions, this would constitute 6 to 7 per cent of the national income.

of additional revenue. Because of personal exemptions and low initial rates, the amount of tax paid by individuals with incomes from $5,000 to $100,-000 is comparatively small. Various estimates have been made of possible increases in revenue to be derived from changes in tax rates and exemption allowances. Of course, the yield of the income tax varies greatly as the size of the national income changes. In the years preceding the depression, only one-fourth of all revenues (Federal, state, and local) was raised through the income tax, and during the depression only one-eighth of all revenues.[1] The higher tax rates of the Act of 1936 and the improvement in business conditions raised this percentage. Dr. Heer estimates that the British tax rates if applied in this country even with our present exemptions would raise about 4 billion dollars on the national income of 1929, or perhaps 2 billion dollars more than what may be considered the normal yield.[2] Prof. Simons who is a very strong advocate of the personal income tax says,

TABLE I.*—ESTIMATED YIELD OF PERSONAL INCOME TAX ON VARIOUS ASSUMPTIONS†

	1928 incomes		1933 incomes	
Exemption:				
Married..........................	$2,500	$1,000	$2,500	$1,000
Single............................	1,000	500	1,000	500
Dependent........................	400	200	400	200
Total tax in millions of dollars:				
1936 act..........................	2,907	3,401	483	689
Schedule A........................	3,397	3,923	591	805
Schedule B........................	4,126	4,681	722	943
Schedule C........................	5,340	6,990	1,077	1,794

* This table is Table 7, p. 74, in *Facing the Tax Problem*, used by permission of the Twentieth Century Fund, Inc., publishers.

† For a normal tax at 4 per cent and for various surtax schedules and for incomes as returned for 1924, 1928, 1931, 1933, and 1934. The net income subject to normal tax and surtax is as defined by the Revenue Act of 1936, except that, up to the last two lines, the taxation of dividends under the normal tax and the effect of the undistributed profits tax are ignored. For details, see the memorandum by Susan Burr and William Vickrey on Federal income and estate tax estimates in the Twentieth Century Fund, *Studies in Current Tax Problems*.

"A personal income tax yielding, say, eight billions annually would represent a most difficult achievement; but it is by no means utopian."[3] He emphasizes that no great increases in revenue can be expected from the

[1] HEER, CLARENCE, "The Place of Personal Income Taxes in a Modern Fiscal System," *Annals*, January, 1936, pp. 78–86. Income taxes play a larger part in *Federal* finances. From 36 per cent of receipts in 1933 they rose to a maximum in the fiscal years 1934–1940 of 45 per cent in 1938. (A correction for a deduction made from total revenues yields a figure of 42 per cent in 1938.) *Treas. Bull.*, September, 1940, pp. 3, 12.

[2] Both American and British rates have been substantially modified since 1936, however, and exemptions have been lowered.

[3] SIMONS, HENRY C., *Personal Income Taxation*, p. 40.

higher income brackets, at least not without a general tightening up of the law and abolition of tax-exempt securities. He advocates an initial normal tax rate of about 20 per cent and a slight reduction in exemptions to $2,000 for married persons (now realized in the Act of 1940) and is of the opinion that the bulk of the increased revenue must come from those with incomes from $3,000 to $20,000.[1]

Prof. Shoup presents some rather elaborate estimates of revenue yields under various alternative schedules and with alternative assumptions made with respect to exemptions. These estimates apply to national incomes of different years. A portion of his table has been copied (Table I), showing the total revenues to be derived from the alternative sets of tax rates for 1928 and 1933 incomes, respectively.

It will be seen that the steepest tax schedule, combined with exemptions of $1,000 for married couples and $500 for single persons, could be expected to yield almost 7 billion dollars from a national income as large as 1928. (Neither Prof. Shoup nor the Twentieth Century Fund recommends the application of such a schedule.)

Prof. Shoup estimates that the total corporation income tax under the Revenue Act of 1936 would yield 2.6 billions in a year like 1928 and 0.6 billion in a year like 1933 (p. 84). (This is on the assumption of the continuance of the undistributed profits tax that was then in force and making certain assumptions favorable to the yield of that tax.)

Below is an abridged table giving revenues to be derived from the estate tax under alternative schedule rates for years similar to 1933 and 1930, respectively.

TABLE II.*—ESTIMATED YIELDS OF FEDERAL ESTATE TAXES ON VARIOUS ASSUMPTIONS†

(Yield figures in millions of dollars)

Rate schedule	Returns filed in 1933		Returns filed in 1930	
	Specific exemption		Specific exemption	
	$40,000	$10,000	$40,000	$10,000
1935 act..........................	180	228	603	685
Schedule A........................	308	380	983	1,107
Schedule B........................	534	671	1,559	1,789

* This table is Table 11, p. 87, in *Facing the Tax Problem*, used by permission of the Twentieth Century Fund, Inc., publishers.

† After deduction of credit for state taxes paid. Net estates are assumed as in returns filed during calendar years 1926, 1930, and 1933. For details, see the memorandum by Susan Burr and William Vickrey on Federal income and estate tax estimates in the Twentieth Century Fund, *Studies in Current Tax Problems*. The net estate, except where the specific exemption is given as $10,000, is as defined in the Revenue Act of 1926 as amended by later acts through 1936.

[1] *Ibid.*, pp. 219–220.

Yield here also depends upon the state of business conditions as is evident from the differences in the totals for 1930 and 1933.

Using the highest of these hypothetical tax schedules on estates and personal income and assuming that national income in 1980 will be *at least as high as that of the late twenties*, the Federal government could raise almost 9 billion dollars from these sources alone. At the present time (1940) they seem to yield only about 1½ billion dollars. The difference would go a long way toward meeting the costs of the social security program, the costs of a much larger debt, and even a small part of defense costs, unless these additional funds are diverted to other uses.[1]

The reader may be misled by the estimate of 9 billion dollars, which is a maximum figure. A more reasonable estimate of the yield of the personal income and estate taxes is 5 billion dollars:[2]

1. Schedule B of income tax for 1928.

2. Schedule B of estate tax for 1926.

3. Reduce to 5 billion dollars to allow for repercussions of rise of yield of one tax upon yield of the other two (see below), reduction of capital gains, etc.

In summary, then, a reasonable estimate of the yield of personal income and estate duties is roughly 3½ billion dollars *in excess* of the yield in 1939, and for corporation income taxes perhaps 1 billion dollars additional in excess of the yield of 1.1 billion dollars in the fiscal year 1939.[3] The anticipated rise of yield for these taxes may be put at 4½ billion dollars.

It is well also to consider the possibilities of a better integration of state, local, and Federal taxes; the plugging of loopholes in our present system; a rise of revenues through excess profits taxes (partly covered by legislation of 1940); the use of business or value added by manufacture taxes; a rise of yield in state and local taxes.[4] Much sentiment has been

---

[1] *Cf.* GROVES, H. M., *Financing Government*, p. 378. Prof. Groves suggests that additional revenues to be obtained from the income taxes will be required to balance the budget and help the states.

On the issues of this section, see especially the following:

Facing the Tax Problem, Twentieth Century Fund Inc.

Studies in Current Tax Problems, Twentieth Century Fund Inc. (Gives raw data and methods for previous volume.)

The National Debt and Government Credit, Twentieth Century Fund Inc.

SIMONS, H. C., *Personal Income Taxation*.

LUTZ, H. L., *Public Finance*, 3d ed.

Annals, January, 1936. Especially an article by Clarence Heer, "The Place of Personal Income Taxes in a Modern Fiscal System," pp. 78–86.

GROVES, *op. cit.*

WITHERS, W., *Financing Economic Security in the United States.*

[2] We are indebted to Prof. Carl Shoup for help with this estimate.

[3] *Treas. Dept. Bull.*, June, 1940, p. 18.

[4] *Cf.* WITHERS, *op. cit.*, pp. 89–101.

expressed for a tax on *value added*. Prof. Studenski, for example, concludes that a 1 per cent tax will yield 500 million dollars today and would be an excellent method of taxation on the basis of actual production which might well (though not always) be passed on to the consumer.[1] Additional yields from the sources enumerated in this paragraph may, however, have adverse effects upon the yields of the income taxes and estate duties; but another billion dollars may be forthcoming. In this discussion one should also keep in mind the relative tax burdens in terms of income and wealth. Both relative to income and wealth, tax burdens (before Second World War) in the United States are light in comparison with those borne in Great Britain and France.[2]

Since the above was written the Revenue Revision Bill of 1941 has been submitted to Congress. On the assumption of a 3.5 billion dollar tax bill, annual revenues should rise to 12 to 13 billion dollars, or 6 to 7 billion dollars in excess of the prewar figure; and even more can be raised. In a great emergency the Treasury may rely heavily on excess profits and excise duties; and moreover, under the stimulus of the war effort incomes have risen more than had been anticipated in these estimates.

11.7. SUMMARY

Future demands on the taxpayer are likely to increase. Two important sources of the increased strain are likely to be subsidies to the old-age account and the cost of servicing of the debt. If we assume that promises are to be kept, then the Federal government will require large additional revenues in the future. It is not clear, however, if we are to draw conclusions from the past, that the government of the future will be able to keep promises. In this connection, the failure to adhere to the original schedule of tax rates and the unwillingness to introduce maximum benefit rates at once are especially ominous.[3] Many reasons may be adduced for the in-

[1] STUDENSKI, P., "Towards a Theory of Business Taxation," *Jour. Pol. Econ.*, 1940, pp. 648–654.

[2] Twentieth Century Fund, *The National Debt and Government Credit*, pp. 99–105. The reader is also referred to the estimates (*ibid.*, pp. 141–155), which have been discussed in the opening chapter, of income, taxes, and expenditures in the forties.

[3] A critic may reply that the failure to pay maximum benefits at the outset is a sign of good faith: more will be available when the burden rises. This argument has some strength. But since the pay-as-you-go school relies on the argument that the burden should be financed out of current revenue and (hence) emphasizes the

troduction of Treasury subsidies which would assure the annuitants of promised benefits. Savings on old-age assistance and the extension of coverage are two points frequently made in favor of subsidies. It is clear now that coverage is more extensive than had been anticipated, and, therefore, the recourse to general revenues carries more appeal. It is said that it would be unfair to tax the many for the benefit of one-third or one-half of the workers. If a much larger proportion of the gainfully employed are covered, it is another matter. I am not, however, convinced by the argument that further subsidies should be forthcoming only if coverage is universal or well-nigh universal. For example, failure to obtain full coverage on account of administrative difficulties should not stand in the way of legislation that is otherwise desirable. Furthermore, now that the large reserve plan has been scrapped, the withholding of Treasury subsidies on the ground of inadequate coverage or on other grounds will jeopardize the program. Extension of coverage, which may well increase costs relative to benefits, is an additional reason for tapping general revenues.

In the not too distant future, the demands upon the state for old-age insurance and debt servicing may well come to 5 to 7 billion dollars. The pay-roll taxes will contribute only a few billions at the most. It is conceivable, however, on very favorable assumptions, that the yield of direct taxes may rise by 4 to 5 billion dollars; and conceivably another billion dollars could be raised through other fundamental changes in our tax system. Part of the slack has been taken up by the Revenue Act of 1940, however. Solvency of the Treasury will then be maintained if we can assume that other demands on the Treasury will be kept in check. On grounds of justice, moreover, it would be well to raise a large part of the required revenue through taxes on the relatively well off. Success in raising the required revenues will depend in no small part upon the use to which the revenue is put and the gradualness of the rise of the tax burden. Transfer expenditures, *e.g.*, old-age insurance and debt payments, will have *less* damaging effects than exhaustive expenditures.

The unfolding of the defense program with its heavy demands on the state suggests a more precarious fiscal position in the future than has so far been assumed. A sustained high level of income

independence of contributions and benefits, and since the cost of maximum benefits today would be small compared with their costs later (the proportion of old is small) they would have shown a more consistent attitude and have given evidence of good intentions had they insisted upon maximum benefits now.

(say at 100 billion dollars) and a radical revision of our tax system may, however, yield the required revenues, which may very roughly be put at 15 to 18 billion dollars. The costs will be even larger in the immediate future.[1]

Finally, one may be too optimistic concerning the beneficial effects of a rise of income. Undoubtedly the defense program will contribute toward a significant rise of income, and purely in terms of the effects upon income and tax capacity, the government's fiscal position may improve greatly. Against the rise of tax receipts, the economist must, however, put the additional burden on the budget both today and tomorrow. No one would be inclined to argue that a rise of income induced through the defense program will contribute toward a solution of the financial problems raised by our social security program in the same manner as an equal spontaneous rise in income. In short, Governor Eccles may compare the income of 40 billion dollars at the low point of the depression and Federal tax yields of 2 billions, and a later income of 70 billion dollars and tax receipts of 6 billion dollars, and in the near future income may well rise to 100 billion dollars or more as some Washington economists now predict. Tax revenues may then rise to 15 billion dollars or more; but how much will be available for social security? Federal expenditures, exclusive of insurance for example, may well rise to 20 billion dollars or more by the fiscal year 1942.

[1] *See* HARRIS, S. E., *The Economics of American Defense* (1941).

CHAPTER 12

SOCIAL SECURITY IN RELATION
TO PUBLIC DEBT

Adherents of the pay-as-you-go plan are naturally on the defensive on the issue of the cost to the national exchequer, for they propose to put the entire cost of old-age benefits on the taxpayer. Interest on reserves is not to contribute. Realizing that the weakness of their plan lies in the potential burden on the taxpayers, they take great pains to demonstrate that the reserve plan is also costly to the taxpayer.[1] Let us consider (1) the effects of the reserve plan on the interest rate paid by the government and (2) the effect upon the magnitude of the public debt.

12.1. EFFECTS OF THE PROVISION OF NEW MARKETS FOR PUBLIC SECURITIES ON THE COST OF TREASURY BORROWING

We turn then to the effects of the accumulation of reserves on the rate of interest.[2] For this discussion, the old-age reserve account

---

[1] It may be noted at this point that supporters of the pay-as-you-go school frequently justify increased participation of the Federal Treasury on the grounds that large savings on noncontributory old-age pensions are effected with the introduction of a contributory plan. Experts (see below) have estimated that the cost of old-age assistance to the Federal Treasury on the assumption that no contributory system is in effect will rise to 857 millions or possibly to 1,294 millions by 1980, the difference being explained by the amount of and conditions for Federal participation. May we also point out here that this particular argument for the pay-as-you-go plan loses force for the following reason. The popularity of the contributory pension plan is explained frequently by the increase of obstacles confronting those who attempt to impose noncontributory plans upon the taxpayer. Financial need then explains in part the increased popularity of contributory systems. Then why support (aside from nonfinancial considerations) a system of finance that puts a greater burden on taxpayers in general and particularly in the future than does the reserve system? *Social Security in America*, pp. 194, 197, 207; M. G. Schneider, *More Security for Old Age*, pp. 9, 29.

[2] *Cf.* Introduction, Secs. 1 and 2 and Secs. 5.1, 5.2 and 5.3.

is of crucial importance; but the growth of unemployment trust funds increases the significance of the considerations introduced here. In this connection, absorption of securities by other government agencies and trust funds is also relevant.

1. The reserve funds may be considered as a sink, which absorbs public securities and keeps them off the market. Interest rates on public securities, therefore, remain lower than they otherwise would be, the net effect being a large net saving for the Treasury on interest on public securities that remain on private *markets*.[1] (Present holders of course obtain a paper windfall as the rate declines; but new issues are made at lower rates and old issues are ultimately funded at lower rates.)

The process may be described in somewhat greater detail as follows. Employers and employees pay into these funds amounts in excess of current disbursements. In addition, public departments receive funds from other sources. The HOLC, for example, may receive cash in repayment of mortgages. In short, net savings rise; and these savings are directed into markets for public securities.[2] It also follows, since the money diverted into the markets for public securities comes from new savings (or new money), that the rate of interest on other securities is probably not affected adversely. Furthermore, the effects on rates in other security markets *may* be favorable because the lower rates stimulate the issue of public securities for the purpose of investment in fields that are competitive with private enterprise.

It seems safe to conclude that the creation of a new market, which may absorb 10 billions of public securities or more, is likely to have the effect of reducing the rate of interest on public securities and will tend to reduce the general structure of interest rates. A tendency toward lower rates in general will follow as those who sell public securities to the insurance funds and other public agencies seek other investments.[3] The problem of the effects of a decline in consumption upon investment and income and, therefore, upon savings via investment and income, is not considered here. This problem is discussed in Part I.

[1] The reader is referred to Sec. 9.4 for a discussion of the fallacy widely held, that the reserves involve the taxpayers in a double cost, *viz.*, the original taxes required in the accumulation of reserves and the taxes required to pay interest on these reserves.

[2] *Cf.*, however, Chap. 3 on Savings.

[3] The reader is referred to the introductory chapter, Sec. 1, for statistical material on cash and investments of governmental corporations and trust funds.

Although the rate of interest on public securities will probably be depressed by the accumulation of reserves, the net effect may not, however, be so great as at first seems probable. (1) Much depends upon the elasticity of private demand for public securities. Should present holders unload large quantities in response to a given rise in their price (decline in yield), the increase in initial demand will be accompanied by a relatively rapid adjustment of demand elsewhere. If, on the other hand, trustee laws and conservatism on the part of investors (for example) and the unavailability of substitutable assets make them reluctant to dispose of public securities, prices will rise rapidly and yields decline precipitously. Sales on the part of present holders are not, however, the only changes possible. The government may be strongly tempted, as we shall see presently, to issue new securities as the price offered becomes more attractive (*cf.* Sec. 5.10).[1] Moreover, private investors may find their requirements for safe, *i.e.*, adequately secured, assets satisfied by new issues on the part of private corporations that now find the gilt-edge market more attractive.

2. The question of monetary policy is relevant here. No one will doubt that the assumed need of keeping the yield on public securities down plays a part in the determination of monetary policy and, hence, of interest rates. As the insurance funds and other government agencies, however, provide a very large and growing market for government securities at a very satisfactory rate of interest, the need of keeping down money rates through monetary policy becomes less pressing. May we say parenthetically that in so far as the objective is cheap rates for the Treasury there is more to be said for a direct attack on the prices of public securities, *e.g.*, through the creation of these new markets, than for a more *general* attack on money rates through reduction of bond rates, lower reserve requirements, and the like. In short, the purchase of securities by official agencies may be considered an instrument for keeping down rates on public securities that may, to some extent, be substituted for direct monetary attacks. It follows, therefore, in so far as the provision of new markets is a substitute for further easing of rates through the intervention of the monetary authority, that the real

---

[1] Critics of the reserve principle, in our opinion, exaggerate the effects on public spending and borrowing of the provision of new markets for social security. *Cf.* Sec. 9.4; T. L. Norton, *Old Age and the Social Security Act*, pp. 91–92; *Hearings*, Ways and Means Committee, House of Representatives, *Social Security*, 1939, pp. 1136, 1271–1272.

effects of accumulation by public departments on yield of public securities will not be so great as they at first promise to be.

Finally, the availability of these artificial but valuable markets for public securities is likely to decrease resistance to a further increase in the public debt and, therefore, is likely to have the effect of increasing supplies of securities and, therefore, to that extent, of offsetting the increased demand. More on this later. We conclude nevertheless that the net effect will be lower rates than would have prevailed had not the Social Security Act (and other legislation having similar effects) provided new markets for public securities through the provision of cash seeking safe investments. Once more the reader is warned, however, that any general deflationary effects will tend to reduce savings and the demand for investments, the net effect on the rate of interest then depending also on the weight of these forces. What is more, a reduction in the rate of interest accompanied by a large decline in the volume of investment should not be considered a favorable outcome. The issues here are, however, the direct effects of the provision of new markets for public securities, not the broader issues of Part I.

Another aspect of the problem of the effects on the rate of interest requires consideration. It has been contended in some quarters that the Fund obtains a subsidy from the Treasury: the Act of 1935 provided a rate of 3 per cent on public securities held by the old-age fund although the rate in the last few years has fluctuated around $2\frac{1}{2}$ per cent. Current yields were, however, taken into account when the rate was set. (It is interesting to compare the 4 per cent rate stipulated on other trustee funds set up at an earlier period when rates were higher.) Although from 1935 to 1939 the stipulated rate on the old-age reserve was above the current rate, the history of rates in the last generation justifies the assumption of a normal rate above $2\frac{1}{2}$ per cent. It is not at all improbable that under the provisions in effect from 1935 to 1939 the Treasury rather than the Fund would ultimately have been subsidized. Unemployment trust funds, it need scarcely be added, receive a return equal to the market rate of interest on government securities.[1] In 1939, let us add, Congress provided for a *market return* on Treasury securities sold to the old-age account.[2]

Treasury subsidies involved in the stipulation of rates above the market (only possible in the years 1935–1939) are in any case

[1] *Cf. Soc. Sec. Bull.*, April, 1937, pp. 74–76.
[2] House Report 728, *Social Security Act Amendments*, 1939, p. 84.

to be set against the lowering of rates that follow the provision of new markets. Our earlier discussion is therefore decisive at this point. The creation of a market for public securities depresses their yield, and, therefore, the market rate is not an accurate guide of the degree of subsidization. Market rates may be 2 per cent and, therefore, it may seem that in paying 3 per cent (say) the Treasury subsidizes the funds to the extent of 1 per cent of its capital, or (say) 200 millions annually on a fund of 20 billions. If, however, the rate on government securities would have been 4 per cent in the absence of artificial support of the public security markets through large purchases by the Fund (or agencies), the Fund actually would have earned 200 million dollars more annually. In other words, the market rate is 2 per cent, the Treasury pays 3 per cent, the rate in the absence of provision of new demand would have been 4 per cent.

Perhaps the term "subsidy" is used loosely here. More accurately, the rate on public securities is depressed through the provision of new markets. This gain more than offsets any loss suffered by the Treasury through the payment of a higher return to the old-age fund than the market rate. Moreover, this reduction of rates applies to all public securities outstanding (not even exclusive of those, e.g., public trustee securities, which earn a fixed return—the rate fixed is related to the market rate which, in turn, has been depressed through the provision of new markets).

12.2. EFFECTS ON THE MAGNITUDE OF THE PUBLIC DEBT

Now let us consider the argument that the accumulation of social security reserves contributes to a growth of the public debt.[1] (1) It is clear that the obligations of the government will grow in so far as Congress fails to appropriate to the old-age account receipts from social security taxes, which are not required to cover administrative expenses, or interest on the reserves of social security accounts. The government incurs at least a moral obligation to meet later deficits of the social security accounts resulting from this failure to appropriate. It does not follow, however, that the Treasury will in fact

[1] See, for example, *Hearings*, Senate Committee on Finance, February, 1937, p. 16; "Old Age Reserve Account," *Quart. Econ. Jour.*, May, 1937, pp. 460–464; P. Douglas, "The United States Social Security Act," *Econ. Jour.*, March, 1936, p. 8.

repay loans obtained through failure to appropriate, for benefits may be reduced, contributions of the insured increased, or, finally, repayment to security accounts may not prove necessary. The last may occur if the estimates of costs of the actuaries prove to be excessive. Again, let us observe here that the appropriation of public security funds by the Treasury for purposes other than social security does not necessarily contribute toward a corresponding increase of public debt even if the government repays the Fund later with interest. Borrowing from other sources will almost certainly be reduced. Danger of misappropriation is reduced for the present, let us add, by the legislation of 1939, which provides for the management by trustees and more or less automatic appropriations.

2. Let us consider the effect on the public debt of the provision that the proceeds of social security taxes not required for current disbursements be invested in public securities. (We now assume that the proceeds are appropriated to social security accounts.) Three possible cases merit discussion. The first is (and this is the current practice) that the government issues securities to the security reserve accounts, the proceeds being used to meet current deficits of the government. Undoubtedly the tendency (though in our view not a very strong one) will be to stimulate recourse to deficit financing. Should the government in the next 10 or 20 years be forced to sell securities in the open markets, which otherwise might have been sold to trust and other departmental accounts, deficit financing would undoubtedly prove somewhat less attractive than would otherwise be the case.

A second possibility is that the social security receipts (in excess of disbursements) are used to buy public securities in the *open market*. Here again the effect is likely to be a stimulus toward deficit financing by the government. In this case, also, the rate of interest will be lower than it would otherwise be. The Treasury will be tempted to raise money and use the proceeds for investment in enterprises which become profitable with the reduction in the rate of interest on public securities. Housing, the substitution of government mortgages for private ones for farmers and home owners and the purchase of railroads are a few examples of the type of investment that may attract the government should the rate on public securities decline to (say) 1 per cent. It is scarcely necessary to add that in appraising the evils of the rise in public debt resulting from this decline in the rate of interest, the economist should consider as offsets the new assets held and any favorable effect of spending by the government on national income. We have now considered two possible cases. In both, the rate of interest tends to become more favorable for the Treasury, and more money is available for the purchase of public securities. In the first case discussed, a reduction of public issues on the market follows; in the second, a rise of demand for public securities on the market follows.

3. Our final assumption relates to the period when all public securities are held by reserve or trustee funds, receipts continuing to exceed current disbursements. In the discussion above, let us observe, it was assumed that the decline in the rate of interest tempted the Treasury to issue more securities, the proceeds being used in the manner indicated. Now we assume that the Treasury does not issue new securities until virtually all securities outstanding have been absorbed by the social security (or other) reserves.[1] At this point the Treasury, fearful of the consequences of hoarding cash, is under pressure to find new outlets of a profitable type for its social security (or other public) receipts. Some suggestions of the type of assets to be purchased are to be found in the preceding paragraph.[2] This solution is not, however, the only possible one. One possibility is a recourse to temporary borrowing from the Fund effected through a remission of taxation. Much is to be said for this solution, for the adverse effects on consumption following the influx of cash to the social security accounts may be offset to some extent by the remission of taxes. (This solution is, however, inconsistent with the assumption of a continued growth of reserves.)[3]

---

[1] *Cf.* ESCHER, G. E., JR., "An Analysis of the Long-term Consequences of the Social Security Act," *Commercial and Financial Chronicle*, December, 1937, pp. 3556–3558. The problem is simple for Mr. Escher. Since the reserve is to come to 47 billions and the current debt is 36 billions, the increase in the debt associated with the Security Act will be 11 billions.

[2] *Cf.* WYATT, B. E., and W. H. WANDEL, *The Social Security Act in Operation*, p. 164.

[3] The disturbing effects upon the money market of a disappearance of public securities are not discussed here. Clearly banks will have to find alternative investments or face bankruptcy. *Cf.* Norton, *op. cit.*, pp. 52–53; and L. H. Kimmel, "Social Security Finances," *N.I.C.B.*, *Bull.* 12, Nov. 19, 1937.

12.3. Effects on Redemption of Debt

It is also frequently argued that the provision of large social security reserves will interfere with the redemption of the public debt and, therefore, will contribute toward its maintenance at a high level.[1] Let us consider this argument which is relevant to the discussion of the effect of social security reserves upon the magnitude of the public debt.

Two possible lines of economic development may be considered. There is the possibility of a continuance of depressions and deficit financing. If the trend of long-term investment is downward and if a deficiency of demand is to continue long into the future, the repayment of public debt will be most unwise. Purchasing power will be taken from taxpayers who are potential purchasers of goods and turned over to the banks and other holders of public securities who, under the assumed conditions, are not inclined to invest these funds. A judicious policy would require at least that the deficiency of total spending should not be aggravated by the collection of taxes from potential spenders and the use of the proceeds for the increase of hoards. Actually, however, a continuance of secular stagnation (?) is likely to be accompanied by a rise of net debt.

The reader may object to the practice of accumulating reserves through the collection of pay-roll taxes in excess of current disbursements for social security in a period of depression on the same grounds on which we now object to the repayment of debt. He may contend that the taxpayer under the Social Security Act is also a potential consumer and, therefore, the use of proceeds of taxes for the purpose of accumulating reserves is to be condemned just as much as the collection of taxes for the redemption of public debt. Much is to be said for this viewpoint as the reader will recall from Part I. One significant point should not be overlooked, however. If the proceeds of taxes are used to accumulate reserves *and finance deficits of the government*, the recipient of the cash, *i.e.*, the government, is not likely to hoard. We assume that the cash paid into the social security reserves is used to buy *new* securities issued by the Treasury, whereas the cash received by the Treasury for debt redemption goes to present holders of public securities, *i.e.*, banks and other investors, who under assumed conditions of depression are

[1] Linton, M. A., "The Problem of Reserves for Old Age Benefits," *Am. Labor Legislation Rev.*, March, 1937, p. 24; Wyatt and Wandel, *op. cit.*, pp. 159–160; Mulford, H. P., *Incidence and Effects of the Payroll Tax*, pp. 45–47.

likely to hoard. Thus in the former case hoarding of tax receipts (in reserves) is offset by deficit spending; in the latter it is not. One further point should be made. It is quite reasonable to assume that the contribution toward inflationary spending, in periods in which secular stagnation prevails and yet reserves of public departments accumulate, will not be so great as when the public departments do not receive more than they pay out.

The main conclusion is that, in the event of a continuance of depressed conditions for many years, the public debt would continue to grow irrespective of any requirements of an adequate volume of eligible assets, *i.e.*, public securities, for investment of reserve funds, and, therefore, the growth of social security reserves would not be a decisive factor in perpetuating a large public debt. At any rate, in such periods should both stagnation and surplus financing by the Treasury be practical, it would be folly to accept this policy of paying off debt at the expense of private spending.

What is to be said concerning the redemption of debt if prosperity rules in the future, and the government is, therefore, able to redeem public debt out of surpluses of revenue? It is contended that if the social security reserves require public securities for purchase the government may well fail to take advantage of favorable conditions for redemption of debt, preferring to provide the social security funds with proper investments. It is even possible that a rise of debt may be involved. Let us consider this argument. (1) It is possible that the security (and other) funds may find adequate public securities on private markets and, therefore, the Treasury may not be under pressure to discourage redemptions or to provide new issues. A most important consideration here is the eventual size of the reserves. (2) Congress may broaden eligibility laws, allowing the reserve accounts, for example, to purchase additional types of trustee assets or keep deposits with banks. (In the latter case, however, earnings may fall greatly.) It would not then be necessary to keep public securities outstanding for the convenience of the social security reserves. (3) The Treasury may yield to the temptation of issuing securities for the convenience of the social security funds, using the proceeds to purchase income yielding assets. A failure to redeem debts under these circumstances is not necessarily unwise: the rise of the public debt may well be fictitious. Against additional debt outstanding, assets of equal value may be held.

The creation of the social security reserves (and other public accounts) may have unfortunate effects upon the magnitude of the public debt, however, if it provides the opportunity for a policy of *tax* reduction when the fundamental economic conditions are appropriate to debt redemption. The redemption of debt is, however, the exception, not the rule, in modern times. A decision to pay off debt or reduce taxes should not be made according as the reserve funds have or have not an adequate volume of public securities at their disposal; and if the decision is made on these criteria, the opponents of the reserves score an important point. It should be noted at this point, however, that the availability of insurance or agency funds as markets for public securities is a factor that weighs against debt redemption.[1] As the market grows, one argument against redemption becomes stronger. It is well to distinguish these two points: (1) The social security reserves constitute an important and more or less permanent market for government securities, and, therefore, the argument of potential depreciation in favor of redemption carries less weight than formerly. (2) The decision, on the one hand, to redeem debts or, on the other, to reduce taxes is to be made on the basis of an examination of numerous considerations including that of the availability of new markets for public securities. In the formulation of this policy, the issue of public securities for the convenience of social security funds should play only a small part.

12.4. The Cost of Retirement of Debt

One further point may be made against debt redemption, *viz.*, the vast cost of a program of debt retirement.[2] Calculations below make it clear that the redemption of debt over a period of 25 years will increase the cost of debt servicing from 1 billion yearly to a sum in excess of 2 billions. Even under relatively prosperous conditions (as viewed from the pessimistic horizon of 1939) the burden of new social security programs and debt retirement may be too much for the taxpayer. [A current debt (net) of 40 billions is assumed.][3]

There are of course many ways of amortizing a given liability over a period of years. A possible method is the liquidation of identical amounts

[1] *Cf.* Hohaus, R. A., "Observations on Financing Old Age Security," *Trans. Actuarial Soc. Am.*, May, 1937, p. 129; Wyatt and Wandel, *op. cit.*, p. 163.

[2] Mrs. Marian Crawford Samuelson did an important part of the work in the next two sections.

[3] The debt in June, 1941, is much larger than when these calculations were made, and therefore the costs of redemption are underestimated here.

of debt each year. This procedure would, however, involve a relatively heavy burden at the beginning of the period, for interest charges would decline *pari passu* with the repayment of debt. It is preferable, therefore, to apply the sinking-fund principle, which provides for an equalization of the total burden over time, the amount of debt retired being small in the early years when interest charges are high and large toward the end when interest charges are low.

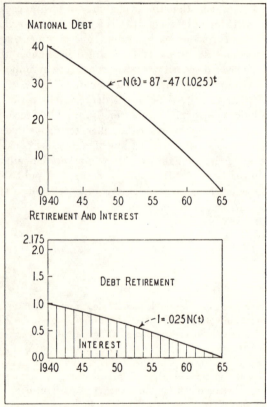

CHART I.—Debt, debt retirement, interest payments.
(Unit: billion dollars.)

Let us set 1940, the beginning, as $t = 0$ and 1965, the end, as $t = 25$. Then the debt will be given by the formula $D(t) = 87 - 47(1.025)^t$.[1] The total will amount to 40 billions at the beginning and zero at the end.

[1] *Cf.* RIETZ, H. L., A. R. CRATHORNE, and J. C. RIETZ, *Mathematics of Finance*, 1932 ed., Chap. VII.

Chart I is appended showing the course of the debt, of interest, and of retirement.

If the debt had not been retired at all, the cost to the Treasury for interest would have been exactly 1 billion per year, or 25 billions over the period. Retirement of the debt in the preceding manner reduces total interest payments for *this period* to 14.375 billions, yielding a net saving in interest of 10.625 billions.

Against the saving in interest, we must add the increase in the total fiscal burden on account of repayment of debt. The total burden on the Treasury for *retirement plus interest* is found to be 2.175 billions per year, more than twice as much as the cost of *interest payments*. For the whole period the Treasury's disbursements for the servicing of the public debt would amount to 54.375 billions of which 40 billions would be for retirement and the remainder for interest.

A summary table presenting the results of this calculation is given.

TABLE I.—COST OF DEBT RETIREMENT
(In billions of dollars)

	If no debt retirement	If debt retirement
Interest payments per year..................	1	Vary according to* 0.025 $[87 - 47(1.025)^t]$
Debt retirement per year..................	0	Varies according to* 0.025 $[47(1.025)^t]$
Total burden per year...................	1	2.175
Interest payments for 25-year period........	25	14.375
Debt retirement for 25-year period..........	0	40
Total burden for 25-year period..........	25	54.375

* Actual yearly figures can be computed.

Savings in interest payments for 25-year period = 25 − 14.375 = 10.625 billions.
Increase in total burden on the Treasury per year = 2.175 − 1 = 1.175 billions.
Increase in total burden on Treasury for 25-year period = 54.375 − 25 = 29.375 billions.

12.5. ESTIMATES OF NATIONAL DEBT ON VARIOUS ASSUMPTIONS

In the preceding chapter the argument proceeded on the assumption that the annual interest charge would not be in excess of 1 to 2 billion dollars. Such estimates may well prove to be optimistic. Public debt may rise at a rapid rate for the next few generations. In view of the growth of debt at an average annual rate in excess of 3 billion dollars since 1933, an estimate of growth by the amount of interest charges does not seem to be unreasonable. In a later part of this section the growth of debt is estimated.

If debt should rise by the amount of the interest charge (*i.e.*, at compound interest and on the assumption of a rate of interest of 3 per cent), it would rise to 130 billion dollars in 1980 and 236 billions in the year 2000, the respective interest charges then being 3.9 and 7 billions (C'' on Chart III). Before the debt attains these heights, however, some form of repudiation may possibly be introduced. For more pessimistic estimates, see A'' and B''. One may also make more optimistic estimates. For example, the debt may be repaid between 1955 and 1960 on the assumption of an annual surplus over all expenditures including interest of 3 billion dollars (F'' in Chart III). These assumptions (F'' and E'') are, however, not to be taken seriously. An annual reduction of but 1 billion dollars seems out of the question now. Whatever the assumptions, the possibilities of a large rise in the public debt which may possibly jeopardize the social security program are not to be dismissed too lightly. Repudiation at a relatively early stage may then be the only means of saving the security program. Social security will undoubtedly contribute greatly, let us add, to the rise of public debt though it may not necessarily be the decisive factor in aggravating the danger of repudiation of debt. These are, however, dangers of the distant future; and, despite the defense program, a public debt of 100 to 200 billion dollars still seems to belong to the future.

We have prepared a number of alternative estimates of the possible magnitude of the national debt at future dates under two general hypotheses concerning the behavior of future expenditure and revenue. Under the first hypothesis we assume that the expenditure of the Federal government, exclusive of interest charges on outstanding debt (E_t), plus such interest charges (iN_t) always exceeds or falls short of tax revenues (T_t) by a constant amount each year, *i.e.*, $E_t + iN_t - T_t =$ a constant (i = rate of interest). The constant can be positive, negative, or zero, and we have chosen round billions varying from -2 billions per year to $+2$ billions per year, giving five estimates in all. For simplicity the interest rate is assumed to be 3 per cent throughout.

In this case the national debt increases or decreases each year by the constant amount so that its behavior through time is linear. In Chart II the national debt is plotted with approximate accuracy. With the aid of the right-hand vertical scale the amount of interest charges can be read off. (In order to save space, the table is not reproduced.)

The second set of estimates is based upon a qualitatively different type of hypothesis. It is now assumed that the total expenditures *exclusive of interest charges* exceed or fall short of tax revenues by a constant amount, regardless of interest charges. ($E_t - T_t =$ constant.) Under the second hypothesis, the expenditures are in excess of those under the first hypothesis by the amount of the interest charge. Thus assume that constant $= 4$ billion dollars, the revenue $= 5$ billion dollars, and the interest charge $= 1$ billion dollars. Then under (1) E_t (8B) $+ iN_t$ (1B) $- T_t$ (5B) $= 4$B. Under

(2) E_t then = 9 billion ($9 - 5 = 4$). E_t under (2) then is 1B > E_t under (1) and the 1 billion = interest charge. If tax revenues exceed expenditures by more than the interest charges on the existing debt at the beginning of the period, the debt will be retired according to sinking-fund principles, *i.e.*, the interest charges of any period plus the debt retirement are equal to a

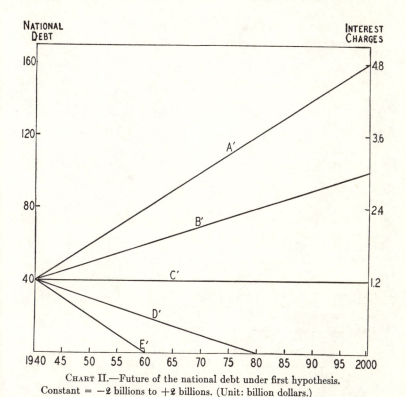

CHART II.—Future of the national debt under first hypothesis.
Constant = -2 billions to $+2$ billions. (Unit: billion dollars.)

constant. In the beginning when the first of these terms is relatively large, debt retirement will proceed slowly. As the outstanding debt decreases, interest charges will diminish and retirement will become more rapid.

If the excess of tax revenues over expenditures exclusive of interest charges falls short of the interest charge on the initial national debt, instead of the debt being retired, it will increase at an accelerated rate as determined by the compound-interest law. The national debt must obey the following law:

[275]

ΔN_t = the same constant $+ iN_t$ where ΔN_t is the increase in the debt from the year t to the year $t + 1$. The second hypothesis perhaps provides the more appropriate basis for extrapolation.

In Chart III estimates of the national debt at the end of each five-year interval following 1940 are represented for numerical values of the preceding

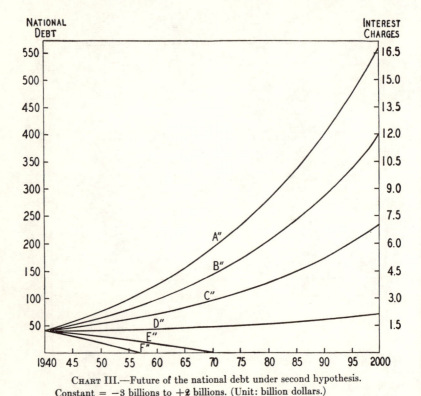

CHART III.—Future of the national debt under second hypothesis.
Constant = −3 billions to +2 billions. (Unit: billion dollars.)

constant ranging from −3 billion to +2 billion per year. The interest charges for each year are also included. In the preparation of this diagram values of the debt for years within the five-year interval have been interpolated by straight lines, resulting in a slight distortion of such intermediate estimates. (Once more the tables are omitted.)

There are various problems of definition that must be faced in the analysis of the national debt and the government budget. For example, how should we treat United States bonds held by the government itself?

What about bonds guaranteed by the government, but issued by special agencies (RFC, etc.)? In computing expenditures, how shall appropriations to accounts be treated? These questions must be answered more or less arbitrarily according to the purpose in view. The answers are not given here.

12.6. CONCLUSION

What are the net results of this discussion? (1) The government undoubtedly gains from the reserve program through a reduction in the rate of interest. Fortunate holders of Treasury issues during the period of appreciation of public securities also gain, however. A decline in the rate of interest associated with the creation of an artificial market for Treasury bonds through purchases by reserve and agency funds, it should be observed, will probably be transmitted to other bond markets. Less government bonds are available for private interests and, therefore, they seek other bonds; and, furthermore, the Treasury may be more disposed to compete in private fields of investment. Again, prices of public securities will rise more, the more inelastic the supplies, *i.e.*, the less the public is tempted to sell and the Treasury to issue new securities in response to the bribe of higher prices. Whatever gains through a reduction in the rate of interest are obtained, may not, however, constitute a net gain; the creation of new markets for Treasury issues may serve in part merely as a substitute for the use of monetary weapons for reducing the cost of Treasury financing.

We have dwelt above upon the effect of the social security funds upon the magnitude of the public debt. Three possible cases may be discussed. First, the Treasury may fail to appropriate to social security accounts the proceeds of pay-roll taxes. The net effect is not necessarily a corresponding rise in debt, for the Treasury may reduce other issues by a corresponding amount. Furthermore, the Treasury may modify rates of benefits and contributions, thus "raiding" the security funds.

2. Assume that the social security funds can purchase required public securities on the market. (No raids are assumed here.) The provision of a new market for Treasury issues may then stimulate deficit financing to some extent, and may induce the government to

embark upon new enterprises. Any relative rise of debt is, however, to be put against the value of new assets acquired.

3. The Treasury may be forced to issue securities to the social security accounts when issues are no longer available on the market. Should a remission of taxation follow, the accumulation of reserves may be held to be the explanation of a growth of the public debt. Another alternative may be suggested here, *viz.*, a broadening of eligibility rules which would make available other investments for the funds, and, therefore, which would remove the need of special Treasury issues for social security. Should the Treasury, however, issue securities to the funds, the rise of debt once more is to be put against any assets acquired with the cash received from the reserve funds.

4. Finally, the problem of the relation of social security funds to debt redemption arises. In periods of depression, the problem of debt repayment is not likely to arise. The provision of a new market for Treasury issues, let us add, is most welcome in a depression. In prosperous periods, it is more likely that debt redemption will suffer. It should be observed, however, that an adequate volume of public securities may be available on private markets for purchase by the Treasury, and, therefore, the pressure to maintain debt for the convenience of the Social Security Board may not be present. Even if the funds require investments in excess of the amounts available on the market, the broadening of eligibility rules may solve the problem, *e.g.*, the funds may be allowed to buy other gilt-edge securities. Treasury expansion in the field of private investments is still another way out. In other words, the public debt may rise; but the favorable terms obtainable as a result of the creation of new markets may justify a rise of debt and the governmental expansion into new fields of enterprise.

Undoubtedly the public debt will rise if large pension and unemployment funds are provided. The net cost may not, however, be great. The policy of debt reduction versus tax reduction should be determined largely irrespective of the availability of these new markets for public securities. But it is necessary to add that the creation of new markets of great significance certainly removes one important argument for debt redemption, *viz.*, a fear for the government credit. A second argument against debt redemption even in periods of prosperity is the cost involved. We estimate the net cost of redemption of 40 billion dollars of debt over a period of 25 years at approximately 30 billions.

In so far as the rising costs of social security are to be put upon the general revenues of the government, the danger of significant increases in public debt grows. Furthermore, the rise of debt may follow from other causes also; and in the general picture, the provision of special markets for public securities may play a relatively small part. Significant increases in the cost of social security may, however, account for an important part of the rise of the debt; and the rise of debt may in turn jeopardize the social security program. Repudiation of debt to which the growth of social security costs contributed may then in some manner or other be the only way of saving at least part of the social security program. My estimates of growth of public debt on various assumptions are not to be taken too seriously in this connection. They do, however, give some indication of the arithmetic of the problem. Long before the public debt would rise to the heights suggested under some of the more pessimistic assumptions, the debt or some of the terms of the social security program would be repudiated.

As I read these lines for the last time in June, 1941, the government announces that the 1942 Federal budget is likely to call for expenditures of 23 billion dollars; and the estimate of revenues is but 11 to 12 billion dollars. At least for a number of years, the debt, under the influence of the defense program, is likely to rise much more than is assumed under the least favorable assumptions in the text.

PART III
INCIDENCE AND EFFECTS OF PAY-ROLL TAXES

INTRODUCTION TO PART III

The nontechnical reader who wishes to skip over technical matters can read this introduction and the conclusion of Part III. He may find Chaps. 15, 19, and 20 troublesome and may be satisfied with reading only the conclusions to these chapters.[1]

Under current legislation, pay-roll taxes will reach a maximum of 9 per cent; but as the cost of the program rises, the maximum may well reach a much higher figure. (Where provision is made for taxes on workers, the maximum is more than 9 per cent even under present legislation.) It is well, therefore, to consider the problem of the incidence of annual taxes of 3 to 4 billion dollars, or (possibly) even more.[2] An *ultimate* pay-roll of 50 billion dollars or more and a tax rate *on employers* of 6 per cent, or even more, is assumed here. In addition there is the problem of the 3 (?) per cent tax on employees. This problem is not without significance for our analysis in Parts I and II. In the former, the issue of deflationary effects of the security program received our attention. For the extent of the deflation will depend in no small part upon the incidence of the taxes. If high-income classes bear the ultimate costs, and if oversavings are characteristic of the period, the effects will be beneficial; but if labor and other poor consumers pay ultimately, the effects on consumption and (then) on investment may well be unfavorable. It will also be recalled that the effects of the program upon the monetary situation, *e.g.*, the distribution of deposits, is related to incidence. In Part II, the issue of reserve financing received much attention. Opposition to reserves has grown partly because they are associated with pay-roll taxes. This opposition would weaken if it became clear that in the long run labor shifts an important part of these taxes to other groups; and less enthusiasm would then be shown for shifting the

---

[1] And Secs. 15.1, 15.2, and 20.1.

[2] The term "incidence" is used rather broadly here. The inquiry is not restricted to an investigation of who pays, but is also concerned with the effects upon demand for commodities and services and upon the supply of the factors of production. In its broadest sense, incidence deals with all the economic repercussions of a tax, and, therefore, an important part of the discussion in Parts I and II may be considered as part of the problem of incidence broadly considered. *Cf.* D. Black, *The Incidence of Income Taxes*, 1939, pp. 119–126.

tax burden directly to income, corporation, inheritance taxes, and the like.

In the opening chapter (13), a survey of the literature on the subject is given. This is followed by an elaboration of the accepted position (which is based on the marginal productivity theory) that the tax is either shifted to labor via a reduction of wage rates, or else employment suffers (14). From this point, the discussion turns to recent developments in the theory of wages, which focuses attention upon the effects of wage movements on monetary conditions, the rate of interest, and effective demand. A rise of the wage rate, unaccompanied by changes in physical productivity, is found to be quite consistent with an unchanged volume of employment (15). Chapter 16 deals briefly with monetary aspects of the problem. In the orthodox treatment, the assumption of an unchanged MV is convenient but not helpful or realistic. In fact, the security program is responsible, in itself, for changes in MV. A discussion of monetary aspects is a good starting point for a consideration of the possibilities of shifts of the taxes forward to consumers (17). Then the effects of the security program upon competitive conditions, output, and employment are given some attention (18). In Chap. 19, we consider the significance of the theory of monopolistic competition for our problem. Since the theory of incidence is generally based on the assumption of competitive conditions, it is necessary to modify accepted conclusions according as supply or demand conditions are less than perfectly elastic. The issues of substitution and complementarity are reserved for a separate chapter (20). Too much has been made of the threat of substitution of other factors for the high-price factor (labor) following the imposition of heavy pay-roll charges; and the presence of complementary relations between factors has been neglected in discussions of incidence. In the last chapter (21), a brief analysis of some of the international aspects of the problem is presented.

CHAPTER 13

A SURVEY OF VIEWS

13.1. CLASSICAL POSITION

Economists who, in the years preceding the introduction of the Social Security Act, had given the problem of incidence careful consideration seem to have been in general agreement that a pay-roll tax, whether levied on the worker or the employer, would be paid ultimately by the worker.[1] These writers were, however, ready to admit that frictional influences ought to be considered. Thus, Prof. Meriam, in a well-balanced statement, pointed out that if wages were tending upward the charge might be absorbed without an increase in unemployment; but if the tendency were downward, the net result might well be a reduction in employment.[2]

Pointing to the presence of frictional influences, Mr. Cohen suggested that the adjustment might be made through changes in the classification of workers, modification in hours, and the like, rather than by a direct assault on earnings. The general position of these writers is, however, that the burden would be put upon the worker, for the wage scale is determined by the net marginal contribution of the worker, and if the employer has to pay insurance or old-age taxes, he would pay as much for labor plus these taxes as previously he had paid for wages alone.[3]

[1] PIGOU, A. C., *Industrial Fluctuations*, 2d ed., pp. 372–373, and *Theory of Unemployment*, pp. 90, 249; BROWN, H. G., *Economics of Taxation*, especially pp. 141–171; MERIAM, R. S., "Unemployment Reserves: Some Questions of Principles," *Quart. Jour. Econ.*, February, 1933, especially pp. 313–319; COHEN, J. L., "The Incidence of the Costs of Social Insurance," *Internat. Labor Rev.*, 1929, pp. 820–836; *Hearings*, Senate Finance Committee (74: 1), *Economic Security Act*, 1935, pp. 448–453.

[2] What Prof. Meriam had in mind at this point was that insurance charges were easily passed on to the worker when wages tended upward; for wages would not rise so much as they otherwise would. When wages tended downward, however, it was difficult to depress wages further than would otherwise have been necessary. A rise of unemployment was therefore associated with the failure in the depression to pass the pay-roll taxes on to workers.

[3] A. C. Pigou (*Theory of Unemployment*, pp. 84–97, 149–153, 249) assumes that the dole (in his terminology the dole includes insurance charges) is passed on to the

[285]

13.2. Recent Views—Emphasis on Short-run Considerations

In the years that have passed since the Social Security Act became law, the weight of informed opinion still seems to be that the pay-roll tax is borne largely by the workers.[1] There seems to be little disposition to question the ultimate incidence on the workers of that part of the tax which is actually assessed on the worker. A distinction may be made according as the employer or employee pays in the first instance. The consensus of views on the tax paid by the employer is that the wage earner pays at least part through a reduction of wages and that the consumer (and wage earner *qua* consumer) pays part through a rise of prices.[2] Writers also occasionally comment on the varying effects on prices according as conditions are competitive or monopolistic, and according to the unequal effects of the tax upon different industries or firms. It may be said also that in the discussion since 1935 the emphasis has been put to a greater extent on short-run considerations, and the importance of

---

workers. Nevertheless when he considers the problem of elasticity of real demand for labor, he argues that the elasticity will be high because the additional wage bill, following a reduction in wages, can be financed to a considerable part by savings on the "dole." If, however, the employer does not bear the cost of the dole, he clearly does not save on the dole through a reduction of unemployment following a cut in wages.

[1] In the most comprehensive statement of the issues in recent years, Prof. Hall concludes that the tax is borne largely by the workers. His position is that the entrepreneur will not pay because, among other reasons, tax-exempt firms do not play an important part in determining prices, and, therefore prices will be determined by taxed enterprises. (The inference is that the bulk of producers will pay taxes and lower wages; and we are told that consumers' freedom to substitute untaxed or less highly taxed commodities is limited.) Yet when the discussion turns to the burden borne by consumers, Prof. Hall rejects the view that consumers pay. Now he emphasizes the fact that the tax is on surpluses as well as on margins; that distributive shares are not rigid and inelastic and, therefore, wage earners pay; and that collective demand for goods and services of taxed industries is not highly inelastic. J. K. Hall "Incidence of Federal Social Security Pay Roll Taxes," *Quart. Jour. Econ.*, November, 1938, pp. 38–63.

[2] *Cf.*, however, the interesting analysis of Prof. Slichter who contends that, in the short run, nonlabor short-period marginal costs and prices rise, output and employment decline, and profits therefore fall. Then a consideration of monetary aspects of the problem and trade unionism confirms Prof. Slichter in his conclusion that employment declines and wages may rise to some extent, and unfavorable effects may also be felt by capital. S. H. Slichter, "The Impact of Social Security Legislation upon Mobility and Enterprise," *Am. Econ. Assoc.*, 1940, especially pp. 52–58.

shifts to consumers in higher prices is stressed much more than in the classical exposition of the pre-Social Security Act era.[1]

13.3. THE POPULAR POSITION—CONSUMERS AND ENTREPRENEURS PAY

A popular position is that the charge on pay-rolls is either borne by industry or that it is passed on by industry to the consumer.[2] Official America frequently takes the position that the pay-roll tax, at least in so far as it is levied on the employer, is not passed on to the wage earner. Popularity of insurance proposals with labor as well as with the government is largely to be explained by the position, taken by these groups, that the pay-roll tax is passed on to the consumer or remains as a charge on industry.[3] Labor spokesmen do not even seem to be aware of the fact that what the laborer

---

[1] On these issues, see "Report of the Committee on Social Security Legislation and Administration," *Proceedings of Thirtieth Annual Conference of the National Tax Association*, 1937, pp. 66–67; BURNS, E. M., "Financial Aspects of the Social Security Act," *Am. Econ. Rev.*, March, 1936, pp. 14–16; *Hearings*, Ways and Means Committee, House of Representatives, *Social Security*, 1939, pp. 956–957; BAUDER, R., "The Probable Incidence of Social Security Taxes," *Am. Econ. Rev.*, September, 1936; MILLIS, H. A., and R. E. MONTGOMERY, *Labor's Risk and Social Insurance*, pp., 162, 177–182; DOUGLAS, P. H., "Payroll Taxes and Coordinated Program for Old Age Protection," *Social Security in the United States*, 1938, p. 142; also his *Theory of Wages*, p. 81; and *Hearings*, Ways and Means Committee, House of Representatives, *Economic Security Act*, 1935, pp. 1087–1088; NORTON, T. L., *Old Age and the Social Security Act*, pp. 38–41; SHOUP, C., "Taxing for Social Security," *Annals*, March, 1939, p. 168. For a skeptical view or at least for one that emphasizes the wide diffusion of the incidence of the tax, see I. M. Rubinow, "State Pool Plans and Merit Rating," *Law and Contemporary Problems*, January, 1936, pp. 78–79.

[2] *Cf. Hearings*, Senate Finance Committee, *Economic Security Act*, 1935, pp. 263–264, 275–276, 285–286; *Royal Commission on Unemployment Insurance*, 1932, Minutes of Evidence, p. 381; CLAY, H., "Unemployment and Wage Rates," *Econ. Jour.*, 1928, p. 3.

[3] Thus Miss Perkins says that the worker is unable to pay, and the implication is that the consumer pays. (*Hearings*, Senate Finance Committee, *Economic Security Act*, 1935, pp. 114–115.) Secretary Morgenthau argues that the masses pay. (*Hearings*, Ways and Means Committee, House of Representatives, *Economic Security Act*, 1935, p. 900.) Workers are unable to pay, according to Mr. Green, and therefore a tax levied on the employer will be paid ultimately by the consumer. (*Hearings*, Senate Finance Committee, *Economic Security Act*, 1935, p. 164; also see p. 229.) The House Committee vacillates between the position that the cost is borne by

gains from benefit payments contributed by other classes he may
lose in part as a consumer through rises in prices. (Prices may rise
because the businessman cuts production and succeeds in passing the
tax on to the consumer.[1]) We do not mean to imply that the workers
who receive no benefits, *e.g.*, the employed, obtain nothing. They
gain because they feel more secure; and note that under the old-age
program survivorship benefits are important. British labor interests, on the other hand, hold that insurance is a charge on industry
and thus contributes toward a reduction of employment and output;
they argue, therefore, that the charge should be distributed widely
through general taxation.[2]

Employers in the United States as well as in Great Britain take
the position that the pay-roll taxes are a charge on industry and
that they are passed on to the consumer and to labor, or (and)
account for the substitution of machines, or result in a diminution
of enterprise. They are especially troubled by the fact that the taxes
are levied on entrepreneurs making losses as well as gains, and by
the fact that these taxes raise serious difficulties for entrepreneurs
selling products for which the demand is elastic, and for those whose

the entrepreneur and that it is passed on to the consumers. House Report 615,
Committee on Ways and Means, 1935, pp. 8, 16.

An agnostic view is taken by Prof. Witte ("Social Insurance and the Price
Level," *Jour. Pol. Econ.*, 1937, p. 26); and in *Social Security in America* (p. 375).
the official commentator merely points out that consumers, employers, and laborers
will share the burden and that the exact distribution of the burden is not predictable.

[1] Thus at hearings on an earlier occasion, Mr. Green offered the parallel of the
workmen's compensation acts which, when they were being introduced, were commonly analyzed as levies that would ultimately come out of wages. They have,
however, in his view, been absorbed by industry. (*Hearings*, Subcommittee of Ways
and Means (73: 2), *Unemployment Insurance*, 1934, pp. 259–260; also see pp. 100–
101.) *Cf.*, however, W. Green, "Why Labor Opposes Forced Worker Contributions
in Job Insurance," *Am. Labor Legislation Rev.*, 1934, pp. 101–105.

[2] *Royal Commission on Unemployment Insurance*, 1931, Minutes of Evidence,
p. 968. The commission seems to have been of a similar opinion. *Report*, pp. 101,
353.

One American writer argues that when profits are large the entrepreneur may
bear the burden of the pay-roll tax (E. L. Dulles, *Financing the Social Security Act*,
p. 55). Another contends that when business is in a strong position, or in the early
stages of the imposition of the taxes, management may absorb the tax (H. P. Mulford, *Incidence and Effects of the Pay-roll Tax*, Social Security Board, Preliminary
Report, pp. 25–27). *Cf.* G. Colm and F. Lehmann, *Economic Consequences of Recent
American Tax Policy*, p. 38. "The possibility that the taxes will be paid mainly
at the expense of profits can be dismissed as improbable, as a consideration of the
sums involved, will show."

wage bills are especially large.[1] These objections may of course be raised against many other taxes.

The results of an interesting questionnaire sent to 200 Texas businesses are of some interest here.[2] One should, however, not rely too much on the 84 replies; for businessmen do not always act in the manner indicated in their replies to questionnaires. Furthermore, those who did not reply may well have been more sympathetic with the Act than those who did. These replies indicate that business is of the opinion that it passes the pay-roll taxes on to labor and consumers, that profits are affected adversely, that the effects are greater in discouraging expansion than in inducing contraction and in preventing increases of wages rather than in making direct assaults on wages.

TABLE I.—REPLIES TO A QUESTIONNAIRE SENT TO 200 TEXAS BUSINESS UNITS

Questions	Yes	No
Has the tax kept you from adding men to your pay-roll?	20	57
Has the tax caused you to reduce your labor force?	13	61
Has the tax caused you to install laborsaving machinery?	26	40
Has the tax caused you to reduce wages?	1	72
Has the tax kept you from raising wages?	25	49
Has the tax reduced your profits?	75	2
Has the tax added to your accounting expense?	71	10
Has it caused you to raise prices?	28	44
Has the tax caused you to abandon or postpone expansion?	32	44
Did the tax help cause the present recession (1937–1938)?	30	31

Economists then have been inclined toward the position that the tax is borne ultimately by labor. Since 1935, they have, however, paid increasing attention to short-run effects though the general position is unshaken. In the short run, part of the costs will be borne by consumers and management. Labor frequently takes the position that consumers or management pays, although its spokesmen seem not always to be aware that in paying higher prices real wages are reduced. Wage earners are likely to evaluate the benefits of in-

[1] See for example National Association of Manufacturers of the U. S. A., *Unemployment Insurance Handbook*, p. 123; *British Commission on Unemployment Insurance*, 1931, Minutes of Evidence, p. 1009; *Hearings*, Senate Finance Committee, *Economic Security Act* (74: 1), 1935, pp. 783, 922–924, 942; and *Hearings*, Ways and Means Committee, House of Representatives, *Economic Security Act*, 1935, p. 1092.

[2] ROOT, T. C., "The Effects of the Social Security Taxes on Business," *Southwestern Soc. Sci. Quart.*, September, 1938, pp. 129–139.

surance at less than their monetary costs and are inclined to feel that they are exploited if their wages are reduced by an amount equal or nearly equal to the payments made by the entrepreneur as an employer or taxpayer. Management contends that labor or the consumers pay and, failing efforts to pass the tax on, enterprise is reduced.

In the discussion of incidence, it is well to distinguish the tax paid by the employer from that paid directly by labor. Undoubtedly labor will find greater difficulties in forcing others to share the latter costs than the former. Under the unemployment insurance, the employer pays 3 per cent and labor as a rule pays nothing. (Actually under experience rating the payments by employers may be more than or less than 3 per cent though the average should be about 3 per cent.) Under old-age insurance, both employers and employees are to pay 3 per cent eventually. The ultimate rates may in fact be much larger or possibly smaller.

CHAPTER 14

THE CLASSICAL THEORY OF INCIDENCE OF PAY-ROLL TAXES

14.1. THE MARGINAL PRODUCTIVITY THEORY

Before proceeding to a brief discussion of the classical theory of incidence of a tax on pay-rolls which has been presented most ably and most lucidly by Prof. H. G. Brown, we discuss the marginal productivity theory, which is the basis of the classical treatment of the subject.[1] It is stated that wages equal the marginal value product of labor (or marginal revenue product), *i.e.*, the difference in the value of the product obtained and that which would have been obtained with an identical number of units of cooperative factors had one less man been employed. As Prof. Hicks points out, marginal product in Marshall's treatment, where the other factors are variable, merely determines the additional value of the block, produced by the *cooperating* factors; but in order to determine the marginal net product (the price to be paid for one component), it is necessary to deduct the prices of additional units of other factors. Thus marginal product is obtained on the assumption of variability in other factors, and marginal net product on the assumption of a fixed supply of other factors. The marginal gross product is, for Mrs. Robinson, the increment in value caused by employing one additional man with the appropriate addition of other factors; and the marginal net increment of value of output is the marginal gross product minus the cost of the additional (other) factors.[2]

That the total productivity curve rises by diminishing increments (other factors fixed) suggests the law of diminishing marginal

[1] HICKS, J. R., *Theory of Wages*, especially pp. 8–17, 23–86, and Chaps. 9–10; ROBINSON, J., *The Economics of Imperfect Competition*, pp. 237–254.

[2] There seems to be some awkwardness in Mrs. Robinson's definition of the marginal net product.

a. Marginal net increment of value of output is the marginal gross productivity (with one workman) with *appropriate addition of other factors* minus their cost.

b. Marginal gross productivity is the increment of value caused by employing one added man with the *appropriate addition of other factors*.

Since marginal gross productivity includes "the appropriate addition of other factors," Mrs. Robinson's definition of the marginal net increment should *not again* productivity; and the curve of diminishing marginal productivity is identified as the ultimate demand curve for labor. Prof. Douglas has made ingenious attempts to measure the slope of this curve. Thus he finds that the flexibility of the marginal productivity curve of labor $= -\frac{1}{4}$: the addition of 1 per cent of labor results in a rise of the product of $\frac{3}{4}$ of 1 per cent. The elasticity of demand for labor is given by the reciprocal of the flexibility value, and hence $= -4$. Should real wages rise by 1 per cent, the amount of labor demanded would therefore fall by 4 per cent.[1] Under conditions of monopolistic competition, however, the elasticity of the productivity function for labor may well have a positive value; *i.e.*, marginal productivity may increase with more laborers. When output has fallen to a value below that for which the plant was planned, the probability of a positive value increases.[2]

It would not be amiss to say a word here concerning the relation of marginal physical product and real wage rates: wages may be expressed in terms of the product of the industry in which the worker is employed. As Mr. Hawtrey expresses it, "each wage-rate is linked to its own product by the appropriate productivity function and the demand for the product is governed by the appropriate demand function."[3] Real wages depend *also*, however, upon the purchasing power in consumption goods of the "product" wage (or money equivalent) of these workers. Despite a rise in the marginal physical product of laborers in a given industry, these workers may be confronted with a reduction in their real wages. This result would follow if the productivity in the industries that provide the goods consumed by workers declined sufficiently. Prices of wage goods, for example, may rise relatively to the price of the goods produced by these workers.[4] Real wages may decline then despite an unchanged money income.

include the italicized words (*op. cit.*, pp. 237–239) in *a*. Otherwise, they are included twice.

Also see *op. cit.*, pp. 240–241. Here Mrs. Robinson's argument is that the change in output will be equal whether the two factors are increased simultaneously or one at a time.

[1] DOUGLAS, P. H., *Theory of Wages*, pp. 151–153; "Wage Theory and Wage Policy," *Internat. Labor Rev.*, March, 1939, p. 330. The reader is referred to the former for definitions and further discussion of the flexibility concept.

[2] ROBINSON, *op. cit.*, pp. 263–264; HARROD, R. F., "Professor Pigou's Theory of Unemployment," *Econ. Jour.*, March, 1934, pp. 26–27.

[3] HAWTREY, R. G., *Capital and Employment*, p. 277.

[4] HAWTREY, *ibid.*, pp. 277–279; KEYNES, J. M., "Relative Movements of Real Wages and Output," *Econ. Jour.*, March, 1939, p. 50.

Entrepreneurs try to keep costs at a minimum. They, therefore, push the employment of each factor until its marginal physical productivity is proportional to its "marginal cost." It follows that the marginal cost of factor a will be in the same ratio to the marginal productivity of factor a as the marginal costs of factors $b \ldots n$ are to their respective marginal productivities; and the marginal dollar spent on the purchase of factors will yield equal marginal products.

In the present discussion, we are more concerned with less fundamental modifications of the marginal productivity theory.[1] In his *Theory of Wages*, Prof. Hicks has commented rather fully on the practical limits of the marginal productivity theory. Some workers, for example, are more efficient than others, and in the practical world it is both difficult to measure the marginal productivity for each worker, and also frequently unwise to pay varying wages based on crude measures of efficiency. Again, marginal productivity fluctuates from moment to moment; but adjustments of wages are made only at long intervals.[2]

In addition to the type of problem adumbrated in the preceding paragraph, Prof. Hicks discusses two problems which are not always clearly distinguished. The first is the failure to adjust wages when marginal productivity has clearly declined or risen. Thus in a depression, employers hesitate to cut wages despite a fall in marginal productivity; and in a period of rising demand, casual laborers do not profit adequately from any rise of productivity. The assumption is, however, that any losses or gains of employers are only

---

[1] See, however, J. A. Schumpeter, *Business Cycles*, 1939, p. 836. " . . . the fundamental theorem about marginal value productivity of labor is an equilibrium proposition that would at best apply (approximately) in neighborhoods of equilibrium, but cannot in the intervals between them."

[2] *Cf.* Pigou, A. C., *Theory of Unemployment*, pp. 254–255; Douglas, P. H., *Theory of Wages*, pp. 69–96; Walker, E. R., "Wages Policy and Business Cycles," *Internat. Labor Rev.*, December, 1938. Prof. Douglas seems to accept the marginal productivity theory; but he is inclined to put more emphasis on the possibilities of exploitation of labor, *i.e.*, payment of wages below the marginal productivity, than does Prof. Hicks. Unemployment, lack of knowledge, and immobility in particular weaken labor's bargaining position. Dr. Walker, on the other hand, does not seem to be disposed to accept the theory. In particular, he emphasizes the failure of the entrepreneur to be motivated exclusively by the profit motive and also his inability to estimate marginal productivity. His position is not, however, convincing. For example, the businessman's failure to follow consistently a profit motive seems a temporary sacrifice made in order to assure larger profits in the long run.

temporary.[1] Exploitation arising from slow adjustment of wages to changes in marginal productivity is, however, to be distinguished from the more important cases of exploitation. In the latter case, the employers, in his opinion, will lose. Workers go elsewhere. Labor markets are not isolated. Employers think of the future and, therefore, do not exploit whenever the occasion arises. We shall return to the problem of exploitation later. Of one conclusion Prof. Hicks seems reasonably sure. A rise of wages above the level justified by productivity will ultimately result in unemployment, though the adverse effects may temporarily be put upon capital. Laborsaving inventions will finally be stimulated and possible adverse effects on the supply of capital may further reduce the level of real wages. These limitations on the marginal productivity theory should be kept in mind when applying it to the theory of incidence.

In the application of the marginal productivity theory of wages to the incidence of the pay-roll tax, one may make some supplementary statements that have not been suggested up to this point. Having been struck by the presence of unemployment in both rich and poor countries and apparently in amounts not related to the demand functions, Prof. Pigou concludes that employment and demand for labor are not correlated. "Changes in the state of demand are, of course, relevant, but when once any given state of demand has become fully established, the real wage-rates stipulated for by workpeople adjust themselves to the new conditions." If this thesis is correct, employers' contributions to insurance, which involve a corresponding depression of the demand function for labor, will have no permanent effect on employment.[2] Workers will adjust their wage demands in such a manner as to leave employment unchanged. Prof. Pigou's interpretation here is clearly that

[1] It should be added that wages are brought into line with marginal productivity not only by cutting them, but also (which is much more likely) by changing the margin of employment, *i.e.*, reducing employment. To give workers less than their marginal productivity means not that the employer is smart but that he is a fool. He would be better off by employing additional workers until the wage equaled the marginal productivity. (Lumpiness and the time factor are left out of account at this point.)

Cf. also WPA, *Survey of Economic Theory on Technological Change and Employment*, by A. Gourvitch, 1940, pp. 154–156. Here the views of Prof. Clark on the relation of wages and marginal product *in a depression* are discussed. Maintenance of prices means that labor is paid less than its full short-run marginal product. In the short run the marginal product of capital, on the other hand, may be nothing or everything.

[2] Pigou, *op. cit.*, pp. 248–249.

the workers pay; and they pay because demand and supply functions are not independent.

A criticism of the *application* of marginal productivity to the problem of incidence arises from the failure to consider the possibility of a rise of wages which does not bring an increase of unemployment, and may even account for a rise of employment.[1] Unfilled vacancies rather than unemployment may be the characteristic of some labor markets. A rise of wages will then have the effect of reducing the number of unfilled vacancies, not the amount of employment. Again, a rise of wages (when the elasticity of demand for labor is >1) will tend to drive workers out of the industry. It is possible that if the industries attracting the workers seeking employment elsewhere have a sufficient number of unfilled vacancies there may be a gain of employment over all industries despite the rise of wages. It is also possible, however, that the increase of unemployment, following a rise of wages, may be in excess of the amount associated directly with conditions in the industry confronted with higher wages. The bribe of possible employment in the high-wage industry may attract workers from other industries, who had previously been employed. They may, however, fail to find employment in the high-wage industry.

14.2. INCIDENCE ON SIMPLIFIED ASSUMPTIONS

The classic treatment of incidence, given for example by Prof. Brown, rests upon the marginal productivity theory of wages.[2] His conclusion seems to be that a tax upon pay-rolls, whether paid in the first instance by the employers or workers, is eventually borne chiefly by the worker, if the long-run supply of labor is fairly *inelastic*. If the long-run supply of labor is very *elastic*, the (net) price of labor falls, the quantity employed (offered) decreases greatly, and the marginal productivity of labor rises until (presumably) the (net) price of labor is back to its original position. If

---

[1] *Ibid.*, pp. 257–262.

[2] *Cf.* first footnote in last chapter. In a more recent study of incidence, Prof. Brown still seems to base his conclusions on the marginal productivity theory of wages. H. G. Brown, "The Incidence of a General Output or a General Sales Tax," *Jour. Pol. Econ.*, April, 1939, pp. 254–256.

the supply of capital is also elastic the tax is, in his view, borne by landowners.

Even under his abstract assumptions of pure competition, three factors of production, no unemployment, etc., we do not think his conclusions are completely justified. For he neglects the fact that the other agents of production may be in complementary (or competitive) relationships with labor.[1] It does not necessarily follow, therefore, that labor will be injured much more or even a little more by a tax on labor than will other factors of production. After all, the important thing is not the object of the taxation, but the adjustments that can be made to it, and these could conceivably involve more pressure on another factor, say capital, than on labor. The discussion of the distribution of the burden among the factors has been reserved for a later chapter (20).

The assumptions underlying the orthodox theory of incidence are of course very restrictive, and not realized in the actual world. There are many points at which they could be relaxed so as to allow for the more realistic imperfections of our economic system. We can drop the assumption of perfect competition in the markets where firms sell their products; we can also dispense with the assumption of perfect markets for the factors of production. We shall return to these problems later. At this point an analysis based upon the marginal productivity theory of wages under competitive conditions is presented. The picture presented is relatively simplified although later lines are suggested along which the marginal productivity theory as used in the orthodox discussions of incidence requires modification.

If now a tax is imposed on pay-rolls for social security purposes, we can imagine two extreme cases:

1. *The net minimum wage that workers insist on getting may decrease by as much as the tax.* If previously workers had insisted on $15 per week, they might now be willing to take 91 per cent of $15 ($15 − 9 per cent of $15). A tax of 3 per cent for unemployment and 6 per cent for old-age insurance is assumed here. This attitude might be explained by the fact that they consider the payments into the reserve funds made for them as an equivalent amount of wages, or simply because they wish to avoid unemployment. Since the minimum level for which they are supposed to hold out is not

---

[1] *Cf. The Economics of Taxation*, pp. 145–146, however. It may be said that at the time he was writing his book the theory of substitution and complementarity had not been advanced very far.

entirely rational in the first place, it is possible that they might consider as part of their wages the amounts deducted from their wages (3 per cent for old-age insurance and in some cases additional amounts for unemployment compensation). Furthermore, they might even consider as part of their wages taxes paid by employers, which the latter in turn attempt to pass on to workers through a cut in wages. (Under the Social Security Act, the taxes *on employers* will eventually reach 3 per cent on account of old-age insurance and 3 per cent more or less on account of unemployment insurance.)

If workers viewed contributions to the social security accounts as wages, the net result would be that the cost of labor per unit to the employer would remain the same; his employment offered would therefore be the same; the net wage of workers would be lower by as much as the tax; in recompense the worker would receive a deferred old-age and unemployment benefit payment. He would be saving part of his income with the government (see chart IV, Fig. I).

2. At the other extreme, workers might still insist on the same *net* rate of earnings. These demands, if granted, would be equivalent to a rise in the level of wages which employers must pay by exactly the amount of the tax. This may roughly be put at 9 per cent and may conceivably reach a higher figure. As a result, less labor will be demanded. Although labor still receives the same net wage, it must accept the additional unemployment which any increase in money wages (as of the same state of demand for industrial products) is likely to entail (see chart IV, Fig. II). The more inelastic the monetary demand for labor (again as of an unchanged state of consumers' demand), the less will be the resulting unemployment.[1] The effects of a rise of money wages on demand are left for later discussion.

3. Between these two extremes lies a whole range of intermediate cases. It is quite possible that the 3 per cent actually deducted from wages in the first instance may tend to fall in the first category; whereas workers may *not* regard the 6 per cent paid directly by the employer as a part of deferred income accrueable later to themselves. As a result, there may be some increase in labor costs to employers, but by less than the whole tax (9 per cent); some unemployment will result, but not so much as in case 2;

---

[1] We leave out of account here any savings to entrepreneurs resulting from the reduction of charges on industry associated with savings on relief and the like that follow the introduction of an adequate security program.

workers will receive a higher net wage than in case 1, but less than in case 2, and less than in the case where there is no tax (see chart IV, Fig. III).

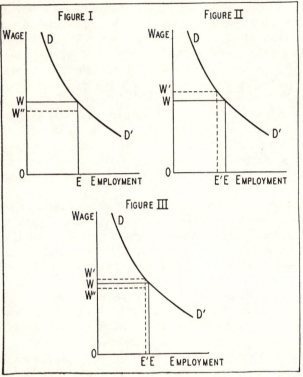

CHART IV.—Pay-roll taxes and employment. Wage before tax = OW. Cost of labor to employer after tax = OW' in Figures II and III and OW in Figure I. Wage received by labor after tax = OW'' in Figures I and III and OW in Figure II. Assumes horizontal supply curve of labor.

In this chapter the marginal productivity theory of wages upon which the accepted theory of incidence of pay-roll taxes is based has been discussed. Important reservations are to be made, however, even to this more or less static analysis. Knowledge is not perfect; labor is not perfectly mobile; and noncompetitive conditions require special consideration. At one extreme, one economist would reject the theory; at another extreme, an eminent economist would accept the theory subject to minor reservations. If the supply and demand functions for labor are dependent in the manner suggested by Prof. Pigou, a reduction of the demand curve for labor following the imposition of new taxes on pay-rolls must result in a corresponding revision of wage rates stipulated, and, therefore, in no net change in employment (case 1). It is also revealed by Prof. Pigou that, under given conditions, a rise in wages does not necessarily entail a rise of unemployment and in fact may have the opposite effect. Finally, the incidence of the pay-roll taxes on simplified classical assumptions is considered here. At one extreme labor pays through an equivalent reduction of wages, and at the other extreme through a reduction of employment.

As we go on, we shall see the limitations of this analysis. In particular the effects upon demand of the disbursements of benefits are neglected.

Chapter 15

GENERAL WAGE THEORY AND THE INCIDENCE
OF PAY-ROLL TAXES

Readers unacquainted with recent developments in general wage theory may find parts of this chapter difficult. Their task may be lightened by the following readings. J. M. Keynes, *General Theory of Employment, Interest and Money* is, of course, the best single source. A briefer and more elementary treatment of Mr. Keynes's views is to be found in J. Robinson, *Introduction to the Theory of Employment*. Chapter VIII of Prof. Gottfried Haberler's *Prosperity and Depression* (1939 edition) gives an excellent summary of the views of Mr. Keynes, his followers, and critics. Many items mentioned in the course of this chapter will also be helpful. Aside from Sec. 15.4, this chapter should not, however, be especially troublesome. The cursory reader, however, may be content with a reading of the introduction and conclusion.

15.1. Introduction

In the past the theory of incidence has been concerned almost exclusively with the problem of the individual firm; and when it has been deemed necessary to take into account the effects on the whole economy, the results of the analysis of one firm have been applied to all firms. That type of analysis has yielded the conclusion that a tax on pay-rolls will result in a curtailment of employment or a reduction of wages. If the theory of monopolistic competition is applied, it will be found that the losses involved in a reduction of output may be tempered for the entrepreneur by an improvement in the price structure or (in some cases) by putting the costs on nonlabor shares. It may be said, however, that the analysis of the individual firm or industry is not applicable without important reservations to the problem of a tax that affects all producers.

In particular, for a decade or more, a controversy has raged on the issue of the relation of changes in the level of money wages to the volume of output and employment. This spirited debate is full of significance for us; for a tax on wages imposed on entrepreneurs

[300]

and not passed on to labor (or in the case of a direct tax on workers, passed on to the entrepreneur through a revision of wage contracts), when the proceeds are to be used for the payment of social security benefits, may be considered analogous to a general rise of wages. If it is true, as the proponents of high wages argue, that a given reduction in wages will fail to increase employment in proportion to the cut in wages and in any case will reduce the total wage bill, or that a rise of wages will not reduce employment appreciably, then, despite contrary evidence given by the incomplete analysis of the individual firm, it may follow that a rise of wages following the introduction of a social security program will improve the position of labor and reduce the volume of output and employment by relatively little, if at all.

One important reservation is to be made. Demand for labor rises on the assumption that the rise of wages brings an increase in monetary supplies and a higher marginal propensity to consume. Accumulation of reserves, however, may (recall Part I) result in a reduction of active supplies of money and therefore in unfavorable effects on the rate of interest; and the favorable effect on marginal propensity to consume may not be had in periods of accumulation of reserves. In other words, though the argument in favor of high wages may prevail in the general case, it may still not be decisive in our case. Much will depend upon the effects of accumulation of reserves upon monetary supplies and demand. Further consideration of monetary problems will be found later in this and the next chapter.

The occasion for the writing of this chapter is that the orthodox association of a rise of money wages and a reduction of employment neglects a significant variable in the picture. It is necessary to take into account the repercussions of a rise of money wages upon monetary supplies and also upon *demand* for commodities and services. If the rise of demand is adequate and the adverse effects via a rise in the rate of interest are not significant, then adverse effects upon employment may be nil or, in any case, will not be so large as will be found under an analysis that neglects the effects upon demand. These considerations of changes in general demand are especially relevant in a discussion of the social security program. That program will influence demand both because it may contribute toward a rise of money wages (inclusive of benefits) and because the accumulation and disbursement of reserves will affect demand. We turn then to the assumptions upon which the argument, that a rise of money wages (inclusive of benefits) may not be so injurious to employment as has been assumed in the literature, rests.

1. Wages constitute but *part* of total costs.[1]

2. Prices are flexible. Then the rise of prices will be given by the proportionate rise of *marginal* costs, which is less than the rise of wages. It is also reasonable to assume that in cases of monopolistic competition the rise of prices will be equal to the *absolute* rise of marginal costs. (The difference between marginal costs and prices should not ordinarily be affected.)

3. The monetary system is sufficiently elastic.

4. The propensity to consume is given. Under the last, the hoarding of reserves is ruled out; and a rise of the propensity to consume (not the total amount of consumption) associated with transfers to wage earners will contribute further toward an improvement in the position of labor, *e.g.*, a rise of real wage rates not offset by a corresponding reduction of employment.

On these assumptions the conclusion is not only that money wage rates will rise but also that real wages will rise. The rise in the latter will, however, probably be of smaller proportions than in the former; for prices will increase. A rise of real wages is then to be explained by (1) a rise in money wages, (2) a rise in output and productivity that accompanies the expansion of monetary demand when economic resources are unemployed and (or) output is below the optimum point. This expansion is to be explained in part by the rise of monetary supplies and in part by the redistribution in favor of low-income groups. Finally, we do not assume that the volume of employment is unchanged. In other words, part of the rise of output may be consumed by additional workers who find jobs with the improvement of demand.

15.2. Wage Theory and Monetary Assumptions

A discussion of the relation of wage levels and output raises the problems of monetary policy and total demand. In the particular-

---

[1] On these issues, *cf.* R. M. Bissell, Jr., "Price Policies and the Theory of Employment," *Econometrica*, July, 1940, especially pp. 199–200, 213–224, 229.

In this interesting article, Prof. Bissell considers the conditions under which Mr. Keynes's findings on the relation of wage rates and employment are valid. (The latter, it will be recalled, holds that any effects must work themselves out through changes in the rate of interest and in the propensity to consume.) A complete analysis would require (1) various assumptions on the flexibility of prices; (2) a consideration of the relevance of "suppliers" who profit from lower prices following a cut in wages and yet do not contribute, via a reduction in wages, toward a diminution of demand; (3) more realistic assumptions than Mr. Keynes makes of the relation of profits and disbursements to owners; and (4) an allowance for substitution effects.

ized analysis each firm or industry occupies our exclusive attention, the changes in the total picture being excluded. Now we concentrate attention on the aggregate demand and consider the manner in which changes in aggregate demand affect n firms. Should the total rise of demand associated with a rise of x wages be ax and should the increase of demand profit each of the n firms (assumed to be of identical size) equally, then the improvement of demand for each firm at a given point will be ax/n. In the controversy over general wage policy, one side has been inclined to take the position that a rise of wages (or a failure to reduce wages in a period of declining demand and prices) has unfortunate effects on output and employment on the grounds that the total demand suffers. These proponents of wage cutting assume that monetary supplies either do not rise or even decline in response to a rise of money wages and do not decline or even rise in response to a cut of money wages; or they neglect monetary aspects.[1]

Supporters of high wages, on the other hand, are inclined to assume a high elasticity of the supply of money upward as money wages rise or downward with a decline. It would, therefore, follow that a rise of wages would yield an equivalent (and later, a much more than equivalent) rise of money demand and a decline of wages a corresponding or even greater decline. This high elasticity upward is to be obtained of course either through the creation of more money or (and) an increased activity of current supplies. In addition to this purely monetary consideration, it is well to consider the effects upon the propensity to consume, which will contribute toward higher wages. Wage earners spend more, others do not spend correspondingly less, and more goods are produced.

Controversy over wage rates has centered around the effects of wage policies upon (1) the supply of and demand for money, (2) monetary demand for output, and (3) the rate of interest. If those who favor high wage policies in prosperity and stability of money wages in depression are right, social security taxes may be absorbed in higher relative wages on both the upswing and downswing. The

---

[1] Prof. Douglas, for example, is critical of Mr. Keynes who, according to the former, assumes that a reduction of wages brings a corresponding reduction of monetary supplies and therefore fails to elicit additional output. Prof. Douglas is dubious that "the money demand curve will shift to the left by precisely the same amount and proportion by which the marginal cost curve has moved downward and to the right."

DOUGLAS, P. H., "Wage Theory and Wage Policy," *Internat. Labor Rev.*, March, 1939, p. 358.

position is, for example, that given a sufficiently high elasticity of the supply of money a rise of money wages through its effects on the rate of interest is not harmful and in its favorable effects upon the marginal propensity to consume may be helpful. These conclusions do not apply to periods of inflation when the marginal propensity to consume is likely to be excessive. In Secs. 15.2 to 15.4, the issues of this controversy are considered briefly and its significance for the social security taxes is pointed out.

This analysis also yields the result that the marginal productivity theory, which has been the basis of the incidence theory of pay-roll taxes, is not adequate. At least it needs some amplification (Sec. 15.5). Marginal value productivity of labor depends, *inter alia*, on the state of the general demand and the rate of interest. These in turn are related to and are not independent of the general level of money wages. Another weakness of the classical wage theory is found in its failure to describe the situation in which employment is not pushed to the point where marginal productivity equals marginal disutility of work. The latter value for a large segment of the population may be below that of the current wage, *i.e.*, below the marginal productivity of the currently employed, and below the potential productivity of the unemployed, and yet additional employment may not be available.

A final issue, which is discussed in Sec. 15.6, is the movement of real and money wages over periods of rising and declining business activity. In the short run, the incidence of pay-roll taxes will depend in part upon the direction of the movement of real wage rates, upon the relation of fluctuations of money and real wage rates, and upon the extent to which workers mistakenly concentrate on money wages. It will surely be easier to ask the worker to pay if his real wage rates are rising than if they are falling, and particularly so if the rise of real wage rates is not based on a corresponding rise of productivity.

Mr. Keynes seems to carry the monetary approach to its logical conclusion when he insists that a reduction of money wages in contributing toward a reduction in the demand for money has effects analogous to those which follow a rise in the supply of money. It is an easy transition then to the position that what is significant is the reduction in the rate of interest; and if the effect via money is not a reduction in the rate of interest, then the cut in money wages will not have the desired result.[1]

---

[1] *Cf.* SCHUMPETER, J. A., *Business Cycles*, p. 843. In commenting on this assumed relation of wage rates and the rate of interest, Prof. Schumpeter writes as follows:

Following in some measure Mr. Keynes's lead, Mr. Hawtrey is optimistic of the results of wage cutting.[1] According to the latter, the sequence will be a reduction of wages, a rise in the relative supply of money, a decline in the rate of interest to the point at which it is both equal to the marginal efficiency of capital and yet assures the country full employment. Mr. Keynes would undoubtedly not go so far. In my opinion the latter's position would be as follows. He would be skeptical of the possibility of an adequate rise in the supply of money following a cut in wages and would emphasize the increased demand for money to satisfy the liquidity motive. Liquidity preference rises as wages decline. Interest rate need not fall, and in any case need not fall sufficiently to assure full employment. Finally, the marginal propensity to consume would be affected adversely.

15.3. WAGE CUTTING AND DEMAND

In the discussion of wage policy, much emphasis has been put upon the effects of changes in wages upon demand for labor. Prof. Pigou finds that a reduction of wages will induce a rise of employment.[2] What the total effect on employment will be depends of course in part upon the monetary system in operation. Aside from the latter issue, the favorable results given by Prof. Pigou follow, as Mr. Harrod has shown, from the assumption that nonwage earners maintain their *money* expenditures. Should the investigator

---

"But the simple nexus alluded to can be asserted to be operative only by means of so unrealistic assumptions and owes the importance attributed to it so exclusively to a theoretical model which excluded all the vital mechanisms through which variations in wage rates act that we need not proceed with it."

[1] HAWTREY, R. G., *Capital and Employment*, pp. 220–226.

[2] In his investigation of the elasticity of demand for labor, Prof. Douglas's conclusions strongly support those of Prof. Pigou. P. H. Douglas, *The Theory of Wages*, especially pp. 151–153.

Cf. also Mr. Robertson's careful treatment of this subject. (WPA, *Survey of Economic Theory on Technological Change and Employment*, pp. 114–115.) (1) It is necessary to consider the movement along the existing curve of demand for labor. A reduction in the number of employed will follow up to the point at which the product of the marginal man equals the artificial wage. (2) With less profits, there will be a cumulative lowering of the curve. It is well to observe that the effects upon demand of a rise of wages are not considered here and that the inference is not drawn that a sufficient reduction of wages will lead to a position of no unemployment.

start with the assumption that *real* (not money) expenditures are maintained by nonwage earners, then following a reduction of money wage rates, prices and nonwage earners' incomes fall in proportion to the decline of wage rates and real incomes of nonwage earners and of wage earners remain unchanged.[1] Prices decline as much as wages (*i.e.*, prime costs), and there is then no inducement to expand output. Nonwage earners' income, on this argument, does not rise. Even if it should increase, however, the effects upon spending may not be so favorable as Prof. Pigou would have us believe. In this connection, Mr. Harrod's emphasis is on the inelasticity of demand of nonwage earners' expenditures and Prof. Pigou's on the high elasticity, which in the latter's view is explained by the nonspecialized character of their consumption.[2]

Many, besides Prof. Pigou, are skeptical of the significance of the "purchasing power" or "increase of demand" theory of high wages. These writers are inclined to emphasize the adverse effects upon costs and profits, the discouragement of investment, the *concentration* of the rise of costs as against the *diffusion* of the increase of purchasing power.[3] It is important, however, to distinguish a *general* from a sectional increase of wages, the latter having the effect of attracting better labor to the high-wage industries and

[1] Dr. Kalecki seems to support Mr. Harrod's position when he argues that nonwage earners will not expand the *volume* of their consumption and investment in anticipation of higher profits associated with a reduction of wages. He goes even further. Monopoly accounts for a failure of prices to decline in proportion to the reduction of wages. As a result, the "real" demand for wage goods falls off, employment and output then declining. M. Kalecki, *Essays in the Theory of Economic Fluctuations*, 1939, pp. 79–84. On the issue of the relation of changes in wages and prices under monopolistic competition, see also Schumpeter, *op. cit.*, p. 839, and the article by Dr. Paul Sweezy in *Proc. Am. Econ. Assoc.*, 1938, p. 156, which the former criticizes.

[2] Pigou, A. C., *Theory of Unemployment*, pp. 100–102; "Real and Money Wage Rates in Relation to Unemployment," *Econ. Jour.*, September, 1937, pp. 405–422; Harrod, R. F., "Professor Pigou's Theory of Unemployment," *Econ. Jour.*, March, 1934, pp. 22–25, 28. Mr. Harrod advances another interesting argument against wage cutting. When conditions of monopolistic competition and output below the level for which the plant has been designed prevail, a rise of wages, (in anticipation of a rise of output) not a decline, is required. *Ibid.*, pp. 26–27.

[3] Clark, J. M., "An Appraisal of the Workability of Compensatory Devices," *Proc. Am. Econ. Assoc.*, 1939, pp. 197–198; Robinson, J., *Essays in the Theory of Employment*, pp. 44–45; Hardy, C. O., "An Appraisal of the Factors Which Stopped Short the Recovery Development in the United States," *Proc. Am. Econ. Assoc.*, 1939, pp. 177–179. Even Mrs. Robinson concludes that a rise of wages through its effects on investment may have an adverse effect on the marginal efficiency of capital.

plants, thus the adverse effects upon costs of the rise of wages being nullified.[1]

Perhaps the strongest case against overemphasis of the significance of wage rates and the importance of high wage rates as a condition of prosperity has been presented by Prof. Schumpeter.[2] Against the argument that a corresponding rise of revenue accompanies a rise of wage rates, he considers the probability of substitution of other factors, with the result that the employment of labor per unit of output is bound to fall.[3] Although his general position is that wage rates are given too much attention, he makes numerous important reservations to this position. He does not, for example, go to the opposite extreme and support the economists who maintain that wage rates are a matter of indifference.[4] Again, he is critical of the high wage rates in the twenties and the high-wage policy in the early years of the New Deal: they had unfortunate effects on employment.[5] On the other hand, he is not too optimistic of the favorable effects of wage cutting upon the wage bill in a depression when the demand for labor shifts downward and becomes less elastic.[6]

15.4. Wages and the Rate of Interest

In the recent literature on the subject, the dominant note has been the effect of a rise or reduction of wages upon the rate of interest. Even so long ago as 1933, Prof. Pigou in attempting to prove that a reduction of real wages would increase both employment and the total wage bill found it necessary to dwell on the effects upon the rate of interest. Since the effects from the rate of interest upon the elasticity of real demand for labor would, under significant conditions, not be adverse, he reaffirmed his conclusion that a reduction in real wages would result in a rise of the total of real wages.[7] The relatively favorable effects upon employment associated

[1] SLICHTER, S. H., "The Changing Character of America's Industrial Relations," *Proc. Am. Econ. Assoc.*, 1939, pp. 127, 131.

[2] SCHUMPETER, *op. cit.*, especially pp. 571–577, 836–849.

[3] *Ibid.*, p. 839.

[4] *Ibid.*, p. 838. Here Prof. Schumpeter is willing to make some concessions. In a decade, an economy will adapt itself to a high wage level.

[5] *Ibid.*, pp. 837, 994, 1009. In one passage, he gives the impression that a rise of wage rates is innocuous only if it is justified by a change in productivity, *ibid.*, p. 577.

[6] *Ibid.*, pp. 953–954.

[7] PIGOU, A. C., *The Theory of Unemployment*, especially p. 87.

with the conditions in the capital market were ascribed largely to the savings on the dole (broadly defined) and, hence, of working capital as employment rises.[1] The impetus given to the high-wage theory by Mr. Keynes's *General Theory of Employment* made it necessary, however, for Prof. Pigou to reaffirm his position and attempt a rigid proof of the validity of his earlier position. He now associates the rate of interest (r) with the rate at which the public discounts real income, and V (velocity) with r and with the proportion of income going to wage earners. He also assumes that $dM/dr > 0$ (M = money). His conclusion is that with output (x) and r unchanged a reduction of wages must result in a reduction of costs.

Under conditions of monopolistic competition, similar conclusions follow: the original position may be put as $p \left(1 - \dfrac{1}{\eta_1}\right) = wF'(x)$ and the position when the wage is reduced as $p_2 \left(1 - \dfrac{1}{\eta_2}\right) = mwF'(x_2)$, where η_1 and η_2 are the elasticities of demand, p = price, and $F'(x)$ = the marginal revenue (dR/dx).[2] Then "if η_2 either exceeds η_1, or falls short of it in less than the critical degree, they earn less than they would do if price were reduced and output expanded."[3] He admits, however, that in some industries the rise of marginal costs would prevent an increase of output. In critical industries, nevertheless, output would rise; and the effects would be magnified as other industries felt the impact of a rise of output in the critical industries. Finally, Prof. Pigou maintains that employment will not rise so much with a reduction of the rate of interest *unaccompanied* by a reduction of wages.

It should be observed that in making $r = f$ (time preference) alone, Prof. Pigou failed to treat one crucial aspect of a general analysis. Despite his association of m with $r[m = f(r)]$, and V with r and with the distribution of income, his analysis remains largely one of the individual firm or industry. Had he, for example, also made $r = f(m)$, then he would have seen more clearly that the changes in wages operate through their effects on the rate of interest.[4] Thus assume that wages fall and output expands. Then it may be held that the demand for money rises and the rate of interest will rise in the absence of an elastic monetary system. A reduction of wages will then stimulate output only temporarily unless favorable effects follow from a rise of MV, *i.e.*, a propensity to dishoard. It may, therefore, be said that it is necessary to take into account the effects of any change in wage rates on the supply of and demand for money and, therefore, upon the

---

[1] *Ibid.*, pp. 94–96.

[2] *Cf.* ALLEN, R. G. D., *Mathematical Theory for Economists*, pp. 255–257.

[3] PIGOU, A. C., "Real and Money Wage Rates in Relation to Unemployment," *Econ. Jour.*, September, 1937, pp. 413–414.

[4] *Cf.* KEYNES, J. M., "Professor Pigou on Money Wages in Relation to Unemployment," *Econ. Jour.*, 1937, pp. 743–745.

rate of interest.[1] In fact, the analysis of the opponents of high wages may easily be put in monetary terms; and the net effects of wage policy may then be put in terms of the resulting change in the supply of and demand for money and hence upon the rate of interest. Thus Dr. Hardy's argument that the manufacturing industries are sensitive to a rise of wages may be put in monetary terms. Entrepreneurs, fearful of a rise of wages, will then increase their hoards and reduce their loans. Output, income, and (therefore) savings will decline. The rate of interest, therefore, rises, despite an initial decline in demand for money for production purposes, because the supply of money and savings decline and the demand for money to satisfy liquidity requirements rises greatly.

Mr. Kaldor in particular made an effective attack on Prof. Pigou with the result that the latter has capitulated.[2] First he pointed out that Prof. Pigou's results rested on the assumption that dS/dr is positive. (S = savings, and r = rate of interest.) Should dS/dr be negative, a reduction of wages and a decline in the rate of interest would be followed by a rise of savings and hence more unemployment. His main criticism follows, however. Employment rises only if the rate of interest declines; and a decline in the rate of interest ensues if $dS/dx > 0$ (x = output). But savings will *then* decline in response to the fall in the rate of interest and also in response to a rise of real balances and a fall of prices accompanying an increase of output. Apparently the decline of prices induces a reduction of real income and then a decline of savings. (Can we be sure of this in view of the favorable factors inducing the decline of prices?) If there is to be a net reduction in the rate of interest, then dS/dx must be sufficiently large (and positive) to bring about a reduction in the rate of interest despite the adverse influence of falling prices and a resulting tendency of savings to fall and (thus) the rate of interest to rise. Should dS/dx be small and dM/dr, dV/dr, and dS/dr be large, the net effect on the rate of interest and employment will be small.

Finally Mr. Kaldor contends that with fixed equipment, savings and investment depend on the rate of interest and the volume of real income. The distribution of income will then be a unique function of real income. There would then be no way in which a change of wages would affect the savings or investment function and, therefore, it could not alter the real output which would secure equality of savings and investment at a given

[1] Prof. Hicks ties up well the effects of a rise of wages with the ensuing changes of production plans, prices, secondary effects on employment, demand for money, and finally the supply of money.

HICKS, J. R., "Wages and Interest: The Dynamic Problem," *Econ. Jour.*, September, 1935, pp. 456–468.

[2] KALDOR, N., "Professor Pigou on Money Wages in Relation to Unemployment," *Econ. Jour.*, 1937, pp. 745–753; PIGOU, A. C., "Money Wages in Relation to Unemployment," March, 1938, pp. 134–138. *Cf.* DOUGLAS, P. H., "Wage Theory and Wage Policy," *Internat. Labor Rev.*, 1939.

rate of interest. (Note that this is on the assumption that the rate of interest is given; and therefore a change in wages will not affect the rate of interest.) " . . . the effect of a wage-reduction on employment will depend upon its effect on the size of idle balances; and that the result on employment and the rate of interest will be exactly the same as if the real value of these balances had been increased by the same amount in some other way."[1]

It must now be apparent that, despite the results obtained in the analysis of the individual firm, it is possible, given a sufficiently elastic monetary system, for a rise of wages to be passed on to the consumer in the form of higher prices. More on this in the next two chapters.

In this connection, we can explain Mr. Keynes's insistence that rigid wages are required to impart stability to the economic system. For his assumption is that the monetary system is elastic and, therefore, a rise in wages tends to send prices skyward and a reduction to send them on a rapid and cumulative descent. Any stability imparted to the price level by rigid wages may, however, be at the expense of employment if the assumption is made that monetary supplies are not of infinite elasticity. What if monetary supplies are of infinite elasticity? Then wages will determine prices (on the assumption of inflexibility in the prices of other factors). Prices will be less stable if wages are flexible than if they remain rigid. Output in the Keynesian system will then be determined by the rate of interest, the schedule of marginal efficiency of capital, and the marginal propensity to consume. What if the elasticity of supply of money is less than infinite and, therefore, the rate of interest is no longer fixed? Then a rise of wages may well tend to increase the rate of interest and money wages will affect the level of output and employment as well as prices. Finally, it should be observed that the effects of any rise or decline of demand, whether it is associated with a change in wage rates or with changes in other variables, will operate through changes in the marginal propensity to consume and the marginal propensity to invest.[2]

[1] KALDOR, op. cit., p. 753. More recently Mr. Lerner has attacked Prof. Pigou's position along similar lines. ("Ex-ante Analysis and Wage Theory," *Economica*, November, 1939, especially pp. 440–451.) Following a reduction of money wage rates, cash requirements to satisfy the liquidity motive rise: it costs less to hold cash with a reduction of the rate of interest, noncash assets are higher priced and hence less desired, and more cash is required for the consummation of transactions. If, however, the propensity to consume is not affected by the decline in the rate of interest, income and employment do not rise and more money is not required to carry through transactions.

[2] See especially KEYNES, J. M., *General Theory, passim;* LERNER, A. P., "The Relation of Wage Policies and Price Policies," *Proc., Am. Econ. Assoc.*, 1939, pp. 158–169; HICKS, J. R., *Value and Capital*, pp. 256–257, 269–270; ROBINSON, *op. cit.*, pp. 105–127. Mrs. Robinson, it should be observed, also seeks a reduction in the rate of interest. Should the elasticity of substitution be >1 and thriftiness excessive, however, then labor, in her view, stands to lose.

In the discussion of the Keynesian position, several economists have commented on his failure to consider substitution effects.[1] Why are not other factors substituted for labor when money wages rise, employment then declining? Keynesians dispose of substitution on the following assumption: factors other than labor are fully employed, and their prices are completely flexible. If, however, other factors do not adjust their rates so that they are fully employed, a rise of money wages may be followed by a reduction of employment of labor: other factors will be substituted at an unchanged price or at a higher price. It is to be observed that to attain their results the supporters of Mr. Keynes are required to assume that, unlike other groups, labor pays excessive attention to monetary rewards.

15.5. LEVEL OF WAGES AND MARGINAL PRODUCTIVITY THEORY

Now that it has been made clear that, given a sufficiently elastic monetary system, real wages, following the introduction of an expansive policy, e.g., the social security program, may be raised, the next question is the manner in which this rise of wages is made consistent with the marginal productivity theory.[2] For it is upon this theory that the accepted theory of incidence of pay-roll taxes is based. Wage earners then obtain an increase of money wages and also, though of smaller proportions, of real wages. Is marginal productivity higher, or does the wage earner obtain the additional wage at the expense of other factors? One possibility is of course that the marginal prime cost curve slopes downward and therefore a rise of demand and output is accompanied by a reduction of cost and a rise of marginal productivity. Economies of management and fuller utilization of fixed resources may account for a net gain despite a tendency to hire less efficient workers as output expands.[3] When

---

[1] For example, Profs. Schumpeter and Bissell and Mr. James Tobin. I am especially indebted to the last for the reservation discussed in this paragraph. Cf. Tobin, J., "A Note on The Money Wage Problem," *Quart. Jour. Econ.*, May, 1941.

[2] In the opening sections the relation of money and real wages was discussed. The increase of *real* wages arises from a failure of prices to rise in proportion to the rise of money wages. In turn, this is to be associated with a redistribution of purchasing power in favor of workers and with the accompanying rise of output.

[3] "This implies that the curve of marginal supply prices, *i.e.*, the (short-period) supply curve, will, in the first part of its course, be descending, then for some time horizontal, then slightly ascending, then steeply ascending, until finally it becomes a vertical straight line." From A. C. Pigou, *Theory of Unemployment*, pp. 136–137,

firms are of less than optimum size, the rise of output, in so far as it is shared by *existing* firms and does not involve an increase in the scale of output beyond the optimum scale, will result in a reduction of unit costs. (We assume free entry and, previous to the rise of demand, production to the left of the optimum point.) A further gain is possible. Labor may gain at the expense of entrepreneurs or other factors. Thus there may be monopsony profits which may be cut to some extent, or other factors may be squeezed; and for short periods, wages may rise to a value in excess of the marginal product.[1]

Wages may be raised to a relatively high level for another important reason, which has been discussed earlier in this chapter. The favorable (?) effects on demand contribute to a rise in the marginal value productivity of labor. It follows therefore that a rise of wages associated with the security program may be accompanied by a rise of demand and of marginal productivity which in turn justify the increase. (The new wage plus the present value of benefits is larger than the wage antecedent to the introduction of the new program.)

This problem should not, however, be confused with another, which by way of digression will be discussed briefly. The latter problem is the maintenance of wages at a level too high to maintain full employment, or, in other words, a wage rate above the marginal productivity of the nth worker when there are n possible gainful workers.

(quoted by permission of The Macmillan Company, publishers). *Cf.* J. H. Richardson, "Real Wage Movements," *Econ. Jour.*, September, 1939, p. 428.

Mr. Harrod comes to similar conclusions. In a depression, output is at a level below that for which the plant is designed. In these circumstances, a strong probability exists that marginal costs will be falling. Harrod, *op. cit.*, pp. 26–27.

Dr. Kalecki (*op. cit.*, pp. 23, 40), however, contends that the short-period marginal cost curve is relatively constant up to a point corresponding to "practical capacity."

[1] Prof. Douglas makes an attempt to study statistically the relation of labor costs per unit of output and the value added by manufacture. His conclusion is that, in general, wages have not been too high in the period 1920–1937 though in 1937 they drew abreast of other costs. The breaks in 1920 and 1929 seem to have come when wages were not relatively high.

Douglas, P. H., "The Effects of Wage Decreases upon Employment," *Proc. Am. Econ. Assoc.*, 1939, pp. 154–157. *Cf.* his *Theory of Wages*, pp. 184–188. Prof. Douglas here is impressed, for the years 1916–1926 (and possibly 1926–1929), by the rise of the average value of physical product relative to real wages. In his view, wages were in these years too low, their insufficiency contributing toward the depression. It should be observed, however, that the low wages thus defined are not necessarily evidence of exploitation. *Cf.* Schumpeter, *op. cit.*, p. 836.

There are numerous reasons why wages tend to stay above the level given by that level of marginal productivity and marginal disutility which would assure full employment. Classicists were undoubtedly aware that monopolistic or restrictive practices on the part of trade unions might keep wages at a level too high to assure full employment. Prof. Pigou reminds us that workers, though aware of the unfavorable effects on employment, may set wages above the level that would assure full employment.[1] Again, workers who set wages above the level determined by their marginal value productivity and who are then excluded from employment, or workers who have no means of giving effect to their wish to cut wages and thus obtain employment are, according to Mr. Keynes, voluntarily unemployed.

Mr. Keynes would distinguish unemployment of this type from what he designates as involuntary unemployment. The evidence of the latter is to be found in the excess of demand for and supply of labor over existing employment which accompanies a slight rise of prices (and a reduction of real wages). Marginal disutility of labor of potential workers may then be at a lower value than that of the marginal product of the employed and of many of the unemployed. In his view, the classical theory, which assumes equality of these two variables, fails to deal with involuntary unemployment.[2]

Mr. Keynes's concept of involuntary unemployment has met with severe criticism.[3] Mr. Hawtrey would not distinguish between Mr. Keynes's involuntary unemployment, the result of miscalculation and change of circumstances on the one hand, and the unemployment that follows the fixation of wage bargains at levels too high to assure full employment, on the other.[4] Others have commented on Mr. Keynes's overemphasis of the concern of workers with their money instead of their real wages.[5] These workers may even be assumed to be voluntarily unemployed. Their plight is explained by their miscalculations.[6] Finally it may be well to observe that economists who, for example, support minimum-wage legislation frequently do so on the ground that the unemployed are *too* successful in

[1] A. C. PIGOU, *Theory of Unemployment*, pp. 252–253; HUTT, W. H., *the Theory of Idle Resources*, pp. 123–131. *Cf.* HABERLER, G., *Prosperity and Depression*, 1939, pp. 233–247, for a survey of some of the issues discussed in this paragraph.

[2] KEYNES, *op. cit.*, pp. 6, 15, 21–22, 128.

[3] A stinging criticism has appeared in a recent book (Hutt, *op. cit.*, especially pp. 95–100, 165–167). In Prof. Hutt's view, economists are not so stupid as to believe that a small reduction of real wages would result in the withdrawal of *all* workers from the labor markets; involuntary unemployment is the *fulfillment* of a preference, not a frustration; and economists in concentrating on "net advantageousness" made it clear that the supply of labor is not a function of the real wages as the sole variable.

[4] HAWTREY, *op. cit.*, pp. 167–170, 225.

[5] *Cf.* CHAMPERNOWNE, D. G., "Unemployment, Basic and Monetary," *Rev. Econ. Studies*, June, 1936, pp. 201, 202–204; HICKS, *op. cit.*, p. 270; HABERLER, *op. cit.*, pp. 233–247.

[6] *Cf.* ROBINSON, *op. cit.*, pp. 10–11.

the act of getting wages down.[1] Through minimum-wage legislation, total wages may be increased and wage rates may be raised to or near the point given by marginal productivity.

Wages may then be maintained at a level that is too high to assure full employment. The explanation may be what economists frequently refer to as voluntary unemployment associated, for example, with wage legislation and trade-union practices. Miscalculation, on the other hand, which Mr. Keynes considers the explanation of involuntary unemployment may also account for a position of less than full employment. Social security taxes, which may increase the wage costs of employers, may then result in a further rise of real wages above the point given by marginal value productivity of all employables, the amount of unemployment being thus increased and the employed being favored against the unemployed. It is another matter, however, if the employed are currently in receipt of a wage below *their* marginal value product. A rise of wages may then not be at the expense of employment. We return to this issue in Chap. 19.

15.6. MONEY AND REAL WAGES AND THE BURDEN OF SOCIAL SECURITY TAXES

We now turn to the cyclical movements of real and money wage rates and their interrelations; for the incidence of social security taxes is not unrelated to these problems.[2] As the volume of output fluctuates, the marginal product and, hence, real wages fluctuate. This problem has received the attention of Mr. Keynes and his critics. They have discussed fully the variations of the marginal product both with a rise of business activity and with a decline. At first, Mr. Keynes was inclined to take the position that real and money wages varied in opposite directions, the former declining on the rise and increasing on the decline, and the reverse for the latter.[3] His explanation apparently was largely that short period

[1] DOUGLAS, P. H., "Wage Theory and Wage Policy," *Internat. Labor Rev.*, 1939.

[2] DUNLOP, J. T., "The Movement of Real and Money Wages," *Econ. Jour.*, September, 1938, pp. 413*ff.*; KEYNES, J. M., "Relative Movements of Real Wages and Output," *Econ. Jour.*, March, 1939, pp. 34*ff.*; TARSHIS, L., "Changes in Real and Money Wages," *Econ. Jour.*, March, 1939, pp. 150*ff.*

[3] For the complications introduced when several wavelike movements are to be considered, see Schumpeter, *op. cit.*, Chap. XI, C and Chap. XIV, F, II. Wage *bills* and *rates*, for example, may well both rise in the depression of the Kondratieff. *Ibid.*, especially pp. 573–574.

Prof. Pigou's position at this point is similar to Mr. Keynes's. "Hence, in general, the translation of inertia from real wage-rates to money wage-rates causes real rates to move in a manner not compensatory but complementary to movements in the real demand function." Pigou, *op. cit.*, p. 296.

marginal prime costs rise with an increase of output. Thus in his opinion marginal user cost rises with an increase in output, and money wages are also likely to rise. When Dr. Dunlop and Prof. Tarshis found, however, that the statistical evidence was that both real and money wages rise with improvement in business and both generally fall on the decline, Mr. Keynes replied as follows:[1] Perhaps previous to an improvement of business employment had been at such a low level that recent increases had not brought output beyond the critical level at which wages and other prime costs rise.[2]

More recently another investigator finds additional support for Mr. Keynes's position.[3] Changes in the cost of living are found to be the dominant element in accounting for movements in real wages; and these variables seem to be correlated inversely. Since the cost of living *generally* (not always) rises in periods of increasing activity, real wage rates decline at such times. Prof. Richardson also finds (and this is not necessarily consistent or inconsistent with Mr. Keynes's conclusions) that *total wage payments* are correlated positively with business activity. Also in support of Mr. Keynes's conclusions, he finds that labor costs per unit of output decline in periods of depression.

A young economist has criticized these statistical studies on the following grounds.[4] (1) He finds that over the 70 years covered by Dr. Dunlop's study, movements of real wages are not highly differentiated. Real wages rise and are unchanged or decline in about the same proportions irrespective of the direction of the movements in the cost of living. (2) The trend of money wages upward is greater than the trend downward. (This fact should be considered in conjunction with our remarks later on technological change.) This trend considered together with the irregularity of the movements of the cost of living may explain the rise of real wages in prosperity and the frequent rise in periods of depression. (3) Economists who are interested in the problem of wage *costs* should concentrate on the relation of money wages to *wholesale prices*, not to the cost of living. Entrepreneurs are interested in the prices they obtain more than in the cost of living.

---

[1] In Prof. Tarshis's discovery of a high negative association between real hourly wages and man-hours of work, Mr. Keynes finds some support for his contention that real wages tend to fall in the period of business improvement. Hours of work rise in these periods and the real hourly wage falls. In a period of improvement real hourly wages decline then despite a rise of weekly real wages.

[2] M. Kalecki (*op. cit.*, pp. 80–88) finds *no* correlation between real wages and the amount of employment. Imperfect competition prevails, and therefore more or less horizontal curves of average wage-costs prevail. *Cf.* International Labor Office *Employment, Wages and International Trade*, 1940, p. 13.

[3] Richardson, *op. cit.*, especially pp. 427–436.

[4] Ruggles, R., "The Relative Movements of Real and Money Wages," *Quart. Jour. Econ.*, 1940, pp. 130–149.

In order to shed further light on these matters, some illuminating figures from American experience are brought together in the following table. The material from the WPA study has but recently become available. The following conclusions emerge.[1]

TABLE I.—EMPLOYMENT, OUTPUT, PRODUCTIVITY, WAGES, AND COST OF LIVING, UNITED STATES, 1919–1936

Year	(1) Production	(2) Employment	(3) Man-hours work	(4) Output per wage earner	(5) Output per man-hour	(6) Same, changing composition	(7) Average hours work per week	(8) Cost of living	(9) Pay-rolls, manufacturing industries	(10) Hourly wages N.I.C.B.	(11) Construction wage rates, skilled workers
1919	63	98	100	64	64	69	48*	102	98	61*	.78
1927	89	96	96	93	93	93	48	102	102	58	1.32
1929	100	100	100	100	100	100	48	100	109	59	1.36
1932	53	64	52	83	103	108	38	78	46	50	1.02
1936	89	91	73	98	122	124	39	85	82	62	1.15

* 1920.

1. Sources: Columns 1–7 from WPA National Research Project, *Production, Employment and Productivity in 59 Manufacturing Industries, 1919–36* (1939), pp. 65–67.

Columns 8–11 from *Survey of Current Business, Supplement,* 1938, pp. 11, 40, 47, 50.

2. Base Periods: Columns 1–6 = 1929; column 8 = 1923; column 9 = 1923–1925; columns 10–11 = absolute figures, cents per hour.

3. Miscellaneous: Columns 8–11 are monthly averages for the year. Columns 5 and 6: the former is based on composition of production of base year, the latter on a changing composition.

1. It is necessary to distinguish (a) total pay-rolls, (b) weekly wages, (c) hourly wages. In drawing conclusions concerning movements of real wages one should distinguish these three variables.[2]

2. A consideration of the movements of output per man-hour in periods of business improvement (1919–1929 and 1932–1935) suggests a rise of hourly real wages in such periods. This conclusion holds even for the years 1927–1929 when the rise of output had reached large proportions. Too much should not, however, be put into a comparison of these variables. Output per man-hour is not merely an indication of labor productivity.

[1] It should be observed that the figures presented in columns 9 to 11 of Table I do not cover the same industries as those in columns 1 to 7.

[2] *Cf.* BELL, S., *Productivity, Wages and National Income,* 1940, pp. 47–51, 173.

Changes 1923–1924 to 1936–1937   Per cent

	Per cent
a. Total wages	−13
b. Hourly earnings, money	+11
c. Hourly earnings, real	+29
d. Weekly earnings, money	−10
e. Weekly earnings, real	+ 4

3. Output per man-hour even rose in the years 1929–1936 despite a reduction of the production index from 100 in 1929 to 89 in 1936.

4. On the basis of output figures per wage earner, one might expect a rise of real *weekly* wages in 1919–1929. In the years 1929–1936, however, a large reduction in weekly hours of work occurred; and, despite the rise of output per man-hour, it is not therefore surprising to find a reduction in the weekly output per wage earner.

5. Even in the great depression of 1929–1932, man-hour output was easily maintained. Output per wage earner fell, however, as might be expected from the large reduction in working hours.

6. Pay-rolls in manufacturing industries rose in 1919–1929, but not nearly in the proportion of the rise of output per wage earner or output per man-hour. The conclusion is then (even allowing for a small decline in employment) that the rise of real wages was not so large as the output figures may suggest. A survey of hourly wage rates for 25 industries supports that conclusion. Skilled wage rates in the construction industry rose, however, more than in proportion to the rise of output per man-hour or per wage earner.

7. Changes in the cost of living do not seem to play the dominant part attributed to them by Prof. Richardson. In particular, the relative stability of the cost of living in 1919–1929, despite a marked rise of output and wage rates, is not what Prof. Richardson would have expected. Even in the years 1929–1932, the decline in the cost of living plays an important, not a decisive, part in the determination of the movement of real wages.[1]

8. We conclude then that real wages rise in periods of increasing activity though the varying proportions of total, weekly, and hourly output emphasize the need of distinguishing total, weekly, and hourly real wages. In the depression period of 1929–1932, hourly real wages apparently rose greatly, weekly real wages moderately, and the total real wage bill declined markedly.

9. On the upswing, the evidence does not support Mr. Keynes; but on the downswing, the hourly figures lend support to his position.[2]

A study of the National Bureau of Economic Research has just appeared which throws further light upon these problems.[3] In par-

[1] *Cf.* RUGGLES, *op. cit.*, p. 134.

[2] *Cf.*, however, CLARK, C., *The Conditions of Economic Progress*, 1940, p. 161. British experience is not always identical with American experience.

[3] MILLS, F. C., *The Anatomy of Prices*, 1890–1940, *Nat. Bur. Econ. Research*, *Bull.* 80.

ticular, one is impressed by the important part played by technological changes which shift the schedule of productivity upward in boom periods even if the nonshifting schedule slopes downward as Prof. Pigou, Mr. Keynes, and others assume. Probably more attention should be paid to the technological trends. It then becomes easier to explain the upward movements of productivity and real wage rates in periods of depression *and* prosperity.

One reservation is required in any discussion of wage rates. The significance of a change in wage rates depends upon the importance of fluctuations in the proportions of workers of various types and skill. What may seem like a rise in wage rates, for example, may in fact be only an increase in the proportion of highly skilled workers. I return to Prof. Mills's study.

A constant amount of *labor time* exchanged for[1] the amounts indicated in the following table:

TABLE II.—TRADING RELATIONS OF MANUFACTURING LABOR

	1933	1937
Manufactured goods...............................	209	219
Commodities in the cost of living index............	152	157
Raw farm products, at wholesale..................	261	232

These figures (compare the base years) suggest that the position of labor has steadily improved since the early years of the century. It is necessary, however, to allow for changes in labor time both for the average worker and for all gainful workers; but a rise of wages per unit of time suggests an additional gain.

TABLE III.—CHANGES IN PRODUCTIVITY AND REAL RETURNS OF WORKERS

	Percentage change		
	1899–1914	1914–1929	1929–1937
Changes in output per worker or per man-hour worked*.......................................	+29.6	+49.7	+24.1
Changes in *real returns* per worker employed or per man-hour worked of wage earners...............	+ 0.7	+31.3	+34.9

* For 1899–1929, figures are on basis of per worker employed, but for 1929–1937, on the man-hour basis.

[1] *Ibid.*, p. 8. 1933 figures (1904 = 100). 1937 figures (1919 = 100).

These figures are used to indicate trends. The reader is warned (above) that the base years are different.

The figures in Table III on productivity and real returns are of some interest.[1]

These figures are subject to this reservation: the year 1899 was a year of prosperity, 1914 a year of depression, and 1929 and 1937 years of prosperity.

Here again a long-run rise of productivity and an improvement in the position of labor are clearly revealed. This long-run rise in the real return per worker or per man-hour worked is to be superimposed upon any cyclical fluctuations. A restriction of changes of productivity to cyclical elements may yield results favorable to Mr. Keynes's original conclusion (for periods of improvement) of a decline of productivity and of real wage rates. It is another matter, however, when account is taken of the secular changes in productivity.

It is necessary to point out that limitations of the measures of productivity ought to be taken into account. Reliance on the input of labor *alone* necessarily detracts from the value of the measure of productivity. That the relative amounts of capital may have declined suggests, however, that the measures of productivity may under- rather than over-state the long-run improvement of labor productivity. Finally, the issue of productivity has not entirely escaped the attention of the economists who have dealt with the subject of cyclical variations in wage rates.[2] It is not, however, clear that the phenomenon of technological advance is merely a cyclical one.[3]

In addition to the changes in real wages associated directly with fluctuations in the marginal physical product, wages may fluctuate for other reasons also. Thus the price of wage goods may diverge from the price of the national composite product, if, for example,

[1] *Ibid.*, p. 9.

[2] *Cf.* DUNLOP, *op. cit.*, pp. 432–433.

[3] *Cf.* WPA, *Survey of Economic Theory on Technological Change and Employment*, 1940, pp. 172, 183. On the statistical aspects of the problem, *cf.* Clark, *op. cit.*, pp. 155–161, 283; and International Labor Office, *Employment, Wages and International Trade*, pp. 13–20. The former finds that from 1850 to 1937 the productivity *per worker* in the United States (assumption of a 60-hour week) rises steadily with very few interruptions, that the rise per worker is not so great or so uninterrupted when the actual hours of work are considered, and finally that the results are less favorable still when allowance is made for unemployment. Differences are to be found, moreover, between British and American experience, and particularly in the last few years.

the prices of imported goods do not fluctuate with the price of the national composite product.[1] Again, wages may diverge from the marginal value product for other reasons. These possibilities were discussed in Sec. 14.1 and in Sec. 15.5 and need not, therefore, be gone into here.

Let us consider further the relation of wage rates and the incidence of social security taxes. The possibilities are presented below.

1. *Business improves*

    a. Assumption of a decline of real wage rates
        Money wages +
        Real wages −

    b. Assumption of a rise of real wage rates
        Money wages +
        Real wages +

2. *Business recedes*

    a. Assumption of an increase of real wage rates
        Money wages −
        Real wages +

    b. Assumption of a decline of real wage rates
        Money wages −
        Real wages −

If real wage movements are in the direction indicated under 1a (periods of improvement), the workers may not be disposed to accept *what they may consider*[2] a further reduction of real wages following the imposition of pay-roll taxes, whether the reduction comes through a direct assault on wages or through a rise in the cost of living. Should wage earners, however, be primarily concerned with their money wages, as Mr. Keynes is inclined to argue, then their resistance to attempts to pass the tax on to them will not be so great as is assumed above. The likelihood of absorption by the workers is greater under the findings presented in 1b than under 1a, for under the former both money and real wages rise.

It is necessary, however, to consider the rewards to the other factors of production. Monetary rewards to those receiving rents and interest may rise though their real rewards are likely to fall. Of particular significance is the rise in profits, both real and monetary, which may well be large. It follows, therefore, that there may be weak resistance on the part of entrepreneurs and owners to a

[1] KEYNES, *op. cit., passim,* and PIGOU, *op. cit.,* p. 64.
[2] Their opposition to a reduction of money (and real) wages will be conditioned of course by their evaluation of the benefits conferred by insurance.

pressure to put the cost on them; and they may, therefore, be forced to pay part of the cost of social security in a period of rising business activity. Supply price of labor then rises; and workers obtain their marginal product at a relatively early point. Profits rise, allow us to observe, because demand and prices both improve. The net effects of the rise of demand and prices plus any accompanying gains from economies of production may then more than offset any rise in the rewards to the factors of production or any other rise in costs associated with an expansion of output. Though real wages rise, they may not rise so much as labor's marginal product.[1] In periods of business upswings, then, the introduction of social security taxes may provide labor with an occasion to obtain its full marginal product. In addition, labor may force entrepreneurs to give up part of their windfall profits. In the absence of monopolistic practices and imperfect foresight, excess profits would soon vanish; but competitive conditions and perfect knowledge are not always present, and adjustments through additional employment require time.

In periods of declining activity, wage earners may be expected to bear the brunt of the taxes if wage movements are in the direction indicated by Mr. Keynes. In other words, their real wages rise and, therefore, they are susceptible to pressure following the payment of pay-roll taxes. Excessive attention to money wages may, however, induce workers to resist further cuts of money wages. The probability of forcing labor to pay the costs of social security increases when attention is given to the very large reduction of monetary and real profits. It may well be that wage earners now receive wages in excess of their marginal product; and any success in putting the cost of social security on entrepreneurs will make the excess even larger. If real wages decline (2b), in the absence of the pay-roll taxes, wage earners will be less disposed to accept the cost of social insurance than on the assumption of a rise of real wages (2a).

We may conclude that with an improvement of business the resistance on the part of all interested groups tends to weaken. Since profits rise much more relatively than the rewards of other groups, it is fair to assume that on the rise a large part of the cost will fall on profits. The extent of the burden of social security to be imposed upon the workers is likely to be greater if our statistical

[1] Entrepreneurs, it should be noted, are interested in the cost of living because it affects the level of money wages; but in dealing with the problem of output, they have to take into account not only money wages but also the prices of their *products*.

findings or those of Dr. Dunlop and Prof. Tarshis are correct (*i.e.*, real wages rise) than if the movements are as indicated by Mr. Keynes. In periods of declining business activity, the possibilities of putting the burden on profits are not great; and the cost to labor will be greater on Mr. Keynes's conclusions relative to the direction of wage movements than on those given in 2*b*. For on Mr. Keynes's assumptions, real wage rates rise in periods of declining activity. If, on the other hand, excessive attention is paid to money wages, workers may resist further cuts in money wages; and they will resist despite an excess of wage rates over marginal product. Finally, workers' reactions will also be determined by movements of real *weekly* wage rates and by the real wage *bill* of *all* workers as well as by hourly real wage rates of the individual worker.

In the task of determining the distribution of the cost of pay-roll taxes, it is always important to distinguish movements in real wage rates that are justified by changes in productivity and those that are not. In the decline, for example, a rise of real wage rates will encounter less opposition on the part of entrepreneurs (and, therefore, they will be more disposed to accept the costs of pay-roll taxes) if the rise is justified by an improvement in productivity than if it is not.

15.7. CONCLUSION

Given a sufficiently elastic monetary system, a rise of money wages may be accompanied by an improvement in monetary demand and, therefore, may not require a reduction of employment. It follows, therefore, that a failure to pass pay-roll taxes on to employees or others is not necessarily harmful to employment. Those who support high-wage policies emphasize the elasticity of monetary supplies (and hence the absence of unfavorable effects via the rate of interest), the favorable effects of transfers of income to those who have a high marginal propensity to consume, and the relative inelasticity of demand for commodities on the part of nonwage earners. In the attack on Prof. Pigou's defense of wage cutting, his adversaries contended that (1) a reduction of wages could affect output via the rate of interest and in no other way; (2) a reduction in the rate of interest would be reinforced if the marginal propensity to consume were affected favorably; and (3) with fixed equipment, savings and investment are determined by the rate of interest and the volume of output, and the distribution of income is a function of the latter. Wage cutting will not contribute toward a rise of output unless the net effects on the rate of interest, marginal propensity to consume, and the marginal efficiency of capital, which jointly determine output, are favorable.

A rise of wages, which is accompanied by a rise of monetary demand, may be quite consistent with the marginal productivity theory; for productivity is not independent of the state of monetary demand. Marginal productivity of labor may also rise if the marginal propensity to consume rises and if, with the resulting increase of output, the productivity function of labor over the relevant area has a positive slope. Wages may of course also increase over the short period despite a failure of marginal productivity to rise. It is also well to note at this point that wages may be at a level or may now be raised to a level too high to assure full employment.

Finally we have dwelt upon the movements of real and money wages over periods of rising and declining activity. The evidence seems to show that real and money wages rise in periods of business activity. It therefore follows that in periods of prosperity the entrepreneur may well succeed in forcing labor to pay the costs of social security. The issues are not so clear in periods of declining activity. It is well to distinguish total, weekly, and hourly wage payments. Real hourly wage rates may fall or rise in such periods, but total real wages are most likely to fall, and weekly wages will probably fall. Labor will resist attempts to put the costs of social security on them, the more so since money wages will probably fall. Entrepreneurs will, however, be much more insistent than in periods of prosperity.

CHAPTER 16

MONETARY ASSUMPTIONS

16.1. INTRODUCTION

In Part I, the monetary aspects of the investment of social security funds were discussed and in Chap. 15 the relation of wage and monetary policy. A successful outcome of a high-wage policy depends in no small part upon its repercussions on the demand for and supply of money and hence upon the rate of interest. The object of this chapter is to deal *briefly* with the direct effects of the social security program upon the supplies of money. If, for example, there are reasons for assuming that in response to the program monetary supplies increase, then the probability of forward shifting to consumers, the issue of the next chapter, increases. In the classical literature on incidence, however, the assumption made is that of unchanged monetary supplies.[1] It follows on this assumption that the expenditure of more money on one commodity will be offset by an equal reduction of expenditures on other commodities. We shall return to the classical position later.[2]

16.2. THE STATE OF THE ECONOMY.

Let us assume for the moment that the annual cost to business of social security of X billion dollars is financed by the creation of X billion dollars of additional purchasing power. Available information on the circulation of money suggests, however, that the required rise of money would be considerably less than X billion dollars.

---

[1] *Cf.* BROWN, H. G., *The Economics of Taxation*, pp. 162–163; MERIAM, R. S., "Unemployment Reserves: Some Questions of Principles," *Quart. Jour. Econ.*, 1933, p. 317; COHEN, J. L., "The Incidence of the Costs of Social Insurance," *Internat. Labor Rev.*, 1929, pp. 827–829.

[2] Consumption expenditures may of course rise at the expense of savings. This diversion may possibly result in a rise of MV and in that case should be considered analogous to a rise in the supply of money.

In the discussion of this and the next chapter, the elastic monetary systems are referred to. They would provide additional supplies of money in response to a rise of total money wages (inclusive of benefits) and spending. Despite the new demands, the rate of interest would go up little, if at all.

1. Let us dwell on a rising economy. A rising economy may be defined as one in which $E = ++$ and $E/Po = +$, where $E =$ output and $Po =$ population. (Others may prefer the definition $E+$ and E/Po not $-$.) Aside from ensuing repercussions upon the supplies of money, which will be discussed immediately, the effect (via the demand for money) would tend to be a decline of prices. Actually money usually rises in such periods in amounts sufficient to overcome the downward pressure and to induce a rise of prices. The latter part of the nineteenth century was a notable exception; and the tendency of prices was slightly downward in the twenties. Any new need for additional supplies of money induced by the security program would have had unfortunate effects in the former period but, in the light of the profit inflation of the twenties, would have been a fortunate factor in the latter period when increased pressure on available supplies of money would have retarded the rise of the twenties. In other periods of rising activity, $e.g.$, 1914–1919, 1933–1937, 1938–1940, the additional supplies of money would probably have been forthcoming. It is well to keep in mind that the required supplies may come from idle balances or from the creation of additional supplies of money which are supported by reserves created through activities of the central banks, devaluation, and the like, or are already available. Clearly when the country has excess reserves of 6 or 7 billion dollars and a large proportion of deposits are idle for long periods, the provision of additional active purchasing power offers no great obstacles. This is, however, subject to reservations to be made later.

2. What of a declining economy? We may define this as one in which $E = -$ and $E/Po = --$. On the assumption of unchanged supplies of active money, prices would rise. The decline in activity, however, induces a reduction of MV adequate to bring a reduction of prices despite further curtailment of activity, which is in turn related to the ensuing decline of prices, and which in itself would tend to raise prices. Any pressure on monetary supplies in periods of depression, which is associated with an upward pressure on prices resulting from forward shifting of taxes, will put an added strain on the economy. One reservation may be made, however. The decline

in prices is explained by (1) inadequate supplies of money resulting
from the contraction of business and (2) excessive demand for money
to satisfy the desire for liquidity. The latter, however, will in large
part account for the former; and the unfortunate effects of the increased demand for money to finance social security will follow
largely from adverse effects upon the demand for money to satisfy
liquidity preference. If the effects via the requirements for cash to
satisfy liquidity requirements are not adverse, the damage done will
not be serious. It is, furthermore, to be kept in mind that there are
important reasons why the effects on liquidity preference may not
be adverse, or greatly so. Expenditures of benefits under the unemployment insurance program in depression periods will be larger
than tax receipts; and the excess of receipts for old-age insurance
will be relatively smaller than in more prosperous times.

Monetary supplies have shown remarkable elasticity in the
United States. At times they have perhaps been too elastic upward,
thus inducing excessive expansion; and in 1929–1932 the decline
was excessive, thus aggravating the depression that accounted for
the initial reduction in the supply of money. In the years 1914 to
1929 (for an example of the elasticity upward) monetary income of
the country rose 50 per cent; and monetary supplies rose sufficiently
to make possible and even stimulate the expansion. Bank debits
in the country were twice as high in 1929 as in 1918; and the supply
of money rose by about one-quarter from 1921 to 1929 and one-half
from 1921 to 1937.[1]

16.3. The Ensuing Rise in Money

On the classical assumption, MV does not change. We may assume either (1) that wages are reduced by the amount of the tax or
(2) that costs rise by the amount of the taxes. No problem arises
under 1. We shall therefore be concerned with 2. If we assume that
prices must still cover costs and that prices rise and MV remains
unchanged, then it is required that T in the quantity equation
$\left(P = \dfrac{MV}{T}\right)$ should fall.[2] Another alternative is to assume that P rises,

---

[1] N.I.C.B., *Studies in Enterprise and Social Progress*, p. 79; *Survey of Current
Business*, 1938, Supplement, p. 53; National Resources Committee, *Structure of
the American Economy*, p. 87.

[2] P = prices; M = money; V = velocity; T = transactions.

T remains unchanged, and MV rises.[1] The proponents of this anti-classical position ought then to account for the rise in the supply of money.

It is in fact not exactly necessary that the supply of money be increased. Consumers may, for example, pay the higher prices asked now by entrepreneurs out of hoards of cash. There will be some difficulties, however, as we shall see in the next chapter. We may go back a step. Entrepreneurs may pay the additional wages out of accumulated balances. They then raise prices by the proportion required by the new taxes and receive back as receipts all or a large part of the additional outlays. Pensioners and the unemployed account for part of the additional monetary demand for goods and services; and in so far as reserves are accumulated, additional demand *may* emanate from investment channels.

What if idle balances are not available and a maintenance of output requires the creation of additional supplies of money? It has been held that when marginal costs rise the incentive to increase supplies of money is not present.[2] This is not necessarily so. The profitability of a business enterprise depends not only on costs but also on demand. If business management appraises the effects on demand correctly, they may well be justified in seeking more funds from the banks. In the absence of deflationary effects of accumulation of reserves and with an improvement in the marginal propensity to consume, the favorable effects upon demand may outweigh the unfavorable effects of a rise of costs. Businessmen, however, may be more aware of the rise of costs than of the ensuing improvement of demand.

A word should also be said of the possible adverse effects of the rise in the demand for active money upon the rate of interest.[3] A niggardly policy on the part of the monetary authority would be unfortunate. A cooperative policy based on the anticipated improvement of demand may even provide the additional supplies without any large net rise in supplies. Confidence may improve, and the

[1] On this question, Ricardo and Trower concluded that a rise in V would allow the price level to rise even in the absence of an increase in the stock of money. *Letters of Ricardo to Trower*, pp. 234–236. (Prof. Shoup brought my attention to this discussion.)

[2] DOUGLAS, P. H., "The Effect of Wage Increases upon Employment," *Proc. Am. Econ. Assoc.*, 1939, pp. 149–150.

[3] *Cf.* ROBINSON, J., *Essays in the Theory of Employment*, pp. 24–29; LERNER, A. P., "The Relation of Wage Policies and Price Policies," *Proc. Am. Econ. Assoc.*, 1939, pp. 159–160, 163–166; and this book, Secs. 15.2 to 15.4.

additional supplies may be obtained at the expense of supplies held to satisfy the speculative *or liquidity* motive.

Difficulties arise in the process of issue of additional credits to producers in order to finance the social security program. It is not easy to issue the amount of money that will prevent a contraction of employment and yet not induce inflation. One is reminded of the difficulties confronted by the monetary authority when it operates on the monetary system via producer credits. Much then depends on the point of injection, the mobility of factors, and the effects on velocity. Space is not available, however, to consider these problems.[1]

Further elucidation of the issues is provided by an examination of Prof. Pigou's standard monetary system. In general, his position is that the aggregate money income available is to be some function of real income.

I define the standard monetary system as one so constructed that, for all sorts of movements in the real demand function for labour or in real rates of wages, whether they last for a long time or a short, the aggregate money income is increased or diminished by precisely the difference made to the number of workpeople (or other factors of production) at work multiplied by the original rate of money wages.[2] (Prof. Pigou italicizes this definition.)

His definition seems to be directed toward the differentiation of monetary and nonmonetary disturbances; but it also seems to suggest the ideal monetary system.[3]

Under Prof. Pigou's standard monetary system, monetary income would be reduced *pari passu* with a reduction of employment following the introduction of a social security program. This is not, however, very helpful, for the effects upon the real demand for labor (and employment) will depend in no small part upon the choice of monetary policies. Acceptance of the classical position would require then that management and the monetary authority agree on a policy that reduces monetary incomes in the proper proportion.[4]

[1] See, for example, DURBIN, E. F. M., *The Problem of Credit Policy*, pp. 43–67.

[2] From PIGOU, A. C., *The Theory of Unemployment*, pp. 205–206. By permission of The Macmillan Company, publishers. *Cf.* also pp. 102, 104.

[3] *Ibid.*, pp. 211–213.

[4] *Cf.* ROBERTSON, D. H., *Banking Policy and the Price Level*, pp. 23–27. Should monetary policy be based upon *effort elasticity* of demand for income, there would seem to be no strong reason why monetary incomes should be reduced following the introduction of a social security program. Misapprehensions concerning the effects of the program may of course have such effects.

Why not, however, act on the assumption that real demand suffers only because monetary policy is not sufficiently expansive and that expansion is justified by inelastic demand for some commodities and shifts of demand following a rise of money wages?

There are then two possible objections to Prof. Pigou's standard system. One is that, at least in this connection, real demand is a function of the monetary policy and, therefore, is meaningless when considered irrespective of monetary conditions. The second objection is raised by Mr. Hawtrey. Correct monetary policy demands not merely passive adjustment to nonmonetary causes of unemployment but attempts to counteract them.[1]

16.4. CONCLUSION

Preliminary to the discussion of forward shifting in the next chapter, some monetary aspects of the problem of social security have been examined. The classical assumption of an unchanged MV is one of many possible assumptions. That the demand for numerous commodities is inelastic and that a rise in monetary demand may follow the introduction of the program are, on the other hand, reasons for assuming a policy of monetary expansion. What are the sources of the additional cash? Disbursement of idle balances in response to a rise of prices in itself constitutes a rise of MV. Furthermore, in periods of increasing activity, the source of *additional* supplies of active purchasing power is readily to be found; and even in depression periods the difficulties may not be so great as is frequently assumed. In general, businessmen may borrow or use their idle balances. The extent of their borrowing will depend upon their ability to envisage the favorable effects upon demand as against the unfavorable effects upon costs. Whether the increased supplies of money will be forthcoming or not without adverse effects on the rate of interest will depend upon the response of the monetary authority and the effects of the program upon the need of cash to satisfy requirements of liquidity. Finally, it should be observed that the real shifts of demand for the factors will depend upon monetary policy and should not be considered irrespective of it.

[1] HAWTREY, R. G., *Capital and Employment*, p. 288.

CHAPTER 17

SHIFT OF TAXES TO CONSUMERS

17.1. INTRODUCTION

Entrepreneurs may attempt to pass pay-roll taxes on to consumers through a rise of prices. In that manner they will indirectly pass the burden on to the most important class of consumers, *i.e.*, laborers and other low-income groups, and to some extent to others. Prices rise as costs rise. The net effect on output will depend upon the elasticity of demand for the commodity and how, as the volume of output changes, unit costs are affected. Resistance by consumers will frequently be weaker than by labor *qua* wage earners. A successful outcome will depend in no small part upon the response of the monetary system. The more elastic the monetary supplies, the more likely that business will succeed in making the consumer pay. Their success will depend also on a related variable, *viz.*, the elasticity of total expenditures of consumers. This in turn will be a function of their income, which again will be influenced by the security program.[1]

In the discussion that follows, we *assume* an employment pay-roll tax of 5 per cent assessed upon employers. At present the tax on employers may be estimated at 3 per cent. It is not, however, unlikely that pay-roll taxes for *both* unemployment and old-age insurance may well ultimately come to 10 per cent or more. At any rate, for illustrative purposes, it is assumed that the total tax will be 5 per cent for unemployment and 5 per cent for old-age insurance. The employment tax is discussed for the most part, though later the old-age insurance tax is considered.

Suppose a tax of 5 per cent of the total pay-roll is levied on employers. They of course may attempt to pass the tax on to consumers through a rise of prices or to wage earners through a reduction of wages. It may be estimated that such a tax would yield approxi-

[1] *Cf.* COLM, G., "Methods of Financing Unemployment Compensation," *Soc. Research*, 1935, p. 156; GILBOY, E., "Income-expenditure Relations," *Rev. Econ. Statistics*, 1940, pp. 117–119.

mately 2 billion dollars in the course of a year.[1] The assumption is also made that a period of prosperity of eight years (say 1940–1947) is followed by a period of depression in the following eight years (1948–1955). In the first period the amount of tax collected is in excess of the disbursements to the unemployed, the rather optimistic estimate of excess of receipts putting the Fund at the end of eight years at 4 billions. In the following four years the accumulations of the preceding years are used up, and in the last four years of the period the Fund borrows from the government.

17.2. Distribution of Incomes, Consumption, and Savings

The following figures form the basis of the discussion that follows.[2] It is scarcely necessary to say that the Resources Committee's conclusions on the distribution of income, which are used here, have been subjected to criticism. According to Dr. Tucker, for example, sampling was deficient, and for that and other reasons the importance of low and high groups has been exaggerated.[3]

Wages and salaries account roughly for two-thirds of the national income;[4] and if we assume that all incomes below $3000 are to be included in these categories, then (5d in Table I) workers and farmers, who may for the purpose of this analysis be treated as workers,

[1] Wages and salaries in 1939 were 44 billion dollars. The assumption that 40 billion dollars would be subject to pay-roll taxes is obviously excessive for 1940 though not for later years. Allowance is to be made for noncovered wages; but on the other hand it may not be unreasonable to assume further extensions of coverage and a rise in the wage bill. In any case the reader who may object to the estimate of a taxable pay-roll of 40 billion dollars for the years 1940–1960 (say) is urged to accept that figure as a pure hypothesis. The preceding figure comes from the *Survey of Current Business, Annual Review Number*, 1940, p. 53.

The President's committee estimated that for the years 1922–1933 coverage of 16 million workers out of 26 millions gainfully occupied would have yielded an average of 825 million dollars if the rate had been 3 per cent. *Report to the President of the Committee on Economic Security*, 1935, p. 12.

[2] National Resources Committee, *Consumer Expenditures in the United States*, 1939, p. 77; *Survey Current Business*, 1939, Annual Review Number, p. 28 for retail sales; Department of Commerce, *National Income*, 1929–36, p. 16, for wages and salaries.

[3] Tucker, R. S., "The National Resources Committee's Report on Distribution of Income," *Rev. Econ. Statistics*, 1940, pp. 165–182 and especially p. 179.

[4] N.I.C.B., *Studies in Enterprise and Social Progress*, 1939, p. 88.

TABLE I.—INCOMES, RETAIL SALES, CONSUMPTION, AND SAVINGS

Billions of dollars

1. Consumers' incomes 1935–1936............................ 59
2. Wages and salaries 1935–1936 (average).................... 39
3. Retail sales, 1937... 40
4. Current consumption, 1935–1936........................... 50
5. Income, consumption, and savings by income classes, 1935–1936

Income classes	Per cent of total number	Aggregate income, billion dollars	Per cent of total income	Current consumption		Savings	
				Billion dollars	Per cent of total	Billion dollars	Per cent of total
a. Income < $780...........	33.3	6.2	10.4	7.2	14.4	−1.2	−20.2
b. Incomes $780–$1,450......	33.3	14.2	23.9	13.9	27.7	−0.3	− 4.2
c. Upper third, $1,450 and over...................	33.3	38.9	65.7	29.1	57.9	7.4	124.4
d. a + b + incomes $1,450–$3,000 (incomes < $3,000)...............	93.0	41.0	69.1	39.4	78.4	0.1	1.2

account for 78.4 per cent of all consumption.[1] Farmers will resist price rises in the same manner as other low- and moderate-income groups. It should be observed, moreover, that any rise in prices of

	Data for 1938	Billion dollars
Department of Commerce.....	Dividends and interest	8.5
	Entrepreneurial income and rents and royalties	13.7*
N.I.C.B....................	*Realized* dividends, interest, rents and royalties	5.0
	Entrepreneurial income	10.4†

* *Survey Current Business, Annual Review Number*, 1940, p. 53.

† N.I.C.B., *Studies in Enterprise and Social Progress*, 1939, p. 85. *Cf.* also, Temporary National Economic Committee, Monograph 4, *Concentration and Composition of Individual Incomes*, 1918–1937, p. 48.

goods bought by farmers will constitute a gain for workers at the expense of farmers. A rise of prices will nevertheless contribute for

[1] The violence done to truth by the acceptance of this assumption may not be great. In a recent year (1938), the total of dividends, interests, and rents and royalties (*realized private production*) was but 5 billion dollars. According to one study, however, roughly one-half (2.4 billion dollars) of all dividends in 1936 was obtained by those whose incomes were below $5,000. Entrepreneurial income (10.4 billions) was the most important type of income other than salaries and wages. The Department of Commerce, however, puts the emphasis upon income *payments* and finds larger amounts of capitalist income (*cf.* above table.)

the most part to a reduction of real wages. Consumption expenditures in the year 1935–1936 amounted to 50 billion dollars, though in the more prosperous year of 1937 retail sales were but 40 billion dollars.[1] (Consumption expenditures are more comprehensive than retail sales.)

It should be observed that consumers will resist any upward revision of prices. Thus the lowest third in the income scale, *i.e.*, those earning less than $780 annually, spend 7.2 billion dollars for consumption (14.4 per cent of all such expenditures) though their income is but 6.2 billion dollars.

A pay-roll tax of 5 per cent on wages and salaries of 40 billion will be absorbed by consumers (on the assumption of forward shifting exclusively) through a rise in the level of prices of consumers' commodities of 4 per cent. (Two billion dollars equal 4 per cent of 50 billion dollars.) Income recipients in the poorest class (5a in Table I) will be confronted with a rise in the sales price of consumption goods of 290 millions (4 per cent of 7.2 billion dollars). They will either cut consumption or require additional relief. (In the latter case the government will then pay out in relief part of the proceeds of the pay-roll tax.)

Resistance will also be offered by the middle third (incomes $780 to $1,450) who account for 28 per cent of consumption and actually dissave to the extent of 250 million dollars. They seem to be faced with the following alternatives in meeting the pay-roll charge of 560 million dollars (4 per cent of 13.9 billion dollars) on their consumption: a reduction of consumption, an increase of dissaving, a rise of income through more work.

The richest third who will be asked to pay 1,160 millions additional (4 per cent of 29.1 billion dollars) if they are to maintain their consumption will offer the weakest resistance. They may maintain their consumption if they cut their savings by one-sixth.

We may assume that, in the absence of additional public aid, the lowest third maintain the dollar value of their consumption unchanged;[2] that the middle third reduce their real consumption, but increase their money expenditures by one-third of the cost of a 4 per cent rise in prices on their original consumption; and that the

[1] The N.I.C.B. seems to estimate consumption expenditures at a higher level than the National Resources Committee. Its estimate *for* 1935 was 57 billion dollars. N.I.C.B., *Studies in Enterprise and Social Progress*, 1939, p. 139.

[2] The National Resources Committee estimates for 1935–1936 that this group spends 98 per cent of the 6.2 billion dollars of its *income* (not *expenditures* note) on

highest third cover the additional cost to the extent of three quarters through a rise of money outlay and one quarter through a curtailment of purchases. Consumers will then pay 1,100 million dollars, or 53 per cent of the taxes; and the remainder will be passed on to workers directly or absorbed by industry. Industry may, however, have to absorb an additional amount in excess of the difference between 2,000 and 1,100 million dollars on account of the decline in the quantity of purchases. How much will depend in part on the slope of the marginal supply curves. We assume that group *b* works

Income group	Additional consumption in millions of dollars*	Effect on savings
a. Lowest third.............................	0	0
b. Middle third†...........................	200	−200
c. Richest third...........................	900	−900
	1,100	−1,100

* Totals in round numbers.

† The net reduction of savings will be somewhat less as this group is assumed to increase hours of work.

harder and increases its income, but group *a* is unable to increase its earnings, and group *c* has no desire to do so. Furthermore, some concessions in prices will be made by entrepreneurs, and, therefore, the reduction of consumption will not be so great as it at first seems.

In this discussion we do not mean to imply that when a group reduces its consumption (its total monetary expenditures unchanged) it does not bear part of the burden: the reduction of consumption is adequate evidence of cost.

The discussion has proceeded so far on the assumption that low-income classes are confronted with a rise of prices and their incomes remain unchanged. It is necessary, however, to allow for any expansion of monetary supplies which accompanies the unfolding of the security program. This was the subject of the preceding chapter. Low-income classes may gain from this expansion as they will gain from any disbursements of the security administration. They will lose, on the other hand, from adverse effects that may follow the accumulation of reserves. The net effect of these considerations is

food, clothing, and shelter. They do, however, spend almost 20 per cent of their total *outlays* on other items of expenditure. *Consumer Expenditures in the United States*, pp. 9, 78, *Cf.* National Resources Committee, *Structure of the American Economy*, 1939, pp. 11, 13; and N.I.C.B., *Studies in Enterprise and Social Progress*, p. 137.

likely to be that consumption will be more nearly maintained than is to be inferred from our calculations.[1]

The following figures may also throw some light on these problems:[2]

TABLE II.—CONSUMERS' OUTLAY, SUBSISTENCE AND MAINTENANCE EXPENDITURES,
1910–1937
(In billions of dollars, except row 3)

	1910	1929	1935–1936	1937
1. Consumers' outlay..........................	26.5	81.4	57.2	71.0
2. Subsistence expenditures.....................	17.4	37.2	27.9	31.2
3. Per cent (2) of (1)..........................	66	46	49	44
4. Maintenance expenditures....................	....	....	35.5	40.5
5. Of families and individuals above maintenance level...............................	....	....	21	26
6. Below maintenance level...................	....	....	15	14

An examination of the N.I.C.B. study will satisfy the reader that these figures give only rough indications of the facts. Furthermore, the definition of subsistence and maintenance expenditures is necessarily arbitrary. "By definition the submarginal or subsistence consumption unit has been placed at the expenditure level corresponding to the mode of prevailing income distributions. . . . The subsistence level of expenditures was determined from the most frequent income in the low-income groups. . . . " The marginal consumption unit (maintenance level) "lies at that income range where savings first appears. . . . "[3] Yet one may draw some conclusions from these figures. The percentage to consumers' outlay

---

[1] Statistical material published in the *Structure of the American Economy* (especially pp. 83–84, 88–91) is of some interest here. (1) It is assumed that since consumers, who have incomes of less than $5,000 and account for 88 per cent of consumption, own but 10 to 14 per cent of bank deposits the stimulation of consumption through disbursements of accumulated cash is not likely to be great. (2) One may infer from the larger decline of savings than consumption in the years 1929–1932 that a reduction of income (or what is similar, a general rise of prices) is likely to result in a *relative* rise of consumption at the expense of savings.

Cf. GILBOY, *op. cit.*, pp. 115–121. Dr. Gilboy finds that the *collective* propensity to consume is 0.74. The propensity to consume is of course found to be much higher in lower incomes, *e.g.*, below $2,000. In other words, a rise of x income for low-income classes will result in a rise of consumption $> 0.74x$. A general rise of prices should then result in a large curtailment of real purchases for the poor. It is, however, necessary to take into account the sluggishness in the change of consumption habits.

[2] Table constructed from materials in N.I.C.B., *Studies in Enterprise and Social Progress*, 1939, pp. 142–153.

[3] *Ibid.*, pp. 143, 149.

of free expenditures, *i.e.*, the excess of consumers' outlay over subsistence expenditures, is much higher than before the war. Thus food expenditures are less important, and the proportion of essential food expenditures declines in significance.[1] It is, therefore, to that extent easier to curtail purchases in response to a rise of prices. In 1910, the excess of outlay over subsistence expenditures was 9 billion dollars, in 1935–1936, almost 30 billion dollars. Another interesting fact is that an excess of consumers' outlay over maintenance expenditures is available to but one-half of all families and units.[2] The others can defend themselves against a rise in prices only in the manner indicated in an earlier part of this section.

17.3. The Extent of the Burden and the Success in Putting the Cost on Nonwage Earners

The immediate effect of the introduction of an unemployment insurance scheme will probably be an attempt to put the burden on the consumer rather than to make an assault on earnings. To a substantial degree the two come to the same thing, of course, for the rise in prices contributes toward a reduction in real wages. Any success in raising prices will to that extent make unnecessary a cut in wages; but it will also result in a reduction of the real income of nonwage earners. The possibility of raising prices against the nonwage earners is particularly great in the industries producing necessities and seminecessities (demand inelastic), and a *strong* possibility exists even in numerous luxury industries. In so far as the nonwage earners accept the rise in prices, continuing to purchase the same quantity of goods, or a smaller quantity at a higher value, the entrepreneur and the wage earner have succeeded in passing part of the monetary cost on to the nonwage earners.[3] The issues are not, however, quite so simple as is here indicated. Assume that output

---

[1] *Ibid.*, pp. 146–147, 153.

[2] *Ibid.*, pp. 147–149.

[3] It is held by the National Resources Committee that price variations account for but a small part of the variations of consumption. In their view, price fluctuations are rare for many commodities and of minor proportions for many others. Prices do not account for variations in consumption of the bulk of industrial products. Fluctuations in buying power are held to be the most significant variable accounting for changes in the volume of consumption; and durable goods are particularly sensitive to fluctuations in buying power. May we observe, however, that a *general* rise of

declines but money value of sales rises. Then the effects upon costs and employment require consideration. Total unit cost for a smaller output may rise, especially if the short-period marginal costs are falling. (The obvious case here is that of monopolistic competition.)

A success in thus diverting the burden will undoubtedly depend to some extent upon the degree of the rise of prices which is necessary in order to compensate for the payments on account of insurance. Should wages, as is suggested above, constitute two-thirds of the total costs and the tax be 5 per cent of the pay-rolls, then the entrepreneur would be compensated adequately if prices were to rise 3+ per cent. That wages are much less than two-thirds of the *value added by manufacture* is not to be taken as evidence that labor costs are much less than two-thirds of all costs.[1] It is necessary to allow for the wages paid in earlier steps of the economic process, and if this allowance is made, a rise of several per cent may be necessary. The tax in any case is not in excess of 5 per cent of the *sum* of all pay-rolls in the industrial process. A rise of prices of 3 to 4 per cent seems a reasonable guess on the assumption of (1) a 5 per cent tax, (2) wage costs equal to two-thirds of all costs, and (3) universal coverage. More success in passing the tax on to consumers will be forthcoming in some industries than in others. Less resistance will be encountered in those, for example, producing commodities for which the demand is inelastic and those in which wages are a relatively small part of total costs. More is said on some of these issues in the next chapter. (The reader is reminded of the assumption made here, *viz.*, the tax is passed on to consumers exclusively.)

Some industries will suffer more than others, In particular those producing wage goods, *i.e.*, goods consumed predominantly by the wage-earning classes (incomes < $3,000) will lose business. Within this group, however, industries producing absolute necessities will not suffer greatly and may well gain: the poor respond to a general rise of prices by redistributing their expenditures in favor of more essential goods. They buy, for example, more energy-producing

---

price is analogous in its effects to a reduction of buying power and, therefore, will have adverse effects on consumption. *Patterns of Resource Use*, preliminary edition, 1939, pp. 8–9; *The Structure of the American Economy*, pp. 18–20.

[1] The House Committee on the *Economic Security Bill*, 1935, was wrong to argue that the burden on consumers would be small because the *direct labor costs* of all manufactured commodities represented on the average about 21 per cent of the value of the product. *The Social Security Bill*, House Report 615 (74: 1), p. 16. *Cf.* Senate Document (73: 2), 124, *National Income 1929–1932*, p. 14, where it was shown that labor income was 65 per cent of all income in 1929 and 1932.

foods (bread, fats) and less protective foods (milk, vegetables). We repeat, however, that the wage-goods industries will probably on the whole suffer more than the nonwage-goods industries though capital-goods and some durable consumers' goods industries may also be affected adversely. Limitation of income plays a decisive part in markets for wage goods. Elasticity of demand is, however, likely to be greater for any one nonwage good, (*e.g.*, automobiles) than for a wage good (*e.g.*, bread).

Wage goods, though a useful, is not an unambiguous term.[1] Wage earners may consume 95 per cent of the market of one commodity and but 1 per cent of another. High-income classes may consume 99 per cent of the latter, *e.g.*, caviar. For the purpose of this analysis, wage-goods industries are those which are largely dependent upon low-income classes for their sales. It is also helpful to distinguish between wage goods and other consumer goods, the latter being consumer commodities largely sold to the high-income classes. Nonwage goods would then include the latter and capital goods.

In this section the argument has been that through a rise of prices the burden may be put upon nonwage-earning classes; but the success will depend in part upon the extent of the rise of prices required. If, for example, a rise of 10 per cent in prices is required, nonwage-earning classes may be called upon to make great sacrifices. Their reduction of purchases may, however, result in the infliction of losses on workers through a diminution of employment, which may offset the gains associated with the higher prices received from nonwage-earners. Industries will be affected in varying degrees by the curtailment of purchases. Wage-goods industries will especially suffer since the low-income classes have not the savings for the maintenance of their consumption; other consumer-goods industries will be affected since demand may well be elastic; and capital-goods industries may also suffer, both in response to a reduction of consumption and in response to a diminution of savings.

17.4. Losses Suffered by Labor and Others

We may now turn to our estimate that in the period of accumulation the unemployment insurance fund collects 4 billion dollars.

[1] Pigou, A. C., *Theory of Unemployment*, pp. 17–20; Hawtrey, R. G., *Capital and Employment*, especially p. 278.

The accumulation of cash may have adverse effects on output as has been suggested in Part I; and the process may be cumulative. As the years go on, employment income, expenditures, and savings may suffer as a result of a curtailment of output. Much depends upon the reaction of the entrepreneur to the reduction of sales and much depends upon the use to which the money accumulated by the Fund is put. Stocks may accumulate in such a period, the *continued* inflow of money into the Fund inducing a reduction of prices from the level determined by costs including insurance and other market factors. If, on the other hand, the money at the disposal of the Fund is invested, output and employment and the prices of consumer goods may all rise, the last even more than might be expected from the amount of the pay-roll tax. Nonwage earners will most likely cut savings (and perhaps, to some extent, consumption of *other* consumers' goods) and will be least likely to cut their consumption of wage goods, whereas wage earners will cut their consumption of wage goods. (The issues are discussed here in terms of effects on prices; for a rise of incomes conceivably resulting from a successful investment of the Fund may in turn stimulate savings.) The sacrifices of the wage-earning class may not, however, be so great as they might at first seem; for should commodities tend to accumulate, they may be recouped for their losses through a reduction in prices below the high level determined by costs including insurance. Unfortunate effects on output may, however, follow.

The nonwage-earning classes save less and spend more but, at the time when the balances in the Fund are growing, they probably do not incur any large part of the *real* costs of the insurance scheme. The explanation of this paradox is that their demand is *relatively* inelastic and they therefore maintain their consumption. (Once more, the relatively low-income groups included in the nonwage-earning groups should be differentiated from the other members of this group.) Whatever sacrifices this group as a whole makes are largely in the consumption of other consumers' goods (nonwage consumer goods) or in a reduction of savings, and therefore, their sacrifices do not make more wage goods available for wage earners, except that any depression in the other consumers' goods or in capital-goods industries will eventually stimulate the movement of the factors of production into wage-goods industries and the absorption of new factors by these industries. (Actually the movement of factors is likely to be out of wage-goods industries.) Finally, nonwage earners' command over goods will be reduced in so far as a reduction in savings contributes to a diminution of investment income.

The wage earners make present sacrifices of wage goods as prices rise, anticipating the maintenance of consumption later when unemployment is at a high level. (Deflationary effects are not considered at this point.) They do not exercise their rights to consumption goods fully and thus cause entrepreneurs' inventories to increase temporarily; or if the entrepreneur cuts prices, then their consumption may not decline so much as they had anticipated (aside from the effects of an ensuing decline of output); or if the money put into the Fund is invested, then they may very well suffer additional losses of consumption goods to the newly employed. Furthermore, they may also suffer if, as the demand for nonwage goods rises with a stimulus to investment, the movements of the factors from wage goods into nonwage goods industries are stimulated.

It is scarcely necessary to add that the greater the amount of unemployment of economic resources, the more can be made available for the newly employed and for production of investment goods without the imposition of sacrifices upon the present employed. Their temporary losses to the newly employed and to the industries producing investment goods are mitigated by the successful outcome of the growth of saving that results from the introduction of the social security program. Wasted savings, *e.g.*, resulting from a failure to find outlets, on the other hand, will be costly in terms of employment.

In the short run, the wage-earning and other low-income groups make the significant sacrifices in consumption necessary to pay benefits for the unemployed and to accumulate resources to be used for the payment of benefits later. Eventually, the burden on other classes may rise above that given by their initial reduction of consumption. This will follow, for example, if they cut consumption in response to a later decline of capitalistic income.

Thus we are reminded in this section again, as we were in Part I, that the accumulation of funds *may* have unfortunate effects upon output and prices. Wage earners may obtain more goods for a given income, following a decline of prices; but the ensuing reduction in employment will more than offset this gain. Against this downward pressure we must allow for upward revisions of prices required in the process of forward shifting. This has been the main topic of discussion here. In response to this rise of prices, nonwage earners will cut their savings and consumption of luxuries. Labor will then gain, through an ensuing rise in the supply of wage goods, tardily if at all; and if investment rises the employed may lose command over wage goods to the newly employed, and wage-goods industries may lose factors to nonwage-goods industries.

17.5. The Extent of the Rise of Prices and the Sacrifices Required

It may also be noted that the more ambitious the insurance schemes put into operation and therefore the larger the ensuing rise in prices and also the more pressed are the nonwage-earning classes, the more likely is it that they will cut their consumption of nonwage goods and even wage goods. When allowances are made for the effects of other insurance proposals, *e.g.*, old-age insurance, and for the large gratuitous payments of all sorts now being made by the Federal government, then the possibility of large increases in prices and economies enforced upon nonworkers becomes very strong. Prices rise not only because these expenditures to some extent involve creations of bank credit, but also because they require for their financing direct taxes on industry, *e.g.*, pay-roll taxes, processing taxes, and income taxes. Limitations of income will, however, hamper the entrepreneur in passing the taxes on, although there is some elasticity in the proportions of income saved and spent. Prices will rise; but sales will decline greatly. It is not amiss here to remind the reader of the discussion of the preceding two chapters. The more the rise of wages is accompanied by a rise of monetary supplies and the less the adverse effects on the rate of interest, the less the ensuing decline in the quantity of purchases.

There is still another reason for expecting higher prices. More and more, consumers are being supported who do not contribute to the productive process and yet add their demands to the market demands for consumption goods. Prices of wage goods are therefore likely to rise more than has been assumed up to this point because the factors of production in wage-goods industries are (*relatively* to other industries) fully employed and because the increase in demand is especially felt by these industries. (The result might be, therefore, a greater reduction of purchases of wage goods by the higher income classes, relative to their curtailment of purchases of nonwage goods, than is indicated by the greater elasticity of demand for nonwage goods than for wage goods. This result will follow because prices of wage goods may rise more than those of nonwage goods.) In this connection it is well to recall, however, that low-income classes economize on wage goods following a rise of prices, and this consideration is to be put against the present issue in appraising the net effect on prices of wage goods. In short, a modest social security program financed by a tax on pay-rolls may, therefore, have a more serious effect on the price level and, to that extent, require greater sacrifices from nonwage earners than would be probable if introduced in a period when public expenditures and the monetary system were normal, and in particular when large expenditures for all kinds of relief, and *hence for consumption goods*, were not so popular.

Under our defense economy, of course, the more intensive pressure may be put upon nonwage-goods industries. Prices will tend to rise especially in industries producing capital goods, war supplies, etc. A correct policy may well require then a rise of prices of consumption goods of more substantial proportions than the rise of incomes: consumption will then be discouraged. It would be better, of course, if economies of consumption could be attained through control of the upward movements of incomes, or, failing that, through canalization of incomes, above amounts required to cover minimum consumption needs, into capital markets that will support war industries.

Perhaps a word should be said here concerning the significance of a rise of prices of 4 per cent relative to other fluctuations. Pay-roll taxes were to reach a maximum within 12 years of the passage of the original act.[1] It is, therefore, interesting to compare the burden of the pay-roll taxes on the assumption that the security program was introduced in 1924 and imposed maximum charges in 1936. I do not reproduce my tables; but the absolute burden of the pay-roll tax does not seem large in relation to other costs; and compared with the large fluctuations in prices, national income, labor income, value added by manufacture, and even weekly factory earnings, the imposition of the pay-roll tax does not seem to be a formidable obstacle to management. Its absorption in higher prices or (for that matter) through a *relative* reduction of wages or even through further economies in operation does not seem to offer insurmountable dif-

---

[1] Senate Report 628 (74: 1), *Social Security Bill*, 1935, p. 12.

ficulties.[1] A sample of figures which gives some indication of the
extent of fluctuations follows. (These cover earlier periods also.)

TABLE III.—VARIOUS COSTS AND PROFITS, 1919–1933 (1914 = 100)*

	1919	1933
Cost of materials.............................	202	85
Cost of fabrication and profits....................	209	120
Labor costs....................................	203	117
Overhead costs and profits......................	213	122

* MILLS, F. C., *Prices in Recession and Recovery*, 1936, p. 551.

TABLE IV.—WHOLESALE PRICES, COST OF LIVING, LABOR INCOME, AND NATIONAL
INCOME, 1925–1937

	1925	1929	1932	1933	1935	1937
Wholesale prices* (1926 = 100).....	104	...	65	..	..	86
Cost of living† (1923 = 100)........	104	...	..	75	..	89
Employees compensation‡ (billion dollars)........................	...	52	..	30	..	47
Factory pay-rolls§ (1923–1925 = 100)............................	...	109	46	..	..	98
National income‡ (billion dollars)...	...	79	..	45	55	..

* *Survey Current Business*, 1936 *Supplement*, p. 12; March, 1938, p. 63.
† *Ibid.*, 1936 *Supplement* p. 11, March, 1938, p. 63.
‡ *Ibid.*, June, 1938, p. 13.
§ *Ibid.*, 1936 *Supplement*, p. 36; March, 1937, p. 3; March, 1938, p. 69.

17.6. TAXES LEVIED DIRECTLY ON WORKERS IN RELATION TO PRICES AND SAVINGS

So far the discussion has proceeded on the assumption that the
tax is levied upon the entrepreneur who then seeks compensation
by raising the prices of commodities. The law may require that at
least part of the tax shall be collected from the wage earner directly
as a tax on wages. Several states impose taxes on workers under the
unemployment insurance program, and of course the workers pay
half the tax under old-age insurance. (We shall return to the latter
below.) The larger the proportion of the tax assessed on labor directly, the more modest the rise of prices, and the less the nonwage-

[1] *Cf.* for example, F. C. Mills, *Aspects of Manufacturing Operations During
Recovery*, Nat. Bur. Econ. Research, Bull. 56, 1935.

earning classes would find it necessary to cut into their savings in order to maintain their consumption. Total savings by the Fund *and* the public would, therefore, probably be larger if a tax were collected from workers than if the tax were collected *in toto* from the employer. Wage earners would reduce their purchases immediately rather than through an enforced curtailment following a rise in prices. The ultimate effects on the output of consumption goods, and their distribution, will depend also upon the use to which the savings are put. It is scarcely necessary to mention once more the fact that a substantial part of the low-income classes can reduce their consumption only at great sacrifices.

17.7. Prices in the Period-of Decumulation

What will happen in depression periods when the payments out of the Fund are likely to be in excess of receipts? Entrepreneurs will continue to collect the tax, and therefore in so far as they are unable to pass the tax on to the worker they will try to pass it on to the consumer. At this point it is likely, however, that the effect of the operation of an insurance scheme will be that monetary expenditures will be in excess of what they would have been in its absence. (The possibility of adverse effects in the decumulation period resulting from *earlier* accumulation is left out of account.) We might assume, as in the prosperous period of the cycle, that nonwage earners respond to any rise in prices imposed by entrepreneurs in an attempt to pass the tax on by spending 900 millions more than they otherwise would have spent and that wage earners spend 200 millions more.[1] (As in the earlier discussion, we include as the wage-earning or low- and moderate-income classes all those who earn less than $3,000 yearly. It will be recalled that wages and salaries account for two-thirds of the national income and that 69 per cent of consumers' income in 1935–1936 was obtained by those with incomes less than $3,000.) The Fund now also spends more than it receives. The decline of expenditures by the insured associated with tax payments is more than offset by payments to the unemployed. An unemployment insurance scheme would, therefore, be more

---

[1] Actually receipts will be less in depression periods for wage payments will be smaller.

likely to contribute *toward* higher prices in a period of depression than it would in a period of prosperity. Prices rise not only because entrepreneurs try to pass the pay-roll tax on, but also because the Fund spends more than it receives. The upward pressure on prices emanating from the insurance program would clearly be greater in the decumulation period. If, however, the money saved by the Fund was promptly invested in the accumulation period, the tendency for prices to rise on the upswing might also be present though it would be checked as new consumers' goods began to appear.

The reader is also reminded that in a period of declining activity there are other forces in operation that tend to induce declining prices, and the resistance to any force that tends to induce a rise is very strong. It, therefore, follows that the consumer will rebel against any price-raising tendency inherent in an insurance scheme operating in depression and therefore will be more inclined to cut his consumption than he would be if confronted with a similar tendency upward in a period of prosperity. In practice this means merely that the consumer in a depression period may not be offered so large a concession in prices as he otherwise would have been offered, and to that extent a stimulus to further production will be lost. On the other hand, sellers of commodities will find a more favorable market for their commodities, although *in so far as* the rise in prices (or rather the failure to decline) is associated with the imposition of a pay-roll tax, the entrepreneur will not find himself in a more favorable position. Expenditures from the Fund contribute toward the more favorable markets, however; and expenditures now are in excess of contributions. Thus it is evident that in periods of decumulation (depression), the insurance program will tend to raise prices though other elements in the situation tend to depress them.

Expenditures of unemployment reserves on consumption goods are additional only if the assets held by the Fund are not disposed of to the public, which then curtails expenditures, or to the banks, which react by reducing their advances to industry by a corresponding amount, and only to the extent that the beneficiaries purchase goods and services that they otherwise would not have purchased. In so far as the payments of benefits are a substitute for a dole financed by bank credit, net expenditures are not increased, but in so far as they are a substitute for gratuitous payments financed by taxation or charity some increase of expenditures is involved.

17.8. In Which the Effects of Taxes for Old-age Insurance Are Considered Briefly

The discussion up to this point has been in terms of unemployment insurance. The introduction of old-age contributory insurance complicates the *quantitative* problem at numerous points. (1) Rates of taxation for old-age and unemployment insurance will be larger than for the former alone. It is well to recall, however, that a rate of 5 per cent on employers, as assumed in the discussion of unemployment insurance, may cover both programs. In our opinion, however, this is unlikely. Pay-roll taxes will probably be higher than even the 5 per cent assumed above, the required rise of prices greater, and, therefore, adverse effects on consumption will be of larger proportions in periods of accumulation. Under the old-age insurance program, workers, moreover, pay one-half of the tax directly, consumption of wage goods in particular suffering from the imposition of taxes directly on workers. Low-income groups, as indicated in the early part of this chapter, will cut consumption, though frequently with great difficulty; but the effect of all these taxes on low-income groups may well be that the government will be forced to increase relief payments greatly in order to maintain consumption of the poor. The Treasury will thus use up part of the proceeds of pay-roll taxes. (2) Part of the burden will probably ultimately be put upon the general taxpayer. A curtailment of savings is likely to follow the imposition of taxes directly upon the wealthy; and the net effect upon consumption and its distribution will depend in no small part upon the effects of a reduction of private savings on investment and income. Furthermore, in so far as the reduction of savings has adverse effects on investment and in so far as the non-wage-earning classes cut consumption, more factors will become available for wage-goods industries. Actually, wage-goods industries will probably suffer a net loss of factors to other industries or compete less effectively for them unless a large part of the tax burden is put upon the general taxpayer.

Finally, it is to be observed that accumulation and disbursement of the two funds do not always synchronize. Thus in a depression period, old-age reserves may continue to grow while unemployment reserves are reduced. The beneficent effects of disbursement of the latter may be offset then by the adverse effects of the accumulation of the former. Old-age reserves are not, however, likely to be large, and if the experience of 1939 is of any significance, adjustments in rates may be forthcoming in periods of depression.

17.9. Conclusion

In this chapter, we have dealt with the problem of a pay-roll tax *universally* applied and have attempted to make some crude estimates of possible effects upon prices. The assumption is, of course, that the monetary system is sufficiently elastic to permit a general rise of prices to follow, and also that the attempts to pass the tax on to the factors of production are beset with great obstacles. (In other chapters backward shifting is dealt with.) At first prices are likely to rise, although the rise may not be adequate to compensate fully for the new taxes. Limitations of income may then prevent the public, and in particular the poor, from maintaining their consumption. Prices may then not rise so much as is indicated by the amount of the pay-roll tax, and (on the assumption that shifting is forward only) output may then decline. A failure of the new savings (net—public and private) to find employment is likely to have unfavorable effects on prices and output; and of course any initial decline of consumption will jeopardize the maintenance even of the past level of investment. Monetary expansion and disbursements of benefits will, however, contribute toward *both* higher prices and maintenance of consumption.

On the basis of studies of the distribution of income, consumption, and savings, it is possible to make some estimates of the effects of a 5 per cent unemployment pay-roll tax upon the latter two variables. In these estimates, universal coverage is assumed or at least a rise in the total wage bill adequate to bring *covered* wages up to the current level of *total* wages and salaries. The main conclusions are that in the case of forward shifting (no backward shifting) consumers will increase their monetary expenditures by 1 billion dollars and cut their savings roughly by a corresponding amount. To some extent, however, price concessions will be made and consumers will respond through an increase of effort and income, aside from the initial rise of wages. Low-income groups will rely mainly on economies of consumption, and high-income groups on curtailment of savings. Effects of taxes on old-age insurance of course are to be added to the effects of the unemployment taxes; and effects in periods of accumulation are to be distinguished from those in periods of decumulation when the upward pressure on prices will be strengthened through the stimulus of an excess of disbursements.

Wage earners and salaried workers pay most of the costs if the security program is financed through a pay-roll tax and if entrepreneurs shift the taxes forward to consumers. Wages and salaries account for two-thirds of the national income; and in the year 1935–1936, those in receipt of consumers' incomes of less than $3,000 accounted for 69 per cent of the income and 78 per cent of the nation's consumption. Moreover, the high-income classes (in excess of $3,000) account for the nation's savings (savings out of incomes from $1,450 to $3,000 offset dissaving of low-income groups) and, therefore, are able to maintain consumption at the expense of savings. Losses of the wage and salaried classes may be recouped to some extent in so far as investment goods and luxury industries feel the decline of demand and hence compete less effectively for the factors of production. (In periods of large amounts of unemployment, this may not be a significant consideration.) These industries may, nevertheless, be in a stronger relative position than before the introduction of the security program. Should the security burden rise to the *equivalent* of a 20 per cent pay-roll tax, then the sacrifices of the nonwage-earning classes (exclusive of low-income groups) may become significant. They will pay more in direct taxes, and the upward pressure on prices will be greater than has been assumed in our discussion. They may not only cut savings, but significant sacrifices of consumption may be forthcoming.

Low-income classes (for the most part labor) lose through rises of prices and a decline of consumption. They gain from any ensuing expansion of money and through any favorable effects on investment of the accumulation of reserves. (In this discussion the possibility of shifts to labor through revision of wage contracts is excluded.) It is possible that in the light of many relief programs (and exclusive of other considerations) the prices of wage goods will rise relatively to those of investment and other nonwage goods. This is not, however, the likely result.

CHAPTER 18

PAY-ROLL TAXES AND THE BURDEN
ON INDUSTRY

18.1. INTRODUCTION

Social security taxes do not bear equally upon all pay-rolls. Various industries are excluded by law altogether from taxation. Others are dominated by independent, self-employed persons. Furthermore, the Federal government *requires* coverage for employment compensation only of enterprises employing eight or more workers for a period of 1 day or more 20 weeks or more per year. This provision discriminates between large and small businesses and those with short seasonal employment. (We assume that noncoverage contributes to a saving in costs.) Discrimination or at least an uneven burden of taxation as between industries and firms in the same industry is to be found for other reasons also.

Preliminary to a presentation of relevant facts, the significance of the uneven distribution of these tax burdens will be commented on briefly. In so far as entrepreneurs succeed in passing the burden on to wage earners or consumers, the problem may not be significant. When we refer to success in passing on to consumers, we mean of course without material loss of markets. It should also be observed that the taxpaying unit may in the long run be affected adversely even if at first it succeeds in making labor pay. If labor does not appraise the benefits of social security as highly as its cost to labor, then wage earners will desert the firms and industries that subject them to these *differential* costs. In the industries subjected to the exodus, wage costs will then tend to rise; and the relevant entrepreneurs will not have succeeded in passing the entire cost of their payroll taxes on to their employees. At present, it is assumed that labor is mobile and that alternative opportunities for employment are open.

Assume, then that at least in part the taxes are not passed on to either consumers or wage earners. It then becomes more profitable relative to the presecurity era to operate in small establishments or in worker-employee establishments. In the economy of the individual firm, further reduction of unit costs as output rises will now be offset by the emergence of social insurance costs. These additional costs arise in many states when the number of employees increases to eight, or, under old-age insurance, when additional employees are hired. Exempted industries and firms now produce at *relatively* lower costs than prevailed in the presecurity period. Factors are then attracted into these industries.

A redistribution of economic resources follows which would not have ocurred in the absence of the new tax program. Security taxes, however, do not have effects significantly different from many other types of taxes, *e.g.*, custom duties, turnover taxes, property taxes.[1] All these taxes weigh unevenly on different industries and on different firms in the same industries. That output for the individual firm is not carried so far toward the minimum unit cost (exclusive of pay-roll costs) as it would have been pushed had there been no pay-roll taxes is, however, a serious matter. At least this conclusion holds in so far as output is reduced below the optimum level.

This chapter deals with the following problems in successive sections: the numbers of excluded workers, the distribution of the burden of insurance and relief,[2] further discussion of experience or merit rating, the significance of the unevenness of the burden, the relation of insurance and output, seasonal industries, statistical aspects—significance of pay-roll taxes to turnover, income, etc.—and the unequal incidence of the burden.

18.2. EXCLUDED WORKERS

Now we turn to a brief discussion of the facts. Mr. Woytinsky estimates that there were about 33.3 million *salary* and *wage earners* in *nonagricultural* pursuits in 1929. Unemployment, illness, etc., reduces this total to between 31.1 and 31.7 millions. After deducting public employment and domestic service the volume of private industrial employment is found to be 25.1 to 25.9 millions. Adjustment for a few minor excluded occupations gives

---

[1] In some quarters in Washington the substitution of a *value added by manufacture* tax is being proposed on the grounds that the effects of this tax will be less erratic than those of a pay-roll tax. *Cf.* G. Colm, "Methods of Financing Unemployment Compensation," *Soc. Research*, 1935, pp. 161, 166.

[2] Other aspects of this problem have been dealt with in Part II, and in the Introduction.

approximately 24.1 to 24.9 millions in insured industries.[1] (Other groups, *e.g.*, self-employed, not covered are mentioned below.)

Of all *gainful* workers, this total comes roughly to about one-half of the gainfully working population *at any one* time.[2] Because of the flux between included and excluded occupations, it is true that a much larger number of workers will be covered at intervals and become eligible to receive benefits. The larger figure, although of extreme importance from the standpoint of computing benefit payments, is of less relevance to the problem of incidence of pay-roll taxation.

Important groups of workers are excluded from both old-age and unemployment insurance. They both exclude agricultural workers, 2.5 to 3.5 millions; farm operators, 6.8 to 7.0 millions; unpaid family workers in agriculture, 3.5 to 4.5 millions; domestic servants in private employment, 2.2 to 2.5 millions; self-employed, 4 to 4.5 millions; public employees, 2.5 to 2.7 millions; casual workers, 1 to 3 millions; work relief, 3.5 to 4.5 millions— these are the largest excluded categories as estimated for 1940.[3] They become eligible for old-age insurance, however, if they meet minimum requirements of employment and amount of pay in covered employments. Furthermore, railroad workers and to some extent public employees are covered through other insurance programs.[4]

In addition, the law stipulates that unemployment insurance taxes are *required* only of firms employing eight or more workers. States may, how-ever, extend the minimum requirement downward. Exclusion of workers resulting from this provision is not serious. (1) It has been estimated that though establishments employing one to eight workers are 74 per cent of all business units they account for but 10 per cent of all wage earners and 9 per cent of the wages.[5] (2) For the purpose of inclusion under the unem-ployment-insurance program, 18 states have set minimum numbers of employees at less than eight. Six states assess taxes for unemployment insurance on all firms with one or more employees.[6] Mr. Woytinsky esti-

---

[1] WOYTINSKY, W. S., *Labor in the United States*, Committee on Social Security, Social Science Research Council, 1938, Chap. XIII.

[2] *Cf.* CORSON, J. J., "Wages and Employment under the Old Age Insurance Program," *Soc. Sec. Bull.*, September, 1938, pp. 20–24. He put the percentage covered at 60 per cent of the gainful workers.

[3] WINSLOW, H. J., and W. K. SHAUGHNESSY, "Estimated Numbers of Persons in Employments Excluded from Old-age Insurance," *Soc. Sec. Bull.*, February, 1939, p. 18.

[4] The following figures are of some interest in that they indicate the changing relationships as between covered and noncovered employment over time. 1929 = 100 January, 1938, wages and salaries: all = 81; covered (old-age insurance) = 74; Noncovered = 99. "Earnings in Employments Covered by Old-age Insurance," *Soc. Sec. Bull.*, March, 1938, p. 83.

[5] CORSON, *op. cit.*, p. 23.

[6] BURNS, E. M., "Unemployment Insurance," *Social Work Year Book*, 1939, pp.

mates that about 1.04 million employees excluded under the Federal act are nevertheless thus included under state excise taxes, about 2.5 millions being still excluded.[1] It is scarcely necessary to add that difficulties will arise in many instances. Thus according to a witness before the Ways and Means Committee, of 79 photoengraving firms in Illinois 59 were subject to the unemployment pay-roll tax and 20 were not.[2]

18.3. The Distribution of the Burden of Insurance and Relief

Under experience (merit) rating, also, the cost of social security as between firms, industries, and areas varies. Employers or communities fortunate enough to have a good employment record then are relieved of part of the costs, and those with an unsatisfactory history are required to pay more.[3] In practice, however, the former may pay less and the latter not pay more, with the result that benefits are reduced or reserves quickly dissipated. The Social Security Board has been aware of this danger.[4] Actually, the result so far indicates a reduction in the average rate of contribution.[5]

449–457; *Hearings*, Ways and Means Committee, House of Representatives, *Social Security*, 1939, p. 2324; Winslow, H. J., "Estimated Volume of Employment Covered by State Unemployment Compensation Laws," March, 1938, p. 30; and Social Security Board, Employment Security Memorandum 8, *Comparison of State Unemployment Compensation Laws as of* Mar. 1, 1940.

[1] Woytinsky, *op. cit.*, pp. 223–231.

[2] *Hearings*, Ways and Means Committee, House of Representatives, *Social Security*, 1939, pp. 1899–1900. According to one writer, 9 per cent of the processing of flour and other grain-mill products in the year 1929 were done by firms with less than eight employees; and 20 per cent of the products were manufactured in bakeries that might thus have been exempted. H. P. Mulford, *Incidence and Effects of the Pay-roll Tax*, pp. 39–40.

[3] From 1921–1931, the days of benefits per insured contributor under British unemployment insurance were as follows: average, 182; shipbuilding, 527; iron and steel, 400; public works contracting, 350; distribution trades, 87. *Final Report of Royal Commission on Unemployment Insurance*, 1932, Cmd. 4185, p. 82. (*Cf.* also amounts of benefits relative to contributions by industries.) *Cf. Report of the New York Unemployment Insurance State Advisory Council on the Subject of Experience Rating*, Part II, pp. 87–99. Large differences in the proportion of benefits to contributions will be found. The analysis applies to industries for the State of New York.

[4] *Cf.* Social Security Board, Bureau of Research and Statistics, *Merit Rating and Unemployment Compensation* by K. Pribram and P. Booth, 1937, pp. 33–35. Haber, W., and J. J. Joseph, "Unemployment Compensation," *Annals*, 1939, p. 26; Nathan, O., "Some Considerations on Unemployment Insurance in the Light of German Experience," *Jour. Pol. Econ.*, June, 1934, pp. 306–308; *Hearings*, Senate Finance Committee, *Social Security Act Amendments*, 1939, pp. 25–29.

[5] *Report of the New York Unemployment Insurance State Advisory Council on the Subject of Experience Rating*, Part II, 1940, pp. 37–46.

At a recent date, 11 jurisdictions had statewide pools with uniform rates in operation, 3 states (including Wisconsin) a merit rating plan with employers' reserves, 2 states employers' reserves and partial pools, and 33 states approved state-pooled funds with provision for merit rating.[1] Since experience is required in order to introduce a scientific merit scheme, the merit plans have not as yet advanced far. In Wisconsin, at a recent date, 2,700 employers were favored with reduced rates and 600 paid in excess of the standard rate; and safeguards have been introduced in order to protect reserves. The Wisconsin authorities prefer merit rating applied to individual employers rather than statewide adjustments of rates applicable to all employers in the state.[2] This is, however, a somewhat unsatisfactory form of merit rating, for workers do not receive adequate protection unless the state supplements the employers' reserve with state funds.[3]

It is not easy to come to a satisfactory conclusion on the issue of the size of the pool and hence on the distribution of costs. At one extreme we may suggest a nationwide pool and a level of rates high enough to cover the costs of unemployment.[4] All unemployed workers would then be provided for through unemployment insurance for indefinite periods of unemployment. On the assumption that the unemployed number 10 millions and that they receive benefits of $10 weekly (roughly one-half the average wage in recent years) the charge on industry would be 5 billion dollars, or the equivalent of a pay-roll tax of 12 per cent or more.[5] This would obviously not be an acceptable solution to industry. Many of the unemployed have never had a job; others have been unemployed so long that they should not properly be considered a charge on industry alone; and the stable elements of the economy would be required to subsidize

---

[1] Social Security Board, *Ann. Rept.*, 1938, p. 65. *Cf. Hearings*, Senate Finance Committee, *Social Security Act Amendments* (76: 1), 1939, pp. 112–113. More recently, 39 states and territories provide for some type of experience rating and 11 others provide for study. But four states (instead of two) have the combined scheme. *Report of the New York Unemployment Insurance State Advisory Council on the Subject of Experience Rating*, Part II, 1940, pp. 18–24.

[2] *Hearings*, Senate Finance Committee, *Social Security Act Amendments* (76:1), 1939, pp. 112–119; KIDD, C. V., "The Administration of Merit Rating under Pooledfunds Laws," *Soc. Sec. Bull.*, Nov., 1938, pp. 3–9.

[3] *Cf. Hearings*, Ways and Means Committee, House of Representatives, *Social Security*, 1939, pp. 2339–2340.

[4] *Cf.* Social Security Board, Bureau of Research and Statistics, *Quantitative Analysis of Enemployment Compensation Simplification Proposals*, 1938, pp. 6–9; HORWITZ, J. W., "The Risk of Unemployment and Its Effects on Unemployment Compensation," *Harvard Business Research Studies* 21, 1938, p. 40.

[5] A taxable wage bill of 40 billion dollars is estimated. This is a reasonable figure for the late thirties on the assumption of full coverage.

heavily the unstable elements.[1] In addition, the cost of unemployment (short and long duration) is so large that the community as opposed to industry should quite properly be assessed a large part of the costs.[2] Then industry would be spared the responsibility of passing the tax on or bearing the entire cost. British experience in the twenties is illuminating on this issue. As the number of unemployed increased, the state raided the Unemployment Trust Fund more and more in favor of those who had exhausted their rights to benefits. In pursuing this policy, the government renounced the principle of an association of benefits and contributions. It was not until 1934 that assistance was once more clearly distinguished from insurance.[3] This discussion does not imply, however, that coverage of all unemployed through insurance is practical.

Actually through careful definitions of eligibility and strict limits on the duration and amount of benefits, the cost of unemployment insurance is kept down to an amount of the order of 1 billion dollars per year. Furthermore, the endorsement of statewide pools and relatively uniform contributions (average) despite the large differences as between states in unemployment experience[4] results, for the states with relatively high amounts of unemployment, in earlier exhaustion of reserves or lower benefits and, therefore, more reliance on government relief and public works. Costs are, therefore, shifted from industry proper to the community. Income, property, and indirect taxes paid by the community are indeed borne in part by industry, but also in part by farmers, and in part by the community as spenders rather than as producers. Furthermore, in shifting the burden to the Treasury, the government relies to a large extent on borrowing, and the result is not only that nonindustrial elements are required to bear part of the cost, but also that present costs are kept down through recourse to deficit financing. Finally, observe that in adopting statewide unemploy-

---

[1] GILL, C., Wasted Manpower, pp. 127–128, 179.

[2] Cf. Final Report of Royal Commission on Unemployment Insurance, 1932, Cmd. 4185, pp. 345–348; Hearings, Ways and Means Committee, House of Representatives, Economic Security Act, 1935, pp. 226, 759, 1087–1088.

[3] DAVISON, R. C., What's Wrong with Unemployment Insurance, pp. 13–15, 21–24, 60–64; Social Security Board, Unemployment and Health Insurance in Great Britain 1911–1937, pp. 32–36; MERRIAM, I. C., and D. BOCHNER, "The Role of Unemployment Insurance and Unemployment Assistance in Great Britain," Soc. Sec. Bull., March, 1940, pp. 3–12, BAKKE, E. W., Insurance Or Dole, pp. 67–76, 85–105.

[4] HORWITZ, op. cit.

ment insurance plans the government excludes the possibility of large subsidies through pay-roll taxation at the expense of sections of the country where unemployment is low. These subsidies are now limited to transfers within state lines. Transfers across state lines are not, however, thus excluded, for what the unemployed in depressed areas fail to obtain through unemployment insurance under a national pool, they may obtain through relief, work relief, and the like.[1]

What the net effect of the pay-roll tax will be depends in part upon the nature of the system to which it is appended. In so far as the unemployed had been provided for through relief, the institution of unemployment insurance shifts the burden at least in part from general revenues to taxes on industry. What of the distribution of the costs of unemployment insurance? Under statewide pools, states with relatively little unemployment may gain a differential advantage, i.e., lower costs, over other states. This will follow if statewide reductions in the rate of tax are allowed. Otherwise, the result will be merely that states with relatively small amounts of unemployment will accumulate large reserves or pay relatively generous benefits, and perhaps obtain some compensation then in lower wages. Under employer pools, the differential again would favor employers with relatively favorable employment records. It is then probable that the costs of unemployment will fall with varying weights upon competing areas and firms. Stipulation of minimum standards of benefits and minimum contributions will, however, prevent excessive differences in costs of insurance.

18.4. The Issue of Merit or Experience Rating

Merit rating raises some questions relating to the optimal allocation of resources. In a world of extremely high effective demand, where an expansion of laborers in one line implies contraction in another, it can be definitely stated that any occupation which offers intermittent and precarious employment might well be required to pay higher hourly rates in order to compensate for the unsteadiness

[1] The Democratic platform (1940) did call for a Federal equalization fund. *Cf.* FELDMAN, H., and D. M. SMITH, *The Case for Experience Rating in Unemployment Compensation and a Proposed Method*, Industrial Relations Counselors, 1939, p. 60.

of employment.[1] This conclusion holds not simply to assure that workers should fare as well in this as in other industries, but more fundamentally because this brings about a maximization of the national dividend through the equating of the marginal productivity of labor in the occupation under discussion, with its opportunity or alternative cost.

In the modern world generally characterized by much unemployment the foregoing principle loses much force. It is quite possible that the alternative to working in a durable-goods industry (say) is being completely unemployed. Increasing rates for such an industry might not be desirable since the opportunity costs of labor may really be nil. On the other hand, if the unemployment reserve fund is to be solvent, somebody must pay higher rates. Considerations of equity being disregarded, a given amount of money should be levied from firms with the most inelastic (long-run) demand for labor. For such a policy will minimize the decrease in employment due to an increase in wage rates. (It is assumed here both that wage costs rise and that in response to this employment suffers.) An alternative is to reduce the burden on industry through a redistribution of the cost of unemployment between insurance and relief. In so far as the charges are thus transferred from a tax on industry to nonindustrial taxes, the effects on employment will be favorable. Any adverse effects on consumption may, however, in turn reduce demand and employment.

Even the very able presentation of the case for merit rating by Feldman and Smith is not convincing.[2] (1) They admit the cogency of the argument just presented. They are apparently not overanxious to force out the

---

[1] It may be said at the outset that little progress has been made in the definition of stabilization; and a careful survey has yielded the conclusion that when allowance is made for stabilization prior to the introduction of insurance the net contribution of the security program toward stabilization so far seems to have been unimportant. In the only significant case quoted, *i.e.*, Eastman Kodak, in the study below, the improvement may well be associated in part with a rise of demand. Furthermore, the security program frequently contributes toward antistabilization policies when they have the effect of reducing benefits. *Report of New York State Unemployment Insurance Advisory Council on Experience Rating*, Part II, 1940, pp. 1–17; C. A. Myers, "Employment Stabilization and the Wisconsin Act," *Am. Econ. Rev.*, 1939, pp. 708–723.

[2] FELDMAN and SMITH, *op. cit.; cf. Hearings*, Ways and Means Committee, House of Representatives, *Economic Security Act*, pp. 872–873, 1002–1004; Evidence before the *Royal Commission on Unemployment Insurance*, 1931, pp. 117–121, 166–167; *Report of the Royal Commission on Unemployment Insurance*, 1927, p. 41; *Report of the Industrial Transference Board*, 1928, pp. 7–8; KIDD, *op, cit.*, pp. 3–9.

unstable or declining industries; for, at this point in the argument, merit rating is to operate only within a very limited scope.[1] A partial subsidization of weak industries will still be effective.[2] In taking this position, they retreat from full acceptance of the merit principle and give up one of the fundamental tenets of the "experience" school: That the employer is to pay what he costs the fund.[3] (2) In advocating a close association of contribution and costs, the authors may be proposing an inadequate pooling of risks.[4] (3) We come to their most fundamental argument. Merit rating is to be supported on the grounds that the maximum incentive for stabilization of employment is thus provided.[5] For numerous reasons, the argument lacks conviction.

Employers with good records operate, to a considerable extent, in industries that are in the process of expansion or they are favored by excellent management which is likely to be related little, if at all, to any incentive provided by experience rating.[6] What is important is that the derived demand for labor varies greatly and is largely outside the control of the individual employer. This position seems to me invulnerable despite the long list of methods of regularization offered by these writers.[7] At best they would thus increase employment in one firm or industry at the expense of others or assure stable employment for X men rather than unstable

---

[1] It is scarcely necessary to point out that concessions to unstable industries will increase the dangers of insolvency of the reserve fund. *Cf.* Pribram and Booth, *op. cit.*, pp. 43–44.

[2] FELDMAN and SMITH, *op. cit.*, pp. 22–23.

[3] *Cf. ibid.*, pp. 29, 41, 49–50.

[4] *Ibid.*, p. 12. The issues here are, however, not so clear. It is possible to pool risks under merit rating. At one extreme we have the Wisconsin plan, which provides for individual employer accounts and a minimum of pooling. At the other extreme, all employers contribute toward a common pool at a uniform rate of taxation. In between it is possible to classify groups homogeneous from the standpoint of exposure to risk, *ex ante*, and to charge them different rates (*e.g.*, the bread and the wine industries). There are dangers here, however, if the classification is carried too far and the number of subgroups is too large. Administration by state agencies increases the risks of inadequate protection or a breakdown. Experience rating that allows limited variations in rates is a compromise between wide sharing of risk, which promotes financial solvency, and the cost principle, *i.e.*, rates charged according to unemployment experience. *Cf.* R. V. Lester and C. V. Kidd, *The Case Against Experience Rating in Unemployment Compensation*, 1939, p. 12.

[5] *Cf.* FELDMAN and SMITH, *op. cit.*, p. 42. "In many situations the stability of employment has less relation to the nature of the industry, product or service than to the employer's attention to the problems and other circumstances peculiar to or favoring the individual business."

[6] *Cf. ibid.*, pp. 18, 40–41. *Cf.* LESTER and KIDD, *op. cit.*, pp. 16, 42–43.

[7] FELDMAN and SMITH, *op. cit.*, especially pp. 5–6, *cf. Report of New York Unemployment Insurance State Advisory Council on the Subject of Experience Rating*, Part II, pp. 14–15.

employment for (say) $\frac{4}{3}X$ men. We are not sure, as Messrs. Feldman and Smith seem to be, that in periods of large unemployment the former is to be preferred to the division of work implied in the latter.[1] In this connection, it is well to observe, moreover, that those employers who experience a favorable employment record, *i.e.*, a large rise in employment or stabilization, frequently induce unemployment elsewhere. Why should they not pay part of the cost? Finally the incentive of a saving of 2 to 3 per cent of pay-rolls (the difference between maximum and minimum rates) to be had under the security program does not seem to be a major factor when compared with other costs and changes in costs and market conditions.[2] Even if it is, moreover, the saving is largely obtained irrespective of any contributions of the individual employer.

In short, merit rating raises not only serious administrative and accounting problems, but also suffers from fundamental weaknesses, and peculiarly so in periods of economic decline. It is well, however, not to follow too closely the British experience in the twenties, when excessive support may have been given to unstable industries and when industry was forced to pay an excessive proportion of the costs of relief. Pooling of insurance risks is one matter; imposing the burden of relief on insurance funds is another.

Experts studying the problem for the Social Security Board have been aware of the weaknesses of experience rating.[3] They distinguish *experience* from *merit* rating; the former requires smaller contributions where the drains on the insurance funds are small, and the implication is at any rate that the gains of these employers are based on experience, not merit. The association of stability of employment (often confused with expansion) with policies of management is not easily revealed. Other objections have also been raised. Pressure has been much stronger to grant concessions than to inflict penalties; the solvency of the fund is jeopardized by that tendency as well as by the reduction of rates early in depressions and in periods of prosperity, the rises frequently coming at the most inopportune time. Employers in stable industries obtain favorable rates despite relatively unsatisfactory employment records, and others in unstable industries are not rewarded for contributions to stability. Finally, administrative difficulties are the despair of all who are interested in experience rating.[4]

---

[1] FELDMAN and SMITH, *op. cit.*, p. 9; *cf.* HABER and JOSEPH, *op. cit.*, pp. 26–27.

[2] *Cf.* FELDMAN and SMITH, *op. cit.*, p. 7; *Report of New York Unemployment Insurance State Advisory Council on the Subject of Experience Rating*, Part II, p. 37.

[3] See especially Social Security Board, Bureau of Unemployment Compensation, *Experience Rating under State Unemployment Compensation Laws*, 1938; PRIBRAM and BOOTH, *op. cit.*, and LESTER and KIDD, *op. cit.*

[4] *Cf.* the above and Social Security Board, Bureau of Research and Statistics, *Wage and Separation Reporting in Unemployment Compensation*, 1938.

18.5. INSURANCE AND UNEMPLOYMENT

Two problems should be distinguished. One is the problem of the treatment of one industry or firm relative to that of another. That issue has been discussed under merit rating. There is, however, a more general (and related) problem, which is of even greater significance. This problem will be dealt with briefly though we hope to treat it more fully in a later study. It has often been said that the availability of relief or insurance funds keeps wages at a level too high to assure full employment and in any case is responsible for a contraction of employment.[1] Workers are more inclined to hold out when they are supported in idleness and when, in fact, idleness is a condition of payment of insurance or relief. Various expedients have of course been tried to reduce this danger: the g.s.w. (genuinely seeking work) condition in the United Kingdom; the fixation of insurance or relief payments at a level below that of wages; the establishment of employment exchanges operating in conjunction with relief and insurance agencies; and many others.[2]

Perhaps the strongest opposition to unemployment pay or insurance on these general grounds is to be found in a recent book by a British economist.[3] The object of unemployment pay, according to this writer, is to secure the consent of those whose labor is displaced by high-wage policy; and yet, unlike cartel agreements, the worker is not at liberty to seek work elsewhere nor does he receive compensation even nearly equal to what he could earn on a free market. State interference in these matters is held to preserve rates of earnings among favored groups of workers. Prof. Hutt's position stands or falls, may we observe, according as his underlying thesis of the inverse relation of employment and wage rates is or is not supported by the facts.

---

[1] *Final Report, Royal Commission on Unemployment Insurance* 1932, p. 101; CLAY, H., "Unemployment and Wage Rates," *Econ. Jour.*, March, 1928, p. 12; CANNAN, E., "The Problem of Unemployment," March, 1930, pp. 46–47; GILSON, M. B., *Unemployment Insurance in Great Britain*, especially pp. 201–210, 226; and more recently SLICHTER, S. H., "The Impact of Social Security Legislation upon Mobility and Enterprise," *Proc. Am. Econ. Assoc.*, 1940, pp. 56–57. *Cf.* also introductory chapter.

[2] Social Security Board, *Unemployment and Health Insurance in Great Britain 1911–1937*, 1938, pp. 29–35; WPA, *A Survey of Relief and Security Programs*, 1938, pp. 47–49.

[3] HUTT, W. H., *The Theory of Idle Resources*, 1939, pp. 127–131.

Some reservations are to be made to the position that, in the manner suggested, insurance benefits have adverse effects. We should first be certain that a general reduction of wages is required to increase employment. Recent controversy in this field leaves the economist less certain than he was even 10 years ago of the inverse correlation of wages and employment. Aside from the general issue, however, there can be little doubt but that in certain crucial industries maintenance of wage rates has been an obstacle to an expansion of employment. Industries in which wage payments are high, relatively to all costs, and which are confronted with a highly elastic demand for their product may fall into this category. The construction industry in the United States is perhaps an example.[1]

Another reservation that has been suggested in this connection relates to the issue of mobility.[2] Relief and insurance payments are held to interfere with that movement of labor which would assure its optimal distribution. Now it has been held (and this is the reservation) that mobility is of secondary or tertiary significance when large amounts of unemployment prevail.[3] Mobility would simply result in the substitution of one unemployed worker for another employed worker who now becomes unemployed, or the attachment of an unemployed worker to industry X instead of industry Y. This reservation to the general position is, however, subject to counter-reservations. (1) Unemployment over a given period (say a year) of X is shared by nx $(n > 1)$ men. An improvement of mobility would clearly result in a quicker and more effective union of the man and the job. (2) Men who are low paid in depressed industries may become attached to rising and relatively well-paid industries. Average productivity and probably employment will rise. In other words full employment is one objective, the optimal distribution of factors is another.

[1] *Cf.* Housing Monograph Series 3, *Land, Material, and Labor Costs*, 1939, especially pp. 78–88.

[2] *Cf.* PIGOU, A. C., "Wage Policy and Unemployment," *Econ. Jour.*, 1927, pp. 355–368; *The Theory of Unemployment*, pp. 269–270; CANNAN, *op. cit.*, pp. 49–52; H. CLAY, "Dr. Cannan's Views on Unemployment," *Econ. Jour.*, 1930, pp. 333–335.

[3] *Cf.* Great Britain, *Report of the Industrial Transference Board*, 1928, p. 19.

18.6. Significance of the Uneven Weight of Pay-roll Taxes

We have seen that at any given time one-half (or somewhat less) of the gainfully employed are excluded from pay-roll taxation, that another few million pay no unemployment compensation tax, and that wide differentials will emerge in the latter tax when experience rating becomes widespread.[1] What is the effect of the introduction of such a system upon the distribution of employment and upon wage rates? We assume that there is mobility between occupations, that each employer uses about the same proportions of labor of various skills, etc. In this case, net wages before and after the introduction of the taxes must be equal in every industry. This implies that wage costs (including taxes) will be higher in those industries which are included in the program and which pay relatively high taxes. The result in such industries will be (1) relative contraction of employment due to substitution of factors of production other than labor, and (2) relative contraction of output due to increased costs with no improvement in demand conditions.

Actually, depressed industries may well pay lower wages for similar work than do the profitable industries. Absence of free movement of labor may explain these differences. Unprofitable enterprises may then gain both from lower wage costs and subsidies on account of insurance.[2] (At least partial subsidization of depressed industries is assumed.) They can then maintain employment at a higher level than would otherwise have been possible. Profitable industries, which carry part of the costs of other industries, would, however, find their demand for labor reduced. If the latter, however, had unfilled vacancies and the depressed industries an excess of labor attached to them, the net results on employment in the short run would be favorable. Then the reduction of demand by the profitable industries reduces the number of unfilled vacancies, not the amount of employment. Furthermore, in so far as these palliatives make it possible for the depressed industries to use up their capital, a net gain is involved.

As soon as we admit the presence of factors of production other than labor, it becomes clear that industries and enterprises may

---

[1] *Cf.* Pribram and Booth, *op. cit.*, pp. 36–38.

[2] It has been estimated that high-wage establishments in one state availing themselves of unemployment benefits would receive 30 per cent less relative to contributions than low-wage firms. *Hearings*, Ways and Means Committee, House of Representatives, *Social Security*, 1939, p. 1898.

differ in the percentage of their total costs represented by the wage bill. The proportion in which the factors of production will be combined at any given set of prices varies in different occupations depending upon the technological production relations within that industry.

The impact of the tax upon different industries will be of varying degree. If no adjustments were made to the tax, those industries with the greatest percentage pay-rolls would find their profits most reduced. Precisely these latter industries will find it to their advantage to make the largest appropriate adjustments. They will first reduce their demand for labor. It is a well-known principle that firms employing a factor of production in very small amounts will have relatively inelastic demands for this factor as compared with firms of the type mentioned above, *i.e.*, it is "important to be unimportant."[1] Therefore, other things being equal, the decline in employment is apt to be larger in industries in which labor costs are an important item. By the same token, the decline in output and increase in price will be relatively greatest in such occupations. Even after all adjustments within the firm have been made, it is likely that profits will be affected unfavorably especially in these lines. The extent to which the primary incidence will fall on profits, prices, or employment depends upon (1) the importance of labor as a cost element; (2) the elasticity of demand for the product; (3) the technological marginal productivity curve of labor including the possibilities for substitution of competing and complementary factors of production; (4) the supply conditions of the factors of production, especially that of labor itself.

Condemnation of pay-roll taxes does not necessarily follow from the fact that they fall with unequal weight on competing firms and industries.[2] Similar indictments may be made of other taxes. Transaction and property taxes, for example, may be criticized on similar grounds. In fact, it would be most difficult to imagine a tax that does not burden some industries or firms more than others. It is, however, partly a matter of degree and, *ceteris paribus*, a tax that varies greatly in its effect upon firms and industries (unless the distribution of the burden is related to capacity to pay, or benefits) is for this reason to be scrutinized with care. An additional difficulty arises

[1] See Hicks, J. R., *The Theory of Wages*, 1932, Appendix, pp. 241–246.

[2] Up to the present, tax costs under experience rating seem to favor large firms. *Report of the New York Unemployment Insurance State Advisory Council on the Subject of Experience Rating*, Part II, pp. 47–56.

under the pay-roll tax. Where unemployment is a peculiarly vexing problem, a tax upon wages may *ipso facto* be accepted with great reservations, and in so far as unemployment is related to high or rigid wages, pay-roll taxes may aggravate the problem of unemployment.[1] The reader is referred, however, to the discussion in Chap. 15.

18.7. SEASONAL INDUSTRIES

Seasonal industries raise questions related to those discussed under merit rating. The discussion will be brief. Three alternative methods may be suggested for dealing with the problem of seasonality under unemployment insurance.[2] These alternatives under unemployment insurance are (1) exclusion of seasonal industries (agriculture, for example); (2) special treatment under merit rating, *i.e.*, higher contribution rates; (3) inclusion under pooled scheme which cautiously defines periods of coverage and provides ungenerous benefit formulas, etc. Under (3), for example, benefits might be limited to the active season.[3] Seasonal workers, it should be observed, may be compensated in part for the lack of continuity in employment by a higher rate of pay. (Evidence that seasonal workers are compensated for their irregular employment in higher rates of pay is not easily obtainable.)

The issues may be put as follows: Should they be subsidized by employers and employees in industries and plants providing regular work, or

---

[1] It is well, however, to take into account the fact that wage costs affect the prices of raw materials. It follows, therefore, that if commodities embodying large amounts of labor at first become relatively more expensive following the imposition of a pay-roll tax the relative effects will become less important as the rise of labor costs begins to be felt in the prices of raw materials. Not only the percentage of labor to all costs but also, in the long run, of labor and materials to all costs may be relevant. This analysis is still, however, of fundamental importance. (1) The rise of labor costs does not affect *all* other costs equally. (2) Prices may rise not by the same *percentage* as marginal costs, but (monopolistic competition) by the same *amount*. Then relative price changes can occur as a result of wage changes even if the proportion of wage to total supply costs is the same throughout the system. On these issues, see R. M. Bissell, Jr., "Price and Wage Policies and the Theory of Employment," *Econometrica*, 1940, pp. 225-226.

[2] Its relevance for old-age insurance is that coverage under seasonal industries is likely to result in relatively small wage credits, and, therefore, in a relatively high rate of benefits to contributors. These gains for seasonal workers will not, however, be so large under the 1939 act as they had been under the 1935 legislation.

[3] *Cf.* MERRIAM, I. C., "Seasonal Workers and Unemployment Compensation," *Soc. Sec. Bull.*, September, 1938, pp. 8-16; BAKKE, *op. cit.*, pp. 57-59.

should they receive compensation in higher wages? Another alternative is that their wages be cut in exchange for larger contributions by their employers and larger benefits.

As an administrative problem, seasonality does not lend itself to easy treatment.[1] A significant proportion of seasonal workers seem at present to be excluded in the United States.[2] All firms that do not employ eight or more employees "on each of some twenty days during the taxable year, each day being in a different calendar week" are excluded from Federal unemployment taxation. Actually only one state defines seasonal trade as one that operates 20 weeks or less. In New York, trades that operate less than 52 weeks are defined as seasonal. Late in 1938, 23 states had provided for special treatment of seasonal unemployment. It is not easy to distinguish between industries like logging which have a fairly definite season and clothing which suffers both from seasonality and uncertainty. One authority would exclude the former but not the latter.[3]

Under the British administration, benefits are provided in the off-season if proof is given that the unemployed had found employment in the off-season in the preceding two years and if the worker proves that he can reasonably expect employment for a substantial part of the off-season. Payment of benefits in the off-season when employment is not to be expected is termed a *subsidy*, not a benefit. Germany and Austria are inclined to emphasize the relief aspects of insurance and are, therefore, less generous in dealing with seasonal workers. These countries restrict benefits to seasonal workers in no uncertain manner.[4]

It is suggested by one writer that "the rights to benefits shall apply only to the longest seasonal period or periods which the best practice of such industry or class of employment will reasonably permit."[5] Workers would however, then be excluded from benefits even if they customarily found employment in the off-season. Ambiguity also arises in the definition of "operation." "Some states have interpreted this to mean that only industries which actually cease operations for a period of time are seasonal; others hold that special provisions should also cover industries in which it is customary to operate at 'greatly reduced levels' during a regularly occurring period."[6]

---

[1] WOYTINSKY, W. S., *Seasonal Variations in Employment in the United States*, 1939, especially pp. 3–8 and Chap. I.

[2] FELDMAN and SMITH, *op. cit.*, p. 26.

[3] MERRIAM, *op. cit.*

[4] Social Security Board; *Seasonal Workers and Unemployment Insurance in Great Britain, Germany and Austria*, 1940, especially pp. 3–15; HUBER, F., "Seasonal Workers and Unemployment Insurance in Great Britain, Germany and Austria," *Soc. Sec. Bull.*, December, 1938, pp. 11–19.

[5] PAPIER, W., "Seasonality in Ohio Canning Establishments in Relation to Unemployment Compensation," *Soc. Sec. Bull.*, October, 1938, p. 6.

[6] WOYTINSKY, *op. cit.*, p. 5.

In short, the problem is beset with theoretical and administrative problems. On the one side, it is necessary to be fair to the seasonal workers; and on the other, the workers in seasonal industries must not monopolize benefit payments.[1]

18.8. STATISTICAL ASPECTS

We turn again to some statistical aspects of the problem. The first problem is the significance of the tax in dollars and cents. One may start on the assumption that the tax is 9 per cent of pay-rolls. At present the assumption is that by 1949 the pay-roll tax on employers for old-age and unemployment will rise to 6 per cent. It would not, however, be amiss to assume that the eventual burden on employers will be 9 per cent (exclusive of the tax on employees). Reserves will not play the important part contemplated in 1935; and costs are likely to be much higher than was anticipated at the time of the passage of the act. In any case, figures in Table I are easily adjusted to smaller or larger taxes than 9 per cent.

In the calculations that follow full coverage is assumed. The cost of the social security program is, therefore, not so large as these figures indicate. It is, on the other hand, helpful to compare the pay-roll taxes (assuming full coverage) with the totals for the other variables. If coverage is but one half, then the burden relative to total income is but one-half (roughly) of the percentage given by the table. Since we include total income, turnover, etc. (and not income relevant to areas where pay-roll taxes are assessed), it seems appropriate to compare pay-rolls on the assumption of full coverage. It still remains true that income which is more or less irrelevant for this problem is included, e.g., farm income; and if the taxes collected in 1937 are but 2 billion dollars (not 4 billion dollars as in table below), then it is well to remember both that the percentage of pay-roll taxes to total income is but 3.0 (not 6.0) and that the percentage of taxes to income *of businesses actually assessed* for pay-roll taxes is much in excess of 3.0. In later years, however, a rise of coverage and pay-rolls may bring the assumed figures close to actual ones.

When we compare pay-roll taxes with turnover (debits outside of New York) the burden seems light.[2] Turnover is roughly (in dollars) five times

[1] KUZNETS, S., *Seasonal Variations in Industry and Trade*, 1933, pp. 124–125, 162, 195. This volume gives some indication of the magnitude of seasonal fluctuations. A comparison of fluctuations of sales and deliveries as against output suggests that corrective measures have been introduced.

[2] For some estimates of the burden of social services in the British economy relative to turnover, wage bill, and output, see Great Britain, Committee on Industry and Trade, *Factors in Industrial and Commercial Efficiency*, 1927, pp. 57–61, 479–491.

as high as pay-rolls. When transactions are numerous, a relatively small addition of prices at each turnover would compensate for the tax. Relative to income, the burden appears much heavier; and its importance rises further if comparison is made with the sales of final consumer goods and (finally) with value added by manufacture. Why should the percentage of taxes to value added by manufacture be so high as 16 to 18 per cent when the pay-roll tax is but 9 per cent? (Wages are but *part* of the value added by manufacture.)

TABLE I.—AMOUNT OF PAY-ROLL TAXES AND PERCENTAGE OF TAXES TO TURNOVER, INCOME, ETC.

9 Per Cent Pay-roll Tax (assumption is full coverage)

	(1)	(2)	(3)	(4)	(5)	(6)	(7)	(8)
	Total pay-roll taxes, billions of dollars	Turnover	Income	Value added by manufacture	Non-wage costs	Sales of final consumer goods	Interest	Profits
1933	2.634	0.018	0.059	0.181	0.157	0.105	0.569	2.677
1935	3.268	0.017	0.060	0.167	0.124	0.099	0.731	0.412
1937	4.205	0.018	0.061	.....	.....	.....	0.903	0.265

Column 1 = 9 per cent of labor income in each year. Columns 2–8 = percentage of column 1 to totals for Turnover, Income, etc.

Sources: *National Income 1929–1936*, pp. 11, 16; *Survey Current Business*, 1936 *Supplement*, p. 44, March, 1938, p. 72, June 1938, pp. 12–13.

Statistical Abstract of the United States, 1937, p. 738.

Census of Business 1935: Retail Distribution, Vol. I., U. S. Summary, June 1937, p. 1–105.

Turnover = bank debits outside of New York City.

Profits = dividends, entrepreneurial withdrawals, net rents and royalties.

The answer in part is that the value added by manufacture applies to a segment of industry that is smaller than that part of the economy which is subjected to the tax. Finally, the high percentage of the pay-roll tax to interest payments and profits (bear in mind the initial reservations) is evidence of the difficulties to be faced in passing the taxes on to the proprietary and management interests.[1] Profits, moreover, fluctuate greatly; and the statistical definition used here is not satisfactory. Entrepreneurial withdrawals are scarcely an accurate index of profits.

Irrespective of the basis chosen, the pay-roll tax falls with varying intensity upon industry. Competing industries and areas do not pay the same proportion of their costs or value added by manufacture. The estimates that follow are largely taken from Social Security Board: *Incidence and Effects of the Pay-roll Tax*, by H. P. Mulford, (1936).[2] In the original tables,

---

[1] *Cf.* SLICHTER, *op. cit.*, pp. 53–54. Prof. Slichter points out that in 1938 the net costs of social security to the railroads were 67 million dollars, or 54 per cent of their deficit.

[2] *Cf. Social Security in America*, pp. 376–377. Here the cost of pay-roll taxes

figures are generally presented for the years 1929, 1933, and 1935. For our purposes, the material for a single year is adequate.[1]

1. In 1935, the ratio of pay-rolls to output or sales for 22 principal industries:

> Minimum = 3 per cent for wholesale trade
> Maximum = 59.5 per cent for anthracite coal (p. 3)

2. Pay-roll taxes of 6 per cent as a percentage of output or sales in the year 1933:

> Minimum = 0.3 per cent for wholesale trade (p. 4)
> Maximum = 3.6 per cent for anthracite coal

The burden relative to output or sales is twelve times as great for the depressed coal industry as for wholesale trade.

3. Ratio of wages and salaries to the value of output for 16 principal manufactured products for 1933:[2]

> Minimum = petroleum and coal products = 10.8 per cent
> Maximum = railroad repairs = 61.7 (p. 5)

4. Ratio of wages and salaries to value added in the process of manufacture for 59 industries for 1933 (p. 7):[3]

Total	= 45.3	
Food	= 32.3 {	Minimum — distilled liquors = 8.3
		Maximum — meat packing = 50
Textiles	= 49.1 {	Minimum — bags = 28.4
		Maximum — hats = 64.0
Chemical and allied products = 27.1		
Transportation equipment	= 50.8 (p. 8)	
Note competitive industries {	Aircraft and parts	= 74.7
	Motor vehicles	= 39.3
	Motor vehicles, parts, and bodies	= 54.3

(1, 3, 6 per cent) in relation to value added by manufacture and value of product is given.

[1] The British also comment on the unevenness of the cost of social services to industry. Great Britain, Committee on Industry and Trade, *Further Factors in Industrial and Commercial Efficiency*, 1928, p. 10; *Appendices to the Report of the Committee on National Debt and Taxation*, 1927, pp. 86–96.

[2] *Cf.* GOODRICH, C., *et al.*, *Migration and Economic Opportunity*, 1936, pp. 452–453. The authors present here the ratio of wages to value added over the period 1923–1933. In general, a downward tendency seems to prevail and large differences among industries are to be noted.

[3] *Cf.* N.I.C.B., *Studies in Enterprise and Social Progress*, pp. 213–218. Wages and salaries are here given as 52 per cent of the value added by manufacture, and 54 and

5. Pay-roll tax (6 per cent) cost per dollar of product for 59 manufacturing industries in 1933 (pp. 9–11):

> Maximum = aircraft and parts = 3.12 cents
> Minimum = distilled liquors = 0.3 cent
> Average = 1.26 cents (thirty-seventh product from highest)

There are 18 items at the modal value of $1\frac{1}{2}$ to 2 per cent; but 8 at less than $\frac{1}{2}$ per cent and $5 > 2\frac{1}{2}$ per cent.

It is observed by Mr. Mulford that those industries which have relatively large wage bills are compensated to some extent through relatively small outlays for raw materials. The price paid for raw materials will to some extent represent a tax on wages[1] (p. 11).

6. It is well to note that the retailer, whose labor costs are relatively unimportant, pays in these taxes a very small part of the dollar value of sales. (Reference is made here only to the pay-roll tax paid by the retailer.) Large differences are to be found, however.

Retail trade: a 6 per cent pay-roll tax cost per dollar of sales in 1933 (p. 14):

> All = 0.7 cent
> Maximum = restaurants = 1.1 cents
> Minimum = farm supply and country general = 0.35 cent

7. Geographical differences are to be found in the following:

RATIO OF PAY-ROLLS TO VALUE OF OUTPUT IN 1933 (P. 17)

Cotton goods		Iron and steel (blast-furnace products)		Aluminum products		Cannery, fruit and vegetables	
State	Ratio	State	Ratio	State	Ratio	State	Ratio
South Carolina	25.0	Pennsylvania	5.7	Wisconsin..	25.9	New Jersey..	10.5
Massachusetts.	33.9	New York....	9.9	Illinois.....	32.5	Washington.	16.4

Naturally these figures are to be used with caution. Identical products are not produced in different states. A stimulus to substitution is, however, to be found in the relative differences in the burden of the tax arising from the varying proportion of labor to total costs.

---

53 in 1935 and 1937, respectively. Wages fluctuate around 25 per cent of the *production value* of manufacturing in the years 1919–1937. It is obvious why wages (and wages and salaries) would be a smaller proportion of this total than of value *added* by manufacture.

[1] *Cf.* BISSELL, *op. cit.*, pp. 225–226.

8. Regional differences are also revealed in the following (pp. 55–56):

> Bituminous coal — 6 per cent tax in 11 areas
> Maximum cost = 11.68 cents per ton in Michigan
> Minimum cost = 4.31 cents in Indiana

The maximum difference for more important competitive fields is, however, less than 3 cents.

9. Ratio of 6 per cent pay-roll tax to 1935 (or 1934) net profits for leading concerns in 15 industries (p. 21):

> Maximum = 3 textile manufacturing firms = 58.6 per cent
> Minimum = banks in Second Federal Reserve District = 9 per cent

10. Ratio of a 1 per cent pay-roll tax to net income for 45 important companies in 1935[1] (p. 23):

> Minimum (when net income is obtained) = 0.2 per cent
> = Texas Gulf Sulphur Company
> Maximum = 215.8 per cent = U. S. Steel Corporation
> American Telephone and Telegraph Company = 3.3 per cent

11. One significant problem is the net effect upon prices of the pay-roll tax which is levied on pay-rolls at all stages of processing. It is an error to assume that the tax can be in excess of a given percentage (6 per cent if the tax is 6 per cent) of the total pay-rolls in *all* stages.

Mr. Mulford finds that in the seven stages of manufacture of a handsaw which sells at $10, total labor costs in all stages are $4.17. A 6 per cent pay-roll tax will then require an outlay of 0.25 cent: 0.0016 cent in the first stage and 0.06 cent in the last stage (pp. 27–28).

A tax of this height will require a rise of prices of but 3 per cent. (This is on the assumption that the entrepreneur seeks compensation through an upward revision of prices.)

A similar study devoted to the four stages of breadmaking gives the following results (pp. 37–40):

> 6 per cent pay-roll tax in the process of making and distributing bread
> = 0.134 cent = 1.5 per cent of 9-cent loaf
> (Another study gives 2.75 per cent in place of 1.5 per cent.)
> Profit per bread (making and delivery) = 0.905 cent
> 0.134 = 14.8 per cent of profit of 0.905

[1] Small business units in recent years seem to have made smaller profits or larger losses than large corporations. In so far as the taxes are not passed on, losses will be increased in the one case and profits reduced in the other. In the longer run, larger firms may obtain some compensation through earlier elimination of the smaller firms. Cf. W. L. Crum, *Corporate Size and Earning Power*, 1940, pp. 17–23; *Hearings*, Ways and Means Committee, House of Representatives, *Social Security*, 1939, p. 793; S. Fabricant, "Profits, Losses and Business Assets, 1929–1934," *Nat. Bur. Econ. Research, Bull. 55*, 1935, p. 3.

12. Labor—per capita annual earnings—nine principal industries in 1932:

Maximum = oil and gas = $1,527
Minimum = bituminous coal = $662 (p. 31)

Large differences are to be found in the average wage level in different industries. High-wage industries subsidize low-paid industries under our social security program. To the extent that the tax cost is later shifted to general revenues of the Treasury, then the cost on high-wage industries will be reduced.[1]

Geographical differences raise many interesting problems. Wages are much lower in some sections of the country than in others.[2] The South, for example, in so far as it is covered under unemployment or old-age insurance then profits from the schedule of benefits, which on the whole favors the low paid. It suffers, however, from the small percentage of the population that is covered.[3] According to a survey by the Social Security Board, covered workers for the country constituted 34 per cent of the estimated population aged 15 to 64. North Dakota's percentage was but 12.1 per cent (a minimum for the country), and Rhode Island's was a maximum at 51 per cent.[4]

Small coverage may be advantageous in so far as it is to be explained by such factors as exemption from unemployment insurance on account of size of plant. Some sections of the country may then gain a competitive advantage. But they may also lose potential subsidies at the expense of taxpayers or possibly at the expense of consumers located in heavily populated sections of the country. Social security is paid in part through a rise of prices imposed on consumers; and in the future the general taxpayer is likely to pay an increasing proportion of all insurance costs. It should be observed, however, that the sections with the lowest percentage of covered workers are those with large numbers of agricultural workers; and the latter obtain subsidies through other programs. Where the proportion of old is low, the losses of small coverage may be considered relatively unimportant. These sectors require little help to take care of their old. Moreover, larger numbers become eligible for old-age assistance when coverage under insur-

[1] On these issues, see, for example, *Hearings*, Ways and Means Committee, House of Representatives, *Social Security*, 1939, p. 1898; WOLMAN, L., "The Recovery in Wages and Employment," *Nat. Bur. Econ. Research, Bull. 63*, 1936.

[2] MURRAY, M. B. and K. D. WOOD, "State Differences in Characteristics and Average Taxable Wages of Covered Employees, 1937," *Soc. Sec. Bull.*, September: 1939, pp. 13–24; *cf.* WASSERMAN, M. J., and J. R. ARNOLD, "Old Age Insurance, Covered Workers and Average and Median Taxable Wages in 1937," *Soc. Sec. Bull.*, April, 1939, p. 6.

[3] CORSON, J. J., "Old-age Insurance and the South," *Southern Econ. Jour.*, January, 1939, pp. 319–335.

[4] MURRAY and WOOD, *op. cit.*, p. 14.

ance is small, and Treasury subsidies contribute toward the costs of assistance.[1]

18.9. CONCLUSION

The burden of pay-roll taxes varies from firm to firm and industry to industry. A large proportion of all workers are still excluded from the benefits of old-age and unemployment insurance. Although entire industries are excluded and, therefore, the issue of competition arises only in an indirect form (*e.g.*, substitution of commodities), exclusion also puts firms and areas at an advantage in relation to competitors. Furthermore, competitive position is affected by the varying proportion of wages to total costs in different industries and areas and even for firms in the same industry.

In the discussion of insurance, much debate has centered upon the load to be carried by insurance funds and the distribution of that burden. At one extreme may be put an unqualified merit program under which each employer pays what he costs the insurance fund. (It is of course not easy to give precision to the clause "what he costs the insurance fund.") At the other extreme, all employers are to pay an equal proportion of their pay-rolls. Under the latter program, risks are pooled and industries and firms with low unemployment ratios subsidize the less stable or declining elements of the economy. Unemployment insurance may of course be given a much larger task if the pay-roll taxes are to be used to finance all unemployment and relief, irrespective of accumulated credits on the part of the participants. Industry and, in particular, the stable elements of industry would then, however, be burdened excessively and the nonindustrial taxpayer let off too easily.

The case for merit or experience rating does not seem strong. It may clash with fundamental principles of insurance: pooling of risks and simplicity of administration. More important, the effects upon stability of employment of the relatively modest savings to be had through minimum assessments on pay-rolls are not likely to be significant. Employment is largely beyond the control of the

---

[1] Federal grants in aid to states under the security program have unfortunately tended to vary *with* per capita income of the state. D. S. Gerig, Jr., "The Financial Participation of the Federal Government in State Welfare Programs," *Soc. Sec. Bull.*, January, 1940, pp. 25–27.

individual employer; and any improvement he shows in response to the stimulus of a relatively small saving on pay-roll taxation will probably be at the expense of another employer or will concentrate unemployment on a smaller group. The latter is a dubious advantage in periods of large unemployment. Furthermore, the cost of insurance must be carried somewhere. The merit system aims to put it upon industries and employers that have unsatisfactory employment records. They are, however, least able to bear the cost; and the imposition of taxes based on their record will give the unstable or declining industries an additional blow. Unfortunately, in periods of large unemployment, the excluded workers will be confronted with almost insuperable difficulties in finding employment in relatively stable industries.

Insurance not only operates as a differential factor but also has general effects on industry. Undoubtedly it contributes toward the relatively high reservation prices by labor in periods of depression. It is not, however, entirely clear that a general reduction in wages will help, though reductions in particular industries may be advantageous. Insurance and relief also may affect mobility adversely; and even in periods of large unemployment, the effects of reduced mobility upon employment and national income will be unfortunate.

Seasonality is another problem in the distribution of the burden of insurance. Seasonal industries may be treated as part of a merit system, additional charges being thus incurred; or they may be given special treatment through the introduction of safeguards against excessive drains. For example, the duration of benefits may be strictly limited, the waiting period extended, the proof of reasonable probability of work in the off-season required, or finally seasonal workers may be excluded. The danger is that seasonal industries may draw excessive amounts relatively to their contributions. The justification of large subsidies to these industries is much less than for other industries suffering from large amounts of unemployment.

Finally, some statistical material relevant to issues discussed in this chapter has been presented. The relation of pay-roll taxes to income, turnover, value added to manufacture and profits suggest some conclusions concerning burden. Material relative to the proportion of wages to total costs in (1) competing industries, (2) firms in the same industry, and (3) in competing geographical areas is also presented. We thus obtain some indication of the effects on competitive conditions of the pay-roll taxes.

CHAPTER 19

THE SIGNIFICANCE OF MONOPOLISTIC COMPETITION

Readers not conversant with the theory of monopolistic competition will find this chapter difficult. They might perhaps read only Secs. 19.1 and 19.10. Those who wish to look into the theory of monopolistic competition may find the following references helpful (also Sec. 19.1). The first seven are general references, listed in the order of the difficulty of the treatment. An elementary knowledge of the theory of monopolistic competition is all that is required to follow this chapter except for Secs. 19.6 and 19.8, and possibly Sec. 19.7. Sections 19.6 to 19.8 rest largely on the analysis of Mrs. Robinson. The second group deals with important matters specifically related to problems of this chapter and should be read after the elements of the theory have been absorbed.

General: MEYERS, A. L., *Elements of Modern Economics*, 1937, Chaps. 5–9; MEADE, J. E., *Introduction to Economic Analysis and Policy*, Part II; CHAMBERLIN, E., *The Theory of Monopolistic Competition*, 1939, Chaps. I–V; TRIFFIN, R., *Monopolistic Competition and General Equilibrium Theory*, 1940, Chaps. 1, 2, and 5; HARROD, R. F., "Doctrines of Imperfect Competition," *Quart. Jour. Econ.*, 1934; ROBINSON, J., *Economics of Imperfect Competition*, 1933, Books I–III; HICKS, J. R., "Annual Survey of Economic Theory—The Theory of Monopoly," *Econometrica*, 1935.

Monopolistic Competition and Distribution Theory: CHAMBERLIN, E., *Theory of Monopolistic Competition*, 1939, Chap. VIII; CHAMBERLIN, E., "Monopolistic Competition and the Productivity Theory of Distribution," *Explorations in Economics*, 1936; ROBINSON, J., *Economics of Imperfect Competition*, Books VI–X; ROBINSON, J., "Euler's Theorem and the Problem of Distribution," *Econ. Jour.*, 1934; MACHLUP, F., "On the Meaning of the Marginal Product," *Explorations in Economics*, 1936; HICKS, J. R., "Distribution and Economics Progress," *Rev. Econ. Studies*, 1936.

19.1. A SUMMARY OF THE THEORY OF MONOPOLISTIC COMPETITION

In the treatment of incidence, it is well to consider the problem of the single firm and the problem of the effects on all firms and industries—the peculiar problems arising from the varying proportions of wages to total costs being reserved for separate treatment. First, some aspects of the theory of monopolistic competition which shed

[373]

light upon the effect of a pay-roll tax on the individual firms will be summarized briefly.

Much of the current theory of monopolistic competition is concerned with the attempts of the single firm to maximize its profits. Output is determined at the point where marginal revenue equals marginal cost. Selling costs, advertising costs, differentiation of product all will be carried to a point where the incremental cost is balanced by incremental revenue. The case of a competitive market requires special assumptions. Infinite elasticity of demand for the product of any firm, large numbers of sellers, standardization of products, or the absence of selling or advertising costs are especially to be noted. Where the elasticity of demand is not infinite, whether the explanation is the fewness of sellers or differentiation of product, marginal revenue is less than price. If e is the algebraic elasticity of demand, the equating of marginal revenue and marginal cost implies that the ratio of price to marginal cost equals $(e + 1)/e$. If demand is infinitely elastic, this equals unity and price is identically equal to marginal cost and marginal revenue. The less elastic is demand, the more will price exceed marginal cost, and the more will output be restricted as compared with competitive output. Once the analysis allows for selling costs and differentiation of product, the definition of an industry and the construction of its supply curve become very perplexing problems.[1]

We turn first to the case of few sellers. This should not, however, be subsumed under monopolistic competition; for in this case the apparatus of demand curves become useless. That indeterminacy is to be found in the oligopoly case, is very important for us. Another source that may finance the tax program is thus suggested.

In the duopoly case, Cournot concluded that the price would settle between the competitive and monopoly price. One of Prof. Chamberlin's solutions is a simple monopoly price even in the absence of an explicit agreement. Much depends, however, on the

---

[1] See the cost controversy in the *Economic Journal*, 1926, 1930, and 1932, carried on by Messrs. Sraffa, Shove, Robertson, Harrod and Mrs. Robinson.

Prof. Chamberlin considers the permutations and combinations possible in the absence of large numbers and undifferentiated products.

In introducing the concept of cross elasticities, N. Kaldor ("Market Imperfection and Excess Capacity," *Economica*, 1935) has attempted to deal with all cases from pure competition to perfect monopoly. Each commodity or firm is regarded as being located on a line or field. The greater the density of the field, the more closely substitutable are the goods, and the higher the "cross elasticities." Pure competition results when the substitutability is infinite, perfect monopoly when it is zero.

assumption made concerning the calculations of each entrepreneur as to the indirect effects of his own behavior on others. Thus if duopolist one (1) changes his economic variable (price, output) from a level x, he expects his rival's output to expand or contract at a rate indicated by the derivative $dx_2/dx_1 = f'(x_1)$. Following Prof. Frisch this may be called the conjectural variation. In one of Prof. Chamberlin's solutions (the above), $f'(x_1) = 1$; *i.e.*, each realizes that both will charge the same price.[1] Analysis of the duopoly case may be helpful in dealing with incidence in cases where price rigidities are great and the demand for the factors extremely inelastic.

Prof. Chamberlin introduces the problem of product differentiation on the initial assumption that the group is large, each business unit being assumed sufficiently unimportant to have negligible effects on the others. Each firm maximizes its profits by equating marginal revenue and marginal costs. When entry is free, new firms enter until abnormal profits disappear. Now not only does marginal revenue equal marginal costs, but average revenue equals average costs; and output is less than that at which costs are a minimum. In Mrs. Robinson's formulation costs include not only normal profits but even excess profits associated with closed entry. It is not likely that taxation, in the long run, will impinge on normal profits (free entry); but we see no reason why the abnormal profits (entry not free) may not be whittled down.

Free entry is frequently not the rule, however. Firms may then not be of optimum size (*i.e.*, produce at minimum cost) for another reason, *viz.*, they may be too large. We shall dwell further on the theory of monopolistic competition in the course of discussion of points of special relevance to the incidence of pay-roll taxes.

19.2. Pay-roll Tax and the Costs of the Firm

It is appropriate to begin with an examination of costs of the individual firm. Therefore a hypothetical cost curve (chart V) is presented showing the relationship between labor costs and other expenditures. In accordance with the usual assumptions, the unit cost curve is U shaped with marginal costs at first falling, later rising. This includes in one diagram the three cases of falling, constant, and rising costs. It has been assumed that labor costs are always 25 per cent of total *variable* costs, this figure being derived

---

[1] Allen, R. G. D., *Mathematical Analysis for Economists*, p. 203.

from the approximate relation between these magnitudes given in the *Biennial Census of Manufactures*.[1] The percentage of labor to total costs rises with increases in output, for a large part of total costs is fixed. (Actually over the entire economy labor costs are roughly two-thirds of *all* costs, as indicated by the relation of wages and salaries to income.)[2] In the present

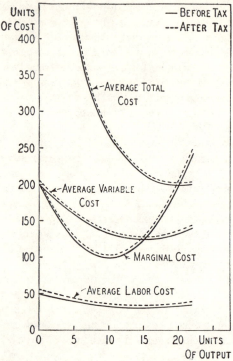

CHART V.—Hypothetical cost schedules. $\left(\text{Equation for total cost} = 1,333 + 200x\right.$

$$- 10x^2 + \frac{x^3}{3}.\Big)$$

calculations, however, we are concerned merely with the value added in the process of manufacture.

Our calculations have been performed on the assumption that a 10 per cent pay-roll tax is assessed. Actually, if any substitution of factors were possible, a 10 per cent pay-roll tax would result in a less than 10 per cent increase in labor cost. Our case, where no substitution is possible, corresponds to a perfectly inelastic demand for labor as of any given output.

[1] Department of Commerce, *Biennial Census of Manufactures*, 1935, p. 22.
[2] *Cf.* calculations in Chap. 17.

Although it is not necessarily true in other cases, it is likely that an increase in labor costs will result in an increase in marginal cost at any given output. There is also some probability in most cases that the imposition of a pay-roll tax will shift the point of minimum average cost to the left, the result being a smaller output by firms producing under perfect competition.

The example presented here is of interest because it is a limiting case. Any actual case will show similar results, but to a lesser degree. A 10 per cent pay-roll tax results here in a 10 per cent increase in labor cost for every output, and in a less than 10 per cent increase in total costs. The ratio of labor cost to total cost for the same output is increased over what it had been before the imposition of the tax. Average variable and marginal costs are each increased by 2½ per cent at each and every output; but marginal costs rise more than average total costs. The point of minimum average cost is shifted very slightly to the left. The points of minimum average variable cost and minimum average labor cost are left unchanged by the imposition of the tax. All these effects are quite small because labor cost, even at the largest output, is only about one-sixth of total cost, and a 10 per cent tax results in a change in total cost roughly of but 1.66 per cent.

The smallness of the effect of a 10 per cent pay-roll tax is somewhat misleading, for in fact the tax would result in an increased cost of materials, fuel, and other nonlabor factors, these being to some degree made by labor in earlier stages of production. Assuming 50 per cent coverage, and total employee compensation of about two-thirds of the national income, one would expect in the final stages of production a 10 per cent increase in pay-rolls to result in an addition of 3⅓ per cent to total costs. One may even put the total rise of cost at 4 per cent or more if allowance is made for a rise of coverage of 60 to 75 per cent.

Mrs. Robinson presents an interesting case of a tax of constant amount per unit of output that fits in well at this point. On the assumption of constant costs and a straight-line demand curve, price will rise by one-half of the rise of marginal costs. Should the marginal cost curve slope downward, the rise (for obvious reasons) will be in excess of one-half of the rise of marginal costs. The reduction of output will be greater, the more concave from above is the demand curve; for the more concave, the farther to the left the intersection of the marginal revenue and marginal cost curves.[1] Should the marginal cost curve be constant and the concavity of

---

[1] ROBINSON, J., *The Economics of Imperfect Competition*, pp. 76–83.

Concavity is defined as $d^2y/dx^2 > 0$. (Concavity as viewed from above, cf. Allen, *op. cit.*, pp. 184–185.) "If $f''(a)$ is positive, then $f(x)$ is changing at an increasing rate as x increases through a and the tangent gradient to the curve $y = f(x)$ increases as we pass through the point with abscissa a. The tangent to the curve turns in the anticlockwise direction and the curve is convex when viewed from below at this point." Quoted from Allen, *op. cit.*, by permission of The Macmillan Company, publishers. (This is concave when viewed from above—Mrs. Robinson's usage.)

the demand curve be so great that the slope of the marginal revenue curve equals or surpasses the slope of the demand curve, the rise in price will equal or surpass the cost increase. If marginal costs are rising with a rise of output or if the demand curve is convex, the effect of the tax tends to be small. This analysis leaves out of account the effects on prices and the demand curves of the imposition of similar taxes on rival firms.[1]

This analysis may be applied to the social security case if the pay-roll tax is assumed to be a constant amount per unit of output. The pay-roll tax may in a general way be considered a tax of this type, *particularly in the range where variable costs are almost constant.*[2] Thus a 10 per cent pay-roll

---

[1] Whether or not the demand and marginal cost curves are straight lines, and regardless of their slopes, the following formula shows the effect on price of a change in tax per unit output (for small changes). I am indebted to Mrs. Marian Crawford Samuelson for this formula.

$$\frac{\text{Change in price}}{\text{Change in tax per unit}}$$

$$= \frac{\text{algebraic slope of demand curve}}{\text{algebraic slope of marginal revenue curve} - \text{algebraic slope of marginal cost curve}}$$

$$= \frac{1}{2 + \text{algebraic adjusted demand concavity} - \text{algebraic ratio of marginal cost and demand slopes}}$$

i.e.,

$$\frac{dp}{dt} = \frac{D'(x)}{2D'(x) + xD''(x) - C''}$$

$$= \frac{1}{2 + \dfrac{xD''(x)}{D'(x)} - \dfrac{C''}{D'(x)}}$$

where

t = tax per unit.

$p = D(x)$ = demand curve.

C' = marginal cost curve.

$D'(x)$ = slope of demand curve.

$2D'(x) + xD''(x)$ = slope of marginal revenue curve.

C'' = slope of marginal cost curve.

$\dfrac{xD''(x)}{D'(x)}$ = elasticity of slope of demand curve or adjusted demand concavity.

If the concavity is zero and marginal cost curve is horizontal,

$$\frac{dp}{dt} = \frac{1}{2 + 0 - 0} = \frac{1}{2}$$

The greater is the concavity from above—the less the convexity from below—and the less is the algebraic slope of the marginal cost curve, the more will price increase, *i.e.,* falling marginal cost and concave demand curves yield the greatest price changes.

[2] Then on the assumption of constancy of variable costs (*e.g.,* below full capacity), we would not contradict the earlier assumptions: (1) labor costs proportional to variable costs; (2) marginal and variable costs U shaped.

tax on a million-dollar pay-roll yielding one million units of goods is equivalent to a tax of 10 cents per unit of output. A reduction of the wage bill to $500,000, output remaining unchanged, would be tantamount to a reduction of the tax per unit of output to 5 cents. Naturally, the smaller the percentage of wages to total costs, or the smaller the charge under merit rating (unemployment insurance), the smaller the tax per unit of output. Let us assume that a pay-roll tax of 10 per cent or 5 cents per unit of output is imposed in this particular case. Then if the slope of marginal cost is upward and the demand curve is convex, the *rise* of marginal costs may be small (they may even decline); and the curtailment of output will be modest.

19.3. TAX ON INDIVIDUAL FIRM

In a discussion of the effect of a pay-roll tax *on the employer* upon an individual firm, it is well to distinguish four cases:

I. Perfect competition in the commodity and factor market.

II. Imperfect competition in the commodity market and perfect competition in the factor market.

III. Perfect competition in the commodity market and imperfect competition in the factor market.

IV. Imperfect competition in both commodity and factor markets.

Case I is dealt with in this section; case II in Secs. 19.4, 19.7, and 19.8; case III (and to some extent IV) in Secs. 19.5 and 19.6.

The first case, *i.e.*, perfect competition in both commodity and factor markets, gives expected results. Previous to the imposition of a tax, workers were employed up to the point where at the margin the value of their product just equaled their wages. Now the cost per unit of labor is raised and a new margin will be reached at a lower level of employment. Prices and wages remain unchanged (on the assumption of perfect competition), and output will probably decline. In fact, this firm should drop out of the market entirely. It is to be emphasized that we are dealing with the economy of a single firm. Should the tax be imposed upon all firms, then it would be well to take into account the effects of the tax on *all* firms upon the demand for the products and prices of the individual firm. In other words, the assumption of fixity of other schedules would then be removed. This problem is treated in Sec. 19.9 (*cf.* Sec. 20.4).

It does not follow, however, that the treatment of the effects upon the individual firm (relations with other firms being put aside) is of no practical significance. The pay-roll tax affects some firms more than others, *e.g.*, those with large proportions of labor costs; and in so far as the tax is larger on one seller than on another, the analysis of the individual firm holds some interest for us. Furthermore, the rise of costs following the imposition of a pay-roll tax is a real one for the individual firm and its effects require study; and repercussions upon demand for the product of the individual firms follow from the collection of taxes, accumulation, investment, and finally disbursement of proceeds. All these problems properly are treated in the analysis of the individual firm. What this analysis fails to handle satisfactorily is the effect upon costs and demand of simultaneous changes in costs of and demand for the products of other firms.

Although somewhat fuller discussion is reserved for a later part of this chapter, it should be observed at this point that a curtailment of output is not so likely to follow in the general case (*i.e.*, a tax on all firms) as in that of the individual firm. Supply of the factors for *all* firms and industries is less elastic than for one or a few firms. It, therefore, follows that a tax on pay-rolls is more easily passed on to the factors of production when the tax is universal than when it is imposed on relatively few firms. In the former case, movements of factors to other firms that have not been subjected to the tax is *ex hypothesi* excluded. The incentive to a curtailment of output through a withdrawal of factors will not be so strong when the tax is universal as when it applies to one firm. In the general case strong trade-unionism may, however, artificially raise the elasticity of supply of factors and strengthen the possibility of adverse effects upon output. Effects from the demand side also require consideration in the general case (*cf.* Secs. 19.9 and 20.4). But it is well to note here that these problems, *e.g.*, the effect of simultaneous changes in costs elsewhere upon the supply and demand conditions of the firm under consideration, do not lie wholly outside the proper field of study of the individual firm. In so far, however, as supply and demand conditions to the individual producers are less than perfectly elastic, these problems are not properly analyzed in this case of perfect competition.

19.4. A Tax under Less Than Perfectly Elastic Demand Conditions

No rise of price was anticipated in the discussion of a tax on an individual firm (differentiated tax) under case I; for under the assumptions of perfect competition, each firm accepts the price of the market for commodities and factors. In the present case (II), however, it is assumed that the demand curve for the firm's output is not of infinite elasticity and, therefore, prices will rise. Output will now suffer less, for part of the cost can be passed on to the consumer. This is subject to the reservation, as Mrs. Robinson has pointed out, that the sales of commodities in rivalry with other firms will result in an upward shift of demand curves and prices. (Once it is assumed that rival firms also raise prices—a uniform tax, for example—then the demand for the products of A will rise as compared with the case usually assumed in which prices of its products alone rise.) Mrs. Robinson's reservation should, however, be considered in conjunction with another, viz., the associated limitation of purchasing power. Inelasticity in the supply of spendable funds will tend to have a depressing effect upon the elasticity and shifts of the individual demand curves (Secs. 17.2, 19.9 and 20.4).

The relevancy of the theory of monopolistic competition for the problem of incidence of a pay-roll tax will now be considered in greater detail.[1] In response to a tax on wages, the entrepreneur increases prices and reduces output. A further question arises, however, viz., the incidence of the restriction of output as between firms. For the net effect on prices will depend in part upon the distribution of the losses of output. Assume that firms are of less than optimum size, i.e., their unit costs are in excess of the minimum. Three possibilities may then be considered: (1) the output of firms that survive remains unchanged, the reduction of output being concentrated on firms now forced out of business; (2) each firm cuts its output by an equal proportionate amount, the result being a rise in average costs; (3) the elimination of firms proceeds further than under (1), the result being an output closer to the optimum than had prevailed

---

[1] In this chapter, our great indebtedness to Mrs. Robinson and Prof. Chamberlin will be evident to the reader conversant with their brilliant works on the theory of monopolistic competition. Since we are here concerned primarily with the rewards of the factors of production, we have relied heavily on Mrs. Robinson's discussion of rents and the rewards to the factors of production.

previous to the imposition of the tax. It is clear, therefore, that the rise of price *in each case*, relative to that indicated by the effects on total output, may be (1) as given by a consideration of the variation in *total* output [as in (1) above]; (2) greater [as suggested under (2)]; and (3) less [as suggested under (3)]. What is significant is that the effect of a tax upon prices will depend upon the distribution of a curtailment of output as between firms. Should the effect be, for example, an increase in the average output of firms that survive, the optimum level being thus approached, part of the tax may be absorbed in a reduction of unit costs.

One may proceed with an analysis along similar lines where the output for individual firms is in excess of the optimum.[1] It may be assumed here that entry is not free, and liquidation of firms following the imposition of taxes is not likely. A tax may then well have the effect of reducing output for all firms, the tendency thus being to bring output closer to the previous optimum level.[2] Part of the cost of social security once more will then be absorbed in a reduction of costs. This is, however, not the only possible result. A reduction of sales may, for example, encourage some sellers to increase their selling and advertising costs in an attempt to maintain the absolute amount of their sales. Their costs may then rise not only in response to the imposition of new taxes but also in response to a rise of selling costs. The aggressive sellers will be confronted with a rise of selling costs which, however, will not be offset by a reduction of unit production costs. Other sellers will, however, find some compensation for new taxes and lost markets in a reduction of unit production costs.

19.5. A Tax When Supplies of Factors Are Less than Perfectly Elastic to the Firm

We now turn to case III: supplies of factors are not perfectly elastic to the unit under consideration. Factors of production, as is

---

[1] Here surplus profits are obtained. The tax may then well fall upon these surpluses. *Cf.* P. H. Douglas, "The Effects of Wage Increases upon Employment," *Proc. Am. Econ. Assoc.*, 1939, pp. 152–153.

[2] This identification of the minimum point of the U-shaped curve as the optimum clashes, however, with the criteria of the social allocation of resources. The latter is achieved whenever (1) output is produced at the lowest *total* cost and (2) price (representing marginal utility) equals or is proportional to marginal costs.

well known, receive rewards in excess of their minimum transfer costs, *i.e.*, the reward required to keep factors from rival uses. In Mrs. Robinson's usage, rent is the compensation over and above what is necessary in order to obtain the cooperation of the factor, *i.e.*, the difference between transfer earnings of inframarginal units and earnings of factors on the margin.[1] When the supply of the factor is perfectly elastic, the element of rent does not arise; but the larger the unit under consideration, the more inelastic in general is the supply of the factors available and, for this reason, the more important becomes the rent element. For other reasons, however, large business units may pay small rents. Acting as discriminating monopsonists they may force the factors to accept rewards that are little in excess of their minimum transfer earnings. More on this later.

Receipts of rents by the factors suggest the possibility that they may pay at least part of the costs of pay-roll taxes. How may this come about? Prices rise following the imposition of the pay-roll tax and, therefore, output declines. Demand for the factors declines, the more expensive units then being dropped. Rents of the inframarginal units now decline as marginal units cost less. Prices finally do not rise so much as they would have in the absence of a cut in rents. It is even possible that labor through an artificially induced elasticity of supply may force the sacrifices largely upon other factors.

One further observation is relevant here. The pay-roll tax affects industries with large wage bills more than others. Should the rents paid by the industries with relatively high labor costs be large, these industries will be in a position to force the cooperating factors, which are now confronted with a relatively large reduction of demand, to accept an important reduction in rents. Furthermore, demand for factors may well suffer all around, although in order to be sure of this conclusion, it is necessary to take into account all the effects of the security program. In summary, pay-roll taxes may be financed in part out of rents.

This discussion of rent brings us to Mrs. Robinson's monopsony case.[2] In her terminology the monopoly buyer is referred to as a monopsonist. The criterion of perfect competition among buyers is that the supply curve to the individual buyer should be perfectly elastic. Perfect competition prevails if the number of buyers is large (or

[1] *The Economics of Imperfect Competition*, especially Chaps. 8–9.
[2] *Ibid.*, Chaps. 17–18, 26 (especially pp. 219–221).

supply is sold under constant price) and if sellers are indifferent as to whom they provide with their wares.

When supply conditions are not elastic, employment of the factors is not likely to be identical with that which prevails when supply conditions are elastic. Thus under perfect competition, employment is given by the intersection of the marginal utility and supply curves. The monopsonist, on the other hand, determines employment at the point where marginal utility and *marginal* cost curves intersect. It follows that employment will be larger than under competitive conditions when the supply curve is falling and less when it is rising. Further, the discriminating monopsonist may increase output beyond that of the simple monopsonist, for he will appropriate rents. He will make the marginal cost of each factor equal and all equal to the derived marginal value productivity of the total. Perfect discrimination requires that the marginal cost of each amount equal the supply price of that amount. The monopsonist will be inclined to buy less where supplies are less elastic and more where supply is more elastic. In the comparison of demand for factors, the *convenient* assumption is made, let us observe, that the marginal productivity and the supply curves are identical under the competitive and monopsonistic conditions being compared. Actually, they will vary. A condition of monopsony, for example, may affect the supply curve of a factor.

Since relative outputs and demand for the factors of production under competitive conditions on the one hand and monopsonistic conditions on the other will be influenced by the slope of the supply curve, any variable, *e.g.*, a tax, that affects the supply curve in such a manner as to change the distance on the X axis between the intersection of (1) the marginal cost and the demand curve and (2) the intersection of the average cost curve and the demand curve, will to that extent affect the relative desirability of monopsonistic and competitive conditions. If the supply curve is a falling one, monopsony employment, it is recalled, will be in excess of competitive employment. At this point the imposition of a pay-roll tax increases the proportion of labor to all costs and thus reduces the proportion of costs that will decline (per unit of output) with a rise of output. The tax increases marginal more than average total costs; and the excess of output, which prevails under monopsonistic conditions with a falling supply curve, now becomes smaller. With a rising supply curve, it is competitive output that exceeds output under monopsonistic conditions. Again a pay-roll tax is likely (except in conditions of output much below capacity) to increase marginal more than average total costs; and the result will be an even greater excess of competitive over monopsonistic output and employment than prevailed prior to the imposition of the tax.[1]

19.6. TAXES AND EXPLOITATION ASSOCIATED WITH IMPERFECT SUPPLY CONDITIONS IN THE FACTOR MARKETS

Another issue raised by the imperfections in the labor market is that of exploitation. We turn to a brief discussion of the issues. For our purposes, it is important to point out that exploitation of this kind is to be found in the real world and that if exploitation is reduced social security taxes may ultimately be paid out of exploitation income formerly received by the entrepreneur. This objective may be achieved through a rise of wages, which may be induced through the imposition of pay-roll taxes. Mrs. Robinson suggests a rise of wages based on efficiency in one case and the imposition of a minimum general wage in the others. In the practical world, however, something may be said for a general rise of wages in the former case, despite unfavorable effects on employment.[2] A social security program may then contribute toward the reduction in the degree of exploitation.

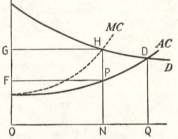

CHART VI.—Monopsonistic exploitation. (*From J. Robinson, Economics of Imperfect Competition, p. 294. By permission of The Macmillan Company, publishers.*)

When the supply of labor is less than perfectly elastic to the unit of control, employment is determined at the point of intersection (H) of the marginal cost and marginal value productivity curves (Chart VI); but the wage will be equal to the supply price (NP) of the amount of labor employed (ON). Exploitation may now be removed by the imposition of a minimum wage (NH).[3] Should the wage be set at NH, the wage would then rise from NP to NH and employment would remain unchanged at ON. Should the wage be fixed at a point $> NP$ but $< NH$, both wages and employment will rise. At the wage QD, employment will be a maximum.

[1] The chart presented in Sec. 19.2 may be helpful at this point.
[2] *Cf.* DOUGLAS, P. H., "Wage Theory and Wage Policy," *Internat. Labor Rev.*, 1939.
[3] ROBINSON, J., *The Economics of Imperfect Competition*, p. 294.

Assume that Mrs. Robinson's solution is not practical. Then a social security program may be helpful. Through the imposition of a wage tax on entrepreneurs paying low wages, the minimum wage will be raised. The tax should, however, be assessed not as a percentage of pay-rolls but on the basis of labor costs per unit of output. For example,

a. Wages = $1   Output = 100 units   Employers' tax = $1
b. Wages = 2   Output = 100 units   Employers' tax = 0

The assumption is that the employers' contribution will be used to provide social security funds for his workers. Under this plan, the best paid workers will, however, not receive any benefits.

Mrs. Robinson then turns from this case of monopsonistic exploitation where firms operate in concert (assumed above) to cases of exploitation where firms do not operate in concert. Profits are assumed to be normal and the selling market perfect. Yet firms are less than optimum size because the supply of labor to the firm is less than perfectly elastic. Workers attached to a particular firm and in a particular area are not numerous enough to assure required supplies at unchanged rates of wages. The wage is of course equal to the average net productivity, and employment is given by the intersection of the marginal net productivity and marginal cost curves. Optimum size is attainable if the imperfections of the labor market are removed. It does not follow, however, that (with a given volume of employment) wages will then rise. Much depends on the effects of the removal of imperfections on the physical productivity of labor, on the prices of cooperative factors, and on the elasticity of demand for the product. What is also clear is that a rise of wages (through social security or any other method) is not likely to be helpful. Profits will fall below the normal level, and output will suffer. A large drop in physical productivity will then be required in order to maintain employment.

Exploitation proceeds farther when discrimination is possible. (1) The supply of men may be perfectly elastic, efficiency varying. Wages are set at the marginal net productivity of the least efficient man. Each receives his transfer wage, and discrimination is perfect. The remedy, in Mrs. Robinson's view, is to pay according to efficiency and not to introduce a general increase of wages, for the latter policy would result in a loss of employment. (2) All men may be of the same efficiency, but employment is adjusted so that the wage of the most expensive man equals the marginal net productivity of the group. Each is once more paid his minimum transfer wage. Exploitation is removed by stipulating that wages of all be raised to those of the most expensive man.

We limit our comments to Mrs. Robinson's first case. In this case, i.e., varying efficiency, more may be said for the solution through a rise of wages than is said by Mrs. Robinson. Payment according to efficiency is frequently not practical. Then a rise of wages may be preferable to no action, and the more inelastic the demand for labor, the less employment will suffer. If the wages, or better, labor cost should be increased through the imposition of taxes, the taxes may largely be at the expense of employers rather than at the cost of employment.

19.7. IMPERFECTIONS ARISING FROM DEMAND CONDITIONS: REMOVE THEM OR RAISE WAGES?

In an earlier section, the case of a falling demand curve for the product of the individual firm was discussed briefly and it was pointed out that the pay-roll tax may, under these conditions, be passed on to the consumer to some extent in higher prices. In this case, the issue of exploitation also emerges. We therefore turn to this aspect of exploitation and inquire whether it prevails, and if it does, whether removal of the imperfections which account for the exploitation will help or injure labor. It is possible that a rise of wages may be a better solution from labor's viewpoint than the removal of imperfections, and in so far as additional wages may be obtained through a removal of imperfections, social security may be financed out of a rise of output or (and) profits.[1]

Exploitation, it has been suggested, arises then not only because the supply of labor is less than perfectly elastic, and the wage is not given by the intersection of the marginal productivity curve and marginal cost curve, but also because the demand for the firm's product is less than perfectly elastic. It follows that wages are given not by the marginal physical product valued at its selling price, but by the marginal physical product valued at its marginal revenue; and the less elastic the demand for the product, the greater the difference between marginal revenue and price, and the greater the excess of the product times selling price over product times marginal revenue.[2] It should be said, however, that exploitation of labor does not arise in the sense that they receive less than workers in competitive industries. They may even receive more than under competitive conditions. But the whole community is exploited in the sense that outputs are not optimal owing to divergence of prices from proportionality with marginal costs.

[1] It should be observed that it is *unequal* exploitation (in Mrs. Robinson's sense) that is bad. If imperfection is everywhere the same, output will be optimal.
[2] ROBINSON, *op. cit.*, Chap. 25, especially pp. 281–283.

Chamberlin quite rightly objects to the use of the term "exploitation" in this connection. Since the entrepreneur is guided in his output policy by marginal revenue, "he will never find it profitable and he will often find it impossible to pay to *any* of the factors the value of their marginal products."[1] He continues that even if surplus profits are earned, the entrepreneur tries to maximize profits and hence will not pay wages equal to the marginal product. The sum of incomes computed on the basis of marginal products may be in excess of the total product. Payment of the marginal product would frequently involve the entrepreneur in bankruptcy. One may therefore well agree with Prof. Chamberlin when he says that the Pigovian criterion of exploitation, *i.e.*, payment of less than the marginal physical product at its selling price, is applicable only to conditions of pure competition.[2]

This reservation may be appended to Prof. Chamberlin's position. It is well, however, to distinguish the monopolistic aspects given by the slope of the demand curve (discussed above) from the monopolistic flavor given by closed entry to which we now turn. There is an element of exploitation under conditions of monopolistic competition where surplus profits are being obtained. Laborers may then have maximum claims given by the value of their physical product multiplied by the difference between price and marginal revenue (which is the version of exploitation applied by Mrs. Robinson at this point) or the amount of surplus profits, whichever is the *smaller*. Possibly exploitation is a strong term even here, though labor may with justice feel that they have claims at least to part of any surplus profits.[3]

Aside from the question of the propriety of considering the difference between the marginal physical product times its selling price on the one hand and times its marginal revenue on the other as exploitable income, it is necessary to consider the effect of the declining demand curve for the product of the individual firm upon equilibrium output. Price depends upon the number of men employed; and the greater the number employed, the

---

[1] E. CHAMBERLIN, "Monopolistic Competition and the Productivity Theory of Distribution," *Explorations in Economics*, p. 241.

[2] CHAMBERLIN, *op. cit.*, especially pp. 241-243. For a view similar to Mrs. Robinson's see Douglas, *op. cit.*

[3] Relative to Prof. Chamberlin's comments it may be well to remember that entrepreneurs seek the maximization of profits, not the social optimum. Furthermore, the payment of additional amounts to factors (profits = 0) would result in a reduction in the number of firms until they were once more breaking even.

more marginal net productivity falls even though physical productivity is unchanged. As output rises, the marginal net productivity of labor will decline not only because the price of the product declines (elasticity of demand $< \infty$), but also because the amount of capital employed tends to fall (or rise less rapidly) with a rise of output and a reduction of prices. Employment will not be at the same level as when the demand curve for the firm's output is perfectly elastic. It is not true, under these conditions, that the number of men whose average net productivity is a maximum will be the number of men that will be employed *at a given wage* by a firm which is of optimum size.[1] Average net productivity is below a maximum at the actual output (which is at a maximum at the given wage) because demand is not perfectly elastic (and therefore output is restricted) and because, with less than perfect elasticity, the amount of capital cooperating in production is not at an optimal level.

It is appropriate at this point to comment on the significance for the problem of the pay-roll tax of the difference between the marginal physical product of *labor* at (1) its selling price and (2) its marginal revenue. In classical theory, a rise of wage costs associated with a pay-roll tax accounts for a reduction of the marginal net productivity of money spent on labor. A dollar of wages now yields less product. The demand for labor falls, and in the absence of trade-unionism and other frictional influences, wages will fall until, to the unit of control, wages plus the tax once more equal the old marginal net productivity of labor; otherwise employment will change. [It is of course also possible even under conditions of perfect competition to assume that the wage tax is applied to *all* competitors and, therefore, that prices rise. The decline in the marginal net productivity associated with a rise of money wages is then offset at least in part by a rise of prices. Money wage rates (exclusive of security payments) will not, therefore, be forced down by a rise of costs so much as in the absence of a rise of prices.]

In the monopolistic competitive case, the imposition of the tax is accompanied by a rise of prices and of marginal revenue even for the individual firm. Thus under these conditions the imposition of a pay-roll tax brings a rise of price, and the more inelastic the demand for the firm's product, the greater the rise of price; and, therefore, the less the need for a cut in wages to maintain the same level of employment. Marginal revenue and marginal costs will be equal at a higher point; but prices will of course continue to be higher than marginal revenue. Marginal net productivity of the wage dollar will now fall less than under pure competition following the imposition of pay-roll taxes not only because of the ensuing rise of prices associated with the falling demand curve for the firm's product, but also because of the more liberal use of capital as the marginal net productivity of capital rises in response to an increase of prices. (In other words, the extent to which the use of capital is reduced by a rise of labor costs is

---

[1] ROBINSON, *op. cit.*, pp. 246–252.

not so great when some compensation is to be had in a rise of prices as when this offset is not available.) Furthermore, the cost of capital may fall if its supply curve at the relevant point slopes upward. On the other side of the ledger is to be put the losses associated with the failure to push economies as far as they would otherwise have been pushed.

Mrs. Robinson considers the possibility of the removal of the imperfections which give rise to the type of "exploitation" associated with a wage less than the marginal physical product at its selling price.[1] It is perhaps indicative of the confusion to which this definition of exploitation leads that, according to Mrs. Robinson, laborers may be better off under imperfect conditions of production, *i.e.*, when labor is being "exploited," than under optimum conditions, *i.e.*, when labor is not being exploited in this sense. Both when the firm is less than optimum size (free entry) and wages are given by average net productivity, and when the firm is more than optimum size and wages are less than average net productivity, Mrs. Robinson's proposed way out is the removal of the imperfections.

It does not follow that the position of labor is then improved when exploitation is removed. A rise of physical productivity, which would probably follow the removal of imperfections, will injure labor because it induces a fall of prices, and any ensuing rise in the cost of other factors will also be injurious to the interests of labor. Thus, should the rise of physical productivity and of the cost of other factors now required to cooperate with labor be large and the elasticity of demand for the commodity not sufficiently high, the employment of labor is likely to suffer. On the other hand, labor gains *qua* consumers from any ensuing decline of prices; and in appraising the net effect, one should take into account the rise of price directly associated with imperfections and an improvement in the terms of labor's bargains with capital. (In this crude form, the last follows, however, only on the assumption that capital's losses of employment are relatively greater than are labor's.)

Perhaps another way out can be found which will improve the position of labor, for it is not clear that labor's position is improved by the removal of imperfections even if we allow that Mrs. Robinson overemphasizes the advantages to labor under imperfect competition. In discussing the case of firms of less than optimum size, she writes as follows: "Exploitation of this type cannot be removed by raising wages, but it would disappear if the market became perfect."[2] Labor's position may, however, improve if the remedy is a rise of money wages. Some unemployment may follow, but total wages may rise. This may be the best possible solution even if imperfections and "exploitation" are not removed. Even in her case 2, *i.e.*, firms producing at above the optimum level, a rise of wages may profit labor. It may be the only practical solution and offers the incentive of an

[1] *Ibid.*, pp. 281–288.
[2] *Ibid.*, p. 284.

erasure of at least part of the abnormal profits and their transfer to wage earners.[1]

Once more a tax on wages (the proceeds to be used for the benefit of wage earners) may result in the improvement of labor's position. In other words, the tax may be absorbed in other quarters. In particular if a removal of imperfections would be followed by a large rise of physical productivity and a rise in the cost of other factors and if demand were inelastic, the correct policy from labor's viewpoint seems to be a rise of wages and prices. Then labor would gain at the expense of consumers (in part nonwage earners) and at the expense of other factors which would find less employment and at lower rates of remuneration per unit.

In this section, the following conclusions stand out. Serious objections may be raised to the use of the term exploitation, when it is associated with a sloping demand curve for the product of the individual firm. Surplus profits may be obtained, however, and labor may have some claims to part of these profits. A removal of imperfections *may* not help labor's position, whereas a rise of wages may prove to be the best policy from labor's viewpoint. A social security program, in offering an excuse for a rise of wages, may contribute toward the consummation of the latter policy. A removal of imperfections may be costly to labor in so far as with a rise of average productivity prices fall and the costs of cooperating factors rise. Labor *qua* consumer gains from a fall of prices, however; and under monopolistic competition, an extension of output by the individual firm frequently brings economies not diseconomies.

19.8. COMPETITIVE AND MONOPOLISTIC DEMAND FOR FACTORS IN RELATION TO PAY-ROLL TAXES

In her *Economics of Imperfect Competition*, Mrs. Robinson deals fully with comparative outputs and comparative demands for labor under monopoly and competition.[2] Her argument may be put briefly as follows. When the demand and supply curves are straight lines and the monopolist pays full rent, monopoly output (and similarly demand for labor) is one-half of the competitive output. If the demand curve is convex (supply

---

[1] *Cf.* DOUGLAS, *op. cit.*, pp. 36–37.

[2] Especially Chaps. 10–12, 14, 23. Prof. Pigou also deals with this problem, though he limits his discussions to linear demand functions and the processing by labor is under constant conditions (ϕ'' is positive). *Theory of Unemployment*, pp. 54–55.

curve a straight line), or the marginal cost curve concave (the demand curve a straight line), monopoly output exceeds one-half of the competitive output. (Concavity as viewed from above $= d^2y/dx^2 > 0$.) Monopolists will then restrict their output as the demand curve becomes more concave, for each successive reduction in output results in a greater and greater absolute rise of prices. Again, the more convex the marginal cost curve, the more they will be tempted to reduce their output. Furthermore, monopolistic output, relative to competitive, will be larger than is indicated by the foregoing in so far as the monopolist is in a position to vary the proportions of the factors, e.g., according to the varying elasticities of the supply curves of the factors; and monopolistic output will also be stimulated by any relief from the payment of rent.

This analysis is of some interest for the examination of the effects of the pay-roll tax. (1) Since monopoly output is most likely to be less than competitive output, the prevalence of monopoly would indicate that the absolute effects on output and, via output on price, of a tax on wages are less unfavorable than the net effect to be found on the assumption of competition. For given demand and supply conditions, an equiproportionate reduction of output will be equal to a smaller absolute reduction under monopoly than under competition. (2) Any effects of a pay-roll tax upon the degree of concavity or convexity of the demand or supply curves (as indicated in the preceding paragraph) will affect monopoly output in a favorable (or unfavorable) manner relatively to competitive output. (3) In response to the introduction of a pay-roll tax, the monopolist may substitute capital for labor if the supply of capital is elastic. He can vary his factors with greater effectiveness than the competitive producer. The imposition of a pay-roll tax would then tend to discourage output under monopoly less than under competitive conditions. Monopoly output will suffer relatively, however, if the factor of more elastic supply (labor, for example) becomes more costly. Further, it should be observed that in so far as the proportions of the factors employed are different under monopolistic and competitive conditions the effects of a pay-roll tax will be different.

In this connection, the following is of some interest. Let us assume that rents play a large part in the rewards to capital and landowners. Monopolists (presumably in general the larger and monopsonistic firms) then will be inclined to use relatively large amounts of capital and land, for large savings on rent are possible as compared with production under competitive conditions when these savings are not to be had. Economies are also obtainable in the cost of entrepreneurship; for the cost per unit of output within limits declines with an increase of size. Labor costs will then be relatively small although large in terms of remuneration per unit, for rents (on our assumptions) play a smaller part in the rewards of labor.[1] The net

---

[1] A smaller amount of employment may, however, contribute toward a reduction of wage rates.

weight of these factors will largely determine the relative importance of labor costs and, therefore, the relative burden of a tax on wages under monopoly on the one hand and competition on the other.

19.9. A Tax on One Firm and a Tax on All Firms

It is well at this point to consider the possibility of a shift of taxes backward to the factors instead of forward to the consumer. It will be recalled that in the consideration of the individual firm it was found that the possibility of passing the tax on to the consumer or to the cooperative factors or to both required very serious thought. Mrs. Robinson sums up the situation well in her excellent chapter on a "World of Monopolies" when she puts monopolistic rewards to the factors of production at $\left(\dfrac{\epsilon - 1}{\epsilon} \cdot \dfrac{E}{E + 1}\right)$ times the competitive reward, where ϵ is the algebraic elasticity of demand for the product and E the algebraic elasticity of supply of the factor. The first part of the first term $\left(\dfrac{\epsilon - 1}{\epsilon}\right)$ depends upon the elasticity of demand and, therefore, indicates the extent to which the entrepreneur may raise prices relatively to the price under competitive (*i.e.*, sales under perfect elasticity of demand) conditions. Should the monopolistic competitor, however, be charging what the traffic will bear, *i.e.*, marginal cost times $\dfrac{\epsilon}{\epsilon - 1}$, then the formula gives some indication of the extent to which he may bear the burden of a new tax. (This is of some significance at least, when entry is not free and monopoly profits are being obtained.) The second part of the first term $\left(\dfrac{E}{E + 1}\right)$ gives an indication of the extent to which the employer may exploit the factors of production as a monopsonist. Employment is determined at the intersection of marginal cost of labor and demand but the payment to the factor is given by the supply price which is less than this marginal cost. Here again the crucial issue is, does the monopsonist exploit the factors to the fullest possible extent as indicated by the formula? If he does not, then the possibility arises that the tax may be an excuse for increasing the degree of exploitation. If he does, then through a reduction of the degree of exploitation, he may pay part of the cost.

[393]

Of what significance are the results, obtained for the individual firms, for an analysis of a tax on all firms? The analysis of the single firm suggests that the *general* tax may be shifted both backward and forward. In the analysis of all firms, so far the consideration of incidence has been limited to the effects upon consumers *qua* consumers. Is it possible that the tax may be shifted backward to the factors as suggested in the analysis of the individual firm? In the discussion of elasticity of supply and elasticity of substitution to which we turn presently, the general problem will be dwelt upon to some extent. Here the task is largely to reconcile the analysis of the individual firm and the general analysis. Elasticity of supply of the factors is presumably greater, the smaller the unit of control under consideration. Thus for the small firm it may be put at infinity and for all firms perhaps at zero. It is not, however, appropriate to put the elasticity of supply for all firms at zero so long as large amounts of unemployment prevail. For the general analysis, nevertheless, the elasticity of supply of the factors may be held to be much lower than for the individual firm.

In this discussion, it is not assumed that the monopolistic competitors operate in concert; for if they did, they might be able to reduce rewards to the cooperating factors to a minimum, *e.g.*, close to a starvation level, or at least to a no-rent level. Even if they act independently, however, the possibility of exploitation is considerably higher in the general analysis than in that of the single firm. Assume that a universal tax is imposed and that the entrepreneurs then squeeze the factors of production. (It is assumed that previously the management had not obtained the best possible terms.) Now the factors have not recourse to employment at the relatively higher and pre-tax return with other firms; for the rewards are universally cut. It follows, therefore, that their reservation price is lower than on the assumption of a tax on a single firm. In the latter case, factors are free to move to untaxed sources. Since the supply price of the factors is lower on the assumption of a tax of universal applicability, the possibility of maximum exploitation, *i.e.*, payment for each unit of each factor at reservation prices, rises. Of course the entrepreneur does not really increase the amount of exploitation. He merely passes the new tax on to the factors. If profits are normal (free entry), the pressure on the factors will probably be greater than if the monopolists are earning profits in excess of normal. In any case, relatively low elasticity of supply under the general analysis suggests stronger grounds for the position that the burden will be passed on to the factors than under an analysis of the single firm. Another alternative is open to the factors, however, *viz.*, an artificial increase in the elasticity of supply through organization and concerted movements, resulting in the maintenance of rewards per unit of supply and (possibly) a rise of unemployment. This rise of elasticity would be induced for occasions when a reduction of rewards threatened.

A word should also be said on the place of demand in the general analysis as compared with the analysis of the individual firm. In her last chapter, Mrs. Robinson puts the elasticity of demand for an individual commodity at more than unity and for all commodities at unity. An elasticity of unity for all commodities rests on the assumption of unchanged amounts of spending. Not only may incomes and hence expenditures vary, however, but they may vary in response to changes brought on by the social security program.

In the analysis of the case of a given commodity and on the *ceteris paribus* assumption, a rise of prices may well induce a rise of total expenditures for the commodity. In the complete analysis of the elasticity of the individual commodity, however, the result obtained depends upon the conditions in other markets. Following a rise in the price of a given commodity, elasticity will be greater or less according as substitute commodities are not or are subject to the tax. It is also necessary to take into account *limitations of* income when the inquiry relates to all commodities; but for individual markets that is not required. If the pay-roll tax is universally applied, elasticity rises above the figure given by the "one-at-a-time" analysis above because of limitations of income; but the unavailability of substitute commodities not subject to the new tax has the opposite effect, *i.e.*, tends to reduce elasticity. Then if the consideration of the elasticity of a single commodity to the exclusion of changes in other markets yields a value of n, the analysis taking into account all markets gives an elasticity $> n$ if the first factor, *i.e.*, limitation of income, carries more weight, and gives an elasticity $< n$ if the second factor, *i.e.*, taxation of substitute commodities, is more important.

19.10. CONCLUSION

A brief summary of issues raised in this chapter is now given.

1. The extent to which prices will rise and output be contracted by the imposition of a pay-roll tax is indicated by a study of average total, average variable, average labor, and marginal costs of a single firm. Relevant variables will be the ratio of labor to total and variable costs, the elasticity of substitution (a subject treated later), the elasticity of demand, and the degree of coverage. On various assumptions concerning the slope of supply and demand curves, some generalizations may be offered concerning the relative effects of a tax per unit of output (a tax in many ways similar to the pay-roll tax) on marginal costs and price.

2. In the purely competitive case, the orthodox position is that since the firm is not in a position to influence prices or the rate of remuneration of factors, the necessary result of the imposition of a pay-roll tax is a rise of marginal costs, intersection of marginal costs and demand to the left of the original position, and a curtailment of output. This leaves out of account, however, a vital factor which should not be excluded even in the analysis of the individual firm. The tax falls on most firms though with varying intensity. In so far as competitors share the tax, the individual firm is in a position not only to raise prices against the consumer but also to reduce the rewards to the factors of production. Labor and capital, even on the assumption of perfect mobility, will not move, despite a reduction of remuneration, if untaxed employments are not available. In other words, their reservation price will probably change.

3. A pay-roll tax is imposed when the elasticity of demand for the firm's product is less than infinite. Here part of the burden may be passed on to the consumer, and the more so, the more inelastic the demand. It is also necessary to consider the distribution of the ensuing change of output. For example, average output may rise for the individual firm, the losses being concentrated on weak firms which now shut down. Then if output has been to the left of the optimum point, part of the tax may be held to have been absorbed in a reduction of unit costs.

4. Supply conditions of the factors of production may be less than perfectly elastic to the individual firm. Output and the demand for the factors are determined at the intersection of the marginal cost of labor and the derived demand curves; but compensation is fixed at the corresponding (lower) point on the supply curve. The

monopsonist may go farther, appropriating part of the rent and even (when remuneration is reduced to the reservation prices of the owners of the factors) the entire rent. On these assumptions, factors are exploited. When the worker is paid the marginal physical product times marginal revenue (the latter instead of the price), the case for exploitation is not so easily made, however; but the laborer may have some claims to surplus profits of the monopolist competitor. This is, however, another aspect of monopoly. What is significant is that the entrepreneur may obtain additional gains at the expense of the factors; and pay-roll taxes might be paid out of these gains. It would only be necessary to raise wages; and pay-roll taxes might be the instrument for achieving this rise of wages. When surplus profits are not being obtained, the shift of costs to entrepreneurs will be temporary, however. In short, both consumers and the co-operating factors may be spared the costs of social security: the entrepreneur may pay.

Another possibility is that the factors will be forced to pay though labor alone will not have to foot the bill. Here the assumption required is that up to this point rents are obtained by the factors. A pay-roll tax is now imposed. Prices rise; output declines; the demand for the factors suffers; more expensive units are thrown out of employment. Entrepreneurs thus save on rents as the difference between low- and high-cost units is reduced.

5. The pay-roll tax will affect the volume of employment and also its distribution. In so far as, for example, the tax affects the relative position of the intersection of the marginal cost and demand curves on the one hand and the marginal cost of labor and labor's supply curve on the other, it will influence the relative values of competitive and monopsonistic demand for the factors of production. Thus if the supply curve is a falling one, monopsonistic employment will be larger than competitive employment. A pay-roll tax increases the proportion of labor to all costs and thus with a falling supply curve reduces the slope of the curve and, therefore, the excess of monopsonistic over competitive output. Again the tax will affect the relative demands for the factors under monopolistic and competitive conditions.

6. In the discussion of incidence, it is necessary to distinguish the case of the individual firm from that of all firms. The tax is imposed on a large segment of industry though with varying intensity. For one important reason, elasticity of demand for the firm's product is less on the assumption of a universal tax than on the assumption of

a tax on a single firm. When prices rise, they rise elsewhere also and, therefore, the substitution of nontaxed commodities is not available. Limitations of income tend to increase elasticity, however. In this connection it is also necessary to consider the effects of the pay-roll tax in all its repercussions on income. The problem of the effects of a widely assessed tax upon prices has been treated fully in an earlier chapter. Similarly, the conclusions relative to the shift of taxes to factors require modification when the assumption of a general tax is made. Factors are more likely to pay, for now they cannot escape through change of employment to untaxed sources.

CHAPTER 20

SUBSTITUTION

Parts of this chapter will be difficult for those who are not familiar with the concepts of elasticity of substitution and complementarity. In particular the reader will find Secs. 20.4, 20.5, 20.10 and (possibly) 20.6 difficult. In Sec. 20.3, I have therefore tried to help the reader with a brief summary of the use of the concept of elasticity of substitution in the literature. For those who would like to delve further into the literature, the most elementary treatment will be found in HICKS, J. R., *Theory of Wages*, 1935, Chap. VI, and MACHLUP, F., "The Common Sense of Elasticity of Substitution," *Rev. Econ. Studies*, 1935. Other references are given in footnotes throughout the chapter. The reader not interested in the technical details may well restrict his readings to Secs. 20.1, 20.2 and 20.11.

20.1. INTRODUCTION

In earlier chapters the alternatives of forward shifting to consumers and backward shifting to the factors of production have been dwelt upon. An obvious solution under the latter is that the tax falls upon wages. This is not, however, the only possible solution. In the preceding chapter, for example, the possibility of the cost being directly borne by nonlabor distributive shares has been suggested. The reward of the nonlabor shares is not fixed, for part of their income is rent; and, furthermore, their reservation prices may change. The issues discussed in this chapter are those which throw light upon the distribution of the costs of social security when the tax is shifted backward to the factors.

Since social security increases labor costs, the effects upon labor will depend largely upon the elasticity of demand for that factor. The latter in turn depends upon (1) the elasticity of substitution of capital (or management) for labor, (2) the elasticity of demand for the commodity, (3) the percentage of labor costs to all costs, and (4) the elasticity of supply of the complementary and competitive factors. In an earlier chapter some space has been given to the general problem of elasticity of demand for labor and (3) above is discussed in Chap. 18. The present chapter is concerned with substitution and complementarity and the variable that is of special significance in their examination, *i.e.*, elasticity of supplies of factors.

It is not necessary to summarize here the results of this discussion. Its main importance is to suggest the relevant variables and to make clear that an important part of the cost may fall on nonlabor distributive shares. Labor will pay less, for example, the less elastic the demand for labor; *i.e.*, the less elastic the demand for the commodity, the less the elasticity of substitution of capital for labor and the less elastic the supply of competing factors.

Later in this chapter the problem of complementarity is dealt with. The factors of production may be competitive as well as complementary, the former being the problem at this point. A rise in the cost of one factor *a* may result in the substitution of another factor *b* for it; or an increase in the supply of factor *a* may result in its substitution for factor *b*. In the consideration of these and cognate problems, Mrs. Robinson and Prof. Hicks formulated their concept of elasticity of substitution. This concept will be discussed in so far as it is relevant to our problems and in particular its relationship to the demand for factors and to their elasticity of supply will be pointed out.

According to Mr. Kahn, cooperation is of more importance than rivalry when there are but two factors. In the actual world, however, there is the possibility that the relation between capital and labor will be predominantly one of rivalry and not one of cooperation. This possibility is stronger, in his view, the more important the part played by other factors and the *less* elastic their supplies.[1]

Surely this is not *always* true. Assume that there are $a, \ldots, n$ factors, the factor a being capital and b labor. Now the supply of a (capital) increases. When there are n factors, complementarity *may* be present not only between a and b, but also between a and any (or all) of the factors $b, \ldots, n$. It is not so clear now, in Mr. Kahn's view, that complementarity will be the dominant relationship between a and b. But surely *inelastic*

---

[1] KAHN, R. F., "Two Applications of the Concept of Elasticity of Substitution," *Econ. Jour.*, June, 1935, pp. 244–245.

More recently Prof. Hicks (J. R. Hicks, *Value and Capital*, especially pp. 92–98) has dealt with this subject. His conclusion for the case of *n* factors and *n* products is that if the fixed resources of the entrepreneur exercise no important effects in limiting production, *i.e.*, the production function is almost homogeneous, complementarity is the rule among productive factors. There are some exceptions when the limited resources of the entrepreneur are sufficiently important.

supply conditions for $c, \ldots, n$ will not always, as Mr. Kahn suggests, increase the probability of rivalry between a and b. The smaller the elasticity of supply of factors $c, \ldots, n$ as the supply of a rises, the more b will profit (*i.e.*, the probability of dominance of *complementarity* increases) from the inelasticity of *rival complementary* (*i.e.*, rival to b in relation to a) factors, and the more so the more elastic the supply of b. In other words, b's complementarity increases (in relation to a) at the expense of $c, \ldots, n$.

20.2. Elasticity of Demand for a Factor

Marshall has dealt fully with the problem of the demand for a factor of production.[1] The demand for a factor is less elastic (1) the less elastic is the demand for the commodity, (2) the smaller the percentage of its costs to total costs, (3) the less elastic is the supply of other factors; and the elasticity of demand is higher, the higher the elasticity of substitution.[2] Mrs. Robinson has demonstrated that (on the assumption of perfectly elastic supply conditions for capital), with an elasticity of substitution in excess of the elasticity of demand for the commodity, the correct conclusion under (2) above is the reverse of that given by Marshall, *i.e.*, the elasticity of demand for labor will be less, the greater the proportion of labor. In this case the aggregate amount of capital decreases with a fall in wages. It should also be observed that (2) is of great significance for the problem of the incidence of pay-roll taxes. When labor costs

[1] Marshall, A., *Principles of Economics*, 6th ed., p. 853; Robinson, J., *The Economics of Imperfect Competition*, pp. 257–262.

[2] Prof. Pigou also follows Marshall closely (A. C. Pigou, *Theory of Unemployment*, especially pp. 43–45; also see pp. 39, 88–89, 112, 118–123). Prof. Pigou goes beyond Marshall in some respects. The elasticity of real demand for labor is a function of time; it varies according to the state of business activity; and much emphasis is put upon "the elasticity of the (short-period) productivity function of labor." In contending that the elasticity of demand for labor is higher the *smaller* is w/q (w = money wage and q = value of net output per head), Prof. Pigou seems to be wrong. (Read *larger* for *smaller*.)

Prof. Douglas also puts much emphasis on the elasticity of the marginal productivity curve. It primarily determines the rate at which the unit return falls when the supply of the factor rises. In his view, this variable is of much more significance than the elasticity of substitution in the determination of the relative or absolute return of the factor. We should be inclined to put it this way: the former accounts largely for the relative change in factor prices which accounts for substitution. (P. H. Douglas, *Theory of Wages*, pp. 58–59.)

are a large percentage of total costs, the imposition of a pay-roll tax is likely to have a more serious effect upon the demand for labor than when labor costs are a small percentage of the total; for the elasticity of demand rises with the rise in the percentage of labor costs. (This is subject to Mrs. Robinson's reservation.) Variations in the percentage of labor to all costs are very large among industries, as we have seen in an earlier chapter.

In discussing the relative weights to be given to elasticity of demand and elasticity of substitution, Mrs. Robinson amplifies Marshall's discussion. Let us assume that wages decline. Then the change in the amount of capital employed will be determined by the relative magnitude of these two elasticities. If the elasticity of demand for the commodity is in excess of the elasticity of substitution, more capital will be employed; and if the latter is in excess of the former, less capital will be used. Following a rise of wages, employment of capital will increase if the elasticity of substitution of capital for labor is in excess of the elasticity of demand for the commodity.

It has been held that σ (elasticity of substitution) will vary with the possibilities of substitution of commodities.[1] Thus the value of σ for a given rise in the supply of labor (fall in its price) may be held to depend not only upon technical conditions, but also upon the extent to which commodities of large labor content will displace those of small labor content in the consumers' budget. An increase in the amount of a commodity demanded, which is associated with a reduction in its price, may, however, more appropriately be considered under its elasticity of demand. Caution is required to avoid double counting in accounting for changes in the demand for a factor. An element of significance for the elasticity of demand for a factor should not be considered *both* under the elasticity of demand for the commodity and under σ.

20.3. ELASTICITY OF SUBSTITUTION—DEFINITIONS

In the sense in which the terms are used throughout most of this chapter, *two factors that are complementary are nevertheless substitutes.* All economic productive factors with positive marginal productivities are substitutes in the sense that one may displace the other the product being left unchanged.

---

[1] MACHLUP, F., "The Common Sense of the Elasticity of Substitution," *Rev. Econ. Studies*, June, 1935, p. 205.

SUBSTITUTION

Prof. Hicks uses complementarity in two different senses: (1) along an isoquant or indifference curve; (2) for changes in one factor, other factors being constant, and product increasing. Complementarity in the first sense is a very esoteric concept involving three factors or goods and is really of no importance from the present point of view. Complementarity in the second sense is what we have in mind throughout most of this paper. In this second sense, complementarity is the rule between factors when entrepreneurial resources are not too important. And the elasticity of substitution σ is a concept applicable to complementary factors as well as those which are not complementary.

The elasticity of substitution or σ is often used simply as a coefficient of relative share. How does labor's share change relative to that of capital *with respect to some change?*

If $\sigma > 1$, the factor which increases in relative supply finds its relative share increasing, etc.[1] Used in this first sense, σ depends upon everything in the economic system—elasticities of supply and demand, interest rate, liquidity preference, etc. It is a net resultant and simply re-asks our original question in a slightly different form. How does the relative share change?

Confused with the preceding concept is the use of σ as a technical measure of some property of a single production function, a measure of curvature of the isoquant, or as used originally by Prof. Hicks as an inverse measure of complementarity. The discussion below relates largely to σ used as a technical measure.

We may now proceed to various definitions of the elasticity of substitution. According to Prof. Pigou, it is the proportionate change in the ratio of amounts of factors divided by the proportionate change in the ratio of their marginal physical productivities.[2] Mr. Lerner's definition is

[1] As so used, the concept is purely formal. It has no definite magnitude but has a different value for every conceivable change (see italicized words above).

The author is indebted to Mrs. Marion Crawford Samuelson for this formulation.

$$\frac{aP_a}{bP_b} = \left(\frac{a}{b}\right)\left(\frac{P_a}{P_b}\right) = \text{relative share of } a \text{ to } b.$$

$$\text{Call } \frac{a}{b} = x; \qquad \frac{P_a}{P_b} = y$$

$$\text{Then } \frac{aP_a}{bP_b} \begin{array}{c}\text{increases when}\\\text{decreases when}\end{array} \frac{d(a/b)}{a/b} \Big/ \frac{d(P_a/P_b)}{P_a/P_b} \begin{array}{c}>\\<\end{array} 1$$

just as total revenue increases when demand is elastic; *i.e.,*

$$xy \begin{array}{c}\text{increases when}\\\text{decreases when}\end{array} \frac{dx}{x} \Big/ \frac{dy}{y} \begin{array}{c}>\\<\end{array} 1.$$

[2] Pigou, A. C., "The Elasticity of Substitution," *Econ. Jour.*, June, 1934, p. 232.

σ (elasticity of substitution) $= \dfrac{\Delta(a/b)}{a/b} \div \dfrac{\Delta(P_a/P_b)}{P_a/P_b}$ when a and b are supplies of factors and P_a and P_b their prices or marginal physical productivities.

[403]

similar. "The elasticity of substitution, it will be remembered, measures the degree to which the substitutability of one factor for another varies as the proportion of the factors varies." The ratio of substitutability is the inverse of the ratio of the marginal productivities of the factors. (He assumes that output remains unchanged.)[1] Again, when an increase in the supply of one factor raises the marginal productivity of all other factors in the same proportion as the increase in the total product, the elasticity of substitution, according to Prof. Hicks, is unity. (Consequential changes in the relative supply of factors are ruled out.) An elasticity of zero is obtained when the unchanging quantities of factors are required to make a unit of output; and the elasticity is infinite when factors are identical.[2]

Mrs. Robinson gives us the following definition. "It appears appropriate to call the proportionate change in the ratio of the amounts of the factors employed divided by the proportionate change in the ratio of their prices to which it is due, the elasticity of substitution by analogy with the elasticity of demand or of supply."[3] Finally, Mr. Champernowne suggests the following definition: "The proportional change in total product F divided by the proportional change in Y, the demand price in terms of product of one factor when the amount y of that factor is held fixed and the amount x of the other factor is varied."[4]

Let us summarize the various definitions:[5]

1. All the writers consider the proportionate change in the ratio of the supplies of factors as one variable.

2 a. Prof. Pigou relates the preceding variable to changes in the ratio of marginal *physical* productivities, whereas Profs. Lerner and Hicks associate it with marginal productivities.

b. According to Prof. Hicks, elasticity of substitution = 1 when the product increases in the same proportion as the marginal productivities of all associated factors. His definition applies only to homogeneous functions of the first degree.

c. In Mrs. Robinson's formulation, the dependent variable is the change in the ratio of supply of factors and the independent variable changes in the ratio of prices of factors to which changes in supply are due. Naturally,

[1] LERNER, A. P., "Notes on Elasticity of Substitution," *Rev. Econ. Studies*, October, 1933, pp. 68–69. *Cf.* SWEEZY, P. M., *ibid.*, pp. 67–68.

[2] HICKS, J. R., *The Theory of Wages*, pp. 116–117.

[3] From ROBINSON, *op. cit.*, p. 256; by permission of The Macmillan Company, publishers. *Cf.* footnote 1, p. 403.

[4] CHAMPERNOWNE, D. G., "A Mathematical Note on Substitution," *Econ. Jour.*, 1935, pp. 247–248.

[5] *Cf.* CHAMPERNOWNE, *op. cit.*, pp. 247–248; KAHN, R. F., "Notes on Elasticity of Substitution," October, 1933, p. 72; MACHLUP, *op. cit.*, p. 205; ROBINSON, J., "Dr. Machlup's Common Sense of the Elasticity of Substitution," *Rev. Econ. Studies*, February, 1936, p. 149.

any ensuing proportionate change in marginal physical productivities of factors through the effects on their prices will influence the proportionate change in the supplies of factors. Both Mrs. Robinson and Mr. Champernowne, however, in concentrating on changes in prices of factors make possible the application of σ outside the field of perfect competition.

d. Mr. Champernowne proceeds from proportionate changes in the supplies of factors to the proportionate change in the price of the factor Y (supply unchanged) and then to the proportionate change in the total product. In his formulation, it follows that the more the demand price of Y declines as the supply of X rises, the less is the elasticity of substitution of X for Y: a rise in the marginal productivity of X is *quickly* offset by a rise in that of Y.

At first high hopes were held for the usefulness and applicability of this concept; but it was not long before economists began to emphasize its limitations. The elasticity of substitution σ depends largely, of course, upon technical conditions. Thus if factor a becomes more plentiful or (and) cheaper, σ will give us the rate at which a will be substituted for b as the ratio of the supply of a and b changes. Prof. Pigou pointed out that a single unambiguous value for σ was to be found only for a homogeneous function of the first degree in two variables—when equiproportionate changes in the quantity of the two factors entail a change in the same proportion in output.[1] A somewhat similar limitation was found by Prof. Tarshis.[2] Thus if the function is not homogeneous, an increase of the factors by a multiple of K will not yield an *identical* rise of output for each *possible* combination.

Prof. Pigou, moreover, denied its applicability when there were more than two factors. As the proportion of *factors* changes, the proportion of the marginal productivity changes according to the nature of the disturbance; and the result is not independent of the shift in the supply functions of the other factors. When there are n factors, there will be $n(n-1)/2$ elasticities of substitution. "Thus, equally whether or not we assume that the productivity function is homogeneous, the elasticity of substitution between A and B in respect of shifts in A does not measure any characteristic either of the general productivity function or of any supply function, but is a complex consequence of interactions between productivity and supply."[3] Mr. Champernowne, however, attempted to save something from the wreckage. The smaller the significance of the third factor and the greater its stickiness in amount, the less the elasticity of substitution will

---

[1] PIGOU, *op. cit.*, p. 233.

[2] TARSHIS, L., "Notes on the Elasticity of Substitution," *Rev. Econ. Studies*, February, 1934, pp. 144–147.

As he puts it, it is the ratio in which factors are combined in the case of any homogeneous production function which determines the ratio of their marginal physical productivities.

[3] PIGOU, *op. cit.*, pp. 233–236.

differ from the elasticity that would have prevailed had there been but two factors.[1]

Further, Mr. Kahn was critical of a tendency on the part of those who consider σ to minimize supply conditions. Thus, when the supply of factor A rises and the supply curve of factor B is a forward falling one (left to right), it is possible that the share of A will decline. It is only required, for the result to follow, that the slope of the falling supply curve be adequate or the demand curve for the commodity sufficiently elastic.[2]

20.4. ELASTICITY OF SUBSTITUTION IN RELATION TO OUTPUT AS A WHOLE

When the analysis of substitution is extended to several industries or output as a whole, difficult problems arise. It was observed by Prof. Pigou that a reduction of the real wage rate in two industries producing competitive commodities would yield a smaller rise in employment than the *sum* of the increase of employment if the reduction had occurred in each of the industries alone.[3] For complementary products, however, the reverse would be true: the increase of employment would be greater than the sum for each industry, when each industry alone is cutting wages.

In some Cambridge circles, it has been fashionable to deal with this range of problems on the assumption that output in terms of itself has an infinite demand, which apparently implies that the entire output finds a market.[4] If the assumptions of equilibrium, full employment, and nonaccumulation of stocks are ruled out and if the elasticity of demand is expressed in monetary terms, the limitations of this approach become evident. In appraising Prof. Pigou's *Theory of Unemployment*, Mr. Harrod has also cast some doubts on this type of analysis. The elasticity of demand for wage goods in terms of wage goods is infinite only on the assumption of a single wage good. When there are numerous wage goods, it is necessary to take into account the effects of a reduction in wages upon the demand for wage goods.[5]

It is necessary also to consider supply conditions. For output as a whole, the elasticity of supply of factors may be put at zero at full employment, and with unemployment, at a much smaller value for all industries

---

[1] CHAMPERNOWNE, *op. cit.*, pp. 246–247.

[2] KAHN, *op. cit.*, pp. 73–74; *cf.* here ROBINSON, J., *Economics of Imperfect Competition*, pp. 262–263.

[3] PIGOU, A. C., *Theory of Unemployment*, p. 66.

[4] ROBINSON, J., "Dr. Machlup's Common Sense of the Elasticity of Substitution," *Rev. Econ. Studies*, February, 1936, pp. 149–150; KAHN, *op. cit.*, pp. 75–76.

[5] HARROD, R. F., "Professor Pigou's Theory of Unemployment," *Econ. Jour.*, March, 1934, pp. 27–28.

than for one or a few industries. σ then becomes a problem of limited significance for industry as a whole. Labor is easily diverted from other firms or industries when the price of capital for a firm or industry rises; but serious difficulties arise when *the increased cost of capital affects all industries*.

It would be helpful to analyze this problem further.

1. First, let us consider Prof. Pigou's statement at the beginning of this section. What his statement implies is that for competitive commodities the net marginal productivity of the labor dollar does not rise so much as is indicated by the reduction of wages. One may, therefore, conclude that in so far as this is thus kept in check the impetus to substitution is reduced.

2. What is the relevance of the assumption of infinite elasticity of demand? Wages decline; output of goods is increased; and, on this assumption, the additional goods find markets. The demand for labor is not reduced because additional units of product are evaluated at a diminishing marginal revenue.

3. The position taken by Mr. Harrod may be interpreted as follows: the reduction of wage rates may well have unfavorable effects on demand and hence on marginal value productivity. The stimulus to substitution is reduced.

4. Finally, it is necessary to consider further the elasticity of demand not for the products of a single firm or industry, but for industry as a whole. Wages are cut. Prices also are reduced. Elasticity of demand is, however, less for all commodities than for a single commodity following a reduction in price. An expansion of sales in the former case is not induced by the substitution of cheap for expensive commodities; and limitations of income now require consideration. In short, the inducement to hire additional laborers following a reduction of wages is probably less than is indicated by an analogous analysis for the single firm or industry.

In this connection, a word should be said concerning the social security program. With a given elasticity of supply of capital, substitution will be greater in the relevant field if the tax is applied over a limited area than if it is universally applied. Furthermore, greater substitution, within the taxed area, will take place in industries that are relatively severely taxed, *i.e.*, those with a large proportion of labor costs. In fact as capital is attracted into the industries with high labor costs, a reverse substitution, *i.e.*, labor for capital, may take place in other industries, *i.e.*, in those in which the relative costs of capital rise in response to the rise of demand for capital and the fall of demand for labor elsewhere. Finally, the rise of prices accompanying the rise of labor costs should be considered. Let us assume complete coverage and an equal tax burden on each firm and each product. Marginal productivity of labor declines. Substitution of *commodities* is ruled out, however, since the tax affects all products. For this reason the decline of labor productivity is less than what it seems to be at first. It is not possible to substitute untaxed commodities. A general rise of prices, on the other hand, will make it necessary to consider income effects. *For this reason*, the decline of productivity of labor (per unit) is greater than in the case of the single commodity. These two variables operating in opposite directions may offset each other. Then the incentive to substitute factors will be given roughly by the increase of labor costs; but the difficulties of substitution of capital over the entire industrial area will still be an obstacle.

20.5. σ AND ELASTICITIES OF SUPPLY[1]

As labor costs rise following the introduction of a social security program, labor's employment will be reduced more the higher the elasticity of substitution σ of capital for labor. But the less elastic the supply of labor, the more labor will lose through a reduction of the rate of remuneration, rather than through a loss of employment. The net increase in the cost of labor will then be less and, therefore, the change in the ratios of the prices of factors which account for substitution will be less than if supply conditions of labor were elastic.

What conclusions are to be drawn on the assumption of a low elasticity of supply of capital? The more inelastic its supply, the more it stands to lose from a rise in the cost of labor; but the higher is σ, the less will be its actual losses. As its price relatively declines, it will be substituted for labor; and its decline in price will of course, on our assumptions, be related to its inelasticity of supply. What of the elasticity of supply of labor? On the assumption that *total* wages are assumed by labor to decline, despite an *actual* rise in costs to the employer, the higher labor's elasticity of supply, the more

---

[1] For discussions of the relation of elasticity of supply and σ, see especially J. Robinson, *The Economics of Imperfect Competition*, p. 261; R. F. Kahn, "Two Applications of the Concept of Elasticity of Substitution," *Econ. Jour.*, June, 1935, pp. 242–246; J. E. Meade, "The Incidence of an Imperial Inhabited House Duty," *Rev. Econ. Studies*, 1934, pp. 249–252.

Mr. Meade's case is especially interesting for our purposes. On his assumptions of unequal elasticities of supply of land and buildings and $\sigma > 0$, the imposition of an inhabited house duty will have the following effect. The greater is σ, the less the disadvantage to the factor in inelastic supply and the less the advantage to the factor in elastic supply. Though the price of the former will fall more, it will recoup more of its losses the higher is σ; for the higher is σ, the more will it be substituted for the factor in elastic supply.

wage rates will rise; the higher is σ, the less will employer wage costs actually rise. A low elasticity of supply of capital for supplies *in excess of those now employed* will, however, tend to reduce σ.

The inquiry now turns to the problem of elasticitities of supply and substitution on assumptions of extreme values. First the problem when $\sigma = 0$ is discussed. The values given below are for the *elasticities of supply* of labor S_l and capital S_c.

$$\sigma = 0$$

a. S_l (Labor) $= 0$; $\quad S_c$ (Capital) $= \infty$

Aside from a temporary decline in the demand for both factors, the net effect will be nil.[1] With $S_l = 0$, the reduction of demand following a rise in labor's cost will result in a reduction of wage rates to the former level. With $S_c = \infty$, the result is doubly assured, for capital will not accept a reduction of its rate of remuneration.

$$\sigma = 0$$

b. $S_l = \infty$; $\quad S_c = 0$

This is an important case, which those who argue that labor must bear the whole burden ought to consider. An issue here is again labor's diagnosis of the direction of wage movements. (1) If the view is that wages have risen, wages will be reduced to their former level. (2) But if labor reacts as though wages had been reduced, then labor may retain a higher wage. Capital is not withdrawn despite a reduction of its marginal productivity; and yet it is not substituted for labor. It follows, therefore, that under *b* (2), employment of capital and labor will be unchanged; but the return on capital will be adversely affected by the social security program.

$$\sigma = 0$$

c. $S_l = \infty$; $\quad S_c = \infty$

Here again the issue of the correctness of labor's appraisal of the situation arises. On the assumption of perfect knowledge and foresight, rates of remuneration and employment will be unchanged. Otherwise no labor at all would be offered since retained wages would fall below the minimum necessary amount.

$$\sigma = 0$$

d. $S_l = 0$; $\quad S_c = 0$

This is a freak case. Since equilibrium is indeterminate prior to the tax, analysis of the effects of the tax is rather futile. In this case, labor neither withdraws nor does it increase its supply, and similarly for capital.

[1] This follows from $S_l = 0$ (labor has no reservation price). Then irrespective of S_c and σ, employment will not change and retained wages will fall by the amount of the tax.

The distribution of the cost of security will then depend on other factors. In this discussion, it will be recalled that we are interested primarily in that part of the cost which is paid by the factors *qua* factors, not *qua* consumers. It is scarcely necessary to recall that the elasticity of demand for the factors is related to σ; and when $\sigma = 0$ the elasticity of demand for labor and for capital is smaller than when $\sigma = 1$. Again, the importance of labor costs to all costs will be a relevant variable in the determination of the distribution of costs.

Finally, we turn briefly to the case where $\sigma = \infty$. In general, the results are similar. It is obvious that when wages rise and $\sigma = \infty$ the gain of labor will soon be lost; but the value of σ will depend upon the elasticities of supply.

20.6. Significance of σ

Of what significance is the elasticity of substitution for our problem? The demand for a factor depends upon the demand for the commodity, the ratio of its costs to all costs, the supply curve of other factors, and the technical conditions of production. It is largely the last that determines the elasticity of substitution. Thus should social security raise the price and thus reduce the profitability of hiring labor, technical conditions will largely determine the extent to which capital and other factors will be substituted for labor. Thus one technical question is the extent of the rise (?) of marginal productivity of labor following a reduction of employment. It is not, however, easy to give precision to the concept when the number of factors is in excess of two; and it is even more difficult to estimate its value.

Too much should not be expected of σ. It is applicable only with reservations when the number of factors is in excess of two and has a single unambiguous value only for a homogeneous function of the first degree. For example, assume that the price of b (labor) rises on the introduction of a social security program. The first question that arises is whether a (capital) is a substitute or complement of b. According to Prof. Hicks, it is more likely to be the latter unless the fixed resources of the entrepreneur are of great importance. Then the question arises whether $c, d, \ldots, n$ are predominantly substitutes or complements of b. If a is a substitute and, therefore, if a larger supply of a is then forthcoming, the next question is what is the effect of the rise in the supply of a upon the supplies of c,

$d, \ldots, n$? Thus a rise in a may induce a rise in c (entrepreneurship), and the latter rise in turn will affect the elasticity of substitution of a for b. These and other difficulties make it impossible to define σ precisely or to give it a precise value. A discussion of σ does, however, attract attention to the relevant variables, and that is of some importance.

In the discussion of the present chapter, it has also been made clear that the demand for a factor depends not only on the elasticities of substitution but also upon the elasticity of demand for commodities and the elasticities of supplies of other factors. The elasticities of supplies of factors, though not a component part of σ, determine the range within which substitutability will operate.

As the price of labor rises, the demand for labor declines. It should be noticed that the introduction of the purchasing-power theory (or the high-wage theory) at this point will not materially change the conclusion so long as contributions for insurance are *used largely to increase reserves*. Then the rise of wages (labor costs) is not offset by an increase in spending by consumers or, so long as investment does not rise *pari passu* with the rise of reserves, by an increase of spending in other quarters.

We turn to a few general remarks. (1) Consider the case of substitutable factors. Wages now (meaning by wages weekly retained earnings plus contributions of employers to insurance) rise. Then the greater the degree of substitutability of capital for labor and the more inelastic the latter's supply, the more labor pays of the tax. Capital will lose less, the more elastic its supply and the higher is σ. (2) Consider complements. Demand for capital *and* labor declines once more. Capital is not in a position to reduce its losses through substitution for labor. It may, however, continue to profit from a higher elasticity of supply than labor; capital will then force labor to pay a larger proportion of the cost of social security, the more elastic supply conditions of capital and the less elastic the supply of labor. Wages will tend to *fall* to their former level and interest and other capitalist incomes to *rise* to their former level.

20.7. Substitution of Machines for Men

Opponents of the social security program have had much to say on the probabilities of substitution of machines for men following an increase in wage costs. In this connection, one should remember that labor costs are not likely to rise in the proportion of pay-roll taxes to former labor costs. Employers recoup their losses to some extent at least, following the disbursements of benefit payments, through a reduction of wages and a marking up of prices. In any case, real wages do not rise to the full extent of the cost of social security. Further, movements in real wages are not as yet associated to a large extent with social security taxes, though in the future their importance will undoubtedly rise. Fluctuations in real wages associated with price movements, the varying fortunes of trade-unionism, public legislation, and changes in labor productivity are more important factors in determining the level of wages than are the costs of social security.

The literature abounds with discussions of the substitution of capital for labor. Prof. Hicks distinguishes autonomous from induced inventions, the former being explained by technical progress alone and the latter by relative movements in the prices of factors. In his view, autonomous inventions are as likely to be capital saving as laborsaving. An invention that induces a rise in the ratio of the marginal productivity of capital relative to labor is held to be laborsaving; and one that induces a relative rise in labor's marginal productivity is held to be capital saving. Both Prof. Hicks and Mrs. Robinson put much emphasis upon the unfortunate effects of laborsaving inventions upon labor. Thus in the view of the latter, both labor's income and employment are likely to be affected adversely although real wage rates of the employed are likely to rise. Labor's relative share declines following the introduction of laborsaving inventions; and the more σ exceeds unity, the greater the loss.[1]

Our problem is the effect of a rise of labor costs, and in particular one associated with social security, upon the substitution of capital for labor.[2] For the following reasons, the dangers are not so great as

---

[1] ROBINSON, J., *Essays in the Theory of Employment*, especially pp. 131–135; HICKS, J. R., *Theory of Wages*, pp. 121–126.

For a complete survey, see WPA, *Survey of Economic Theory on Technological Change and Employment*, especially pp. 84–122, 158–200. In particular the author of this study clarifies the assumptions on which unfavorable effects on employment are ruled out; and he explains the manner in which technological change induces unemployment, notably in contraction periods. *Cf.* H. Jerome, *Mechanisation of Industry*, especially pp. 344–346.

[2] Many economists are skeptical of the relation of high labor costs to the introduction of laborsaving inventions. E. Lederer, *Technical Progress and Unemployment*, International Labor Office, Studies and Reports, Series C., p. 33.

might be inferred from current discussions in some quarters and from the preceding paragraph.

1. Laborsaving inventions may be *autonomous* or may be *induced;* and, moreover, if induced, may be explained by a reduction in the rate of interest as well as by a rise in labor costs. In recent years, the cost of obtaining capital has been reduced greatly; and in so far as laborsaving inventions are in vogue, part of the explanation may be found here.

2. Lately capital-saving inventions seem to have been prominent in industry. According to one survey covering the most important inventions of the last generation, the proportion of laborsaving inventions has been small indeed.[1] Again, an important public document of very recent date goes on as follows: "There is little doubt, however, that depression stimulates efforts to reduce unit labor requirements, particularly by speeding up operations and introducing technical and managerial improvements which require little capital outlay."[2] These improvements of recent years save not only labor but also capital. They represent the response of management to a decline of demand and to business losses. They are not associated with high labor cost alone any more than they are associated exclusively with high taxes, with high fixed charges, or with lack of confidence. All these factors and others account for industrial changes that result in economies of *both capital and labor.*[3]

3. A rise in wages will not result in the displacement of labor by capital unless several conditions are satisfied. Capital must be available at relatively favorable prices; businessmen must be optimistic of the net returns of the future, and risks, relative to expected returns, must not be excessive. Furthermore, time is required to increase the supply of capital, though more intensive use of existing plant provides some elasticity and monetary expansion may stimulate capital expansion in the short run.

[1] DOUGLAS, *op. cit.*, p. 214. *Cf.* also WPA, *op. cit.*, pp. 93–96. Cannan and Taussig, and Dr. Kaldor emphasize the prominence of capital-saving improvements.

[2] WPA, *Production, Employment and Productivity in 59 Manufacturing Industries*, Part I, 1939, p. 74; also see National Research Project on Reemployment Opportunities and Recent Changes in Industrial Techniques, *Unemployment and Increasing Productivity* by D. Weintraub and H. L. Posner; and D. Weintraub, "Effects of Current and Prospective Technological Developments upon Capital Formation," *Proc. Am. Econ. Assoc.*, 1939, pp. 15–31, *Hearings*, Temporary National Economic Committee (76: 1), 1940, Investigation of Concentration of Economic Power, p. 3511.

[3] *Cf.* SCHUMPETER, J. A., *Business Cycles*, p. 841.

4. Economists who emphasize the likelihood of substitution of capital for labor following increases in the cost of labor do not offer convincing evidence that wages are too high. Thus for the years 1922–1929 Mr. Jerome compares a rise in average earnings of laborers in manufacturing of 17 per cent with a reduction of the price of goods used to produce capital equipment of 3 per cent on the one hand and with relatively low money rates in these years on the other.[1] The inference is that the substitution of capital for labor would be stimulated under these conditions. We should, however, know more about the productivity of labor to draw such inferences.

5. As has been indicated above, factors other than social security play a decisive part in determining the level of real wages.

6. It is generally maintained that wages are too high in depression periods; but at such times, confidence is at a low ebb and substitution of capital is, therefore, not easily made. In periods of prosperity, on the other hand, the additional cost of labor, or that part associated with social security, is easily absorbed.

7. A rise in labor costs also contributes toward a rise in the cost of capital equipment and to that extent discourages substitution. One should not, however, go so far as to argue that the ensuing rise in the cost of manufacturing capital equipment will make the substitution of capital unprofitable. Economies of labor are still to be had.[2]

20.8. Elasticity of Supply of Labor and Capital

The problem of elasticity of supply of the factors of production is now taken up in so far as it is relevant to the problem of incidence. In this discussion the assumption is that the government imposes a large tax on wages in order to finance the social security program. *Current* real wages then decline as entrepreneurs attempt to recoup their losses through a rise of prices and a reduction of wages. Total wages, *i.e.*, current wages plus present value of future benefits, will probably rise. Two considerations support this position. (1) The financing of social security in part through taxes other than those on workers (directly or indirectly, inclusive of later contributions by

---

[1] Jerome, *op. cit.*, p. 346. *Cf.* pp. 262–270, however.

[2] *Cf.* Lehmann, F., "The Role of Social Security Legislation," *Proc. Am. Econ. Assoc.*, 1939, p. 221.

the Treasury) implies that the nonlabor population will pay part of the cost. (2) And more relevant here, part of the pay-roll taxes will be passed on to nonlabor groups. Labor in general gains though particular groups of laborers may gain little or even lose. These facts should be kept in mind in the discussion that follows, for in concentrating upon the total effects of social security, one may be justified in assuming that wages rise as evidenced in the cost of labor to employers; but in concentrating on the pay-roll taxes and the imperfect vision of laborers (they estimate future benefits at less than full value), one may well assume that wages decline as evidenced in the reduced supply of labor. Workers sensitive to any reduction of current money wages and a rise of prices, *i.e.*, decline in real wages, imposed by entrepreneurs in response to new taxes may react as though wages had fallen.

Should the elasticity of supply of labor be high in the short run, a reduction of the real wage would be followed by a large reduction of the supply of labor offered on the market, and a rise of real wages, by an increased offer of labor. With the introduction of New Deal policies, *e.g.*, relief, insurance, encouragement of unionism, the elasticity of supply in the short run is likely to be higher with a given decline of real wages (real or imagined) than it otherwise would have been. On the other hand, the existence of unemployment means that wages need not rise to call out new workers.

Economic literature is not very helpful in throwing light on the relative elasticities of supply of labor on the one hand and other factors on the other. Many, for example, have contended that the short-run supply curve for labor is negatively inclined: an increase in real wages induces a reduction of hours of labor and of the length of the working life and of the percentage of population gainfully employed, the leisure of workers being thus increased.[1] The Cambridge view seems to have been that since the marginal disutility of labor increases with increases in its amount workers will increase (or reduce) their exertions with a rise (or fall) of remuneration offered them.[2] A more modern view is that the supply curve of labor at first rises and at some point begins to turn back on itself (Chart VII).[3]

[1] See the excellent survey in Douglas, *op. cit.*, pp. 269–314; also see F. H. Knight, *Risk, Uncertainty and Profit*, p. 117; *cf.* L. Robbins, "On the Elasticity of Demand for Income in Terms of Effort," *Economica*, 1930, pp. 123–129.

[2] MARSHALL, A., *Principles of Economics*, 8th ed., pp. 141–142; *cf.*, however, A. C. Pigou, *The Economics of Stationary States*, p. 163.

[3] KALDOR, N., "A Classificatory Note on the Determinateness of Equilibrium," *Rev. Econ. Studies*, February, 1934.

It is not necessary to dwell at length upon the long-run supply of labor. Classical economists (Malthus, Ricardo, *et al.*) thought that the supply curve was horizontal, of infinite elasticity, and at a level just sufficient to induce the population to reproduce itself. All that can be said in connection with this theory is that a reduction of wages, whether induced by a social security program or some other cause, would be corrected ultimately by changes in the rate of population growth. It is not helpful, however, to consider a social security program in relation to the classical theory of wages. At present it is generally recognized that standards are above the minimum level and population growth is determined only in small part by changes in real wages, particularly by such changes associated with social security.[1]

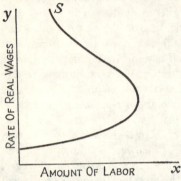

CHART VII.—Supply curve of labor. (*From J. Robinson, Essays in the Theory of Employment, p. 166. By permission of The Macmillan Company, publishers.*)

Now we turn to the elasticity of supply of capital. Annual changes in the stock of capital are a very small percentage of the accumulated stock of capital.[2] In the very short run the stock of capital may be considered constant, for it takes time to reduce it through depreciation or increase it by investment. There is, however, a rate of growth or decline at any instant of time, and this is related to the rate of interest.

Classical economists embraced the hypothesis of a constant supply or cost schedule of savings of infinite elasticity.[3] Böhm-Bawerk, Landry, and Prof. Fisher and others argue that an increase in interest rates will call forth additional savings.[4] In 1867 Sargent presented the view that the supply curve of savings is negatively inclined: at lower rates of interest, the public saves more; and at higher rates, they save less.[5] Profs. Knight and Kleene and others argue that these tendencies will cancel out, the result being a perfectly inelastic curve.[6] Mr. Keynes more recently has

---

[1] See DOUGLAS, *op. cit.*, Chaps. 13–16. Prof. Douglas finds that a rise of real wages seems to be accompanied by a reduction in the birth rate. " . . . there is a tendency for an increase in real wages greater than the average, to be accompanied by a fall in the net growth rate by more than the average." (*Ibid.*, p. 400.)

[2] KNIGHT, F. H., "Interest," *Encyclopedia of the Social Sciences*, vol. VIII, pp. 131–143; DOUGLAS, *op. cit.*, pp. 421–422.

[3] *Cf.* TAUSSIG, F. W., *Principles of Economics*, 1918 ed., vol. II, pp. 24–28.

[4] FISHER, I., *The Theory of Interest*, pp. 120–121.

[5] DOUGLAS, *op. cit.*, p. 429.

[6] KNIGHT, F. H., "Professor Fisher's Interest Theory—A Case in Point," *Jour. Pol. Econ.*, April, 1931, vol. 39, p. 202.

given us a more complicated relationship: he considers the effects of a movement in the rate of interest upon investment and income and through these *upon savings*. He denies the validity of the classical (?) assumption that a rise in the rate of interest necessarily induces more savings; for through adverse effects on investment and income, savings may actually decline.[1]

Finally, a word may be said concerning the long-run problem of the influence of the rate of interest upon capital growth. On this problem the views of Prof. Fisher, Pigou, Cassel, and Hicks are to be contrasted with those of Profs. Schumpeter, Lange, and Wicksell.[2] The former are inclined to assume a positive rate of interest in a stationary state, whereas the latter hold that at any positive rate of interest there will still be net savings. Equilibrium will be

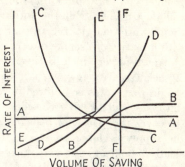

CHART VIII.—Rate of interest and volume of saving. (AA) Classical School; (BB) Taussig; (CC) Sargent; (DD) Landry, Böhm-Bawerk; (EE) Cassel; (FF) Webb-Knight. (*From P. H. Douglas, Theory of Wages, p. 457. By permission of The Macmillan Company, publishers.*)

attained, provided technology is constant, only at zero rate of interest. Chart VIII illustrating the various short-run supply curves of savings concludes this section.[3]

20.9. ELASTICITY OF SUPPLY OF FACTORS IN RELATION TO SOCIAL SECURITY

In the short run, the supply of capital goods is relatively fixed; and what is more, it is not at all clear that a reduction in the rate of interest will reduce the supply. What then is to be said of the incidence of a pay-roll tax in the short period on the assumption that the net effect is to increase the cost of labor? We assume here that

---

[1] *Cf.* Robinson, *op. cit.* Mrs. Robinson, a close follower of Mr. Keynes, shrinks from the advocacy of low rates of interest. In her opinion effects on consumption and, therefore, ultimately upon incomes and savings may be adverse.

[2] HICKS, J. R., *Value and Capital;* PIGOU, *op. cit.*, p. 55; LANGE, O., "The Place of Interest in the Theory of Production," *Rev. Econ. Studies*, June, 1936, p. 190.

[3] DOUGLAS, *op. cit.*, p. 457. Prof. Douglas finds little help in empirical data in resolving these problems, *ibid.*, Chap. 18.

capital is complementary to labor. A rise in labor costs will result in a reduction of the quantity of labor demanded. The marginal productivity of capital (on the assumption of complementarity) will then decline. But the withdrawal of capital is most difficult. (Some variations in the rate of use, *i.e.*, depreciation associated with intensity of use, are of course possible.)[1] In general the supply of capital is very inelastic in the short run and, therefore, the costs of social security may in part be put upon capital. Furthermore, should wage rates be reduced in response to the imposition of payroll taxes, should labor consider the reduction of the weekly wage (to cover the insurance benefits) a cut in total wages, and should the supply of labor be elastic, the cost of social insurance may clearly be put in large part upon capital.

Moreover, the possibility of shifting to other capitalist interests should also be considered. Elasticity of supply of land in use and even of entrepreneurial services (the assumption is that the tax is general) is very low in the short run; and the difference between reservation price and current reward may be very large for the entrepreneur.

We may assume then that the cost of labor rises and that in the short run the supply of capital, entrepreneurship, and natural resources are highly inelastic. Labor may then put a large part of the cost of social insurance upon these shares on the following assumptions:

1. Despite a rise of total wages, labor concentrates upon its weekly wages and, therefore, considers that its wage has been reduced. If, on this assumption, the supply of labor is elastic, the burden will be shifted to the other shares.

2. Labor appraises the situation correctly and reacts as though wages had risen. Then the burden may largely be shifted to other shares if the supply curve of labor is negatively inclined: a reduction of supplies follows a rise of wages. It will be recalled that Prof. Douglas's investigations point to a negatively inclined supply curve for labor.

Ultimately the imposition of unexpected losses upon the non-labor shares following the introduction of a social security program will have adverse effects upon their availability. This is likely to follow even if the supply curve for capital is negatively inclined. Expectations of return on capital have been disappointed: the pos-

[1] See BAUER, P. T., and P. R. MARRACK, "Depreciation and Interest," *Econ. Jour.*, June, 1939, pp. 237–243.

sibility of a new tax program had not been taken into consideration. Rentiers and perhaps entrepreneurs may, in truth, now have to accustom themselves to a lower rate of return. They will not, however, replace plant or embark on new enterprises so long as the expected net return is not in excess of the current (and expected) rate of interest. The latter may decline; but it must decline adequately to cover the change for the worse. Ultimately, therefore, the capitalist groups may force upon labor acceptance of a larger part of the cost of social security, or more unemployment. It is also conceivable that adverse effects upon the supply of capital are not necessarily injurious to the economy. Much depends upon the current state of consumption demand and of savings.

In the short run, then, elasticity of supply is likely to be greater for labor than for the capitalistic factors. Labor refuses to accept a cut (or what appears to be a cut) below the current weekly wage level; and if demand for *all* factors is elastic, the complementary agents, the marginal productivity of which would be reduced if labor withheld its cooperation, will pay a large part of the costs of social security; and their contribution will be larger, the more inelastic their supply. Should demand for the products (or for the complementary factors) be inelastic or should the social security program account for an increase in total demand, the costs of the program to that extent would be absorbed by consumers and come out of additional income. Finally, in the longer run, the nonlabor shares may succeed in retransferring part of the burden to labor.

20.10. COMPLEMENTARITY

We now turn to the influence of complementarity and the elasticities of supply of the factors of production upon the process of tax shifting. In the previous section the latter problem was discussed but it is also considered here relevant to the problem of complementarity; now more attention is paid to the distribution of losses between employment and rates of remuneration. In classical discussions of incidence, the possibility of complementarity has received scant attention.

What do we mean by complementarity? Y is complementary with X in a consumer's budget if a rise in the supply of X (Y constant) raises the marginal utility of Y; and Y is competitive with

X if the rise in the supply of X lowers Y's marginal utility. Similarly, the coefficient of complementarity of capital and labor may be given by the degree to which the marginal productivity of capital is increased when the amount of labor cooperating with it is increased.[1] Prof. Hicks is inclined to emphasize the likelihood of complementarity rather than of competitiveness. Even if productive opportunities limit the scale of output greatly, rivalry between some of the factors is not ruled out. Even in the case of many products and many variables, however, Prof. Hicks seems to emphasize the possibilities of complementarity rather than competitiveness.

In Prof. Hicks's view, a rise in the supply of factor A is more likely to result in a rise in demand for factor B and a rise in the production of X (complementarity) than it is likely to result in a decline in the demand for B and (1) a rise in the production of X (substitution) or (2) a decline in production (his regressive curve).[2] Following Prof. Hicks (though the case here is one of increased costs, not as above, a rise in supply) we may say that as the price of A (labor) rises upon the introduction of a wage tax, the likely result is a reduction of the demand for the *other* factor B (capital) and a decline in the output of product X. A rise in the demand for B accompanied by a rise or decline in output X is less likely.

Should substitution be the dominant relationship, capital will now be substituted for labor. Should complementarity be the dominant relationship, capital will stand to lose as the demand for labor declines. Further, should the supply of capital be inelastic and that of labor elastic, the former will suffer the larger losses. Should the supply of both be inelastic, their rates of remuneration rather than the amount of employment will decline. The problem of substitution has been discussed in the earlier part of this chapter and now a more extended discussion of complementarity is given.

Assume that the national dividend is the product of labor and capital and that to each factor is imputed its marginal physical productivity, constituting the demand schedules for the factors of production. If we assume supply schedules for labor and capital in terms of their respective real earnings, we get a determinant system. Now if we introduce a tax on the real wages leaving all other schedules intact, the resulting effects on the real wage, employment, remuneration, and employment of capital can be determined. In this discussion, it should be observed, the assumption is that wage

[1] HICKS, *op. cit.*, p. 92; *cf.* PIGOU, A. C., *Theory of Unemployment*, p. 66.
[2] HICKS, *op. cit.*, Chap. VII, especially p. 97.

costs for the entrepreneur actually rise. In so far as the proceeds of
the taxes are used for benefit payments (now or later), in so far as
workers evaluate these benefits at their proper value and *accept*
proportionate cuts in wages, and in so far as entrepreneurs in a
money economy pass the tax on in higher prices (or even in lower
wages in addition to a reduction to be associated with the foregoing
consideration), the tax does not constitute a burden on the entrepreneur. A tax on wages, for example, does not leave the other
schedules intact if the proceeds of the taxes are used to finance
benefits (now). A rise in costs is offset at least to some extent by a
rise in demand. We go on, however, subject to these reservations
and proceed on the assumption that the *net cost* of labor rises following the imposition of the tax.

In this discussion it is assumed throughout that the supply
schedules of both capital and labor are positively inclined, *i.e.*, a
rise in remuneration is accompanied by an increase in supply.[1]
The imposition of a tax on labor will result in decreased employment
of labor and capital and a reduction in the rate of remuneration for
both factors. The amount of the decrease in these variables will
depend on the elasticities of supply of labor and capital, their elasticities of demand, and the coefficient of complementarity between
capital and labor;[2] *i.e.*, the degree to which the marginal productivity of capital is increased when the amount of labor cooperating
with it is increased.

1. The exact direction of the dependence is as follows:[3] The more
elastic is the supply of labor, the more elastic the supply of capital, and

---

[1] Should the supply curve for capital, for example, be a backward rising one, then
a rise of labor costs and a reduction in the demand for labor would, for a given coefficient of complementarity, result in a larger proportion of the loss being imposed
upon labor than would be the case if the supply curve of capital were positively
inclined. This conclusion follows because with a backward rising supply curve for
capital a reduction in the demand for capital will be accompanied by a rise in the
return per unit of capital.

[2] Elasticity of demand for labor gives us the proportionate reduction in employment of labor associated with a small rise in the cost of labor. The coefficient of
complementarity gives us the associated decline in marginal productivity of capital
and this, with the elasticity of supply of capital, gives the change in employment of
capital. Obviously the larger the decline of marginal productivity and employment
of labor for a given coefficient of complementarity, the larger the corresponding
declines for capital.

[3] The author is largely indebted to Mrs. Marian Crawford Samuelson for this
formulation.

the less the downward shift in the demand for capital, the greater will be the decrease in *employment* as the result of the imposition of a tax on labor.

2. The more inelastic is the supply of labor the more elastic the supply of capital, and the less the downward shift in the demand for capital, the greater will be the decrease in the remuneration of labor as the result of the imposition of a tax on labor.

Perhaps a word should be said here concerning the relevance of the elasticity of supply of labor for cases (1) and (2). Assume that wages = $2, and the tax = 50 cents.

a. Then if the supply of labor is absolutely elastic (and future benefits are not considered as part of wages), current wages will remain at $2 and total wage cost will be $2.50. Employment will then suffer as is indicated in (1) above.

b. If the supply of labor is absolutely inelastic, wages fall to $1.50 (+50 cents) and employment is unchanged. This result is possible under (2) above. In other words, the remuneration of labor will depend not only on the elasticity of supply of and demand for capital but also on the elasticity of supply of labor.

Another relevant variable is the elasticity of demand for labor. Yet that variable is not discussed under (1) or (2) except implicitly. It is clear that the more elastic the demand for labor, the more labor will suffer from an imposition of a wage tax. What is not clear is the extent of the loss to labor and its *distribution* between employment and the rate of remuneration of labor. These effects will depend upon the elasticity of supply of labor and capital and the elasticity of demand for capital.

3. The greater the degree of complementarity between labor and capital, the more elastic the supply of labor, and the more elastic the supply of capital, the greater will be the decrease in the employment of capital as a result of the imposition of a tax on labor.

4. The greater the degree of complementarity between labor and capital, the more elastic the supply of labor, and the more inelastic the supply of capital, the greater will be the fall in the *remuneration* of capital as a result of the imposition of a tax on labor.

Here again under cases (3) and (4) the elasticity of demand for labor is a relevant variable. The more elastic the demand for labor, the more costly a given rise in wages will be for labor; but the distribution of losses of labor between rate of remuneration and employment is not revealed. The more employment of labor is reduced (and the extent to which the loss is felt in a reduction of employment will depend partly on the elasticity of supply of labor), the greater the range within which the elasticity of the supply of capital and the coefficient of complementarity operate. Thus the more elastic the demand for labor, the greater the losses of capital for a given elasticity of supply of capital and a given coefficient of complementarity. The division of losses of capital between employment and return per unit for a given elasticity of demand for labor is not thus revealed, however.

Elasticities of supply of labor and capital and the coefficient of complementarity determine the effects on employment of capital on the one hand and rates of return on the other. Furthermore, we may say this in amplification of (3) and (4) above. When the supply of capital is absolutely elastic, the result will be a maximum decline in the employment of capital. When the supply of capital is absolutely inelastic, employment remains at a maximum and rate of remuneration a minimum.

20.11. CONCLUSION

In this chapter the three related problems of substitution, complementarity, and supply have received our attention. The following conclusions emerge.

1. In so far as the costs of social security are shifted backward to the factors (and forward shifting in higher prices is not an irrelevant consideration in the bargaining process) the factors in inelastic supply are likely to pay a large part of the cost of the social security program. If, as seems likely, the supply of capitalistic factors (including capital, entrepreneurship, and land) is relatively inelastic in the short run and that of labor elastic, then labor may succeed in putting a large part of the burden upon the former. Under the social security program, costs of labor will rise and, therefore, demand will fall. But if labor withdraws readily and substantially in response to the curtailed demand at a higher price and capitalist factors do not, the latter will bear a large part of the cost. This does not mean that it pays labor to put this burden on capital; labor loses through a reduction of employment.

Two reservations should be made here. First, much depends upon the attitude of labor toward the program. Total wages rise, and by total we mean weekly retained wages (even if reduced somewhat) *plus* present value of benefits. An elastic supply may then be costly to labor if in response to an actual rise in total wages, and (therefore) a reduction in demand, the supply of labor now increases. If, however, workers concentrate on their weekly wages and assume that their wages have been cut, the high elasticity of labor will contribute toward the maintenance of high wage rates. They will reduce their offers of work.

The second reservation relates to the supply of capital. In the very short run, it is inelastic though monetary resources and variations in the rate of consumption contribute toward a higher elasticity. As to what happens in the long run, however, economists are not by any means in agreement. On the classical position, a reduction of return (following the introduction of social security) would result in a withdrawal of capital. But at the other extreme is the view that supplies rise with a fall in the return. In the latter case, labor's gains would be greater than is assumed here. In between these extremes numerous other positions are taken.

2. We may complicate the problem further by introducing additional variables, *e.g.*, the elasticity of demand for capital and for labor and the degree of complementarity. The latter is peculiarly important, if, as is generally maintained, complementarity is of more importance than substitution. It is not necessary here to repeat the conclusions given in the text (Sec. 20.10). An examination of the relevant variables, at a given coefficient of complementarity, will suggest (1) the relative losses of capital and labor, (2) the relatives losses of both or either as between employment on the one hand and remuneration per unit on the other.

3. In the problem of social security, one of the main issues is that of the substitution of competing factors for labor when the latter becomes more expensive. Hence the attention to the elasticity of substitution σ, which gives us the changes in the ratio of factors in response to a change in relative marginal productivities or prices of the relevant factors. It would be very helpful if, in the actual world, we could obtain σ for all changes in the price or marginal productivity of labor. Unfortunately, the concept is defined precisely only for two factors and even then only when the production function is homogeneous and of the first degree. Complications arise in the case of n factors; for the supply conditions of $n - 2$ factors may change in response to interaction between the subsets of variables, and these changes will in turn influence the substitutability of any two factors. Yet the concept is useful in focusing attention on relevant variables; technical conditions in the industry, which put limits on substitutability; supply conditions in the factor markets—when elasticity of supply = 0, substitution is not possible; and its relation to the elasticity of demand for the factors. In particular, the last is a crucial problem. Our problem is the effect of a rise in the price of labor on the amount of labor demanded. Elasticity of substitution, the percentage of labor to all costs, and the elasticity of supply of factors are all relevant variables. One final point. On neither theoretical nor empirical ground is much evidence found

that technological changes, *e.g.*, substitution of capital for labor, are largely explained by increases in the cost of labor.

4. On the assumptions that $\sigma = 0$ and ∞ and that the elasticities of supply of labor and capital $= 0$ or ∞ (these are the only factors), the effects of the social security program have been considered. On these extreme assumptions, the results are similar with $\sigma = 0$ as with $\sigma = \infty$, though at the latter value, substitution may contribute toward the outcome that follows in the other case with no substitution. (1) The elasticity of supply of labor is put at 0 and that of capital at ∞. Then wages are reduced to their former level, and the employment of capital is unchanged. (2) The elasticity of supply of labor is ∞ and that of capital is 0. On the assumption that wage earners are informed of the true state of affairs, *i.e.*, an increase of their wages, the supply of labor will rise until wages are depressed to their former level. Capital's position is unchanged. The outcome is not so favorable to capital, however, when labor's position is that wages have been cut; and this is an important case. (3) The assumption is zero elasticity of supply of labor and capital. Here the outcome will depend on extraneous considerations, there being an indeterminancy of the intersection of supply and demand. (4) The elasticities of supply of labor and capital are both infinite. If wages do not fall to their previous level, because labor does not recognize the full value of benefits, employment of labor will fall to zero. Any attempt to squeeze capital will necessarily be unsuccessful. (5) In general this may be said. The more elastic the supply conditions of labor, and the less is σ (substitution of capital for labor), the more successful will labor be in putting the costs of social security on capital.

5. The relevance of elasticities of supply may be explained as follows: Wage costs rise. Then the more elastic the supply of labor in response to lower demand at the higher cost, the more the cost of wages to the entrepreneur, and hence the greater the proportionate change in the ratio of factor prices, which induces substitution. But much substitution will not take place if the elasticity of supply of capital is 0.

Chapter 21

SOCIAL SECURITY IN AN OPEN ECONOMY

21.1. Introduction

So far nothing has been said concerning the international aspects of social security costs. Yet any program that enhances the costs of industry is likely to have repercussions on foreign markets, which are more sensitive to rises of prices than are domestic markets. The significance of this analysis is related to the cost of the program and to the costs of other programs that tend to raise prices for the producer. It would not be unreasonable to estimate the long-range costs of the security *programs* at 10 per cent of the national income. On the assumption that the costs are put directly on industry, the required rise of prices would be 10 per cent or thereabouts. Actually, the government will put part of the burden on surpluses and (or) on factors. Furthermore, though social security may seem to be a matter of secondary importance for our international trade position, its significance rises when considered as one of numerous high-cost policies, *e.g.*, wage legislation, defense programs, and restriction of output. Finally, one important reservation is to be made. Foreign competitors are subjected to similar charges; and the total effects upon international trade of the American program are to be distinguished from the *differential* effects.

We are here concerned with that part of the cost of social security which the entrepreneur is unable to pass on to the wage earner or to recipients of other shares of the national income. For the purposes of this discussion the entire cost of social security, whether assessed on pay-rolls or upon the general taxpayer, is relevant. We assume that failure to pass taxes on to the nonentrepreneurial recipients of income accounts for a corresponding rise of wages and prices; and this rise of prices may be particularly upsetting to the foreign trade of a country. (It is scarcely necessary to add that temporary burdens on entrepreneurs, rentiers, and other groups may frequently affect costs adversely through the effects on the contributions of the relevant factors to industry; but this is an effect that will be discussed briefly farther on.)

The following issues will be treated briefly. (1) In 1921–1933, the British discussed the pros and cons of wage policy in relation to international trade. High wages were associated by many with vexatious social legislation. Here the British debate is commented on. (2) The issue of the relation of wage costs and trade arises. (3) The conditions under which American losses in trade are a maximum are examined. (4) There follows an examination of the way out if security charges prove to be disastrous for our export trade.

21.2. THE BRITISH CONTROVERSY

It is interesting in this connection to consider the debates in Great Britain in the *twenties* and *early thirties*. In international markets or even in domestic markets where foreign competition, actual or potential, is a serious matter, the possibility of passing the costs on to the consumer is not so great as in purely domestic markets. A rise of costs is a more serious matter in international than in domestic trade.[1] The demand for the products of any one country, except those for which the country has a virtual monopoly, is highly elastic, a rise in prices being followed by losses of markets to competitors. On this score Great Britain's experimentation with social legislation has, therefore, been a matter of concern to many, and the depression in the export trade has been evidence to many that their misgivings were not wholly without justification.[2] Wages in the nonsheltered international industries, it is to be noted, were low relatively to the general wage level; but prices in the export industries have generally been much higher relatively to 1914 than the wholesale price level.[3] It does not therefore fol ow, however, that these industries had succeeded in passing on to the foreigner the burden of insurance and other social legislation through a rise in prices, for the wholesale price index number has been depressed by the large weight given to raw materials and foodstuffs which have

---

[1] Contrast *Royal Commission on Unemployment Insurance*, Final Report, 1932, pp. 101–102 and J. L. Cohen, "The Incidence of the Costs of Social Insurance," *Internat. Labor Rev.*, 1929, p. 836.

[2] GILSON, M., *Unemployment Insurance in Great Britain*, p. 156; CLAY, H., *The Post-war Unemployment Problem*, pp. 96–98.

[3] *Ibid.*, p. 83; CLAY, H., "Unemployment and Wage Rates," *Econ. Jour.*, 1928, pp. 1–7; Committee on Industry and Trade, *Survey of Overseas Market*, pp. 2–7.

suffered severe declines in prices, and furthermore, any rise in prices of exports has to be considered in conjunction with the large drop in the quantity of exports. In some industries, cotton textiles for example, where combination has been popular, the prices charged to foreigners have been too high, inadequate weight being given to the elasticity of demand for the products of any one country on international markets.[1]

A reduction in wages will undoubtedly make possible a quantitative extension of foreign trade.[2] The purchasing-power argument loses its force when applied to wage cutting in export industries; for the reduction of demand associated with a cut in wages is of secondary significance for foreign demand for exports. The need of such a reduction is not any less because Great Britain has been losing competitively on foreign markets.[3] In the early thirties, Mr. Keynes and Mr. Clark maintained that the level of output, both past and present, seemed to justify the current wage levels; but the high level of unemployment and the stagnation in the export trade industries are not irrelevant considerations.[4]

21.3. WAGES AND TRADE

There may be some difference of opinion as to whether a reduction in money wages will contribute toward a rise in foreign trade,

[1] CLAY, H., *The Post-war Unemployment Problem*, p. 88.

[2] *Cf.* the next section however.

[3] Committee on Industry and Trade, *Survey of Overseas Market*, pp. 2-8, 21-24; CLARK, C. G., "Statistical Studies Relating to the Present Economic Position of Great Britain," *Econ. Jour.*, September, 1931, pp. 355-361.

[4] Limitation of space prevents a fuller discussion of the wage controversy. Those who opposed the reduction of wages drew attention to the marked rise of productivity, the high standard of living despite the unusual amount of unused capacity, the inelasticity of demand abroad for British exports, and the unfavorable effects on domestic demand of a reduction of wages. Proponents of wage cutting pointed to the large amount of unemployment, the need of a reduction of prices and wages for retention of foreign markets, and the large increase in the cost of social services. On the one hand, see *Report of Committee on Finance and Industry*, 1931, pp. 194-198; J. M. *Keynes, Treatise on Money*, vol. II, pp. 183-189; C. G. Clark, *op. cit.*, pp. 355-361; on the other, Sir W. Beveridge, *Unemployment: A Problem in Industry*, 1931, pp. 365-367; A. C. Pigou, "Wage Policy and Unemployment," *Econ. Jour.*, September, 1927, and *The Theory of Unemployment*, Part II, Chaps. 9, 10, and Part V, Chaps. 9, 10.

or a rise reduce it. Mill argued, it will be recalled, that a reduction of money wages will not enable producers to undersell foreign competitors. Edgeworth, on the other hand, contended that in Mill's usage a reduction of wages meant only a reduction of the *share* of the national income going to labor. Edgeworth's position was that if workers in any country are willing to produce goods for foreign markets at a greater sacrifice, *i.e.*, work harder for a given supply of foreign goods, *i.e.*, accept lower money wages, foreign trade of that country will be extended.[1]

Mill's assumption was that as wages decline other incomes rise and therefore a reduction of wages results in neither a reduction of prices nor an extension of trade. Edgeworth, on the other hand, assumed that nonlabor incomes do not rise *pari passu* with a cut in money wages. Prices drop, and foreign trade rises. Let us comment further on Edgeworth's case. Not only would sales of A, a commodity of large labor content, rise but the total sales of A plus B (the latter of small labor content) would rise. (But two commodities are assumed.) On Mill's assumptions, gains in sales of A would be offset by losses in sales of B. It should be noted that the extension of trade in Edgeworth's case is quantitative though the dollar value of trade may also rise.

Edgeworth assumed, let us note, that a reduction of wages in his case was tantamount to an offer of more goods for a given amount of foreign goods. Actually, a reduction of wages and a resulting rise in output may be felt largely in domestic industries; and its effects may be felt in an increase in domestic demand for the output of export industries. It is not necessary to discuss here later repercussions on prices and the balance of payments.

21.4. Effects of Social Security upon American Exports

Let us assume that wages and prices both rise following the introduction of a security program and, therefore, that the rise of wages is not obtained through a *direct* reduction of other distributive shares.

1. Sales of American products abroad will decline more, *the more inelastic the demand at home.* Americans then maintain their consumption well despite the rise of prices, and, therefore, the diver-

[1] Edgeworth, F. Y., *Papers Relating to Political Economy*, vol. II, p. 24.

sion of export commodities to foreign markets will be modest. Foreign markets are not then inundated with commodities previously sold at home. It is necessary, however, here to distinguish the state of demand from elasticity. The more important *domestic* sales of exports to *all* sales, the more significant the elasticity of demand at home. On the present assumptions of inelastic demand at home, the more important domestic relative to all sales, the *greater* the effects of the inelasticity of domestic demand in preventing diversion to foreign markets. The rise of prices abroad will be a minimum, on the other hand, if domestic sales are a large part of total sales and domestic demand is highly elastic and foreign demand highly inelastic.

Shifts of demand are also of some significance here. A rise of wages may be accompanied by a shift of demand to the right, and, therefore, any decline of foreign sales may not be a cause for anxiety. But the accumulation of reserves is a relevant issue here: the rise (?) of wages is largely represented by claims to future consumption, and in the absence of successful investment of reserves may not give rise to an improvement of demand currently.

2. We now come to the second condition for maximizing the loss of foreign sales: this condition is related to (1) above. Elasticity of supply for foreign markets (2) is related to elasticity of demand at home. Sales will fall more, *the more elastic American supply conditions for foreign markets, i.e.*, the more easily output is curtailed or sales diverted to domestic markets when the rise of wages and of prices encounters strong resistance abroad. The smaller the percentage of sales abroad, the greater the elasticity of supply for foreign markets: as foreigners are confronted with higher prices and reduce purchases, Americans withdraw supplies from foreign markets the more easily the less important foreign sales are relative to American sales. Elasticity of demand is likely to be higher abroad than at home, and, therefore, the domestic market improves relatively following a rise of prices of American commodities. It is clear that the goods excluded from foreign markets will be sold on domestic markets with less pressure on domestic prices, the more important are domestic relative to foreign sales.

Elasticity of demand abroad for American commodities may not, however, remain so much higher than the elasticities at home after the imposition of social security taxes as before. The social security program raises prices of most commodities in the United States, and, therefore, demand for any one commodity becomes more elastic.[1] Limitations of income and of total expenditures now become a significant factor in the determination of elasticities of demand for individual commodities on the American market. Since foreigners spend a relatively small part of their income on American exports, their elasticities are not affected in the same degree. This factor will tend to increase the elasticity of supply for foreign markets and, therefore, to reduce the losses of sales on foreign markets. (As domestic consumers reduce purchases in response to higher prices, more becomes available for foreign markets: Foreign buyers tend to absorb a larger part of total sales.)

Finally, it should be observed that the more comprehensive the social security program and the more inelastic supply conditions at home, the more pressure there is to put the costs on the factors and to depress prices toward the presecurity level. When discrimination is possible, the reduction in prices to the former level will be greater in markets of elastic demand, *e.g.*, foreign markets, than in those of inelastic demand.

3. Losses of foreign sales will be greater, *the more elastic are foreign sources of supply* for commodities competing with American commodities. American sales abroad will suffer more, the larger the percentage rise of foreign supplies in response to a given rise of prices of American products. Elasticity of supply abroad will be a function *inter alia* of the amount of unemployment of factors, mobility of factors, and accumulation of stocks. In this connection, the normal relation of the magnitude of sales abroad to that of American sales abroad is of some significance. The larger are foreign sources of supply, the larger the new contributions abroad in response to a rise of price from American sources. Thus an increase of output by 10 per cent in response to a rise in the American price of 10 per cent will yield 1 million units if foreign contributions had been 10 million units and 2 million units if they had been 20 million units.

4. A final condition for maximization of losses of foreign sales is that the *demand abroad for American products be elastic*, *i.e.*, the reaction abroad to a rise of prices should be a large reduction of purchases. Elasticity of demand abroad is of course related to the elasticity of *foreign* sources of supplies for commodities (or their substitutes) sold abroad by Americans. The more elastic the foreign sources of supplies (or the more important relatively), the more elastic the demand for American products.

---

[1] One offset is relevant here. Elasticity of demand is reduced at home by the unavailability of untaxed commodities to which the consumer may now turn.

The effect upon the total export trade and trade of individual commodities will be related to the varying ratios of wages to total costs. The less the ratio of wages, the less the social security taxes and, therefore, the less the rise of prices. Assume the following:

TABLE I.—EFFECT OF SOCIAL SECURITY TAXES ON PRICES OF EXPORT COMMODITIES
(Commodities listed in order of costs as percentage of foreign costs. No transportation costs, duties, etc., assumed)

Commodity	Costs as per cent of foreign costs	Per cent of wages to total costs	Per cent rise of prices following imposition of 15 per cent pay-roll tax
Exports			
a.	90	40	6
b.	95	50	7½
c.	96	60	9
d.	96	70	10½
Nonexport			
e.	99	80	12
f.	102	20	3

It is at once apparent that commodities b to d may cease to be export commodities after the imposition of the tax, and f (a nonexport commodity) may become an export commodity. The final result will of course depend upon the numerous elasticities discussed above. Thus if, within the relevant ranges, supply conditions for d are inelastic at home and abroad, and demand conditions at home elastic and abroad inelastic, losses of sales of d abroad may be relatively small. But *ceteris paribus*, sales abroad will suffer more, the larger the percentage of labor costs.

A general decline of exports may be expected to follow the rise of prices of American exports though the effects on sales will not be uniform.[1] In classical theory, the loss of exports would be followed by price and income adjustments, tending to recoup these losses and reduce imports. If recovery in the export trade and restriction of imports are not easily effected, adjustments may conceivably be made in other items of the balance of payments. In the American economy of the thirties, a stoppage of the inflow of gold alone would have sufficed to reestablish equilibrium. The United States would then ultimately have profited from monetary expan-

---

[1] It is of course possible that the net effect of the social security program may be lower rather than higher prices. Much depends upon the so-called deflationary effects of the accumulation of reserves. I assume here that the secondary effects are neither inflationary nor deflationary.

sion abroad and from higher incomes and prices following expansive monetary policies abroad; but the loss of foreign markets would largely have been concentrated in the United States in the first instance. Gains from monetary ease, on the other hand, would have been distributed over most of the world.

21.5. ALTERNATIVES

In the discussions of the social security program and of the various so-called Townsend proposals, fear of foreign competition has frequently been expressed. Estimating the increase of prices, following the acceptance of their proposals, as high as 50 per cent, the Townsendites would protect the American producer against low wages abroad through an upward revision of tariffs.[1]

We may distinguish four positions on the relation of higher wages (or higher costs as proposed by the Townsendites) and the balance of payments. (1) Mill's position as presented above. A rise of wages is assumed to be at the expense of other groups and hence does not require a rise of prices. On his assumptions, varying ratios of wages to total costs do not affect total exports or those of any industry. (2) An application of Edgeworth's position would indicate that higher wages, *i.e.*, smaller sacrifices for the acquisition of foreign goods, would reduce export trade. Both Mill's and Edgeworth's position may be considered as classical. (More recently the position taken by Taussig on reparations is reminiscent of Edgeworth's position.)[2] (3) Mr. Keynes has tended to put the emphasis on conditions affecting movements toward a position of equilibrium. In his view, wage rates are of little importance, elasticity of demand is small, obstacles to trade are decisive, other items in the balance of payments are relatively fixed in value. It follows that a reduction of wages is not likely to increase exports significantly and a rise of wages is not likely to reduce exports to any important extent. Finally, the politicians (in the discussion of the NRA bill and the Social Security Act, for example) also put the emphasis on conditions of disequilibrium. But in their view, a rise

[1] *Hearings*, Ways and Means Committee, House of Representatives, *Social Security*, 1939, pp. 438–439, 640–641, 863.

[2] Prof. Ohlin's conclusions are not unlike those of Edgeworth and Taussig; but he puts emphasis on shifts of demand.

of wages induced by wage or social security legislation or in any other manner is harmful. They would immediately raise tariffs. They leave out of account the possibility that industries in which labor costs are relatively a small part of total costs may improve their export position and that adjustments in imports may follow any reduction of exports. In the peculiar conditions of recent years, however, a large loss of exports may be at the expense of other items in the balance of payments rather than at the expense of imports.

What are the alternatives if a rise of prices associated with social security taxes meets strong resistance abroad? At present the cost of security may not be a vital factor; but when the cost rises to 10 per cent of the national income, its significance for these problems will become great. A tendency to divert sales to domestic markets is most likely to appear in the manner of British economic development in the postwar period. Such movements may be accentuated by the introduction of artificial restraints, e.g., tariffs. Should foreign markets be of great importance and domestic demand at a low point, these adjustments may fail to prevent large losses. When price discrimination is possible, of course, a larger part of the additional costs will be put upon domestic purchasers: prices rise less where demand is more elastic, i.e., in foreign markets. Where product differentiation is widespread, price discrimination among national markets is effected with ease. Still another alternative is to shift capital to non-taxed industries. But if coverage of the security program is extensive or exportation of capital fraught with danger, this method of escape or evasion may not prove to be feasible. Then the owners of capitalist shares may accept lower rates of remuneration or (and) gradually consume their capital. Business then fails to meet its fixed charges.[1]

It ought to be pointed out, however, that the possibility of maintaining foreign or domestic trade through living on capital is open only for relatively short periods and that costs are likely to rise in

---

[1] A few additional comments are required on the problem of fixed costs. (We are not discussing all overhead costs.) Capital plant loses value for the following reasons: (1) deterioration with the passage of time; (2) more effective methods of production, changes of taste, etc.; (3) use; (4) failure to maintain in good repair. Fixed costs include the going return on the investment and an amount adequate to cover depreciation under (1) and (2) and part of the repair bill. (Part of the repair bill is incurred irrespective of use.) Even this relatively fixed part of the repair bill is in a sense variable, however. Thus should prospects of net revenues decline on account of the introduction of a social security program and, therefore, should the possibility of obtaining revenues adequate to cover fixed charges vanish, repairs in order to maintain plant for future use would be reduced.

the future just because fixed costs have not been met in the past.[1] The persistence of a practice of not meeting fixed costs, and to a greater degree in foreign than in domestic trade, may well result in higher costs in international industries later and a stimulus to factors to move into industries serving domestic markets. Losses on foreign sales will be greater because elasticity of demand is higher in foreign markets. The more important the foreign markets, *ceteris paribus*, the greater the losses that may be attributed to foreign sales. Losses on foreign sales may be greater whether price discrimination is possible or is not. In one case, *i.e.*, nondiscrimination, diversion of sales to domestic markets depresses prices, and in the other, price concessions are made directly.

[1] A lower limit to the losses on capital is set by (1) an increased demand for capital to replace the high-cost factor, *i.e.*, labor, and (2) a downward revision of the supply price of labor following a decline of employment. Any concessions made by labor must be adequate not only to cover any additional costs associated directly with the security program but also to offset the decline in marginal productivity of labor associated with a reduction of capital.

CONCLUSION TO PART III

From the previous discussion it appears that the problem of incidence is not simple. Adherence to the theory that the tax is passed on to the worker in a reduction of wages has been general; but it becomes necessary first to delve into the theory of marginal productivity. Even its supporters agree that wages merely tend toward the marginal productivity of labor, that the marginal product is not easily revealed, that payment of wages according to the contribution of *each* worker is not practical, that exploitation is quite prevalent. The marginal productivity theory requires amplification for another reason. It has generally been assumed that if wages rise through the imposition of taxes upon business for social security the marginal profitability of hiring labor declines. A general movement of wages has, however, repercussions on the monetary system, and vice versa. Marginal productivity is affected by fluctuations in the rate of interest and in monetary demand that accompany wage movements.

Supporters of the orthodox theory contend that wages will be reduced *pari passu* with the imposition of social security taxes; or employment will decline by the amount required to make wages and marginal productivity equal once more. On the assumption that these are the only alternatives, which will labor choose? Much depends upon the rigidity of the reservation prices for wages currently received. If labor is determined to maintain wage rates, the loss will be felt largely in a reduction of employment. Other considerations are also relevant, however. In periods of rising demand, the burden may be passed on to employers in the sense that workers thus obtain a rise of remuneration sooner than they otherwise would have received it. Within limits, employers or employees will absorb the charge, the effect on employment being nil. Much will depend upon the movement of money and real wages and the current relation of wages and marginal product.

Prof. Pigou seems to put the emphasis on the first solution, *i.e.*, shifts to wage earners in a reduction of wages, when he argues that labor adjusts the wage rate stipulated for to any change in the demand function for labor. When employers are assessed for social security, for example, the demand curve for labor falls. Workers respond, in his view, by reducing their supply price. Economists who dwell upon the stability in the proportion of labor income to total income would seem to lend support to the productivity theory; but the adjustment may come in a reduction of wages to their former level or in a reduction of employment at the higher level of wages.[1]

In popular discussion and even in professional circles since 1935, increasing emphasis has been given to the possibility that the consumer may pay. Assumptions of fixed supplies of money and inelasticity of total disbursements exclude this solution for those who follow the usual pattern of the marginal productivity theory and the wage theory of incidence. That the consumer may pay a large part of the cost of social security is not necessarily incompatible with the productivity theory. It can be made quite consistent with it: labor pays through a reduction of *real* wages, *and* marginal productivity rises in response to a rise of general demand evidenced in an increase of monetary expenditures. In other words, employment may be maintained because on the one hand real wages decline, and on the other marginal productivity rises. This approach does not, however, give the answer usually given by the adherents of the marginal productivity theory. Labor may account for two-thirds of all consumption, not all. On the basis of current distribution of income and savings, one may make some rough guesses concerning the distribution of the burden of a pay-roll tax shifted forward. Perhaps one-half of the tax may be financed through a rise of monetary expenditures. Low-income classes will increase their debts and cut their consumption; but the well-to-do will impinge on savings. The net effect will also depend upon whether accumulation or decumulation of reserves is current, upon the effects of other taxes on business costs and prices, upon the relative effects on demand for different types of goods, and upon the ensuing movements of factors. Sacrifices of *consumption* will, however, *largely* be made by the low-income classes. Others may pay later as the effects of a curtailment of savings begin to be felt. Nevertheless, labor succeeds in passing part of the burden to nonlabor elements.

Imperfect conditions in the commodity or labor market require further revisions of the accepted theory. It is here necessary to consider the economics of the individual firm.

[1] *Cf.* DOUGLAS, P. H., *The Theory of Wages*, pp. 221–224, and KALECKI, M., *Essays in the Theory of Economic Fluctuations*, especially pp. 29–34.

In order to make the behavior of the firm determinate, we must know (1) the technological conditions of production relating inputs and output as of a given state of knowledge, (2) the demand conditions for the finished goods produced by the firm, (3) the supply conditions to the firm of the factors of production. In connection with (2) and (3) there exist at least four possibilities.

1. There may be perfect competition in the commodity market with perfect competition in the factor market.

2. There may be imperfect competition in the commodity market with perfect competition in the factor market.

3. There may be perfect competition in the commodity market with imperfect competition in the factor market.

4. There may be imperfect competition in both commodity and factor markets.

The following table shows the final results of the effect of a payroll tax on employment, output, and price.[1] A $+$, 0, or $-$ sign, respectively, indicates that the tax results in an increased, unchanged, or decreased amount of the variable. It should be observed, however, that these results are based on the assumption that the rise of costs

TABLE OF RESULTS

Case	a_1 (labor used)	w_1 (wages)	X (quantity of finished goods)	p (price of finished goods)
1	$-$	0	$-$	0
2	$-$	0	$-$	$+$
3	$-$	$-$	$-$	0
4	$-$	$-$	$-$	$+$

affects only the individual firm. Should, for example, the rise of costs affect the position of the vast majority of the firms then even under case 1 (perfect conditions in both factor and commodity markets) prices may well rise. Analysis of the economy of the individual firm may, therefore, be held to be applicable to our problem in so far as differentials in the tax burden are felt.

These four cases are, however, of great interest. It will be observed, for example, through a comparison of case 1 and the three imperfect cases that prices rise *or* wages decline in the latter cases; and in case 4 prices rise *and* wages decline. That wages decline is explained by the fact that as output is reduced the demand for labor falls. The supply curve of labor is on these assumptions a rising one,

---

[1] We are indebted to Mrs. Marion Crawford Samuelson for this formulation.

a reduction in the amount demanded requiring, therefore, a reduction in the wage rate. To the extent that the supply curve rises, then, the losses to labor are greater than they otherwise would be. Other shares may also suffer, however, from a reduction of output in the face of rising supply curves.

It is also well to observe that imperfections may frequently be reduced through a rise of wages whether this rise is brought on through the introduction of a social security program or some other factor. It is possible then that the security program will be financed in part through a reduction of surplus profits or at the expense of other factors. It is well also to recall that the marginal product is not, as under perfect competition, the physical product times price, but the former times marginal revenue, which is less than price. It does not follow that workers are exploited because they obtain less than the physical product times prices. Entrepreneurs may in fact receive but normal profits despite the apparent exploitation of workers. The latter may, however, have some claims to part of the surplus profits, available when entry is not free. This aspect of monopoly should be distinguished from the problem of the slope of the demand curve.

In numerous other aspects, the theory of monopolistic competition and (to some extent) of pure competition is relevant. Here we mention the fact that fluctuations in the volume of output associated with social security will result in changes in the costs per unit of output. Much will depend upon the manner in which the reduction (?) of output is shared. Should the net result be a reduction of costs per unit of output, part of the costs of social security may thus be absorbed.

Finally, it should be observed that a tax widely applied would affect most firms. Supplies of factors then become relatively inelastic as alternative (untaxed) employment is not available. The possibility of putting the tax on factors of production is thus increased. Taxes may be shifted backward to the factors or forward to consumers. Under backward shifting the crucial question is the distribution of the costs between labor and other factors. In general it may be said that the factors in inelastic supply will suffer more than those in elastic supply. If capital[1] is more inelastic than labor

---

[1] One may include here all capitalistic shares, not excluding entrepreneurship. The difference between the return for entrepreneurship and its reservation price may be very large indeed; and this is an additional source from which taxes may be financed. Indeed a universal tax, which implies absence of evasion through move-

(especially in the short run), labor may place a large part of the cost on capitalistic shares.

Factors are competitive or complementary. In recent literature the dominance of the latter has been emphasized. Any rise of costs of labor and ensuing reduction of demand will then have the effect of reducing the marginal productivity of other factors. And under relatively simple assumptions, the distribution of labor's and capital's losses as between employment and rate of remuneration may be indicated.

Much has been said of the probability of substitution of machines for men if the cost of labor should rise on account of the introduction of a social security program or some other factor. But numerous factors other than social security play a part in the determination of labor costs and of technological advance. In recent years, wage costs seem to have been one of the *many* factors determining the advance of technology; and capital-saving improvements seem to have been as prominent as laborsaving improvements.

It was hoped that the concept of elasticity of substitution would throw much light on these problems. Unfortunately it is applicable only under very simple and unreal conditions. The discussions have, however, brought attention to the relevant variables: technical conditions, elasticities of supplies, the relation of elasticity of demand for the factor to elasticity of substitution and to the ratio of labor to all costs. In this book a large part of a chapter is devoted to a discussion of the effects of a pay-roll tax under varying ratios of labor to all costs.

In summary, the more or less accepted theory that labor ultimately pays the cost either through a reduction of money wages or of employment is subject to *important reservations. A substantial part of the burden falls elsewhere.* The marginal productivity theory upon which the theory of incidence has been based is, itself, subject to reservations and amplifications. A rise of the cost of labor may be accompanied by a rise of prices, by an increase of monetary supplies and monetary demand, and, therefore, by favorable effects upon marginal productivity. Social security costs may thus be absorbed, employment and wage rates to that extent not suffering. Furthermore, the theory of monopolistic competition with its concentration on imperfect elasticity of supplies of factors and of de-

ments to untaxed sources, suggests the possibility of a large difference between current returns and reservation prices.

mand for commodities also suggests to the student of social security the possibility of putting part of the burden on the consumer and factors of production other than labor. Finally, the presence of complementary relations between labor and other factors and the limited significance of substitution are additional reasons for the anticipation of shifts to nonlabor elements.

AUTHOR INDEX

A

Allen, R. G. D., 308, 375, 377
Altman, O. L., 30, 85
Altmeyer, A. J., 27, 57, 164, 169, 174, 193, 194, 242, 247, 251
Andrews, J. B., 75, 111
Armstrong, B. N., 247
Arnold, J. R., 251, 370

B

Bakke, E. W., 48, 52, 354, 363
Ballantine, A. A., 210, 213
Bauder, R., 287
Bauer, P. T., 418
Bell, S., 316
Beveridge, W., 428
Bigge, G. E., 53
Bissell, R. M., Jr., 302, 311, 363, 368
Black, D., 13, 283
Bochner, D., 354
Böhm-Bawerk, E., 416, 417
Booth, P., 352, 357, 358, 361
Bowers, E. L., 151
Brown, D., 243, 246
Brown, H. G., 285, 291, 295, 324
Brown, J. D., 68, 161, 169, 218, 219, 246
Bruere, H., 31
Burns, A. E., 35–37
Burns, E. M., 47, 50, 72, 165, 168, 185, 192, 212, 229, 246, 249, 287, 351
Burr, S., 256, 257

C

Cannan, E., 359, 360, 413
Cardozo, B. N., 252
Carr-Saunders, A. M., 235
Cassel, G., 417
Chamberlin, E., 373–375, 381, 388
Champernowne, D. G., 313, 404–406

Clague, E., 47, 51, 52
Clark, C. G., 28, 317, 319, 428
Clark, J. M., 36, 38, 71, 77, 109, 110, 151, 294, 306
Clay, H., 287, 359, 360, 427, 428
Cohen, J. L., 285, 324, 427
Cohen, P., 56
Colm, G., 38, 39, 75, 82, 83, 89, 102–104, 288, 330, 350
Corson, J. J., 251, 351, 370
Cournot, A., 374
Coyle, D. C., 212
Crathorne, A. R., 272
Crum, W. L., 369
Currie, L., 30, 85, 139

D

Davison, R. C., 49, 56, 163, 354
Dewhurst, J. F., 58, 169, 246, 249
Director, A., 148
Dirks, F. C., 97
Doane, R. R., 58
Douglas, P. H., 52, 72, 75, 110, 148, 151, 154, 186, 210, 222, 248, 266, 287, 292, 293, 303, 305, 309, 312, 314, 327, 382, 385, 388, 391, 401, 413, 415–418, 437
Dublin, L. I., 187, 188, 235, 236
Dulles, E. L., 27, 42, 72, 73, 75, 161, 162, 166–168, 173, 181, 184, 199, 228, 229, 247, 288
Dunlop, J. T., 314, 315, 319, 322
Durbin, E. F. M., 133, 328

E

Eccles, M. S., 27, 35, 44, 46, 75, 261
Eddy, G. A., 83, 86
Edgeworth, F. Y., 429, 433
Eliot, T. H., 199
Engels, F., 125

AUTHOR INDEX

[445]

SUBJECT INDEX

A

Accounting problems, appropriation and nonappropriation of reserves, 200–203

Actuarial soundness, 181

Actuarial status, of funds, 181–183
of present covered vs. future entrants, 189–192

Amendments of 1939 (*see* Social Security Act)

Average wage, principle of, 195–196, 245

B

Banks, investment of reserves in, 137–147
(*See also* Deposits)
Reserve, investment of reserves by, 147–150

Benefits, adequacy of, 246–247
under amendments of 1939, 165, 167–171, 193–198, 230, 243–246
and average earnings since 1936, 230
and average wage principle, 195–196, 245
and consumption, 76–78
and experience rating, 352
future, capacity to pay, 228–231, 241–261
and insurance principle, 194–195, 244–245, 249
and need, 194–198
present and future, 55–56, 189–193, 195–198, 228–231, 234–240
and price movements, 219–221, 226–227
in program introduced in 1850, 225–227
and Treasury subsidy, 246–248, 259–261

Benefits, unearned, 57–60
unemployment, and wages, 47–52

Birth rate, 187, 228, 235–236

Burden of social security, on community, 354–355
distribution of, 125–127, 168–169, 231, 247, 285–441
and experience rating, 352–358
in future, 212–214, 222–224, 234–240
on industry, 349–372
and money and real wages, 314–323
on present vs. future generations, 66–68, 206–211, 217–221
and reserve plan, 209–211, 217–221, 224
(*See also* Incidence of pay-roll tax)

Business conditions, and effect of security program on consumption and savings, 78–80
and effect of security program on demand for money, 324–326
and effects of wage cutting, 304–307
and incidence, 300–323
and investment of reserves, 132, 150–156
and reserves, 215–217

Business deposits, 137–142, 145, 147–148

C

Capital, living on, 434–435

Capital formation, 26, 81–86
(*See also* Investment)

Capital goods, 119, 122–124

Capital investments, governmental, 38–39

Compensable wage loss, 56

Competition (*see* Imperfect competition; Monopolistic competition; Perfect competition)

[447]

SUBJECT INDEX

Prices of consumption and investment goods, of wage goods and others, 124–126

Productivity of labor and wages, 316–319, 321–322
  (*See also* Marginal productivity theory)

Profits (*See* Incidence of pay-roll tax)

Propensity to consume, effect of taxes on, 28, 254–255
  and expenditures, 254
  optimum, 80
  and oversavings, 94–95, 254–255
  and reserve accumulation, 301
  and wage changes, 303–304, 322–323
  (*See also* Consumption)

Propensity to save, 28–30, 94–95, 100
  (*See also* Savings)

R

Real vs. financial problems, 66–68

Receipts under security program, 40–43, 55–56, 254–259

Relief and works programs, 23, 47–52, 359–360

Reserves, abandonment of, 63–65
  accounting problems, 200–203
  actuarial status, 181–183
  alternative plans, 1935, 161–165, 177–179
  amendments of 1939, 165, 168–171, 178, 197, 201
  and burden in future, 212–214, 219–221, 224
  and consumption, 75–76, 78–80, 118, 153–155, 212, 215–216, 338–344
  contingency, 166–167
  deflationary effects of, 95–96, 208–209
  in depression, 269–270
  and different classes of goods, 122–124
  and distribution of taxes over time, 205–206, 222–223
  earnings, 166–167
  earnings on, 165, 178, 209–211, 221, 238
  and effective demand, 130
  estimates of, 183–186, 197
  failure to appropriate, 266–267
  and Federal debt, 218, 262–279

Reserves, under hypothetical 1850 program, 224–227
  and incidence, 301–302
  and income, 205
  and inflation, 213–214
  and insurance funds, 65–66
  and insurance principle, 249
  interest on, 165, 178, 209–211, 221, 223, 238
  and interest rate on public securities, 262–266, 277
  investment of (*see* Investment)
  and investment, 105–113, 118, 127–128, 153–155, 215–216
  and justice in taxation, 248–249
  management of, 215–217, 224
  and merit rating, 352–358
  monetary aspects, 206–208, 215–217
  and monetary policy, 264–265
  opposition to, 165–171, 229
  and output, 127–128
  and pay-as-you-go plan, 66–68, 97–101, 113, 177–179, 208–209
  plan of 1940, 172–173
  and prices of assets, 135–137
  and private insurance analogy, 221–224
  and propensity to save, 100
  real and financial aspects, 203–209
  and rentier income, 128–130
  and savings, 78–80, 97–113, 127–128, 204–207, 338–341
  of securities, 201–203, 216–218, 267–268
  superreserve plan, 173–177, 179–180
  and supply of Treasury issues, 265, 267–268, 277
  and tax reduction, 270–271, 278
  theory of, 199–224
  unemployment (*see* Unemployment reserves)

Revenue in future, 44–46, 176, 212–214, 222–224, 230–233, 241–261
  (*See also* Receipts; Taxation)

S

Savings, and amount and distribution of income, 102–106, 113

[453]